RAJASTHAN Delhi and Agra

Note to readers

The table of contents on p 4 will help you to find your way around the guide.
The guide also contains information on Delhi, Agra, Fatehpur Sikri and Mathura, which are not part of Rajasthan but which are often visited on the same trip.
A word of explanation concerning the practical information sections: the information in the "Practical Information" section is of a general nature and designed to help you plan your trip and find your way around once in the country. Then, after each town or itinerary description, there is a "Making the most of…" section (eg "Making the most of Jaipur", p 220) intended to provide practical details about the place: access, useful addresses, accommodation, restaurants, leisure, shopping etc.
The itineraries described and the maps will give you ideas for excursions off the beaten track. The ■ indicate possible overnight stops. To get an idea of how long your excursion is likely to take, refer to the itinerary map on the inside front cover.
In this guide, hotels and restaurants have been ranked by price (in US$) in order to help you budget your trip. It is however essential to remember that both changes in the cost of living and almost permanent changes brought to opening and closing times make it more than likely that this type of information will have changed since publication.

Michelin Travel Publications
Published in 2000

NEOS

New – In the NEOS guides emphasis is placed on the discovery and enjoyment of a new destination through meeting the people, tasting the food and absorbing the exotic atmosphere. In addition to recommendations on which sights to see, we give details on the most suitable places to stay and eat, on what to look out for in traditional markets and where to go in search of the hidden character of the region, its crafts and its dancing rhythms. For those keen to explore places on foot, we provide guidelines and useful addresses in order to help organise walks to suit all tastes.

Expert – The NEOS guides are written by people who have travelled in the country and researched the sites before recommending them by the allocation of stars. Accommodation and restaurants are similarly recommended by a on the grounds of quality and value for money. Cartographers have drawn easy-to-use maps with clearly marked itineraries, as well as detailed plans of towns, archeological sites and large museums.

Open to all cultures, the NEOS guides provide an insight into the daily lives of the local people. In a world that is becoming ever more accessible, it is vital that religious practices, regional etiquette, traditional customs and languages be understood and respected by all travellers. Equipped with this knowledge, visitors can seek to share and enjoy with confidence the best of the local cuisine, musical harmonies and the skills involved in the production of arts and crafts.

Sensitive to the atmosphere and heritage of a foreign land, the NEOS guides encourage travellers to see, hear, smell and feel a country, through words and images. Take inspiration from the enthusiasm of our experienced travel writers and make this a journey full of discovery and enchantment.

B. Brillion/MICHELIN

Rajasthan

Setting the scene 8

Setting the scene

B. Koch/DIAF

The Thar desert

From the River Yamuna to the Thar Desert

The state of **Rajasthan**, located in northwestern India just to the north of the tropic of Cancer, ranges over 342 000sqkm. From border to border, it spans some 700km. To the west lies Pakistan, India's lifelong enemy and the border between them continues to be fraught with conflict. Elsewhere, it is surrounded by five neighbouring Indian states. **Delhi**, less than 100km to the northeast, is India's capital city. Located between the states of Haryana and Uttar Pradesh (commonly known as U.P.), it has the status of a Union Territory.

Natural regions

See the map on the inside cover

Rajasthan is cut in two along a diagonal line created by the Aravalli Range of mountains which run from the northeast to the southwest. The Aravalli separate the state's different climates and create three vast natural regions: a zone composed of tablelands and fertile plains in the southeast (which extend into the alluvial plain of Delhi and Agra), a mountainous region in the centre and a semi-arid zone of desert steppe to the west.

Delhi and the Yamuna Valley

Throughout India's millenniums of history, western invaders traditionally approached the sub-continent via the famous Khyber Pass (between Afghanistan and Pakistan). Their progression eastward was hampered by the Himalayas to the north, the Thar Desert and the last outcrops of the Aravalli Range to the south, forcing them to approach through the plain of Punjab and head for the first water point to the east, **Delhi**, situated on the sacred river Yamuna, a tributary of the Ganges. This fertile alluvial plain is densely populated, but its monotonous, dusty landscape renders it singularly unappealing.

The Indies – India, Hindus – Indians

These terms tend to be used in a rather haphazard way by many English speakers. Their origin goes back to the name the Aryan invaders gave to the River Indus, and as a result, to the land beyond to the east: "Sindu", which the Greeks subsequently deformed into "Hind". The Persians called it "Hindustan" and 19C Europeans renamed it the "Indies" (because it was broken down at that time into a multitude of kingdoms and trading centres). Once independent, the Indies united and became "India", officially, the "Indian Union" or "Bharat", after a legendary king and wise-man (India is traditionally known as the "land of the sons of Bharat"). The word "Hindu", formerly used to designate the inhabitants of "Hind", now refers to all followers of "Hinduism" (a name invented by the Western world to designate the modern form of Brahminism), while "Indian" refers to a citizen of India, whatever his or her religion. However, Indians from the North continue to call themselves "Hindustani", whether Hindu or Moslem...

The Aravalli Range

When driving from Delhi to Jaipur, travellers first cross an agricultural plain of well-tended fields. Shortly before the border of Rajasthan, on either side of the road, a daunting range of hills suddenly becomes visible, which as you get nearer reveals itself as the Aravalli Range. Formed from sedimentary rocks which were subjected to folding-in during the Precambrian period,

these mountains are among the oldest in the world. They cut Rajasthan in two, from the north-east to the southwest. Erosion has taken its toll, particularly around the area north of Jaipur. The highest peak, Mount **Guru Shikhar** (1 721m) rises imposingly in the south between Udaipur and Mount Abu. The beauty of this hilly, green landscape adds great charm to the eastern part of Rajasthan.
Modest though it is in height, the Aravalli Range plays a determining role as a frontier. It checks the monsoon rains arriving from the southeast, which break against the eastern flanks, leaving the west of Rajasthan gasping for water. In the opposite direction, it acts as a screen against dust storms from the desert. Furthermore, in ancient times it provided protection against invasions from the West, further reinforced by forts built in its valleys and passes: Jaipur, Alwar, Ranthambore, Kumbhalgarh.

The south-eastern plains and tablelands

To the southeast of the Aravalli lies a region of alternating hills and basalt table-lands, separated by alluvial plains. Two main rivers, the Banas and the **Chambal** (tributary of the Yamuna), Rajasthan's only perennial river, flow through it. The rich black soil of the fertile **Hadoti** plain is well-drained. Cotton, linen, ground-nuts, barley, wheat and basmati rice all grow in this relatively humid climate, similar to that of the Yamuna valley.

Semi-arid steppe

To the west of the Aravalli Range, a semi-arid region of dry, saline soil scattered with thorny scrub continues on towards Pakistan, finally drying up completely to form the **Thar** Desert. It is difficult to imagine that some two billion years ago it was covered by a vast sea, a fact confirmed by the discovery of shell fossils. Its sand dunes, sculpted by erosion and south-westerly winds, make the Thar very similar to the Sahara. It is however really a desert only on the Pakistani side. On the Indian side, as much as 40% consists of a rocky landscape covered in bushes and acacia, which is far from uninhabited, because tribes of nomads continue to roam across the region with their herds of camels and goats.
A vast semi-arid plain of gneiss forms a transition zone between the Thar Desert and the Aravalli Range. This plain encompasses the **Marwar** steppe (around **Jodhpur**, the region's only large city) and the sandy plains of **Shekhawati**, where millet and oilseeds are cultivated. A few rivers drain into the area from the Aravalli, including the Luni, which rises near Pushkar, but all dry up well before the dry season.

The monsoon: a reprieve

The warm climate of the whole region is subject to the **"summer" monsoon** winds: the rainy season (July-September) accounts for 90% of the yearly rain-fall. This season provides the majority of work and economic activity in the region. However the monsoon, which moves from south to north, is almost over by the time it reaches Delhi and only really affects Rajasthan superficially (primarily in the west). The summer is followed by a mild **autumn** season and then **winter** (December-February), with cold nights (it has been known to freeze). During this period, it is coldest in Delhi and warmest in Udaipur. Temperatures rise suddenly in mid-February to reach heat-wave proportions at the end of April. The **summer** temperatures are unbearable, and by the end of June the whole region anxiously awaits the first rains, which are always greeted with relief.

Flora and fauna

Despite its dense population, and with the exception of its bustling conurbations, India is a distinctly rural country, in which the flora and fauna continue to thrive, despite the steady loss of habitat. Rajasthan, which is relatively sparsely populated, has retained a noticeably bucolic flavour, bordering on wilderness in places.

Sacred trees

Less than 10 % of Rajasthan is covered in **forest**, and what remains lies mainly to the south and east of the Aravalli Range, whose peaks and monsoon rains encourage growth. It is a dry forest comprising both evergreen and deciduous (bare from March to May) species, such as **teak**, whose gigantic leaves are partly mottled as a result of a parasite, **mango**, several species of **tamarind** (members of the leguminous group of plants) and of course, **bougainvillea**, whose bright colours are as visible in the undergrowth as they are in gardens.

Little more than xerophilous plants grow in the semi-drought conditions of the **scrubland** in the western and northern regions of Rajasthan, in particular **babul** *(mimosa arabica)*, the most widespread species of acacia and **khejri** *(prosopis cineraria)*, which the Bishnois (a tribe from the region of Jodhpur) hold to be sacred. Its pods, prepared with spices, can be found in restaurants. A large variety of shrubs thrive in the sandy soil and dunes, stabilising the soil with their root systems. In addition, their roots, branches, leaves and fruit are all used, whether as firewood, food or for medicinal purposes.

Since ancient times, trees have been venerated in India, to depict the cosmos and also as symbols of everlasting fertility and immortality. Among the most sacred are the **banian** or Indian fig tree *(ficus indica)*, whose air-borne roots hang over the leafy branches like creepers. They provide shade in large numbers of Indian village squares, except in western parts of the Aravalli Range, where it is too dry for them. Buddha is said to have reached enlightenment under the shade of a **pipal** or pagoda fig tree *(ficus religiosa)*, the heart-shaped leaves of which are silver coloured on one side. Hindus sometimes blend it with a **neem** *(azadirachta indica)*, to produce a mixture whose incalculable medicinal and germicidal properties have been common knowledge in India for centuries (*neem*-based toothpaste can be found in all grocery stores). An American company has even patented the product. The slender silhouette of the **ashoka** or "mast tree" (family of *Annonaceae*) is easily recognisable, its long, narrow, shiny green leaves often serve as a model for the festoons over temple entrances.

Jungle dwellers and city guests

Forget any ideas of luscious rambling forests that the word "jungle" may evoke. In Hindi, this word actually designates a woody area, dense or sparse, inhabited by wild animals. Rajasthan's jungle most definitely veers towards the sparse rather than the dense, and its undisputed king, the **tiger** *(sher)*, who, at the beginning of the century, reigned over the whole length of the Aravalli Range, now only survives in reserves in Ranthambore and Sariska. Rajasthan is also home to a certain number of other predators: **panthers** (also known as leopards or *cheetah*), **wild cats, hyenas, wolves,** together with hordes of **jackals**, which have been known to approach the suburbs of large cities at night.

The shy **cervidae** (with antlers or horns) are represented by the **sambar**, the largest stag in India, the smaller, spotted **axis stag**, and the **chital** fallow deer. Travellers are however more likely to come across **antelope** (with hollow spiral

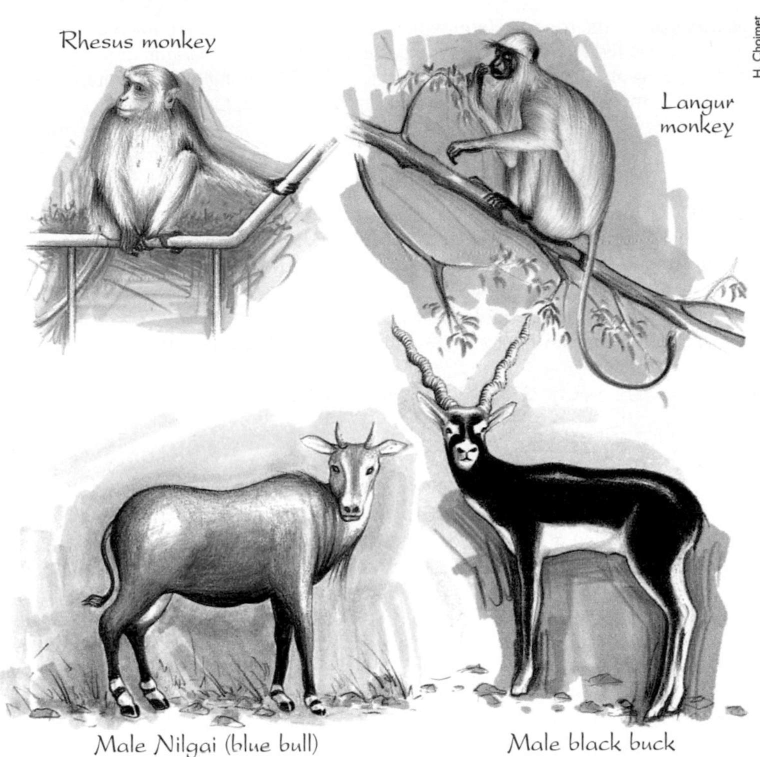

antlers), among which are the **nilgai** or bluebull, a large grey-black (male) or beige (female) antelope, four-horned **sambar**, **blackbucks** so beloved of painters and the **chinkara** gazelle. The latter two can be found in the steppe region around Jodhpur, where they are protected by the Bishnoi from poaching, sometimes at the risk of their lives. Despite the fact that hunting has been banned since the 1970s and that blackbucks and *chinkara* gazelles are now classed as endangered species, they both remain the target of wealthy city dwellers, industrialists or movie stars in search of fresh venison or thrills. Among other jungle inhabitants, visitors should have no difficulty catching glimpses of **wild boar** in the foothills of the Aravalli Range.

Hordes of **semi-wild animals** co-exist alongside humans. The largest group is the monkeys which have set up home in all the large city bazaars, where their constant pilfering is more or less tolerated by the Hindu population, who view them

Peacocks and other winged creatures

The peacock was chosen as the symbol of the Indian Union and its ear-piercing calls will soon become familiar to every visitor. The sight of these magnificent birds strutting their stuff in the Indian countryside is a spectacle that never fails to amaze. Rajasthan is a stopping point for many migratory birds and some 350 species nest in Bharatpur bird sanctuary. Among the most frequently seen, in town and country, are the easily recognisable mynah birds, with bright yellow or orange eye contour and upper legs, little long-tailed green "tota" budgerigars, the symbol of true love, and the crow.

as members of the tribe of Hanuman, the monkey king. The **rhesus monkey**, with its distinctive red face and rump, is stockier than the gangly **langur** monkey, which has a grey coat and black face and hands. Adorable mongoose can often be seen during the monsoon season, when their lairs are flooded. Little **squirrels**, with three or five stripes, said to be the mark of Shiva's trident, are also visible everywhere, even on the pavements in Delhi, while at nightfall, **geckos** (lizards) start hunting insects on bedroom walls (except during the winter, when they hibernate).

Among the animals used by man, **elephants** are surely the most prestigious, but no wild elephants survive in Rajasthan's jungles, which are not humid enough for them. Among the million and a half **camels** in India, nearly a third can be found in Rajasthan (the remaining two-thirds are in the Gujarat). Both a pack and a riding animal, it is also used to haul heavy loads and can be seen yoked to a plough in the sandy Shekhawati plains or pulling heavy cartloads in the streets of Jaipur.

An endangered environment

Over-exploited countryside

Although the daily spectacle of groups of women walking along the roadside with bundles of twigs on their heads may seem picturesque to tourists, it actually masks one of Rajasthan's most serious threats to the environment. Every day millions of women strip the trees of their branches in order to find fodder for animals or firewood for cooking. Trees are being decimated faster than they are being replaced. In addition, the **deforestation** and clearing of land, made necessary by demographic pressures, is fast encroaching on natural land features, which are dwindling by the day. This is further exacerbated by the **intensive grazing** of sheep, goats and camels of nomadic tribes on uncultivated land. There is too much livestock to give the grass time to grow, with the result that the thin covering of vegetation is gradually disappearing and desertification is increasing.

Smoke-filled cities

Most studies on pollution spotlight Calcutta, Delhi and Bombay (in that order) among the ten most polluted cities in the world. Unfortunately even medium-sized cities such as Agra, Jaipur, Jodhpur and Kota are little better. The primary cause of urban pollution is **traffic**: exacerbated by poor quality fuel and badly maintained exhausts and engines. In addition, **industrial waste and smoke** are unscrupulously poured into the air, soil and rivers. The almost total lack of any ecological lobby has done little to encourage the Indian government to take any real measures and only disasters such as **Bhopal** seem capable of having a real effect. (In 1984, an explosion in a Union Carbide chemical factory at Bhopal, capital of Madhya Pradesh, produced a toxic cloud that poisoned and killed over one thousand people in just a few hours and left hundreds of thousands with long-term health problems.) The use of **dustbins** is practically unheard of in India, as a glance at the state of the streets, more akin to gigantic public tips, quickly reveals. Cows and pigs, left to roam free by their owners who don't have to feed them, forage among the rubbish: leftovers, but also newspapers and other more or less "eatable" rotting waste is in this way recycled willy-nilly. Furthermore, the current increase in consumerism has led to the proliferation of all types of non-recyclable household waste: batteries and piles of plastic bags can be found littered around even the most isolated hamlets. In India, quality of life has yet to be measured by the cleanliness of the streets or the purity of the air and water.

Over 4 000 years of history

Ancient times

BC

2600-1800	Peak of the Indus civilisation. Cities of Harappa and Mohenjo-Daro established.
1600-1000	Aryans move into the northwest of India.
6C	Buddha and Mahavira (founder of Jainism) lived.
268-231	Reign of Ashoka the pious. Unification of the north of India. Spread of Buddhism.

AD

1-3C	"Indo-Scythian" Empire. Kushan dynasty.
4-5C	Gupta dynasty.
End 5C	The Huns invade northwestern India.
8C	First Rajput dynasties emerge. Foundation of Chittaurgarh, capital of Mewar.

Moslem India

1026	Mahmud of Ghazni raids northwestern India.
1192	Mohammed of Ghor crushes the Rajput coalition at Tarain and takes over Delhi.
1206	Qutb ud-Din Aibak founds the Sultanate of Delhi.
1290-1413	Khilji then Tughluq dynasties of Turkish descent.
1398	Tamerlane raids northwestern India.
1413-1526	Sayyid, then Lodi dynasties of Afghan descent.
1526-1530	Reign of Babur, founder of the Mughal dynasty.
1530-1556	Reign of Humayun, interrupted by the usurper Sher Shah (1540-1555).
1556-1605	Reign of Akbar. Foundation of Fatehpur Sikri.
1605-1627	Reign of Jahangir.
1627-1658	Reign of Shah Jahan. Construction of the Taj Mahal at Agra.
1658-1707	Reign of Aurangzeb. Many Hindu and Jain temples are destroyed.
1727	Jai Singh II, maharajah of Amber, founds Jaipur.

Colonial era

1498	Vasco da Gama reaches the coast of Kerala.
1818	The British move into Rajasthan
1857	Sepoy mutiny.
1877	Queen Victoria is proclaimed "Empress of India".
1920	Gandhi organises the first campaign of "non-co-operation".
15 August 1947	Partition and independence of India and Pakistan.
1948	Assassination of Mahatma Gandhi

Modern India

1948	First war against Pakistan.
26 January 1950	Official proclamation of the Republic of India.
1962	War against China.
1965	Second war against Pakistan.
1971	Third war against Pakistan. Bangladesh is created.
1974	First nuclear tests at Pokaran.
1984	Assassination of Indira Gandhi.
1991	Assassination of Rajiv Gandhi. Economic liberalisation.
1998	The BJP Hindu party joins central government. More nuclear testing at Pokaran.

From Aryans to nuclear power

The history of Rajasthan, Delhi and Agra follows for the most part that of northern India and its scattering of more or less long-lasting invasions. The essence of Rajasthan, "Abode of Kings", lies in the existence of a mosaic of small rival kingdoms which lived side by side in more or less constant opposition up until the 19C. The chaos produced by their constant rivalry explains why the region is so rich in forts: Jaisalmer, Jodhpur, Chittaurgarh, Amber. The historical and legendary wealth these names evoke is unsurprising in a country so adept at marrying past and present, indeed a single word *"kal"*, means both "yesterday" and "tomorrow".

A land of gods and kings

First inhabitants (4th millennium-1600 BC)

Five thousand years ago, northwest India was inhabited by tribes called **"Proto-Australoids".** As a result of waves of invasions, many of these populations found refuge in the forest and mountain regions. Some still form significant minority populations in Rajasthan today (**Bhils** and **Meenas**). The oldest civilisation discovered in northwestern India is the **Indus civilisation**, which emerged during the 4th millennium, reaching its apogee between 2600 BC and 1800 BC. The use of bronze and copper, sophisticated planned cities, which depended both on agriculture and trade, all characterise this civilisation. Large numbers of seals, covered for the most part in still undeciphered pictograms, have been found as far away as Mesopotamia. Excavations at Harappa and Mohenjo-Daro (now in Pakistan), Lothal (Gujarat) and Kalibangan, near Ganganagar (northern Rajasthan), would seem to indicate that this amazing civilisation extended over the whole region. Towards 1600 BC however, for some unknown reason (climatic disaster, alteration in river courses, increasing saline content in soil…), it abruptly broke down.

Advent of the Aryans (towards 1600-1000 BC)

Around 1600-1500 BC, **Aryans** ("noble" in Sanskrit), a light-skinned people of nomad farmers from the coasts of the Caspian sea, crossed over the Iranian tablelands and reached the plain of Punjab via the traditional invasion route formed by the northwestern passes. They progressed on towards the Ganges Plain which they occupied around the 11C BC, building cities such as Indraprashta (Delhi) and either crushing local populations or forcing them southwards into the forests. During their stay, the invaders began in fact to assimilate certain aspects of local culture, leading to the emergence of a new civilisation, of which, however, no archaeological traces have been found. The only knowledge we have of them has been gleaned from sacred books, the **Vedas** (meaning "knowledge"). These manuscripts tell of an organisation divided into hierarchies or classes, **varnas** *(see Religion, p 46)*.The Aryans also introduced the use of horses and war chariots, as well as their language (Sanskrit) and religion (Vedism), essentially based on rites and sacrifices offered to gods who personified natural elements.

First unifications (c 600 BC-600 AD)

The little we know of the history of the numerous Aryan kingdoms has often been picked up from bewildering accounts of ancient legends. However, in the 6C BC, there are clear accounts of emerging protest movements that began to oppose the ritualism and power of the Brahmins, giving birth, in the kingdom of **Magadha** (current state of Bihar), to reformist religions that were to become Buddhism and Jainism.

Around 518 BC, Darius the Great, emperor of Persia, invaded the northwest peninsula via the Khyber Pass and founded the Achaemenian satrapies or provinces. Two centuries later, in 327 BC (first certain date in Indian history), **Alexander the Great** crossed the Khyber Pass and conquered the Punjab. His death, three years later, prevented him from consolidating this conquest. His governors and their successors were ousted by Chandragupta, a native of Magadha and founder of the **Mauryan** dynasty (4-2C BC), who conquered all of northern and a large part of southern India. The height of this empire was reached during the reign of Chandragupta's grandson, **Ashoka** (3C BC). Ashoka was the first sovereign to undertake political unification in India. These attempts were however short-lived and Ashoka's heirs were unable to withstand either the creation of **Indo-Greek provinces** (2-1C BC) along the northwestern border, or the invasions of nomad peoples from the Iranian plateau: **Parthians**, then **Scythians** *(Sakas)* during the 1C BC, followed by the **Kushanas** (1-3C, who chose Mathura as their winter capital and Begram (in Afghanistan) as their summer capital. In turn, the impressive **Gupta** dynasty, also from Magadha, managed to unify northern India into a single empire, from the 4-5C, but the **Hun** raids (end of 5C) were to annihilate this new-found unity. In their wake came the **Gurjuras** clans, from whom the Rajputs are partly descended.

Lion capital, Ashoka's column, Mauryan period

The mythical Rajput heritage (6C-10C)

As the Gupta empire began to disintegrate, the Hindu Gurjara vassal kings and clan chiefs saw their opportunity to take control of Rajasthan and the Ganges Plain. They created hosts of mini kingdoms, rivals but also united by brotherhood clan and vassal ties. The lack of

Ashoka the pious, a Buddhist emperor

During the 3C BC, Buddhism spread throughout the greater part of the peninsula and even further afield. The main instigator of this missionary work was emperor Ashoka, despite having been born Hindu. At the beginning of his reign, he set out to conquer the kingdom of Kalinga (current state of Orissa), but such was the cruelty of his campaign, he was struck with remorse and began to question the meaning of power. Attracted to Buddhism, he encouraged its propagation, establishing monasteries and erecting edicts on the roadside and in cities to encourage his subjects to develop religious tolerance and universal compassion.

any real historic substantiation has given rise to all sorts of legendary interpretations of how they came to power. Self-appointed members of the *Kshatriya* caste of warriors, they proclaimed themselves Rajputs ("sons of kings") and endeavoured to trace their lineage back to mythical times in order to mask their somewhat unorthodox rise to power. Some claimed to descend from the "Race of the Sun" **(Suryavansa)**, descendants of Surya, by way of the god Rama; others from the "Race of the Moon" **(Induvansa)**, descendants of Krishna. A third branch claimed to be "Fire Born" **(Agnikula)**, because they were said to have been born in the sacrificial fire on one of the peaks near Mount Abu. All the Rajput clans claim to be descended from one or other of these three dynasties, of which the Agnikula is thought to be the most recent. However, attempts to draw up any serious sort of chronology prior to the 10C are a delusion.

The Rajasthan kingdoms (8C-13C)

From the 8C to the 10C, the **Gurjuras-Pratiharas** clan reigned, controlling almost all of northern India, but this did not prevent smaller clans from asserting themselves and growing in influence, thereby giving birth to dynasties that were to dominate Rajasthan. Hence the emergence of the **Chauhans**, in the region of Ajmer as early as the 7C (their kingdom extended as far as Delhi in the 12C), the **Sisodias**, who ruled over Mewar (southern Rajasthan) from the 8C, with Chittaurgarh as their capital. Arab incursions into the Indus plain in the 8C were to force the **Bhattis** clan eastwards into the desert in the 11C, where they founded Jaisalmer (12C). The **Kachwahas** were driven from the banks of the river Yamuna and retreated to Amber (near Jaipur) at the end of the 11C. Finally towards the end of the 12C, the **Rathores**, defeated by invaders from Afghanistan, left the Ganges Plain for the heart of Rajasthan where they founded Mandore and the kingdom of Marwar. In this way the main Rajput clans formed a **Rajputana** (group of princely states), protected by the steep, arid landscape whose natural defences they reinforced by forts. Proud, quarrelsome and extremely independent, the Rajputs were to prove almost incapable of joining forces against a common enemy, thereby leaving themselves vulnerable to invasion. Furthermore, Rajasthan's position, on the route between Delhi and Gujurat's ports, made it a prize coveted by many assailants. Luckily, the sheer number of kingdoms combined with the fiercely independent nature of the Rajputs made any hope of definitive conquest unfeasible. Hardly was one kingdom overcome, when another was already up in arms and on the road to revolt.

Islam

First Moslem invasions (711-1192)

In 711, Arab hordes from Damascus made a brief incursion into the peninsula, but progressed no further than the Indus valley. However, 300 years later, **Mahmud of Ghazni**, a Turkish sultan who had settled in Afghanistan, launched some 15 raids between 1001 and 1027. After conquering the Punjab and founding Lahore (first Moslem capital of the sub-continent), he reached the Ganges, ransacking the region of Mathura. The threat and consequences of these initial Moslem incursions were not however long-lived, because Mahmud's goal was not to conquer, but simply to pillage and carry his booty home to Ghazni.

Akbar passing the crown of India to his son, miniature by the Mughal School (1605)

The Sultanate of Delhi (1192-1526)

Mohammed of Ghor's invasion at the end of the 12C was however a totally different story. He began by invading the Punjab, before decimating the armies of the last Hindu sovereign of Delhi, the Chauhan Rajput, **Prithviraja III**, at the battle of Tarain (1192). Unlike his predecessor, his goal was to conquer and not to pillage, even if he governed from his distant throne in Ghazni, Afghanistan. On his death in 1206, all the Rajput kingdoms of northern India were dismantled, with the exception of those of Rajasthan. One of his lieutenants, **Qutb ud-din Aibak**, a former Turkish slave, proclaimed himself "sultan of Delhi", inaugurating India's first Moslem dynasty, known as the **dynasty of slaves** (1210-1290). This meant that power was derived by divine right, as in Persia, and the sultan was considered to be the "Shadow of God" on earth. Ala ud-Din Khijli, of the **Khijli dynasty** (1290-1320), of Turkish origins, carried out frequent attacks on his neighbouring Hindu sovereigns, sacking Jaisalmer and seizing Ranthambore and Chittaurgarh. Encouraged by these victories, he even pushed southwards into India. A number of despotic and unstable sovereigns were to mark the **Tughluq dynasty** (1320-1413), also Turkish. However, under Mohammed ibn Tughluq (1325-1351), the Sultanate of Delhi reached the peak of its territorial grandeur, comparable to that of Ashoka's, with the exception of the majority of the Rajputana who appear to have remained independent. Revolt after revolt however undermined the Sultanate, which began to fall apart, failing to defend itself against a raid by the Mughal-Turk, **Tamerlane** (Timur Lang) in 1398. After six months of carnage, leaving millions dead and the Sultanate on its last legs, he left the country. Over the next century power was to swing between a handful of Afghan dynasties of minor importance (**Sayyid** then **Lodi**). This left the Rajput sovereigns a free hand to take advantage of the situation and reinforce their control over Rajasthan.

Beginning of the Mughal era (1526-1556)

From his kingdom in Kabul, **Babur**, a descendant of Tamerlane on his father's side and Genghis Khan on his mother's, launched his troops against the subcontinent in 1526. After invading the Punjab, he defeated the armies of **Ibrahim Lodi**, sultan of Panipat (80km north of Delhi). He then pushed south, seizing Delhi where he proclaimed himself *padishah* of Hindustan. Confronted by the Moslem threat, for once the Rajputs managed to join forces under the command of *rana* Sanga Singh of Mewar. But the Mughal army, more powerful, better organised and equipped with modern artillery, crushed the Hindu coalition at the battle of Khanwa in 1527. Following the death of Babur (1530), his son **Humayun**, the first real sovereign of the Mughal dynasty, was ousted from power by the Bihar Afghan chief, **Sher Shah Sur** (1540-1555), proving himself to be a great reformer. Humayun, exiled in Persia, only regained his throne in 1555, a year before his death.

Prestigious emperors (1556-1707)

Emperor **Akbar** (1556-1605), the first Great Mughal, succeeded his father Humayun at the age of 13 and was to dominate the Mughal dynasty. Both intelligent and tolerant, he was the first Mughal to realise that the only way to successfully govern this foreign land was to become accepted and he began to form political alliances with the Hindus. He abolished the tax on non-Moslems and outlawed the slaughter of cows. Ajmer, a Moslem pilgrim city, became an imperial province where he set up his headquarters, a Mughal enclave in the heart of

Rajput territory. His political acumen enabled him to transform conquered enemies into loyal allies by arranging strategic marriages: his wives and daughters-in-law were chosen from among the princesses of Rajasthan. In this way, his grandson, the future Shah Jahan, was three-quarters Rajput. The maharajas recognised the emperor's sovereignty, who in exchange guaranteed their autonomy and granted them imperial offices (military or government positions). Only the maharana of Mewar, the indomitable **Pratap Singh** held out, resisted the Mughal movement and resolutely maintained his independence right up until his death. His son however was forced to pledge allegiance to the emperor. The Indo-Moslem culture reached incomparable heights of sophistication and luxury during the reigns of Akbar and his successors: **Jahangir** (1605-1627) (an aesthete, alcoholic and opium-addict who left his wife to rule) and **Shah Jahan** (1627-1658), who was an art lover. The Rajputs, inspired by their sovereigns, also built gracious Moslem-style palaces within their strongholds.

Mughal dagger

R. Marca

The beginning of the reign of **Aurangzeb** (1658-1707) was to end this period. The empire had never been so vast – in fact, so vast, it had become quite unmanageable from Delhi. To compound the situation, the last Great Mughal, a bigoted zealot, ordered harsh measures of austerity and re-established political discrimination against non-Moslems (reintroducing the non-Moslem tax and destroying temples). This tyrannical backwards step led to the uprising of the Deccan Marathas (led by Shivaji), the Sikhs from the Punjab, the Jats of Mathura, and of course, the Rajputs. Always quick to react, the latter adopted guerrilla tactics in 1679 when Aurangzeb attempted to take control of the kingdom of Marwar (Jodhpur). Right after his death, the three most powerful Rajputs – **Jai Singh II** of Amber, **Amar Singh** of Mewar and **Ajit Singh** of Marwar – formed an alliance and signed a truce that would protect them from the crumbling Mughal empire.

Colonial times and the road to Independence

Europeans in India (1498-1818)

Right up until the early 16C, the Middle East was a strategic exchange zone between the West and Asia, and the safety of convoys was dependent on the prevailing political situation. On the far side of the sub-continent, Portuguese born **Vasco da Gama** reached land at Kerala in 1498 after a 10-month voyage round the Cape of Good Hope. In so doing, he opened up a maritime route to the Indies for the West so eager for exotic goods – silk, cotton, spices, indigo. The majority of European expeditions were for trade purposes at this time and the main action took place along the coasts, far from Rajasthan and Delhi. Trading posts were opened: the Portuguese made **Goa** their capital (1510), British merchants and the **British East India Company** settled first in **Bombay** (1534-1661) before moving to Calcutta (1690), while the French East India Company set up shop in **Pondichery** (1674). India became the backdrop of fierce rivalry among European powers (primarily between the French and English). These incessant struggles for influence and wars to obtain territorial rights gradually enabled the East India Company to take control of practically the whole country.

The British in Rajasthan (1818-1857)

Following the death of Aurangzeb (1707), the Mughal empire rapidly declined. Delhi, weak from repeated pillaging, no longer had any authority. For their part, the Rajput princes, too busy with never-ending wars of succession, internal struggles and feuds, became weaker and more vulnerable to attack. Incapable of defending themselves against the raids of the **Maratha Confederation** in the early 19C, they requested the protection of the British who had already taken over Delhi, any remaining emperors serving merely as figureheads. Their new masters required the Rajput princes to sign individual treaties of assistance (1818), thereby recognising British sovereignty. The British, quick to begin organising, very soon ensured that the Rajputs became, to all intents and purposes, fully dependent. They astutely placated the maharajas however by guaranteeing them semi-independence and a carefree life of luxury.

The Indian Mutiny (1857-1858)

In the mid-19C, the British controlled most of northern India, from the North West Frontier with Afghanistan to Burma. Although the majority of India's sovereigns had adapted to the presence of these polite foreigners, who were keen hunters and horsemen, and excellent business entrepreneurs, this was not the case for the rest of the population. Their reticence and aloofness from the general population gradually gave rise to antipathy and discontent. This lack of contact between the British and ordinary Indians produced ignorance and was most probably the source of the legendary Indian Mutiny. In the spring of 1857, a rumour, which the British failed to adequately deny, began to circulate among the Sepoy (Indian conscript) battalions stationed in northern India that the new cartridges supplied by the army were supposed to have been rubbed in cow or pork fat. Cows are held sacred by Hindus and pigs are considered impure by Moslems. On May 10 1857, mutiny broke out at **Meerut** (now in Uttar Pradesh). Three battalions massacred the Europeans living there, before heading for Delhi where Emperor Bahadur Shah came out on their side. Practically the whole of northern India was up in arms. Only the Punjab Sikhs remained loyal to the British. In Rajasthan, although the population turned against the western colonists, most of the Rajputs, aware of what they owed the British, stood up to the rebels. Thanks to the support of the Sikh battalions, the British managed to rescue the situation. One month later, the uprising was quashed. **Bahadur Shah II**, last great Mughal, was exiled to Burma, where he died, and his sons were executed.

The opulent Raj (1876-1947)

The 1857 uprising revealed how fragile the British East India Company was and how incapable it was of administering such a vast territory. Thus in 1858, the British crown took over official control of the country and in 1877, Queen Victoria was proclaimed "Empress of India". For the first time, the sub-continent was to be unified and ruled by a single power for a long period (with the exception of the Portuguese and French trading posts), known as the Indian Empire (*the Raj*). This encompassed all the provinces directly controlled by the British, together with some 550 princely states who were awarded statutes of semi-independence under British protection. A period of opulence for the Rajput sovereigns commenced. Their loyalty during the uprising had earned them this semi-autonomy, although the British retained the right to ratify the inheritance of thrones.

The new masters' mistrust of the Indian population led them more and more to resort to local intermediaries to administer the vast territory, creating a middle-class elite whose role was to run the empire. Little by little, the traditional sphere of power (maharajas, princes and nawabs) broadened to encompass a genuine middle-class (civil servants, lawyers, businessmen), with the result that the latter began to aspire to creating a modern state, inspired by the example of western democracies.

The Gandhian era (1914-1947)

As early as 1885, these emerging aspirations led to the foundation of the **Indian National Congress**, which was to play a vital role in the struggle for Independence. As Bengal became a hotbed of political unrest, in 1911 the British transferred their capital from Calcutta to Delhi. The Rajput princes did not however feel at all inclined to react to calls for independence, preferring their silver-lined state of dependence to the uncertainty of a future democracy. The spearhead of the movement for independence was a lawyer from a middle-class family, **Mohandas Karamchand Gandhi**, soon known as **Mahatma** ("great soul") or **Bapu** ("father"). In 1914, he began to organise non-violent resistance to the British occupier. "Non-cooperation", "civil disobedience", peace events and marches began to spread the concept of independence through all classes of Indian society. The Congress Party, presided over by Jawaharlal Nehru, officially requested India's independence. In 1935, the British government, aware of the urgent need for concessions, proposed the creation of an Indian legislative assembly, with limited powers. The Congress was unsatisfied and pursued the struggle. When, in 1942, Japan invaded Burma, some Indian nationalists, such as Subash Chandra Bose, decided to support Japan rather than their colonial government. At the end of the Second World War the British still ruled India, but it had become clear that the British Empire's control was seriously undermined and could not last.

The father of the nation

Mohandas Karamchand Gandhi was born on October 2 1869 in Porbandar (Gujurat), into a wealthy middle-class "vaishya" Hindu family. After law studies in England, he set up practice in South Africa for 20 years. On returning to India in 1914, he threw himself into the struggle for Independence, as a result of which he was regularly imprisoned. His loyalty to Hindu values, such as fasting and his attachment to the concept of non-violence ("ahimsa") of Jainist origins (of which there were many followers in Gujarat), made him very popular. He campaigned for the development of villages, also defending the lot of the "untouchables" (without though, questioning the caste system). However his desire to reconcile India's different religious communities earned him the hostility of extremists. He was assassinated, in Delhi on January 30 1948, by a member of a Hindu nationalist organisation, who claimed that Gandhi was responsible for the division of India.

Independence (August 15 1947)

In February 1947, the British government officially declared its intention of withdrawing from India. Lord Mountbatten, appointed viceroy of India in March, was to supervise the transition to Independence, a particularly delicate operation given the inter-religious conflicts. The Congress supported the creation of a secular nation, the Moslem League, led by Ali Jinnah, and called for the creation of two States, separated on the basis of religion: a Hindu-dominated

India and a Moslem-dominated Pakistan. Partition seemed inevitable. The British, anxious to rid themselves of what had become a burden, hastily drew frontiers, giving the Moslems Sindh, northern Punjab and 900km away, eastern Bengal. On August 15 1947 the States of India and Pakistan were born. The declaration of Independence was the scene of a vast migration of populations across both borders. Some 10 million Hindus and Sikhs left Pakistan for India, while some 8 million Moslems took the opposite route. On both sides of the border, exiled minorities were assaulted, leading to the bloody massacre of some 300 000 victims in just a few months.

The world's largest democracy

Neighbours in conflict (1947-1966)

The 562 princely states also achieved Independence with the rest of India. One after another, Rajasthan's 18 maharajas, like most of the other sovereigns, recognised the Indian Union and the existence of their kingdoms within it. The borders were to be the scenes of major tensions, as India embarked on four wars in 25 years (three against Pakistan and one against China). In 1948, Pakistan threatened **Kashmir**, whose Hindu maharaja had elected to be part of India. Delhi's troops managed to push the Pakistani forces back over the border, known as the "cease-fire" line, which the UN are in charge of patrolling, but which is recognised by neither country. The Kashmir issue is far from solved and to this day, continues to poison relations between the two countries.
On January 26 1950, the **Republic of India** was proclaimed officially. The head of the Congress Party, **Jawaharlal Nehru**, became Prime Minister. As he set about introducing the first phase of modernisation, another conflict emerged, this time with China. In 1959, India welcomed the Dalai Lama, fleeing the invasion of Tibet by Chinese troops. The Peking government despatched troops to the Himalayas, past the Mac-Mahon Line (a border established by the British). Although they defeated the poorly-equipped Indian forces, the invaders withdrew, content to have inflicted a humiliating warning. In 1964, Nehru died. The following year, his successor, **Lal Bahadur Shastri** had to deal with new clashes over Kashmir. A temporary truce was signed at the Declaration of Tashkent (January 1966) but Lal Bahadur Shastri died the day after the signing. He was replaced by Nehru's daughter, **Indira Gandhi** (married to a Jain businessman and with no family ties to Mahatma).

The maharajas and democracy

With the advent of Independence, each Rajput sovereign was free to choose to be part of either India or Pakistan. Within the space of two years, they had all joined democratic India, thereby relinquishing all rights over their kingdoms. In exchange, Delhi granted them privileges, such as pensions ("privy purses") and tax exemption of their fortunes. The region, now controlled by Delhi, became a new Indian state with a new name, Rajasthan. Its final make-up became definitive in 1956 when Ajmer and Mount Abu were also annexed. Some maharajas became members of parliament, others diplomats. In 1970 when Indira Gandhi revoked their pensions, many started up businesses, turning their palaces into luxury hotels.

One woman's power (1966-1984)

The **Green Revolution** emerged during the second half of the 1960s, with the backing of middle-class farmers (introduction of high-yield cereals, irrigation, use of fertilisers and pesticides). **Indira Gandhi** resolutely adopted a policy of social protection, with severe controls on banks and large companies. Outside of India, tensions were still strong. In 1971, Delhi backed "Eastern Pakistan's" (future **Bangladesh**) struggle for independence. As a result, Pakistan once again attacked northwest India. This time India was victorious, but the permanent threat of Pakistan drove the Indian government to modernise its army. In 1974, the first nuclear tests carried out in the sub-continent took place at **Pokaran** (between Jaisalmer and Jodhpur) in Rajasthan. The domestic situation was no better. Guerrilla attacks in northeastern states (Nagaland, Mizoram), ethnic and linguistic rivalries and **Naxalite** violence (linked to left-wing extremists) incited Indira Gandhi to proclaim a **"state of emergency"** in June 1975, leaving her free to govern without the control of Parliament. She outlawed strikes, banished extremist organisations, muzzled the press and embarked on a programme of forced sterilisation. India's hopes for democracy appeared doomed. To prove her popularity, Nehru's daughter organised general elections but her Congress Party was defeated in March 1977 and she was forced to resign. **Morarji Desai**, a Gandhian veteran, became head of a coalition government, led by the **Janata Dal**, ("People's Party"), but the shaky alliance soon faltered and the next general elections in January 1980 returned Mrs Gandhi and Congress to power. The government now had to deal with a Sikh independence movement in the **Punjab**. In June 1984, troops were sent into the **Golden Temple** at Amritsar, the Sikh's most holy shrine, which had become a base for militant activists backed by Pakistan. The Sikhs never forgave Indira this sacrilege and four months later, she was assassinated in Delhi by two of her Sikh bodyguards.

Rajiv's tragic destiny (1984-1991)

Indira Gandhi's son, **Rajiv Gandhi**, a pilot educated in the West and married to an Italian, Sonia, then became head of Congress, winning the elections in December 1984 with a large majority. Rajiv pledged to pursue India's route towards modernity, developing information technology and introducing widespread reform. The first home-grown "yuppies" emerged. Although nicknamed "Mr Clean", his reputation was sullied by the **Bofors scandal**, involving kickbacks regarding a Swedish armaments contract, which contributed to toppling his government in the 1989 elections. During the following two years, two coalition governments got bogged down in domestic issues: quotas set aside for the low castes in administrations and universities, a fast-declining economic situation and unrest among radical Hindus concerning the **Ayodhya** mosque in Uttar Pradesh (built by Emperor Babur on the birth place of Rama). Then, when the Spring 1991 elections seemed to suggest an easy victory for Congress and the return of Rajiv Gandhi, he was assassinated in southern India, in May 1991, by a Liberation Tiger of Tamil Eelam **(LTTE)** terrorist. LTTE was the most extreme Tamil organisation for independence of Sri Lanka and they had never forgiven Rajiv his decision to send peace-keeping forces into northern Sri Lanka.

Nationalism and liberalisation (1991-1999)

Congress won a clear victory in the 1991 June elections. **Narasimha Rao**, a native of Andrha Pradesh in southeast India, became Prime Minister. Within two years his liberalisation campaign (tax cuts, encouragement of foreign investment, devaluation of the rupee) managed to boost the economy. But while middle-class India discovered the new-found joys of consumerism, rural India lagged a long way behind. In December 1992, armed right-wing Hindu

M. Deville/Gamma

Sonia Gandhi and her daughter on an electoral poster

extremists destroyed the **Ayodhya** mosque, causing a wave of violence in its aftermath (at least 700 killed) and very real fears about a possible civil war between Hindus and Moslems. Taking advantage of the tense atmosphere and weariness with the Congress Party, the **BJP** ("Bharatiya Janata Party" or "Indian People's Party") whose credibility was on the rise, carried off several regional elections, gaining a foothold in the local government of Delhi, Rajasthan, Uttar Pradesh, Gujurat, among others. Even though it was to become the largest party represented in Parliament following the May 1996 elections, it failed to form a viable government. For a year, a left-wing coalition government (led by HD Gowda then by IK Gujral) took the reins, but the investigation into Rajiv Gandhi's death was to compromise the DMK Tamil organisation, whose support was vital to the coalition. The latter fell in the autumn of 1997.

In spring 1998, new elections saw the relatively clear victory of the BJP. **Atal Behari Vajpayee**, the party's most credible member, took the head of a coalition government. In May of the same year, India once again carried out nuclear tests at **Pokaran** in the Rajasthan desert. Pakistan immediately followed suit. Although tensions were lower between the two countries, the economic climate was rocky and inflation high. Local elections in November 1998 witnessed the downfall of the BJP and the return of Congress, notably in Rajasthan and Delhi, but the Hindu party nonetheless retained central power. Its position however grew more and more insecure. A few months later, the Tamil DMK withdrew its support of the BJP and the coalition government promptly collapsed. **Sonia Gandhi**, Congress president since 1998, stood for election in **September 1999**, but growing tensions on the Kashmir border were favourable to the BJP, whose firm position regarding Pakistan reassured electors. The 24-party coalition, led by the BJP, took the majority of votes and Atal Behari Vajpayee was once again elected Prime Minister.

INSTITUTIONS

India is a federation of 25 states and seven territories, including Delhi and the former French and Portuguese possessions (Pondichery, Daman and Diu). The State of Rajasthan is itself divided into some thirty districts, each named after its capital city (Jaipur, Udaipur, Jodhpur).

R. Marca

Indian flag

A federal constitution

Officially proclaimed on January 26 1950 (Republic Day), the **Constitution** created the Indian Union or Bharat, a democratic, federal, secular republic. The constitution defines the institutions and their role, both centrally and regionally.

Central government, or federal government, is in Delhi. It has sole responsibility for defence, foreign affairs, currency, etc. The **President**, head of executive power, is elected for five years by an electoral college (composed of members of federal government and state legislatures). In reality his role is negligible (except in times of crisis), because real executive power is in the hands of the **Prime Minister** and his cabinet. The head of the parliamentary majority is automatically the Prime Minister. Ministers are appointed by the President on recommendation of the Prime Minister.

Legislative power belongs to the **federal parliament** which is made up of two houses. The upper house, or **Rajiya Sabha** (Council of State) has some 250 members elected by state legislatures, 12 of whom are appointed by the President. It ratifies legislation voted by the **Lok Sabha** (House of the People), this lower house comprises some 545 members elected by democratic elections every five years. (Rajasthan has 25 seats in the *Lok Sabha*.)

The High Court acts as a check on legislative power. Independent of government, it is the guardian of the constitution and arbitrates in conflicts between central government and the States, or between States.

Local government, or State government, resides in the capital of each State, and is responsible for local affairs, health, agriculture, etc. Power is organised on the same lines as federal government. The Governor, appointed by the President, has no direct executive power, which is in the hands of the Chief Minister (head of the majority party) and his cabinet. Legislative power belongs to one or two houses depending on the State. The lower house or Legislative Assembly *(Vidhan Sabha)* is elected democratically on the same day as elections to the *Lok Sabha*).

Presidential Rule can be declared by the president if he or she considers that order and safety can no longer be guaranteed within a State. The local assembly is then dissolved and the running of the State is entrusted to the Governor of that state.

Administration is the responsibility of the **Indian Administrative Service** (IAS), whose top civil servants are part of an elite. In villages, administration is carried out by town councillors, called **panchayat**.

The economy

Over 75 % of Rajasthanis live in the country. This percentage, slightly higher than in the rest of India (70 %) illustrates the preponderance of the role of agriculture within the State's economy. The maharajas derive the majority of their revenue from taxes paid by peasants and tradespeople; hardly any have invested in industry, thereby leaving Rajasthan sorely behind the rest of the other more well-developed States. Today it is still one of the least developed regions of India.

Demographic strength

As of 2000, India, the second most populated country in the world after China, had 1 billion inhabitants. This population increases every year by some 18 million. Its density varies widely (average of 288 inhabitants per sqkm), from almost deserted regions such as the Thar Desert to the densely inhabited coastal regions of Kerala where it reaches 800 inhabitants per sqkm. Rajasthan's statistics are modest in comparison: a population of 50 million and an average density of 160 inhabitants per sqkm.

Living traditions

The most fertile and the most populated areas of the state are in the east and south. In most cities the majority of middle-class Hindus have adopted the "two children per family" policy, hence a birth-rate of 29 per thousand. However in Moslem culture (8 % of Rajasthan's population), large families are frequent, even in urban contexts. In rural areas, ignorance of contraceptive techniques and the deep-rooted desire for a son (who will traditionally remain with his parents and

An avenue in the old district of Jaipur

B. Perousse/HOA QUI

care for them) are behind the large families (where the birth-rate is 35 per thousand). The birth of a girl continues to evoke negative reactions. The **dowry system** *(see Daily Life, p 61)* partly explains why there are fewer women than men (913 per thousand men in Rajasthan compared to 929 per thousand throughout the rest of India), and the infanticide of baby girls unfortunately remains a reality.

Monsoons vs. Agriculture

Rural life in India remains precarious, conditioned by the monsoons and handicapped by weak infrastructures.

Agriculturally top-heavy

Plagued by an arid climate, Rajasthan's agriculture has remained traditional and for the most part outmoded. **Millet** is the most widespread cereal crop due to its hardy, undemanding nature and ripening season of just three to four months. The most common species in Rajasthan are *bajra* ("mil" in Africa), which grows in the driest areas, and *jowar* (sorgho), which prefers more humid conditions. Both are grown during the rainy season, from June to October. In semi-arid zones, such crops are combined with chick peas and oilseeds (groundnuts, sesame, mustard). In irrigated zones, to these can also be added lentils, corn and barley. The rich black soil of the well-watered **Hadoti** lava (in the southeast) make richer crops possible (wheat, corn, rice, sugarcane, cotton), with two harvests a year. Rajasthan's overriding agricultural problem is lack of fresh water: the groundwater is saline and rainfall insufficient. Irrigation systems remain few and far between, despite the construction of the **Indira Gandhi Canal**, or Rajasthan Canal, that has transformed the desert area it irrigates.

Rajasthan has to import rice and vegetables from neighbouring states. Semi-nomadic camels, cattle and sheep are allowed to graze on all non-cultivated land and by the roadsides, because proper grazing land, as such, is almost nonexistent: agricultural yield is low, thereby forcing farmers to cultivate every last centimetre of available land. Cattle destroy precious vegetation for little benefit. However the issue of whether animal husbandry should in fact persist, although often questioned by agronomists, is never broached in villages. Cows produce milk, albeit in small quantities, and their manure is a precious substitute for firewood in a region so poor in forests.

Industry

Rajasthanis at the origins of Indian capitalism

Rajasthan, on the traditional route of the **caravans** between the Middle East and southern Asia and between the ports of Gujurat and Delhi, has produced particularly successful merchants and bankers, most of whom were from the *Banya* (trades people) communities, both Jain and Hindu. Towards the end of the 19C, the arrival of the British and the advent of new trade routes spelled the end of the caravans. The Shekhawati *Banyas* (northeastern Rajasthan), reputed to be clever and enterprising, set out to make their fortunes leaving the isolated Rajasthani desert behind them. They settled in the ports of the Indian Empire, where they began to be known as **"marwari"** *(see p 248)*. They were behind some of India's largest industrial firms (Birla, Goenka, Bajaj, Poddar, Modi, etc). Two other communities which also contributed, with the Marwari, to the development of modern Indian capitalism and who today control the majority of India's industrial concerns (around 80 %), are the Jains, often from Rajasthan (Jain, Mahindra, Mafatlal, Dalmia, Walchand, etc) and the Parsis (Tata, Godrej, Mody, etc).

Colonial legacy

During their occupation of India, the British sought to develop sectors which were both profitable in trade terms and which didn't compete with British manufactured goods. This led them to encourage the production of raw materials (cotton, silk, tea, etc) to the detriment of local industry and crafts which were practically asphyxiated. When the British left India in 1947, some of the country was nonetheless left a good road, rail and port infrastructure, a unified administration, a rigorously educated elite, together with a few major industries. The majority of the country however, and Rajasthan with it, remained sorely under-developed.

The success of the Birla

Natives of the little city of Pilani in Shekhawati, the Birla family symbolises the success of the "marwari" businessmen. Shiv Narayan Birla is thought to have left northern Rajasthan on camel in 1857 for Ahmedabad (in the current State of Gujurat), then in its heyday, before reaching the port of Bombay (now Mumbai). His descendants made their fortunes from the cotton industry. The Birla group has since extended its activities to a wide number of sectors (finance, insurance, press, etc). Ghanshyam Das Birla (1894-1983) provided financial support for several of Mahatma Gandhi's projects to aid the untouchables and develop rural areas and this philanthropic ethic remained strong in his family who had temples and schools built in several Indian towns.

Indian socialism and liberalism

After Independence, **Nehru** embarked on a vast national project to develop heavy industry, electricity and agriculture, but progress was severely hampered both by the delicate border situation and by the degree of backwardness into which the country had fallen. **Indira Gandhi** adopted the socialist model (nationalisations and advantages for the public sector). **Rajiv Gandhi**, in power from 1984-1989, attempted to implement a modern economy, but it was not until 1991 that any real liberal measures, so awaited by business, saw the light of day. **Narasimha Rao**, with the blessing of the International Monetary Fund, devalued the rupee, making it convertible, abolished certain State monopolies, enabled foreign investors to invest in Indian companies and awarded expatriate Indians tax rebates (NRI) to encourage them to invest in India. Little by little, multinational corporations began to take an interest in the country. However, eight years after the first measures, results are far from clear cut. While towns had no compunction about adopting the consumerist system, administrative hassles, political instability and weak infrastructure continue to discourage many potential investors. In addition, the disparity between rich and poor continues to grow, creating an ever-growing estrangement between urban and rural inhabitants.

Textiles, tourism and crafts

The main economic sectors in Rajasthan are **textiles** (cotton and synthetic), **cement** (general trend throughout India), and **marble** and **sugar** production. The state is banking more and more on **tourism** and **craft** activities, which can be developed both in towns and in the countryside. Every year, three-quarters of the two million or so tourists visiting India also stop in Rajasthan. With a good hotel network, the region is currently actively promoting itself abroad. Crafts, the majority of which are made for export, enable the creation of jobs in isolated areas, which are unlikely to be the target of multinational corporations for many years yet.

ART AND ARCHITECTURE

The incalculable number of palaces, forts and *haveli* (merchant dwellings) undoubtedly explains much of the popularity of the Rajasthan-Delhi-Agra trio. Visitors may however be surprised to discover that only very few remains of ancient Hindu art still exist in the area. This is due to the turbulent past of northern India and the consequence of repeated looting and pillaging. As early as the 11C, Moslem invaders set about razing any monument or building that failed to comply with Islam. Many Hindu and Jain sanctuaries were laid waste under the reign of the sultans of Delhi (12C-16C), followed by Emperor Aurangzeb. No pre-18C temples exist in the holy cities of Mathura or Pushkar and even less in the former capitals of the empire, Delhi or Agra. It is almost a miracle that a few remaining statues dating from the Kushana period (2C-3C) have emerged unscathed from these ordeals

Ancient India

The Indus civilisation

The highly-sophisticated urban civilisation, known as the Indus civilisation (the peak of which extended from 2600 BC to 1800 BC), has left pottery, jewellery and baked earthenware figurines, together with some splendid **engraved seals** featuring pictograms and animal silhouettes (most probably religious symbols), illustrating an exceptional gift for observation. A few rare bronze and copper statuettes, including the famous "dancer" from Mohenjo-Daro (in the National Museum in Delhi) have also been discovered. The archaeological heritage left by the subsequent civilisation of invading Aryans (1600-1000 BC) seems quite paltry by comparison. The lack of significant objects or monuments from this era has also considerably reduced any possible speculation relative to "Aryan art".

J.L. Nou/AKG PARIS

Seal from Mohenjo-Daro

Mauryan art

The development of Buddhism and Persian influences would seem to be behind Mauryan art (4C-2C BC). The columns erected by Ashoka (3C BC) intended to spread Buddhist Law (such as those found at Feroz Shah Kotla, in Delhi), illustrate the influence of Hellenised Iran: polished stone, the formal severity of capitals, either bell-shaped or with lateral volutes, stylised palmettte motifs, groups of statically depicted animals… *(see illustration p 17)*. On the other hand, Mauryan animal art, more life-like than Persian, displays a more specifically Indian sense of observation.

Early Buddhist iconography

The first Buddhist monuments materialised during the **Shunga dynasty** (2C-1C BC), which followed that of the Mauryan. Among them, the **stupas**, semi-spherical tumulus, burial or reliquary mounds. Initially very basic, they became gradually more embellished with carvings on the surrounding fences or railings *(vedika)* and on the **toranas** (monumental archways) set into the barriers at the four cardinal points. This sculpture reveals generously-rounded human shapes typical of the Indian love of full-bodied silhouettes, together with a meticulous sense of detail. Naturalistic scenes, still full of life, depict Buddha's life. The latter is not represented as such, but symbolised: umbrella, throne, *svastika* (swastika), *harma* wheel, footprints... This resulting iconographic library was in turn adopted by Hindu sculptors.

The **yaksha** and **yakshini**, protective genies and nymphs, are associated with fertility. They are depicted carrying royal fly-swatters or as seductive beauties, languorously draped over the branch of a tree. These Buddhist genies can also be found in the form of **gandharva** and **apsaras** in Brahmin and Jain iconography *(see "Rankapur" p 329)*.

Mithunas, entwined lovers, symbolise fertility. Later on in Brahmin temples, they come to symbolise the mystical fusion of soul and god. They are also felt to symbolise Tantric thought, whereby the female force (energy or *shakti*) is dominant and alone has the power to move the dormant male force to action. Yet another interpretation is that they represent the purely carnal union of devotees with *devadasi* (sacred dancers, who are thought to have also doubled as prostitutes).

The **naga** and **nagini**, water genies, are represented in Brahmin iconography with a man or woman's torso, terminating in a snake.

The **makara**, aquatic monster, part crocodile, part elephant and part fish, is associated with water fertility. He becomes the "vehicle" of the goddess Ganga (Ganges), who, with her counterpart, the goddess Yamuna (mounted on a tortoise) is depicted at the entrance to Brahmin sanctuaries.

The **vahana** are animals nestling at the feet of the genies and nymphs. In Brahmin iconography, they become the gods' "vehicles", each god having his or her own *vahana* which symbolises them (thus the bull Nandi of Shiva).

Gandharan art and the Mathura school

The **Kushan** dynasty (1C-3C AD) saw the emergence of two schools: the Mathura school and the "Greco-Buddhist" school of **Gandhara** (Afghanistan and Pakistan). The Gandharan school was apparently the first to depict Buddha in human form. This figurative revolution gave rise to a whole new iconography that has marked Buddhist art up until the present day. The face of the "Enlightened One" acquired its distinctive features: elongated ear lobes, protuberance on the skull, neck with three-circular folds... He was often represented draped in a heavy monastic garment, covering both shoulders like a toga. At **Mathura**, on contact with Indian art, this garment became flimsier and revealed a bare right shoulder. The face became more rounded and the lips fleshier.

J.L. Nou/AKG Paris

Buddha. Kushan art of the Mathura school (2C AD)

Gupta classicism

The depiction of Buddha underwent a further transformation during the reign of the Guptas (4-6C): the silhouette under the folded robe grew taller while his face became more

distinguished and his expression more serene, as artists sought to achieve a classical harmony and purity of forms. At the same time a canon emerged of **asana**, attitudes and hand gestures, **mudra**, that subsequently influenced Brahmin sculpture.
Parallel to this, the *tirthankara* of the Jain religion began to evolve on the same lines as the Buddha model, depicted either standing or sitting in the lotus position, but devoid of any expression or individuality as the saintly figures retreat into a sublime conformity of expression. Brahmin sculpture in the meantime developed, endowing its divinities with definite strength of character and authority, yet retaining their humanity and grace. Standing figures began to illustrate the famous **three-body bends pose** *(tribhanga)*, in which the head is slightly tilted at an opposite angle to the torso and hips sway voluptuously *(see illustration p 34)*.

The temple

See architectural illustrations p 42.

Mountains and caves

Based on sacrifice, primitive Brahminism involved no community rituals so there was no need for communal places of worship. Furthermore, Brahmin temples, built around an altar, were not intended for mankind but for gods, whose dwelling they were. Very little is known about the early wooden or bamboo shrines, all the more so as the science of architecture, considered a sacred and esoteric doctrine, is traditionally passed on orally and any rare remaining manuscripts, still in existence today, are jealously guarded by priestly architects. Mountain symbolism, the prototype of which is **Mount Meru**, abode of gods and axis of the world, is a distinctive feature of temple architecture. Mountains are represented by a tower raised above the shrine. The latter's square-design is considered to be a perfect shape and to symbolise the heavens. Its small dimensions evoke a womb-cave, meeting point of gods and men. The pyramid structure, so typical of Hindu temples, is visible throughout the whole subcontinent.

The Nagara or Indo-Aryan temple

The first temples built of permanent materials date from around the 6C. Each course of brick or stone was corbelled out over the previous one, permitting the construction of ever higher towers. In southern India, these took the form of triangular pinnacles (Dravidian style), whereas in the north, they are more circular (*nagara* or Indo-Aryan style).
Until the 10C, *nagara*-style temples consisted of a single element: an inner shrine or womb chamber **(garbha-griha)**, the abode of the god and place of sacrifice, was set on a base, above which rose a circular spire, **shikhara**. A door opened into the inner sanctum which held an image of the god. At the beginning of the 10C, a square outer hall was added, the **sabha-mandapa** (meeting room), *mukhashala* or simply *mandapa*. This primitive design became more sophisticated with the addition of an ambulatory passage around the inner shrine and of halls and vestibules on the axis defined by the inner sanctum and outer *sabha-mandapa*. A small shrine, opposite the temple, also frequently housed the god's "vehicle" (Nandi the bull or Garuda the bird).
At this time, exuberant ornamental sculpture and **high relief** carving began to invade the outer and inner walls, with the exception of the *garbha-griha*.

Apsara of the temple at Menal

The Jain temple

Jain sanctuaries can be distinguished from Brahmin temples by both the quantity of ornamental sculpture and by the venerated image in the inner sanctum, except in Gujarat and Rajasthan, where a specific form of Jain temple architecture developed. The temple was set in a rectangular courtyard, lined with alcoves, each of which housed the statue of a meditating *tirthankara*. The temple was composed of an inner shrine, surrounded on three sides by porticos and hypostyle halls (whose roof is supported by columns), leaving them exposed to the outer world to a far greater extent than their Hindu counterparts. Some typically Jain halls *(mandapa)* have pillars which support a false or flat dome, obtained by corbelled masonry courses *(see p 324)*. Other distinctive features of Jain temples are the exclusive use of white marble and the incredible profusion of carving, the intricacy, transparency and fluidity of which have no equal.

Moslem architecture

See architectural illustrations p 42.

Indo-Moslem art (13C-16C)

The first act of the Moslem troops who invaded northwestern India at the end of the 12C, was to destroy all temples and colleges of Sanskrit, which they replaced with mosques and *madrasa* (Koranic schools), hence the scarcity of ancient Hindu temples still intact in the north. Islamic law, which forbids any representation of living creatures, was to call a halt to the development of Indian figurative sculpture. Nonetheless, Moslem architecture introduced new forms that were to breathe fresh life into local art. The invaders, of Turkish and Monghol blood and Arabic-Persian culture, brought with them the architectural Seljuk tradition. They replaced the entablature and the corbelling of Indian architecture with **keel arches** (which in India became ogee arches) and **domes on pendentives**. And the craftsmanship of exuberant Indian sculptors – similar to the Persian painters' distaste for empty space – was employed in ornamentation, dearly loved by Moslems: human and animal figures were replaced by superbly calligraphed Koranic inscriptions, complex geometric filigree work, derived from star-shaped polygons or by arabesques and undulating tracery.

Thus the early Indo-Moslem style combined the Moslem love of geometry and linear forms with the decorative excesses characteristic of Indian art. At a later stage, during the Tughluq dynasty (14C), architecture became more austere and adopted more traditional "Iranian" forms. Other characteristic features of Indo-Moslem decoration were multicoloured red sandstone façades inlaid with white marble or porcelain tiles, blind arcades of *mihrabs* and **muqarna (honeycomb of arches)**, alcoves used to support corbelled galleries and which rapidly evolved into a fretwork of interleaved arches whose function was purely decorative.

Mughal art (16C-19C)

The first two centuries of the Mughal era constitute a period of incomparable artistic achievement. Iranian forms dominate the reigns of the first sovereigns (Babur and Humayun). The **iwan** of Sassanid origins (vaulted space) and the **pishtaq** (large doorway into the *iwan*) make their entrance and become unavoidable architectural features. The third Mughal, Akbar, imposed his eclectic taste in architecture as elsewhere, combining, as at Fatehpur Sikri, Persian elements (arch, *iwan*, clearly-ordered volumes) with Indian characteristics (red sandstone, pillar and entablature, canopy and corbel, extravagant ornamentation, etc). The reign of Jahangir marked the return to a more traditional Persian style of architecture, bordering on classicism under Shah Jahan (who built the Taj Mahal). It was characterised by the adoption of the **multifoil arch** and a distinctly Persian decorative repertory, marrying floral motifs with outlines of flasks and vases and by the overwhelming use of **white marble**, into which fine stones were inlaid using the Italian **pietra dura** *(see p 195)* technique. The overall result, while highly elegant, in fact conveyed less energy and strength than that expressed by earlier architecture. Under Aurangzeb, Moslem architecture declined: the lines became more baroque and the overall clarity was diluted in a surfeit of decoration. In the 18C, this decline accelerated: superfluous ornamentation, elaborate plasterwork…

Moslem monuments

The mosque *(masjid)* is a place of assembly and prayer. Each city possesses its own **juma masjid** (Friday mosque), where the imam preaches to the assembled community.

The design of Indian mosques was based on that of the central courtyard mosque that emerged in 12C Iran: a **vast courtyard** with a central pool for ablutions, surrounded on three sides by cloisters. The fourth side, facing west (direction of Mecca), is closed by a **prayer room**, flanked by **minarets** *(minar)*. The room's façade is pierced with arches, of which the central, most important one, leads into the **mihrab**, an alcove which indicates the direction of Mecca *(qibla)*. The *mihrab* is empty but profusely ornamented in such a way that one's vision is drawn inwards, as if to pierce the wall and take flight towards Qaaba. There is no furniture in the prayer room, with the possible exception of a **minbar** (pulpit) to the right of the *mihrab*, from which the preacher delivers his sermon. On the floor the limits of each person's appointed praying place are often visible. Sometimes, part of the room is given over to a **dikka**, set aside for women.

The arcades or cloisters around the courtyard often house a **madrasa**, the school where the precepts of the Koran are taught in Arabic.

The mausoleum is the abode of the deceased, who lies, with his or her head facing Mecca, shown by a *mihrab* in the centre of the *qibla* (west-facing wall). Early Indo-Moslem tombs *(rauza)*, called **gumbad** or *gumbaz* (domes), were square-shaped monuments, covered by a dome on pendentives. The slightly-pointed semi-spherical dome was sometimes set on a drum. At the time of the Sayyid and Lodi sultans (15C) an octagon-shaped tomb, rising from a drum and surrounded by little kiosks *(chhatri)*, a legacy of Hindu architecture, were added. In **1565**, a Persian architect designed a new type of tomb, of monumental dimensions for Humayun, which was to mark a break with past traditions. The funeral chamber, covered with a slightly bulb-shaped dome, was buttressed by four secondary chambers. The whole edifice was set on a raised platform within a walled garden. All tombs built after 1565, including the Taj Mahal, take their inspiration from Humayun's mausoleum. Interestingly, the Mughals adopted a concept common to the Steppe peoples, of a double burial place; a commemorative cenotaph was placed in a central chamber, but the real burial place was in an underground chamber or secret place. In addition, according to Tartar tradition, they erected their tombs during their lifetimes.

The Mughal palace, set behind ramparts, comprised administrative buildings (archives, etc), a public audience hall **(diwan-i am)** for formal receptions and the emperor's private apartments. The latter were divided into two distinct sections: the men's quarters, **mardana** and the **zenana**, for the wives and concubines, which could only be entered by women, eunuchs and the emperor. The *mardana* comprised a set of pavilions arranged around a garden, possibly linked by a covered gateway, and completed by mobile elements: awnings, canopies and tents. The main buildings also held the private audience hall **(diwan-i khas)** where friends and council ministers were received, the **sheesh mahal**, a chamber covered in convex mirrors designed to reflect and magnify the flickering lamp light, and **hammams**. A typical Mughal pavilion would have been designed around a hypostyle hall open on three sides. These openings were shielded by elaborate stone screens or **jali**, intricately carved screens, often of hexagonal motifs. The shade and the breezes they created would not only keep rooms cool, but also enabled the women in *purdah* to observe, without being seen, what was going on in the men's quarters. Mughal pavilions had either flat roofs or arched **Bengali**, also called "half-moon", roofs, borrowed from Bengali architecture.

The Mughal garden, or **chahar bagh** (quadripartite garden) provided both relief against the dust and the arid landscape and was designed to refresh and relax, conveying an image of Paradise. Introduced into India by the first Mughal, Babur, it is walled and typically features two canals of running water with little fountains, dividing the garden into four equal parts, planted with a profusion of star or octagonal-shaped clumps of flowers.

Itimad ud-Daula's mausoleum at Agra

Rajput architecture

See architectural illustrations p 42.

While they remained fiercely attached to Hindu tradition, as early as the end of the 16C, the Rajput princes, who for the most part pledged allegiance to the emperor, were to adopt the architecture, taste for decoration and opulence of the Mughals.

Forts and palaces

Unlike the Mughals who built their palaces in the plains, the Rajputs preferred setting their forts on hilltops, like eagle's nests keeping watch over the valleys below. Although from the outside, the stark, impressive walls illustrate the Rajputs' military preoccupations, once inside, the visitor is often stunned by the elegance of their graceful palaces divided into *mardana* and *zenana*, around inner courtyards. From the end of the 16C, the Mughal influence is visible in the decorative style: multifoil arches, bulbous columns, flower and flask motifs... In eastern India, the Mughal influence was stronger, leading to the construction of flat-roofed pavilions in the purest Mughal style, but in the deserted western regions, the well-entrenched Rajput style continued to remain predominant. Among the most distinctive aspects of the Rajput style is the **jharokha**, a projecting balcony screened by a *jali* and covered with a half-dome or a "Bengali" roof, with sharp, over-hanging gables. The **chhatri,** a little pavilion crowned with a semi-spherical dome and a sharply-protruding awning or overhanging roof, is another immediately recognisable Rajput architectural element.

The **Durbar Hall** (reception rooms where the lord convened his assembly of nobles or *durbar*) was often richly decorated, with a play of mirrors enhanced by coloured cut-glass mosaics *(see illustration p 215)*, porcelain Delft tiles brought by caravans and vividly coloured frescoes in which human and animal figures prevail, because Hindu Rajasthan did not feel itself compelled to respect the Islamic ban on figurative painting.

The haveli

The rich merchants and nobles of Rajasthan built magnificent family residences or **haveli** in the cities. Those built in the 19C by the Jain merchants of Jaisalmer are among the most beautiful: in particular the profusion of finely sculpted *jharokha* and *jali*. The Shekhawati *haveli*, less flamboyant architecturally, are famous for their murals.

Havelis were built around two inner courtyards, **chowk**, onto which all the residence's rooms opened, the upper floors featuring a gallery that went right round the courtyard. The first *chowk* was the public area. The *bhaitak* (reception room), equivalent of the palace *durbar hall*, opened onto the courtyard via three doors or archways. It served to welcome visitors who were not part of the family, who would have been seated on thin mattresses covered in white sheets, made more comfortable with thick cushions. The second courtyard was for the family and close friends.

The cenotaph (burial place)

The mortal remains of Rajputs were incinerated according to Hindu tradition. However, under the influence of Mughal emperors and sultans who had tombs erected, the Rajput princes took to building cenotaphs on the place of their incineration. Hence the common sight in Rajasthan of little canopied pavilions,

S. Held

Krishna and the gopis, Bikaner Fort

composed of a raised platform and four or eight pillars upholding a dome, called **chhatris,** which means both umbrella and "*kshatriya*" (the protection of an umbrella is a royal privilege, *see p 289*).

The dome was placed over a flat corbelled cupola, built using the same technique employed in the *mandapa* of Jain temples.

Occasionally the *chhatri* also housed a commemorative stele with a sculpted image of the dead person, often riding a horse (*see p 294*), while another stele might depict a feminine silhouette or footprints, thus evoking the sacrifice of wives who committed *sati*, throwing themselves onto their husband's funeral pyre.

The well

Given the arid desert climate, water has always been held almost sacred and consequently, building a well or a reservoir for the community was considered to be a pious act. Rajasthan, together with Gujarat and Kamataka, has the largest number and widest variety of these ornate edifices financed by rich donors. Their ingenious constructors endeavoured to find the best solutions for easily reaching the water table, whatever its depth, and then preventing it from evaporating: a natural or artificial lake, covered underground reservoir or drilled well, etc. The variety of forms and names, is baffling. The most common name is **baori** for stepwells (*baoli* in Delhi), but *kund, vav, johad* (in Shekhawati) are also used. A number of superb examples can be found in the little town of Bundi. Some wells in Shekhawati can be seen from far away since they are covered by a raised platform with canopied kiosks as well as two or four towers, to which systems of pulleys are attached, enabling vast water-skins to be raised with the help of oxen.

Miniature painting

The tradition of miniature painting in Rajasthan dates back to the 11C. At this time, the Jain community added illustrations to their sacred texts, written on narrow bands of palm leaves, then on paper (a technique imported from Persia in the 14C). Miniature illustrations in red and yellow were inserted into the text: lacking in perspective, they concentrated above all on clear, precise lines. In the 16C, blue pigments became available in India. From then on, the backgrounds of miniatures, up until then always red, became blue.

The Mughal school

In 1555, Humayun's retinue included two painters of the Shiraz school, a souvenir of his exile at the Persian court, who began to initiate Indian artists into the techniques of Persian miniature painting. When Akbar founded the first state workshop of painting, these two masters were appointed to run it. Indian miniatures thus gradually adopted a Persian style. However, Indian artists, gifted with an innate sense of observation, rapidly broke free of the idealism and traditional Persian calligraphic drawing techniques. They added their taste for naturalism, combined with a spontaneity and sense of detail, which, encouraged by Akbar's decision to lift the ban on figurative representation (human and animal), led them to create works of art of a realism as yet unheard of. The precision, delicate drawing and subtle use of colour produced art that leaves a general impression of harmony. These Mughal artists were to excel in the art of portrait painting, to which they added genuine psychological insight *(see p 19)*.

Rajput schools

The Mughal court's pictorial style was to spread rapidly through Rajasthan, influencing local workshops (particularly in the field of perspective). The latter did not, however, succumb to slavish imitation and retained their quality of refreshing naivety. Despite differences in style between the Rajput schools, called *kalam* ("quill and brush"), there remains a series of common traits: attention to thousands of anecdotal details, a taste for bright, vivid colours, stylised forms outlined in black and an overall simplicity of line, all of which is set on a coloured background.

At the close of the 17C, Emperor Aurangzeb, a bigot and an iconoclast, dismissed large numbers of painters, who turned to the Rajput princes for work, thereby helping to make this epoch the apogee of Rajput painting. The oldest miniatures come from **Mewar** (16C-18C). The 17C and 18C were the heyday of the **Marwar** (Jodhpur and Bikaner) School, heavily influenced by the Mughal style, then of the **Bundi** and **Kota** schools *(see p 358)*, and of the **Kishangarh** school (Ajmer region) which focused on Krishna. The **Jaipur** *kalam*, also heavily inspired by Mughal art, was to emerge later (18-19C) *(see p 191)*.

Rajput miniature art is deeply symbolic, expressed in analogies and parallels. Thus, changing times of the day or the seasons are reflected in the sentiments and psychological states of the characters, whose moods are depicted by *ragas* (musical modes) and also in poems. Different series of miniatures, such as the **raga mala** ("wreath of musical modes"), the **barah mesa** ("twelve months") or the **nayaka nayika** ("the hero and heroine"), reveal the infinite parallels between these complementary art forms. Religion remains the primary theme of Rajput painting, even if the life of Krishna, depicted as a young herdsman head over heels in love with Radha and the *gopis*, might be construed as simply a pretext for illustrating the sentiments of love and desire, as the god becomes a *nayaka* and his lovers innumerable *nayika*. Apart from religious themes, portraits of powerful nobles, snippets of life inside the palaces, with their feasts and entertainment, hunting scenes in lovingly illustrated landscapes constituted the other main domain of miniature painters at the time. At the end of the 19C, the advent of photography did away with one of the prime raisons d'être of miniature painting – portraits of the sovereign and his court – and little by little the schools disappeared.

British influence

Indo-Saracennic style

Indo-Saracennic art mixed western, Mughal and Rajput influences on the same building with no qualms: domes, *chhatri*, gothic arches and even very British clock towers. The most famous instigator of this hybrid style was **Sir Samuel Swinton Jacob** (1841-1917) *(see p 213)*. An engineer-cum-architect settled in Rajasthan, he would appear to have had a hand in almost every project: Rambagh Palace and the Albert Hall in Jaipur, Lalgarh Palace in Bikaner and Mayo College in Ajmer, to name just a few.

An Art Deco legacy

At the end of the twenties, **Sir Edwin Lutyens**, initially inspired by Sir Samuel's architectural endeavours, designed monuments for the new capital, New Delhi, before returning to a more classical approach: Art Deco was now in vogue. This style was most appreciated by Rajasthan's maharajas who embarked on Art Deco renovation of their palaces, calling upon some of Europe's most talented designers. Umaid Bhawan, the maharaja of Jodhpur's gigantic palace, undoubtedly remains the most extravagant example of this style. It was the work of **H.V. Lanchester** and was one of the world's largest private residences at the time.

Pietra dura at the Taj Mahal, Agra

J.L. Nou/AKG PARIS

Glossary of art and architecture

Apsara	Celestial dancing girl who lives in water, forests, the air...
Arayish	or "goutai". Glossy wall surface made of powdered marble, crushed limestone, egg, yoghurt and honey.
Bagh	Garden.
Baori	Stepwell. Called "baoli" in Delhi.
Bhawan	Building, palace.
Burj	Tower, spire.
Chahar Bagh	Walled Mughal garden, divided into four parts by channels and enclosed by walls.
Chaumukha	Literally "four sides". Refers to the cruciform design of some Jain temples, laid out around a shrine with four openings.
Chhatri	Canopied pavilion or kiosk, crowned with a dome. By extension: cenotaph.
Chowk	Courtyard of a haveli. Square or roundabout.
Dargah	Tomb of a Sufi saint.
Darwaza	"Door" in Urdu. Equivalent of "pol".
Dharmshala	Inn for Hindu or Jain pilgrims.
Diwan-i Am	Public audience hall in palaces.
Diwan-i Khas	Private audience hall.
Durbar	Group of a sovereign's noble vassals. By extension, a Rajput palace's reception hall. Equivalent of the Diwan-i Am.
Gandharva	Heavenly attendant and musician, consort of the "apsaras".
Garbha-griha	Inner shrine of Hindu temples, abode of the god and place of sacrifice, into which only appointed servants are admitted.
Ghat	Steps leading up to water point, used to carry out ritual ablutions and to incinerate bodies.
Gumbad	or "gumbaz". Square-shaped Moslem mausoleum, covered with a dome.
Gurdwara	Sikh temple.
Hammam	Bathroom of Turkish origins.
Haveli	Richly decorated residence of a wealthy family.
Iwan	Vaulted hall or recess, open on one side and closed on the other.
Jali	Lattice or filigree-patterned screen.
Jharokha	Covered protruding balcony supported by brackets.
Linga	Phallic symbol of the god Shiva, often represented with the "yoni", its female counterpart.
Madrasa	Koranic school.
Mahal	"Palace" and by extension, a lavishly decorated chamber.
Mandapa	Hall in Jain and Hindu temples.
Mandir	Temple.
Masjid	Mosque.
Mardana	Men's quarters in "havelis" and palaces.
Minar	Minaret, spire.
Mihrab	Recess in main wall of mosque, showing the direction of Mecca.
Mithuna	Entwined couple, symbol of mystic union.
Muqarna	"Stalactite" formations decorating the underside of a dome or arch.
Panchayatana	Temple with a main sanctuary, surrounded by four smaller shrines.
Pishtaq	Portal of the "iwan".
Pol	Gateway to a city or fort.
Qibla	Direction of Mecca. The "qibla" wall faces West.
Shikhara	Spire erected over a temple's inner sanctum.
Stupa	Semi-spherical reliquary or burial tumulus or mound.
Svastika	Sign of prosperity and good fortune.
Tirthankara	Ascetics who "pass fords" (also called "jina"), of which there are 24.
Torana	Ceremonial porch or archway.
Zenana	Women's quarters in palaces.

Hindu architecture

The Hindu temple (mandir)

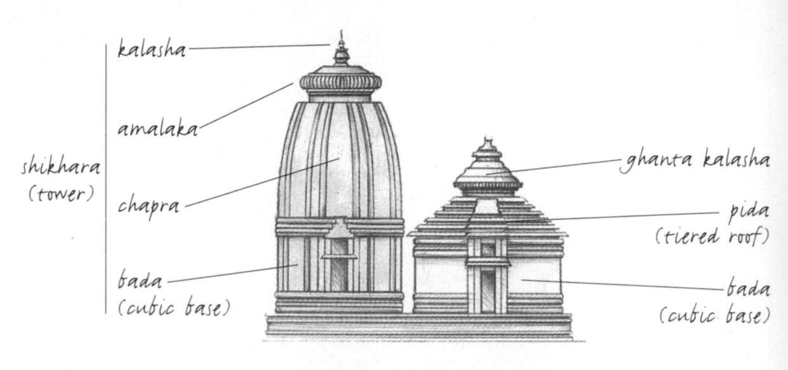

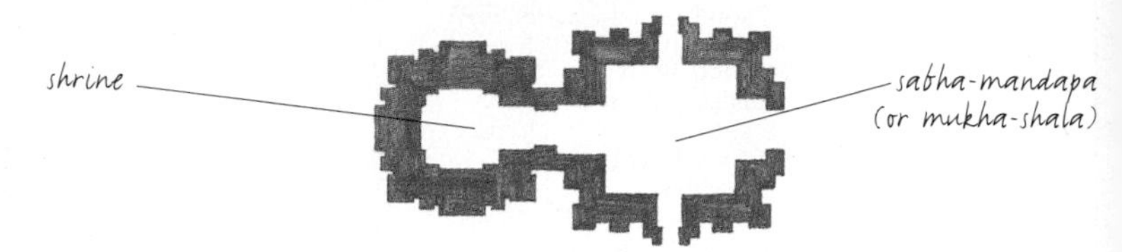

Nagara style temple (Indo-Aryan)

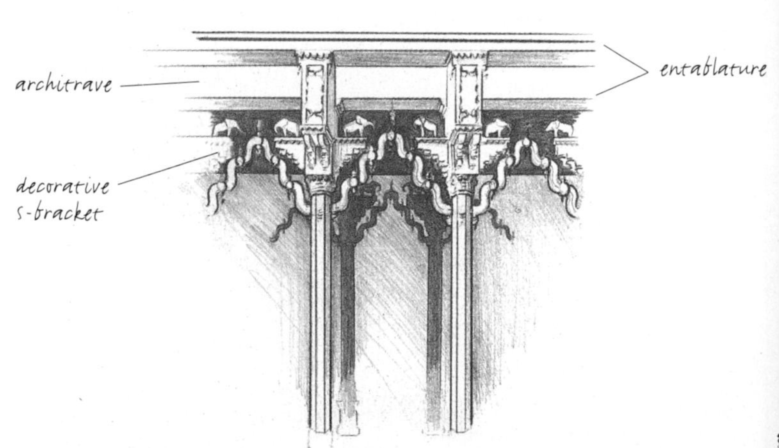

Torana (archway)

Rajput architecture

Façades

JHAROKHA (COVERED BALCONY)

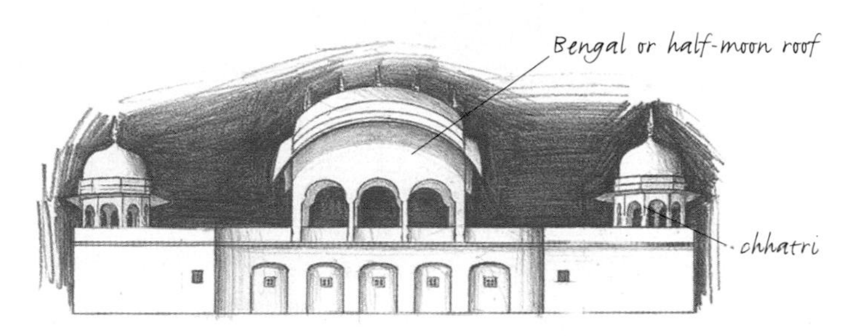

PAVILIONS

The cenotaph

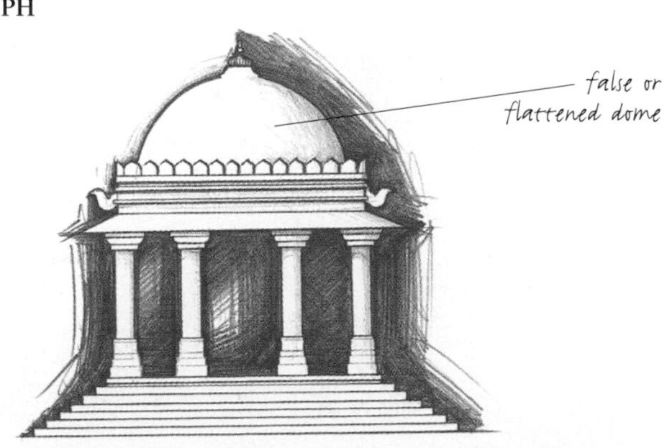

CHHATRI (PAVILION WITH BALDACHIN OR KIOSK WITH DOME)

H. Choimet

Indo-Islamic architecture

The tombs (rauza)

TOMBE OF SULTAN ILTUTMISH
(DELHI, 1235)

TOMB OF THE LODIS PERIOD
(1494)

TOMBE OF ITIMAD UD-DAULA
(AGRA, 1628-1630)

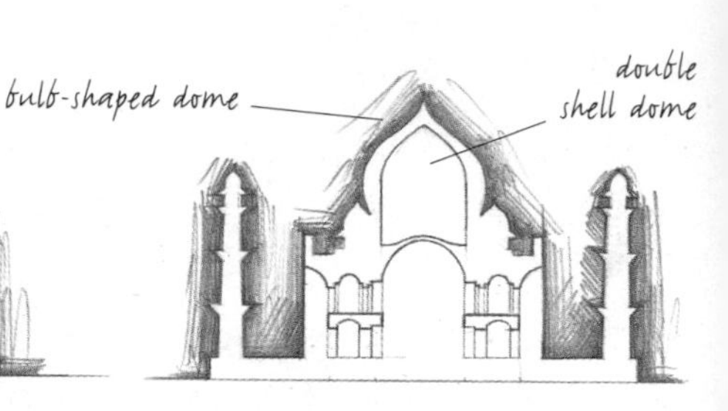

THE TAJ MAHAL
(AGRA, 1632-1644)

The mosque (masjid)

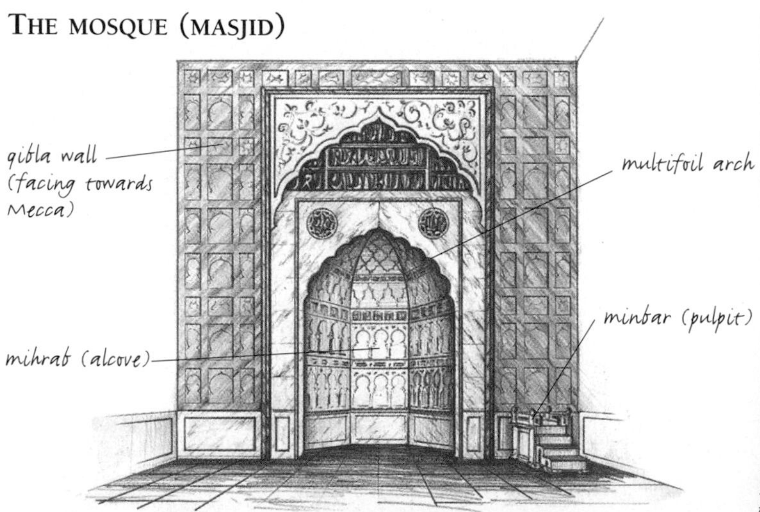

MIHRAB

H. Choimet

OGEE ARCH

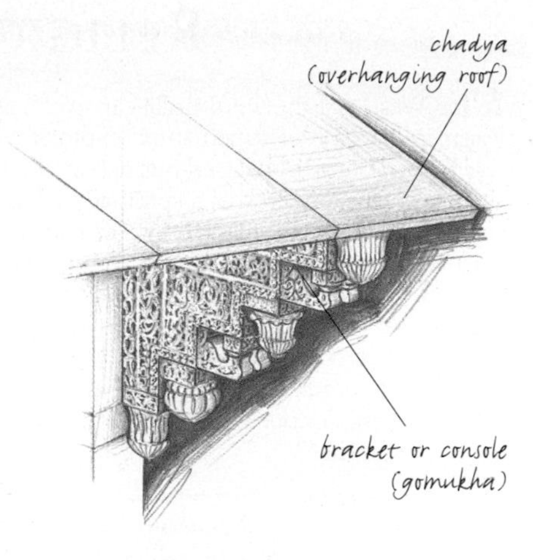

MULTIPOIL ARCH

MUQARNA
(STALACTITE ORNAMENT)

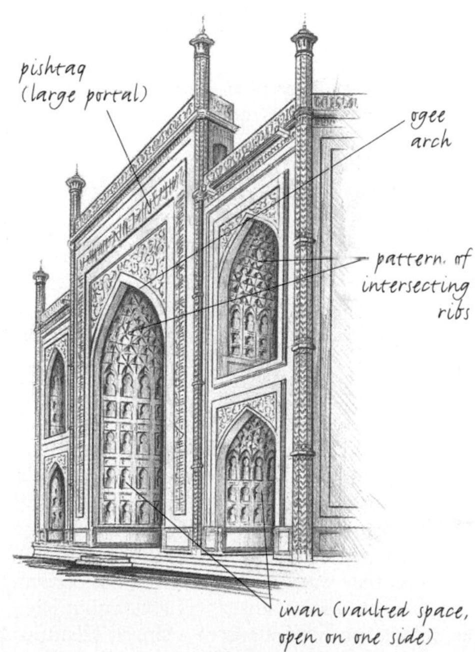

DOOR
(DARWAZA)

H. Choimet

Religions

To the West, just the word India can evoke an image of a nation of mystics and wisemen, capable of supernatural exploits, whose teachings would perhaps be able to turn our own stressed businessmen into paragons of meditation. The idealistic traveller in search of a spiritually-advanced nation may well be surprised, even shocked by the superstition, credulity, fanaticism and inter-religious violence encountered. However, a closer look would reveal that Hinduism is situated on two very distinct planes: one concerns daily life and rituals, while the other encompasses metaphysical reflection on the Absolute. Most Hindus, unable to live on an Absolute plane, where all differences vanish, live ordinary lives, full of contradictions, just like their western counterparts, with the exception of a few *sanyasin*, who have withdrawn from the world and who live in caves and forests.

	Rajasthan Pop 44 million	**Delhi** Pop 9.4 million	**India** Pop 844 million
Hindus	89%	84%	82.4%
Moslems	8%	9%	11.7%
Sikhs	1.5%	4.8%	2%
Jains	1.3%	1%	0.5%
Christians	0.1%	0.9%	2.4%
Buddhists	0.01%	0.05%	0.6%

These are the figures of the latest ten-yearly census (February 1991), although more recently, it was announced that India's total population had reached 1 billion in 1999.

Hinduism

Despite its size and ethnic, linguistic and political diversity, India is a cultural entity with a common base: the Brahmin religion (also called "Hinduism") and its conception of the world. Foreign domination has never succeeded in undermining the vitality of Indian culture, its tales or legends – everything that makes up its inner unity, over and above the apparent disparities.

Hinduism is not, strictly speaking, a religion, but a socio-ethnic-religious system which encompasses all aspects of human life. One of its characteristics is the division of society into hereditary and hierarchical communities (called "castes" by the West). One is a Hindu if born of Hindu parents, one cannot be converted to Hinduism. All the more so, as there is no single dogma or a centralised clergy available to teach or enforce an "orthodox" religion as such. Hindus only have to recognise the division of society into castes, the Brahmins' supremacy and the sacred nature of the *veda* (holy books). Apart from that, they can believe whatever they want, to the extent of not believing in God. Varying conceptions and doctrines, some atheist, cohabit within Hinduism, where they are accepted as different manifestations of a single, identical reality. This sense of relativity and spirit of tolerance and syncretism, from which nothing is excluded and everything assimilated, is characteristic of India.

The caste system

Introduced by the Aryans around 1600-1500 BC, this hierarchical, hereditary system comprises several distinctions which the 16C Portuguese categorised as "caste". The first division is into four **varna** ("colour" or "race"); at the top of the ladder are the **Brahmins** (whose role it is to carry out rites, study and teach), next come the **Kshatriya** (whose mission is to fight and protect), they are followed by **Vaishiya** (merchant class), lastly the **Shudra**, whose role is to serve the former three. This four-varna system does not comprise the **caste-less** ("pariahs", "untouchables" or "Hajijan"), who are generally natives of non-assimilated ethnic groups or tribes at the time of the Aryan invasions (17 % in Rajasthan). This division into *varna* in theory overrides that of the concrete **jati** ("caste through birth"), but the latter is in fact the only one that really counts in India. There are around 3 000 *jatis* in India and Hindus live in their *jati*. The *jati* is a Hindu's homeland, it is where he or she is born, marries and dies. Members of a *jati* share the same outlook, the same type of occupation, the same food, the same rites. Within their own *jati*, Hindus do not run the risk of being polluted by any person or thing less pure than themselves. In fact the whole system of social division which keeps society separated and everyone in their place, is based on **religious notions of pure and impure**, in which ritual and bodily impurities are confused. Anything to do with death (corpses, leather, etc), bodily secretions and impurities (saliva, dirty washing, cut hair...), waste (remains of food, dust), alcohol, etc is considered impure. By extension, any activity requiring contact with that which is impure makes those involved so polluted that they literally become "untouchable". The members of these untouchable *jatis* are least likely to be polluted – already being so to such an extent – so they are able to live much less restricted lives than those of other *jatis*: They are allowed to consume meat and alcohol, widows can remarry, etc. However at the other end of the scale, the Brahmins, the purest *jati*, run the constant risk of pollution, hence the innumerable caste taboos they must respect in order to remain pure.

The Constitution of India does not recognise the caste system. They are nonetheless essential to India's social (marriages, professional relations) and political life. Since Independence, the government has attempted to favour the lower castes (euphemistically known as "scheduled castes and tribes"), of which there are respectively 140 million and 70 million members, by reserving places for them in universities and in local government. Such partiality, however, is felt to sanction rather than weaken the system's survival, giving rise to the jealousy of other castes and even sporadic outbursts of violence.

From Vedism to Hinduism

As soon as they arrived in the sub-continent, some 3 500 years ago, the Brahmins set about formalising the hymns and liturgies brought with them from Iran, which had, up until then, been passed down orally. They comprise the four **Vedas** (knowledge).

The Vedic pantheon is comprised of gods *(deva)* who embody natural forces. It is dominated by **Indra** (god of lightning and war), **Varuna** (who sits at the zenith and sees all), **Agni** (fire) and **Surya** (sun). Around these forces is gathered a whole host of celestial nymphs (**apsaras**), snake-divinities (**naga**) and the gods' enemies (**asura**).

During the later hymns of the *Vedas*, the idea of a supreme being, soul of the world, emerged. This notion was to be developed in the **Bhramana** (around 10C BC), a collection of texts which refined and interpreted the hymns, evolving into

Ramayana and Mahabharata

Composed between the 4C BC and the 4C AD, the "Ramayana" relates the exploits of Rama, 7th incarnation of Vishnu. Driven from his kingdom by palace intrigue, Rama, crown prince of Ayodhya (now in Uttar Pradesh), hid in the forest in the company of his brother and his wife, Sita. The latter was kidnapped by the devil-king, Ravana, who held her prisoner on his island, Lanka. With the help of the loyal Hanuman and his army of monkeys, Rama managed to free Sita and recaptured his throne at Ayodhya. Dating from roughly the same period, the "Mahabharata" recounts the war that occurred between two rival clans of the region of Indraprashta (Delhi): the five Pandava brothers and the Kaurava. The work includes several poems, among which is the masterpiece of philosophy, "Bhagavad Gita".

complex rituals (hence the origins of the name "Brahminism"); the **Upanishad** (10-5C BC), treaties on metaphysical speculation, further completed this work. In the **Purana** (6-2C BC), which relate the lives of the gods, the Vedic hymns lose most of their meaning. Superstition, pre-Aryan beliefs and hero worship all contributed to multiplying the gods – even their arms! – endowing the most popular with fantastic legends. This gave rise to two epic tales, the **Ramayana** and **Mahabharata**, in which the ancient gods of the *Vedas* are relegated to second place and Brahma, Shiva and Vishnu move to the forefront.

In parallel, six philosophical systems (**darshana**), orthodox "points of view", emerged, which were variations on the same basic doctrine developed in the *Vedas*. Among these were **yoga**, a practical discipline of control of the mind and body and the *vedanta* ("end of the Vedas"), a genuine doctrine of pure metaphysics.

Hanuman temple at Galta (Jaipur)

A. Perigot/HOA QUI

Seven key words of Brahminism
(or "Hinduism" as it is now more often known)

Atman	The individual, innermost self or the soul.
Brahman	The Absolute, unique and eternal, supreme cause of the universe. The *Upanishad* developed the concept of identity between *atman* and *brahman*. The ultimate goal of human life is the integration of *atman* into *brahman*.
Dharma	Order which reigns over the universe and the notion of individual duty within this cosmic context.
Maya	The illusion which masks reality and makes the One appear multiple.
Samsara	The transmigration of the individual (*atman*), caught up in the perpetual cycle of reincarnation, from existence to existence.
Karma	The consequence of acts that leads the *atman* into *samsara*. These acts automatically condition the next reincarnation.
Moksha	The final liberation giving freedom from *samsara*. The equivalent of achieving identity between *atman* and *brahman*, and the main preoccupation of all religious and philosophical systems.

The faithful can develop spiritually and attain salvation through different **pathways** (also called *yoga*). Depending on their inclination, they can choose the pathway of philosophical enquiry *(jnana)*, devotion *(bhakti*, *see p 190**)*, good deeds *(karma)* or physical training (*raja yoga* and *hatha yoga*).

A profusion of divinities

The Hindu pantheon is dominated by three gods: **Brahma**, **Vishnu** and **Shiva**. The first, Brahma, emanation of metaphysical Absolute, remains little known. However, Vishnu and Shiva have both become objects of intense cults, the devotees of either god proclaiming that "their" god is the greatest. Despite squabbles between the followers of Vishnu (who paint a v between their eyebrows) and the followers of Shiva (who paint three stripes on their forehead), the three gods continue to remain part of a trinity, **trimurti**, thereby reconciling them in a conveniently established syncretic order. Newcomers should be warned: these gods are neither Three nor any other number! Hindus appear to have a bewildering quantity of names for God (Vishnu, Krishna, among many others), who is represented with a thousand faces, but over and above the variety of names and forms, there exists an eternal, unique God who can be neither named nor represented.

Duty according to the Bhagavad Gita

In the final battle related by the "Mahabharata", Krishna acted as coachman to Arjuna, one of the five Pandava brothers. Before the combat, seeing that his cousins and former friends had joined the enemy ranks, Arjuna hesitated before going into battle. This prompted Krishna to reveal his message to the quaking hero: whatever the situation, one must have confidence in God, remain true to one's own personal "dharma" (duty) and not seek personal gain (independent of the consequences of an action). This philosophical treatise, in 700 verses, comprises the Bhagavad Gita, and is the text most revered by Hindus. It is part of the group of sacred books, including the Vedas and the Upanishad.

Daily rites and modern trends

First thing in the morning, after washing and purifying rituals, Hindus are required to carry out **puja** ("worship") of their personal gods on the family or temple altar: incense sticks are lit, flowers, *ghee* and rice offered and *mantras* (sacred verses) are recited. The most pious

The Hindu triad (trimurti): Brahma-Vishnu-Shiva

In blue, main name of the god and his associated gods

In black, other names and incarnations of the god

Brahma

Creator of the universe and its dual nature. Brahma is represented as a bearded man with four faces, sitting on a lotus flower that emerges from Vishnu-Narayana's navel. He holds a copy of the *Vedas* and a vase of water. He rides a **goose** (*hamsa*).

Sarasvati – Brahma's wife. Goddess of language and knowledge, patron of arts and science. She plays the *vina* and holds a book, a rosary… She rides either a **swan** or a goose.

Vishnu and Brahma

R. Marca

Vishnu

Preserver and restorer. He wears a cylindrical tiara. His attributes are the discus (weapon), conch shell, club and lotus flower. His vehicle is **Garuda**, part-bird (eagle or vulture) and part-man.

Narayana – Represented lying on the snake **Shesha** or **Ananta**, floating on a cosmic ocean between two cycles of creation.

Vishnu's ten main avatars – These are the forms adopted each time he comes to save the earth from destruction: fish (Matsya), tortoise (Kurma), boar (Varaha), lion-man (Narasimha), dwarf (Vamana), Parasurama (Rama with an axe), Rama, Krishna, Buddha and the white horse Kalki (yet to come). The most well-known are:

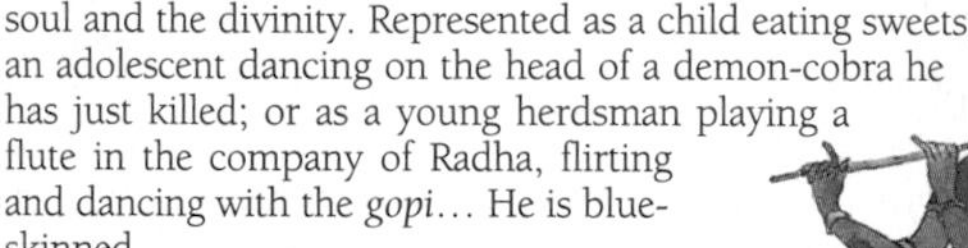

Rama – 7th incarnation. Consort of **Sita**, depicted with bow and arrows.

Krishna (the dark) – 8th incarnation. **Radha's** lover. His trysts with the *gopi* (shepherdesses) symbolise the union of the soul and the divinity. Represented as a child eating sweets; an adolescent dancing on the head of a demon-cobra he has just killed; or as a young herdsman playing a flute in the company of Radha, flirting and dancing with the *gopi*… He is blue-skinned.

Krishna and Radha

R. Marca

Lakshmi (or Shri) – Vishnu's consort. Goddess of fortune and prosperity. She is depicted as a woman framed by two elephants who shower her with water from their raised trunks.

Hanuman – General of the monkey army who helped Rama release Sita, held prisoner by the demon Ravana. He is the perfect follower and loyal servant. Depicted as a monkey or with a man's head and a monkey's tail, he has only two arms, in which he holds a club and a rock.

Shiva

Both destroyer and creator. He is sometimes depicted with three or five heads, seated in meditation, attired in a tiger skin. He has three eyes and his hair is arranged in a coil of matted locks (to lessen the fall of the Ganges when it came to earth) and decorated with a crescent moon. He carries a cobra and a trident (*trishul*), (in the south: a deerskin and an axe) and rides the bull **Nandi**.

Mahadeva (great god) – Creator. He is symbolised by an erect lingam (phallic symbol), over the *yoni* (female genitals).

Nataraja (king of dance) – This god spreads his power throughout the world. He is represented with four arms dancing the cosmic *tandava* dance of destruction and recreation, within a circle of fire, to the beat of a drum in the shape of an hourglass.
Devi (or Mahadevi, the great goddess) – Wife of Shiva and daughter of the Himalaya. Mother-goddess, Shiva's *shakti* (brings him the energy to act).
Durga (the inaccessible) – Demon (*asura*) slayer. Represented as a woman slaying Mahisha, a demon who can be either elephant, giant or buffalo. She can have between eight and ten arms and carries a trident, axe, bow, she rides a **tiger** or a lion.
Kali (the black-skinned) – Destroyer of illusions. Represented as a hideous, threatening black-skinned fury, complete with tongue dripping in blood. Wearing a necklace made of snakes and human skulls, she brandishes a sword, trident, fire and the severed head of a giant.
Parvati (mountain dweller) – Shiva's chaste wife. Depicted either seated in state next to her husband on Mount Kailasha, or alone on a lotus. Accompanied by the bull Nandi.
Gauri (the light-skinned) – The matron of marriage, associated with harvests.
Ganesha (or Ganapati) – Son of Shiva and Parvati, this chubby elephant-headed divinity is god of knowledge, overcoming all obstacles. He holds a bowl of sweetmeats, an elephant spur, a rosary, the *Mahabharata* (it was recited to him)... He rides a **rat**, who is as greedy and clever as he is.
Karttikaya (or Skanda) – God of war. Son of Shiva and Parvati. This six-headed youth carries a bow and arrow and is accompanied by a **peacock**.
Harihara – Composite image, the left-hand side is Hari (Vishnu) and the right-hand side is Hara (Shiva).

go to the temple every day in order to have a **darshan** ("vision") of God (whose energy they can use), to take part in the **arti** (fire ceremony) or to receive **prasad** ("grace", food offered to the gods and eaten by devotees). At various times, followers will also undertake pilgrimages to a series of sacred cities (Mathura, Ayodhya, Pushkar, Haridwar, Varansi, etc).
From the 19C, contact with the West and Christianity gave rise to reformist movements, all of which originated in northern India. In 1828, Mohan Roy founded **Brahma Samaj** which contested certain notions such as untouchability, *sati*, marriage of children. At the same time, **Arya Samaj** attacked the caste system while developing a strongly nationalistic Hindu movement that was eventually to result in the emergence of fundamentalist parties such as the present day BJP *(see p 26)*. Parallel to these developments, mystic leaders such as **Ramakrishna**, **Vivekananda** and **Shri Aurobindo** focused on the concept of universal mysticism, freed from a purely Indian context.

Rajasthani heroes and goddesses

In Rajasthan, several local heroes, who had become the object of popular cults, were promoted to the rank of saints and assimilated into the Hindu pantheon. This was the case for **Tejaji** and **Gogaji** who heal snakebites. The first is depicted as a horseman, the second as an entwined snake. **Baba Ramdev** (Ramdeo), champion of the untouchables, is associated with Krishna and is often symbolised by footprints. **Pabuji**, a Rathore warrior, is the appointed protector of livestock and the sickly. Also revered are **Karni Mata**, a mystic, who became the guardian goddess of the Bikaner royal family, **Shitala Mata** who protects against smallpox and the Bishnoi community's spiritual guide, **Jambhaji**.

Buddhism

Nowadays Buddhism has very few followers in India, except in Tibetan regions such as Ladakh and Sikkim. Yet it was here that Prince Siddartha Gautama Shakyamuni, who became **Buddha** (the "Enlightened one") was born in the 6C BC (at Lumbini, just north of the current border between the state of Bihar and Nepal). He lived in the ancient kingdom of Magadha (now Bihar).

Buddhist doctrine emerged in reaction to Brahmin domination and the ritualism so prevalent at the time. It owes no allegiance to Brahmin texts or to ritualism, and denies the existence of *atman*, however it does recognise *samsara*, made up of successive temporary states of being. To break free of *samsara* and attain **nirvana** (non-being), followers seek to extinguish all desire (source of suffering and illusion) through meditation. Buddha's message was initially a philosophy, but through teaching, it gradually evolved into an authentic religion. Under the influence of Emperor Ashoka (3C BC), it spread throughout India and even further afield, but by the 6C AD had almost died out in its native land. This was due in part to the reaction of the Brahmins, the deep-rooted nature of the caste system and the assimilative ability of Hinduism. Hinduism was willing to integrate external concepts providing they did not question the caste system or the superiority of the Brahmins. Consequently, many 'lost sheep' were admitted into its fold and Buddha was recognised as the ninth incarnation of Vishnu!

Jains

Jainism was founded by **Mahavira** ("the great hero"), a noble and a contemporary of Buddha, who also lived in the kingdom of Magadha and revolted against Brahmin ritualism. He advocated a new path that would break free of the cycle of reincarnation in favour of asceticism and the sanctity of life (*ahimsa* "universal love", hence the rigid vegetarian diet). Self-control, virtue and charity form the basis of the moral values of Jainism; its followers seek to extinguish all passion and by extension, become detached from the world. They do not believe in a creative god but they revere the 24 jinas ("conquerors") who definitively annihilated the *karmas*. The jinas are also known as **tirthankaras** ("finders of the path"). Chronologically, Mahavira was the last tirthankara. In principle, Jains spurn the caste system. Since the 1C BC, Jain monks and nuns (muni) are divided into two sects: the more rigorous **digambara** ("sky clad" or, in other words, naked), most of whom live in southern India, and the white-robed **svetambara**, who are more numerous, particularly in Gujarat and Rajasthan. They wear a mask over their mouths, carry a woollen duster (both of which items are intended to prevent them from inadvertently swallowing or sitting on an insect) and a begging bowl for food.

Paradoxically, the members of this outwardly so austere community in fact developed vast fortunes and are reputed for their business acumen and success. This is in part because of the numerous bans in their religion preventing them from adopting any profession that does not enable them to respect the essential principle of *ahisma* (agriculture, rearing of livestock, etc).

Pilgrim in the Jain temple at Dilwara (Mount Abu)

Sikhs

A visit to a Sikh temple or *gurdwara* is necessary to better understand this dynamic, colourful, hospitable community, which although it only represents some 2 % of India's population, plays a significant role in the country's economy. In the Punjab, cradle of their faith, they are however in the majority (60 %).

Nanak (1469-1539), generally held to be the founder of Sikhism, was born into a Hindu Punjab family. Influenced by Hindu and Moslem mystics, such as Kabir (late 15C), who were focusing on the fundamental similarities between both religions, Nanak left home, embarking on a pilgrimage during which he preached that there is "neither Hindu, nor Moslem", that the love of God should be expressed through brotherly love and that salvation was not to be found in rites or asceticism, but through virtuous deeds. The spiritual leaders or gurus who succeeded Nanak, transformed his teachings into a religion and created a community based on the concept of a single, transcendent God. Sikhs ("students") also rejected the harsher Hindu traditions: caste system, widow sacrifice, marriage of children… When their ninth guru was beheaded by Emperor Aurangzeb for refusing to convert to Islam, in 1699, his successor, **Guru Gobind Singh** founded the **Khalsa panth** ("sect of the pure"), a martial brotherhood intended to defend the community against oppressors. On his death, the **Guru Granth Sahib**, or Adhi Granth, the sacred scriptures containing the work of gurus with texts by Moslem and Hindu saints, occupied the central position of Sikh faith.

The Five K's

The bearded and turbaned Sikh is possibly one of the most familiar images westerners have of India. The hair and beard ("kes") are never cut and this vow is one of the Five K's that all members of the "khalsa" swear to obey. The other four are wearing a "kangha" (comb), a "kara" (bangle), a "kachna" (short breeches, a very uncommon hygienic measure in 16C India), and the famous "kirpan", originally a sabre to defend the oppressed, but now more often a small dagger.

Islam

Islam, brought to the north of the sub-continent by invaders from Afghanistan, has always been considered a "foreign religion" imposed by the sword. But even following Partition in 1947, there is still almost one Moslem for every seven Hindus and India possesses the second largest Moslem population in the world. Ninety percent are **Sunnites** (faithful to the orthodox teachings passed down by the three first Khalifs). Ten percent are **Shiites** (who follow the descendants of Ali, Muhammad's son-in-law), and live in the north, mainly in Uttar Pradesh. Influenced by the Hindu *bhakti* and the *Upanishad*, **Sufism** (a mystic Islamic movement) developed in northern India at the time of the early Moslem invaders. The most eminent of the India Sufi brotherhoods, the Chisti Order, was founded by the Afghan, Khwaja Main ud-Din Chisti (1142-1236) who lived in Ajmer where his *dargah* (tomb of a *pir*, Moslem saint) lies today. The *dargahs* of Nizam ud-Din Aulia (13C) at Delhi and of Sheik Salim Chisti (16C) at Fatehpur Sikri also belong to this order. Many northern Hindus feel affinities with Sufism and occasionally go to the *dargah* to pray with Moslems.

Islam does not of course recognise the caste system, but as a result of their contact with Hindu society, the Moslems structured themselves in endogamic (forbidding marriage outside one's social group) social groups, on the basis of

The key-words of Islam	
Koran	The Holy Book containing God's words to Mohammed via the Archangel Gabriel, set out in 114 chapters or surahs.
Five religious duties	Declaration of faith ("The only god is God and Muhammad is his prophet"), prayer five times a day, alms, fasting during Ramadan, pilgrimage to Mecca which every believer must undertake at least once in his or her life (those who have undertaken it can be recognised by their hair dyed with henna).
Sharia	Islamic Law considered to be the expression of the will of God.
Purdah	The "curtain" that separates the women's quarters from the rest of the world. "To be in purdah" means remaining behind the curtain and not showing one's face to strangers. On contact with their Moslem invaders, northern Hindus also adopted this custom of keeping women within the home and veiled, particularly in Rajasthan. However, even if the lot of Indian Moslem women is hardly an enviable one, Indian Islam is infinitely less rigorous than that practised in the Middle East.

ethnic and economic similarities. The **Ashrafs** ("notables") comprise the Sayyids, said to descend from Fatima, the prophet's daughter and Ali; the Sheikhs, who claim Arabic ancestry and the Pathans, who descend from the Afghan chiefs. The **Ajlafs**, or the plebeians – in other words all the rest – make up the vast majority. They are descended from Hindus who converted, by force or choice, during the Middle Ages: essentially craftsmen (mainly Mumin weavers) or untouchables. The Moslem community speaks Urdu which is close to Hindi but written with an Arabic-Persian alphabet. The liturgical language, that of the revelation, remains Arabic. Arabic is taught in the *madrasa* (Koranic schools), which are often located in the cloisters bordering the mosques.

Christians

Following a venerable tradition, **Thomas** the apostle, one of Christ's twelve disciples, is said to have brought the Gospel to southern India before being martyred at Madras. The Nestorian (or Syro-Chaldean) church may thus have existed in India since the 1C. Whatever the case, the presence of Syriac churches in Kerala can be found as early as the 3C. Catholicism was introduced by the Portuguese at the end of the 15C and the Jesuits of Saint **Frances Xavier**, known as the apostle of the Indies, made Goa a haven of the Roman faith. Rajasthan – and northern India generally – was relatively ignored by passing missionaries, as British colonists, contrary to their Latin counterparts, came to India for the sole purpose of trading and making money. Happy to take advantage of religious divisions, they saw no reason to spread a doctrine which preached equality and which was likely to undermine their exploitation of India's population.

Most of the Christian converts in northern India came from the lower classes of Hindu society, eager to escape from the caste system. Christianity is most visible in India through its social work. The best hospitals, dispensaries, schools and colleges are often those founded by Christian communities, and they continue to reflect favourably on their communities, 50 % of whom are Protestants.

Meeting the people

R. Mattès

Red turbans
and white dhotis

The peoples of Rajasthan

The Aryans, from central Asia, settled in northern India between 1600 BC and 1000 BC *(see p 16)*. They mixed with local ethnic groups to form today's **Indo-Aryan population**, which constitutes the majority of the region's inhabitants.

Tribal populations

While some tribes were assimilated by the Aryan invaders, others were driven southwards. Some also sought refuge in the region's mountains and forests, where they still live and practise some of their ancient customs and beliefs. These tribes, which existed prior to the Aryan invasions, now live in the mountainous regions in South and East Rajasthan, representing some 12 % of the population (higher than in the rest of India). The Indian government, conscious of their plight, created a specific category for them, **scheduled tribes,** entitling them to certain advantages: student grants and fixed quotas in universities and public administrations, for example.

The Minas are the largest of the scheduled tribes in Rajasthan (over 50 %). They were a fierce warrior tribe driven from Amber by the Rajput Kachhvahas in the 12C when the latter established their capital there. They live in the east, around **Jaipur**, Alwar and Shekhawati. For many years they maintained close links with the Kachhvahas dynasty, serving in its army and acting as guardians of its treasury. Tall and fine-featured, they are reputed for their excellent agricultural skills.

The Bhils, one of the largest aboriginal tribes of India, live in the area around Gujarat, Madhya Pradesh and in South Rajasthan, and around Chittaurgarh and

A Rebari caravan

Udaipur. Admired for their archery skills and bravery, they were the backbone of *Maharana* Pratap Singh's struggles against the Moguls, retaining close links with the Sisodias dynasty. Slightly more thick-set than the Minas, they believe in marrying for love and sometimes practise polygamy. Magic and witchcraft remain deeply-rooted in their culture.

The Grasias represent some 5% of Rajasthan's tribal population. This tribe of ancient warriors, now farmers and followers of Krishna, is famous for its marriages by elopement. They live primarily around **Mount Abu**.

The main communities

The Rajputs (10% of Rajasthan's population) make up the *kshatriya* caste. The precise origins of the Rajputs are obscure, but they are thought to descend from the **Gurjaras**, a clan people who arrived in India in the wake of the Huns (end of the 5C) *(see p 17)*. The dominant families of each clan formed the dynasties that were to reign over the region in some twenty or so kingdoms until the advent of Independence. The Rajputs were linked by a sort of feudal system: in thanks for services rendered the princes distributed strongholds in *jaghir*. In return, their vassal lords *(jaghirdar)* administered the lands, collected the princes' taxes and supplied them with armed troops. The system was abolished in 1954 and this landed class was only allowed to retain land it farmed itself.

The Jats (10%) are one of the largest farming communities and are represented throughout the whole of north-western India. In Rajasthan, they live mainly in the area of **Bharatpur**. Good farmers and brave warriors, they succeeded in establishing their own kingdom in the 18C, of which Bharatpur and Deeg were the capitals *(see p 234)*.

Opium drinkers

The use of opium, grown primarily in Mewar, is quite common among the Bishnois who regularly offer it to guests as a token of hospitality. The opium is kept in the form of a little ball cooked in milk and sugar. When consumed, this ball is crushed in an oval shaped mortar and then mixed with water and filtered. Everything relating to opium (and to hemp) is associated with Shiva.

The Bishnois, famous for their love of nature, live in the region of **Jodhpur**. They are organised in a sect, whose origins can be traced back to the 15C, when their master **Jambhaji** devised a list of some twenty bans including, among others, wood cutting or taking life. The Bishnois, unlike other village communities, hold trees sacred, particularly the *khejri*, which is why they don't cut off branches. On their death, they are buried rather than incinerated, again to save wood. In the 18C, over 300 Bishnois sacrificed themselves in an attempt to protect the trees against the axes of Jodhpur's soldiers. This peace-loving community also venerates deer and the *chinkara* gazelle, whom they consider to be reincarnations of particularly "worthy" Bishnois. They live in hut villages and farm their own land. The men wear distinctive white garments *(see p 315)*.

Nomad communities

The Rebaris, a shepherd community, live in the arid desert regions of Rajasthan and Gujarat. The women wear brightly-coloured costumes and magnificent jewellery and the men are dressed in white tunics with red turbans. They raise camels and small livestock. Their standard of living and education are noticeably lower than the rest of the country, but as members of the scheduled tribes, they have certain quota advantages.

The Gadia Lohars are Rajput blacksmiths *(lohar)*, devotees of Vishnu. They move around in groups of 20 or 30 families in carts *(gadi)* covered in hammered sheets of copper, setting up camp on the edges of cities. News of their arrival spreads fast and they are quickly inundated as village and city dwellers bring them tools or utensils for sharpening or repair. They claim to be natives of Chittaurgarh where they were armourers. Legend has it that when the fort was captured by Akbar, they vowed to return to Chittor in the company of *Maharana* Pratap who would conquer the Mughals. They pledged to become nomads, refusing a roof over their heads or a candle at nightfall, for as long as this vow remained unfulfilled. In the 1950s, Nehru offered them plots of land so that they could settle down, but they refused as they had not yet honoured their pledge. The women's distinctive red clothing makes them easily recognisable.

The Banjara, who live in the region of Chittaurgarh, could be the ancestors of gypsies. They were travelling salespeople, transporting the goods of other merchants, supplying the armies with grain, salt, *ghee* and fodder… from the Punjab right to the south of the peninsula.

The Kalbeliyas move around in small groups, with their chickens, goats and greyhound-like dogs. They are snake-charmers *(sapera)*, tradesmen, healers and are also reputed to be petty thieves. Their camps, set up in the heart of the countryside, can be a pitiful sight.

Daily life

Economic liberalisation in the early 1990s and access to consumer goods were to transform many aspects of daily life for the wealthier urban classes. Rural India, singularly unaffected, still appears entrenched in century-old traditions. The arrival of a jolting bus, bursting at the seams, often continues to be the only event of the day for many rural Rajasthanis. The difficult, precarious existence of the peasant classes, for the most part illiterate and still exploited by a wealthy elite, hardly affords them the luxury of questioning ancestral values. Social prejudice, strongly influenced by the caste system, continues to play a major role in the fundamental aspects of most people's daily life: choice of suitor for one's child, choice of profession, choice of restaurant or even public park.

Family portraits

The hopes of a rural family

Rajendra, 33 years old, lives in a tiny hamlet just off the road between Udaipur and Nathdwara. His mud hut is next door to more recent and affluent concrete-built dwellings. This relatively poor farmer only possesses one-tenth of an acre of land on which he grows lentils and vegetables. This is not enough to feed his wife and three children (two boys and a girl), so he works on the land of a neighbouring wealthy landowner. "He pays me 25Rs a day (just over 50 cents)", Rajendra says. "With that, I can buy seed and clothes for the children..." He can hardly read but is conscious of the gap between his standard of living and that of the urban middle classes. One look at the bright billboards lined up along the main highways is enough to reveal a world of ease and luxury. His dearest wish? "That my children are able to raise a family and live near me. To find a good husband for my daughter..."

A village in eastern Rajasthan

T. Bognar/LA PHOTOTHEQUE SDP

When he has the chance, he pulls out a *charpoy* (wooden bed strung with rope) in front of his house and has a short rest. In the evening, his wife prepares *chapatis* and a vegetable curry. After the meal, everyone sleeps in their dwelling's single room, on mats laid on the ground, untroubled by the endless howls of the neighbourhood dogs. At daybreak, his wife rises to fetch water for the day from the village fountain which she carries back in an enormous aluminium jar on her head.

By the mosque at Ajmer

Ghulam Mohammed, 45 years old, is a tubby little bearded man who runs a restaurant in the working-class area around the Adhai-din ka Jhonpra mosque at Ajmer, the most famous Moslem pilgrimage site in all India. Sitting behind his counter, he shouts orders to his staff: "Three mutton *biryani*! A jug of water! Clean that table!..." The customers, almost all bearded men wearing the traditional Moslem skullcap, eat without exchanging a single word, noisily chomping on their food. Once the meal is over, they go the washbasin and wash their hands, rinse their palate and throat and let rip a few ear-splitting belches. Despite the dark, uninviting walls and with the kitchen situated practically in the street, the visible lack of luxury or comfort does not appear to have impaired the restaurant's success. Indeed, Ghulam Mohammed and two of his brothers have just bought a little hotel, already very popular, in a nearby street to provide accommodation for pilgrims for whom comfort and cleanliness are not the highest priority. Ghulam Mohammed has just extended his own home, a two-storey concrete cube, located in a residential quarter of Ajmer. He lives there with his wife, three children, elderly parents and youngest brother. The house is decorated with wall-hangings which depict mosques and Koranic inscriptions and are souvenirs of his eldest brother's pilgrimage to Mecca. Despite this somewhat blatant traditionalism, progress has made incursions into the household: a television blares out all day long, often so loudly that it drowns the muezzin's call to prayer.

A born tradesman

Rajesh Agarwal is a happy man. At 25, he has at last got married. His parents, prosperous shopkeepers in the bazaar at Kota, arranged his marriage to the daughter of a clothes merchant from Jodhpur. "We met twice before taking the final decision" comments Rajesh, seated in the entrance to his shop amidst piles of colourful fabric. The newly-weds will live in the Agarwal's family house, a large building covered in damp spots, just a few minutes from the shop. All the rooms open onto an inner courtyard which resounds to the noisy shrieks of the games of the many children. "Nephews, cousins, neighbours... there are so many, it's difficult to say" jokes Rajesh. The children, intrigued by the foreign visitors, chatter excitedly in Hindi. "They have come to buy scarves and silk, which they will sell in their own country to make lots of money", declares one of the children, just 10 years old, proud to reveal his business acumen. Rajesh notices that we've understood. "In our family, business is in the blood!" he bursts out laughing.

A wealthy district in Delhi

Vasant Vihar is a wealthy district in south Delhi, with one- or two-storey houses set around shady squares of acacias and other flowering trees. Sanjay Mehta, 37, in charge of sales for a computer firm lives here with his wife, Sujata, 33, who is a picture of elegance and beauty: graceful smile, glossy hair, perfect figure and dressed in a magnificent fuchsia pink *shalwar kamiz* (tunic and trousers). Their two daughters, Rina, 10 years old and Kavita, 8 years old, are glued to the television, hopping from one satellite channel to another in an effort to see as many cartoons as possible, nibbling on *namkin*, snacks and savoury seeds the Indians so enjoy. The furniture – chairs and table – all stand against the walls, which are covered in framed family photos. Although apparently very Westernised, the kitchen, which is out of bounds, is far more rustic and the domain of the servants. Although Sujata only enters to distribute orders, she is proud to speak of women's growing emancipation. Married just after graduating from university, she has never worked and devotes herself to the education of her children, who attend a private Protestant school and study in English. While they are at school, she may drive her little Maruti 800 car to visit her friends.

Family

Families are essential to India's social and economic life. In case of disaster or need, an Indian looks first to his family – or possibly his *jati* (sub-caste) *(see Religions p 47)* – for help. Individually, unless wealthy, Indians are doomed to an old age of poverty and abject indifference. Hence the importance of marriage and of keeping one's children close by.

No major decisions (choice of profession, moving, etc) can be taken without consulting one's parents, the head of the family in particular, who can go so far as making decisions without consulting the 'interested party'. The Western model of an individual who controls their own destiny, while the object of growing envy among educated classes, disturbs the majority of Indians. Urban youth, although eager to take part in material progress and fascinated by the Internet, remains surprisingly conservative with regards to family and marriage. A poll carried out in 1998 among young people aged between 18 and 28 in five major Indian cities, revealed that 80 % shared practically all their parents' opinions and 86 % felt that they should, under no circumstances, defy their parents' authority.

Marriage

"Love" matches remain an exception and as a general rule, marriages are organised by parents, uncles and aunts, who set out on the quest for a suitable son- or daughter-in-law. This quest for a suitor, who must be from a similar background, will take into consideration the *jati*, religion, social and economic situation and reputation of any prospective candidate. When suitable suitors cannot be found by the family, adverts will be placed in newspapers to broaden the choice. Skin colour (the lighter the better), profession, salary, etc are all examined in relation to the **dowry** that the daughter-in-law's family will have to pay to her prospective future husband's family. The dowry is often responsible for life-long debts on the part of the girl's family, and while officially banned, it is still common amongst Hindu families, both in cities and in the countryside. A glance at the **matrimonial small ads** section of the Sunday edition of the Hindustan Times – now also on the Internet – reveals how singularly devoid of romanticism Indian betrothals can be. Entire pages of offers and proposals, listed by caste, professional standing or linguistic group, are a sober reminder of the overriding priorities. "Seek young Brahmin man, earning over 10 000Rs per month, for beautiful young Brahmin girl of 21, five feet four inches..." or

A wedding in Jhalawar

Traditionally, a great number of weddings take place in November. On this particular Saturday evening, several weddings are being celebrated in Jhalawar. One noisy wedding procession gaily marches around the city to the sound of a fanfare and lit up by neon lights. Parents and friends of the groom lead him to the home of his future wife. Riding a white mare and proudly attired in a turban and wreathed in bank notes, he reaches his fiancée's home, also ablaze with lights. The groom then pierces the "torana" arch above the door with a sword, indicating his conquest and intention to sweep off the young girl. The latter awaits dressed in a red silk sari and with eyes lowered. A Brahmin is called upon to carry out the religious rituals around a sacred fire. Parents and friends then bless the newly-weds.

"Brahmin family seek spouse of same caste, beautiful, light-skinned, 25 years maximum, speaking Hindi and English for a 29-year old doctor, five feet six inches, who works in Canada and will be visiting India next month..." No traditional Hindu marriage would be planned without the approval of an **astrologer**. Any incompatibility of birth charts would lead to the marriage being called off, or persuading the astrologer to produce more optimistic calculations!

After the ceremony, the young wife becomes a possession of her in-laws and the couple move in with the husband's parents, living with all the other sons and daughters-in-law. There is very little place within this **joint family** for any privacy and this practice is slowly dying out amongst the more Westernised classes, particularly as professional constraints now require young people to move round the country and sometimes around the world.

The door of Tila ki Pol at Jaisalmer

Birth

In Hindu families, a birth gives rise to rituals intended to chase away malevolent spirits, responsible for the deaths of new-born children: an astrologer is consulted for the choice of name, first meal of solid food, shaving the head... Modern India has often forgotten the full religious meaning of such rituals, which have now become social conventions.

The birth of a boy is an occasion for rejoicing and a matter of great pride for his parents, because a grown-up son will be able to care for his parents in their old age, perpetuate their lineage and increase the family's wealth. The birth of a girl, on the other hand, gives rise to no rejoicing and is a portent of future sacrifice. Girls will leave their families and will not contribute to its wealth or prosperity. On the contrary, their families have to provide a dowry upon their marriage. In the words of a rural proverb: "Bringing up a girl is like sowing one's neighbour's field".

Death

Washed and scented, the corpse is wrapped in a cloth (white for men and red for women) and then laid on a stretcher. While the womenfolk remain at home, lamenting the deceased, the men carry the body in procession to the place of incineration, near a river or water of some sort. Once the body is cremated, the family scatter the ashes in the nearby water, unless they are kept for dispersal at some later date in a particularly sacred spot, such as the confluence of the River Yamuna and the River Ganges. Ten days or so after the death, a commemorative ceremony is organised by the family.

In poor areas, funeral ceremonies often bring about long-term debts; the wood for the funeral pyre is very expensive, especially in arid regions. Poverty-stricken Hindu families have been known to throw half-burnt bodies into the river.

A woman's lot

Right from birth, a little girl is made to understand that she will leave her family when she marries. This explains why she receives much less attention than her brothers, she is less well-fed, less cared for and less educated. Once married, she moves into her in-laws' home where her main duty is to bear children and humbly serve her husband and his family. The tradition of **purdah**, whereby women live hidden by the family "curtain", introduced by invading Moslems centuries earlier, is slowly dying out in the North of India. However, in some of the more conservative regions of Rajasthan, which remains an incredibly backward State, women still avoid going out and hide their faces behind an *orhni* (or *odhni*) whenever they leave the family home. Although India's constitution has recognised

Murder for a dowry

The father of the bride must pay his in-laws vast sums in lieu of a dowry, sometimes as much as 50 000Rs (over $1000) in certain rural areas. Any default of payment or the in-laws' one-sided decision to increase their claim, suddenly demanding a scooter or a refrigerator not initially agreed in the marriage contract, results in quarrels, and can occasionally lead to the murder of the young bride. Such cases are not unheard of even in large cities, where the newspapers occasionally publish such grim tales: a daughter-in-law is burnt alive because her clothes apparently "caught" fire while she was cooking. If a complaint is lodged and the accident hypothesis is not accepted, a guilty party still has to be found. In such cases, the mother-in-law generally gives herself up in order to spare the male members of her household.

women's right to vote, to divorce and to remarry, the ancient *Manu Laws*, sacred texts which determine a person's caste and rights, continue to prevail in Rajasthan.
Even if the lot of Hindu women has improved immeasurably of late, that of Moslem women remains dependent on their family, where they are considered as secondary beings and kept indoors. A husband has only to pronounce the word "talak" (divorce) three times, for his wife to have to quit the home instantly. Any visit to a Moslem area never fails to give rise to the age-old question "Where are all the women?"

Education

In Rajasthan, only 38 % of the population is literate (55 % of men and 20 % of women) compared to the national average of 52 %. In the district of Barmer, to the south of Jaisalmer, only 8 % of women know how to read and write – the lowest rate in India. This backwardness is partly explained by Rajasthan's traditional conservatism – "Too much learning is bad for traditions" – partly due to the resigned attitude of vast poverty-stricken groups and partly the result of the cynicism of the dominant classes, happy to maintain the masses in servile ignorance.
The country may well be an international player in terms of nuclear power and privately educated middle-class children may be renowned for their academic excellence, but these aspects do not reflect the position of the majority of the population in India's rural regions. State schools are of course free and, in theory, all children are required to attend, but many parents can simply not afford the exercise books and textbooks. Most families find it difficult enough to feed their children regularly, let alone send them to school. Indeed, many Rajasthani schools don't even have blackboards or chalk.

A school outing in Amber

B. Perousse/HOA QUI

INDIAN COOKING

Indian restaurants, long since established in Britain, are multiplying all over Europe and North America to such an extent that any prospective visitor to the sub-continent should not find it difficult to get a foretaste of some of the spices and terms of Indian cooking. Indeed a 1997 poll revealed that over one-quarter of Britons ate curry at least once a week and that Marks & Spencer sells 18 tonnes of chicken *tikka masala* each week. However, just as the fact that this particular dish is virtually unheard of in the sub-continent, it should be noted that many Indian restaurants outside India, perhaps in an attempt to cater to a "Western" palate, serve dishes that are overwhelmingly fake and which bear no resemblance to a proper banana leaf or *thali* meal as served in India. What's more, even the term "curry" is primarily Western and although it is now used in India, it can refer to any number of very different types of dishes.
Again, once in India, anyone who limits their choice of restaurants to hotel dining may well be very unimpressed by what is often a highly mediocre rendering of a varied and subtle gastronomy. Such meals are often stereotyped and the ubiquitous Indian Rail curry, designed to cater to all tastes, often turns out to be totally tasteless. Any real taste of authentic Indian cooking must either take place in a family home or in one of India's better restaurants.

Dangerous food

"Food is God" say the Vedas, because it maintains life. Food should thus be venerated as sacred. Taboos are attached to food and water depending on the person's caste and on the Hindu notion of purity, physical and spiritual purity being one and the same thing to a Hindu. Hindus cannot, for example, accept food prepared or offered by someone from a caste beneath them, for fear of being polluted. Again, food prepared in "ghee" (clarified butter) is considered to be less likely to lose its purity, and thus less "dangerous" than food prepared in oil, roasted, or even worse, boiled.

Indians and food

Indians have a very special relationship with their food, which differs according to the region and also caste and religion. Moslems and Sikhs eat meat, whereas Jains are vegan, eating neither meat, fish nor eggs (occasionally not even onions or garlic). Ten percent of Hindus are also vegan and half are vegetarian. Whatever the case, even if meat is not taboo, it is generally only served on special occasions and even then will usually be chicken or goat, less expensive than mutton.

Tandoori or tikka?

Whatever the region, a traditional meal, served on a tray called a **thali**, is almost always composed of vegetables *(sabzi)* and lentils *(dal)*, served with rice *(chawal)* or wheat pancakes (*chapati* or *roti*), yoghurt and spicy **pickled** vegetables or fruit (*achar* conserved in oil, vinegar or lemon or sweet and sour **chutney**).
Each recipe requires a specific blend of spices (**masala** or *garam masala* in the case of very hot spices) which is prepared individually and the secret of which is jealously guarded by cooks. Stooping to use shop-bought *masala* would bring shame on any self-respecting chef.
Northern India primarily cooks with *ghee* and the region has devised numerous recipes based on Persian cooking such as the delicious **Mughlai cuisine**. Dishes of Afghan origin are also served under the banner "North-West Frontier cooking". Millet or **bajra** is the staple element of **Rajasthani** diets. It can be served with beans *(mogri)*, capers *(kher)* or acacia pods *(khejri)*. The most famous Rajput dish is **sula**, a goat's meat or chicken kebab, marinated in spices and cooked in a *tandoor* clay oven.

Bread – Most of the bread eaten consists of **chapati** or **roti**, unleavened bread made from whole flour. The former are cooked on a metal sheet *(tawa)* and the latter are baked in a *tandoor* oven. Generally made out of wheat-flour, they can also be made from millet *(bajre ki roti)* or corn *(maki ki roti)*. **Naan** is leavened bread made from white flour mixed with milk and oven baked. **Paratha** are thicker and pan-fried, often stuffed with vegetables. Before meals, many restaurants also serve **poppadum** (or *pappad*) which are like gigantic crunchy crisps made from lentil flour. Originally a southern Indian speciality, they are now available everywhere.

Desserts – Many Indian desserts are based on milk, cardamom and pistachio nuts, among which **kheer**, rice pudding, **firni**, a sort of custard and **kulfi**, soupy ice cream, are great classics. Favourite sweetmeats, made for the legendary Indian

Main dishes	
Curry	A very wide-ranging term referring to chicken, mutton, fish or vegetables which are cut into small pieces and simmered with a blend of spices *(masala)* in a sauce based on vegetable oil or *ghee*.
Dal	Made from lentils and pulses, *dal* is served with almost all Indian meals. Favourites include *dal maka-hani* (buttered lentils) and *rajma* (lentils and red beans).
Dosa and idli	Both are made from the same basic mixture of rice and lentils fermented in buttermilk. *Dosas* are thin pancakes. *Idli* is steam-baked fluffy milk bread. Originally from southern India, these dishes are served with *sambar*, a hot lentil and vegetable based stock-soup.
Kofta and kebabs	Recipes of Turkish-Afghan origins. Minced meat *(kima kofta)* or vegetable *(malai kofta)* balls are cooked in a sauce of yoghurt and dry fruit. Kebabs are made from minced chicken or mutton barbecued on skewers.
Korma	*Kormas* are pieces of chicken or mutton cooked in a sauce of yoghurt, cashew nuts, almonds, saffron and seeds.
Namkin and chaat	A mixture of grilled and spiced or sweet-and-sour seeds that the Indians adore nibbling all day long. The most popular *chaat* is *blel puri*, originally from Bombay but now available everywhere. It is eaten either as a snack or served before meals. It consists of a mixture of rice crispies, peanuts, fried lentils and grilled chickpeas, served with chutney or lemon juice.
Pulao and biryani	In these two *mughlai* dishes, rice, meat and vegetables are cooked together. The former (whose name is derived from the Persian "pilaf"), is cooked in a saucepan, whereas the second is steam-baked.
Pakora	Chickpea flour *(besan)* balls served in a yoghurt sauce.
Paneer	Means "fresh cheese" and frequently appears as *palak paneer* (spinach in cheese) or *matter paneer* (peas in cheese).
Raita	Yoghurt with spices and vegetables (cucumber, tomatoes and potatoes).
Samosa	Small deep-fried savoury pastries stuffed with meat or vegetables, available on most street corners.
Tandoori	This term refers to all dishes cooked in a *tandoor* clay oven.
Tikka	A Punjab recipe of chicken or fish, cut into small boneless pieces, marinated in spicy yoghurt and cooked on a skewer in a *tandoor* oven.

sweet tooth, include **laddu** (made from chickpea flour and melon seeds), **gulab jammun** (made from flour, sour milk and pistachio nuts served in syrup) and **rasgulla** (a white ball made from fresh cheese blended with flour and served in syrup).

Drinks – Since the introduction of tea plants from China by the British in the mid-19C, **tea** has become the national drink. However what is also Britain's national beverage is a somewhat murkier concoction under India's skies. Tea now refers to a half-water half-milk mixture to which is added tea powder, sugar and spices (ginger, cardamom…). This is then boiled three times to produce **chay**, which north Indians can be found drinking all day long.

Lassi is another classic, made from beaten yoghurt, it can be savoury, sweet or spicy. Summer drinks include **thandai** (milk flavoured with crushed almonds and cardamom) and **jira pani** (water flavoured with cumin, mint and lemons). Indian **beer**, served chilled, is a pleasant surprise in a country where alcohol is often relegated to the position of a hateful foreign import. "Kingfisher" and "Black Label" are common brands.

Paan – No decent meal can end without chewing *paan*, supposed to improve the digestion and freshen one's breath. To make your own *paan*, take a betel leaf, coat it in lime paste, add areca nut or other ingredients of your choice (aniseed, cardamom, coconut, tobacco…), fold into a triangle and fasten with a clove. Wrap in thin silver paper *(vark)* and your *paan* is ready. Most people however get theirs made up by a *paanwaller* as they leave the restaurant. Chewing real *paan* involves frequent spitting of bright red saliva, so you may prefer to buy pre-wrapped *supari*, a mixture of digestive spices covered in coloured sugar, and

A namkin merchant

Costumes and Jewellery

From the turban down to the tips of the shoes

The increase in off-the-peg clothing has done little to undermine the importance of the *darzi* (tailor) who continues to make the clothes of many city and rural dwellers. Traditionally, everyday working clothes are made from cotton, but synthetic fabrics are making more and more headway, and silk is only bought by the wealthy urban classes.

Men's dress

In cities, men have largely taken to wearing Western-style trousers and shirts to work. But once back in their homes, whether in Delhi or Udaipur, they will generally revert to a more comfortable garment which they will wear in the evening and to bed. This can be a *lungi*, a chequered loincloth from South India, but is more likely to be a **kurta-pyjama**, a thigh-length tunic worn over loose-fitting trousers. The cut of the *kurta-pyjama* can vary from region to region: tight-fitting in Uttar Pradesh and looser among Sikhs and Jats. When the pyjama is loose around the thighs but tight around the calves, like jodhpurs, it is called a **churidar**. In the winter, nifty dressers may also wear an **achkan,** coat made famous by Nehru, over their *kurta churidar*.

Peasants and farmers in Rajasthan's countryside still often wear a **dhoti**, a long piece of fine white fabric which is attached to the waist and passed between the legs. This is often worn with a *kurta* or an *angrakha*, a short white shirt, tight-fitting around the chest and more flowing around the waist.

Turbans *(pagri, safa…)* which can be between eight and eleven metres long, symbolise a Rajput's honour and are also worn by Jats and Sikhs. The way it is tied and its colour will vary depending on the region, the community, the season and also a man's family situation.

Women's dress

Most Western images of Indian women will invariably bring to mind a figure in a sari. However this rectangular piece of fabric, which can be over five metres long and makes for such an elegant silhouette, is in fact very little seen in Rajasthan, apart from among the urban middle-classes. Since the 1980s, most of India's young city women have adopted the **shalwar-kamiz**, the traditional costume of northern Moslems: loose trousers, tight around the ankles, partly hidden under a long tunic. To this they generally add a **dupatta**, a large scarf worn over the chest. The Hindu equivalent of the *shalwar-kamiz*, the **kurta-churidar** (identical to the men's *kurta-churidar*) is making a timid comeback. In more conservative circles, the *shalwar-kamiz* or the *kurta-churidar* are not worn after marriage, when only saris should be worn. Punjabis – Sikhs and Hindus – are an exception; they wear a Punjabi suit, similar to the *shalwar-kamiz*, but looser.

For maharanis just as much as for peasant women, traditional Rajasthani dress is composed of a full, ankle-length skirt (**ghaghra** or **lehanga**), worn with a short tight-fitting bolero-type blouse, which covers the shoulders and chest (**coli** or **kanchli**), and a looser blouse, called **kurti** (often dispensed with, leaving the bolero visible). This is then completed with a veil (**orhni** or **odhni**) which is worn over the head and shoulders and tucked into the skirt's waist.

Shoes

Just as the turban symbolises the dignity and honour of its wearer, shoes are considered to be objects of pollution. Made from leather (felt to be impure by Hindus), even one's own shoes are handled at arm's length, and touching those belonging to someone else (at least for the higher castes) is quite out of the question. Buffalo, cow or camel hides are tanned by one of the casteless communities, **Chamars**, using successive baths of lime, acid and *babul* bark (acacia). Styles have changed little over the centuries, as 2C statues of Buddha, wearing **chappal** (sandals), reveal: a wide leather strap over the main part of the foot and a smaller one around the big toe. **Jutis**, typical Rajasthani footwear for peasants and city dwellers, are a sort of slipper with a slightly-raised pointed toe. The most lightweight models are made by *mochi* (Moslem cobblers). *Chappal* and *juti* are hand-stitched and left either natural-coloured or dyed and are then embroidered or decorated with velvet and gold thread appliqué.

Gold, silver and precious stones

In Rajasthan's countryside, as in the rest of India, jewellery continues to represent the only investment which is safe, easy to convert and to pass on. Jewellery is considered part of one's inheritance, in particular, that of women, for whom it used to be the only property they were able to possess in their own right, until the Hindu Marriage Act (1955) enabled them to inherit normally. Hence the custom of wearing all one's treasure at one time, necklaces, bracelets, earrings, etc.

Traditionally both men and women used to wear jewellery, but most men seem to have ceded their beautiful pearl necklaces to their wives. However Rajasthan once again proves to be an exception and it is quite common to meet men, even in the cities, with earrings which designate their community, or peasants wearing necklaces and ankle bracelets – all of this would be in silver, because only the purest castes are allowed to wear gold.

Gold and silver jewellery

Although jewellery is always representative of a community and a region, whether in gold or silver (or decorated with precious stones), several styles can be found throughout Rajasthan. Both men and women wear **amulets** (in which a lucky charm is placed) around the neck or upper arm and **patri**, small medal-like pendants of one's personal god – Ganesha, Durga or a local deity. Men and women also wear neck-rings *(hansli)*, armbands *(bajuband)* and ankle-rings. Although ankle-rings are apparently losing favour with many men, in south-western Rajasthan (districts of Jalor and Sirohi) they are still very common. **Nose-rings** *(nath)* and **pendants** worn on the forehead *(bindi, rakhi, borla...)* are commonly only worn by women, together with toe-rings, in theory worn only by married women. This is also the case of **ivory bracelets** (often plastic now), dyed red, to symbolise marriage.

It is well-nigh impossible to find any antique gold or silver jewellery over 50 years old, because old jewellery was traditionally melted down to make new.

The art of jewellery

Traditional belief holds that the energy of the planets and of the gods which rule them is expressed by a vibration of colours. Each colour has a corresponding precious or semiprecious stone which acts as a source of energy. Indians firmly believe that each metal and stone is possessed of a power with influence over a person's (even an animal's) health and destiny. Accordingly each person possesses his or her own special stone, but to be on the safe side, many people often wear a complete range of colours. **Navratan** jewellery ("nine stones") feature the nine basic stones, including a pearl, set in a single jewel, generally a ring or a pendant. Jaipur's goldsmiths *(sunar)* are reputed for **kundankari** ("art of pure gold") which involves embedding polished precious stones into gold. Stones are inlaid to form shapes: stars, Islamic crescent moons, peacocks, budgerigars, fish. People without the means to invest in precious stones resort to coloured cut-glass instead. The apogee of *Kundan* art occurred from the 17C to the 19C. Many ancient pieces still exist and any self-respecting Jaipuri jeweller will have a treasure or two locked away in some secret casket.

In the early 17C, a few master enamellers from Lahore (Punjab) were enticed by *Maharaja* Man Singh to settle in Jaipur and teach their art of **meenakari** (*champlevé*, which is a type of enamel work). As a result, in the 18C and 19C, Jaipur, and Alwar to a lesser extent, were to become, and still are today, the heart of enamel art in India. Although bright green, red and white are among the most frequently used colours, little touches of blue can occasionally be seen. One of the most popular models is a wide, rigid bracelet of Mughal origin that finishes in two heads of fighting animals. The back of *kundan* jewellery is often covered using the *meenakari* technique to protect the gold from wear. The enamel is decorated with incredibly detailed pictures inspired by nature: leaves, flowers, birds, etc.

One technique can be found only in Rajasthan: pendants decorated using the **thewa** technique, as practised in the 16C by a few goldsmiths at Pratapgarh, south of Chittaurgarh. A sheet of gold, finely sculpted in the shape of animals or people is applied to a base of red or green coloured glass. *Thewa* art is also used to make caskets and jewel cases.

The handles of **ceremonial daggers** also called upon the art of fine jewellery, made out of jade for example, encrusted in rubies and emeralds set in gold. The love of jade and precious gems was inherited from the Mughals. The taste for precious stones led certain wealthy princes as far as ordering ceremonial bridles and harnesses inlaid with costly gems for their favourite horses.

Sarpech: a turban ornament

Arts and crafts

It is true that when the princely States were abolished, a whole class of wealthy patrons of local arts, whose demanding standards and good taste inspired many craftsmen to create elegant, innovative objects, also disappeared. Nowadays, connoisseurs are too few and far between to impose their taste over that of foreign buyers. The latter buy up whole containers of "local craftwork" intended solely for a "cheap and cheerful" market niche, with no pretensions of quality. To satisfy this ever-growing market, Rajasthan has become used to producing goods with little or none of their former charm or artistic qualities. The situation is not however as bleak as it might appear, and several sectors have remained creative or have evolved. This is the case of the textile and blue pottery industries, which since the end of the 1980s, have experienced a new creative boom.

Painting

Miniature painting is still very well-established in Rajasthan, although today's quality is not a patch on that of former times. Large numbers of artists carry on traditional methods, but most of the painting produced goes little further than stale reproductions of ancient works of art *(see p 39)*. However, the presence of this elitist form of classical art has not prevented the development of more popular painting such as the often garish representations of the Hindu pantheon of deities, which can be found on the walls of houses and cafés everywhere.

Behind the statue of Krishna-Nathji in the temple at **Nathdwara** *(see p 349)*, hangs a blue painted picture known as a **pichhwai** ("which is behind") depicting the blue god in one of the episodes of his life. The *pichhwai* is changed with the seasons and to reflect current or approaching festivals. In response to demands from pilgrims as early as the 18C, regional artists have reproduced various forms of *pichhwai*, printed, embroidered or painted, depicting Nathdwara's very distinctive Krishna: a dark perfectly oval face, eyes like slits, left arm raised to support Mount Govardhan and a flowing robe, partly hidden by garlands of flowers.

Bhopas, travelling priests or bards, who sing the legends of Pabuji *(see p 82)*, use painted canvas some five metres long, **phad** or *phar*, to illustrate their ballads. The hero's adventures are depicted in a brightly-coloured cartoon-style, by painters from the region of Chittaurgarh and Bhilwara, members of the Joshi clan of dyers *(chhipa)*.

Mandana are ritual paintings that Rajasthani village women paint on the ground of their courtyards at each festival or special occasion. Over a base of dung mixed with ochre, they dip their fingers into white lime to paint geometric motifs mixed with lotus flowers, stars, peacocks – designed to attract the gods' benevolence on their household. Called **rangoli** in the region of Delhi, they are more colourful and can even be found on the landings of blocks of flats.

Pietra dura

Pietra dura, a technique whereby semi-precious gems are inlaid in marble, was introduced into Indian monumental art in the early 17C under the reign of Emperor Jahangir *(see p 195)*. Highly characteristic of Mughal art, it is still used by Agra's craftsmen today who produce marquetry work with tiny inlaid stones for objects and table tops.

Textiles

Rajasthan is without doubt India's richest cotton textile producing region. The vivid hues, daring juxtapositions of colours and extraordinary variety of decorative techniques and motifs make it a paradise for fabric lovers. Although the traditional vermilion red, indigo blue and saffron yellow have given way to more synthetically produced dyes, during the late 1980s a trend back to more traditional pigments began to make headway.

Rajasthan's rivers, rich in salt, are partly responsible for the early development of textile dying in the region. **Tie-dye** techniques, whereby the cloth is knotted before being dyed, were already practised in pre-Christian times. Two techniques are currently used: **bandhani** ("tying") which produces the classic white circles on a coloured background and **loharia** ("ripples") which creates zigzags, stripes or checks. *Bandhana* fabrics are commonly used for women's clothes, whereas *loharia* textiles are used for *orhni*, *dupatta* and turbans.

Wooden block printing, even older than tie-dye techniques, is carried out by *chhipa* (printers), either by directly applying a wooden block, dipped in dye, to the fabric, or by first covering parts of the fabric with a dye-resistant substance (such as wax) and then dying it. Motifs and colours vary from region to region. The areas around Jodhpur, Jaisalmer and Barmer are famous for their block-printed fabrics. Bagru and Sanganer, near Jaipur are also renowned, the latter in particular for its highly elegant calico prints.

Embroidery is also a popular craft in Rajasthan, of which **shishadar** is undoubtedly the most striking example: it consists of brightly-coloured embroidered fabric onto which are stitched tiny mirrors *(shish)*. This technique is practiced all over western Rajasthan, in Gujarat and in the Pakistani Sindh regions. Used to decorate skirts, boleros and the skull-caps of Moslem shepherds, it is however mainly found on wall-hangings over doors or on the walls of village huts.

Zari is another embroidery technique, which uses gold or silver threads to embellish ceremonial uniforms or costumes and mural tapestries and hangings. This technique is still highly popular among Moslems and Jaipur and Agra remain major centres of this art.

Drying saris

J. Horner/HOA QUI

Gota, **appliqué embroidery** involves stitching gold and silver thread into haberdashery items, such as fringes, braids and other trimmings which are then used to decorate ceremonial costumes. The everyday clothes of women in a few communities commonly feature such details. Take a close look at the bright red or yellow *orhnis* worn by the women on the roadsides around Shekhawati or Mewat and you may see large embroidered silver *gota* circles.

The freezing winter nights of the western desert regions have inspired superb hand-spun woollen **shawls and blankets**. Clearly hand-made, they often feature coloured stripes of geometric motifs set on a black or white background. Those woven in the region of Jaisalmer, onto a black background, are among the most attractive.

Wood

Woodwork and wood carving has always been a particularly refined art in an area so lacking in such natural resources. Teak, imported from other states, was finely carved into doors, windows or balconies (those of Shekhawati and Jaisalmer are particularly rich in detail); it was also inlaid with sandalwood, rosewood or ivory to produce exquisitely carved inner door panels.

Sculptors also exercised their talents on **pidas** (low folding chairs), bed frames and wooden boxes.

Large carved and painted wooden statues of **Ishar** and **Guari**, popular Rajput deities who are incarnations of Shiva and Diva, stand at the entrance to almost all forts and *haveli* inhabited by Rajputs. Most of these statues, often draped in magnificent robes, were made at **Bassi**, a village east of Chittaurgarh, where the few remaining sculptors now produce wooden toys. Heads of Ishar and Gauri made out of copper or pottery and dressed in richly brocaded garments can also be found. Today's **wooden puppets** *(katputli)* worked with two strings are still based on traditional models, but mass production has considerably altered their quality.

Carpets

The carpets produced in Rajasthan are essentially reversible cotton **dhurries**. Out of favour in the early 1920s, they have undergone a revival since the 1980s. They are woven on horizontal looms by village families, mainly in the regions of Jaipur and Jodhpur, and geometric motifs and pastel colours predominate. The villages near Jodhpur and Barmer also produce some non-reversible cotton **kilims** in brighter colours than those of the *dhurries*. **Knotted** carpets were first introduced by the Mughals to Agra and then later to Jaipur in the 17C.

Metalwork

Rajasthan's metalwork (copper, bronze and brass) developed as early as the Indus civilisation due to the region's deposits of copper, tin and zinc. In a land where war was part of everyday life, anything relating to **arms** was of prime importance and Rajasthan developed a particular talent in the art of decorative weapons, the main centres for which were at Jaipur, Alwar and Jodhpur.

More everyday examples of metalwork can be seen in large lattice-work coffers made to keep *paan* utensils *(see p 69)* or little travel betel or opium boxes, nutcrackers, *huqqa* (water pipes) and oil lamps, occasionally beautifully-sculpted in the shape of a peacock or Lakshmi (goddess of good fortune).

Pottery

Molela, a village to the north of Udaipur, continues to uphold the tradition of carved **earthenware** votive plaques of appealingly naïve, plump gods or mythical heroes. These steles are either left clay-coloured or are painted in white, vermilion, bright yellow, light blue and black, and then varnished in oil.

Glazed blue pottery, of Chinese origins, was brought to India by the sultans of Delhi, via Persia. It only became a popular art form under the patronage of the maharaja of Jaipur, Ram Singh II, in the 19C, when he invited potters from Delhi to his School of Fine Arts, founded in 1866. This pottery tradition underwent a further revival in the 1960s as a result of the combined efforts of *Maharani* Gayatri Devi and the potter Kripal Singh Shekhawat. Floral or geometric motifs are painted primarily in blue, which is obtained from copper and cobalt oxides. Green, yellow and white, together with little touches of pink, complete the spectrum.

J.L. Nou/EXPLORER

Ganesha, a clay sculpture from Molela

A GARLAND OF FESTIVALS

The sight of men sporting saffron, fuchsia or bright yellow turbans and of women dressed in the most vividly-coloured skirts and shirts, bedecked in jewellery can bring to mind images of a lavish celebration, such as a royal wedding. Festivals attract a sudden influx of brightly-dressed villagers and can turn what is a dusty little backwater into a scene from the Arabian Nights. Booths spring up everywhere, selling pastries, jumbo glasses of sugarcane juice, gadgets for the children and ribbons of every imaginable colour. Music blares out all around, whether from the strident loudspeakers of the cassette seller or played by the traditional musicians accompanying puppet shows or dancers. Indians love a good show and festivals are always enjoyed and appreciated by young and old. In fact the simplicity of such events is precisely what never fails to charm even the most cynical hearts of well-travelled tourists.

Sacred and secular

Almost all Indian festivals manage to combine purely religious events with the trappings of an enormous popular gathering *(mela)*, with dances, puppet shows and fairground attractions. In rural areas, *melas* have gradually become cattle fairs, such as at Pushkar, Nagaur or Jhalrapatan, occasions to meet old and new acquaintances, do business and, of course, contract marriages. Despite the crowds and ear-splitting decibels, they cannot however be compared to the carnival atmosphere of places like Brazil. Alcohol is almost unheard of and communication problems between different social groups combine to make Indian festivals on the whole pretty well-behaved. Only Holi, a festival which borders on boisterous madness, remains an exception to this decorum.

Calendar of the main religious festivals

State-administered bodies and the business world follow the Gregorian calendar. However, the religious life of each community is based on the traditional calendars of their respective religions.

Hindu, Jain, Buddhist and Sikh festivals

Calculated on the basis of **lunar-solar calendars**, the exact dates of these festivals vary from year to year, but they always occur in the same season. Since 1957, Hindu festivals have been officially calculated according to the calendar of the **Shaka era**. Year 1 started on 22 March 78 (2000 occurred in 1922-1923 of the *Shaka* era). Each year is divided into twelve months, each of which is divided into two fortnightly periods. The **waning fortnight** (the first) begins on the day after the full moon and finishes on the night of the new moon. Few celebrations occur during this period, except those in honour of Shiva. The **waxing fortnight** runs from the day after the new moon until the night of the full moon *(purnima)*.

The **Jain calendar** starts with the death of Jina, founder of the Jain religion, in 524 BC (2000 occurred in 2524-2525 of the Jain calendar).

December-January

Camel festival at Bikaner Full moon. The camels take part in parades, competitions, races over a two day period.

January-February

Republic Day January 26. Commemorates the declaration of the Republic (January 26 1950).

Nagaur Fair (Between Jodhpur and Bikaner.) Cattle fair, in honour of Baba Ramdev.

Jaisalmer Desert Festival Full moon. Three days of cultural shows and competitions.

February-March

Mahashivaratri (or *Shivratri*, "night of Shiva") New moon. Shivaites commemorate the night when Shiva is said to have danced the "tandava" dance of destruction and recreation. Fasting, worship of "linga.

Holi Full moon. Most important Hindu festival. Marks the end of winter. The day before bonfires are lit on which effigies of the demoness, Holika, are burnt to the accompaniment of ribald songs. The next morning, everyone "plays Holi", becoming the demon themselves and dousing each other with a mixture of coloured powder or coloured water. Everyone is quickly soaked and soaked in colour (old clothes are recommended). This widespread exuberance sometimes gives rise to violence, particularly in Agra or parts of Delhi and many participants traditionally consume "bhang" (derivative of cannabis) in milk or cakes. In the afternoon, dressed in clean clothes, Hindus pay visits on parents and friends taking offerings of sweetmeats with them. The **Elephant Festival at Jaipur** takes place at Holi.

March-April

Rishabdevji Festival Takes place between the 6th and 8th day of the month, at Rishabdev (near Udaipur). Gathering of Jains, Vishnuists and Bhils in honour of Rishabdev.

Gangaur Between the 3rd and 4th days after the new moon. Rajasthani women give praise to Gauri (Devi). Young women pray to the goddess for a husband as perfect as Shiva. The Mewar Festival at Udaipur and Gangaur Fair at Jaipur also take place during this festival.

Ram Navami 9th day after the new moon. Birth of Rama, incarnation of Vishnu. Theatrical adaptations of the *Ramayana* and the *Ram-Lila* are staged during the preceding 8 days.

Karni Mata Festival at Deshnok (Near Bikaner). The faithful converge to celebrate Saint Karni Mata and bring sweetmeats to the rats.

Mahavira Jayanti 12th day after the new moon. Birth of the Jain *tirtankara*, Mahavira.

Vaishakhi Sankranti April 13. Punjab new year's day, marks the start of the harvest. Sikhs commemorate the foundation of *Khalsa-panth*, the communities of the pure.

Buddha Jayanthi (or *Buddha Purnima*) Full moon. This Buddhist festival celebrates Buddha's birth, enlightenment and attainment of nirvana all in one day.

July-August

Teej 3rd day after the new moon. Young girls dream of Teej (Parvati) getting ready to welcome home her husband, Shiva. **Teej Fairs at Jaipur and at Bundi.**

Nag Panchami 5th day after the new moon. Tribute is paid to snakes, especially in Jodhpur: milk is offered to their effigies or placed in front of their lairs.

Raksha Bandhan (or *Rakhi Purnima*). Full moon. Women tie a *rakhi* round their brother's wrist (a thread decorated with paper flowers) to protect them during the coming year.

August-September

Krishna Janmashtami 8th and 9th day of the month. Krishna's anniversary is the occasion for plays to be put on by children of the *Ras Lila*.

Independence Day August 15. Prime Minister's speech at the Red Fort at Delhi.

Ramdevji Festival at Ramdevra (Around Jaisalmer). 2nd-11th days after the new moon. Ramdev, a local hero who defended the oppressed, is celebrated.

Ganesh Chaturthi 4th day after the new moon. Anniversary of the birth of Ganesha, the elephant-headed god.

September-October

Nav Ratri ("nine nights") 1st-9th nights after the new moon. Fasting and *puja* (worship) in honour of Devi – mainly represented as Durga. The last four days are called **Durga Puja**. Rama, an incarnation of Vishnu, is also celebrated. Each district organises *Ram-Lila* and puts up enormous effigies of the demon Ravana and his two henchmen.

Dasahra (or *Vijay Dashami*) 10th day after the new moon. This "10th day victory" of Rama over Ravana is celebrated by the burning, just after nightfall, of the effigies of the three demons who are stuffed with firecrackers.

Marwar Festival at Jodhpur At the full moon. Parades, competitions, cultural events.

October-November

Divali (or *Dipavali*) New moon. This, with Holi, is the other major Hindu festival. Houses are cleaned from top to bottom in order to welcome Lakshmi, goddess of good fortune, in true style. Firecrackers, Roman candles and other pyrotechnical wonders all invade the bazaars which are also stocked to the brim with little candles and earthenware lamps: Rama's triumphant return to Adyodhya after 14 years of exile must be celebrated with a maximum of noise and light. Houses are ablaze with lights – little oil lamps or strings of electric lights – strung across windows and along garden walls. The children set off firecrackers and the night sky is lit up by exploding rockets. In small towns, the night of Divali is quite magical, in large cities, such as Delhi, it may feel more like a bomb attack than a religious festival.

Bhai Duj 3rd day after the new moon. Brothers call on their sisters to bring them a new sari and offer them gifts of money. In exchange, the sisters paint a red spot (tika) on their brother's forehead.

Pushkar Camel Fair and Chandrabhaga Fair Full moon. Cattle market and cultural events at Pushkar and at Jhalrapatan (near Jhalawar).

Guru Nanak Jayanti Full moon. Anniversary of Guru Nanak, founder of the Sikh community. Verses of the Nanak are recited and there is a procession in honour of Granth Sahib.

Moslem festivals

In the Islamic calendar, based solely on the moon, each new year starts between 10 and 12 days before the previous one. This means that the dates of festivals are far from fixed and can occur at any time during the year.

Muharram 10th day of *muharram* (1st month of the year). After nine days of fasting in honour of the martyr Hussein, Mohammed's grand-son, Shiites take *tazia* (paper replicas of Hussein's tomb) to a river where they are immersed.

Id-i Milad 12th day of *rabi ul-awwal* (3rd month). Mohammed's anniversary.

Ramzan During *ramzan* (9th month) adults fast all day from dawn to dusk (Ramadan). The 27th night commemorates the day when the Koran came down from the sky.

Id ul-Fitr 1st day of *shawwal* (10th month). Day of festivities at the end of the ramzan fasting.

Bakr Id (or *Id ul-Zuhara*) 10th day of *zil-haj* (12th month). The sacrifice of Ismael, son of Abraham, is celebrated by killing thousands of goats.

Urs of Sufi Saints (at various times), anniversary of the death of Hazrat Nizam ud-Din Auliya at **Delhi** and Khwaja Main ud-Din Chisti at **Ajmer**.

INDIAN CULTURE

In India, culture is not restricted to the more scholarly forms that have been exported to the West (classical music and dance or Satyajit Ray's movies) and which are more representative of an urban elite. While India's larger metropolises are gradually yielding to the onslaught of Western culture, conservative rural Rajasthan, still light-years away from Hollywood and Techno music, remains a stronghold of time-worn traditions. A puppet show in a tiny isolated village in the Thar or the nostalgic drone of a *sarangi* in a side-street of Jaisalmer soon make visitors forget the strident bad taste of modern Indian television. In fact, once back home, many people often find themselves strangely pursued by haunting desert melodies which tap into a universe of dreams and energies hitherto unknown to consumers of synthetic modern music.

Music and dancing

From Mughal and Rajput courts...

In addition to its complexity, another distinctive feature of classical Indian music is the fact that it is not written, but passed on from master to pupil. Based on a heptametric register (Sa-Ri-Ga-Ma-Pa-Dha-Ni), musical modes or **ragas** express different moods or atmospheres *(rasa)*, which are in turn reinforced by a highly-complicated rhythmic pattern, known as **tala**. An accompanying bass instrument provides a background melody similar to the distinctive drone of ancient Western music.

Although southern India's music traditions ("Carnatic") have remained faithful to their original religious inspirations, northern Indian ("Hindustani") music evolved on contact with artists brought by the Moslem sultans and emperors from Persia. This is also the case for northern dancing traditions, such as the **kathak**, which, while retaining its original theme – Krishna – also assimilated other Middle-Eastern influences. It is based on rhythmic foot beats, reinforced by the tinkling of the little bells *(ghungru)* fastened round the dancers' ankles. As in other Indian dances, body and hand *(mudra)* gestures and expression *(abhinaya)* are based on an age-old symbolism to express distinct feelings and emotions *(bhava)*.

A typical Hindustani music group would comprise three musicians: a soloist, a drummer and a **tamboura** player (a four-stringed instrument which produces the steady background drone). Rhythm is provided by a **tabla**, a percussion instrument composed of two drums of varying sizes, beaten with the palm of the hand or the fingers. Such groups also often feature a **sitar** and a **sarod** (stringed instruments), a flute and the human voice.

As well as the more scholarly forms of singing (**dhrupad**, **khayal**, etc), an Indian's daily life will be surrounded by other semi-classical forms, such as **ghazal**, **thumri**, etc, and songs of worship, **bhajan** for Hindus and **qawwal** for Sufis.

... to the Rajasthani countryside

No family or village ceremony or festival would be complete without the presence of musician-singers, **Dholis**. These communities of travelling professional musicians are, for the most part, members of the lower castes or Moslem converts, as is the case of the **Manganiyars, Langas** and **Kalbeliyas**. Their powerful, husky voices can be heard chanting the religious poems of leading mystics or singing popular ballads in an easy-to-understand, no-fuss manner. A more

Dhola-Maru

The love affair between prince Dhola and princess Maru is one of the favourite subjects of Rajasthan's ballad singers (and painters). Just before her marriage to prince Umra, Maru eloped with her beloved Dhola. The betrayed fiancé pursued the lovers relentlessly through forests and over deserts. During their flight, Dhola was bitten by a poisonous snake and died, but Shiva took pity on him and resuscitated him. From then on the young couple lived an idyllic life such as is the dream of all young Rajasthanis.

elaborate version, **mand**, also emerged in princely courts, intended to immortalise the chivalrous and amorous exploits of their Rajput patrons.

The **Charans**, musicians, singers, storytellers and bards, are also genealogists, while the **Bhopas**, travelling priests, relate the tales of warrior saints, in particular of Pabuji. Before singing, a Bhopa minstrel brings out a painted canvas (*phad* or *pharh*) which illustrates the saint's life, then as he chants the saint's exploits, he points to the appropriate picture. The **Bhats**, also of troubadour tradition, but non-religious, traditionally put on **puppet** *(kathputli)* shows. The puppets are made of wood and fabric, and worked with two strings and their shows are accompanied by a drum and a bamboo whistle.

Among **folk instruments**, the **sarangi** undoubtedly takes place of honour. This bowed instrument is held vertically on the right thigh and played sitting down. In common with the majority of India's stringed instruments, as well as 3 or 4 gut strings, it possesses sympathetically vibrating strings which resonate to the vibrations of the bow and the fret. The **rawanahattha**, also a bowed instrument (the body is made out of a coconut shell and the rest out of bamboo), produces a bewitching sound, in perfect harmony with the mysterious desert atmosphere. The **shenai** is a double-reeded oboe-like instrument found throughout India. Its cheerful, distinctive notes make it particularly popular in parades and processions. Rajasthan also boasts a number of flutes found only within the region, such as the **algoza**, a double-flute on which musicians can play both the melody and the accompanying drone, and the **narh** (or nad), desert flute, played vertically. The **poongi,** with its distinctive bulge, is the famous instrument of the snake charmers of the Kalbeliyas' community. Rajasthan's most common drum is the **dhol**, beaten with one or two sticks. The smaller **dholak** is struck with the flat of the hand or the fingers. Lastly, the **morsing** is a small iron instrument similar to a mouth organ or Jew's harp found throughout India.

Rajasthan's **traditional dances** are often carried out in groups: **dandia**, **ger** and **gidar** are danced by men only, armed with sticks or swords, while **ghoomar** are danced by circles of women, whose swirling skirts create a magical, quite thrilling effect. One of the most spell-binding dances is the **terahtal** which is carried out by women clenching a sabre between their teeth or balancing an oil lamp on their heads. Thirteen small cymbals are attached to their waist, wrists and elbows and further accentuate the dance's beat. Finally, there is a **fire dance**, a speciality of the members of the religious Siddh Nath sect.

Living literature

Over the centuries, Rajasthan's legends, popular fables and epic tales have traditionally been handed down by word of mouth. The oldest written work known today is the tale of a 9C Mewar hero, **Kuman Raso**. The **Prithviraj Raso**, another epic poem, relates the story of Prithviraj III, the Chauhan sovereign defeated by the Moslems in 1192.

Hindi literature is relatively poor by comparison with that of other Indian languages, it has nonetheless produced great poets such as **Amir Khusau** (1253-1325), who also wrote in Persian, and mystics such as **Kabir** (15C) and **Mira Bai** (16C *(see p 355)*, whose works are still very well-known because they are sung as *bhajan* or *ghazal*. This is also the case with Urdu poetry and authors such as **Mir** (18C), **Ghalib** (19C) and **Iqbal** (20C). The contribution of **Premchand**, a major Hindi novelist (1880-1936) and large numbers of Indian writers writing in English marked the 20C. Since the 1980s, the latter have reached world-wide recognition, with authors such as **Vikram Seth** *(A Suitable Boy)*, **Amitav Ghosh**, **Amit Chaudhuri**, **Upamanyu Chatterjee** among others.

"Bollywood" cinema

"Masala movies"

India is famous abroad for its classic films, but such films and their directors remain practically unknown within India, because they fail to appeal to the majority of India's cinema-goers. The latter have little time for deep meanings or realism, they are interested in entertainment, escape and action. Over one-third of the **850 films** produced in India every year are made in "Bollywood" (the nickname for Bombay's film industry). A stunning mixture of music, tragedy and slapstick comedy, these "masala movies" last three hours and despite the fact that the outcome of the eternal confrontation between the goodies and the baddies is obvious right from the start (even to non-Hindi speakers), they continue to enjoy widespread popularity. A whirlwind of genres, **dancing and singing** is followed pell-mell by action and drama, combining to produce the essential mixture for success. The songs are promoted on the market before the film hits the box-office, and in fact, their success or failure actually conditions whether or not a film is released. Consequently, some of the more popular melodies are so well-known that the whole audience launches into heart-felt renderings of them when the film actually reaches the cinemas.

Typical "Bollywood" billboard

J. Horner/HOA QUI

SOCIAL ETIQUETTE

Tourism is not new to Rajasthan, even in the most isolated hamlets, and tourists shouldn't be surprised when greeted with choruses of "One pen, one pen" or "Five rupees" by hordes of mischievous little children.
The diversity of peoples and cultures in India is such that a foreigner may easily find it difficult to make any real contact with Indians. One often feels trapped between seeming too patronising or too aloof, and whatever the case, the breadth and intricacy of the culture make it difficult for foreigners to relate to new found friends. Chance encounters in markets or on streets with locals happen all the time, but remain, of course, superficial, and often somewhat bewildering. Although making real contact with well-educated Indians is apparently easier, Westerners may soon become uncomfortable with what can be perceived as a somewhat callous approach to their country's plight. The only rule is perhaps to remember that this is a land whose history dates back over several millenniums and as such getting to know the people requires not only time, but patience.

Forewarned is forearmed

Greeting – To show respect, place both hands together at chest level. Such politeness is however out of place in everyday situations (when entering a shop, for example). If so greeted, you should however return the compliment. Do not attempt to shake hands, if not invited to do so. While this Western custom is growing more common, it is only practised among people of the same sex.

Language – If your knowledge of Hindi goes beyond "Namaste. Aap ka shubh naam kya hai?" ("Hello. What's your name?"), you will encounter great success, particularly among less well-off folk, who are always an appreciative audience. It is even a good idea to try and make yourself as entertaining as possible. You will at least avoid being considered like the more upper-class Indians, who have a reputation for being snobbish, boring and generally overbearing.

Interpreting "No problem" and head-shaking – Polite behaviour in India, which involves always answering what you think someone wants to hear, is a source of great misunderstanding for many tourists. One soon learns to be wary of promises and the eternal "No problem...", which are more often than not portents of major problems. It is also essential to understand that head-shaking does not necessarily mean "no", but rather "OK" or "Alright".

Shoes – Shoes must be removed before entering any religious building. When visiting Indians, make sure you look at their feet before entering their home to see whether you should remove your shoes or not. If you make the mistake of touching your shoes while taking them off, make sure you don't attempt to shake hands with this (polluted) hand.

Clothes – Women should avoid bare shoulders, low necks and wearing anything that doesn't cover their legs. If wearing trousers, these should be ideally covered by a tunic or a long shirt. Men should wear only trousers (shorts are considered underclothes).

Alcohol – As the consumption of alcohol is discouraged in Indian culture as a rule, people sometimes have trouble handling it when they do have a drink. If you are invited round for a cocktail, be aware that things can get a bit out of hand.

R. Mattès

"General stores" at Bikaner

Meals – If there is no cutlery, only eat with your right hand. If invited to a traditional Indian family, you will eat alone while the masters of the house serve you. The pre-dinner period can often last for what might seem a very long time, but this is because people rarely speak during the meal and guests all leave immediately after the last mouthful.

Discussions – There is no point in launching into major philosophical debates, and avoid religion at all costs.

Breaking down caste barriers – There is also no point in trying to encourage Indians from different classes to mix with each other, such attempts will only result in clumsy blunders. Someone from the Brahmin caste cannot for example eat food prepared by someone from a lower caste.

Gifts – If offering a gift, don't expect it to be opened in front of you or to be thanked on the spot. Your host will put it to one side and only open it after your departure. If invited to dinner, sweets are always a safe bet.

Photography – Most children and young men adore being photographed and will often throw themselves in front of your camera, generally managing to prevent you from taking the little girl you were patiently trying to photograph. Most women will not allow themselves to be photographed and you should always ask their permission.

Queueing – Queueing in Indian cities is far from an orderly, well-organised affair. There can often be two queues, one for men and one for women (and the disabled). If there is only one queue, women are allowed to jump the queue.

Public transport – If attempting to board a bus or train without a reservation, do it Indian style: barge your way on. Any pretence at polite behaviour will leave you standing on the platform.

Languages

India has 18 "constitutional" (also known as "regional" or "major") languages and 1652 dialects. Such statistics may prove daunting to a prospective visitor. **English** is however spoken throughout the country and was declared an "associate" language, together with Hindi, and continues to remain, over half a century after Independence, one of the few languages in which Indians of different mother tongues can communicate among each other.

Indian mosaic

Shortly after Independence, the Indian Union was divided into states on the basis of linguistic practices. In Gujarat, Gujarati is spoken, Punjabi in Punjab, etc. Most of the North's languages belong to the **Indo-Aryan family**, derived from Sanskrit which was introduced by the Aryan invaders. In the south, **Dravidian languages** such as Tamil, Malayalam, Telugu and Kannaa are spoken by some 230 million people. These languages have existed in India for longer than their Aryan counterparts and are as such considered to be the only languages of solely Indian origins. After Independence, the Delhi government attempted to impose Hindi, an Indo-Aryan language, in schools and administrations throughout the country, but it came up against resistance on the part of the southern states and the programme of linguistic standardisation was abandoned. Two other linguistic families exist in India: in the Himalayan borders and in the outlying northeastern states, the inhabitants speak **Sino-Tibetan languages** (Tibetan, Lepcha, Manipuri, Mizo), while some of the aboriginal tribes of central India speak **Austro-Asiatic languages**, or munda, which are closer to Khmer dialects, such as Santali or Khasi.

Sanskrit

Sanskrit (from "samskrta" – "perfect") was the cultural language of the Aryan invaders, spoken only by an elite. The masses spoke languages derived from Sanskrit, but which were grammatically simpler, called "prakrit" ("natural"). Sanskrit was the language of the sacred texts, rituals, philosophical and spiritual speculation and also scientific knowledge and it was to play a major role in the spread of classical Indian civilisation. Through the diffusion of myths, basic ideologies and a concept of the world, Sanskrit brought India a unity it would not otherwise have achieved. Recognised as one of India's 18 official languages, it is now only used by an elite and even then not on an everyday basis, and today plays a purely cultural-religious function. Nonetheless national radio broadcasts news twice daily in Sanskrit. Furthermore all the Dravidian and Indo-Aryan languages contain innumerable Sanskrit words, thereby helping to maintain this language's role as a form of cultural glue.

Sanskrit is written in **devangari** script, the "writing of the gods". The alphabet (34 consonants and 14 vowels and dipthongs) is written from left to right and the words are linked by a continuous horizontal line. *Devangari* script is used to write other distinct, yet related languages, such as Gujarati, Punjabi and Bengali.

Hindi

The most commonly spoken language in northern India, spoken by Hindus and Moslems alike, is now called Hindustani. It emerged during the 13C around Delhi and Agra at the same time as the Indo-Islamic culture began to spread.

Based on a local language, **Braj** (spoken in Braj, a region of Mathura) it evolved on contact with **Persian**, spoken by the Mughal emperors and sultans and their administrations, from which it was to borrow many Persian, Arabic and Turkish words.

In the early 19C, Hindu circles saw the emergence of a literary form of Hindustani, which began to show a distinct preference for Sanskrit rather than Arabic-Persian words. It was named Hindi. Since Independence and Partition, Hindi has sought to favour more and more Sanskrit words, thus asserting its Hindu origins and setting itself apart from a more Islamic Arabic-Persian style. Such Sanskritisation is particularly noticeable in Hindi literature, but in everyday Hindi (Hindustani), Arabic-Persian terms continue to crop up as reminders of the deep-rooted influence the Moslems had on culture, independent of religion.

Hindi is written in **devangari**. The fourth most spoken language in the world, it is used by **400 million** Indians located in the "Hindi Belt": Delhi (it is the mother tongue of 77 % of Delhi's inhabitants), Rajasthan (33 %), Haryana, Uttar Pradesh (85 %), Bihar and Madhya Pradesh. It is also spoken in the Punjab (56 %) together with Punjabi.

Family likenesses

Many Hindi words will seem familiar to Western ears. Consider, for example, the likeness between the "name" of a royal "king", from the Latin "rex, regis" and the "nam" of a "raja" rajput, or Rome's "pater" and "mater" and Delhi's "pita" and "mata"... Similarly, the presence of the British in India has led to many Hindi words being adopted by the English language: bungalow, curry, jodhpurs, chutney... Indeed, Indians may be very amused to find that the battle cry of some British football crowds is "Vindaloo"...

Urdu

This word appeared in the 18C and initially referred to the scholarly form of Hindustani, steeped at that time in Persian, Arabic and Turkish words. In the early 19C when Hindi, the Sanskritised form of Hindustani began to develop, "Urdu" began to refer to purely Islamic Hindustani literature. By adopting a growing number of **Arabic-Persian** terms, Urdu differentiated itself more and more from Hindi, finally to become irrevocably associated with Islamism. It is one of the rare languages not to be based on geographic factors, and is spoken by some 100 million Moslems over Northern and Central India. The percentage of the population for whom Urdu is the most commonly used language is 6 % in Delhi, 11 % in Uttar Pradesh and 3 % in Rajasthan. The morphology and syntax of Urdu are identical to Hindi. The only difference with its sister-language lies in the vocabulary and script which are of Arabic-Persian origins.

Rajasthani dialects

Rajasthani is a language very close to Hindi, but with neither literature nor a scholarly form, and it is commonly used by over 55 % of Rajasthan's population. Rajasthani dialects vary greatly from one region to another and even from village to village. The most common is **Marwari** (in the northwest), followed by **Mewari** (in the southeast) and **Shekhawati**. The various tribes (Bhils, Minas, Rabaris...) also have their own dialects, but **Bhili** is the most common (4 %).

Practical information

B. Pérousse/HOA QUI

A bus trip

Before going

• Local time

India is 5hr30min ahead of standard GMT / UTC time, 10hr30min ahead of American EST and 4hr30min behind Australian EST. Officially referred to as Indian Standard Time, the time is the same throughout the country. When it is noon in Delhi, it is 6.30am in Britain (5.30am in the winter), 1.30am in America and 4.30pm in Australia.

• How to call India

To call India from abroad, dial 00 + 91 + the regional code (without the 0) + the number you wish to call.

• When to go

The best season to visit is from **mid-October** to **March**, when the sky is blue and the temperatures are pleasant. At this time, the days are relatively short (the sun rises around 7am and sets around 5.30pm) and the chill of the night only fades slowly. As a general rule the weather is dry and sunny, but a combination of very low night-time temperatures and relatively high day-time temperatures means that Delhi, Agra and Jaipur can become swamped in a thick morning fog which severely disrupts traffic. This is also the height of the tourist season and hotels are sometimes fully booked. However it is always possible to find some sort of accommodation if booked a few days in advance. Whatever the case, avoid the heat-wave summer period of May and June, when Delhi has been known to reach temperatures of 46°C and Bikaner and Jaisalmer have had record highs of 50°C.

During the **monsoon** season, heavy rains occur during July and August but have almost dried up by September. Disruptions due to torrential rainfall do occur and heavy showers are frequent. Roads can often be closed and rail and air traffic affected. Rainfall always leads to a sudden drop in temperature and to a rise in the level of humidity in the air.

Average daily and nightly temperatures in Rajasthan.

	Jan	Feb	Mar	Apr	May	June	July	Aug	Sept	Oct	Nov	Dec
Max (°C)	22	25	31	37	42	42	38	34	36	34	30	25
Min (°C)	8	10	15	22	27	28	27	25	24	19	13	10

• Packing list

Clothes

Take lightweight, comfortable, easy-care clothing, preferably in cotton or linen. A woollen jumper is a must for mid-season evenings, if you plan to visit Mount Abu or when staying in air-conditioned hotels. Temperatures can be cold during the winter period, particularly from December to mid-February and many hotels are not heated, so take warm socks, trousers and a jumper. Out of respect for local traditions, women should avoid low necks, bare shoulders, legs should be covered and, as a general rule, gauzy or tight-fitting garments are not recommended. Men should not walk around bare-chested and shorts should be no higher than knee-length.

It is not essential to pack too much because clothes generally dry during the night (except during the monsoon season or in the winter) and it is easy to buy inexpensive, well-made clothes on the spot.
All packing-lists should include a pair of slip-on shoes, because one finds oneself slipping them on and off constantly, particularly when visiting religious sites. You will also need socks to protect your feet from the hot or dirty floors, in fact a pair of plastic flip-flops are a good idea, even in some showers, which can be of dubious cleanliness. Don't forget some sort of dressy outfit if eating out in one of the larger hotels, where such ceremony is still common, sunglasses of course, an umbrella (for the monsoon season), a cotton hat and a swimsuit.

Extras

Take a strong, waterproof bag or suitcase which can be locked, together with one or two little padlocks when travelling by train or if staying in hotels with unlocked doors. It is recommended to carry any valuables in a body-belt and to have photocopies of all important documents: air ticket, passport, visa, insurance, what to do in case of theft of your credit cards and a numbered list of travellers' cheques. This may prove invaluable if the originals are mislaid.
A sleeping-bag will prove useful if planning a camel-trek and sleeping in the desert. It will also make rail travel more comfortable and come in handy in some of the smaller or less well-equipped hotels where the bedding or the heating is not adequate. During the hot season, a single sheet or sheet sleeping-bag will be sufficient. A torch will help out during power cuts and ear-plugs are recommended for light sleepers.

• A trip for everyone

Travelling with children

Indians adore children and will often come up and talk to them or pat them affectionately on the head, particularly if they are blond. Some children can get a bit irritated by such interest. Children are more sensitive to the heat and the sun than adults, who should ensure that they drink sufficiently – dehydration can occur much faster than one would think. Hotels will generally add an extra bed or two so that children can sleep in their parent's room at an extra charge of around $4 per bed in an average hotel. If travelling with a baby, take a kangaroo pouch or back-sling, because pavements are not only few and far between but difficult to manoeuvre with a pushchair. Disposable nappies are relatively scarce, but can be found in chemists.

Travelling in a couple

Indian society continues to impose a clear demarcation between the sexes. Men and women, even married, do not hold hands, touch or kiss when in front of someone else, and especially not in public. Such customs should be respected in order to avoid shocking those around you.

Women travelling alone

A woman travelling alone or who smokes or drinks alcohol in public is commonly felt by most Indians to be a "loose woman". That said, a woman alone in India runs absolutely no risks providing she exercises a minimum amount of common sense and respects local customs. The sexual revolution which took place in the late 80s has perhaps made India less "inhibited" than formerly. Men have become more enterprising, sometimes even aggressive – especially in the north – and because they are convinced that westerners have an unbridled approach to sex, can be over-pushy. If travelling alone, a woman will need to pay special attention to her clothing *(see Packing list)* or run the risk of a great deal of unwanted attention. Whatever the case, even if covered from head to foot, a woman alone will be scrutinised and probably accosted – you will unfortunately have to get used to it. Two golden rules may guarantee a minimum amount of peace: never look a man in the eye and ignore anyone who accosts you. It is also a good idea to avoid guesthouses or hotels with poorly-locking doors, walls full of little spy-holes or with fanlights, popular among "peeping toms". When travelling on a bus, don't be surprised if your neighbour slyly slides his hand onto your lap. React immediately and firmly. Above all, don't be naïve and don't believe everything you are told.

Elderly people

Travelling in India should pose no problems at all to elderly people who are as a general rule respected and venerated. It is however clear that the noise, pollution and long, bumpy journeys make for a tiring trip. The best option is either an organised tour or renting a car (with driver).

Disabled travellers

Facilities for the disabled are non-existent and only a tiny percentage of hotels have lifts (except in Delhi and Agra). It is advisable to rent a car and travel with a friend or relation who can help overcome the numerous difficulties, such as potholed or overcrowded pavements.

• Address book

Embassies and Consulates

Australia – High Commission, 3-5 Moonah Place, Yarrelumla, ACT-2600, ☎ (02) 6273 3999, Fax (02)6273 1308, hicanb@ozemail.com.au

Canada – High Commission, 10 Springfield Rd, Ottawa, Ontario K1M 1C9, ☎ (613)744 3751, Fax (613)744 0913, hicomind@ottawa.net

New Zealand – High Commission, 180 Molesworth St, Wellington, ☎ (04) 473 6390, Fax (04) 499 0665, hicomind@clear.net.nz

United Kingdom – High Commission, India House, Aldwych, London WC2B 4NA, ☎ (020) 7836 8484, Fax (020) 7836 4331, www.hcilondon.org

USA – 2107 Massachusetts Ave NW, Washington, DC 20008, ☎ (202) 939 7000, Fax (202) 265 4351, www.indianembassy.org

Indian Tourist Information Offices

Australia – Level 2, Piccadilly, 210 Pitt St, Sydney NSW-2000, ☎ (02) 92 64 4855, Fax (02)9264 4860, sydney@tourismindia.com

Canada – 60 Bloor St West, Suite No 1003, Toronto, Ontario M4W 3B8, ☎ (416) 962 3787, Fax (416)962 3788, toronto@tourismindia.com

United Kingdom – 7 Cork St, London W1X 2LN, ☎ (020) 7437 3677, Fax (020) 7494 1048, 24 hours brochure line ☎ 01233 211999 www.indiatouristoffice.org

USA – Avenue of the Americas, Suite 1808, NY-10020, ☎ (212) 751 6840, Fax (212) 582 3274, ny@tourismindia.com

The **Rajasthan State Tourism Dept** may also be worth contacting to help plan your trip: Department of Tourism and Culture, Government Hostel Campus, M.I. Road, Jaipur, India, ☎ (91) 141 376362, Fax (91) 141 376362, www.rajasthan-tourism.com

Web sites

Government of India Tourist Office – www.indiatouristoffice.org

Hindu Online – www.hinduonline.com

Indian Government – www.nic.in

Ministry of Tourism – www.tourismindia.com

Times of India – www.timesofindia.com

Bookshops

Given the quantity of specialised bookshops both in North America and Britain, the following are intended purely as starting points and are by no means exhaustive.

Stanford's Map and Travel Bookshop, 12-14 Long Acre, Covent Garden, London WC2E 9LP ☎ (020) 7836 1321.

India Bookhouse, 2251 West Devon Avenue, Chicago, Illinois, 60659 ☎ (773) 764 6567, Fax (773) 764 7195, www.indiabookhouse.com

The following websites may also prove useful:

www.amazon.com

www.booklook.com – specialising in out of print books with some 700 titles relating to India.

www.firstandsecond.com – which claims to be India's biggest online bookshop.

• Formalities

The details given below are purely for information and are likely to undergo changes at any time. It is recommended that you contact the Indian consulate closest to you at least one month before leaving.

Identity papers, visa

All visitors to India must have a **visa**. This will not be delivered when you arrive in the country and must be requested, at least one week before leaving, from the Indian consulate *(see above)* nearest to you. A **passport**, valid for at least six months after your intended arrival in India, two passport photos, a return ticket (or proof of repatriation insurance) and an amount in cash that will vary depending on your nationality are also required. In most cases your passport can be collected the following day. Requests can also be made by mail; contact the nearest Indian consulate for the appropriate procedure.

Extensions can only be requested once in India and are rarely granted for over a month. Application forms are available from the Home Office in New Delhi, which once filled in, must be returned with four passport photos to the Foreigners' Registration Office.

In theory, foreigners intending to remain in India for over four months will need to present a Tax Clearance Certificate to customs on leaving. This can be obtained from the Income Tax Office in New Delhi, but is, in practice, never actually demanded.

Customs

Imports – When arriving in India, you will not need to declare anything if carrying less than 200 cigarettes (or 50 cigars), one or two bottles of wine or spirits, one or two cameras and 25 films, a 16mm camera and five reels and a video recorder. However, video cameras, professional equipment and laptop computers must be declared on the Tourist Baggage Re-Export Form that will be stapled to your passport. On departure, these items must be shown as proof that they haven't been sold. Imports of Indian rupees are not permitted, but you can bring in as much foreign currency as you wish. If travelling with over US$10 000, fill in a Currency Declaration Form and keep any exchange slips to prove that you didn't change money on the black market.

Exports – Indian rupees cannot be taken out of the country and must be converted before leaving (with proof of exchange). Visitors can leave India with souvenirs of unlimited value and jewellery worth a maximum of 100 000Rs. Otherwise an export permit must be obtained from the Reserve Bank of India. Items made from ivory, animal fur, snake skin or any other wild animal, whatever their value, cannot be exported, nor can anything over 100 years old. Export Clearance Certificates must be requested either from the shopkeeper or from the Museum Department (Archaeological Survey of India, Janpath, New Delhi, ☎ (011) 301 72 20). It is also worthwhile checking what can be imported back into your own country by contacting your customs department.

Health regulations

Tourists from Europe, North America and Australia are not subject to any particular health regulations.

Vaccinations

Although none are compulsory, vaccination against hepatitis A and B, tetanus, polio and typhoid, are advised and, if intending to stay for a long time in any rural areas, against Japanese encephalitis (during the monsoon period) and rabies (particularly if staying in an area which doesn't have an anti-rabies centre) is recommended. Even if you've left it until the last minute, it is still better to be partially vaccinated rather than not vaccinated at all. It is a good idea to have all vaccinations recorded on an International Health Certificate (available from your doctor or health department) which you should take with you. Advice can be obtained from doctors, telephone information centres, international vaccine centres and airline companies. The World Health Organisation (www.who.org), together with the US State Department (www.travel.state.gov) and the British Home Office (www.fco.gov.uk) also have useful web sites.

Driving licence

An International Driving Licence is essential to drive a car or a motorbike in India.

• Currency

All everyday expenses can be paid for in Indian rupees but the larger hotels will require bills to be paid in foreign currency, generally with a credit card.

Cash

The currency in India is the **rupee** (Rs). At the time of publishing, US$1 equalled around 45Rs.

The rupee is divided into 100 *paise*. There are 25 and 50 *paise* **coins** and 1, 2 and 5 rupee coins. 5, 10 and 15 *paise* coins can only be found in the tiniest towns. Small change is the bane of Indian life; shopkeepers almost never have any and taxi and rickshaw drivers never have any. Any small change you come across should be treasured.

10, 20, 50, 100 and 500Rs **notes** exist. Although 1, 2 and 5Rs notes are no longer printed by the Reserve Bank of India since 1996, they are still in circulation in the provinces. Damaged notes are almost always refused by shopkeepers but can be changed in banks.
The Indian numbering system counts in tens, hundreds, thousands, hundred thousands and ten millions. A hundred thousand is a *lakh* and ten million is a *crore*. Both words are almost always used in place of their English equivalent. Thus you will see 10 *lakh* rather than one million and one *crore* rather than 10 million. Furthermore if something costs five *crore* or is worth 10 *lakh*, it always means 'of rupees'.

Money exchange

Buying rupees is impossible abroad, but it is possible to change money on arrival at all international airports. Money can also be changed at some main banks: State Bank of India, Bank of Rajasthan, State Bank of Bikaner and Jaipur and the Bank of Baroda. It is quicker to change money in foreign exchange offices, but these only exist in the major tourist centres. The simplest solution is often to change money in your hotel because many medium and luxury class hotels buy foreign currency or exchange travellers' cheques. The tiny commission charge more than compensates for the time lost. Changing money on the black market is not recommended because of the risk of forged notes. Keep all proof of exchange operations (Encashment Certificates), because they will be demanded when changing rupees back into foreign currency on leaving, if you want to pay your bill in rupees in hotels that request payment in foreign currency or to obtain a Tax Clearance Certificate *(see "Customs")*. **US dollars** are always a good idea and less hassle than other currencies.

Travellers' Cheques

The most widely accepted travellers' cheques are **American Express** and **Thomas Cook** in **dollars** or **pounds sterling**. Other currency travellers' cheques are accepted but may prove more difficult.

Credit cards

Take a **MasterCard** or a **Visa** card. Any other cards will prove a problem anywhere other than Delhi. Many restaurant and hotel bills in medium and upper category establishments accept credit cards, which in theory, does away with the 10% charge *(see "Taxes")*. However, an extra 5 to 10% may be added by shops if paying with a credit card. It is always advisable to obtain a receipt and tear up the carbon slip to avoid any fraudulent usage. Withdrawing money with a credit card is only possible in the large cities from the Bank of Baroda or Andhra Bank. ATM machines can only be found in Delhi.

Transferring money from abroad to India

It is possible to arrange for a transfer in less than 24 hours, by contacting someone at home and asking them to contact their local branch of either Western Union or Thomas Cook.
Western Union – Offices in Delhi, Agra, Jaipur and Udaipur.
Thomas Cook – Offices in Delhi, Agra, Jaipur.

• Spending money

As would be expected, Rajasthan offers good value-for-money, though Delhi is relatively expensive. A tight budget will require a minimum of **$10** per day per person, including a single room in a modest, but decent hotel (from $3 for a double room), dining out in small restaurants (around $1) and using auto-rickshaws, buses or trains (non air-conditioned second class compartments) to travel. It is possible to spend even less if dormitory-style accommodation and the cheapest eating-houses don't put you off.

For **$75** per day, one has a choice of heritage hotels or 2- or 3-star hotels ($40), while meals in a good restaurant cost around $4, with the possibility of dining out in a luxury hotel from time to time. You can travel in second class air-conditioned rail compartments or rent a non air-conditioned car with chauffeur ($30).

By spending a minimum of **$120** per day, you can stay in 4-star hotels ($80), eat in the smartest restaurants ($10) and travel by air or air-conditioned car ($45). Palatial-style accommodation will cost around $250 per room.

The above prices are purely for information and are calculated per person sharing a **double room** (not including trips, visits or shopping).

• Booking in advance

Domestic airline tickets should be booked well ahead of departure as should the first few nights hotel accommodation in Delhi. Booking can be made either through a travel agency *(see p 97)* or by directly contacting the hotel by fax. Make sure you enquire about the price of rooms and taxes and take a copy of your confirmation with you. It is also recommended to book the rest of the trip if travelling during the peak season (December-February) or during India's national holidays *(see p 101)*. At these times, finding a hotel in Delhi, Agra or Udaipur will prove most difficult. If intending to brave India's roads and reckless drivers, self-drive cars can be booked by faxing a local agent or by contacting your local Hertz Reservations Centre. Alternatively Rajasthan can also be visited aboard one of the legendary Maharajas' Trains, bookings from *Palace on Wheels* or *Royal Orient (see p 105)*.

• Repatriation insurance

Travel and repatriation insurance covering theft, loss and medical costs is essential and should be taken out if it is not already covered by your credit card, airline ticket or package holiday. Travellers from the US, where medical costs are high, should pay special attention to the small print clauses. It is worth checking that activities such as scuba diving, motorcycling or even trekking are also covered.

• Gifts to offer

A guest *(atithi)* is considered to be an envoy from God and visitors may well get the chance to appreciate the hospitality of an Indian family during their trip. To thank one's hosts, take along good quality gifts that are difficult to find in India (possibly with London or New York printed on them), while leather goods, toiletries or perfume are also very acceptable.

GETTING THERE

• By air

Scheduled flights

Air India operates seven regular flights via New York/London/India per week and three flights via Chicago/London/India, also per week. The London-Delhi flight lasts around nine hours. Singapore Airlines (Air India's carrier), British Airways and Air France also operate several direct weekly flights from North America and the UK to India. There are no charter flights as such to India but many travel agents and tour operators offer interesting rates and it is well worth shopping around before booking.

Air India – Landsdowne House, 55 Berkeley Square, London WIX 5DB ☎ (020) 7495 7950/51, Fax (020) 7495 1401, www.airindia.com

Air India – 570, Lexington Avenue, 15th floor, New York, NY 10002, ☎ (212) 407 1300, Fax (212) 838 9533, www.airindia.com

British Airways – Information: callers within the UK ☎ 0345 222 111, callers outside the UK ☎ 44 141 222 2222, www.britishairways.com

Singapore Airlines – 143-147 Regent St, London W1R 7LB ☎ (020) 7439 8111, Fax (020) 7437 6856, www.singaporeair.com

Singapore Airlines – 55 East 59 St, Suite 20B, New York, NY 10022, ☎ (800) 742 333, Fax (212) 319 6139, www. singaporeair.com

Air France – Landsdowne House, 55 Berkeley Square, London WIX 5DB ☎ (020) 7495 7950/51, Fax (020) 7495 1401, www.airindia.com

Air France – 570, Lexington Avenue, 15th floor, New York, NY 10002, ☎ (212) 407 1300, Fax (212) 838 9533, www.airindia.com

Confirmation

Return flights should be confirmed at least 72hr before the departure date, possibly even on arrival, if certain of the return flight date.

Airport

The majority of international flights land at night at Indira Gandhi International Airport at Delhi *(see "Making the most of Delhi", p 151)*.

Airport taxes

On leaving India, travellers are required to pay a 500Rs airport tax in cash. Check however with your airline or travel agency to see whether this is included in the price of your ticket.

• Package deals

Many tour operators offer highly competitive rates for airline travel, combined with a choice of classical group tours or made-to-measure individual programmes. It is also possible to book a wide range of other services through them: hotels, car rentals, air tickets, etc.

There are simply hundreds of tour operators located in the UK, North America and India of course, catering to all tastes and budgets. It is possible to find operators which specialise in rail travel, culture, accommodation, off the beaten tracks, educational tours, wildlife safaris, sports and adventure holidays, charters and cruises among others. The choice is endless and the best option is to contact your nearest Indian tourist office *(see p 92)* who will send you a fact-finder file with the details of current reputable tour operators either in India or near you. Another possibility is to contact the Rajasthan State tourist office *(see p 92)*. When planning a trip to Rajasthan and to India in general, it is also a good idea to remember that getting from A to B always takes on average three times longer than it would when travelling in Europe or North America.

The basics

• Useful addresses

Tourist offices

The **Government of India Tourist Office** is the official Indian government national tourist office. There is a branch in each State capital, and in Delhi, Jaipur and Agra (even though the capital of Uttar Pradesh is Lucknow). All branches have efficient staff and a good selection of brochures on India.

Each State also has its own specific network of tourist offices, Tourist Reception Centres, located in all the main tourist centres. The quality and actual usefulness of such centres however varies widely. Most will be able to provide a map of the town, occasionally a few brochures and a list of government-authorised guest houses and guides.

Tourist Reception Centres are managed by an independent government agency, the **Tourism Development Corporation** (TDC) which also runs the State bus company and hotel chain. You will come across the Delhi TDC (Delhi Tourism), Uttar Pradesh TDC (U.P. Tourism) and the Rajasthan TDC (RTDC); the latter can be found in the local TDC hotel.

Embassies and consulates

All the embassies are located in the Chanakyapuri district of New Delhi.

Australian Embassy – 1/50-G Shantipath, ☎ (011) 688 8223, Fax (011) 688 7536.

British Embassy – 50 Shantipath, ☎ (011) 687 2161, Fax (011) 687 2882.

Canadian Embassy – 7/8 Shantipath, ☎ (011) 687 6500, Fax (011) 687 6579.

New Zealand Embassy – 50-N Nyaya Marg, ☎ (011) 688 3170, Fax (011) 688 3165.

United States Embassy – Shantipath, ☎ (011) 688 9033 (30 lines), Fax (011) 611 3033 (20 lines).

• Opening and closing times

Although Indians get up early and many households and residential areas are busy from daybreak, most working days start much later.

Tourist offices

10am-1.30pm/2pm-5pm; closed Sundays. Jaipur's and Jodhpur's offices open earlier and close later.

Banks

10am-2pm Monday-Friday; 10am-12noon Saturdays; closed on Sundays.

Bank branches in the large hotels and foreign exchange offices stay open later, sometimes until 7pm.

Post Office

10am-5pm Monday-Saturday; closed Sunday. Some branches close at 12noon on Saturdays. The central post offices (GPO) in some of the larger towns have longer opening hours, at least at some counters. The Central Telegraph Office is open 24 hours a day.

Shops

Modern retail shops are open 10am-6.30pm, booths and stalls from 9am to 8pm. Closing days will depend on local customs, but are often on Sundays, Mondays or Tuesdays.

Restaurants
Indians eat quite late but meals are generally served from 12.30pm-3pm and from 7.30pm-11.30pm. Most town restaurants open as early as 10am, serving cooked meals at meal times and snacks the rest of the time. Hotel coffee shops are open from 7am to 11.30pm, sometimes even 24 hours a day in the 4- or 5-star establishments.

Offices
10am-5pm Monday-Friday; 10am-1pm Saturday; closed on Sunday and every second Saturday of the month.

• Museums, monuments and sites
Opening times
In Rajasthan, government museums are open every day except Fridays and public holidays, 10am-4.30pm. The others are open from 10am-5pm, closed Mondays. Monuments are open from 9am-5pm (closing day variable), but many sites can be visited from daybreak onwards.

Entrance fees
The entrance fee to most museums and monuments is rarely more than 10Rs, very occasionally 150Rs (in some of Delhi's museums). Government-run museums are free in Rajasthan on Mondays. An extra charge (50Rs) will be made for cameras, more for video cameras.

Religious sites
Temples and mosques are open from daybreak to nightfall, but mosques are closed to tourists during prayer times and the tombs of Moslem saints are generally out-of-bounds to women. Some rare Hindu temples refuse access to non-Hindus, but providing tourists are correctly dressed, priests may waive this ban, in which case donations are most appreciated. Before entering a religious monument or edifice, always remove your shoes and ensure that your legs are covered. In *gurudwaras* and some mosques, men and women must wear a hat or scarf. Leather articles are not permitted within Jain sanctuaries and some Hindu temples.

Guided visits
The Tourist Reception Centres organise guided tours in Hindi and in English. The list of government-authorised English-speaking guides can be obtained from tourist offices. A four-hour visit for a party of one to four people will cost around 250Rs.

• Postal service
Mail can be sent from the **General Post Office** (GPO). Allow between one and three weeks for mail to reach its destination, depending on whether the town it is posted from has an airport or not. Stamps can be bought from the post office and in hotel boutiques. It costs 6Rs to airmail a postcard and 11Rs for a letter. Avoid putting letters in the red letter boxes (strangely familiar to British visitors) that can be found almost everywhere, because the stamps are frequently stolen. Post offices generally have a special counter for airmail. Pre-stamped international airmail letters are both inexpensive (6.5Rs) and save time. Parcels should be sent by **registered mail** (600Rs by sea and 850Rs per kg by air). **Philatelic** counters exist in the Delhi, Jaipur and Jodhpur GPOs.

R. Marcà

Letter box

Express post

To send express mail or parcels within India or abroad, go to the **EMS Speed Post** counter available in most post offices (640Rs for 500gr and 900Rs for a 1kg parcel) or contact **DHL**, very reliable, who can deliver within three to four days (1 320Rs for 500gr and 1 900Rs for 1kg). For parcels weighing over 10kg, contact a travel agency who will arrange air-freight delivery.

Poste restante

Most of the GPOs in the larger towns have a *poste restante* service. People wishing to send you mail should print the address as follows: last name in capital letters and underlined, first name, *Poste Restante*, GPO, GPO address. To pick up mail, you will need your passport. Check that mail hasn't been misfiled under the initial of your first name. Mail is generally held for two weeks, sometimes longer. If you have an **American Express** or **Thomas Cook** card, mail can also be sent to either one of the latter's addresses in Delhi, where it will be kept for you.

• Phone and fax

It can often be quicker to get an immediate connection with an international number (generally instantaneous) than with a neighbouring town. Neither telephone boxes nor telephone cards are very common in India. However the tiniest, most remote hamlets often have private booths with one or two telephones. Clearly indicated by large **STD/ISD/PCO** signs, they are open late and some operate 24 hours a day. Between 2 and 3Rs for a local call and 60Rs per minute to call the UK or 78Rs for the US. Post offices also have coin-operated boxes for local calls (1Rs) but these are notoriously out-of-order. Go to the **Central Telegraph Office** to call abroad.

International calls

To call abroad, dial 00 + the country code + the number you wish to dial without the 0. A reverse charge call can be made by dialling 000 + the country code + 17. You will obtain an international operator in your home country who will put you through. You will be charged the price of a local call for the connection.

Local calls

To make a local call, dial the number directly. If you are calling another town, add the town code and a 0 in front of the number.

There are cheap rates for domestic calls: 50 % reduction from 7am-8am and 7pm-8.30pm; 60 % from 6am-7am and 8.30pm-11pm; 75 % from 11pm-6am. Over the last few years, vast improvements have been made to the Indian telephone network, resulting in a proliferation of changes to telephone numbers, to which one or two figures are regularly added. It is thus inevitable that a percentage of the numbers indicated within this guide will no longer be correct when you reach India. If this is the case, call local directory enquiries ☎ 197.

Fax

Faxes can be sent from the private **STD/ISD/PCO** booths (around 150Rs per page) or from the **Central Telegraph Office** which is cheaper (100Rs).

• Internet

Private booths can be found in many bazaars of large cities, with Internet access and email facilities (40Rs to send a page, 25Rs to receive and print or 160Rs per hour).

• Public holidays

Each State has its own set of public holidays: those which are celebrated throughout India and those which only exist within the State. Some are days off for everyone, while others are only holidays for administrations and businesses. Finally, some of the more minor religious festivals are only celebrated by followers of that particular religion, who are allowed to take the day off.

Main public holidays

26 January	Anniversary of the Constitution (1950).
March-April	Good Friday.
15 August	Independence Day (1947).
2 October	Anniversary of the birth of Mahatma Gandhi.
25 December	Christmas.

Not included above is a whole range of religious holidays whose dates vary from year to year depending on the lunar calendar, Holi (full moon in February-March) and Divali (new moon in October-November). To find out the dates of other religious festivals, see p 78.

• School holidays

Christmas holidays	Two weeks in December-January.
Summer holidays	May and June.
Durga Puja and Dasahra holidays	One week in September-October.
Divali holidays	Two weeks in November-December.

GETTING AROUND

• By car

Travelling by car is the best way to get to know India in-depth. It also saves time and, providing you don't have to drive yourself, helps keep you sane.

Car rentals

Self-drive rental – To rent a self-drive car, one must be over 21 years old, have an International Driving Licence and a certain daredevil type of nature. This form of transport is only recommended to drivers with excellent reflexes, infinite patience and a distinct taste for danger. Europcar has offices in Delhi and Jaipur. Allow around 1 300Rs per day for an air-conditioned Maruti 1 000, unlimited mileage up to 150km, 7Rs per extra km. From Europe and the US, Europcar only offers car rental with chauffeurs at rates that are higher than those practised in India. Hertz also has agencies in Jaipur, Delhi and Mumbai (around 2 000Rs per day for a Maruti 1 000 with 200km per day and 12Rs per extra km).

Car rental with chauffeur – Information can be obtained from either private or state-run travel agencies, such as Ashok Travels & Tours at Delhi or RTDC counters in Rajasthan. Hotels can also lay on chauffeur driven cars, either via their own rental counter or via companies with whom they regularly work. There are three or four categories of vehicles: Maruti or Ambassador non air-conditioned vehicles (around 1 000Rs per day all inclusive), air-conditioned Ambassador cars (1 250Rs per day), Contessa or Esteem cars (1 500Rs per day) or a Daewoo Cielo/Ford Escort (3 000Rs per day). The price is based on

An Ambassador

The Ambassador:
one of India's idiosyncrasies

All 1950s car enthusiasts will instantly fall in love with the voluptuous curves of the "Ambassador", so frequently seen both in towns and in the countryside, where she has proved her ability to withstand wear-and-tear. Experts may recognise the distinctive body shape, an almost identical replica of a 1956 Morris Oxford, with however one notable difference. After Independence, the "Ambassador" became Indian and it was widened, unfortunately without altering the steering system. As a result, the driver's seat and the steering column are no longer aligned. To get round this problem, the constructor mounted the steering wheel at an angle, thereby forcing the driver to sit in a crooked position, often bent half out of the window. The "Ambassador" is manufactured by Hindustan Motors, which belongs to the Marwari Birla family. Unfortunately its days may be numbered, because a new "Ambassador" mark 6 should soon be released, minus the familiar curves of yesteryear.

a fixed mileage rate with a minimum number of kilometres (between 250 and 300km per day), inclusive of petrol, taxes and road tolls, but to which must be added a set rate for the driver (150Rs per night). If you wish to leave the car in a town other than that from which you hired it, you will need to pay the driver for the number of days necessary to return it to its place of origin. The prices indicated in the different "Making the most of..." sections of each town refer to a non air-conditioned Ambassador. Negotiation is quite permissible.

Don't accept cars whose windows are covered in a coloured protective plastic film (you can't see out of them) and make sure your driver speaks English and knows the region. It is possible to ask to meet the driver with the car the night before leaving and to only pay the deposit when you actually set off.

Road network

It will soon become clear that India's road network is not the country's pride and joy. There are no motorways and only 880km of 4-lane highways, some of which can be found between Delhi, Jaipur and Agra (under construction). On National Highways, (only 2 % of the road network), speeds rarely exceed 60kph, and then only when there aren't too many lorries; average speeds are more likely to be around 40kph. Single lane roads, comprising a 3-metre wide band of tarmac, constitute over 65 % of the network, which, due to the number of potholes, make for top speeds of 25kph.

Distances are indicated in kilometres. Signposts are generally only in Hindi, rarely in English, but as most are covered in posters, they are often unreadable anyway. If you notice that your driver hesitates over a direction, insist that he stops and asks directions (many are reluctant to admit they are lost).

Driving
In theory, cars drive on the left-hand side, but it doesn't take a visitor long to appreciate the rift between theory and reality. Anarchy and the survival of the fittest are the rules of the game on Indian roads and drivers place more faith in their instincts than in any hypothetical highway code. Traffic signs are few and far between and those that do exist are ignored. Any crossroads should be approached with great care. Cyclists and scooters often drive on the right-hand side, whether in town or on the open road. Pedestrians should pay particular attention when crossing any busy street.

Fuel
Finding petrol stations is well-nigh impossible except in cities and on National Roads (30Rs per litre), though diesel is easier to obtain (15Rs per litre). Delhi only has unleaded fuel.

Parking
With the exception of Delhi, which is choked with cars, it is easy to park. No-parking zones are unheard of and everyone stops exactly where they want.

In case of accidents
If someone is hurt by your car, you will be immediately surrounded and hassled, even if you're not at fault. It is best not to stop but to drive to the nearest police station. If the affair gets nasty, call your ambassador. If your victim was a goat, expect to pay a sizeable compensation to the owner.

• By taxi
Delhi has two sorts of taxi. The most common are black and yellow Ambassadors: rudimentary comfort and sluggish, but quite cheap rates. Drivers are often loath to start their meters and engage in endless haggling. If you can't convince them to switch the meter on, make sure the price is agreed before you set off. There are also white Ambassador Tourist taxis, which are more comfortable, don't have meters and with higher prices. Elsewhere, jeeps frequently serve as makeshift taxis.

Taxi drivers regularly refuse to take you on excursions unless you agree to pay three times the normal price. In this case, contact your hotel or the tourist office who will hire the taxi for you. Railway stations always have taxi ranks often with pre-paid taxis. Taxi drivers are notorious smooth-talkers and gleefully embark on all sorts of horror stories to lure you away from your proposed hotel to one where they will get a commission. This is all the more true at night-time, when fatigue can make one more disoriented and credulous than usual. If things get difficult, call the hotel and ask them to send a taxi.

• By group taxis
Group taxis, called *tempos*, operate as little buses and cost just a few rupees more. Routes are fixed and they are supposed to transport up to six passengers, but squeezing in three times more is not unheard of.

• By rickshaw
Black and yellow **auto rickshaws** (engine powered, as opposed to the man-powered cycle rickshaws) are a familiar sight in all towns and cost half what a taxi does. Only Delhi's rickshaws have meters, but these are always mysteriously out-of-order when a tourist approaches. It is often cheaper and easier to rent one by the day. All the major cities' railway and bus stations have

An auto rickshaw

pre-paid rickshaw ranks (red on blue signs). **Cycle rickshaws** are bicycles with a rear seat and cost between 20 and 25 % less than an auto-rickshaw.

• By train

Indian Railways, the world's largest employer with some 1.7 million employees, runs the second largest railway network in the world. Although rail travel is not the best way of getting acquainted with Rajasthan's countryside, life on board a train is an adventure in itself and an excellent way of getting to know India at first hand. The diversity and scope of life on board will help make you forget the excruciatingly slow speeds and frequent delays.

Train categories

Indian Railways has four train categories: passenger trains (best avoided), mail trains, express trains and super-fast trains. Of the latter, the fastest are the Rajdhani (which run between Delhi-Jaipur-Abu Road and Delhi-Kota) and the Shatabdi (Delhi-Jaipur-Ajmer and Delhi-Agra lines). Railway fares progressively decrease: the longer the distance, the lower the price per km.

Most trains have several classes:

AC First class, air-conditioned, with comfortable seats, bunks and free bedding. Trains which operate exclusively in Rajasthan do not have this class (around 950Rs for 300km).

AC Second class sleeper (also called an *AC 2-Tier sleeper* and *AC 3-Tier sleeper*). Compartments comprise four or six seats, turned into bunks at night-time, separated from the corridor by a curtain. Bedding will be supplied on request to the wagon manager (20Rs, free in the 2-Tier), but ask as soon as you leave because stocks are limited. Second class sleepers are the most popular and need to be booked well in advance. Fares in the 2-Tier and 3-Tier class are respectively a half or a third of the cost of AC first class.

First class, non air-conditioned, with closed compartments and convertible seats. Bedding (20Rs) must be requested when the ticket is purchased. Prices are equivalent to an AC 3-Tier Sleeper.

Sleeper class, non air-conditioned, open compartments, squatted in all day long by travellers without reservations who will attempt to share your seat, by force if necessary. A great way of mixing with ordinary Indians, it is not however the most comfortable form of travel. The seating transforms into bunks, but bedding is not available. Costs approximately half the above class. Each wagon has a ladies' only compartment which can be locked.

Second class, best avoided. Very cheap rates (40 % less than the former), but very uncomfortable and always packed.

Shatabdi trains only have either **AC executive chair cars** (first class, air-conditioned) or **AC chair cars** (second class, air-conditioned).

Bookings

Bookings are recommended (essential for some trains such as the Rajdhani and the Shatabdi trains) for all trips of over three hours. You will definitely save time and energy if you ask a travel agency to book your seats, which they will do for under 100Rs *(see the "Making the most of..." sections)*. Seats can also be booked from the **computerised reservations counter** (8am-8pm Monday-Saturdays, 8am-2pm Sundays). There is a special queue for women and foreigners, but expect to wait around an hour. If the train you want is full, consult the **Tourist Quota Office**: a certain number of tickets are reserved for foreign travellers, enabling them to get a reservation a few days or even hours before a departure on otherwise full trains. Such tickets must be paid for in dollars.

Indrail Pass

The *Indrail Pass*, on sale at Delhi, Agra and Jaipur railway stations, gives you the right to take as many trains as you like over a 7, 15, 21, 30, 60 or 90 day period and gives you priority status for reservations. Prices vary depending on the class ($440, 220 or 110 for 21 days). There is however no point if just touring Rajasthan.

The Maharajas' trains

The Rajasthan Tourism Development Corporation (RTDC) offers 7-day trips of Rajasthan on board the **Palace on Wheels**, a replica of the former luxurious maharajas' trains. Trains leave Delhi every Wednesday, from September to April. The price per day and per person, in a double compartment, meals included, is around $330.

Bookings can be made in Delhi or Jaipur at RTDC counters *(see p 153 and 222)* or on www.palaceonwheels.net

The **Royal Orient** takes you on a week-long trip through part of Rajasthan and Gujarat. Departures from Delhi, from September to April. Around $250 per person/per night in a double compartment. Contact Gujarat Tourism, A/6 Baba Kharak Singh Marg, at Delhi, ☎ (011)373 4015, Fax (011)373 2482 to book.

• By bus

Bus companies are individually managed by each State Transport Roadways Corporation (STRC), this means that you will travel on either the very well-organised Rajasthan STRC or the less reputable Uttar Pradesh STRC. Rajasthan also has a number of **local bus** companies, which operate uncomfortable and over-crowded services to the more out-of-the-way places – short distances only.

Express buses – decrepit bodywork, windows that shudder with every jolt, incessant, ear splitting klaxons, noisy, if not deafening, neighbours – are identical to their regional counterparts but stop less often. Tickets can be bought 30min before departure or directly on the bus, only trips over 6 hours are booked. **Express deluxe** buses provide more comfortable transport with individual, padded, reclining seats (130Rs for 300km), **Silver Line** buses (Super Deluxe of the RSTRC, 250Rs for 300km) or air-conditioned **Pink Line** buses which only run between Delhi and Jaipur (300Rs for 250km). Book the day before at the latest. Inner city buses are exceedingly cheap and very over-crowded.

• Domestic air services

Indian Airlines, India's domestic airline (and its subsidiary **Alliance Air**), together with **Jet Airways**, **Jagson Airlines** and Sahara Indian Airlines (all private companies) operate regular flights between Delhi, Agra, Jaipur, Jodhpur, Udaipur and, more recently, Jaisalmer.

Air travel within India is notoriously unreliable, particularly in terms of timetables and flights are often suspended, particularly in April and May. It is essential to check with a travel agency and book as early as possible. Return flights must be confirmed at least 72hr ahead, when you should also check that flight times haven't been changed.

A Delhi-Jaipur ticket costs around $45 and Delhi-Jaisalmer, around $100. Children under two travel free on Indian Airlines, children between 2-11 years get a 50 % reduction and young people between 12-29 years a 25 % reduction. The other companies' rates are pretty similar. Tickets can be paid by credit card or in rupees with an Encashment Certificate.
Indian Airlines also has "Discover India" **passes**, valid for 15 days ($500) or 21 days ($750). Unlimited flights and priority reservations, but no stopovers twice in the same town. Only really worthwhile if intending to travel further than just Agra and Rajasthan.

• Two-wheel rentals

To say that riding a bicycle, scooter or a motor-bike on Indian roads is foolhardy is an understatement by any standards, but die-hard fanatics can rent or buy a *Kinetic Honda* scooter, a 100cc *Yamaha*, *Suzuki*, *Honda* or *Kawasaki* motorbike, or even a 350cc or 500cc *Enfield Bullet*, with the legendary throb of its exhaust. Contact a garage.

• Hitch-hiking

Given the ridiculously cheap prices of public transport, hitch-hiking is relatively uncommon and definitely to be avoided by women.

• Organised tours

Several well-established, reliable agencies organise individual tours, from one-day excursions to complete trips around Rajasthan. The best and most widely represented include: Rajasthan Tours, SITA World Travel and Travel Corporation India (TCI). Many hotels and government agencies also offer tours ranging from a few hours to a day.

BED AND BOARD

Rajasthan, with the exception of a few rare towns such as Deeg, Ajmer or Chittaurgarh, whose facilities are almost non-existent, has good accommodation facilities, with something to suit all budgets. Accommodation in Delhi, and to a lesser extent, Agra, is more expensive.

• Prices

The range of prices indicated in this guide is based on a double room in the peak season (except for Mount Abu); they do not include breakfast but taxes are included. Single people will pay less, except if staying in a suite. During the low season (May-June), hoteliers readily grant at least 15 % reductions, but prices can also rise dramatically in some of the more popular areas during holiday periods or major festivals (Mount Abu, Pushkar). Rates generally go up on October 1st.

Taxes

Rooms are subject to two taxes: **luxury tax** (between 5 and 10 % depending on the State) for all double rooms over 1 200Rs, and **expenditure tax** (10 %) on rooms over 4 000Rs. In theory, foreigners paying in foreign currency or by credit card don't pay the latter, but many hoteliers often neglect to apply this regulation. Check your bill.

Food and drink is subject to a **sales tax**, which also varies from state to state: 7 % in Delhi, 5 % in Uttar Pradesh and 6 % in Rajasthan. Tax on beer and alcohol is between 5 % and 12 %, but this can easily go up to 12 %, 32 % and 55 % on imports. More high-class establishments may also add a 10 % expenditure tax. When eating at your hotel, it is worth asking whether the luxury tax applies only to the room or to the whole bill. In the latter case, don't sign meal bills but pay them after each meal. If on the other hand, the hotel is subject to expenditure tax and you intend paying by credit card or with foreign currency, sign your meal bills.

• Various types of accommodation

Rajasthan is very well provided for both in terms of the quantity and the diversity of accommodation available. Furthermore the charm of many of its hotels makes the blandness of Delhi's and Agra's accommodation all the more noticeable.

The degree of comfort and price of rooms vary depending on whether or not they are equipped with fans, an air "cooler" or air-conditioning **(AC)**. **Coolers** are large boxes, similar to portable air-conditioners, fixed outside the window, which produce cooled air by the circulation of water rather than by a refrigeration system. During the monsoon season, coolers primarily contribute to raising the degree of humidity of an already over-humid atmosphere and do very little in the way of cooling. From mid-November to mid-February the nights are particularly cold and most hotels **lack heating**. Check to see if you can have a back-up heater (sometimes at a charge of 100Rs). In some establishments, **hot water** is provided in basins. Make sure that you have hot running water in your bathroom. Most rooms must be vacated by 12noon.

Hotels

India's 4- and 5-star hotels (from $80-500) are excellent and more than bear comparison with their western counterparts. Lower category hotels, equally numerous, are also very decent, but the standards of the smallest establishments (under $15) leave a lot to be desired in terms of cleanliness, bedding and bathroom facilities. The top-bracket establishments insist on payment either in foreign currency or in rupees on condition of being able to produce an Encashment Certificate of the appropriate amount.

Bookings are advisable, particularly in Delhi, Agra and Udaipur, if you're travelling during the peak period or during the Indian school holidays. Once in the country, you should also book one stop ahead, possibly seeking the help of your hotel.

HRH Group of Hotels – At Delhi, ☎ (011) 631 4401 and 691 9116, Fax (011) 682 2856, delhi@hrhindia.com. At Udaipur, ☎ (0294) 52 8001/ 02/03, Fax (0294) 52 8006/12, resv@hrhindia.com

Neemrana Hotels – At Delhi, ☎ (011) 461 6145 and 462 5214, Fax (011) 462 1112, del.wag@axcess.net.in and neemrana@fwacziarg.com

The Oberoi – At Delhi, (011) 436 3030, Fax (011) 436 0484.

The Taj Group of Hotels – At Delhi, ☎ (011) 332 2333, Fax (011) 331 0750. At Jaipur, ☎ (0141) 37 1616, Fax (0141) 37 1640.

WelcomHeritage Hotels – At Delhi, ☎ (011) 686 8992/3, Fax (011) 686 8994, welcomheritage@bigfoot.com

Other useful links are www.fhra.com and www.hotelsofindia.com

RTDC and ITDC hotels

RTDC hotels are tourist establishments run by the state of Rajasthan. Quite the antithesis of charm, they are impersonal, unattractive and offer only basic comfort and poor service, they are however dependable and very cheap. To book contact a RTDC hotel or the central booking office in Jaipur, Swagatam Hotel, Station Rd, ☎ (0141) 31 9531 or 20 3531, Fax (0141) 31 6045 or 20 1045, rtdc@jp1.vsnl.net.in

The **ITDC hotels of the** Ashok Group are similar but slightly more luxurious and are run by the India Tourist Development Corporation. Only in Delhi and Agra.

Palace hotels

Most of the palaces, forts or *haveli* (homes of wealthy middle-classes) that have been turned into hotels are members of the **Heritage Hotels Association of India**. Even if on a tight budget, it ought to be possible to enjoy a night from time to time in one or two of these magical establishments. Some have rooms at $25 and it would be a great pity to miss out on staying in one of these picturesque residences, so replete in Rajasthan's distinctive charm and history. Bookings are recommended: either the place is well-known and generally fully-booked, or it has only recently opened and not yet able to cater for impromptu guests.

To locate the Heritage Hotels outside of towns, *see the regional maps, p 200-201, 318-319, 247.*

Guesthouses

Rajasthan's vast assortment of guesthouses, half-way between the small hotel and the bed and breakfast concept, are an ideal way to get to know the country.

Bed and breakfast

Rajasthan was the first Indian State to pioneer the bed and breakfast concept. Each tourist office has a list of families who are members of what is called the Paying Guest House Scheme.

• Eating out

All the prices in this guide refer to a meal for one person, inclusive of taxes, comprising a meat dish, such as chicken *tikka*, a vegetable dish, *dal makhani* (lentils in butter) and two *chapatti*.

In hotels

Although all hotels are open to non-residents, this is rarely true of guesthouses. Hotels have coffee shops, sometimes open 24 hours a day, which serve food, snacks and tea and coffee, and most also have one or two restaurants, often the most elegant of the area – and the most expensive (around $10, more in Delhi). The "buffet" formula is also widespread, particularly in hotels which cater to groups. Guesthouses and heritage hotels provide fixed menus or buffets for residents, which are often over-priced given the variety and quality (between $3 and $10).

In restaurants

Classic restaurants, known as **multi-cuisine**, offer a wide range of Indian specialities together with a selection of Chinese and Western dishes. From $1-8. Many Hindus and Jains are vegetarian and there are many vegetarian (veg) restaurants. Those which indicate **pure veg** only cook with *ghee* (clarified butter) and do not use eggs, onion or garlic.

In the street

In bazaars, **sweet shops** with tables and chairs, serve local sweets, vegetarian snacks from southern India ($0.5-$1) and fresh fruit juice ($0.5). They are a good idea for a light snack. There are also no end of street stalls selling all sorts of basic meals for under $1 – to be avoided by easily upset tummies! The more daring (or those with iron stomachs) may want to try the snacks also on sale from street vendors.

R. Marca

Alcohol

Although Gujarat still operates total prohibition, Delhi, Uttar Pradesh and Rajasthan only have a few dry days per year, primarily January 26, August 15, October 2 and election days. Local spirits can be bought from *Beer and Wine Shops*, of which there are very few and then, only open a few hours each day. Spirit licences are expensive and many smaller hotels and restaurants don't have one. Others may have a bar but not a restaurant licence. It is however almost always possible to find a solution and you can always get a beer in your room.

SPORTS AND PASTIMES

• Treks

It is possible to plan an "adventure" holiday, before leaving, by contacting a specialised agency (*see p 97*), but once there, the choice of activities, whether walking, horseback, camel or jeep treks, is both vast and easy to find, either from local agencies or hotels.

Horseback

Equestrian sports are still very popular in Rajput regions. Even today the most lowly *thakur* (lord) keeps at least three horses to take part in polo matches – either thoroughbreds or *marwari*, small horses with lyre-shaped ears. Some of the heritage hotels organise treks on horseback (300Rs an hour), often around Udaipur, some can also provide four- or five-day treks, with accommodation in castles or luxury camps (between 4 000Rs and 5 000Rs per day, per person, more if organised by an agency). Contact **The Shekhawati Brigade Horse Safari** at Nawalgarh or the **Royal Equestrian and Polo Centre** at Dundlod (*see "Making the most of Shekhawati ", p 259*), **Fort Chanwa** at Luni and **Rohat Garh** at Rohat (*see "Making the most of Jodhpur", p 312*), **Pratap Country Inn** at Udaipur (*see "Making the most of Udaipur", p 347*) or **Kotri Raola** at Kotri (*see "Making the most of Ranakpur", p 331*).

By camel

Camel safaris have long been the exclusive domain of Jaisalmer, but other tourist centres, such as Jodhpur, Bikaner and Shekhawati have recently started organising such activities. A wide range of possibilities exists, from a few hours (350Rs

for three hours), to a two- or three-day circuit to a one-week trip from one town to another (not recommended for beginners). If intending anything over a day trip, only contact a reputable agency (especially if a woman travelling alone), as swindles, robbery and other mishaps are not unknown. The best period is from October to March. Choose a circuit off the main tourist routes and **check a few points** before setting out: how many people are on each camel (only one person per camel), sleeping arrangements (open-air or in tents), number of blankets per person, how will water and luggage be transported (on your steed or by cart), quantity of drinking water (organised or not by the agency, included or not in the price), type of menus (*dal* and *chapatti* at all meals or varied dishes with fresh fruit and vegetables), distances covered each day (22km maximum). Your packing list for such an outing should contain a pair of sturdy trousers, light clothing for the day and very warm clothing for the night, a wide-rimmed hat, sun glasses, sunscreen, moisturiser and lip cream. A sleeping bag is a good idea if not taking one of the more up-market treks.
Prices range from 800Rs to 3 000Rs per day per person for an excursion of between five and ten people with tent and cart, and as little as 500Rs if sleeping out of doors and transporting your own luggage. Anything costing less should be avoided! **Prices** may vary depending on the number of participants, and a party of under five may have to pay an extra 10%. Furthermore, one-week safaris are slightly more expensive than four-day trips and as a general rule, rates are somewhat lower at Jaisalmer.

In a jeep

The most classic excursion is a four- or five-hour jeep "safari" tour round the tribal villages and some of the more out-of-the-way temples, or perhaps to see the craftsmen and the wildlife of the region. Around 450Rs per person.

• Sports

Swimming

Most of the medium and upper category hotels have an outdoor swimming pool, open from March to November. Most are open to non-residents for a fee, approximately 100Rs (300Rs minimum in Delhi).

Horse-riding and polo

Polo takes pride of place in a Rajput aristocrat's life, all the more so as modern day nobles no longer go warring or hunting. Imported from Central Asia by the Mughals, this breakneck sport was brought back into fashion at Manipur by the British soldiers, who then spread it all over India. Jaipur, Jodhpur and Udaipur have the best teams. Basic lessons can be had from the **Royal Equestrian and Polo Centre** at Dundlod *(see "Making the most of Shekhawati", p 259)* or the **Pratap Country Inn** at Udaipur *(see "Making the most of Udaipur", p 347)*. Matches take place during the polo season (October-November and February-March).

Golf

Jaipur and Delhi both have splendid golf courses. New Delhi's is ranked among the world's top hundred.

Cricket

Cricket is the national sport (if not an obsession), quite as popular as football. Children play it on every street corner and the best players are national heroes and stars, constantly in the headlines. Jaipur's Sawai Mansingh Stadium *(see p 228)* is an international stadium and often stages World Cup matches (only during the winter). Tickets go on sale 10 days before the match and are advertised in the English-speaking press *(see p 116)*.

• Night life

With the exception of Delhi, which does have a few night-clubs, nights out in India have a tendency to be cosy and intimate, consisting of drinks at the hotel bar or moonlight strolls...

Cinemas

Forget about catching up on Satyajit Ray's films or other's of his ilk – such films are almost invisible in India. Rather, go and see the latest box-office hit, the songs of which you will hear in all the bazaars. Films are always in Hindi, but don't worry, the images speak for themselves. Ask your hotelier to suggest a film and give you the address of the cinema. Take a balcony seat, it's more expensive, but the spectators have a tendency to be slightly less hysterical than those in the stalls.

Concerts and shows

If in Delhi from November to March, there is a wide range of classical dance and music concerts (far fewer performances from May to September). Elsewhere, guests are treated to a variety of folk-type performances by hotels and also during religious festivals, cattle fairs and weddings.

SHOPPING

• What's on offer

See also the "Crafts" and "Costumes and jewellery" sections p 70 and 74.

Crafts

Carpets – Rajasthan and Agra are India's main manufacturing and export centres. Expect to pay around 500Rs per sqm for a woven cotton rug *(dhurry)* and around 1 000Rs per sqm for a knotted wool carpet of average quality. Antique carpets are rare and most of those presented as such have been "aged". Silk carpets are the most expensive.

Fabric – Good quality, printed or tie-dye cotton fabric costs around 70Rs per metre and plain or printed silk between 100Rs to 500Rs a metre. Silk saris (5.5m long) are generally sold by weight (from 700Rs to 2 500Rs), whereas embroidered saris, which are more expensive, are sold by the metre. Wool shawls from the desert are particularly good value in Jaisalmer (around 400Rs).

Leather – Leather slippers (*juti* and *mojri*) and sandals *(chappal)* in embroidered leather are available almost everywhere. The best quality ones are from Jodhpur.

Paintings – It is practically impossible to find any genuine antique miniature paintings. Delhi and Udaipur specialise in miniature paintings on silk and marble, and more rarely on pages out of old manuscripts. Most artists reproduce large quantities of paintings designed to cater to the tastes of the average tourist. *Pichhwai* (painted wall-hangings of Krishna) are industrially manufactured whereas printed *phad* (canvas illustrations featuring local heroes) have remained more hand-crafted.

Hand-made paper – Stock up on writing paper made from fabric remnants, to which natural items have been added (leaves, grasses, etc).

Pottery – All craft shops stock glazed blue pottery items (glass mats, little boxes and candle-sticks) from Delhi and Jaipur. Unvarnished votive terracotta plaques from Molela can be found at Udaipur.

Wood – Finding good-quality puppets is unfortunately impossible, but it is still possible to find beautiful carved wooden blocks used to print fabric.

Pietra dura – Agra specialises in stones inlaid in marble. Good quality items are expensive.

Antiques

A wide variety of reproduction works of art, sometimes very well-imitated, exist, but originals are very rare. Finding any real antiques will take time and luck, often in the most banal *kabariwalla* (junk shop). Ask to look round, go and rummage about in the rear-shop... Anglo-Indian colonial-style objects and furniture, recently back in fashion, are easy to find, but sometimes at ridiculous prices.

Jewellery

To avoid nasty surprises, only buy silver, gold, precious and semiprecious stones from authorised dealers.

Silver jewellery – Silver is extremely cheap and sold by the gram, based on its alloy (three-figure hallmark). Three types of alloys are used in India varying between 300 to 950 thousandths, meaning that they contain between 30 to 95 % of silver and 5 to 70 % of copper (in Europe only 800 and 950 thousandths are legal). Hall-marked silver under 500 thousandths goes black and some more disreputable dealers willingly stoop to mixing alloys within the same piece of jewellery, which in time produces a mottled effect. Tribal jewellery, whether originals or copies, is sold according to weight and quality.

Other jewellery – Only buy from reputable shops. Large numbers of tinted glass or synthetic imitations of gems, particularly precious stones, are in circulation. Even more difficult to detect is the technique by which stones are heated or irradiated, thereby improving their colour, but making them more fragile. Stones should always be examined by daylight if possible at different times of the day. If in doubt, have stones assessed by the **Gem Testing Laboratory** of Jaipur or Delhi's Ministry of Trade *(see the "Making the most of..." sections regarding both towns)*. All the major jewellers will have some antique jewellery but it will not be exhibited. You must ask to see it, in which case you will be taken to the back of the shop and it will be taken out of the safe, item by item. However appealing the offer might seem, systematically refuse any proposals regarding wholesale purchases of stones or exports on behalf of Indian jewellers. Nine times out of ten you'll be on the losing end.

Clothes

The choice is enormous, from traditional Indian garments, possibly revamped by young Indian designers, to major European brand names or "ethnic"-type hippy trends. Tailors are cheap, but the result may not always live up to your expectations. The best solution is to take one of your favourite, simply-cut garments with you and have it copied.

Scents

Flower essences *(ittar)*, much less volatile than our perfumes, are made to be smelled at close-range. Specialised boutiques sell them, together with fragrant soap and incense sticks.

Food

Namkin (spicy or sweet-savoury snacks) is bought from sweet-shops, which also sell locally produced sweets. The latter can be kept for three days in a fridge. Confectionery made from cashew nuts or hardened condensed milk *(barli)* travels better than the others. These shops also sell tinned confectionery. Tea is also a good gift idea: Assam, Nilgiri or Darjeeling, plain or "masala" (with spices).

Tapes and CDs

If attracted by Indian music, buy it while in the country as it is almost impossible to find elsewhere. The best labels are Music Today and HMV.

• Where to shop

Which towns

The best place to shop is Delhi, which has the widest choice in all of India. However, Jaipur cannot be beaten for precious and semiprecious gems, jewellery and Rajasthani fabric, Udaipur is best for miniature paintings.

Shops

Each town has a traditional bazaar and a modern bazaar, which between them should be able to satisfy all your wants. Many private boutiques are self-proclaimed "Government Approved" or "Emporiums". Don't be misled, this does not mean that prices are fixed. Large hotels generally have a shopping mall and their bookshops are often the best in town.

Emporiums

The only real emporiums (state-run shops) are **Rajasthali** (Rajasthan crafts), **Handloom House** (hand-woven fabrics) and **Khadi Gramodyog** (homespun fabric woven according to Mahatma Gandhi's precepts). Goods are labelled and prices are fixed, which if nothing else, enables visitors to get an idea of prices.

• Goods with specific taxes and regulations

See the "Customs" section, p 93.

• Sending goods home

It is recommended to personally supervise the postage of goods home *(see "Postal services", p 99)*, or one runs the risk of paying the carriage costs and customs taxes twice, not to mention the fact that the goods may never even arrive. The only shops that can be trusted to organise postage are state-run emporiums.

HEALTH

• Illnesses

Before leaving, make sure your vaccinations are up to date *(see p 94)* and possibly start anti-malarial medication. That said, the most common upsets encountered are due to the heat or the food.

Sun

To avoid any risk of **heat-stroke** or **dehydration**, sunbathe gradually, always wear a hat, apply sunscreen and drink regularly. In the summer, **prickly heat**, due to poor evaporation of perspiration, can be avoided by applying an anti-fungal talcum powder after bathing. Also beware of air-conditioning in hotels, trains and aeroplanes. Although extremely pleasant at the time, it can have after-effects (colds, sore throats); always keep a warm jumper close at hand.

Food

One out of two tourists suffers from intestinal upsets – the legendary "tourista" – very soon after arriving, due to the change in climate and food, further exacerbated by the fatigue of the journey and jetlag. Although not serious, the consequences are bothersome. In case of diarrhoea, eat white rice, avoid fruit and vegetables, drink as much as possible (salt-enriched) to avoid dehydration and, if necessary, take an intestinal antiseptic and a diarrhoea "blocker". If things have not improved within three days, or if there is blood in your stools, contact a doctor. Some illnesses, due to infected food or water, such as **giardiasis**, **dysentery**, **cholera**, **typhoid** and **hepatitis A**, are far more serious. They can be avoided by respecting a few basic rules.

It is of course more sensible to only stay or eat in hotels or restaurants which at least appear to be hygienic, to wash one's hands before every meal, to use purified water to brush teeth, to peel all fruit and raw vegetables, only drink boiled or disinfected water or bottled **mineral water** that is opened in front of you. Tea and coffee can, in theory, be drunk everywhere. Drinking water in the main cities is chlorinated, as is that served in the large hotels, but is best avoided. Avoid ice-cubes, hand-made ice-creams, fruit juice with added water, shellfish or anything that is only lightly cooked, and be particularly wary of un-pasteurised (the norm) or un-boiled milk. This does not at all mean you have to forgo Indian's wonderful cuisine: yoghurt is excellent for upset stomachs, as are raw onions, and spices have many excellent digestive properties. What's more, hot chilli peppers kill any amoeba before they've even had a chance to start developing.

Mosquitoes

The best way of preventing mosquito-borne illnesses is not to get bitten, primarily by protecting oneself when mosquitoes are most active, from dusk to dawn. Wear long sleeves, trousers, socks, cover your neck and apply a mosquito-repellent to any exposed areas. Avoid dark clothes and perfume. Sleep with the air-conditioning on, buy an electric diffuser (on sale from all Indian chemists and grocery stores) or use a repellent-impregnated mosquito net. Mosquito activity is minimal during the winter and maximal during the monsoon season.

Paludism (malaria) – Even though none is 100 % effective, anti-malarial medication is still recommended. The mosquitoes in northern India have developed a resistance to chloroquine, so you will need to investigate a specific anti-paludal drug. Treatment should start the day before leaving and continue for four weeks after returning from the infected region. There are fewer risks in Rajasthan than in Delhi.

Dengue fever – The symptoms of this endemic illness, similar to a severe bout of flu, are joint and muscle pains and extreme tiredness, lasting for several weeks. Some attacks can involve haemorrhaging and require hospitalisation. Otherwise no preventive treatment is available, other than avoiding mosquito bites.

Japanese Encephalitis – A very dangerous brain infection. Vaccination is essential if intending to spend any length of time in rural areas.

• Medical kit

A standard kit should contain a wide spectrum antibiotic, a diarrhoea "blocker", an intestinal antiseptic, water purification tablets and possibly an antiseptic cream and plasters. Most medicines can be found in India so there's not much point in weighing yourself down needlessly.

Also pack a good sunscreen, mosquito repellent, tampons (sporadically available in chemists) and condoms (local brands aren't very reliable). Hepatitis B and AIDS are as rampant in India as they are elsewhere and common sense should prevail. Likewise, body-piercing and tattooing are also potentially dangerous, as is going to a barbers' shop for a shave.

• Health services

All the hotels can provide the services of an English-speaking doctor who will come to the hotel at any time of the day or night.

Hospitals

Opt for private health establishments (hospitals, nursing homes, clinics) which are much better equipped and maintained than the state-run Government Hospitals. If you encounter any serious health problems, avoid being hospitalised anywhere other than Delhi and attempt to contact your insurance company and get yourself repatriated.

Doctors

Again opt for a private doctor in a clinic (around 100Rs) or in a surgery (around 200Rs). Your hotel or the chemist will be able to advise you.

Chemists

Every bazaar has at least one chemist and there are also a few dispensaries near the hospitals. Almost everything is available, including antibiotics, at very low prices and without prescriptions. Although highly effective on certain illnesses, **ayurvedic** medication, based on minerals and plants, is not recommended for serious illnesses. Although this type of medication can be found in ayurvedic chemists, it is better to buy the brands sold by allopathic chemists which are more carefully controlled.

Dentists

Avoid if at all possible consulting a dentist, because of the risks due to poor sterilisation.

• Emergencies

Police ☎ 100 Fire brigade ☎ 101 Ambulance ☎ 102

From A to Z

• Bartering

Prices in India serve primarily as an introduction to an interminable session of bartering. Bartering takes time, patience and infinite good humour, and don't think twice about offering half the initial price or less. Dollars in cash often win over seemingly inflexible shopkeepers.

• Beggars

Although giving coins away may relieve our conscience, it in fact only serves to encourage begging and all the associated practices (networks which exploit children, mutilation, etc). It is however difficult to remain indifferent. Without falling into the trap of becoming blind and uncaring, try to remember that when you give out a coin or a sweet to a lone child, you will more than likely be swamped by hordes of turbulent outstretched, sometimes aggressive, hands. Extricating oneself from such forays requires a good deal of authority and good humour. Always think twice before opening your bag. Making a donation to any one of the large numbers of reputable charities which exist may constitute a much more worthwhile contribution to the plight of India's needy.

• Commissions

One of the most irksome aspects of tourism in India. All the railway and airport tourist offices, taxi or rickshaw drivers and touts of all sorts earn commission from the hotels, restaurants and shops to which they take you. Make sure that the shopkeeper knows that it was your decision to come to his shop otherwise your bill will be increased by a commission (around 20%). If you decide to go to a hotel that doesn't play the game, it can be almost impossible to find a taxi or a rickshaw willing to take you there. They will pretend that the place is disreputable or has gone out of business.

• Drugs

Unless you fancy ending your trip in an Indian prison, bear in mind that the dealing, transport and consumption of any drugs, including hashish, is totally prohibited.

• Electricity

Electricity is 220V. Power cuts are common, particularly during the summer, and especially in Delhi and Agra. Sockets are similar to the European three round-pin variety, but not identical, meaning that they don't fit as well and the connection is not always guaranteed. If you really want your appliance to work, take one that is battery operated.

• Laundry service

All hotels provide a laundry service. Only 4- and 5-star hotels have their own in-house laundry service, the others all give out laundry to a member of the *dhobi* caste who takes it down to the river for washing. There, it is twisted, wrung, beaten against stones and left to dry on the grass in the harsh sunshine. After a few days of such harsh treatment, most fabrics are noticeably thinner, colours more faded, buttons broken and many stains still present... It is better to wash any delicate clothes oneself using the mini-packs of washing powder available from all grocery stores. Dry-cleaners can only be found in the main towns, and are best avoided.

• Mineral water

"Mineral" water (in fact purified water) has become very widespread, particularly in places like Rajasthan, where the water reservoirs are salty (hence the strange taste of some tea or coffee). Bottled mineral water is on sale in all the tourist centres and prices, fixed by the government, vary from 15Rs to 30Rs a litre. Check that the bottle top is properly sealed and that it hasn't been filled with tap water using a syringe: turn upside down to see if it leaks.

• Newspapers

All the main American and British newspapers and magazines are available almost everywhere. The English-language Indian press (*The Times of India*, *The Hindustan Times*, *The Indian Express*) is of a very high standard, but covers very little international news. *India Today*, a weekly, and *Frontline*, a fortnightly review, are also excellent. Rajasthan only has one daily newspaper, the *Rajasthan Patrika* (in English and Hindi), but other national newspapers can be found, if a little late. In the main towns, newspapers can be bought from street-vendors, bookshops and in the main hotels, as well as in railway stations.

• Photography

Colour slide film is rare, but print film *(Kodak, Fuji)* is easy to find and often less expensive than in Europe. Only purchase from proper shops, because those from street vendors have often been exposed to excessive heat or tampered with. Development is cheap, but again, only give your films to proper laboratories, if possible in Delhi. Equipment needs to be protected against dust and humidity.

• Prices

Some industrially produced goods (medication, biscuits, fizzy drinks, etc) have labels which indicate a Maximum Retail Price (MRP) (inclusive of taxes). Whatever the shopkeeper tries to tell you, never pay more than the amount indicated.

• Radio and Television

All India Radio, or Akashvani ("voice from the sky"), is a national company which broadcasts in all the languages spoken in India, including English and Sanskrit. **Doordarshan** ("vision from afar") is also a state monopoly (news in English around 9.15pm). **Cable channels** have been authorised since 1992, the most widespread of which are BBC World, CNN, Star TV and ZTV (a Hindi channel).

• Theft

You are unlikely to encounter problems if you respect a few common-sense rules. Be particularly wary in railway and bus stations and never accept tea or sweets from a stranger in the street or a public place, especially if travelling alone; cases of tourists who have been drugged and robbed are not rare. In case of loss or theft, fill in a "First Information Report" (FIR) at the nearest police station and inform your consulate if you have lost your passport. Contact your bank within 24 hours if you have lost your credit card and travellers' cheques and send your insurance company a copy of the FIR within 48hr. Always keep photocopies of all important documents.

• Tips and baksheesh

Tips are always welcome, even if not common. Tip a hotel porter between 5-15Rs, more for special help. As for baksheesh (a mild and very common form of bribery), it will enable you to open doors that would otherwise have remained closed, such as gaining entry to a palace.

• Tobacco

Smokers should taste a *bidi* (or *biri*) – small cigarettes in rolled tobacco leaves, with an acrid odour and high in nicotine and tar. Mild cigarettes are those most commonly available, stronger brands include *Charminar* and *Charms*. In Delhi, smoking is not allowed in public places, including restaurants and bars. You may also get the chance to taste a *huqqa* (hookah pipe), generally only found in villages or private gatherings. Subject to strict caste taboos, it is not shared freely.

• Units of measurement

India has adopted the metric system, but continues to use the Imperial system. 1 inch = 25.4mm; 1 foot = 304.8mm; 1 yard = 0.9144m; 1 mile = 1.609km. Indians have also remained faithful to two traditional units of measure: the *lakh* (10 thousand) and the *crore* (10 million).

Distances in this guide are given in kilometres. As a rule of thumb, one kilometre is five-eighths of a mile: 5 miles is therefore about 8 kilometres, 10 miles is about 16 kilometres and 20 miles is about 32 kilometres.

LOOK AND LEARN

• History and politics

BASHAM AL (edited), ***A Cultural History of India***, Oxford India Paperbacks, 1975.
CAMPBELL Christy, ***The Maharajah's Box***, HarperCollins, 2000.
KATHURIA Ramdev P, ***Life in the Courts of Rajasthan, during the 18C***, 1987.
KEAY John, ***Into India***, John Murray, 1999.
KEAY John, ***India: A history***, HarperCollins Publishers, 2000.
LAPIERRE Dominique and COLLINS Larry, ***Freedom at Midnight***, Harper Collins, 1997.
MATHESON Sylvia A. and BENY Roloff, ***Rajasthan, Land of Kings***, 1984.
ALLEN Charles, ***Soldier Sahibs Land***, John Murray, 2000.
SINGH Raghubir, ***Rajasthan; India's Enchanted Land***, 1981.

• Human sciences

DEVI Gayatri, ***A princess remembers***, Rupa and Co., 1996.
DEVI Phoolan, ***I, Phoolan Devi,*** Warner, 1997.
HARDY Justine., ***Scoop-Wallah – Life on a Delhi Daily***, John Murray, 1999.
MUJEEB M, ***The Indian Muslims***, 1967.
NAIPUL VS, ***India, A million mutinies now***, Random House, 1990.
SAINATH P, ***Everybody loves a good drought***, Headline Book Publishing, 1996
SCINDIA Vijayaraje, ***Princess: Autobiography of Dowager Maharani of Gwalior***, Century Hutchinson, 1985.
SINGH GALOT Sukhvir, ***Rural Life in Rajasthan***, 1982.
SINGH GALOT Sukhvir and DHAR Banshi, ***Castes and Tribes of Rajasthan*** 1989.

• Classical works

BABUR (translator BEVERIDGE AS), ***Babur***, Low Priced Publications Board, 1996.
BHAGAVADGITA (translator EDWIN Arnold), ***Bhagavadgita***, Dover Publications, 1994.
NARASIMHAN CV (translator), ***The Mahabharata***, Columbia University Press, 1998.
DANIELOU Alain, ***The complete Kama Sutra: The first unabridged modern translation of the classical Indian text***, Inner Traditions International, 1995.
DHARMA Krishna, ***The Ramayana***, Torchlight Publishing, 1998.

• Art

CRAVEN Roy C, ***Indian Art***, Thames and Hudson, 1997.
GILLOW John, BARNARD Nicholas, ***Traditional Indian Textiles***, Thames and Hudson, 1993.
KRAMRISCH Stella, ***The Art of India***, 3rd edition, 1987.
MICHELL George, MARTINELLI Antonio, ***The Royal Palaces of India***, Thames and Hudson, 1999.
NATH Aman and WACZIARG Francis, ***Arts and Crafts of Rajasthan***, 1987.
SANKALIA HD, ***Archaeology in Rajasthan***, 1988.
TADGELL Christopher, ***The History of Architecture in India***, Phaidon, 1998 (reprint).
WALKER Daniel, ***Flowers Underfoot***, Thames and Hudson, 1998. (This book is about carpets and not about flora.)

• Fiction

ALI Ahmed, ***Twilight in Delhi: a novel***, WW Norton, 1994.

ANAND Mulk Raj, ***Untouchable***, Phoenix Press, 1994.
BANERJEE DIFAKARUNI Chitra, ***Sister of my heart***, Black Swan Press, 1999.
DAS Prodeepta, ***I is for India***, Frances Lincoln, 1999, (photographic alphabet).
FARRELL JG, ***The Siege of Krishnapur***, Phoenix Press, 1996.
FORSTER EM, ***A passage to India***, Penguin, 1998.
KAYE MM, ***Enchanted Evening***, Viking, 1999 (last of a trilogy).
KIPLING Rudyard, ***The Jungle Books and Just so stories***, Bantam Books, 1986.
MEHTA Gita, ***Raj***, Minerva, 1997.
ROY Arundati, ***The God of Small Things***, Flamingo, 1998.
SCOTT Paul, ***The Jewel in the Crown, etc*** (The Raj Quartet), Panther Books, 1977.
SETH Vikram, ***A suitable boy***, Phoenix Press, 1994.
SETH Vikram, ***An equal music***, Phoenix Press, 1999.
SINGH Khushwant, ***Train for Pakistan***, Greenwood, 1976.

• Travel

DALRYMPLE William, ***The Age of Kali (Travels and Encounters)***, HarperCollins, 1998.
KAUL HK (editor), ***Travellers' India***, OUP, 1979.
LEWIS Norman, ***Norman Lewis Omnibus***, Picador Press, 1995.
NAIPUL VS, ***An Area of Darkness***, Penguin, 1970.
TULLY Mark, ***The Heart of India***, Penguin, 1996.

• Coffee-table books

NATH Aman, SING JODHA Samar, ***Jaipur***, Tauris Parke, 1996
SINGH Raghubir Singh, ***Rajasthan***, Thames and Hudson, 1995.
WHEELER Sarah, CHOPRA Tarun, ***Majestic Jaipur***, Local Colour Publications, 1997.

• Fauna and flora

ALI Salim, ***The Book of Indian Birds***, OUP India, 1997.
THAPAR Valmik, ***Natural World: Tiger***, Hodder Wayland, 1996.
TRAVERS Will, ***Natural World: Elephant***, Hodder Wayland, 1992.

• Music and cinema

BHAVNANI Enakshi, ***The Dance in India***, 1979,
COOPER Darius, ***The Cinema of Satyajit Ray***, Cambridge University Press, 2000.
FARRELL Gerry, ***Indian Music and the West***, Clarendon Press, 1998.
MASSEY Reginald and MASSEY Jamila, ***The Music of India,*** Kahn and Averill, 1994.
RANGOONWALLA Firoze, ***Indian Cinema***, 1983.

• Cooking

CHOPRA Veena, ***Veena Chopra's Real Indian Cookery***, Fousham, 1999.
FERNANDEZ Rafi, ***Taste of India***, Lorenz Books, 1997.
HUSAIN S, FERNANDEZ R, ***Complete Book of Indian Cooking***, Hermes House, 1998.
HUSAIN Shehzad, ***Vegetarian Indian Cooking***, Hamlyn, 1999.

• Health

LEAK John, ***Travellers' Survival Kit: India***, Vacation Works Publications, 1997.

• Maps

India & Bangladesh, Lonely Planet, Travel Atlas.
Northern India and ***Western India***, Nelles Maps, Nelles-Verlag.
World Map: India North Eastern Region, GeoCenter International Ltd.

GLOSSARY

Numbers

one	ek	eight	aath
two	do	nine	nau
three	teen	ten	das
four	char	fifty	panchas
five	panch	hundred	so
six	chhe	hundred thousand	lakh
seven	saat	ten million	crore

Everyday expressions

Mr (Mrs) you...	bhai sahab (bahanji), aap...
Mr (Mrs) Gupta, you...	Gupta sahab (sahiba), aap... ou Guptaji, aap...
Mr (Mrs) Gupta	shri (shrimati) Gupta
Miss Gupta	kumâri Gupta
Yes, Mr (Mrs)	ji haan
No, Mr (Mrs)	ji nahin
Hello	namaste
Hello (Hindu, rural)	Ram
Thank you	shukriya
Please	meharbani seh
Excuse me	maaf kijiyeh
How are you?	Aap kaiseh hain?
(Very) good, fine	(bahut) accha
I see, I understand	acchaa!
Enough!	bas!

Finding your way

Where is...?	kahan hai?
Which direction is Jaipur?	Jaipur kahan hai?
How far is Udaipur?	Udaipur kitni dur hai?
Is the post office far (nearby)?	kya daakghar dur (paas) hai?
Near the hotel	hotel ke paas
Straight on	(bilkul) sidha

Time

When?	kab?	This (the) evening	shaam ko
Today	aaj	This (the) night	raat ko
Tomorrow, yesterday	kal	Tomorrow morning	kal subah ko
This (the) morning	subah ko	Quick	jaldi

colours

blue	nilaa (nili)	orange	naarangi
white	safed	pink	gulabi
yellow	pilaa (pili)	red	laal
black	kaala (kâli)	green	haraa (hari)

In the restaurant

water, drinking water	paani	spinach	paalak
lemon juice	nimbu paani	peas	matar
tea	chay	radishes	muli
without sugar	binaa chini	aubergine	bengan

and without milk	or binaa dudh
hot	garam
cold	thandaa
"non-veg", meat eating	maansaahari
vegetarian	shaakahari
full meal	thali
snacks	chat
rice	chaaval
egg	andaa
yoghurt	dahi
yoghurt with cucumber	raita
cheese	panir
butter, in butter	makhan, makhani
clarified butter	ghee
oil	tel
Meat	mans
chicken	murg
mutton	gosht
goat	bakri
fish	machhli
Vegetables	sabzi
potatoes	aalu
carrots	gaajar
cauliflower	phulgobhi
peppers	mirch
"ladies' fingers"	bhindi
onions	pyaaz
garlic	lahsun
Spices	masala
Hot pepper	lal mirch
pepper	kali mirch
salt	namak
ginger	adarak
cumin	jira, zira
mint	pudina
Fruit	phal
papaya	papita
mango	aam
guava	amrud
lemon	nimbu
banana	kela
pineapple	ananas
grapes, raisins	angur, kishmish
apple	seb
orange	santarâ, nârangi
cashew nuts	kaaju
almonds	baadam
pistachio nuts	pista

Shopping

How much is it?	kitneh ke hai?
It's too expensive	bahut mahanga hai
(very) beautiful	(bahut) sundar hai

Body language

Whether you speak Hindi or not, everyone relies on body language and it is worthwhile knowing what various gestures may mean.

A slight shake of the head generally replaces thanks, because people rarely use "excuse me", "please" or "thank you" in India, even when offered gifts. Don't interpret the lack of such words as impoliteness.

Moving the head from right to left means the familiar "no". But this gesture is, in fact, little used, because, Indians, eager not to disappoint, avoid whenever possible saying "no" or admitting that they don't know, preferring any answer, however improbable, to no answer at all. When asking directions, beware of answers: if the person asked shows the slightest hesitation, all answers should be taken with a pinch of salt.

Finally, don't misinterpret the head shaking which often accompanies conversations with Indians. Contrary to what one might think, gently shaking the head from side to side is a form of agreement: "OK then", "I understand", "As you wish".

Exploring the Mughal towns

R. Haidinger/ANZENBERGER-COSMOS

The Diwan-i Am
at Agra Fort

DELHI★★★

Capital of the Indian Union
Pop 9.4 million – Alt 290 m
200km from Agra – 250km from Jaipur – 650km from Udaipur
See map p 200

Not to be missed
The Red Fort. Juma Masjid mosque.
Humayun's tomb. Qutb Minar.

And remember...
To avoid getting stuck in traffic in Old Delhi, walk.
Hire a taxi for a day and visit the southern part of the city.
Allow three days to explore Delhi and to shop.

The capital of the Indian Union, the third largest city after Mumbai (formerly Bombay, population 12 million) and Calcutta (10 million), represents such historic and artistic diversity and such vitality that it is one of the most interesting cities in the whole of southern Asia. It immediately brings home the contrasts of modern India, so extolled by travel brochures. It takes just 15 minutes to leave the wide, open avenues of New Delhi and become engulfed in the dark, little lanes around Chandni Chowk bazaar. While the former are reminders of a wealthy elite, keen consumers in true "Western" style, the latter summon up a more traditional picture of oriental legend. An untrained eye has no hope in attempting to pick out differing physical traits or manners of dress in this incredible bedlam. Even an anthropologist would only stand half a chance. All around people are engaged in a multitude of tiny occupations and tasks with an enthusiasm and a faith which leave the observer both intrigued and amazed.
First contact with what feels like pandemonium often drains many visitors, accustomed to a more ordered environment. It is difficult to resist the temptation to flee, to seek calm... and oxygen (according to the WHO, Delhi is the seventh most polluted city in the world, just behind Calcutta and Mumbai). Refuge can perhaps be sought in one of the parks built around the incredible Indo-Moslem monuments in the southern part of the city. A stroll through Lodi Garden or that of Humayun's tomb should reconcile any exhausted visitor to the turmoil of Delhi.

A city created ten times over

The home of Indra – The creation of Delhi is steeped in myth and attributed to the Pandavas, heroes of the Mahabharata. It was then known as **Indraprashta** ("home of Indra", who was one of the main gods of the Vedic era). This first Delhi may in reality not be as mythical as was once believed. Pottery dating back to around 1000 BC has been recently unearthed at Purana Qila, proof of the existence of an ancient city. Seven centuries later, it was a sufficiently imposing centre for Emperor Ashoka to deem it worthy of erecting a column carved out of sandstone and inscribed with his edicts. One millennium later, the Rajputs of the **Tomar** clan built **Dilli** fortress around the 8C AD, a few kilometres south of Indraprashta.

Moslem invasions – From the 12C, Dilli was under the control of the Rajputs of the **Chauhan** clan, based in Ajmer (Rajasthan), but the Moslems were soon to come onto the scene: in 1192, **Mohammed of Ghor**, from Afghanistan, was hammering at the doors of Delhi, and, at the battle of Tarain, he defeated the army of Prithviraja III – Delhi's last Hindu monarch. Before returning to his mountainous home, the conqueror entrusted the city to his general, **Qutb ud-Din Aibak**, a former Turkish slave, who proclaimed himself "sultan" on the death of his master, inaugurating the dynasty of the "Mameluks" ("slaves"). He founded his capital on the site of what is today the Qutb Minar: the first "Moslem Delhi" was born.

The Sultanate succumbs to dynastic quarrels – In one century (from 1290 to the late 14C), two new Turkish dynasties followed one after another, the **Khilji** and the **Tughluq**, between them creating four new cities in Delhi. The sultans' power was already considerably weakened in 1398 when **Tamerlan** (Timur Lang or Timur Lane), the Turkish-Monghol, ransacked the capital, leaving it in such ruin that over a century was to pass before it regained its former splendour. One of Tamerlan's lieutenants moved into the city and founded the **Sayyid** dynasty (1414-1450), soon followed by the **Lodi** dynasty (1450-1526), which governed from Agra. Sapped by incessant clan quarrels, the sultans were unable to resist **Babur**, a new invader from Afghanistan: a descendant of Genghis Khan on his father's side and Tamerlan on his mother's side, he was to found the illustrious **Mughal** dynasty.

Capital of an empire – After conquering Sultan Ibrahim Lodi at the battle of Panipat (1526) and the Rajput confederation at Khanwa (1527), Babur settled in Agra, but his son **Humayun** (1530-1540 and 1555-1556) was to make Delhi the capital once again, fortifying Indraprashta. Humayun was unable to defend his throne though, and was ousted for 15 years by Sher Shah, an Afghan lieutenant. While the Great Mughals, Akbar and Jahangir, chose to govern from Agra and Lahore, their successor, **Shah Jahan** (1627-1658), once more elected to make Delhi the capital. He built the ninth city "Shahjahanabad", now Old Delhi, endowing it with two of its most famous monuments: the Red Fort and Juma Masjid mosque.

From one empire to another – The Mughals' power almost ceased with the death of Emperor Aurangzeb in 1707. Delhi, capital of a feeble, divided empire, was looted and pillaged three times, first by the Persian king Nadir Shah (1739), then by Ahmed Shah, an Afghan chief (1756), and finally by a *raja* Jat from Bharatpur in 1764. The Mughal emperor had become no more than a puppet

Raisina Hill: the presidential palace and ministries

figure and the British gradually took control of the sub-continent, leaving the Mughal on his phantom throne, while installing a resident, whose job it was to govern the capital. During the **Indian Mutiny** in 1857, **Bahadur Shah II**, an 80-year old emperor-cum-poet, stood up for the mutineers. After violent battles, the British overcame the mutiny and captured Bahadur Shah Zafar (Zafar, "the sword" was his pen name), who had sought refuge within the walls of Humayun's tomb. He was exiled to Rangoon and his two sons were publicly executed.

From the 18C the new masters governed from Calcutta (in Bengal), but, wary of the political unrest rife in Bengal, they decided to transfer the capital to Delhi, which was after all, the country's legitimate capital. The decision was announced in 1911 by King George V and the construction of the tenth Delhi, **New Delhi**, was entrusted to architect Sir Edwin Lutyens, assisted by Herbert Baker. From 1918 onwards, a whole new city began to rise from the ground, in honour of the power and influence of the Indian Empire (the *Raj*). It was officially inaugurated in 1931.

Capital of the world's largest democracy – When India acquired Independence in 1947, the creation of the predominantly Moslem Pakistan engendered vast population transfers within the Indian Union. Thousands of Moslems left their homes in Delhi for Pakistan, while Hindus and Sikhs also left almost all their belongings behind in Pakistani Punjab and moved to the capital with the sole desire of starting afresh. Once Moslem, Delhi now became a Punjabi capital. Since 1956, the city has had **Union Territory** status, distinguishing it from its neighbouring states (Uttar Pradesh and Haryana). Politically, it wavers between the BJP (the nationalist Hindu "Bharatiya Janata Party") and the Congress Party.

Growth and shanty towns

India's economic capital is Mumbai (Bombay), headquarters of Indian and foreign multinationals and the sub-continent's most Westernised megalopolis. However, Delhi is an astonishing example of dynamism, quite comparable to that of her rival on the Arabian Sea. The two cities are traditional antagonists: tropical Mumbai is a cosmopolitan, modern city, overlooking the sea and open to foreign influences, yet sorely lacking in greenery, whereas Delhi, far inland, has the reputation of upholding traditions and of rough, provincial customs, despite its ministries and ambassadors. The city claims some 90 000 industrial and craft firms. They produce absolutely everything – from household appliances to medicines, from clothes to religious artefacts. Encouraged by the economic liberalisation of the 1990s, Delhi's middle-class has embarked on a euphoric bout of consumerism. Yet with its sprawling shanty towns and regular power cuts, Delhi remains a third-world city. A bad monsoon season, poor crops in nearby rural areas or food shortages can throw the population into disarray, causing the economy to slump and resulting in massive influxes of poverty-stricken villagers.

Urban violence...

Delhi is not a dangerous city; even if recent polls rank it as last of the five Indian metropolises in terms of women's safety (and the courtesy of its inhabitants. It is ranked second before last in terms of quality of life and facilities...). It does however suffer from an "illness" rife throughout all of India: that of inter-religious, known as "communalist", violence. The bloodiest crisis of recent date was the massacre of at least 2 000 Sikhs following the assassination of Indira Gandhi (31 October 1984) by two of her Sikh bodyguards. An emerging phenomenon of the 1990s is mafia violence, most often wielded by Mumbai "godfathers" and their legendary organiser, Dawood Ibrahim, a Moslem Indian currently in hiding in the Gulf.

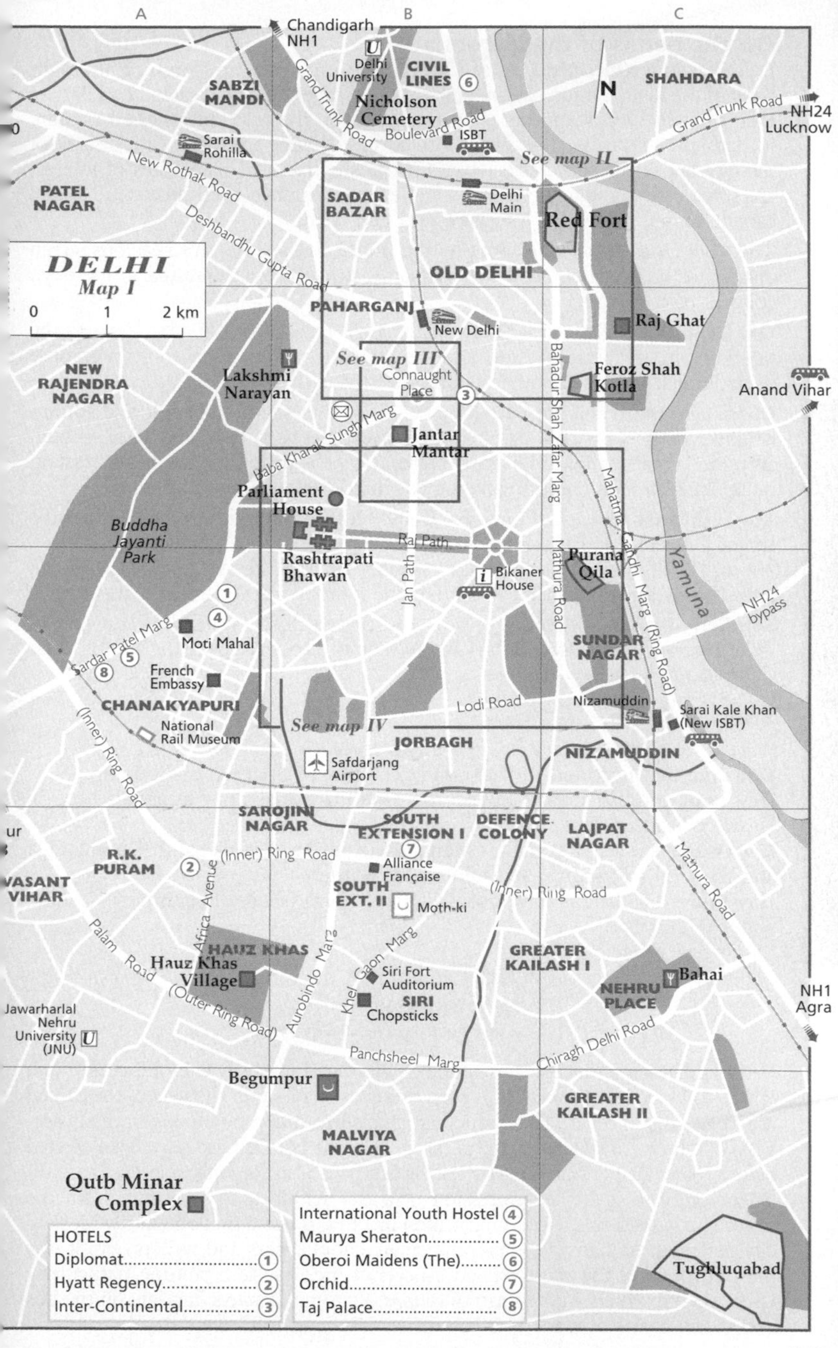

A
B
C
DELHI
Map I
0 1 2 km
Chandigarh NH1
Delhi University
CIVIL LINES
SABZI MANDI
Nicholson Cemetery
Grand Trunk Road
Boulevard Road
ISBT
SHAHDARA
N
Grand Trunk Road
NH24 Lucknow
Sarai Rohilla
New Rothak Road
See map II
PATEL NAGAR
SADAR BAZAR
Delhi Main
Red Fort
Deshbandhu Gupta Road
OLD DELHI
PAHARGANJ
New Delhi
Raj Ghat
NEW RAJENDRA NAGAR
Lakshmi Narayan
See map III
Connaught Place
Feroz Shah Kotla
Anand Vihar
Bahadur Shah Zafar Marg
Baba Kharak Sungh Marg
Jantar Mantar
Parliament House
Buddha Jayanti Park
Raj Path
Rashtrapati Bhawan
Jan Path
Bikaner House
Mathura Road
Purana Qila
Mahatma Gandhi Marg (Ring Road)
Yamuna
NH24 bypass
Moti Mahal
Sardar Patel Marg
French Embassy
SUNDAR NAGAR
CHANAKYAPURI
Lodi Road
Nizamuddin
Sarai Kale Khan (New ISBT)
National Rail Museum
See map IV
JORBAGH
NIZAMUDDIN
(Inner) Ring Road
Safdarjang Airport
SAROJINI NAGAR
SOUTH EXTENSION I
DEFENCE COLONY
LAJPAT NAGAR
R.K. PURAM
(Inner) Ring Road
Alliance Française
VASANT VIHAR
SOUTH EXT. II
Moth-ki
(Inner) Ring Road
Mathura Road
Africa Avenue
Palam Road
HAUZ KHAS
Hauz Khas Village
Aurobindo Marg
Khel Gaon Marg
Siri Fort Auditorium
SIRI
Chopsticks
GREATER KAILASH I
NEHRU PLACE
Bahai
NH1 Agra
(Outer Ring Road)
Jawarharlal Nehru University (JNU)
Panchsheel Marg
Chiragh Delhi Road
Begumpur
GREATER KAILASH II
MALVIYA NAGAR
Qutb Minar Complex
Tughluqabad
HOTELS
Diplomat 1
Hyatt Regency 2
Inter-Continental 3
International Youth Hostel 4
Maurya Sheraton 5
Oberoi Maidens (The) 6
Orchid 7
Taj Palace 8

On the banks of the Yamuna

Delhi lies in a rocky plain, spread over 30km from north to south on the right bank of the River Yamuna. A tributary of the Ganges, it is held sacred by Hindus, even though the city appears to turn its back on the river, or at least to ignore it, perhaps due to its close links with former Islamic invaders. The history of the city and of its successive rebuilding means that the major sites of interest are spread throughout the town, some a great distance from the centre. Delhi cannot simply be divided into New and Old Delhi.

The Civil Lines (Map I B1) – Built by the British in the 19C, this spacious, green district to the north of Delhi will primarily attract those interested in the city's colonial past.

Old Delhi (Map I B/C 1/2) – South of the Civil Lines, the 17C city contains the Red Fort, Juma Masjid Mosque and the bustling bazaars. Ideal to get a glimpse of traditional India and some picturesque streets.

Connaught Place and Raj Path (Map I B2) – Further south, this trade and administrative centre of the city, designed by Lutyens between 1910 and 1920, is built around Connaught Place (airlines, banks, shops with luxury goods and restaurants) and Raj Path (central government buildings, National Museum).

The residential district of Lutyens' Delhi – Just to the south of Raj Path lies the capital's quietest and most spacious district. To the west Chanakyapuri (Map I A3), or "Diplomatic Enclave" is the embassy zone. To the far south, Lodi Road (Map I B3) is set in the heart of gardens built around the Moslem mausoleums.

Southern districts – A series of new, ill-assorted districts, for the most part of little interest, except for one or two havens of peace such as the Qutb Minar Complex (Map I A5).

Stays in Delhi

What to see if staying in the city for between 1 and 4 days.

Day one: Red Fort and Juma Masjid. The Qutb Minar. And shopping...
Day two: add Chandni Chowk, the National Museum, Humayun's tomb, Hazrat Nizam ud-Din's "dargah".
Day three: add a visit to Jantar Mantar, Gurudwara Bangla Sahib, Purana Qila and the Crafts Museum, as well as Lodi Garden.
Day four: visit Safdar Jang's tomb, Hauz Khas Village, Begumpur Mosque, and Tughluqabad

Old Delhi★★★ (Map II)
(Shahjahanabad)

One day visit on foot and by taxi.

Delhi's inhabitants call the part of the city founded in the 17C by Emperor Shah Jahan, "Old Delhi" *(Purana Dilli)*, even though several other districts of the capital are in fact much older. This particular area, surrounded by ramparts, many sections of which are still standing (in the east), is the last Delhi to have been erected before "New Delhi" was built by the British. It is also the only one that has sufficient unity to give the impression of a city within a city, distinct from the neighbouring districts. Up until Partition in 1947, it was a predominantly Moslem city of Turks, Afghans, Persians, craftsmen, shopkeepers and writers, etc. It was the birthplace of the most refined aspects of Indo-Moslem culture, particularly Urdu poetry, which, in the form of *ghazals*, the semi-classic songs still on the lips and in the hearts of many North Indians, continues to thrive today.

Red Fort*** (Lal Qila) (Map II D1-2)

10am-5pm. Entrance fee. 2hr. In 1638, Emperor Shah Jahan transferred his capital from Agra to Delhi and immediately began building a fort designed along the lines of a "forbidden city". It housed the imperial residence and government and administrative buildings. In order to build the Red Fort, he had to raze an 11C fortress built by the Tomar Rajputs. Looking at the building now, it is difficult to get an idea of the extent of luxury in which the emperors and their courts lived in this palace, which was to be their residence up until Bahadur Shah Zafar, the last Mughal, was exiled after the Indian Mutiny in 1857. Repeated looting throughout the 18C together with demolition work undertaken by the British after the revolt have greatly reduced the buildings. To make defending the fort easier, the British knocked down the entire district which surrounded it, building a spacious esplanade (current entrance to the monument) in its place. Inside, they destroyed part of the palaces, replacing them with ugly barracks, still in use by the army today.

The **red stone ramparts** stretch for over two kilometres. Entry is via **Lahore Gate**, with its barbicans (watchtowers). This impressive ogee archway, topped with small white domes, has a symbolic value: it was here that India's flag of Independence flew for the first time on 15 August 1947, and it is also here that the Prime Minister reads his speech to the nation every 15 August. The doorway opens onto a covered gallery, **Chhatta Chowk**, which now houses souvenir stalls, but which was a bazaar at the time of Shah Jahan. At the end is the **Naubat Khana** or Naqqar Khanna, "Drum House", where the musicians used to stand and play during ceremonies. The first floor of the main building houses a small **military museum** *(India War Memorial, 10am-5pm, entrance free)*. The emperor convened his court or received his subjects and foreign diplomats in the **Diwan-i Am** (public audience hall), situated at the end of the garden. Damaged during the various ransackings of Delhi in the 18C, the entrance into this red sandstone edifice is through elegant Moorish multifoil arches. Inside is a marble **throne** over which hangs a Bengali-style canopy. Note the intricate *pietra dura* (inlaid semi-precious stones) work which continues around the back of the throne: floral scrolls, birds, even an Orpheus, said to be the work of a Florentine or French artist.

Continuing left around the Diwan-i Am are the gardens of the **private quarters**. The latter originally comprised a series of six palaces facing eastwards, overlooking the Yamuna. Five remain. They must be imagined in their former glory, decorated with costly, precious carpets and red silk hangings stretched between walls to create inner courtyards and overhead, to protect from the sun's rays. Directly opposite the Diwan-i Am is the **Rang Mahal**. Divided into six apartments, it was here that the emperor's first wife lived. A basement area afforded relief from the heat-wave temperatures before the monsoon season. The Nahar-i Bihisht ("stream of paradise") ran through all the fort's private palaces. The water was perfumed, providing both pleasure and refreshment.

The next palace (northwards, to the left when in front of the Yamuna) is the elegant **Khas Mahal** where the emperor lived. Its spectacular *jali* (ornamental lattice screens) depicting scales of justice, one of Shah Jahan's favourite motifs, are still intact. From the balcony of the octagonal tower overlooking the Yamuna, the "shadow of God on earth" appeared in public, offering his *darshan* ("vision") to the people. Further north is the **Diwan-i Khas** (private audience hall), the fort's masterpiece. Its white marble walls used to house the famous "peacock throne",

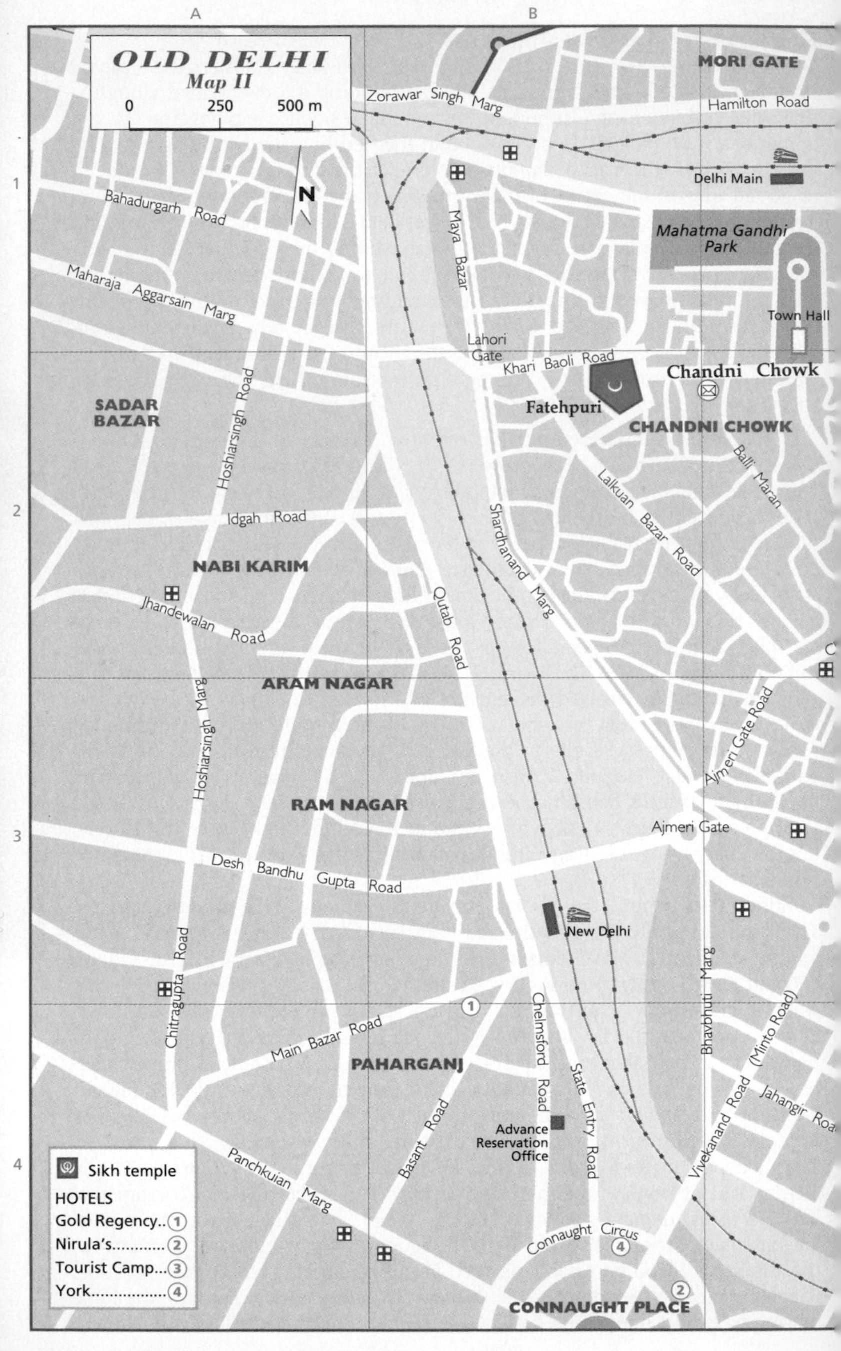

OLD DELHI
Map II
0
250
500 m
N
A
B
1
2
3
4
MORI GATE
Zorawar Singh Marg
Hamilton Road
Delhi Main
Bahadurgarh Road
Maharaja Aggarsain Marg
Maya Bazar
Mahatma Gandhi Park
Town Hall
Lahori Gate
Khari Baoli Road
Chandni Chowk
Fatehpuri
CHANDNI CHOWK
SADAR BAZAR
Hoshiarsingh Road
Balli Maran
Lalkuan Bazar Road
Shardhanand Marg
Idgah Road
NABI KARIM
Jhandewalan Road
Qutab Road
ARAM NAGAR
Hoshiarsingh Marg
Ajmeri Gate Road
RAM NAGAR
Ajmeri Gate
Desh Bandhu Gupta Road
New Delhi
Chitragupta Road
Bhavbhuti Marg
Main Bazar Road
PAHARGANJ
Chelmsford Road
State Entry Road
Vivekanand Road (Minto Road)
Jahangir Road
Basant Road
Advance Reservation Office
Panchkuian Marg
Connaught Circus
CONNAUGHT PLACE
Sikh temple
HOTELS
Gold Regency..1
Nirula's...........2
Tourist Camp...3
York.................4

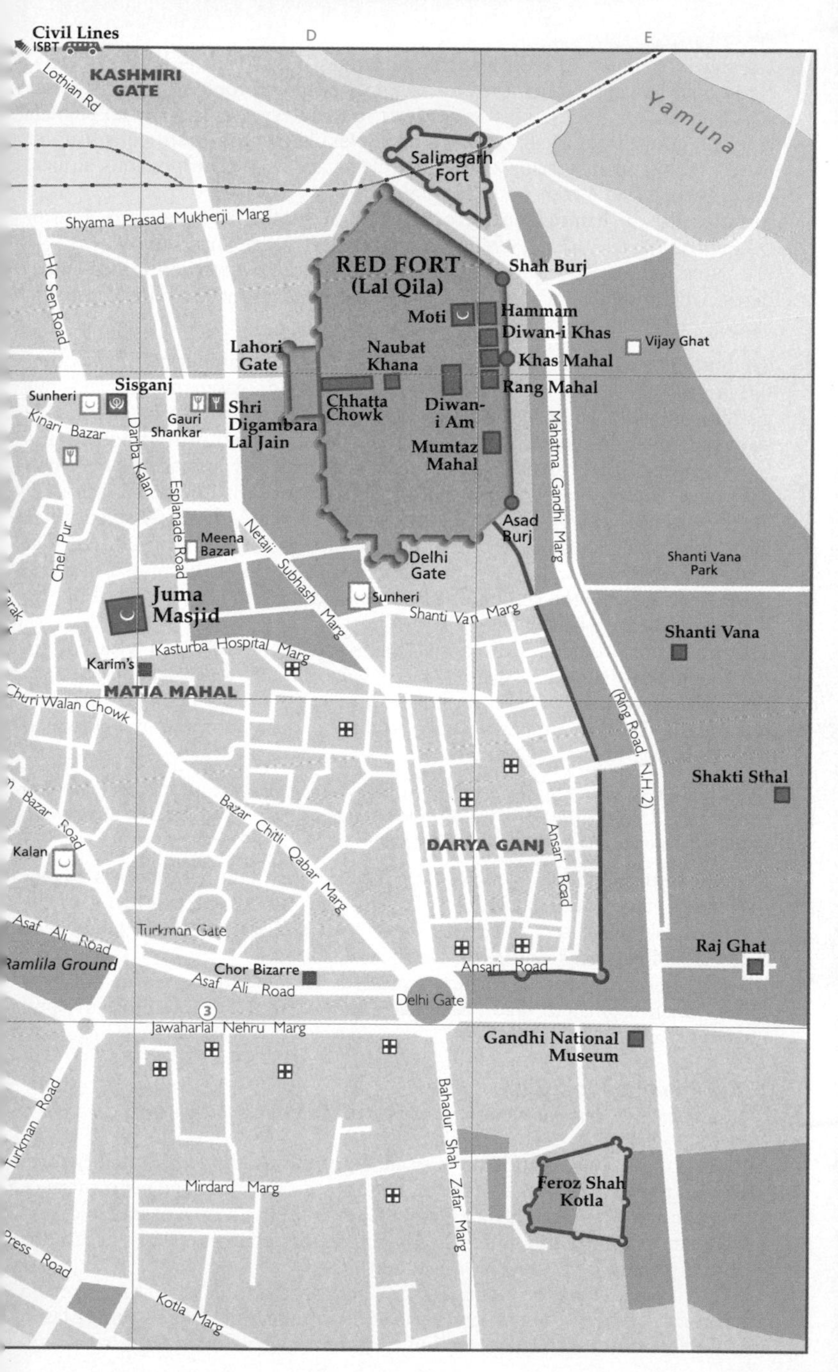
Civil Lines
ISBT
D
E
KASHMIRI GATE
Lothian Rd
Yamuna
Salimgarh Fort
Shyama Prasad Mukherji Marg
HC Sen Road
RED FORT (Lal Qila)
Shah Burj
Moti
Hammam
Diwan-i Khas
Vijay Ghat
Lahori Gate
Naubat Khana
Khas Mahal
Rang Mahal
Sisganj
Sunheri
Gauri Shankar
Shri Digambara Lal Jain
Chhatta Chowk
Diwan-i Am
Mumtaz Mahal
Kinari Bazar
Dariba Kalan
Esplanade Road
Mahatma Gandhi Marg
Chel Pur
Meena Bazar
Netaji Subhash Marg
Asad Burj
Delhi Gate
Shanti Vana Park
Juma Masjid
Sunheri
Shanti Van Marg
Shanti Vana
Kasturba Hospital Marg
Karim's
MATIA MAHAL
Churi Walan Chowk
(Ring Road, N.H.2)
Shakti Sthal
Bazar Road
Bazar Chitli Qabar Marg
DARYA GANJ
Ansari Road
Kalan
Turkman Gate
Asaf Ali Road
Ramlila Ground
Chor Bizarre
Ansari Road
Raj Ghat
Asaf Ali Road
Delhi Gate
Jawaharlal Nehru Marg
Gandhi National Museum
Turkman Road
Bahadur Shah Zafar Marg
Mirdard Marg
Feroz Shah Kotla
Press Road
Kotla Marg

a priceless treasure covered in precious stones. In 1739, the king of Persia, Nadir Shah, seized it when the city was ransacked and took it back to Tehran where it remains today. Fifty years later, on the very same spot, an Afghan chieftain gouged out Shah Alam II's eyes. Next is the **hammam** consisting of three bathing rooms, made out of marble inlaid with semi-precious stones, one of which had a rose-water fountain.
Just opposite the hammam is the opulent **Mothi Masjid mosque** (Pearl Mosque) *(recently closed to the public)*, which Aurangzeb, the "bigot", had built for his sole use. Note the excessively baroque style and almost overpowering decorative detail which denote a decadence very removed from traditional Islamic classicism.

Continuing further north, the **Hayat Baksh Bagh**, "garden which gives life" *(on the left)*, revealed the Persian taste for walled, geometrically laid out gardens, intended as images of Paradise. Introduced into India by Babur, this style gave birth to many "Mughal" style gardens, divided in four equal parts by two right-angled canals. Further on past a small pavilion stands the **Shah Burj** tower jutting out of a corner of the wall. Part of this tower was set aside for the emperor to work in. At the foot of the edifice, a device enabled water from the Yamuna to be brought up to supply the Nahar-i Bihisht. On returning, there is a walk through a garden with pavilions decorated in a late baroque style. Note the central one, surrounded by water, which was built by the last Emperor, Shah Zafar.
The private apartments should not be left without paying a visit to the **Archaeological Museum** *(right to the very south, after the Rang Mahal. 10am-5pm, closed Fridays. Entrance included in entrance fee to the fort)*. A collection of artefacts, relating the life of the imperial court, is housed in the **Mumtaz Mahal**, which used to be the harem's apartments.

Leave and make your way towards the eastern door of Juma Masjid Mosque, the one opposite the Red Fort (about 800m away), but stop on the way at the Shri Digambara Lal Jain temple, at the corner of Chandni Chowk.

Shri Digambara Lal Jain Temple (Map II D2), which faintly resembles a colonial house, was founded in the 17C. This Jain sanctuary, belonging to the *digambara* (sky-clad) sect is famous for its **bird hospital**, to which Jains, keen defenders of all forms of life, bring wounded birds.
Behind stands a tower *(shikhara)*, typical of Hindu sanctuaries in northern India, which belongs to **Gauri Shankar Mandir** temple, devoted to Shiva and his wife, Gauri.

Juma Masjid Mosque*** (Map II C-D2)

Closed to non-Moslems during noon prayers. Remove shoes before entering. Charge for cameras.
The "Friday Mosque" stands on a small hill opposite the Red Fort. Begun in 1644 and finished in1658, it is the biggest mosque in India. The main entrance is through the open-air stalls of **Meena Bazaar** selling a host of knick-knacks for Indian pilgrims and tourists. An impressive staircase leads up to the gateway, pierced by a deep *iwan* (vaulted recess).
On entering the **courtyard**, one is struck both by the building's sheer size and the contrast between the red sandstone and white marble. Delhi's Juma Masjid was the last major mosque to be built by the Mughals. Its design is the cul-

mination of the Indo-Islamic style of mosque with courtyard: a large courtyard surrounded on three sides (north, east and south) by identical arcades, each with an imposing central portal. The arcades contain small alcoves where professors of Islam can meditate and children can learn the Koran. A pool for ritual ablutions before prayer *(namaz)* is set in the centre of the courtyard. On the western side – towards Mecca – is the **sanctuary** itself, flanked by two minarets and crowned by three enormous white bulbous domes. The large central portal *(pishtaq)* merits a closer look. Pierced by a multifoil Moorish archway, it leads into the prayer room, the walls of which are covered in calligraphed Koranic inscriptions. The rear wall, called *qibla*, indicates the direction of Mecca. In its centre is a *mihrab*, an empty recess highlighted by the contrast of the white marble on red sandstone, which represents a symbolic gateway to God. A superb **view**★★ of Old Delhi can be had by climbing the steps of the **southern minaret** *(turn right on leaving the prayer room)*.

Leave the mosque by the south gateway. From the top of the monumental staircase, there is a wonderful view over part of the district surrounding the mosque on two sides with narrow lanes, frequented mainly by men, and with shopfronts and posters in Urdu, the Arabic-Persian script used by India's Moslems. The fish and meat market *(on the left)* is next door to the little bistros of **Matia Mahal**, a district which serves one of the most authentic tastes of *Mughlai* cooking in all India. Delicious mutton *korma* simmering in gigantic black cauldrons, freshly baked *naan* (white flour pancake-shaped bread), straight out of earthenware ovens and mouth-watering kebabs dripping with oil.

After exploring the narrow lanes of Matia Mahal, either go back into the mosque and cross the courtyard to leave by the northern entrance (opposite), or walk around the outside of the mosque.

Chandni Chowk★ (Map II C2)

To reach Chandni Chowk, the main east-west thoroughfare of Old Delhi, take Dariba Kalan, formerly the jewellers' road (a few jewellers still remain). At the end, on the corner of Chandni Chowk, it is worth stopping for a minute at the Old Famous Jalebiwala where they are said to make the best *jalebi* in the capital (deep-fried pastries dripping in syrup).

Chandni Chowk, the "chowk of moonlight", is so named because the moon used to shine on the canal water running through its centre (today filled in). It was the Nahar-i Bihisht, a derivation of which was seen in the fort. At the turn of the last century, Chandni Chowk was still a peaceful, elegant avenue, lined by tall shady trees... Nowadays, it is a bustling, busy bazaar crammed with gaily jostling, shoving shoppers and tradesmen. Foreigners are often stunned by the vision of mayhem produced by cycle-rickshaws darting among ox carts and *tongas* pulled by half-starved horses. The furore is further increased by spluttering, hooting scooters and auto-rickshaws weaving in and out of the motley collection of stalls offering cheap jewellery, shoes, crockery and gadgets for only a few rupees. No district better symbolises the demographic pressure and back-breaking labour of India's sprawling cities than Chandni Chowk and its nearby lanes.

Turn into the avenue and walk left. The presence of bearded men in turbans indicates that **Gurudwara Sisganj**★, the largest Sikh temple in Delhi, is not far away. *(Wear a hat or scarf and remove shoes.)* The temple was built on the spot where the Sikhs' ninth guru, **Teg Bahadur**, was decapitated in 1675, by order of Emperor

P. Horree/ANA

Crossroads in Old Delhi

Aurangzeb for remaining true to his faith. The faithful meet together in the main room to pray, and *kirtan* (religious hymns) are chanted all day long, to the accompaniment of a *tabla* and a portable harmonium.

Continue on Chandni Chowk. Go past the little square with a fountain (on the right-hand side) and turn left into **Paranthewali** Gali, a narrow lane where three families have for several generations specialised in parantha (fried wheat pancakes). It is impossible to miss the distinctive round-bottomed *kadai* used to fry the cauliflower or potato *parantha*. The tiny lane continues left into **Kinari Bazaar**, dominated by red and gold colours. Here Hindus come to buy all the accessories and haberdashery items necessary to a wedding: ceremonial turbans, garlands of bank notes for the husband, red clothes (brides wear red) with gold tassels and braids… Also note the disguises: monkey and bird masks, Rama's quiver and arrows and the gigantic, charmingly naive, *papier-mâché* reproduction of his trusty ally, the monkey-god Hanuman.

The lane leads into Dariba Kalan, so turn back the way you came. On reaching the crossroad with Paranthewali Gali, continue left and wander through the maze of tiny lands and *katra* (covered alleys). Watch the *baniya* (Hindu shopkeepers) unfolding yard on yard of fabric before the insatiable eyes of their customers,

Welcome to a gurudwara

One of the major appeals of Sikh sanctuaries is their distinctive blend of fervour and good-natured welcome. The purpose of a "gurudwara" ("door to God") is to bring together people of all walks of life, castes and religions, uniting them in their common adoration of a unique, eternal God. The "langar" symbolises this unity: a communal dining room where you may be invited to share a meal. The congregation serves at the tables (serving the community is an essential aspect of the Sikh faith). Visitors will be invited to sit on the ground, with the other pilgrims – unthinkable in the Hindu religion where people of different castes cannot eat together. The menu will comprise "dal" (lentils) and "roti" (wheat pancake).

who generally leave without purchasing. The incessant hooting of the scooters can be annoying and tiring but the reward is well worth the effort. Lose yourself in this labyrinth of hectic, busy lanes interspersed with unexpectedly peaceful courtyards, reminiscent of a medieval East. The following landmarks may reassure timid adventurers. Nai Sarak, the road where the students buy their exercise and school books. **Chawri Bazaar**, mainly devoted to paper. Most of the shops are run by Jains. Note the printers and their wedding invitations or greeting cards covered in good-luck signs such as the *swastika* (ancient sun symbol). The elegant **Fatehpuri Masjid** mosque (Map II B2) is at the westernmost edge of Chandni Chowk. It was built in 1650 by the Begum Fatehpuri, one of Shah Jahan's wives. Just behind, **Khari Baoli Road** and the neighbouring streets comprise one of Asia's largest spice markets.

To the south of the Red Fort

Take a taxi or an auto-rickshaw to Raj Ghat. This wide boulevard runs round the Red Fort to the east. It leads to Shanti Vana Park, which borders the River Yamuna, and to monuments which mark the spots where various personalities were incinerated. The most visited cenotaphs are **Shanti Vana** (that of Jawaharlal Nehru, who died in 1964), followed by **Shakti Sthal** further south (of Indira Gandhi), then **Raj Ghat**★ (Map II E3) *(5.30am-7.30pm)*, which is Mahatma Gandhi's monument. The *samadhi* (memorial) to the "nation's father" is one of Delhi's most moving sites. The black marble plaque, decorated in flowers, bears the inscription *"He Ram"* ("Oh God"), Mahatma's last words when he was assassinated on 30 January 1948. The small **Gandhi National Museum** (Map II E4) *(9.30am-5.30pm, closed Monday, no charge)*, located on the opposite side of the boulevard, contains a few relics of Gandhi's era, photos and personal belongings, including his spinning wheel.

To the south of the museum lie the ruins of **Feroz Shah Kotla** (Map II E4), the fortress of Ferozabad, a short-lived city built in 1354 by Sultan Feroz Shah Tughluq. The peaceful park makes a pleasant interlude. **Ashoka's Column**, a pillar on which Emperor Maurya had his famous edicts engraved in the 3C BC, stands in the middle of the derelict palaces and mosques. Feroz Shah is said to have brought it back as a trophy after a campaign against Hindu sovereigns.

Connaught Place and its surroundings★ (Map III)

3hr on foot, not including the visit to Lakshmi Narayan temple and the station.

"Connaught Place" is in fact the name of a square, but it generally refers to Connaught Circle (or the Outer Circle) and the surrounding area. Considered to be the capital's nerve centre and showplace, it inevitably attracts hordes of dealers, touts, fortune-tellers and other petty crooks all intent on gleaning a few rupees from the wealthy passers-by – foreign and Indian. Connaught Place's elegant arcades and the neighbouring streets, particularly those near the station, constitute a paradise on earth for these well-practised swindlers, who home in on unsuspecting naive tourists, fresh to Delhi and its ways.

Connaught Place (Map III B2) is a vast circular square, whose incessant turmoil and cacophony of traffic perfectly symbolise the wheeler-dealer aspect of India's middle class. Surrounded by colonial-style buildings, it was inaugurated in 1931 in honour of the Duke of Connaught, King George V's uncle. In 1995, the square itself was renamed "Indira Chowk" and Connaught Circus became "Rajiv Chowk", but Delhi's inhabitants stubbornly persist in using the original names, or the familiar nickname "CP". CP's traffic-jams differ from those of Old Delhi by the modernity of their vehicles. No cycle-rickshaws or ox carts are allowed, only auto-rickshaws or ancient, badly-tuned *Padminis* which drive side by side with *Daewoos*, *Hondas* or *Fords*, made in India since the 1990s.

Jantar Mantar★ (Map III B4) *(open from dawn to dusk, no charge)* is an early 18C **astronomical observatory**. It was designed by Jaipur's founding Maharaja, Jai Singh II, who was a keen astronomer. He had noticed that brass measuring instruments lacked reliability due to their small size and the play of their axes and thus decided to build fixed instruments 100 times larger. This resulted in the creation of *Jantar Mantars* in Delhi and Jaipur *(see p 207)*, as well as less grandiose ones at Varansi (Benares), Ujain and Mathura (the latter no longer exists). These incredible structures proved to be so functional and reliable that they revealed errors in the astronomical charts of some of the leading astronomers of the period. Nowadays, the proximity of the surrounding modern buildings, with which they mingle almost surrealistically, makes it impossible to use them. Note the **Samrat Yantra**★, an enormous sundial (gnomon) with a central staircase. Just next to it is the **Jai Prakash Yantra**, which Jai Singh II invented to check the measurements of the other instruments.

Return to Connaught Circus and turn left. Take the first road on the left, Baba Kharak Singh Marg, for 150m.

Built by Jai Singh, Jaipur's astronomer-maharaja, and modified several times, the **Hanuman Temple** (Map III B3) *(remove your shoes before entering)* is dedicated to Hanuman, the monkey-god. Although devoid of architectural interest, the shrine is close to the hearts of Delhi's inhabitants, and provides an excellent example of the extent of Hindu fervour and worship. Tuesdays, Hanuman's day, are particularly crowded. Stalls sell carnations and puffed rice which is offered to the gods before climbing the sanctuary's steps. There are no fixed times or days for going to temples, and the faithful go whenever they feel like it, to get a *darshan* (vision) of the gods and become filled by their energy. In thanks, the believer places an offering in front of their chosen god, without forgetting to pay their respects to the others.

Further on Baba Kharak Singh Marg, the gold dome of **Gurudwara Bangla Sahib**★ (Map III A4), Delhi's largest Sikh temple can be seen *(wear a hat or a scarf and remove your shoes)*. It was built in the 18C on the site of the house where the eighth guru, Harkishan Dev, lived when he was in Delhi (1664). The entrance to the temple is lined by stalls selling copies of the **Granth Sahib** or cassettes of devout songs, as well as turbans, sabres and metal bracelets – the traditional attributes of a Sikh. Follow the crowds of pilgrims, particularly numerous on Sundays, into the prayer room which resonates to the hymns *(kirtan)* intoned to the glory of God, unique and boundless, and to the community's ten founding gurus. Note the screen which protects the holy book, the *Granth Sahib*. Before leaving the temple, the faithful wash in an immense pool. Ever since it was blessed by Harkishan Dev, it has been said to cure cholera and smallpox.
Next to the temple's main entrance a staircase leads down to a basement, which has been turned into a museum *(Baba Baghel Singh Museum, no charge)*. It houses a series of colourful pictures illustrating the edifying, often dramatic and bloody, story of the community's ten gurus.

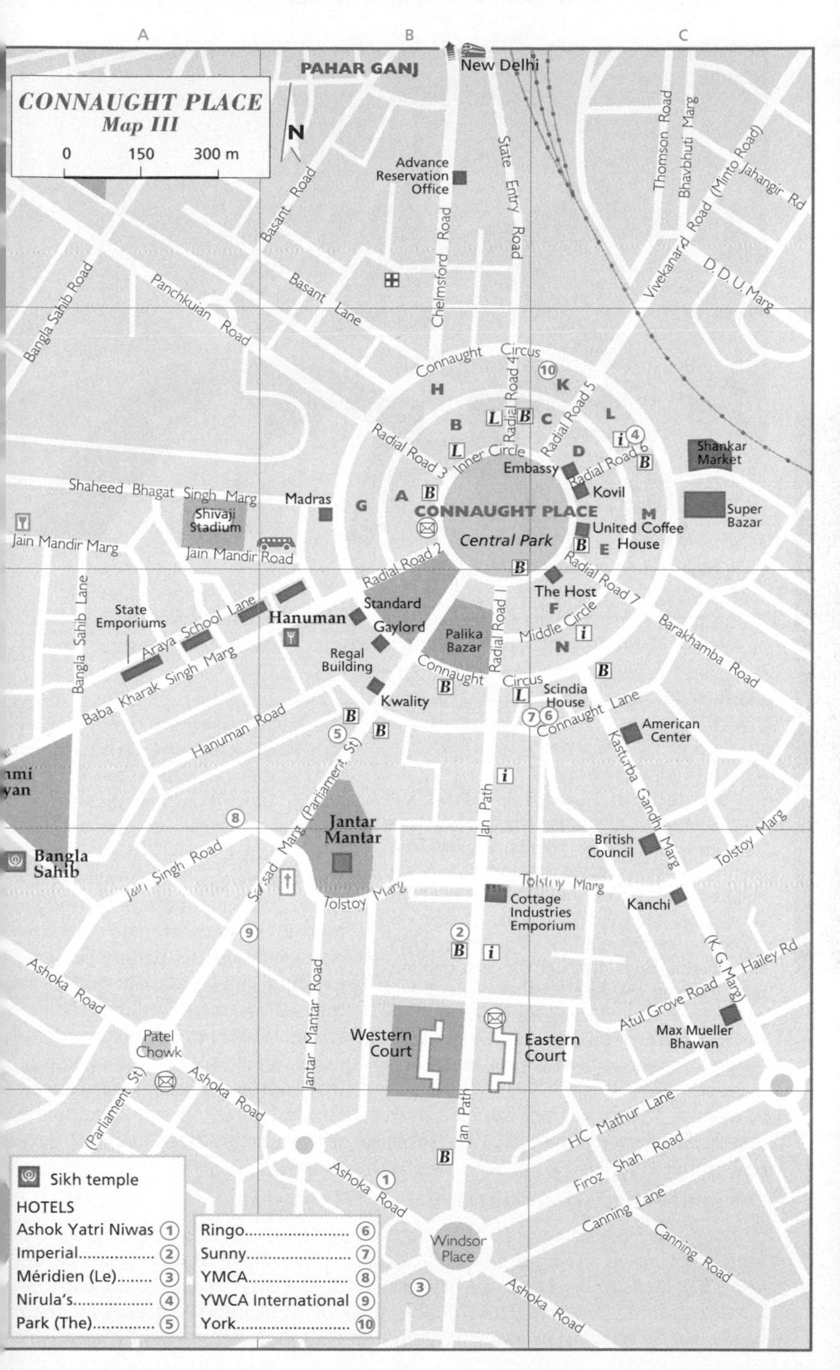
CONNAUGHT PLACE
Map III
0 150 300 m
N
PAHAR GANJ
New Delhi
Advance Reservation Office
Basant Road
Basant Lane
Chelmsford Road
State Entry Road
Thomson Road
Bhavbhuti Marg
Vivekanand Road (Minto Road)
Jahangir Rd
D.D.U. Marg
Bangla Sahib Road
Panchkuian Road
Connaught Circus
Radial Road 4
Radial Road 5
Radial Road 6
Radial Road 3
Inner Circle
Embassy
Kovil
Shankar Market
Super Bazar
Shaheed Bhagat Singh Marg
Shivaji Stadium
Madras
CONNAUGHT PLACE
Central Park
United Coffee House
Jain Mandir Marg
Jain Mandir Road
Radial Road 2
Radial Road 7
The Host
Bangla Sahib Lane
State Emporiums
Araya School Lane
Hanuman
Standard
Gaylord
Palika Bazar
Radial Road 1
Middle Circle
Barakhamba Road
Regal Building
Kwality
Baba Kharak Singh Marg
Scindia House
Connaught Lane
American Center
Hanuman Road
(Parliament St)
Kasturba Gandhi Marg
Jan Path
Jantar Mantar
Sansad Marg
Bangla Sahib
Jai Singh Road
British Council
Tolstoy Marg
Kanchi
Cottage Industries Emporium
(K.G. Marg)
Hailey Rd
Atul Grove Road
Max Mueller Bhawan
Ashoka Road
Jantar Mantar Road
Western Court
Eastern Court
Patel Chowk
(Parliament St)
HC Mathur Lane
Firoz Shah Road
Canning Lane
Canning Road
Windsor Place
Sikh temple
HOTELS
Ashok Yatri Niwas 1
Imperial 2
Méridien (Le) 3
Nirula's 4
Park (The) 5
Ringo 6
Sunny 7
YMCA 8
YWCA International 9
York 10

B. Kaufmann

Delhi observatory

At this point, either move on to the next visit ("Raj Path and its surroundings", p 131) or continue on towards the Lakshmi Narayan temple (particularly if you are interested in Hinduism), then to New Delhi railway station.

Lakshmi Narayan Temple (Birla Mandir) (Map I B2) *(1km from here: go back along Baba Kharak Singh Marg to the left until you reach a roundabout, turn right into Kali Bari Road; at the end, turn right (in front of a small Buddhist temple) into Mandir Marg. Take your shoes off before entering.)* Built by the wealthy Birla family, originally from Shekhawati *(see p 29)*, this Hindu shrine, made entirely out of white marble, is dedicated to Vishnu-Narayana and his personification, Lakshmi, the goddess of good fortune so revered by *marwari* merchants. Mahatma Gandhi agreed to inaugurate it in 1938, on condition that "untouchables" were allowed to enter it, which was not the case in many Hindu temples. A sign outside the temple does however indicate that "those suffering from infectious diseases" (lepers) cannot enter.

The end of a tyranny

On the death of Aurangzeb (1707), the Mughal empire declined rapidly, but northern India regained little by little its religious freedom. The Hindus seized the opportunity and rebuilt their temples. The Sikhs attempted to do likewise for their "gurudwaras", but not without a certain amount of strife. In 1783, Baba Baghel Singh, head of the Sikh community, stormed the Red Fort and forced Emperor Shah Alam to negotiate. To retrieve the Fort, the latter had to grant the Sikh community the right to build temples in Delhi.

Take a rickshaw to New Delhi Station.

Nothing can be compared to the sensation of being caught in the overexcited frenzy of a crowd attempting to catch a train at **New Delhi Station** (map I B2 and map II B3). It has to be seen to be believed. As do the easily recognisable, red-uniformed porters, balancing improbable piles of trunks and suitcases on their heads, whilst weaving in and out along the platforms crammed with travellers and their families. The departure of a son, in-laws or distant cousins would not be complete without the ultimate family meeting on the platform and sometimes in the over-crowded compartments themselves.

Opposite the station is **Pahar Ganj** (map II B3-4 and map III B1), whose main road, Main Bazaar Rd *(opposite, slightly to the left leaving the station)*, contains budget hotels, second-hand clothing shops and cheap arts and crafts. In the neighbouring lanes, clients of the tiny *chay* shops – a portable stove and two wooden benches – sip milky tea while the soundtracks of local films blare out of a few television sets.

"New-wave" hippies

Pahar Ganj is one of the spots favoured by foreigners to India intent on reliving the former hippy years. A number of hotels and restaurants are packed with long-haired, shabbily dressed Westerners, covered in extravagant body piercing and waiting to leave for Goa or Nepal. However they do not seem to appreciate Indian food, and have a tendency to consume spaghetti bolognese, chips or veggie burgers... Thus, this marginal clan spends the cold winter abroad in warm, comfortable idleness. The gulf separating them from what is a fundamentally conservative society gives rise to all sorts of tensions and misunderstandings.

New Delhi★★ (Map IV)

5hr in a rickshaw.

This tour through spacious, green districts – or museum rooms – starts at **Raj Path**, the former King's Way or the "Road of Power": a vast 2.5km-long avenue that leads westwards to a series of symbolic monuments of India's democracy: the Presidential Palace, main ministries and the Parliament building. Built by the British at the turn of the last century according to plans by **Lutyens**, the buildings were originally intended to house the administration of the British Raj. The view initially culminated in the east with the Purana Qila, but this was blocked in the 1930s when a stadium was built. To the south lies a district, hidden amongst trees and greenery, of 1920s white bungalows with verandas built in long, **straight, tree-lined avenues**. Here, the term bungalow refers to spacious residences, surrounded by elegant verandas, now the official homes of ministers and generals.

Go to **Vijay Chowk** (Victory Square) (Map IV B2). Opposite stands the **Head of State's Palace**★ (Rashtrapi Bhawan) (Map IV A2) *(closed to the public. The Mughal gardens can be visited in February-March. Changing of the guard on Saturdays, 8.30-9.15am in the summer and 10.30-11.10am in the winter.)* set on Raisina Hill. Finished in 1929, it was initially the home of the viceroy. Since 1947, it has been the official residence, (which most people simply call "Raisina Hill") of the President of the Republic. **Government buildings** and ministries stand neatly on either side of the avenue, as if on parade *(see p 125)*. The drive up to Raisina Hill is impressive and reveals the palace's large dome, inspired by the Buddhist stupa (reliquary) at Sanchi (State of Madhya Pradesh).

Parliament House (Map IV B1-2), set slightly off the main road to the north of Raj Path, is a vast circular edifice surrounded by an arcade of columns. Completed in 1927, it briefly housed meetings of the "Chamber of Princes" and the "Assembly", the two, totally symbolic, legislative bodies granted to India by Britain in 1935. It is now the seat of the Union's two assemblies: the **Rajiya Sabha** (Council of State) and the **Lok Sabha** (House of the People).

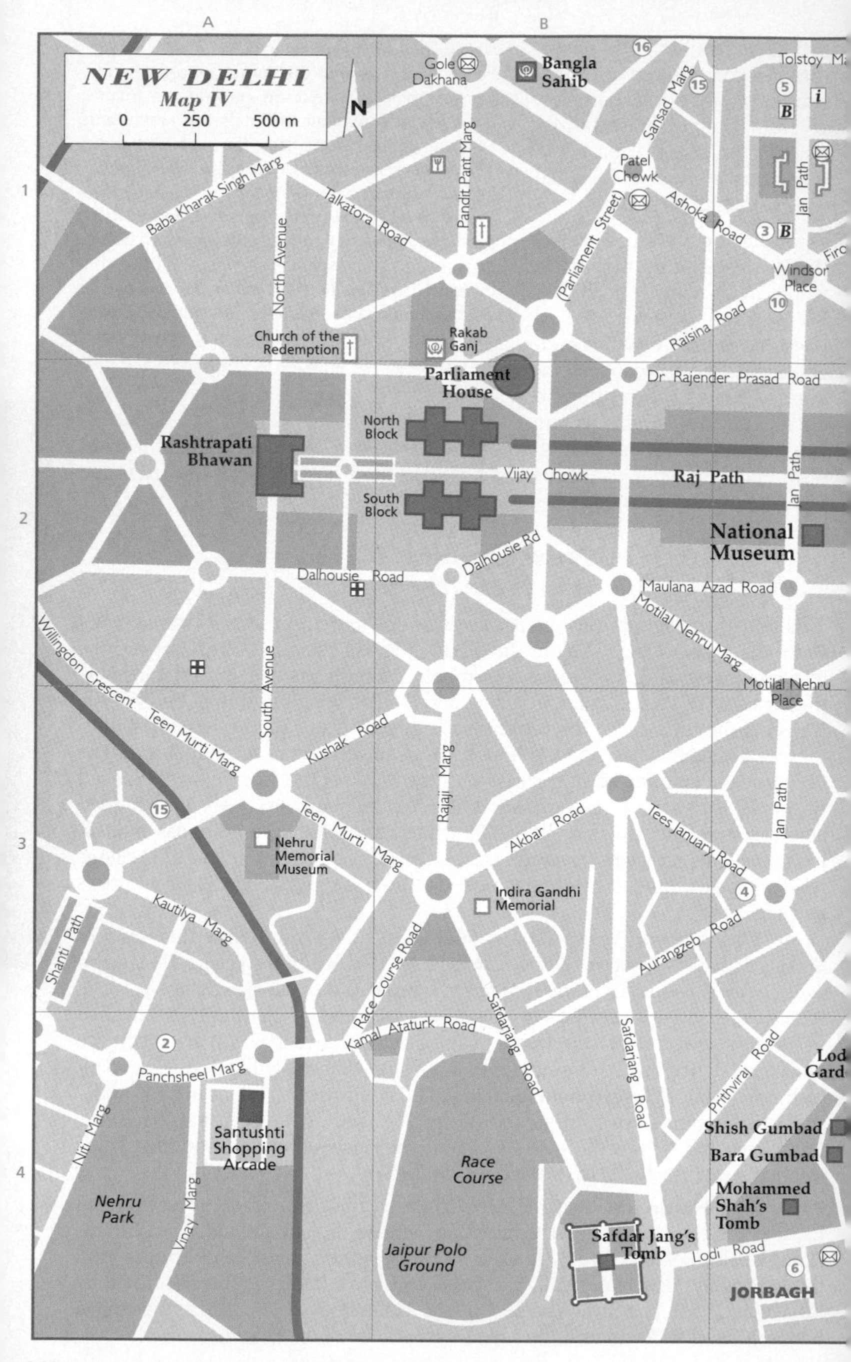
NEW DELHI
Map IV
0 250 500 m
N
A
B
1
2
3
4
Gole Dakhana
Bangla Sahib
Tolstoy M
Sansad Marg
Patel Chowk
Baba Kharak Singh Marg
Talkatora Road
Pandit Pant Marg
North Avenue
Ashoka Road
Jan Path
(Parliament Street)
Windsor Place
Raisina Road
Church of the Redemption
Rakab Ganj
Parliament House
Dr Rajender Prasad Road
North Block
Rashtrapati Bhawan
Vijay Chowk
Raj Path
South Block
National Museum
Dalhousie Road
Dalhousie Rd
Maulana Azad Road
Motilal Nehru Marg
Willingdon Crescent
South Avenue
Motilal Nehru Place
Teen Murti Marg
Kushak Road
Rajaji Marg
Akbar Road
Tees January Road
Nehru Memorial Museum
Indira Gandhi Memorial
Kautilya Marg
Shanti Path
Aurangzeb Road
Race Course Road
Kamal Ataturk Road
Safdarjang Road
Prithviraj Road
Panchsheel Marg
Santushti Shopping Arcade
Niti Marg
Vinay Marg
Nehru Park
Race Course
Jaipur Polo Ground
Safdar Jang's Tomb
Lodi Road
Shish Gumbad
Bara Gumbad
Mohammed Shah's Tomb
Lod Gard
JORBAGH

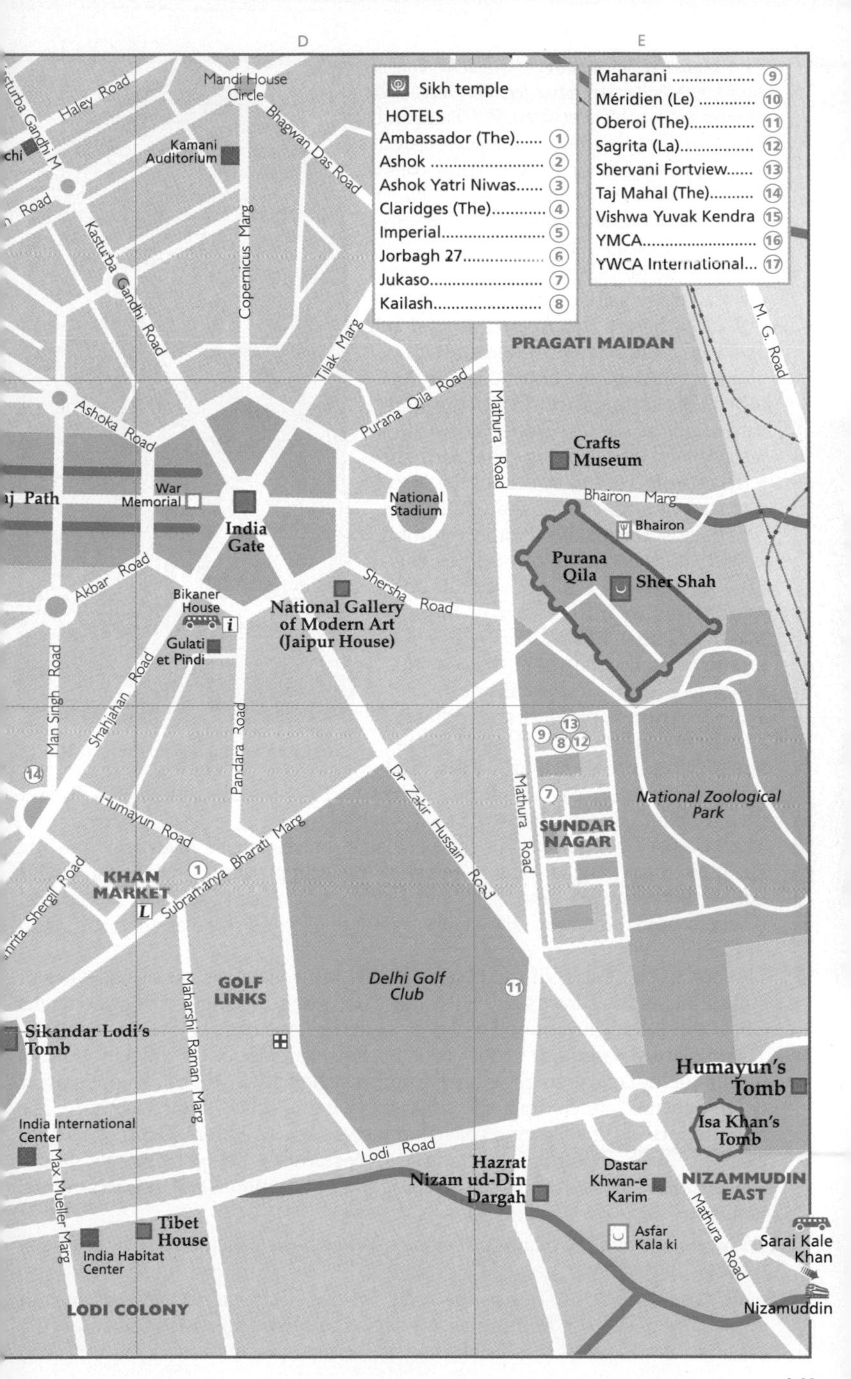
D
E
Sikh temple
HOTELS
Ambassador (The)...... 1
Ashok 2
Ashok Yatri Niwas...... 3
Claridges (The)............ 4
Imperial...................... 5
Jorbagh 27................. 6
Jukaso........................ 7
Kailash....................... 8
Maharani 9
Méridien (Le) 10
Oberoi (The).............. 11
Sagrita (La)................ 12
Shervani Fortview...... 13
Taj Mahal (The).......... 14
Vishwa Yuvak Kendra 15
YMCA......................... 16
YWCA International... 17
Mandi House Circle
Haley Road
Kamani Auditorium
Bhagwan Das Road
Copernicus Marg
Kasturba Gandhi Road
Tilak Marg
PRAGATI MAIDAN
M. G. Road
Ashoka Road
Purana Qila Road
Mathura Road
Crafts Museum
War Memorial
India Gate
National Stadium
Bhairon Marg
Bhairon
Purana Qila
Sher Shah
Akbar Road
Bikaner House
Shersha Road
National Gallery of Modern Art (Jaipur House)
Gulati et Pindi
Man Singh Road
Shahjahan Road
Pandara Road
Dr Zakir Hussain Road
National Zoological Park
SUNDAR NAGAR
Humayun Road
Subramanya Bharati Marg
KHAN MARKET
GOLF LINKS
Delhi Golf Club
Maharshi Raman Marg
Sikandar Lodi's Tomb
Humayun's Tomb
Isa Khan's Tomb
India International Center
Max Mueller Marg
Lodi Road
Hazrat Nizam ud-Din Dargah
Dastar Khwan-e Karim
NIZAMMUDIN EAST
Asfar Kala ki
Sarai Kale Khan
Tibet House
India Habitat Center
LODI COLONY
Nizamuddin

The National Museum*** (Map IV C2) *(10am-5pm; closed on Monday, entrance fee, 2hr visit)* is situated on the crossroads between Raj Path and Jan Path (the "People's Path"), formerly Queen's Way. It is famous for its wonderful **collections of statues***** which are exhibited on the ground floor and cover all the periods of Indian history. The first room is devoted to the Mohenjo-Daro and Harappa civilisations which dominated northwestern India before the Aryans' arrival in 1600 BC. Showcases contain statuettes, including the famous copper "dancer" and other objects found during excavations carried out in 1921 in Sindh (now Pakistan). Among the following collections, the terracotta objects and statues of the Mauryan and Shunga eras (3 and 2C BC) are particularly remarkable. Some beautiful Greco-Buddhist heads of Buddha illustrate Gandharan art (1C and 3C AD) which was to influence the famous Mathura School. Buddhist art is also present in the collections from the Nagarjunakonda site in Andhra Pradesh (3C sculpted friezes, plaques and pillars) and the Gupta era (5C terracotta objects and 6C sculptures). The following rooms are devoted to statues from southern India of the Chhalukya (8C), Pallava (9C), Chola (11C) and Hoyshala (12C) periods.

Statue of Vishnu, Pala dynasty (11C)

The **jewellery** collection contains necklaces, bracelets and diadems, from the Harappa to the Mughal eras. A series of interesting pictures relates the evolution of **Indian scripts** from India and southeastern Asia. (The Thai, Khmer and Burmese alphabets were all largely based on scripts originating from south India.)

The first floor starts with the **Marine Room**, with paintings telling the story of Hindu imperialism from the 7C to the 11C, when the ships of the monarchs Chola and Pallava adventured out as far as the distant coasts of Java and Sumatra. The **miniature paintings**** room contains fine examples of the different schools (kalam) of Indian painting, grouped together regionally – Mughal, Rajput, pahari or "mountains" (including the amazing Kangra school) and Deccan. The **manuscripts** of the following collection contain an 8C Koran. The second floor rooms contain collections of traditional **costumes***, weapons, some superb **woodwork** from south India and a collection of traditional **Indian instruments**: *sitar, sarod, tabla, etc.*

On leaving the museum, return to Raj Path and follow it round to the right until you reach the roundabout.

India Gate (Map IV D2), set in the centre of this octagonal square, was put up in memory of the 100 000 Indian soldiers who died fighting for Britain during the First World War. It is a favourite gathering spot for Indian families who come to enjoy the cool of the evening among ice-cream and balloon sellers. On the right of the roundabout *(with your back to Rashtrapati Bhawan)* are the former town houses of the maharajas of Bikaner and Jaipur: Bikaner House (now Rajasthan's tourist office) and Jaipur House, now the **National Gallery of Modern Art** *(10am-5pm, closed Monday, entrance charge)*, home to the works of contemporary Indian artists such as Amrita Sher-Gil and Jaya Appasamy.

The Old Fort, **Purana Qila**** (Map IV E2) *(to the east of Raj Path, on the other side of Mathura Road. Open from dawn to dusk, entrance fee, extra charge for cameras and video equipment)*, built up on a hill, is a favourite Sunday outing spot with Delhi's inhabitants, who come here to picnic with their families in the fort's park or to go boating on the water at the foot of the city's walls. This hill is said to be the legendary site of **Indraprashta**, as mentioned in the *Mahabharata*, in other words, the first Delhi. Recent archeological excavations seem to confirm this myth. Furthermore a village called Indrapat situated in the ruins existed up until around 1910. The ruins date back to the period of Humayun, the second Mughal emperor, who built the fort at the beginning of his reign, naming it Dinpanah ("refuge of the faith"). However in 1540 the city, as well as most of the rest of the empire, fell into the hands of a usurper, Sher Shah. Humayun finally managed to recapture his inheritance in 1555, but was killed, just the year after, when he fell down the stairs in his library, (still visible in the Purana Qila).

Four **monumental doors** are set in the walls. The fort itself now only contains three monuments, including **Sher Shah's attractive mosque**, which illustrates the architectural transition from the time of the Lodis, still dominated by Hindu techniques, to the Mughal era and its Persian influences. The importance accorded the façade's central arch is an example of this Persian influence with an archway that is much higher than the others and surrounded by a decorative frame of epigraphical banners, which protrude, forming a real *pishtaq* (monumental portal). Note the incredible detail of the decorative mosaic work and multicoloured ceramics. The nearby tower, **Sher Mandal**, decorated with *iwan* arches and topped with a *chhatri*, housed Humayun's library (closed to the public). In between these two monuments is a graceful **baoli** (stepwell).

The tastefully designed **Crafts Museum**** (Map IV E2) *(10am-5pm; closed Monday, no charge. Allow at least an hour)*, provides a fascinating step back in time into Indian crafts and rural arts and traditions of yesteryear. It is laid out in the form of a village with a series of houses laid out around courtyards. There are many fine examples of mural decorations, woodwork and intricately carved doors.

A first room *(on the right)* houses changing exhibitions of the work of folk artists. The adjoining room has some wonderful **bronze statues** and **sacred wood panelling** from southern India. The latter's bright colours exemplify the exuberant fervour so typical of Dravidian temples.

The **courtly crafts** room features an 18C **jharokha**, an exquisitely carved wooden balcony, adorned with *jali* (lattice screen) from a *nawab's* palace in Gujarat. The same room also contains the replica of a **Gujarati haveli** (residence) with superb wood panelling. Upstairs, an interesting **textile collection** features different weaving techniques, together with some splendid saris, cashmere shawls and printed cotton fabrics from Bagru and Sanganer (Rajasthan).

Finally the **park** provides the opportunity for a leisurely stroll. In the winter, it is also the scene of exhibition-sales of work by well-known artists from various Indian States. It also contains reconstructions of the **traditional dwellings** of some of India's tribes.

Along Lodi Road** (Map IV)

Allow 4hr with a rickshaw, not including Tibet House.

A walk that leads through a series of well-maintained parks (the flower borders are a pure delight in February-March) that line the south of the residential area built by Lutyens. The tombs and mausoleums along the way give visitors a good idea of how Indo-Moslem architecture evolved between the 15C and 18C. The tour concludes with a trip to the heart of a picturesque district, a particularly popular Moslem pilgrim centre.

Safdar Jang's Tomb** (Map IV B4) *(from dawn to dusk, entrance fee, extra charge for cameras and videos)* is often described as the last masterpiece of Mughal art. It is the tomb of one of the emperor's prime ministers *(wazir)*, who was given the honorary title of **Safdar Jang**. Built in 1754, it is typical of all the Indo-Moslem tombs built after 1560 (of which you will see a prototype during this visit in Humayun's tomb). Built within a walled Mughal garden *(chahar bagh)*, and divided into quarters by two canals, it is imposingly set on a raised platform with the tomb in full view, to create the effect of a pyramid. In truth, a lack of proper proportion, overly high façades and an excessively bulbous dome remove much of the monument's overall majesty, but it nonetheless remains a remarkable work. The decorative features (marble mosaics on the corner towers and stucco moulded ceilings) are particularly worthy of note.

Continue on down Lodi Rd for around 300m, on the left-hand side.

Lodi Garden** (Map IV C4) *(from dawn to dusk, no charge)*, a truly peaceful haven of greenery, contains tombs *(rauza)* dating back to the eras of the Sayyid and Lodi sultans. The southern entrance leads *(to the left, past a clump of bamboos)* to **Sultan Mohammed Shah's tomb** (1450), formerly walled, today dominated by royal palm trees. It is the first example in Delhi of an **octagonal tomb**: a central chamber with eight sides, topped with a spherical dome *(gumbad)* and surrounded by a gallery supporting eight kiosks *(chhatri)*, a legacy of Hindu architecture. It can be noted that the sharply protruding awning *(chadya)* is typically Hindu, whereas the ogee arches are clearly Persian.

Towards the centre of the park, two, almost identical, square-shaped *rauza* mark the burial places of influential members of the Sultanate. The first is the **Bara Gumbad** (1494). The door frames are typical of Pre-Mughal architecture: a lintel supported by two opposing corbels. A mosque attached to the tomb turns out to be a simple prayer room. Opposite, on the other side of the pool, is a hostel for pilgrims. Next to this, the **Sheesh Gumbad** still has a few of its original blue tiles. Inside, the western wall has a pretty *mihrab* (recess indicating the direction of Mecca).

Right to the north of the garden **Sultan Sikandar Lodi's Tomb** (1517) is hidden behind a crenellated wall. Although also octagonal in shape, it has lost its *chhatri*. It is an ideal place to stop for a quiet rest, under the shade of the *chadya* and the large trees, which provide a refreshing curtain of leaves, and are full of twittering budgerigars.

Continue down Lodi Rd as far east as it goes. If you are keen on Tibetan art, stop along the way and visit Tibet House.

Tibet House (Map IV C4) *(Monday-Friday, 9.30am-1pm/2pm-5pm)* has a library of over 4000 books and a small museum with *tangka* (pious paintings on fabric), cult objects, jewellery.

Humayun's tomb

Humayun's Tomb*** (Map IV E4) *(from dawn to dusk, entrance fee, extra charge for video filming)*, which lies in the midst of greenery, also has several other tombs of important people. Just before the entrance, a door set in a crenellated wall *(on the right)* leads into **Isa Kahn's tomb** (1548), a dignitary of the time of Sher Shah. The work faithfully reproduces the now-familiar octagonal model with veranda (already seen in Lodi Garden), adopted a century earlier.

Return to the main path leading to **Humayun's tomb** and go into the enormous walled Mughal garden *(chahar bagh)*, in the centre of which is the tomb, built in 1565, almost like a residence of bliss in Allah's paradise. One is immediately struck by the perfection of the proportions and the sober contrast between the red sandstone and white marble, and also by the leaps and bounds made architecturally since the construction of Isa Kahn's tomb just 20 years earlier. The emperor's heartbroken widow entrusted the monument to a Persian architect, who created a tomb so perfect that it became a prototype for all Indo-Moslem tombs. First, the large tomb is placed, as an object to be admired, on a raised platform, surrounded by a spacious central *iwan* (vaulted recess), which creates an impression of space and light. Finally, four *chhatri* are positioned around the dome, which is placed at the top of the pyramidal construction, and to which all eyes are drawn. It should be noted that the inner, flatter dome is set inside the outer, slightly bulb-shaped dome, creating a vast inner empty space between the two shells. This is the first example of the use in India of the "double shell". The many typically Persian additions are very clear from a distance: ogee arches have definitively replaced the traditional Hindu lintel and corbel construction and the series of vaulted *iwan* recesses and bays create a permanent movement of light and shade.

In the centre of the platform, a staircase leads to a terrace. Inside, the octagonal mortuary chamber is a model of sober harmony. A series of vestibules surround it, separated by monolithic *jali* which enhance the play of the shadows within.

From the terrace, two domes can be seen rising from the eastern wall; the one on the right, covered in blue ceramics, protects a 17C tomb, while on the left, a white marble one belongs to the *gurudwara* which commemorates the visit of guru Gobind Singh in 1707.

On leaving, walk towards the roundabout with the 17C Sabza Burj tower (green tower), turn left into Mathura Rd and take the first lane on the right.

The dargah of Hazrat Nizam ud-Din** (Map IV E4) provides a glimpse of the heart of one of Delhi's most picturesque, predominantly Moslem, working-class areas. Hazrat Nizam ud-Din Auliya was a mystic saint of the Chisti brotherhood of Sufis, who died in 1325, and has remained extremely popular among Moslems and Hindus. His *dargah* (tomb of a Sufi saint) can be reached through a winding lane that becomes gradually narrower, initially weaving its way past little restaurants, which soon give way to stalls selling religious cassettes and books. *Qawwals* (pious Sufi songs) blare out all around, Pakistani-style. The atmosphere becomes almost austere and one is surrounded by bearded men and beggars. The stalls selling rose and jasmine petals (which the pilgrims use to decorate the tomb) add a touch of gaiety, further enhanced by the bright green *chadors* displayed around the stalls, waiting to be placed over the saint's tomb. The lane leads into the **courtyard of the dargah** *(wear a hat or scarf and remove your shoes)*. Many famous people expressed a wish to be buried close to the saint to whom many miracles are attributed. There are three tombs in particular: that of the famous poet Amir Khusrau (1253-1324) *(opposite the entrance)*, one of the saint's disciples; the tomb, screened by **jali**, of Jahanara, Shah Jahan's favourite daughter; and that of Emperor Mohammed Shah (18C) *(opposite the previous one, on the right)*. The **saint's tomb** (1562) is on a raised platform in the centre of the mosque's courtyard, next to the prayer room. Large numbers of pilgrims visit it every year to be blessed or to make a wish (symbolised by a cotton thread tied to the tomb's *jali*) and every day, exalted *qawwal* are sung to the accompaniment of a harmonium. Ignore the various beggars and hawkers who will present books with the names of imaginary famous donors in the hope of receiving some sort of donation.

The southern districts** (Map I)

6hr in a taxi for the whole visit,
3hr 30min if you miss out Tughluqabad or the Bahat temple.

Lower- and middle-class residential areas alternate with smart new districts and old villages, without any attempt at order or harmony, in what has become a form of urban anarchy. A few pleasant exceptions subsist in what, to many foreign eyes, resembles pandemonium.

On the road to Qutb Minar

Up until the end of the 1980s, **Hauz Khas Village*** (Map I A4) was a village with buffaloes and *charpoys* (string beds) like any other, hidden in between residential districts. Then the designers moved in, turning it into a centre for smart ethnic fashion *(see the shopping section in "Making the most of Delhi")*. In the early 14C, Sultan Ala ud-Din Khilji dug a reservoir here *(hauz)* to supply water to his new city of Siri (Map I B4). On its banks a few 14C **tombs** remain, in particular that of Sultan **Feroz Shah Tughluq**, which is built in the Persian style, with a dome supported on squinches. These sober, austere monuments are just next to the well-conserved ruins of a **madrasa**. Tamerlane set up camp among these monuments before attacking Delhi in 1398.

Begumpur Mosque* (Map I B5) *(follow Aurobindo Marg southwards. Once past the Outer Ring Rd crossroads, take the first left; this takes you into a residential area and gets suddenly narrower before it reaches the mosque. No charge)* is a peaceful haven that has retained its village character. On Sundays, *charpoys* are pulled in front of the mosque and the men sit out and play cards or smoke their *hookahs*. This is the best preserved monument of the former **Jahanpanah** (14C), one of the three cities founded by the Tughluq dynasty. The fortified mosque, built on a raised platform, now serves as a playing field for the village children and grazing for the goats who nibble on weeds that grow between the roughly-laid stone slabs in the spacious courtyard. Two minarets formerly flanked the central archway into the prayer room. On climbing the stairs, a glance over the outer walls reveals the ruins of the old fort at Jahanpanah just a few hundred metres further north.

Qutb Minar Complex*** (Map I A5)

(From dawn to dusk, entrance charge, free on Friday, extra charge for videos. At least 1hr.)

The pleasant park encloses a mosque, tombs and various monuments most of which date back to the 13C and 14C. The most famous of them is the Qutb Minar, Delhi's emblem. This minaret-tower commemorates the victory of Mohammed of Ghor – and of Islam – over the Hindu monarch Prithviraja III at the battle of Tarain (1192). It is named after General **Qutb ud-Din Aibak** who led Mohammed's troops and who was to become governor and then sultan of Delhi (1206-1210). Qutb ud-Din built a city next door to Prithviraja, which underwent considerable enlargement and embellishment for over a century. Two earthquakes however (14C and 19C) substantially damaged the Qutb Minar and the nearby building.

Visit – The main pathway opens onto an esplanade, dominated *(on the left)* by **Qutb Minar**. Every Indian is familiar with its slightly conical outline. 73m-high (the tallest edifice in India), it consists of five superimposed sections which are separated by *muqarna (honeycomb of arches)* supporting a gallery. Bands of Kufic calligraphy decorate the tower like scrolled banners. Just behind the minaret is a cube-shaped building with an archway called **Ala-i Darwaza**. Walk through and turn round to have a view of what the faithful would have seen when entering the mosque. This door was added in 1310 by Sultan Ala ud-Din. Koranic inscriptions, scrolls and interlaced characters and motifs were sculpted by local Hindu artists. Every square centimetre is covered, as is generally the case with Indian art which cannot abide any empty space, however small. The familiar alternating red sandstone and white marble add a degree of order to the monument's exuberant ornamentation. On the right is the attractive **tomb of Imam Zamin**, early 16C.

Turn back towards Qutb Minar. A few steps *(on the left)* lead down to India's oldest mosque, **Quwwat ul-Islam** ("the might of Islam"), begun in 1193 and enlarged twice within a century. It was built with materials removed from some twenty Hindu and Jain temples, destroyed in the name of Islam. Hence, the gallery's pillars comprise two superimposed, square-shaped columns, typical of 8C-10C Hindu art. An iron pillar – without a single rust spot – stands practically in the centre of the courtyard. The last surviving trace of the Hindu period, it was dedicated to Vishnu in the 4C and, according to the Sanskrit inscription, is said to have been used as a flagpole. All that remains of the former prayer room are the entrance's stately ogee arches, covered in entwined vines and Koranic inscriptions. Both the profusion and intricacy of the carving denotes the workmanship of Indian master craftsmen.

Walk through the arcades and bear left. The ruins of **Ala ud-Din Khilji's tomb** (early 14C sultan) are located in a **madrasa**. This association of a tomb and a school, typical of the Seljuk tradition, is a throw-back to the Turkish origins of India's early Moslem rulers.

Walk back to the arcades, but don't go through them, keep straight on. The **tomb of Iltutmish**, successor to Qutb ud-Din, was built during his lifetime in 1235. This square building was originally crowned with a dome that rested on squinches. It was the first monumental tomb built in India and served as prototype for Indo-Persian mausoleums up until the Mughal era. Once again the abundance of intricate sculpture reveals the workmanship of local artists.

In the centre of the lawn, a vast and unsightly heap of stone *(on the left when walking towards the exit)* is a reminder of Ala ud-Din's aborted attempt to build a minaret, **Ala-i Minar**, which was to have been twice as high as the Qutb. On the death of the sovereign in 1316, no one had the courage to pursue his extravagant project.

Other monuments

Perched on a rocky outcrop, **Tughluqabad's gigantic citadel*** (Map I C5) *(on the southeastern limits of Delhi? 8km from Qutb Minar by Marhauli Badarpur Rd)* was founded in 1320 by Sultan Ghiyas ud-Din Tughluq, but was abandoned several years later, so the legend goes, due to a curse thrown on it by the Sufi saint Nizam ud-Din. Visible from afar *(on the left-hand side of the road)* due to its impressive outer walls, where hordes of monkeys greet callers. The almost derelict interior of shapeless ruins will probably only appeal to the more imaginative visitors. Opposite *(right-hand side)*, **Ghiyas ud-Din's tomb** was erected by his son after the latter had assassinated his father in 1325. It is hidden behind a crenellated wall and surrounded by a now dried-up lake, as if it were a mini-fortress. Built out of red sandstone and white marble, its slanting walls further accentuate the defensive style of the building.

Bahai Temple* (or Lotus temple) (Map I C4) *(From Tughluqabad, drive north and turn left into Chiragh Delhi Rd and continue on until Nehru Place. 9.30am-5.30pm from October to March, 9am-7pm from April to September, no charge)* is set in a superbly well-cared for garden, rising like a gigantic lotus bud. Finished in 1986, it symbolises the unity and peace advocated by the followers of Bahaism. In the basement, a bookshop and museum provide information about this religion that appeared in Iran in the 19C, which preaches religious unity based on tolerance and personal mystical experience.

Quwwat ul-Islam, Qutb Minar mosque

Civil Lines

90min is more than sufficient for this "short" visit.

Throughout the whole sub-continent, the British, not wishing to mix with the locals, built themselves districts, known as "Civil Lines", outside the main city centres. These districts contained administrative buildings, a church and residential bungalows. A stroll through Delhi's Civil Lines, evokes memories of what life must have been like for the families of the British residents in the 19C, at the time of the Mutiny (or war of Independence) that broke out in 1857 and which almost tolled the death knell of European domination in north India. This tour is limited to the southern approach to Civil Lines, which although the least pleasant, is, in fact, the most interesting.

St James' Church (Map I B1) *(east of Lothian Rd)*, surrounded by a garden and a small cemetery, it only dates back to 1835 but is nonetheless the oldest church in Delhi. It was born out of a pledge made by an adventurer born of a Scottish father and a Rajput mother, Colonel James Skinner, whose Skinner's Horse was rapidly to become an elite regiment, distinguishing itself regularly on the battlefield up until the Second World War. Skinner's home, a vast semi-spherical dome, lies just behind the church *(not open to the public)*.

Kashmiri Gate (Map I B1) *(some 100m north, along Lothian Rd)* is a vestige of Shahjahanabad's original ramparts. It marked the starting point of the Kashmiri Route, and today, acts as southern border to Civil Lines. During the Mutiny, violent battles took place here and part of it was destroyed by an explosion.

Continuing northwards, you reach the busy, congested crossroads between Lothian Rd and Boulevard Rd.

Qudsia Bagh *(on the other side of Boulevard Rd, on the right)*, an old Mughal-style garden, contains the ruins of a mosque, but the ear-splitting racket of the nearby traffic somewhat detracts from the place's overall charm.

Nicholson Cemetery (Map I B1) *(from Kashmiri Gate: on the other side of Boulevard Rd, on the left)*, is one of oldest British cemeteries in the whole sub-continent. Today it is primarily home to weeds, brambles and monkeys. It was named after General John Nicholson, who lost his life defending Kashmiri Gate and who lies in the cemetery. Abandoned and forgotten, it exerts a poignant appeal.

The walk can be continued towards the old ministry, now seat of the Council, the Mutiny Memorial and Ashoka's column.

Making the most of Delhi

Getting there

By plane – *Indira Gandhi International Airport (IGI)* (just off Map I A4), called ***Terminal 2***, is 20km southwest of Connaught Place. ☎ (011) 565 20 11 and 569 60 21. On arrival, exchange bureaux are open 24 hours a day and there is also a computerised reservation terminal for train tickets (8am-8pm). The ***India Tourism Development Corporation (ITDC)*** may be able to supply useful information about Delhi, but cannot be depended on for accommodation: it only sends visitors to hotels that pay it a commission, systematically denigrating the others.

To take a taxi into the city centre (around 280Rs), go to the "pre-paid" taxi counter, also called "Delhi Traffic Police", which is outside the main building. The fare is paid before getting into the taxi and customers are given a receipt indicating the amount paid and the taxi number. It must only be given to the driver on arrival at the hotel. Most international flights arrive at night-time and some taxi drivers take advantage, on the way in, of their passengers' fatigue and lack of familiarity with India, to make them believe that their hotel is either disreputable, full or even that there is rioting in the area. The purpose of such stories is to entice travellers to hotels which pay the drivers a commission, possibly even taking them as far as Agra or Jaipur… If you don't have a hotel reservation or don't feel confident about setting out at night, wait until daybreak before leaving the airport.

The Ashok Travel & Tours car rental agency provides "tourist taxis" from 350Rs to the town centre. There is also a non-air-conditioned minibus run by EATS (Ex-Servicemen's Air Link Tourist Service) that runs a shuttle service between the airport and Connaught Place, via the domestic airport. A shuttle in theory leaves every hour. The bus will stop, on request, at hotels on its route. If arriving at Connaught Place at night, it may be difficult to find a rickshaw willing to take you to the hotel of your choice.

When leaving Delhi, if you have to leave your hotel early in the morning for the airport, reserve a taxi the day before or take the EATS bus which has ten departures between 4am and 10.30pm (35Rs), Block F, Radial Rd 1, Connaught Place, ☎ (011) 331 65 30. To get to the international or the domestic airport (7km), either take the free Airport Authority of India (AAI) shuttle or the EATS bus.

Only travellers with tickets can enter the airport. There is a departure tax of 500Rs, unless it is included in the price of the airfare (check when confirming the flight).

Indira Gandhi Domestic Airport is called ***Terminal I*** of IGI, around 13km southwest of Connaught Place (off Map I A4), ☎ (011) 566 51 81; flight information, ☎ (011) 566 51 21.

In the arrival hall, there is a reliable, efficient "pre-paid" service (150Rs to the town centre) and an Ashok Travel & Tours car rental counter. Outside, there are EATS buses.

Daily flights to Agra (35min) on Alliance Air, subsidiary of Indian Airlines. 2 or 3 daily flights to Jaipur (50min), run by Alliance Air, Jet Airways and Jagson Airlines. Jagson Airlines runs four weekly flights to Udaipur (2hr15min) and Alliance Air runs three. The latter also offers three weekly flights to Jodhpur (1hr) and to Jaisalmer (2hr). Check the regularity because timetables are frequently changed. Flights need to be booked well in advance.

By train – Four stations run services to Agra and Rajasthan:

Delhi Main Railway Station, in the north of Old Delhi (Map II C1). Getting there from Connaught Place means crossing Old Delhi, with its frequent traffic jams. Departures primarily for Alwar, Jaipur, Ajmer, Abu Road and Jodhpur.

New Delhi Railway Station, 700m north of Connaught Place (Map II B3). On the same line as Delhi Main, but also runs services to Mathura, Agra, Bharatpur, Sawai Madhopur and Kota. The "Shatabdi" trains leave from New Delhi, a little more expensive than the others, but more comfortable, quicker and air-conditioned. There is a service to Alwar, Jaipur and Ajmer (every day except Sunday), another to Agra (every day), arriving around 8am, which is perfect for spending a day before catching the evening train back to Delhi at 8pm.

Nizamuddin Railway Station, east of New Delhi (Map I C3). A peaceful station compared to the former two. Trains for Mathura, Agra, Bharatpur, Sawai Madhopur and Kota; some leave from New Delhi and stop at Nizamuddin, others leave directly from Nizamuddin.

Sarai Rohilla Railway Station, around 5km northwest of Connaught Place (Map I A1). Trains to Bikaner and via Jaipur-Ajmer-Chittaurgarh-Udaipur leave from here.

The best way of booking a train ticket is to contact a travel agency, who for only 50Rs, will save you much time and energy. It is also possible to book from the computerised reservation desks, available in all stations (8am-8pm, Sundays 8am-2pm). The main desk is in the IRCA Building, Chelmsford Rd, between

New Delhi and Connaught Place (Map II B4), ☎ (011) 334 86 86 and 334 87 87. Allow at least an hour to queue for tickets. There is also a special desk for foreigners at the ***International Tourist Bureau*** in New Delhi Station, on the 1st floor, ☎ (011) 334 68 04 and 373 41 64. 8am-1.30pm/2pm-5pm; closed Sunday. This desk is always crowded, particularly on Mondays, but Indian Railways have a quota of train seats reserved for foreigners. Tickets must be purchased in US dollars or pounds sterling. This desk also sells "Indrail Passes", which can also be purchased from the computerised reservation desks.

Check which station your train leaves from. Finally, beware of the pickpockets and touts who roam the premises: don't listen to or follow any of the advice from so-called well-wishers keen to help you on your journey, particularly around New Delhi Station or Connaught Place. In recent years, growing numbers of credulous tourists have been taken in by crooks and petty criminals of all sorts.

Information and bookings on the Maharajas' Trains can be obtained from Rajasthan Tourist Office for the "Palace on Wheels" (see "Tourist Offices") and from Gujarat Tourism for the "Royal Orient", A/6 Baba Kharak Singh Marg, ☎ (011) 373 40 15.

By bus – ***Bikaner House***, Pandara Rd (Map IV D2), ☎ (011) 338 34 69; reservations 6am-7pm. "Super deluxe" buses run by Rajasthan State Transport Roadways Corporation (RSTRC): twenty "Silver Line" (non air-conditioned) and 5 "Pink Line" (air-conditioned) buses leave every day for Jaipur between 6am and midnight (6hr). This is the best way of getting to Jaipur, apart from the "Shatabdi" train.

Inter-State Bus Terminal (ISBT), Kashmiri Gate, Old Delhi, north of Delhi Main Station (Map I B1); reservations at Bikaner House or ☎ (011) 296 12 46, 5pm-7pm. "Pre-paid" taxis and rickshaws available. The private lines leave from here (avoid the ones with a video on board or take earplugs), as do a few of the ordinary RSTRC lines, primarily those to Shekhawati.

Sarai Kale Khan Bus Terminal (new ISBT), Mahatma Gandhi Rd, east of Nizamuddin Station (Map I C3), ☎ (011) 464 37 31. Buses to all Rajasthan's cities and to Agra, via Mathura and Vrindavan.

Anand Vihar Bus Terminal, Trans-Yamuna (off Map I C2). This particularly difficult to find bus station in the east of the city is run by Uttar Pradesh State Transport Roadways Corporation (UPSTRC). State buses leave for Mathura, Agra, Bharatpur and Sawai Madhopur. The train is a much better option.

Getting around

By bus – Delhi has three types of buses: "Green Line" buses run by Delhi Transport Corporation (DTC) which follow a fixed route and are numbered (but no map of the routes exists), and private "Blue Line" and "White Line" buses. Prices range from 1-6Rs. Always bursting at the seams, giving some men the opportunity of practising their favourite sport "Eve teasing...", particularly on foreign women...

By rickshaw – Delhi is the only city in which the auto-rickshaw drivers use their meters – even if they often dither about starting it up. Delhi government regularly raises the fixed starting rate (5.50Rs in 1990) and the mileage rate, but many meters are rarely updated. It is worth checking at the beginning of the trip to see whether the meter has been brought up-to-date (the current starting rate is published in the weekly "Delhi Diary"). If it hasn't, expect to have some serious calculations/negotiations on arrival, or consult a chart that provides comparisons between the old and the new rates. All rickshaw-drivers have such a chart but many will present false charts or no chart at all. From 11pm to 5am, add 20 % to the normal rate. "Prepaid" rickshaw ranks are available on Jan Path (opposite the market) and in front of stations. Cycle-rickshaws are practically forbidden in Connaught Place and in the south.

By taxi – Delhi's black and yellow "Ambassador" taxis, non-air-conditioned and generally falling to bits, soon become a familiar sight. Fares can be calculated by checking the equivalence chart. White, non-air-conditioned Ambassador "tourist taxis" also exist with DLY number plates, often in better condition and also more expensive. Taxis can be rented by the day, either from taxi ranks or from an agency (400-800Rs for 8hr and 80km). From 11pm to 5am, add 25% to the normal rate. "Pre-paid" taxi ranks can be found in front of stations.

Vehicle rental – Between 1 000 and 1 600Rs, sometimes more, for a non-air-conditioned "Ambassador" with driver. ***Europcar***, Vins Overseas India, T-2 Community Centre, Sheikh Sarai phase I, New Delhi, ☎ (011) 623 03 81 and 623 08 08, Fax (011) 622 45 43. Branches in Park and Maurya Sheraton hotels. Prohibitive if travelling around town, but reasonable for trips outside Delhi under 150km per day. Self-drive cars available for the rash and daring.

Address book

Tourist information – Many travel agencies, particularly around Connaught Place and Paharganj call themselves "Tourist Information Centres" in an attempt to entice unsuspecting tourists, sometimes for dishonest purposes. Beware and only trust the addresses indicated below:

Government of India Tourist Office, 88 Jan Path, New Delhi 110001 (Map III B3), ☎ (011) 332 00 05/08. 9am-6pm; closed Sundays. Supplies brochures and information for all of India, including Delhi, together with a list of English-speaking guides and the permit required to visit Rashtrapati Bhawan Garden.

***India Tourism Development Corporation Offices* (ITDC)** at the airports and at L-1 Connaught Circus, Radial Rd 6 (Map III C2), ☎ (011) 332 03 31. Every day from 6am-10pm. Organises three interesting visits everyday for those with little time to spare: New Delhi (8am-1pm, 140Rs), Old Delhi (2.15pm-5pm, 110Rs) or New and Old Delhi (8am-5pm, 220Rs). Excursions to Agra (see "Excursions".)

***Delhi Tourism Development Corporation* (DTDC)**, N-36 Connaught Place, Middle Circle (Map III C3), ☎ (011) 331 53 22, Fax (011) 331 36 37. 7am-9pm; closed Sundays. Of limited usefulness except for the fact they provide information about the city and the "son et lumiere" show at Purana Qila (in English, starts between 7.30 and 9pm depending on the season, lasts 1hr). Reservations from the Central Reservation Office, Coffee Home, Baba Kharak Singh Marg, opposite Hanuman's Temple (Map III B3), ☎ (011) 336 53 58. Every day from 7am-9pm. Offices in New Delhi and Delhi Main Stations.

Rajasthan Tourist Office and ***Rajasthan Tourism Development Corporation* (RTDC)**, Bikaner House, Pandara Rd (Map IV D2), ☎ (011) 338 38 37 and 338 95 25, Fax (011) 338 28 23. 10am-1.30pm/2pm-5pm; closed on the 2nd Saturday of the month and on Sundays. Information about Rajasthan and reservations for the "Palace on Wheels" luxury train and Rajasthan's RTDC hotels.

Uttar Pradesh* (UP) *Tourism, Chandralok Building, 36 Jan Path, rear staircase, 2nd floor (Map III B4), ☎ (011) 332 22 51. 10am-5pm; closed Sundays. Information about Agra and Mathura.

Banks and money – Most ATMs are located around Connaught Place (Map III). They take Visa or MasterCard, sometimes both: ***ANZ Grindlays Bank***, E-10 Connaught Place (C2); ***Hongkong Bank***, ECE House, 28 Kasturba Gandhi Marg, corner of Connaught Circus (C3); ***Bank of America***, Hansalaya Building, 15 Barakamba Rd; ***Standard Chartered***, 17 Parliament St, next to Park Hotel (B3); three branches of ***Citybank***, Jeevan Bharati Building, Connaught Circus (B3); DCM Building, 16 Barakamba Rd; F-41 South Extension I.

To change money, either cash or travellers' cheques, contact one of the following. Most are closed on Sundays.

Central Bank of India, Ashok Hotel. 24 hours a day (B5).

Gold Regency Hotel, 4350 Main Bazaar, Paharganj. 24 hours a day (Map II B3-4).

Bank of Baroda, 16 Parliament St, 1st floor, opposite Park Hotel (B3). 10am-2pm, Saturdays 10am-12noon. Withdrawals by card.

STIC, Jan Path Hotel, Jan Path (B5). 9.30am-6.30pm.
Thomas Cook, Imperial Hotel (B4), ☎ (011) 334 05 61, Fax (011) 334 05 63. 9.30am-6pm, Saturdays 9.30am-6pm. Another branch C-33 Connaught Place, Radial Rd 4 (B2), ☎ (011) 335 65 75/78, Fax (011) 335 65 80. 9.30am-6pm. Withdrawals with a Thomas Cook card.
American Express, Wenger House, A Block, Connaught Place (B2), ☎ (011) 332 52 21 and 332 47 65, Fax (011) 371 53 52. Exchange and reimbursement of stolen cheques. 9.30am-6.30pm. Withdrawals with an American Express card. 9.30am-5.30pm, Saturday 9.30am-12.30noon.
SITA World Travel, F-12 Connaught Place, 9.30am-7pm, Saturday 9.30am-6pm.
LKP Merchant Financing, M-56 Connaught Circus, Radial Rd 6 (C2), 9.30am-6.30pm.
To have money sent to India in a few hours:
Western Union, at SITA World Travel, ☎ (011) 331 11 22, Fax (011) 332 46 52, and ***Thomas Cook***.

Post Offices and Telephones – ***GPO***, Dak Bhawan, Parliament St (Map III A4). 10am-6pm; closed Sundays. EMS Speed Post (10am-6pm), registered mail (10am-4.30pm), philately desk (10am-1.30pm/2pm-5pm) and private fax service. Postal code: 110001.
Eastern Court Post Office, Jan Path, opposite Janpath Hotel (Map III B4). Sale of stamps and stamping letters (10am-8.30pm, Sundays 10am-12.30noon), packets (10am-5pm), registered mail (10am-8.30pm, Sundays 10am-12.30noon), EMS Speed post and fax (24 hours a day).
Connaught Place Post Office, A Block, Connaught Place (Map III B2). 10am-5pm; closed Sundays.
Express mail by ***EMS Speed Post***, in post offices or via ***DHL***, 74-75 Scindia House, Connaught Circus, via Jan Path and Connaught Lane, then 1st lane on the left (Map III C3), ☎ (011) 331 66 75 /76. 9.30am-8pm, Saturdays 9.30am-4pm; closed Sundays. Other branch at 111 Ashirwad, D-I Green Park, ☎ (011) 913 480 00/01. 24 hours a day.
To send cargo parcels contact ***SITA World Travel*** (see "Banks and money").
Poste restante service at the ***Foreign Post Office***, c/o Post Master, Bhai Vir Singh Marg, New Delhi 110001 (Map I B2). 9am-5pm, Saturdays 9am-1pm; ***Government of India Tourist Office***, c/o Regional Director (see "Tourist information"), but the mail is not watched when left at the entrance; ***American Express*** (see "Banks and money") for Amex card holders.
To send and receive faxes: ***Central Telegraph Office***, Eastern Court (Map III B4), Fax (011) 331 34 11/12. 24 hours a day.
There are growing numbers of boutiques offering Internet access in Main Bazaar and at Paharganj. ***Simla Studio***, 4 Regal Building, Parliament Street. 9.30am-9pm.

Health – ***Ambulances***, ☎ 102. ***Accident & Trauma Service***, ☎ 10 99.
East West Medical Centre, 38 Golf Links (Map IV D4), ☎ (011) 462 37 38 and 469 92 29. Private clinic.
Two good ***chemists*** at Connaught Place: ***Nath Brothers***, G Block, Radial Rd 3 and ***Chaturbhuj & Bros***, G Block, G-45, outer circle (Map III B2). Also at Khan Market: ***Crown Drug Store***, 28-B (Map IV C-D3).
Dentist: Dr. S. Mehta, 41 Khan Market (Map IV C-D3), ☎ (011) 461 59 14.
Optician: Lawrence & Mayo, 76 Jan Path. Bon-Ton, 13 Jan Path, opposite the other one. And A-5 Connaught Place, next to the post office.

Safety – ***Police***, ☎100 and (0141) 56 55 54/55. ***Fire Brigade***, ☎ 101.

Travel agents – ***Ashok Travels & Tours***, in hotels belonging to the Ashok group, primarily Ashok Hotel, ☎(011) 611 01 01, ext 21.56 (every day 7.30am-8.30pm), and Ashok Yatri Niwas Hotel, ☎ (011) 334 45 11, ext 225 (7.30am-9.30pm). English-speaking guides (500Rs for 8hr) and taxi service. Relatively expensive rental cars.
Nexus Tours & Travels, The Connaught Hotel, Shaheed Bhagat Singh Marg (Map III A2), ☎ (011) 334 58 60,

☎ and Fax (011) 374 78 15, ntt@nda.vsnl.net.in This small agency offers hotel reservations at very competitive prices. Some of the cheapest car rentals available.

Merrygo Travels, 3 Municipal Market, Connaught Circus, opposite K Block (Map III B-C2), ☎ (011) 334 73 64 and 334 82 93, Fax (011) 334 73 65, travels.merrygo@axcess.net.in 9am-6pm, Sundays 9am-4pm. Good value car rentals.

Thomas Cook, C-33 Connaught Place, Radial Rd 4 (Map III B2), ☎ (011) 335 65 75/78, Fax (011) 335 65 80. 9.30am-6pm; closed Sundays. Reservations of tickets and organised excursions and trips. Another branch in Rishyamook Building, 85-A Panchkuin Rd (Map III A1), ☎ (011) 374 74 04/13, Fax (011) 334 62 88 and 334 67 55. Reasonably priced car rentals.

Paul Tours, York Hotel, K Block, Connaught Circus (Map III B-C2), ☎ (011) 332 30 19 and 332 37 69. Totally reliable agency in terms of hotel bookings and tickets. Relatively expensive car rentals.

SITA World Travel, F-12 Connaught Place (Map III B-C3), ☎ (011) 331 11 22, Fax (011) 332 46 52, and 4 Malcha Marg Market, Chanakyapuri (Map I A3), ☎ (011) 611 11 22, Fax (011) 687 01 23, sitadel @sita. sprint-rpg.ems.vsnl. net.in 9.30am-6pm, Saturdays 9.30am-1.30pm; closed Sundays. Has several agencies in Rajasthan. Relatively expensive car rentals.

Travel Corporation India (TCI), Metro Hotel, 1st floor, N-49 Connaught Circus, Radial Rd 1 (Map III B3), ☎ (011) 331 51 81 and 331 58 34, Fax (011) 331 67 05, tci.delhi@speed.spintrpg.ems.vsnl.net.in. 10am-5.30pm, Saturdays 10am-2pm; closed Sundays. This excellent agency is well-represented all over India, but their car rental charges in Delhi are far too expensive. Good for train and air tickets.

International airline tickets at cut-price rates: ***Tripsout Travels***, 72 Jan Path, ☎ (011) 332 26 54 and 372 26 16, Fax (011) 332 18 63. 9.30am-6pm. The agency is in a little side street off Jan Path.

Airline companies – ***Air India***, Jeevan Bharati Building, Connaught Circus (Map III B3), ☎ (011) 373 64 46/47/48, Fax (011) 373 97 96. This branch is located in the building designed in the 1980s by Charles Correa. Airport ☎ (011) 565 20 50 and 145 (departure information).

Air France, 7 Scindia House, Connaught Circus, Kasturba Gandhi Marg (Map III C3), ☎ (011) 331 17 05 and 373 80 04 to 07, Fax (011) 371 62 59. 9am-5.30pm; closed Sundays. Airport, ☎ (011) 565 20 99. Cargo service at IGI Cargo Complex, room 205, ☎ (011) 565 22 76/78.

Air Canada, Alps Building, 56 Jan Path (Map III B3-4), ☎ (011) 373 7263/4, Fax (011) 373 7262. Airport, ☎ (011) 565 28 50. Cargo, ☎ (011) 565 29 56.

British Airways, DLF Plaza Tower, DLF Qutab Enclave, Phase-1, Gurgaon, Haryana, ☎ (091) 359 911 from Delhi and ☎ (01324) 359 911 from outside Delhi, Fax (01234) 59 926.

Canadian Airlines, 66 Jan Path (Map III B3-4), ☎ (011) 371 33 66, Fax (011) 371 27 66. 9am-5.30pm; closed Sundays.

SwissaIr, DLF Centre, 1st floor, Parliament St, opposite Park Hotel (Map III B3), ☎ (011) 332 25 21 and 332 55 11. 9.15am-5.15pm; closed Sundays. Airport, ☎ (011) 565 25 31/35.

Indian Airlines, Malhotra Building, F 27 Connaught Place, Radial Rd 1 (Map III B3), ☎ (011) 331 05 17. 10am-1.15pm/2.15pm-5pm; closed Sundays. Safdarjang Airport, ☎ (011) 462 05 66. 24 hours a day. Airport, ☎ (011) 548 35 35 and 566 54 33/34. Information, ☎ 140. Reservations, ☎ 141. Arrival ☎ 142 and departure information ☎ 143.

Jet Airways, 3-E Hansalaya Building, 3rd floor, 15 Barakamba Rd (Map III C3). 9am-6pm; closed Sundays. Another branch at Jetair House, 13 Community Centre, Yusuf Sarai, ☎ (011) 685 37 00 (24 hours a day). 8am-11pm. Airport, ☎ (011) 566 54 04/05.

Jagson Airlines, 12-E Vandana Building, 11 Tolstoy Marg (Map III C4), ☎ (011) 372 15 93/94 and 332 85 79 /80, Fax (011) 332 46 93. Airport, ☎ (011) 566 55 45.

Embassies and consulates – Most are located in Chanakyapuri district (Map I A3):

American Embassy – Shantipath, ☎ (011) 688 9033 (30 lines), Fax (011) 611 3033 (20 lines).

Australian High Commission – 1/50-G Shantipath, ☎ (011) 688 8223, Fax (011) 688 7536

British High Commission – 50 Shantipath, ☎ (011) 687 2161, Fax (011) 687 2882.

Canadian High Commission – 7/8 Shantipath, ☎ (011) 687 6500, Fax (011) 687 6579.

New Zealand High Commission – 50-N Nyaya Marg, ☎ (011) 688 3170, Fax (011) 688 3165.

Miscellaneous – ***Archaeological Survey of India***, Jan Path, next to the National Museum (Map IV C2), ☎ (011) 301 72 20. To extend your visa, contact the ***Ministry of Home Affairs***, Lok Nayak Bhawan, Khan Market (Map IV D3), ☎ (011) 469 33 34, then the ***Foreigner's Regional Registration Office (FRRO)***, Hans Bhawan, Bahadur Shah Zafar Marg (Map I C2), ☎ (011) 331 94 89. 9.30am-1.30pm/2pm-4pm. To obtain a "Tax Clearance Certificate". If staying in India for over 120 days: ***Income Tax Office (ITO)***, Foreign Section, Indraprashta Estate (Map I C2), ☎ (011) 331 78 26.

Press – One weekly, ***Delhi Diary***, two twice-monthlies ***Delhi City*** and ***Metro Today*** and two monthlies, ***First City*** and ***Here***. The ***Eicher City Map*** is a good map of the city.

WHERE TO STAY

If you haven't reserved a room (sometimes even if you have), the rickshaw and taxi drivers will try their utmost to take you to a hotel that pays them a commission, most often in the Karol Bagh district. Stick to your guns, especially if arriving at night, or wait until daybreak to find a hotel. Low season from mid-April to September.

• North of Connaught Place

Under $7

Tourist Camp, Jawaharlal Nehru Marg, New Delhi, around 1.5km northeast of Connaught Place, opposite L.N.J.P.N. Hospital (Map II), ☎ (011) 327 28 98 and 328 66 94, Fax (011) 326 36 93 – 97rm 12rm with bath and 18 with cooler. Accommodation is in somewhat basic, windowless cabins dotted about a garden. Good way of meeting fellow travellers and soaking up a bit of sun. Camping available.

From $15-30

Gold Regency Hotel, 4350 Main Bazaar, Pahar Ganj, New Delhi, about 100m from the station (Map II), ☎ (011) 354 01 01, Fax (011) 354 02 02, goldregency@hotmail.com – 34rm. TV CC Internet access available. The only real hotel in Pahar Ganj, it is modern and well-looked after even if the finishings are not all they could be. Pity that most of the rooms are windowless. The only distinction between a standard and a deluxe room is the size, which hardly justifies the difference in price.

From US$100-150

The Oberoi Maidens (The Oberoi), 7 Shamnath Marg, Delhi, 10km from Connaught Place, in Civil Lines (Map I), ☎ (011) 291 48 41, Fax (011) 398 07 71 – 54rm. TV CC Located in a handsome colonial-style building that has retained a feel of its former atmosphere, this hotel combines charm and style, without being luxurious. Suites available. 35 % discount in the low season.

• Connaught Place (Map III)

Practically all of Delhi's cheap little hotels are located around New Delhi station, in the busy, congested district of Pahar Ganj, renowned for its traffic. Comfort and cleanliness are minimal and charm non-existent. It is safe and can be recommended. Connaught Place on the other hand has hotels of all types of categories and has the advantage of being close to restaurants, banks, travel agents and shops.

Under US$7

Ringo Guest House, 17 Scindia House, Connaught Circus, via Jan Path and Connaught Lane, ☎ (011) 331 06 05 – 18rm 4rm with a tiny bathroom.

Individual rooms and nine-bed dormitories. Popular among young people with tight budgets: close to the city centre, the rooms, while basic, are clean and the courtyard provides an opportunity to meet other travellers.

Sunny Guest House, 15 Scindia House, Connaught Circus, ☎ (011) 331 29 09 – 20rm. 14rm. with bath, 7 individual rooms. Almost identical copy of the former, its next-door neighbour. Similar prices.

From US$15-30

Ashok Yatri Niwas (Ashok Group), 19 Ashoka Rd, ☎ (011) 334 45 11, Fax (011) 336 81 53 – 547rm. 120rm. with cooler. Hot water from October to March, 3hr in the morning and 3hr in the evening. Somewhat neglected concrete building whose lobby and dirty, depressing corridors have about as much charm as a railway station. The rooms are however clean and excellent value for money. Fixed price (US$15). Women travelling alone should be wary of room service.

YMCA Tourist Hotel, Jai Singh Rd, ☎ (011) 336 18 47 and 336 19 15, Fax (011) 374 60 32 / 35 – 112rm. Several rooms with bath, AC and television. The comfort is nothing to write home about, but the atmosphere is lively and pleasant. 15-day maximum stay and bookings need to be made at least a month ahead, due to its popularity.

YWCA International Guest House, 10 Parliament St, ☎ (011) 336 15 61 and 336 16 62, Fax (011) 334 17 63 – 24rm. Same style as the former but not quite as good and less lively. Spacious, relatively clean rooms, but minimally decorated. 7-day stay maximum. Book at least a month in advance.

From US$40-70

York Hotel, K-10 Connaught Circus, ☎ (011) 332 30 19/69, Fax (011) 335 24 19 – 27rm. This well looked-after establishment has really quite well-decorated rooms. Ask for one with a bath – they are larger and have better facilities than the rooms with shower. 40 % discount for people travelling alone.

Nirula's Hotel, L Block, Connaught Circus, Radial Rd 6, ☎ (011) 332 24 19, Fax (011) 335 39 57, delhihotel@nirula.com – 28rm. The corridors are decorated with engravings and the courtyard is full of plants. The standard rooms are tastefully decorated and comfortable, but small and often windowless. 40 % discount for people travelling alone.

Over US$150

Imperial Hotel, Jan Path, ☎ (011) 334 12 34, Fax (011) 334 22 55 – 265rm. Opened in the 1930s, the hotel has a drive which is lined with royal palm trees. Recently renovated, it is now very cosy but not half as smart as it used to be. The lawn is as pleasant as ever. Suites available.

Inter-Continental Hotel, Maharaja Ranjeet Singh Marg, ☎ (011) 332 01 01, Fax (011) 332 53 35, newdelhi@interconti.com – 391rm. A modern (1980s) high-rise tower, located in the business district, that seems to change owners every three or four years. (It has successively belonged to Holiday Inn and Hilton). 53 suites. The coffee shop serves excellent all day buffets and the restaurant-grill on the 28th floor is both smart and very decent.

The Meridien, Windsor Place, ☎ (011) 371 01 01, Fax (011) 371 45 45, meridien@nda.vsnl.net.in – 355rm. Coffee-shop open 24 hours a day. Steel and glass construction built towards the end of the 1980s. The inner central tower is definitely worth a look. "Club" rooms and suites.

The Park Hotel, 15 Parliament St, ☎ (011) 373 37 37, Fax (011) 373 20 25 resv.del@park.sprintrpg.vsnl.net.in – 224rm. Business centre. The closest 5-star hotel to Connaught Place, although not as stylish as most hotels of its category. Suites. The city's only Mexican restaurant (dinner only).

• South of Connaught Place

(Map IV)

From US$30-40

Jorbagh 27, 27 Jorbagh, ☎ (011) 469 44 30 and 469 86 47, Fax (011)

469 84 75 – 18rm. 5km from Connaught Place, but only 1min from Lodi Garden in a smart residential zone, this house and small garden has pretty rooms and a relaxed friendly atmosphere. Jorbagh market is a 3min walk away.

From US$40-70

Orchid Hotel G-4 South Extension I, ☎ (011) 464 35 29, Fax (011) 462 69 24 – 18rm. Situated in the heart of south Delhi's most animated markets. The rooms are perfectly kept and much better than a first glimpse of the reception would lead one to believe. The more basic rooms are windowless. New bathrooms.

From US$70-150

The Ambassador Hotel (Taj Group), Sujan Singh Park, Khan Market, ☎ (011) 463 26 00, Fax (011) 463 82 19 – 88rm. The welcome is somewhat frosty and the cheaply-decorated corridors (false wood panelling) don't add to the overall charm. The rooms are however spacious and light and the hotel is well-located, just on the edge of Lutyens' Delhi. Suites.

Over US$150

The Claridges, 12 Aurangzeb Rd, ☎ (011) 301 02 11, Fax (011) 301 06 25, claridges.hotel@gems.vsnl.net.in – 162rm. Situated in the heart of Lutyens' wide avenues of vast, white bungalows, this hotel, renovated in 1994, has kept some of the former charm and intimacy of yesteryear. Suites.

Hyatt Regency, Bhikaji Cama Place, Inner Ring Rd, ☎ (011) 616 12 34, Fax (011) 618 68 33 – 517rm. Big shopping mall. This excellent 5-star establishment, always very busy, has become one of the liveliest centres of the capital. "Club" rooms and suites.

The Taj Mahal Hotel (Taj Group), often called Taj Mansingh, 1 Mansingh Rd, ☎ (011) 301 61 62, Fax (011) 301 72 99 – 300rm One of Delhi's liveliest and most pleasant 5-star establishments, just 400m from Khan Market.

The Oberoi Maidens, Dr. Zakir Hussain Marg, ☎ (011) 436 30 30, Fax (011) 430 40 84 – 290rm. Boutiques. The hotel overlooks the Golf Club, where most business people stay. Elegant, sophisticated restaurants, including an excellent Thai establishment.

• Sundar Nagar (Map IV)

This pleasant, quiet, green residential area, just 4km southeast of Connaught Place, has several small hotels situated in former private homes. All of them make visitors welcome and all have perfect lawns for relaxing. 10-15 % discount during the low season and 20-30 % discount for people travelling alone.

From US$40-70

Kailash Inn, 10 Sundar Nagar, ☎ (011) 462 50 47, Fax (011) 461 74 01 – 16rm. Not particularly welcoming and with rooms that are not as well looked-after as they could be, it remains the cheapest address in the area.

Sagrita Tourist Home, 14 Sundar Nagar, ☎ (011) 460 12 49 and 469 45 41, Fax (011) 463 69 56 – 19rm. The rooms are similar to those of the above establishment, but the reception is better.

Jukaso Inn, 50 Sundar Nagar, ☎ (011) 469 03 08/09, Fax (011) 469 44 02 – 49rm. Near the market, this hotel is well-run and maintained. The corridors and reception are in marble. Can be somewhat noisy.

Maharani Guest House, 3 Sundar Nagar, ☎ (011) 469 31 28/29, Fax (011) 462 45 62 – 24rm. Very pleasant welcome by a Franco-Indian director. Pretty, comfortable rooms.

Shervani Fortview Inn, 11 Sundar Nagar, opposite the zoo, ☎ (011) 461 17 71 and 461 96 70, Fax (011) 469 42 26 star@del3.vsnl.net.in – 16rm. Reliable, well-kept establishment with tastefully decorated rooms. The bill can be paid in foreign currency.

• Chanakyapuri (Map I)

5km southeast of Connaught Place. The embassy district, often called the "Diplomatic Enclave". Malcha Marg Market, to the northwest, has a few shops and three good restaurants.

Less than US$7

International Youth Hostel, 5 Nyaya Marg, ☎ (011) 611 62 85, Fax (011) 611 34 69 – 9rm 5rm. with AC. 6 air-conditioned dormitories with 4 beds and 8 non-air-conditioned dormitories with 10 beds. Hidden within a nest of greenery, this establishment provides clean, well-looked after accommodation and a smiling welcome. Non-youth hostel members can join for 250Rs (year's subscription) or pay an extra 50Rs per night. Maximum stay 3 nights and rooms must be vacated by 10am. Booking advisable. Around 30Rs in a rickshaw from Connaught Place.

From US$15-30

Vishwa Yuvak Kendra (International Youth Centre), Circular Rd, Chanakyapuri, ☎ (011) 301 36 31 – 35rm. A concrete block located right at the end of the 2km-long green esplanade that traverses Chanakyapuri. Lukewarm welcome, minimal service and non-existent decoration, but the rooms are reasonable.

From US$70-150

Diplomat Hotel, 9 Sardar Partel Rd, ☎ (011) 301 02 04, Fax (011) 301 86 05 – 25rm. TV CC This very well-run establishment is located in a modern bungalow set in pleasant green surroundings. Quiet, intimate atmosphere. Eight suites.

Over US$150

Ashok Hotel (The Ashok Group), 50-B Chanakyapuri, ☎ (011) 611 01 01, Fax (011) 687 32 16 – 563rm. TV CC Shopping mall. This mammoth establishment is state-owned. The rooms were recently renovated but the bathrooms are tiny.

Maurya Sheraton Hotel & Towers (WelcomGroup), Sardar Patel Marg, ☎ (011) 611 22 33, Fax (011) 611 33 33, maurya@cyber-club.com – 440rm. TV CC Boutiques. A permanently busy 5-star establishment, one of the capital's best.

Taj Palace Hotel (Taj Group), Sardar Patel Marg, ☎ (011) 301 04 04, Fax (011) 301 12 52 – 421rm TV CC Not quite as lively as the above establishment. Suites. Three restaurants including a great French and an excellent Chinese one.

Where to eat

Delhi's cuisine is mostly a mix of Punjabi and Mughlai cooking, the great classics of which are "dal makhani" (lentils simmered in spices and butter), "rajmachawal" (lentils and red beans cooked in tomatoes and spices, served with rice) and "tikka" (boneless chicken or fish cooked on skewers).

The 4- and 5-star hotels all have a coffee shop, open 24 hours a day. Meals cost around US$10 but helpings are plentiful and one dish is often more than enough. Most also lay on buffets with a large choice of Indian and international dishes. Hotels also have at least three sorts of good-quality restaurants, serving a variety of Mughlai, North-West Frontier, Chinese, Thai, French cooking or grilled dishes.

• North of Connaught Place

(Map II)

Less than US$4

Karim's, 16 Jama Masjid, Gali Kababiyan, Old Delhi (D2), ☎ (011) 326 98 80. 7am-12noon. Open since the 1930s, this restaurant is right in the heart of the traditional working-class Moslem district. Serves the best Mughlai cooking around, delicious and very rich. Don't miss the "burra kebab", "biryani" and particularly the "mutton pasanda". A real treat!

From US$4-10

Chor Bizarre, Broadway Hotel, Asaf Ali Rd (D3), ☎ (011) 327 38 21/25. CC 12noon-3.30pm/7.30pm-11.30pm. Unusual, highly original decoration and very smart atmosphere. The menu includes a good choice of excellent Kashmiri and Mughlai dishes.

• Connaught Place (Map II)

For a light snack or sudden craving, choose between the excellent **Wengers** (A16) bakery, which sells the most amazing spicy chicken and mushroom pastries or taste one of the delicious desserts at **Nirula's**, Delhi's best ice-cream parlour (just next door to Wengers).

Fast-food addicts will be able to assuage withdrawal symptoms at the packed and noisy **Wimpy** (N Block, Radial Rd 1), or the not unattractive **Pizza Hut** (E3).

Pizza Pizza Express (D10) is expensive, but very good and also serves alcohol. The ***Cafe 100*** (B-20) also serves a few Indian dishes.

1.5km east of Connaught Place, Bengali Market has two very well-known pleasant, spacious sweet shops ***Nathu's Sweet*** and ***Bengali Sweet House***, which are ideal to stop at before going to an exhibition or a concert at Mandi House.

Less than US$1.5

Madras Hotel, P-23 Connaught Circus (B2). 7.30am-8.45pm; closed Sundays. Two "pure veg" rooms on the 1st floor overlooking the street. South Indian-style snacks in a somewhat rundown setting, albeit reasonably clean. Queues are normal at meal times and customers have to leave as soon as the last mouthful is finished.

Kanchi, Centre Point Hotel, 13 Kasturba Gandhi Marg, corner of Tolstoy Marg (C4). Every day from 10am-10.30pm. Well-kept "pure veg" establishment is the only rather cheap address within a radius of 500m. As such it is often packed.

Kovil, E-2 Connaught Place (C2). "Pure veg" cuisine in a functional, clean setting. Classic southern dishes served on banana leaves. Don't bother with the coffee, expensive and disappointing.

Between US$5-10

Nirula's Pot Pourri, next to Nirula's Hotel, on the 1st floor, over the ice-cream parlour (C2) 🍷 CC Every day from 7.30am-midnight. The dining room is decorated in straw, bamboo trellis and artificial green plants. The atmosphere is young, lively and relatively noisy. Pizzas, burgers, Indian dishes, wonderful ices and a decent salad buffet. Often full.

Standard, 44 Regal Building, Connaught Place (B3), ☎ (011) 336 00 48. 🍷 CC 10.30am-11pm; closed Sundays. The entrance is via a tiny bakery shop, but the 1st floor room proves to be smart and spacious and its wide bay windows provide an unusual view over Connaught Place. Open since 1952, it is a favourite among Delhi's inhabitants. A somewhat dingy room in the back serves south Indian dishes at very cheap prices.

York's, York Hotel (B2-C2) 🍷 CC Although the room itself is comfortable, it is nothing to write home about, the food however is among the best to be found on Connaught Place. Chicken kebab is the house speciality.

Embassy, D-11 Connaught Place, Radial Rd 6 (C2), ☎ (011) 332 04 80. 🍷 CC Every day 10am-11pm. Founded in 1948, it continues to welcome Delhi's politicians and upper middle-class in a hubbub of noisy conversations. The tables, too close together, make intimacy impossible. Steer clear of the dishes in sauces, a bit too rich, and opt for the tandoori specialities or the "chicken chaat".

United Coffee House, E-15 Connaught Place (C2), ☎ (011) 332 20 75. 🍷 CC Daily 9.30am-midnight. Frequented by regulars who come and read their newspaper or talk politics all day long, although rapidly becoming more and more popular among foreign tourists. Excellent coffee and a delicious cinnamon apple pie with fresh cream. The meals compare rather poorly.

The Host, F-8 Connaught Place (C2-3), ☎ (011) 331 63 81. 🍷 CC Daily 10am-11.30pm. Comfortable room, decorated with mirrors and rough stone walls. Same style as the above, also frequented by regulars, but somehow not quite as "authentic". The meals are however better.

Gaylord, 16 Regal Building, Connaught Circus (B3), ☎ (011) 376 07 17. 🍷 CC Daily 10.30am-midnight. A "multi-cuisine" restaurant opened in 1952, along the lines of a smart teashop. Excellent for teas, but the other meals are somewhat ordinary.

Kwality, 7 Regal Building, Parliament St (B3), ☎ (011) 373 23 10/52. 🍷 CC Daily 12noon-11pm. Prettily decorated pink and apricot rooms. Not exactly spacious and the service is a little slapdash, but the tandoori cooking is good and their "chhola bhatura" is excellent.

Coconut Grove, Ashok Yatri Niwas Hotel (B5) CC Daily 12noon-3pm/7pm-11pm. It is nice to discover that south Indian cooking is not restricted to "dosa" and "idli" from Tamil Nadu. This restaurant offers excellent specialities from Kerala in a very pleasant setting. Delicious, if very spicy curries. Try the "thoran" or "aviyal" (vegetables cooked in coconut) served with "appam" (soft pancakes made out of fermented rice).

From US$4-7

Garden Party, Imperial Hotel (B4), ☎ (011) 334 12 34. 🍷 CC 24 hours a day. A smart, yet relaxed coffee shop with a clientele of regulars. Its terrace and lawn provide a welcome open-air pause and are worth the stop, compensating for the somewhat ordinary cooking and limited menu.

• South of Connaught Place (Map IV)

From US$3-4

Dasaprakash, The Ambassador Hotel, ☎ (011) 463 26 00. CC 12noon-3.30pm/7.30pm-11.30pm. Authentic "pure veg" cooking from southern India, served in an impressive rotunda, complete with mast and bronze bells. The *thali* comprises Tamil Nadu specialties.

Pindi, 16 / 17 Pandara Rd Market, behind Bikaner House (D2), ☎ (011) 338 87 03. CC 12.30noon-midnight. The market of Pandar Park's residential area has several restaurants one next to the other, renowned for their rich Punjabi and Mughlai cooking. Butter chicken is the Pindi's speciality. Served at all times and people often buy it while waiting for the bus.

Gulati and ***Veg Gulati***, 8 Pandara Rd Market (D2), ☎ (011) 338 87 03. CC 12noon-4pm/8pm-1am (Veg Gulati 7pm-11pm). Same style as the former. Very popular among cinema stars.

Dastar Khwan-e Karim, 168/2 Jha House, Nizamuddin West, next to the mosque (E4), ☎ (011) 469 83 00. CC Branch of the famous Karim's, in Old Delhi, of which it is a replica. Smarter interior but its Mughlai cooking is not quite as good.

From US$4-7

Chopsticks, Siri Fort, Khel Gaon Marg (Map I B4) 🍷 CC Highly popular Chinese restaurant and well situated after a concert at Siri Fort Auditorium. Try the fish in ginger or shrimp in garlic.

Machan, Taj Mahal Hotel (C3) 🍷 CC 24 hours a day. One of Delhi's most pleasant coffee shops with an airy, animated atmosphere in an attractive safari setting (a "machan" is a platform hidden in the trees to observe animals).

• Chanakyapuri (Map I A3)

From US$4-7

Moti Mahal, 20/48 Malcha Marg Market, ☎ (011) 611 56 25 🍷 CC 12.15noon-3.15pm/7pm-midnight; closed Tuesdays. Pleasant room if somewhat excessively decorated. Serves tasty tandoori and Punjabi cooking. Their "dal makhani" is quite delicious.

Over US$14

Bukhara, Maurya Sheraton Hotel, ☎ (011) 611 22 33 🍷 CC 12.30noon-2.30pm/7.30pm-midnight. Renowned for its Mughlai cooking and kebabs. The decoration reproduces a Peshwari inn. A glass window enables guests to watch the food cooking in clay ovens. Limited choice, but excellent cooking. Bookings essential.

Dum Pukht, Maurya Sheraton Hotel, ☎ (011) 611 22 33 🍷 CC 12.30noon-2.30pm/7.30pm-midnight. Elegant, refined basement room where they serve "awadhi" cooking (from the region of Lucknow), in particular "dumpukht", which as it name suggests, is steamed in earthenware dishes, sealed with a dumpling/pastry mixture. Other specialities include "koh-i awadh" (chicken with cardamom and saffron), yoghurt and garlic dal, mushroom rice and kebabs.

WHERE TO GO FOR A DRINK

Nirula's Pegasus, next to Nirula's Hotel (Map III C2). 🍷 CC 11am-midnight. Anglo-American bar decorated with dark wood panelling, old photos and background music. On the menu are snacks, sandwiches, pizzas, fried chicken, onion soup and draught beer.

Garden Party Bar, Imperial Hotel (Map III B4). 🍷 CC 11am-11.30pm. The bar is one of the hotel's few spots that has escaped renovation, retaining a flavour of good taste and its Louis XVI armchairs. The place for a quiet chat over a drink, not for a party. The hotel also has another bar, opened in 1998, the ***Patiala Peg***. Draught beer served in a teak panelled décor of prints relating the exploits of the famous Maharaja Bhupindra of Patiala and his cavalry.

Djinn's, Hayatt Regency (Map I A4). 4pm-midnight. The liveliest and most "in" place in Delhi. An orchestra plays every night, from 8.30pm, except Tuesdays and changes every three months. The bar is located in the centre of a vast room, around which are dotted little alcoves where one can have a quiet drink or game of darts. Lebanese cooking, Mexican, Australian and Japanese draught beer. From 7pm onwards, all guests are required to spend a minimum of US$14 each on Wednesdays, Fridays and Saturdays, US$10 each other evenings.

Most of the large hotels have a ***night-club***, open from 10pm to dawn. ***My Kind of Place***, at the Taj Palace Hotel is the only one open to non-residents (500Rs per couple). They all have a "Ladies Night" at least once a week (free entrance for unaccompanied women).

Entertainment

Cinema – The capital's 70 or so cinemas show typical box-office Hindu hits. Foreign films are shown at the ***Priya***, Community Centre, Vasant Vihar (CP) and in other community centres. The ***International Film Festival*** (January) and the ***National Film Festival*** (June-July), devoted to Indian classical films, are held at Siri Fort Auditorium at Khel Gaon Marg (Map I B4).

Concerts and dance – During the season (October-April) several performances of Indian dance and music are put on every evening. They start around 6.30pm and free tickets can be obtained from a selection of places indicated in the press. Most concert and dance halls are located in the Mandi House Circle area, southeast of Connaught Place (Map IV D1): ***Kamani***, ***FICCI***, ***Triveni Kala Sangam***, ***Shri Ram Centre***. 5km south, the ***India International Centre (IIC)*** is located on Max Mueller Rd and the ***India Habitat Centre*** is on Lodi Rd (Map IV C4). Even further south, on Khel Gaon Marg is ***Siri Fort Auditorium***, Delhi's largest concert hall (Map I B4). "Son et lumière" shows are also put on at the ***Purana Qila*** (Map IV E2) (tickets on sale there or from Delhi Tourism) and at the ***Red Fort*** (Map II D1-2) (tickets available there).

Cultural centres – All have an auditorium, an art gallery and a library which one can join as a temporary reader. ***American Center***, 24 Kasturba Gandhi Marg (Map III C3), ☎ (011) 331 68 41. ***British Council***, 17 Kasturba Gandhi Marg (Map III C4), ☎ (011) 371 14 01. ***Max Mueller Bhawan***, 3 Kasturba Gandhi Marg (Map III C4), ☎ (011) 332 95 06.

Music and dance lessons – Around Mandi House Circle (Map IV D1), ***Sangeet Natak Akademi***, Rabindra Bhawan, ☎ (011) 338 72 46 and ***Kathak Kendra***, Bahawalpur House, ☎ (011) 338 50 65.

Sports – ***Swimming pools***: hotel swimming pools open from Holi (end of January-early February) until November. They rarely accept non-residents for the day. The cheapest is Claridges Hotel (300Rs for a day).

Riding and ***polo***: if there during the season (October-November and February-March), don't miss a match at the ***Jaipur Polo Ground***, Kamal Ataturk Rd (Map IV B4). Information from ***Delhi Polo Club***.

Delhi Golf Club on Dr Zakir Hussein Marg is a superb 24-hole course, featuring monuments dating back to the Lodis, (Map IV D3), ☎ (011) 436 27 68. *Around US$40 per day.*

Gliding and ***parapent***: ***Delhi Gliding Club***, Safdarjang Airport (Map I B3), ☎ (011) 463 12 36.

Sports' articles can be found at ***Pioneer Sports***, F-21 Connaught Place (Map III B-C3).

Yoga – ***Central Research Institute for Yoga***, 68 Ashok Rd (Map III A4), ☎ (011) 372 14 72. ***Shri Aurobindo Ashram***, Aurobindo Marg (Map I B4-5), ☎ (011) 66 78 63.

Excursions

Coach trips to Agra are organised by the India Tourism Development Corporation (see "Tourism Offices"). They include Agra Fort and Sikandar (6.30am-10pm, every day except Monday, 660Rs in AC coach). It is best to avoid the tours organised by the smaller Jan Path companies, because they invariably miss out parts of the tour in favour of shopping halts. Travelling alone, one can visit Agra in a day by train.

Holidays and festivals

Republic Day (January 26). Military parade, including armoured vehicles, along Raj Path.

Beating of the Retreat (January 29). Military music and firework display opposite Rashtrapati Bhawan.

Nizamuddin Urs (April-May and November-December). At dusk, singers and musicians celebrate the memory of the Sufi saint Nizam ud-Din at the dargah in the Nizamuddin district.

Independence Day (August 15). Speech by the Prime Minister at the Red Fort.

Gandhi Jayanti (October 2). Anniversary of the birth of Mahatma Gandhi is commemorated at Raj Ghat.

Phoolwalon ki Sair, the "florists' procession" (end September-early October). At Mehrauli, near the Qutb, floral fans, symbolising the traditional bonds between Moslems and Hindus, are distributed at the Khawa Qutb ud-Din Bakhtiyar dargah and the Hindu temple at Jogmaya.

Shopping

Old Delhi (Map II) is of course one of the capital's busiest shopping centres, full of traditional stalls, most of which are closed on Sunday, with the exception of ***Chor Bazaar*** (Map II E1-2), the "thieves' market", also known as Kabadi or Lal Qila Bazaar, held every Sunday between the Red Fort and the Yamuna (carpets, furniture, books and knick-knacks). ***Connaught Place*** (Map III) is where the majority of Delhi's smart modern shops, offices and banks are situated (closed Sundays), ***Khan Market*** (Map IV C-D3), the most popular among Delhi's wealthy citizens, is also here, as is ***South Extension*** (Map I B4), fashionable among Delhi's young middle-classes (closed Monday).

Smart "ethnic" fashion and home decoration centres comprise ***Santushti Shopping Arcade***, on Kamal Ataturk Rd (Map IV A4) and ***Hauz Khas Village*** (Map I A4), started at the end of the 1980s by a group of young designers, but prices have rocketed of late (closed Sunday). The Qutb area (Map I A5) has just begun to replace the latter with two new centres not far from each other: ***The Qutb Colonnade***, H-5/6 Mehrauli Rd, in the northwest corner of the Qutb Minaret's enclosure, and the ***Ambawatta Complex***, at the entrance to the village of Mehrauli (both are partially closed on Sundays and Mondays).

Crafts – Delhi specialises in high-glaze blue pottery small lacquered objects, decorated with fragments of mirror and animals made out of black fabric and gold trimmings, and the work of Rajasthan's Bhat community in Delhi. However, Delhi being the capital, it also provides – with labelled prices – an excellent range of crafts from the rest of India.

Cottage Industries Emporium, Jan Path, corner of Tolstoy Marg (Map III B4).

State Emporia, Baba Kharak Singh Marg (Map III A3). Comprises 18 state shops, including Rajasthan's, ***Rajasthali***.

The ***Craft Museum*** offers a good selection of objects in its museum boutique and regularly has a dozen or so good-quality craftsmen working in its courtyard for the benefit of visitors.

If in town in February, stop by the open-air ***Surajkund Crafts Mela*** fair, at Surajkund, just past Tughluqabad (towards Map I C5), and the ***Indian Handicrafts & Gift Fair***, Pragati Maidan, on Mathura Rd (Map IV E1-2).

Chatta Chowk Bazaar (Map II D2) is a 17C shopping gallery in the Red Fort offering tourist-type souvenirs, as well as Indian and Tibetan "antiques".

Hanuman Mandir Mela, Baba Kharak Singh Marg, on the esplanade in front of Hanuman's temple (Map III B3), is a relatively small fair held every Tuesday (Hanuman's day) and Saturday, with local crafts.

Tibetan market, Jan Path, to the north of Imperial Hotel (Map III B3-4).

Fabric and clothes – ***Janpath Lane***: Rajasthani and Gujarati fabrics, embroidered and encrusted with mirrors, are sold both on the pavement by women from Rajasthan as well as in Jan Path's boutiques. On Connaught Place, ***Khadi Gramodyog Bhawan***, 24 Regal Building (Map III B3), has homespun cottons and hand-woven silks, as does

International Handloom, 49 Shankar Market, 3rd alley (Map III C2), which has a cotton fabric, that once washed, looks as if it was hand-woven silk. Two other good addresses for silk are ***Handloom House*** (A-9) and ***Kalpana*** (F-5). If in Delhi in January, don't miss the annual Fabric Fair at Pragati Maidan (Map IV E1-2), ***Tex-Styles India***.

Good quality bedding or table linen, scarves, bags, Indian or Western clothes made out of traditional fabrics, are available at the following shops: ***Anokhi***, Santushti Shopping Arcade and 32 Khan Market; ***The Shop***, 10 Regal Building, Parliament St; ***Tulsi***, Santushti Shopping Arcade and 30 Hauz Khas Village; ***Fabindia***, Archana Shopping Centre, Greater Kailash I (Map I B-C4), closed Tuesday; ***Good Earth***, Santushti Shopping Arcade, The Qutb Colonnade, and Ambawatta Complex (fabric, decorative objects and pottery); ***Shyam Ahuja***, Santushti Shopping Arcade and Greater Kailash II (Map I C5) (silk and dhurries).

For clothes, try ***Krishna***, 26 Hauz Khas Village (antique and modern shawls). ***Anmol***, The Qutb Colonnade (evening jackets and shawls). ***Crama***, H-5/6 Mehrauli Rd, near The Qutb Colonnade, has a selection of most of India's fashion designers' work. ***Ensemble***, Santushti Shopping Arcade, and Ambawatta Complex (silk and linen shirts). ***Christina***, Santushti Shopping Arcade (brightly-coloured printed silk shirts).

For "zari" work, pearl embroidery or gold or silver thread, go to Hauz Khas Village: ***Theme for a dream***, ***Neelam Jolly's*** and ***The Marwari's***.

Connaught Circus and Connaught Place also have one or two Western boutiques: ***Lacoste*** (N-3, Radial Rd 1) and its famous 1 000Rs shirt, ***Levi's*** (N-13), ***Lee*** (L-7B), ***Reebok*** (B-12), ***Nike*** (F-7), ***Adidas*** (F-28, Radial Rd 1). At South Extension I: ***Arrow***, Ring Rd, F South Ext I.

Leather and footwear – Traditional "chappal" sandals from Kolhapuri, at Maharashtra, and "jutis" (with upturned toe), are on sale along Jan Path, in boutiques nos 61 and 62. European brands on Connaught Place: ***Woodlands*** (F-18) for shoes and ***Da Milano*** (E-12) for clothes, bags and accessories.

Jewellery – In Old Delhi, ***Dariba Kalan*** (Map II C-D2) is the traditional jewellers' lane, but very few in fact still remain here. Go to ***Hanuman Mandir Mela*** (Map III B3) for glass bracelets. ***Sundar Nagar Market*** (Map IV E3) has a few jewellers who offer tribal and antique jewellery, as well as copies. The best, although also the priciest, is ***The Studio***, at no 4 (closed Sunday).

Old and modern jewellery also from ***Kanjimull & Sons***, Scindia House, Jan Path (Map III C3), ***Sumtidass & Bros***, 18 Regal Building, on Connaught Circus, ***Bharany's***, in the Hyatt Regency Hotel (Map I A4), and ***Nirmal Vijay & Co***, (B-7) Connaught Place, Radial Rd 3, whose modern work is designed by Nirmal, formerly employed by Cartier.

Carpets – "Dhrurries" from ***Shyam Ahuja***, Santushti Shopping Arcade, and Greater Kailash II.

For Indian and Persian carpets, old or new, go to the ***Carpet Cellar***, 1 Anand Lok, Khel Gaon Marg, to the north of Siri Fort (Map I B4), ***The Treasure*** and ***Turkish Bazaar***, 10 and 26 Hauz Khas Village, or to the ***Cottage Industries Exposition (CIE)***, DCM Building, 16 Barakhamba Rd, corner of Tolstoy Marg.

Antiques – ***Gupta Brothers Art Gallery***, K-3A Aurobindo Marg (Map I B4), 1km before the Qutb Minar, on the right, opposite the road from Gugaon. 10am-6pm; closed Tuesday. Good antiques, reasonable prices. ***Indian Arts Palace***, 19-E Connaught Place, Radial Rd 7. Quite high prices for objects and curios.

Toiletries and beauty care – Plant-based products from ***Biotique***, D-5 Connaught Place, and 29-A Khan Market, as well as from ***Shanaz Husain Herbal***, B-13 Connaught Place; 12-B and 33-B Khan Market.

Most of the large hotels have a beauty salon. The ***Vogue***, at the Ambassador Hotel, (10am-6.45pm; closed Monday) offers scalp and face massages, shampoo and blow-dries at reasonable prices, but the salon itself is not very inspiring.

On Tuesdays and Saturdays at the ***Hanuman Mandir Mela*** (Map III B3), "mendhiwali" will cover your palms or the soles of your feet with henna scrolls and arabesques ("mendhi"), as fine as a spider's web.

Perfume – "Ittar" (perfume essences), incense sticks, soaps and fragrant candles are on sale from ***Gulabsingh Johrimal***, 320 Dariba Kalan, Old Delhi (Map II C-D2) and ***Natural Perfume Oils***, 1115 Main Bazaar, Paharganj (Map II A4-5), next to the mosque (everyday 11.30am-8pm).

Culinary specialities – An enormous spice, dried fruit and condiments market, said to be the largest in Asia, is located in the west of Old Delhi, on Khari Baoli and the two neighbouring roads (Map II B2). Around Connaught Place: ***Bharat Dry Fruit Mart***, 3-MM Jan Path; ***Cheap Dry Fruit Mart***, 5 New Janpath Market.

"Mithayan" and "namkin" (confectionery and spicy or savoury-sweet snacks), particularly those from Bengal, said to be the best, because not so sweet and more delicately scented, can be found at ***Nathu's Sweet*** and ***Bengali Sweet House***, at Bengali Market, 1.5km east of Connaught Place, and at ***Annapurna Bhandar***, Chandni Chowk, Old Delhi (Map II C2). Delhi-style confectionery from ***Haldiram Bhujjiawala***, Chandni Chowk, Old Delhi, near Annapurna, and ***Ghantewala***, opposite the former (founded in 1790).

Photography – ***Delhi Photo Company***, 78 Jan Path, just south of the tourist office.

Indian musical instruments – The most reputable is ***Rikhi Ram***, Marina Arcade, Connaught Circus, ☎ (011) 332 76 85. ***Yamaha***, G-14 Connaught Circus, outer circle. ***A Godin & Co***, 1 Regal Building, Parliament St.

Records – ***Blue Bird & Co***, 9 Regal Building, Parliament St ***The Music Shop***, 18-AB Khan Market, ☎ (011) 461 84 64.

Art galleries – Most galleries open from 11am to 6pm and are closed on Sunday. ***Art Today***, A-1 Connaught Place; ***Dhoomimal Art Gallery***, A-8 Connaught Place, 1st floor, India's oldest established modern art gallery; ***Kumar Gallery***, 11 Sundar Nagar Market; ***Triveni Kala Sangam***, Mandi House Circle; ***Lalit Kala Akademi***, Rabindra Bhawan, Mandi House Circle; ***Galerie Romain Rolland***, Alliance Française.

Bookshops – Jan Path has quite a few little bookshops one after the other. Good bookshops on Connaught Place: ***ED Galgotia & Sons***, B-17, ☎ (011) 332 28 76; ***The New Book Depot***, B-18; ***The Bookworm***, B-29, Radial Rd 4, ☎ (011) 332 22 60; ***Oxford Book***, Scindia House, Connaught Circus, ☎ (011) 331 53 08. Khan Market also has a number of good shops: ***Times Book Gallery***, 25-A, ☎ (011) 462 50 66; ***Bahri Sons***, ☎ (011) 469 46 10; ***Faqir Chand***, 15-A, ☎ (011) 461 88 10; ***The Book Shop***, A-14, ☎ (011) 461 10 08. At South Extension II: ***Crossword***, book department of the Ebony Department Store, D-4.

Stationery from ***New Delhi Stationery Mart***, C-8 Connaught Place, Radial Rd 4 and ***Snow White***, 14-B Khan Market, and G-16 South Extension I.

Agra★★★

Uttar Pradesh State
Pop 1 100 000 – Alt 180 m
205km from Delhi – 58km from Mathura
See map p 200

Not to be missed
The Taj Mahal. Agra Fort.
Itimad ud-Daula's tomb.
Akbar's tomb at Sikandra.

And remember...
Allow at least a day.
Rent a car for a half-day and combine a visit to Sikandra, with Mathura and Fatehpur Sikri.

The celebrity of the **Taj Mahal** has made Agra famous throughout the world. Some visitors to India only come to admire this mausoleum, built by Emperor Shah Jahan in the 17C solely out of love for his deceased wife, **Mumtaz-i Mahal**. At the time, Agra was one of the Mughal empire's most beautiful cities (the other two being Delhi and Lahore, now in Pakistan) and its architectural wealth was not limited to the Taj. Some of the finest 17C buildings can still be admired, including palaces, mosques and tombs, all featuring the traditional marriage of white marble and red sandstone, set in a backdrop of gardens inspired by the Paradise of Allah. Unfortunately, the city centre, now a filthy metropolis, disfigured by anarchic building and totally submerged by the noisy cacophony of scooters and rickshaws, somewhat detracts from the sublime beauty of its monuments. Petrochemical and leather factories both swamp Agra and the Taj with their obnoxious fumes. Some days, the latter is even invisible from the fort, which is only a few kilometres away. Visitors would do better to remain in the tourist district, to the south of the city, which is still relatively quiet and airy.

The city of the Taj Mahal

An intermittent capital – Mentioned in the *Mahabharata* under the name of Agrabana as well as in Ptolemy's *Geography*, the city only emerged from the shadows in 1492, when the Sultan of Delhi, **Sikandar Lodi**, set up court here. Although his successors preferred Delhi, Agra was once again capital in 1526, under Babur, the first Mughal. His son Humayun returned to Delhi, before being ousted by Sher Shah, but under the reign of **Akbar** (1556-1605), a golden age commenced for Agra, attracting merchants, artists and scientists from the world over. In fact, Akbar only governed from Agra for the first 15 years of his reign and transferred his capital first to the brand new city of Fatehpur Sikri (38km to

An ungrateful son

In 1657, Emperor Shah Jahan almost died of a heart attack. The false rumour of his death quickly spread through northern India. Three of his sons, Murad, Shuja and Aurangzeb, immediately began a merciless struggle for the throne. When the truth emerged, Shah Jahan's youngest son, Aurangzeb, nonetheless seized power. In 1658, he imprisoned his father in Agra Fort and disposed of his brothers. The death of Shah Jahan in 1666 marked the end of the grand epoch of Mughal architecture. Aurangzeb's main influence, architecturally speaking, was to destroy all Hindu temples and to replace them with somewhat mediocre mosques.

the west of Agra), before finally establishing it in Lahore. He was only to return to Agra at the end of his life. Akbar's son, **Jahangir** (1605-1627) somewhat neglected the banks of the Yamuna, oscillating between Lahore, Delhi and Agra. **Shah Jahan** (1627-1658) finally re-established the empire's capital at Delhi. However, his passion for lavish architecture was to enrich Agra with a number of gems, including the Taj Mahal.

An era of looting and pillaging – After Aurangzeb's austere reign, the empire began to decline and its sovereigns, who governed from the Red Fort at Delhi, had great difficulty maintaining any proper control over the capital, let alone over the rest of the empire. Agra was ransacked by the **Jats** from Bharatpur (1761) and again by the **Marathas** in 1770, before the British stepped in to take control of the region in 1803. After Independence, the former capital was little more than an average-sized city, suffering from urban chaos, unemployment and sulphur dioxide fumes. During the early 1990s, the Indian government took measures to clamp down on the polluting factories and workshops and launched a somewhat utopian campaign in favour of a "Green Agra". It would probably be easier for UNESCO to take down the Taj Mahal, stone by stone, and rebuild it on some Californian beach, than it would be for the Indian government to vote for and enforce any law in favour of the environment.

The town★★★

Allow 4hr and hire a rickshaw to get from the Taj Mahal to the Fort.

The Taj Mahal★★★ (Map II E2)

8am-4pm from October to March, 5am-5pm from April to September, closed Monday, entrance fee, extra charge at dusk; tax for video cameras. Allow 1hr.

To do it full justice, India's most beautiful monument should be visited at different times of the day. It is said to pass through a range of colours, from peach to pearl according to the light of the sun, the moon and the stars, every variation of light revealing a different aspect of this fairy-tale monument.

A coloured photo of the Taj Mahal (1906)

W.Abbeg/AKG PARIS

A beloved wife – In 1631, Shah Jahan's favourite wife, Mumtaz-i Mahal, "the palace's chosen one", died giving birth to their fourteenth child. The emperor decided to build a mausoleum of such dimensions as would reflect the depth of his sadness, conceiving it as a sort of monument to love: "Mumtaz Mahal" or the "Chosen One's Palace". At some later point, the name became deformed into "Taj Mahal" ("Crown Palace"), because the Hindi "z" and "j" are written almost identically. Work began in 1632 and continued for twelve years but the identity of the main architect remains a mystery today. A 19C tradition mentions the Persian Ustad Isa Khan. One thing is certain, Shah Jahan took an active interest in all the stages of the monument's construction. A legend, brought back by modern European travellers, has it that Shah Jahan intended to build a replica of the Taj Mahal on the opposite bank of the Yamuna, which would have been his own mausoleum, but was to have been made out of black marble.

The mausoleum – Enter the monument by the red sandstone and white marble **west gate**. As one emerges from the dark archway, the white Taj appears, looking almost unreal. Sit for a moment on one of the benches around the gate and admire the mausoleum before venturing closer. A water channel, lined with cypress trees (formerly alternating with orange trees) leads the visitor's eye towards the Taj. The Taj itself is set – like an object in a museum – on an immense platform, based on the prototype invented some 70 years earlier for Humayun's tomb in Delhi *(see p 145)*. The latter was however located in the centre of the garden, while the Taj is set at the rear of the splendid **Mughal garden** (chahar bagh), an image of Paradise where the souls of the emperor and his beloved now reside. Another difference with the prototype is the position of the four **minarets** flanking the tomb, which are isolated, set on the four corners of the platform. This in fact is a re-use of a formula tested a little earlier, on Jahangir's tomb (Shar Jahan's father) at Lahore. Their effect is to "anchor" the central monument onto the platform, which would otherwise give the impression it was going to topple backwards. Like Humayun's tomb, the central building is square shaped and divided into vestibules. A central *iwan*, surrounded by a *pishtaq* and by two storeys of recesses, give an overwhelming impression of space and emptiness. The whole result is however more graceful than Humayun's, partly due to the bulb-shaped dome, placed on a raised drum of the same width as the *pishtaq*, giving an extraordinary impression of upward movement. Note, the four *chhatri* (little kiosks) around the dome, forever faithful at their posts...

Walk to the pool, located in the exact centre of the garden. Its width was calculated to provide a complete reflection of the Taj. In fact, the tomb and its eerie shadow seem to stand out, almost freed, highlighted against the blue of the sky and the water.

On reaching the tomb's platform *(take your shoes off before going up)*, admire the stunning whiteness of the marble from quarries at Makrana (near Ajmer). The elegance of the ornamentation combines floral motifs carved in low relief and scrolls, wreaths and Koranic inscriptions, inlaid with semiprecious stones, using the *pietra dura* technique. The entrance leads through the central *iwan* whose arch is covered in a fretwork of filigree carving. In the octagonal mortuary chamber the false tombs of the imperial couple lie beneath a flat dome (their real tombs are in the crypt). Originally, they were surrounded by a protective railing, made out of gold and precious stones, but financial worries led Aurangzeb to sell the railing and replace it with the current exquisitely carved marble balustrade.

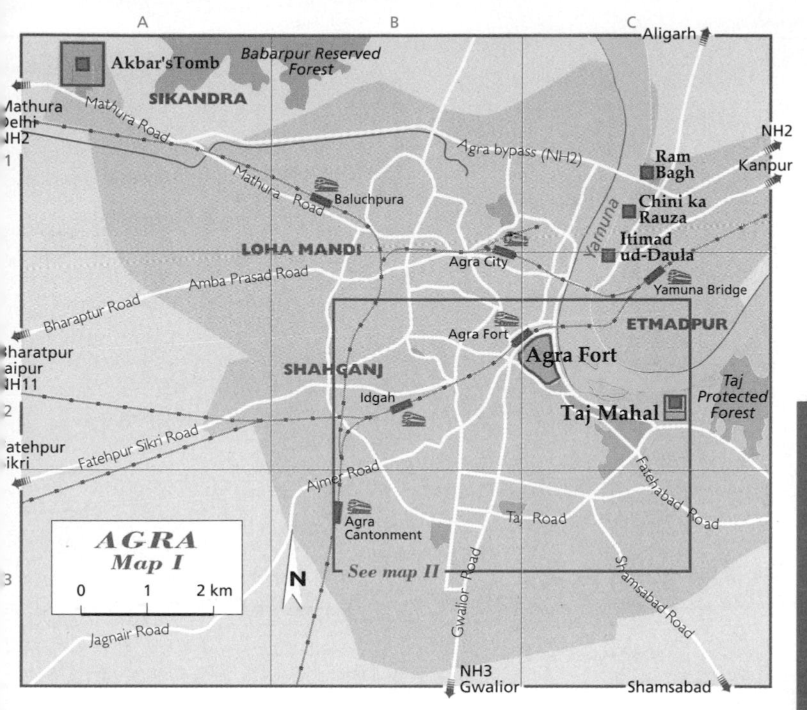

On leaving the mausoleum, note the **two identical buildings**, in red sandstone, set on either side of the Taj and separated by a pool wide enough for both monuments to be reflected in their entirety. These two edifices alone would constitute the pride and joy of a host of Indian cities, but the proximity of the Taj has relegated them to second place. In fact, only the building on the left, facing west, is a mosque. Its double, which lacks a *mihrab* (showing the direction of Mecca), served to shelter pilgrims or poets and musicians who came to pay homage to the deceased and proclaim the greatness of Allah, during ceremonies and firework displays that were staged in the gardens of this residence of beatitude.

Take a rickshaw from the south gate to Agra Fort, some 2km further up on the Yamuna.

Agra fort*** and mosque (Map II C1)

6am-6.30pm, entrance fee, free on Fridays, charge for video cameras. Allow 1hr.

Agra Fort, also known as the "Red Fort", with its double row of red sandstone **ramparts** separated by a deep moat, was clearly built for military purposes. Akbar had it built in 1565 on the site of the Chauhan Rajputs' fortress and his grandson, Shah Jahan, added to and embellished the edifice with white marble palaces and mosques. The complex has however greatly suffered as a result of ransacking. The fort's last siege was in 1857 at the time of the Mutiny, when the British held out for four months in the shelter of the ramparts, before reinforcements arrived from Delhi to relieve them. Nowadays, the site belongs to the army and only the southeastern section, the most interesting part, can be visited.

A
B
1
2
3
4
ASHOK NAGAR
NAI KI MANDI
HING KI MANDI
MANTOLA
Juma Masjid
DHAULIKHAR
PANCHKUIYAN
SHAGANJ
CHHIPITOLA
RAKABGANJ
CHILGARH
MOHANPURA
KATLAPURA
IDGAH COLONY
MODEL TOWN
NAMNER
SADAR BAZAR
SULTANPUR
PURWA NAULAKHA
Subash Park
Sikandra
Mathura
Delhi
NH2
Bharatpur
Jaipur
NH11
Fatehpur Sikri
Karauli
NH3
Gwalior
Ghalibpura Road
Hing ki Mandi Road
Kinari Bazar Road
Mantola Road
Juma Ma
Mahatma Gandhi Road
Saiyad Ali Nabi Road
Police Lines Road
Fatehpur Sikri Road
Rakabganj Road
Chhipitola Road
Kutchery Road
Gwalior Road
Ajmer Road
Nammer Road
Prithviraj Road
Mahatma Gandhi (M.G.) Road
Gopi Chand Shivhare Road
The Mall
Station Road
Taj Road
Sadar Bazar
Grand Parade
Power H
Idgah
Digambar Jain
Kohinoor
Baptist
St Mary
RSRTC
Dasaprak
Zorba the Buddha
Agra Cantonment
Petals
Sardar Pa Park
HOTELS
Agra Ashok 1
Amar 2
Amar Yatri Niwas 3
Atithi 4
Clarks Shiraz 5
Grand 6
Laurie's 7
Mansingh 8
Mughal Sheraton 9
Mumtaz 10
Oasis 11
Park Plaza 12
Taj View 13
Tourist Rest 14
Trident 15

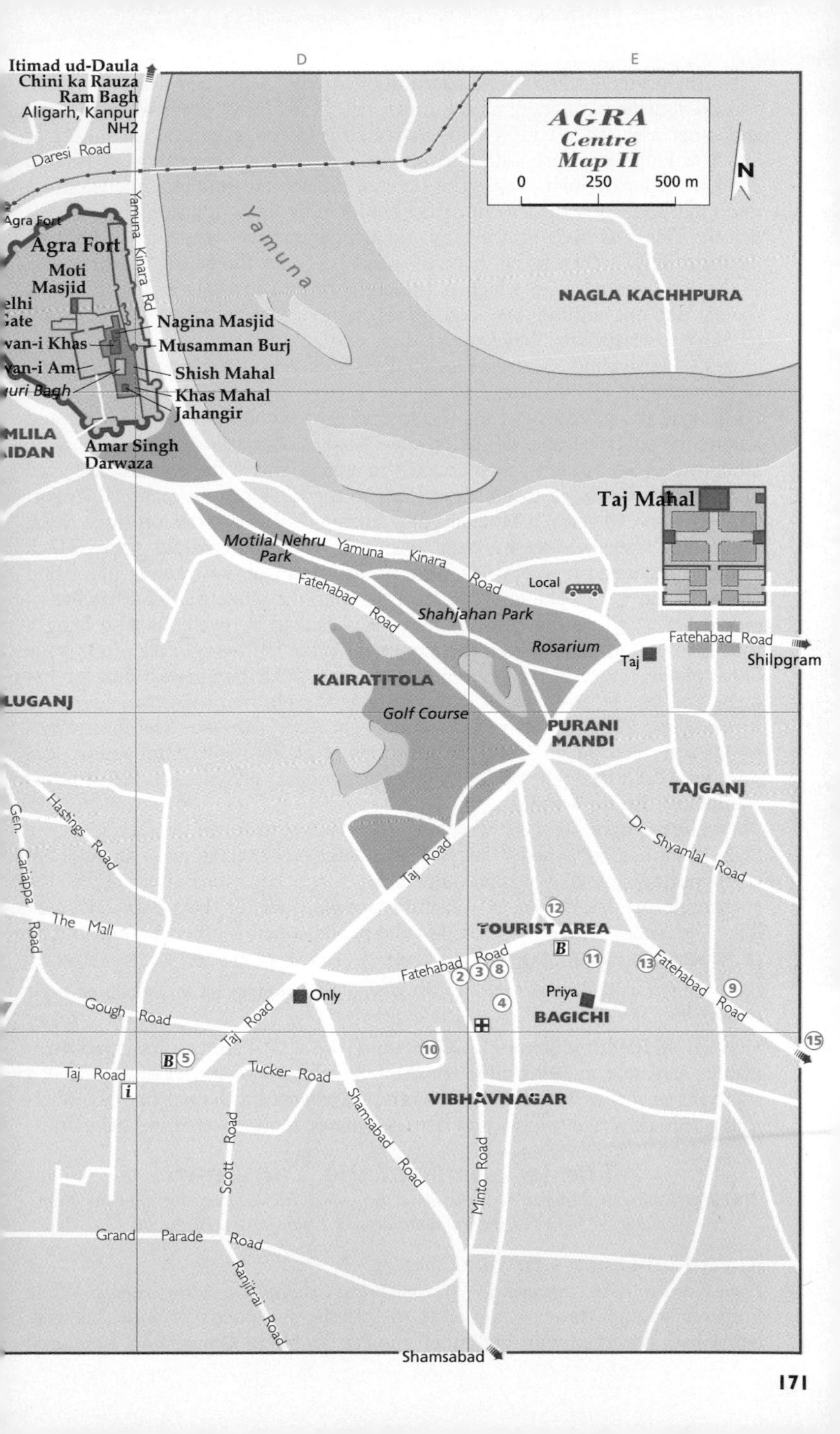
AGRA
Centre
Map II
0 250 500 m
N
D
E
Itimad ud-Daula
Chini ka Rauza
Ram Bagh
Aligarh, Kanpur
NH2
Daresi Road
Agra Fort
Agra Fort
Moti Masjid
Nagina Masjid
Musamman Burj
Shish Mahal
Khas Mahal
Jahangir
Amar Singh Darwaza
Yamuna Kinara Rd
Yamuna
NAGLA KACHHPURA
Taj Mahal
Motilal Nehru Park
Yamuna Kinara Road
Fatehabad Road
Local
Shahjahan Park
Rosarium
Taj
Fatehabad Road
Shilpgram
KAIRATITOLA
Golf Course
PURANI MANDI
TAJGANJ
Dr Shyamlal Road
Hastings Road
Gen. Cariappa Road
The Mall
Taj Road
TOURIST AREA
Fatehabad Road
Priya
BAGICHI
Only
Gough Road
Taj Road
Tucker Road
Shamsabad Road
VIBHAVNAGAR
Scott Road
Minto Road
Grand Parade Road
Ranjitrai Road
Shamsabad

Cross the bridge leading to the south door, **Amar Singh Darwaza** (Map II C2), and do your best to ignore all the touts, rickshaw drivers, souvenir merchants and other assorted pseudo-guides in search of a few generous clients. Amar Singh, a Jodhpur prince with anti-Mughal inclinations, was executed here in 1644 by order of Shah Jahan. The door of the second ramparts opens onto a ramp that leads to a garden-courtyard bordered by the red façade of **Jahangir's palace**. This was built in 1585 by Akbar and was the residence of his son, Jahangir. Blind arches in the shape of *mihrabs* decorate the façade on either side of the deep central *iwan*, which is the entrance into the palace. Inside, in the rooms laid out around two courtyards, note the joint existence of Hindu (awnings, protrusions, brackets…) and Persian architectural features (ogee arches…), providing once again an illustration of the syncretic nature so typical of Indo-Mughal architecture.
On leaving the palace, head for the second garden-courtyard *(to the right)* and admire the sober elegance of the **Diwan-i Am** (public audience hall) *(on the right)*, a hypostyle room in sandstone covered in stucco, where the emperor received his subjects. A passage to the right leads to the fort's private quarters. **Anguri Bagh** (garden of grapes), a Mughal patio surrounded by arcades on three sides, was named after the three hundred or so gold, ruby and emerald grapes which formerly decorated it and which were probably part of the treasure plundered by the Jats in 1761. The fourth side opens onto the white marble **Khas Mahal** (private palace) where the emperor lived. It is flanked by pavilions with Bengali roofs (half-moon) overlooking the Yamuna. On the left *(opposite the river)*, is the **Shish Mahal** (palace of mirrors) comprising two small hammams: one for hot baths and one for cold. Behind the baths is the **Muthamman Burj** (octagonal tower) where Mumtaz-i Mahal lived and where Shah Jahan was later imprisoned by his son. Shah Jahan spent the last years of his life here, entertaining, it is said, the courtesans who added a little gaiety to his gilded cage. His window overlooked the Taj Mahal.
The staircase, opposite the tower, leads to a patio overlooked by a terrace. Here Shah Jahan had a **Diwan-i Khas** (private audience hall) built in order to entertain distinguished guests. On the other side of the courtyard, upstairs, is the enchanting **Nagina Masjid**, a miniature mosque built for the palace's women-folk. The section of the fort closed to the public contains other monuments, in particular, the **Mothi Masjid** (Pearl Mosque) (1646), renowned for its elegance.

Leave the fort and take a rickshaw to the Juma Masjid mosque, on the other side of the railway line.

Finished in 1648, the **Juma Masjid mosque** (Map II C1) is much less spectacular than its namesake in Delhi, although also built by Shah Jahan. Set in the rear of a courtyard surrounded by multifoil cloisters, it is crowned with three domes of alternating red and white colours and houses a prayer room covered in blue paint…

The left bank of the Yamuna★

Hire a rickshaw or a taxi to visit the three sites which are located, one after the other, along the banks of the Yamuna, around 1.5km apart. Allow 2hr.

Itimad ud-Daula's tomb★★ (Map I C1-2)

From dawn to dusk, entrance fee, free on Friday, charge for video cameras. While Emperor Jahangir devoted himself to the pleasures of poetry or wine, his wife, Nur Jahan, governed with her father, the Persian **Mirza Ghiyas Beg**, honoured by the title of Itimad ud-Daula ("pillar of state"). On his death in 1628 – four years before the construction of the Taj Mahal – his daughter had a tomb built for him which is a pure marvel *(see illustration p 36)*. It immediately brings to mind images of a precious ivory coffer. Square-shaped, flanked by four relatively squat minarets, it is reminiscent of the formula adopted by Jahangir at Lahore, but smaller (Ghiyas Beg was not of royal blood!). Hindu-style awnings protrude around the ground floor and the upper level, blending admirably with the Persian arches. The **façades**** give the impression of having been painted by a pointillist artist or sewn by a lace-worker: the ornamentation flows freely, uninterrupted, across delicate *jali* screens and **multicoloured marquetry** work of inlaid stones and white marble. This mausoleum is held to be the first example of a Mughal monument made entirely out of white marble, inlaid using *pietra dura*. Note the grace and elegance of the motifs, all of which are images of Paradise: irises, cypress trees, pomegranates, bottles of the elixir of immortality, etc. The sarcophagi of Nur Jahan's parents lie in the ground floor funerary room, while upstairs, false tombs are laid on stones, whose arabesques reproduce a carpet. A residence of beatitude fit to spend eternity in!

From here, a country lane through fields leads to **Chini ka Rauza's tomb** (Map I C1) *(dawn to dusk, entrance free)*, known as the "porcelain mosque", where **Afzal Khan**, the Persian poet and Shah Jahan's prime minister, was buried in 1639. Only a few of the porcelain tiles still remain on the walls of this abandoned tomb.

Ram Bagh Garden (Map I C1)

From dawn to dusk, entrance free. Emperor Babur, pining for his Afghan parks, had this walled garden built as soon as he arrived in Agra. His body was buried here in 1530, before being removed to Kabul. Enjoy the pleasant walk through this typical Mughal garden or *chahar bagh* ("quadripartite garden"), one of India's oldest, and admire the pleasure pavilions and hammams. The *chahar bagh* takes over the Iranian symbolism of the garden as an image of paradise, but instead of being divided into eight, like its Persian model, the Indian *chahar bagh* is in four sections, divided by two water channels which meet at right angles in the middle.

Excursion

Allow 1hr.

Akbar's tomb at Sikandra** (Map I A1)

10km from the centre, on the road from Mathura to Delhi. 5am-7.30pm, entrance fee, free on Friday, charge for video cameras.

Here lies, on the site of the capital founded by Sikandar Lodi, one of the major figures of India's history, **Emperor Akbar**, in a monument fully worthy of his legend and which he designed himself. Work began in 1602 and was completed in 1613 – after Akbar's death – by his son, Jahangir.

The park is entered by a lavishly decorated **door**, entirely covered in multicoloured marble, inlaid in red sandstone, featuring purely geometric motifs. Among the octagonal motifs, note the Hindu *svastika* (symbol of good fortune) *(in a square half way up, repeated on either side of the iwans)*. Once inside, enjoy a leisurely stroll through the gardens, in the company of *langur* monkeys or shy deer.

The **tomb**, set in the centre, is the last of the Mughal era to have been built in red sandstone. It is a stepped pyramid, embellished with *chhatri*, very different from the classical Persian style despite the four *pishtaq* (doors with vaulted recesses – *iwan*) on either side. The last floor, entirely in white marble, comprises a terrace screened by a *jali*.
Inside, the **first room** reveals mural paintings, gilt-work and Koranic inscriptions. A dark corridor leads down to the **crypt**, which is entirely bare except for the tomb: it was originally decorated with frescoes illustrating the world's different religions, but Aurangzeb, a notorious fundamentalist, had them erased. Akbar's remains were scattered by the Jats in 1761, but the site still inspires great emotion – with the exception of a few disrespectful visitors who insist on trying out the vault's echo effect... In line with the double burial practice common to steppe peoples, a false tomb lies in view on the top floor.

400m further on, towards Delhi, on the right: note the **tomb of Mariyam** (also known as "Mariam") where Akbar's first Rajput wife, daughter of the maharaja of Amber and whose Moslem name was Mariyam, is buried.

Making the most of Agra

Getting there

By air – *Kheria Airport*, 8km to the south-west of Agra, in a military zone. Alliance Air, a subsidiary of Indian Airlines, ☎ (0562) 30 22 74, operates daily flights (35min) between Agra and Delhi. Take a taxi from the airport to the town centre.

By train – *Agra Cantonment Railway Station* (Map II A3), located in Sultanpur district, ☎ 131. Computerised reservation desk, ☎ (0562) 36 41 31. 8am-8pm, Sundays 8am-2pm. The best way to get to Delhi is to take one of the thirty or so daily trains going to the capital (3hr30min), via Mathura (50min). Most arrive at New Delhi Station and some continue onto Nizamuddin (20min away). If possible, opt for the morning "Kamataka Express", the "Taj Express" which leaves around 6pm or the "Shatabdi" which leaves around 8pm – more expensive (400Rs) but comfortable, air-conditioned and rapid (2hr).

Agra Fort Railway Station (Map II C1), near the Fort. Information, ☎ 132; bookings, ☎ (0562) 36 41 63. Supposed to provide connections with Rajasthan, but these have been suspended for an indefinite period due to rail work. Two daily departures for Mathura, but leaving from Agra Cantonment Station is really a much better idea.

By bus – The state's bus company, Uttar Pradesh State Roadways Transport Corporation (UPSRTC), has two main bus stations, the largest of which is ***Idgah Bus Stand*** (Map II A3) on the corner of Ajmer Rd and Fatehpur Sikri Rd, ☎ (0562) 36 75 43. 24 hours a day. Reservations, 8am-8pm. Departures for Delhi (5h), via Mathura, every 30min, from 5am to 8pm, and for Fatehpur Sikri (1hr) every 45min, from 6am to 8pm. Coach to Jaipur (6hr), via Bharatpur (90min), every hour, from 6am to 11.30pm; 5 coaches continue on to Ajmer and one goes as far as Bikaner. An express coach leaves for Udaipur around late afternoon (12hr).

Other buses leave from ***Power House Bus Stand*** (Map II C1), Gwalior Rd, to the west of the Fort, ☎ (0562) 36 45 57, 6am-10pm. Reservations impossible. Coaches for all the towns of Uttar Pradesh leave from here in a filthy, noisy cacophony. Express coach every hour for Delhi (6hr), via Aligarh, local buses to Mathura (2hr).

The Rajasthan State Roadways Transport Corporation (RSRTC) buses leave from ***RSRTC Bus Stand***, in front of Sakura and Sheetal Hotels on Ajmer Rd (Map II A3), ☎ (0562) 36 94 20. A dozen "Silver Line" buses leave daily for Jaipur (5hr30min), via Bharatpur, between 6.30am and midnight. Reservations advisable.

By taxi – The extent of traffic jams on the roads out of Agra is such that it takes an hour to get to Fatehpur Sikri by car. Rates vary from agency to agency, from 300 to 600Rs for 4hr and between 650 to 950Rs for 8hr. For Mathura, allow 2hr for travelling and between 600 and 1000Rs for a day (Vrindavan included) and for Bharatpur, allow 75min and 560 to 950Rs.

Getting around

Using some form of transport to get from one site to another is advisable, given the distances involved. Traffic flows quite smoothly in the Cantonment residential area along the "Mall" and between the Taj and the Fort, but gets much heavier towards the areas north of Ajmer Rd, to the east and north of the Fort.

By rickshaw – There is a "prepaid" rickshaw stand at Agra Cantonment Station. Allow 40Rs to the Taj Mahal. Agra is the city where the commission system, paid by merchants, hoteliers and restaurant owners to rickshaw and taxi drivers is by far the most developed. Visitors must assert themselves and remain firm, categorically refusing any detour not requested. It should cost around 320Rs to rent a rickshaw for a day (8hr).

By taxi – The taxi drivers of Agra Cantonment Station have formed a union offering fixed price rates. While perhaps not the cheapest, they are at least practical. If coming from Delhi for the day on the Shatabdi, you can rent a taxi on arrival for 950Rs that will stay with you all day until the train leaves (around 11hr).

Car rental – Prices range from 1 000 to 1 450Rs per day. Add another 450Rs if you intend crossing the border with Rajasthan.

Bicycle rental – At Sadar Bazaar (Map II B3). 25Rs per day.

Address book

Tourist Offices – ***Uttar Pradesh Tourism***, Agra Cantonment Station, platform n° 1 (Map II A4), ☎ (0562) 36 85 98, daily 8am-8pm. Also located at: 64 Taj Rd (Map II C4), ☎ (0562) 36 05 17. 10am-1.30pm/ 2pm-5pm; closed Sunday and the 2nd Saturday of every month. Provides information about Agra and Uttar Pradesh. It is possible to make reservations for the two daily guided visits: one for the Taj, the Fort and Fatehpur Sikri (8hr, 190Rs), the other just for Fatehpur Sikri (4hr, 150Rs). Both leave from Agra Cantonment Station at 10.15am.

Government of India Tourist Office, 191 The Mall (Map II B3), ☎ (0562) 36 39 59, Fax (0562) 36 33 77. 9am-1pm/1.30pm-5.30pm, Saturdays 9am-2.30pm; closed Sundays. Provides friendly, useful information about Agra and the rest of India, together with a list of English-speaking guides. Also at the airport.

Banks/Money – ***Bank of Baroda***, 13 M.G. Rd (Map II B2). Accepts travellers cheques and bank cards. ***Canara Bank***, M.G. Rd, Sadar Bazaar (Map II B4). Accepts cash and travellers' cheques in dollars and pounds sterling, as well as Visa cards. ***Allahabad Bank***, Clarks Shiraz Hotel (Map II D4), 1pm-4pm, Saturdays 1pm-2pm; closed Sundays. Cash and travellers' cheques. ***Clarity Financial Services***, Fatehabad Rd, opposite the Park Plaza Hotel (Map II E3), everyday, 9am-9pm. Cash and travellers' cheques. To have money sent to you from abroad in just a few hours, ***Western Union***, located in SITA World Travel agency.

Post Office/Telephones – ***GPO*** (Map II B3), Gopi Chand Shivhare Rd 10am-5pm; closed Sundays. One counter for the sale of stamps and mail opens from 8am. The poste restante service is renowned for being singularly incompetent. Postal code: 282 001. Express mail by ***EMS Speed Post***, in post offices, or by ***DHL***, Plot 3-4, Nehru Nagar Shopping Complex, M.G. Rd, ☎ and Fax (0562) 35 05 17. To send or receive a fax: ***Central Telegraph Office***, Gwalior Rd (Map II C3), Fax (0562) 36 11 46. 8am-9pm, Sundays 10am-6pm.

Health – ***Ambulances***, ☎ 102. ***Amit Jaggi Memorial Nursing Home***, Minto Rd (Map II E3), ☎ (0562) 33 06 00. Private clinic.

Safety – ***Police***, ☎ 100 and (0562) 36 11 20; Tajganj, ☎ (0562) 33 10 15. ***Fire brigade***, ☎ 101.

Travel agents – ***Eagle Tours & Travels***, Tourist Rest House, ☎ (0562) 36 39 61, ☎ and Fax (0562) 36 69 10. Hotel bookings and air, bus and train tickets. Car rentals at moderate prices (only non air-conditioned Ambassadors).

Travel Corporation India (TCI), Clarks Shiraz Hotel, ☎ (0562) 36 11 21, Fax (0562) 26 95 60. 10am-1.30pm/2pm-5.30pm, Saturdays 10am-2pm. Excellent agent, well represented all over India. Tickets, hotel reservations, taxi and car rentals at competitive rates.

Touraids, A-17 Shopping Arcade, Gopi Chand Shivhare Rd (Map II B3), ☎ (0562) 36 18 20, ☎ and Fax (0562) 26 56 24. Also at: 46 Gopi Chand Shivhare Rd, ☎ (0562) 36 99 41, ☎ and Fax (0562) 36 34 07, touraids@nde.vsnl.net.in Everyday, 10am-5.30pm. Reputable agency providing hotel, train, bus and air reservations. Taxi rentals at reasonable rates, but car rentals are relatively expensive. Can change cash and travellers' cheques in dollars.

SITA World Travel, A-2 Shopping Arcade, Taj Rd, Sadar Bazaar (Map II B3), ☎ (0562) 36 31 81, ☎ and Fax (0562) 36 30 13. A good, well-represented agency throughout India, however the car rental rates of the Agra branch are far too high.

Airlines – ***Indian Airlines***, Clarks Shiraz Hotel, ☎ (0562) 36 01 90 and 36 09 48. Everyday, 10am-1pm/2pm-5.30pm.

Miscellaneous – ***Archaeological Survey of India***, 22 The Mall, opposite the Tourism Office of India (Map II B3), ☎ (0562) 36 35 06. ***Antique Registration Office***, 19 MIG, New Shahganj. To extend a visa, contact ***Foreigners Regional Registration Office***, 16 Idgah Colony, Ajmer Rd (Map II B3), ☎ (0562) 26 95 63 and 36 75 63.

WHERE TO STAY

None of the hotels, except in the 4-star category, can be said to be really pleasant. There are however masses of low-budget guest houses, most of which are located in the roads and lanes to the south of the Taj Mahal. None of these establishments has been selected, primarily because it was in this area in 1998 that a few hotels were found guilty of several cases of poisoning of foreign guests and insurance swindles with the complicity of doctors and hospitals.

Power cuts are frequent in Agra and it is recommended choosing a hotel with its own generator, or making sure you have a torch and candles to hand. Most hotels grant a 10-20% reduction between April and September.

• Around Sadar Bazaar (Map II)

Under US$7

Tourists Rest House, Kutchery Rd, Baluganj, ☎ (0562) 36 39 61, Fax (0562) 36 69 10 – 27rm. Cooler. Agra's best low-budget address. The rooms are set in a U-shape around a central courtyard. The upper rooms are lighter and provide the use of a balcony. Friendly and decently maintained. The owner can organise trips to Rajasthan.

From US$15-30

Lauries' Hotel, M.G. Rd, Pratap Pura, ☎(0562) 26 61 53 and 36 45 36, Fax (0562) 26 80 45 – 12rm. Cooler. A large, white, yet somewhat dishevelled bungalow, that looks as if it has seen better times. All rooms are the same price and are spacious, if not very well maintained. A reliable, safe hotel, with friendly, respectful service. Campsite available.

Grand Hotel, 137 Station Rd, ☎ (0562) 36 40 14 and 36 43 20, Fax (0562) 36 42 71 – 72rm. Cooler. Same style as the above: not particularly inviting, but reliable. Ask for a room with a tiled floor, the carpeted rooms tend to have a funny smell. Campsite.

From US$40-70

Agra Ashok Hotel (Ashok Group), 6-B The Mall, ☎ (0562) 36 12 23 and 36 12 32, Fax (0562) 36 16 20 – 55rm. Boutiques.

The lobby looks very smart, but the rooms and corridors, which look half-finished, are a let-down. Very reasonable for a state hotel. 40 % reduction for single travellers.

• Fatehabad Road (Tourist Area)

(Map II)

The western section of Fatehabad Rd, 5km from Agra Cantonment Station, turns out to be an unending string of hotels, restaurants and boutiques for tourists.

Under US$7

Mumtaz Guest House, 3/7 Vibhav Nagar, South Area, ☎ (0562) 33 15 75 – 8rm. In a residential haven, this private house offers a few spacious, light rooms, but cleanliness and general decoration are not all they might be. A radiator or a cooler can be added for a small charge.

From US$7-15

The Oasis Hotel, 44 Bansal Nagar, Fatehabad Rd, ☎ (0562) 33 03 45 and 33 14 30, ☎ and Fax (0562) 33 12 86 – 18rm. Cooler. Just off Fatehabad Rd, this hotel puts on a warm welcome. The rooms are decorated with posters of cars, animals or landscapes, but otherwise are clean and airy.

From US$15-30

Amar Yatri Niwas, Fatehabad Rd, ☎ (0562) 33 38 00/04, Fax (0562) 33 38 05 – 33rm. This recently built hotel is well-maintained, clean and friendly, if somewhat lacking in the bustling atmosphere of its parent establishment, the Amar Hotel. The standard rooms, just a little smaller than the "deluxe" ones, are US$4 less. Pity that the finishings are not better.

From US$30-40

Atithi Hotel, Fatehabad Rd, in the little street just next to the Pizza Hut, ☎ (0562) 33 08 79 and 33 08 84, Fax (0562) 33 08 78 – 25rm. Clean with a friendly welcome, but the rooms are all totally identical and somewhat devoid of warmth.

Amar Hotel, Fatehabad Rd, ☎ (0562) 33 18 85/89, Fax (0562) 33 02 99 – 68rm. Don't be put off by the pandemonium or crowds sometimes found in the lobby. This hotel is perfectly well run and provides excellent value for money, particularly the more expensive rooms. Twelve large and garishly furnished suites.

From US$40-70

Mansingh Palace (Mansinghgroup), Fatehabad Rd, ☎ (0562) 33 17 71, Fax (0562) 33 02 02 – 97rm. Beauty salon. A modern, well-established, lively hotel, even if the rooms are relatively ordinary. Choose a "deluxe" room, which is much better and only US$4 extra. 30 % discount for single travellers.

Park Plaza Hotel (sometimes called the Howard Plaza), Fatehabad Rd, ☎ (0562) 33 18 70 to 78, Fax (0562) 33 04 08, hppi@nde.vsnl.net.in – 83rm. Good restaurant, beauty salon. Modern and equipped with all the modern comforts, yet a little forlorn, especially compared with the above.

From US$70-150

Clarks Shiraz Hotel (Clarks Group), 54 Taj Rd, ☎ (0562) 36 14 21, Fax (0562) 36 14 28, clarkraz@nda.vsnl.net.in – 220rm. Shopping mall, beauty salon. Not as luxurious as some of the more modern establishments, but this old, recently renovated hotel, set in a vast park, is undoubtedly one of the town's smartest. 50 % discount for single travellers.

The Trident (The Oberoi), Fatehabad Rd, Tajnagri Scheme, ☎ (0562) 33 18 18, Fax (0562) 33 18 27, ttag@tridentag.com; bookings from Delhi (see p 107) – 140rm. Boutiques. Formerly the Novotel, located in a lush, green area, 2km from the tourist area. Prices drop considerably from April to September making a stay in luxurious surroundings a feasible proposition.

Taj View Hotel (Taj Group), Fatehabad Rd, Taj Ganj, ☎ (0562) 33 18 41 to 45, Fax (0562) 33 18 60; bookings from Delhi (see p 107) – 100rm. Shopping mall. Poorly organised but friendly reception service. The rooms are quite expensive but do offer a view of the Taj.

Over US$150

Mughal Sheraton (WelcomGroup), Fatehabad Rd, Taj Ganj, ☎ (0562) 33 17 01, Fax (0562) 33 17 30, mughal@welcomgroup.com; bookings from Delhi (see p 107) – 287rm. Billiards, beauty salon, shopping mall. Half the rooms overlook the Taj Mahal from a distance.

WHERE TO EAT

• Sadar Bazaar (Map II)

From US$3-4

Dasaprakash, Meher Theater Complex, Gopi Chand Shivhare Rd (Map II C3), ☎ (0562) 26 02 69. 12.30noon-3.30pm/6pm-10.30pm; closed from May 1 to July 5. A branch of the Dasaprakash establishment in Delhi which provides a comfortable, pleasant stopping place with vegetarian specialities from the South. A few European dishes and a wonderful choice of ices and "lassi". Excellent service.

Petals Restaurant, Taj Rd, Sadar Bazaar (Map II B4). 12noon-10.30pm. A brand-new, airy, clean "multi-cuisine" restaurant, popular with local people working in the area.

Zorba the Buddha, E-13 Shopping Arcade, Sadar Bazaar (Map II B3), ☎ (0562) 36 77 67. 12noon-3pm/6pm-9pm; closed from May 1 to July 5. The 'New Age' temple frequented by disciples of Osho and "bacteriaphobes". Vegetables and fruit are soaked in boiling water before being prepared "meditatively". As a result the salads are tasteless, the portions are as tiny as the room and the prices are exorbitant. A real curiosity.

• Fatehabad Road (Tourist Area) (Map II)

Pizza freaks will be overjoyed to find a ***Pizza Hut*** – faultlessly clean – on Fatehabad Rd, next door to the Amar Yatri Niwas Hotel, while the more famished will prefer to tuck into one of the buffets provided at the Clarks Shiraz or the Taj View (only when there are groups, around US$10), or at the Mughal Sheraton (US$12 at lunchtime and US$15 in the evenings).

From US$3-4

Only Restaurant, 45 Taj Road (Map II D3), ☎ (0562) 26 65 08 and 36 43 33. 5pm-10pm. Depending on the weather, you can choose between the lawn or a spacious, cane room. A little noisy and the tablecloths are far from immaculate, but the place is lively and the Mughlai cuisine very tasty, if adapted to Western palates.

Priya Restaurant, off Fatehabad Rd (Map II E3), ☎ (0562) 33 01 49. 5pm-10.30pm. This austere dining room is decorated with just three rather unappealing garish paintings, but the lawn is very pleasant and the service is attentive. Classic, very decent Mughlai cooking, particularly the mutton "shahi korma gosht" with cream and dried fruit.

From US$4-7

Ripples, Mansingh Hotel's coffee shop. 6am-midnight. Renowned above all for its ambience and the cool, airy decoration (green fabric and cane furniture), because the Indian and international dishes served are relatively nondescript. Just next door is the hotel's restaurant, the Sheesh Mahal, which serves Mughlai cooking, to the accompaniment of "ghazals" from 8pm.

Mughlai, the Clarks Shiraz Hotel restaurant. 7.30pm-11.30pm. Pleasantly decorated and very stylish service. Taste the "murgh begum bahar", stuffed chicken with a cashew sauce. "Ghazals" in the evenings or a sitar concert on Tuesdays.

• Around the Taj Mahal (Map II)

A host of "German Bakeries" line the little streets to the south of the Taj, and innumerable little eateries, whose hygiene standards most often don't bear thinking about, can be found perched on terrace-roofs or in courtyards. Popular among young travellers on low budgets. Most menus offer "thali", macaroni, banana pancakes, Israeli dishes, etc.

Under US$3

Taj Restaurant, Fatehabad Rd, west of the Taj Mahal, (Map II E2). 10am-6pm. A spacious, functional and perfectly clean cafeteria. Unfortunately the choice is limited: "thali", a few sandwiches, toast and drinks.

Where to have a drink

Agra's night-life is restricted to a visit to the Taj Mahal on nights with a full moon.

Bagh-e-Bahar, Mughal Sheraton Hotel. 🍷 CC 6am-11pm. Comfortable seats and a relaxing ambience make this a welcome halt in the early evening for a quiet beer or cup of tea.

Pastimes

Sports – Some hotels, such as the Amar, Atithi, Agra Ashok and Mansingh, admit non-residents to their swimming pool (from 110 to 170Rs per day).

Shopping

Sadar Bazaar (Map II B3), the Cantonment's largest shopping centre, has all you might need in the way of day to day necessities.

Crafts – The crafts and souvenir shops for tourists are all located to the south of the Taj Mahal in the "Tourist Area" (open everyday). Beware when making purchases because swindles and frauds are unfortunately very commonplace in Agra.

Shilpgram, 1km east of the Taj Mahal. Complex of open-air stalls, set up by the UP Tourism Office and intended to provide an outlet for a fresh set of craftsmen every month. Unfortunately it is neglected and more often than not, deserted, except during the annual Taj Mahotsav festival (18-27 February).

Cottage Industries Exposition (CIE), 39 Fatehabad Rd (Map II D3). An attractive bungalow perched up on a hill, between Amar Hotel and the only restaurant. Offers crafts from Agra and Kashmir (shawls, embroidery, carpets).

Inlaid marble work – Beware of imitations of real marble or alabaster inlaid with precious stones using the pietra dura technique. These imitations made with worthless stones or cut glass are sold in a certain number of unscrupulous souvenir shops. The real materials are fine, the work is detailed and lengthy and the prices are accordingly quite high. Boxes, glass mats, table tops are all available. Craft stalls are located in a small lane to the south of the Taj. Sadar Bazaar has two reputable manufacturers, both of whom are open everyday, ***Subhash Emporium***, 18/1 Gwalior Rd and ***Oswal Emporium***, 30 Munro Rd.

Carpets – Since the time of the Great Mughals, Agra has manufactured and continues to manufacture woollen and silk carpets – more often than not synthetic rather than natural whatever the merchants may say. Carpets and dhurries can be found at Main Bazaar and in the Tourist Area.

Jewellery – ***Kohinoor***, 41 M.G. Rd, corner of Chhipitola Rd, ☎ (0562) 36 88 55/56. Jewellers for over five generations, renowned for their high-quality gems.

Embroidery – Moslem craftsmen developed an embroidery of gold or silver thread on black velvet, known as "zari". Another speciality, very popular in the Middle East, is 3-D embroidery. One of the best known craftsmen, Sheikh Shasuddin, displays some of his work at Kohinoor (above).

Culinary specialities – Agra's specialities can be obtained from "namkin" or confectioners: "dalmoth", a mixture of fried, savoury yellow lentils, "petha", preserved pumpkin pulp and "gazak", based on brown sugar and sesame.

Bookshops – ***Modern Book Depot***, Taj Rd, Sadar Bazaar (Map II B4). 10am-9pm; closed Tuesdays. The Clarks Shiraz, Mughal Sheraton and Taj View hotels also have good bookshops.

Photography – ***LBG Sons*** and ***Agra Colour***, Shopping Arcade, Gopi Chand Shivhare Rd, Sadar Bazaar (Map II B3).

FATEHPUR SIKRI★★★

Uttar Pradesh State
Former Mughal capital 38km to the west of Agra
See map p 200

Not to be missed

Everything!

And remember...

Come for a half-day excursion direct from Agra.
If travelling by car, combine this visit
with that of Akbar's tomb at Sikandra (Agra).

The road from Agra winds through a fertile, well-cultivated plain, where travellers occasionally chance upon the strange sight of a man leading a black dancing bear, always ready to launch into a few dance steps for a few rupees. Perched on a rocky outcrop, the town's red walls loom suddenly ahead. Fatehpur, the "city of victory", seems very peaceful and rightly so. Emperor Akbar's short-lived city has been uninhabited for the last four centuries and the only life left here now takes place around a tomb. It is a ghost town. Only a little village survives, just outside the town walls, inhabited by stonemasons whose ancestors built these astonishing red sandstone palaces.

A fleeting Mughal capital

In 1570, Emperor **Akbar** (1556-1605), who was at the height of his glory, decided to transfer his capital from Agra to this site at Sikri, despite the absence of any real strategic or economic reasons. His main desire, apart from the prestige of founding a new city, was to move closer to a Sufi saint he venerated, **Sheikh Salim Chisti**. The latter had announced the birth of three sons to the emperor, who at the time still had no descendants, so when the following year, a son was born (the future Jahangir), he was named Salim after the saint.

Akbar, an enlightened sovereign

At the head of a territory as vast as Europe with a hundred million inhabitants, Akbar is considered the greatest sovereign of North India, after Emperor Ashoka (3C BC). An astute politician and great reformer, he centralised power and unified the currency, the language (he imposed the use of Persian at court), and even his subjects; reducing differences between Moslems and non-Moslems, he removed the tax on the latter, abolished Islam as the state religion and authorised inter-religious marriages. Both curious and deeply tolerant, he sought to surround himself with philosophers and theologians of all religions, organising great ecumenical debates among them. One of his sons had a Christian tutor. Under the guidance of a Zoroastrian master, he even considered developing a religion to synthesise all the existing religions.

Akbar had an entire city built on the promontory at Sikri, encircled by ramparts on three sides and protected on the fourth by a lake, now partially filled in. It proved difficult however to supply water to the city, it was also too far from the Empire's main routes and its sensitive borders. As early as 1585, Akbar abandoned Sikri and transferred his court to Lahore (now in Pakistan). In the early 17C, plague swept through the city, emptying it of its final inhabitants.

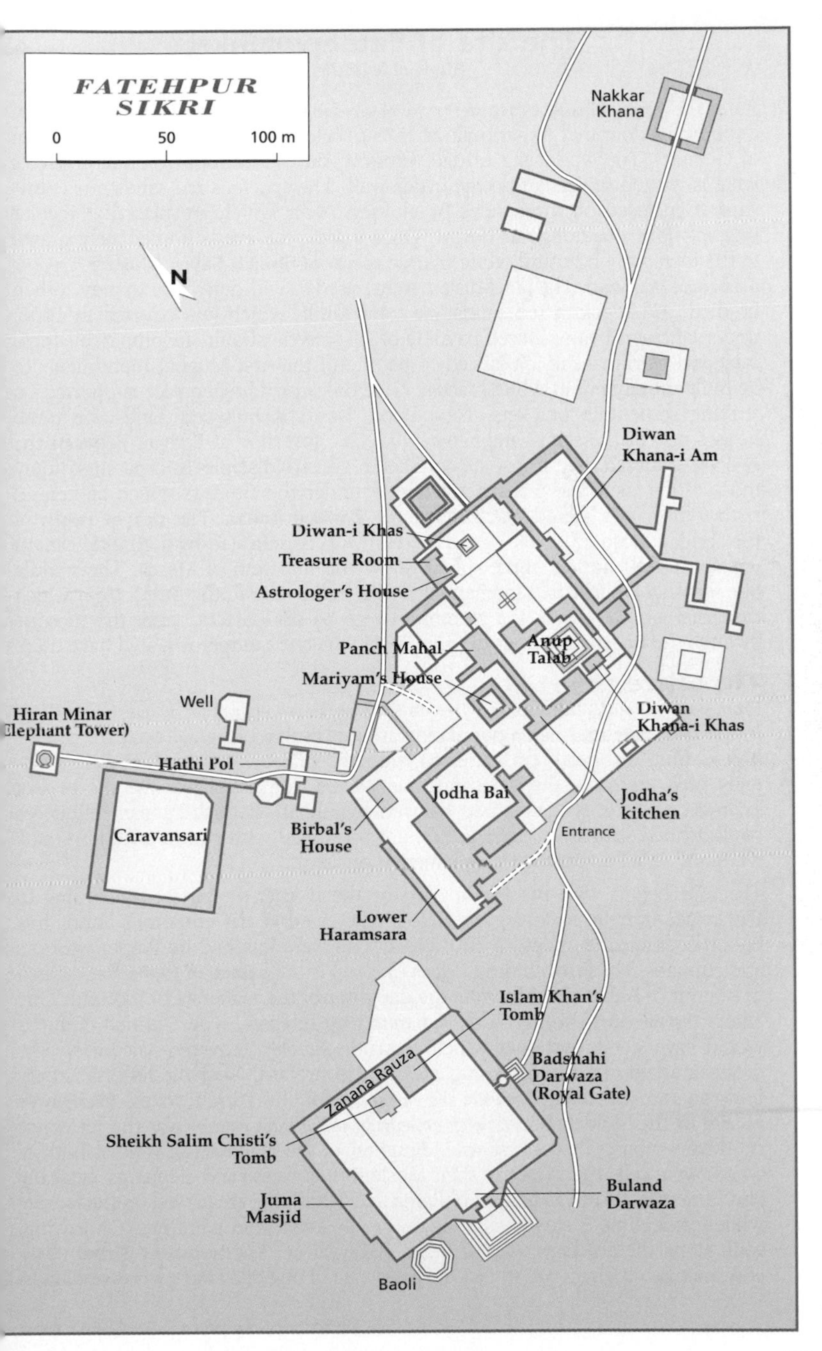
FATEHPUR SIKRI
0
50
100 m
N
Nakkar Khana
Diwan Khana-i Am
Diwan-i Khas
Treasure Room
Astrologer's House
Panch Mahal
Anup Talab
Mariyam's House
Well
Hiran Minar (Elephant Tower)
Diwan Khana-i Khas
Hathi Pol
Jodha Bai
Jodha's kitchen
Caravansari
Birbal's House
Entrance
Lower Haramsara
Islam Khan's Tomb
Zanana Rauza
Badshahi Darwaza (Royal Gate)
Sheikh Salim Chisti's Tomb
Buland Darwaza
Juma Masjid
Baoli

The site of Fatehpur Sikri

Allow at least 2hr.

Enter the **Juma Masjid Mosque***** *(remove your shoes)* via the **Buland Darwaza**, a triumphal door that Akbar built in 1575 to celebrate his victory over the Sultan of Gujarat. "The world is a bridge. Cross it, but build nothing underneath" is what is written in Persian on the inside wall. The spacious red sandstone courtyard is enclosed on three sides by cloisters, over which are placed at regular intervals four quadrangular *chhatri*. Once inside, the eye is immediately drawn to the incredibly beautiful white marble **tomb of Sheikh Salim Chisti**** *(opposite the Buland Darwaza)*. The *pir* (Moslem saint) used to withdraw here to pray. When he died, Akbar had a red sandstone tomb built, which was covered in 1606, under Jahangir, by this closed pavilion of *jali* screens of quite incomparable intricacy and workmanship. It is said to be one of the first Mughal monuments to be built entirely out of white marble. Note the protruding cornice supported on striking serpentine brackets. Next door, **Islam Kahn's** red sandstone tomb houses one of the saint's nephews, who was governor of Bengal. Between the two are scattered the tombstones of Sheikh Chisti's disciples and parents – only those of the men; the women are buried under the cloisters which lie behind both tombs, in a sacred place called the **Zanana Rauza**. The **prayer room** of the "Friday Mosque" *(to the west of the courtyard)* is indicated by a gigantic central *pishtaq* (portal). Inside, three *mihrab* show the direction of Mecca. The middle one, lavishly embellished in enamelled tiles, has a *minbar*, the pulpit from which the *imam* would deliver the sermon. To go to the palaces, leave the mosque through the **Badshahi Darwaza** (royal door) which the emperor would have used.

The palaces***

From dawn to dusk, entrance fee, free on Fridays. Extra charge for video cameras.

In the 16C, Fatehpur had a population as large as that of Agra. Today the private houses built of brick have vanished from the hillsides where they were originally built and only the red sandstone palaces remain. These are the perfect expression of the syncretism so beloved by Akbar: Turkish-Persian influences (well-defined structures, ogee arches) are combined with Hindu traditions (cornices and brackets, excessive ornamentation, etc).

The tour begins with the **Haramsara** or the women's quarters. According to Father Monserrate, a Portuguese Jesuit who lived at the emperor's court, this harem contained as many as 300 wives, who were guarded by Rajput warriors and eunuchs. The first building *(left on entering)* is the **palace of Jodha Bai**, named in honour of Akbar's Hindu wife, the daughter of the maharaja of Jodhpur. One enters *(by the east)* through a door flanked by recesses, where armed eunuchs would have stood, and over which protrude *jharokha* (covered balconies). The rooms are laid out around a single, central courtyard. Note the little sanctuary built on the west side *(opposite the entrance)* for the Hindu wives. **Mariyam's House** or the "golden house" *(left on leaving Jodha Bai's palace)* was the residence of Akbar's mother or his first wife, daughter of the maharaja of Amber, both of whom were called Mariyam in their Moslem title. Geese and elephants, typically Hindu motifs, as well as images of Rama and Hanuman are carved on the façade, while inside, time is slowly wearing away the lavish gold paintings. On leaving, walk along the northern wall of Jodha Bai's palace. The **house of Birbal** *(name of the emperor's advisor)* was in fact the residence of one of Akbar's wives or daugh-

In front of the jali of Salim Chisti's tomb

ters. An extraordinarily intricate pattern of arabesques and scrolls covers the whole building, resembling carving in wood. To the south of the courtyard, the **lower Haramsara** was probably used by the harem's servants and not as stables as is sometimes claimed.

Turn round and go back down the passage behind Mariyam's house. It leads to the women's garden and then onto the men's quarters.

The strange triangular outline of the **Panch Mahal** (five-tiered palace) is easily recognisable: composed of five-tiered hypostyle floors, each one slightly smaller than the first, placed on top of each other, like a house of cards. It is said that none of the building's 176 columns is identical. The edifice would originally have been closed off by *jali* which would capture the breeze and transform it, making the palace an ideal place to sleep during the hot summer nights.

The **Diwan-i Khas** (private audience hall) stands in isolation to the north of the esplanade. Four free-standing *chhatri* are posted at each corner of the roof-terrace which no doubt originally surrounded a central larger kiosk (no longer in existence). The four main doors open onto a room whose main feature is a quite extraordinary **column**. This branches up into an incredible capital, composed of radiating serpentine brackets, supporting a circular platform. From this central platform, where the emperor would have sat enthroned, master over the four parts of the world, four narrow bridges lead to the surrounding gallery. Installed on a dais, he would have received distinguished guests or presided over religious or philosophical debates. On leaving note the stone rings at the top of the façade. Others can be found on other buildings throughout the city. They were used to attach canopies, awnings, tents, screens which were stretched between the buildings, in order to protect from the sun or create smaller, more intimate alcoves. This mobile architecture is strangely reminiscent of the Turk-Monghol nomad way of life of Akbar's ancestors.

The **treasure room** consists of three basement rooms where the state's gold was stored. Legend tells that the emperor used this pavilion to organise vast games of hide-and-seek with his courtesans, hence his nickname of "Ankh Michauli" ("closed eyes"). The next-door kiosk, called the **"Astrologers Lodge"**, features delicately carved **arches** *(torana)*, based on work by Jain sculptors. Was it really the abode of the court's astrologer or did the emperor use it himself, to observe the movements of the pawns on the giant chess board *(pachisi)* that can be seen marked out on the stones of the esplanade *(centre)*? This is in fact a *chaupar*, a game played on board similar to a chess-board. Once again, legend relates that naked slaves and prisoners of war were used as pawns.

A door at the east of the esplanade leads to the **Diwan Khana-i Am** (public audience hall), a court surrounded by portals, where the emperor would have dispensed justice.

Return to the esplanade. The first building encountered on the left is the enchanting **palace of the Turkish sultan**, made to look like a wooden cabin and surrounded by a quite exquisitely worked veranda. The square pool, the **Anup Talab**, divided into four like an inverted *chahar bagh* (Mughal garden), features a stage where musicians and dancers would have put on performances to entertain the emperor. The **Diwan Khana-i Khas** (private apartments), which dominates the pool, was where the emperor worked, dined and retired. He would also have received his advisors in private, on a raised dais covered in carpets. From the window looking over the courtyard of archives *(to the south)*, he was able to present himself to his subjects every morning, offering them his *darshan* to bring them good health.

If you still have a little energy, go to the northwest of the site *(through a door to the north of Jodha Bai's palace)*. The path leads under the **Hathi Pol**, past the caravanserai, before reaching **Hiran Minar** tower, decorated with stone elephant tusks, in memory of Hiran, Akbar's favourite elephant, who is buried beneath it. Beyond stretches the polo field.

Making the most of Fatehpur Sikri

Getting there

Fatehpur Sikri is included in many excursions leaving Agra or Delhi. Enquire at travel agents in both towns.

By train – The station is located 1km to the southeast of Juma Masjid mosque. There are however no rail connections with Agra at present due to rail works.

By bus – Buses stop in the main street, a 5min walk from Buland Darwaza (the mosque's southern door). Irregular services run from Agra, from 6am to 8pm, but you rarely wait for more than 45min. Allow an hour due to heavy traffic on the way into Agra. Also 6 buses a day to Bharatpur (1hr).

By taxi – It is possible to hire a taxi from Agra Fatehpur (see "Getting there" in the "Making the most of Agra" section).

Where to stay

Under US$7

Maurya Rest House, just beneath the Buland Darwaza, ☎ (05619) 23 48 – 7rm. 2rm without bathrooms. At the price one can hardly expect a palace, but the family is friendly and meals can be taken on the roof terrace.

Goverdhan Tourist Complex, Buland Darwaza Rd Crossing, 400m from the bus stand, ☎ (05619) 88 22 22 and 88 26 43 – 9rm Its situation near to the crossroads of the main street make it noisy, but the rooms are reasonably clean given the price. Tiny bathrooms and hot water in basins.

From US$15-30

Gulistan Tourist Complex (UPTDC), first hotel on entering Fatehpur, turn left after Agra Gate, 1km from the bus stand, ☎ (05613) 88 24 90 – 24rm. Cooler. This hotel is run by Uttar Pradesh State and you can tell: no care has been taken over the finishings and maintenance is sloppy. It is nonetheless one of the best addresses in the area. The ground-floor building, set around a courtyard, is damp. A pity, because with a little more care it would be quite pleasant.

Joshi Tourist Complex, Agra Rd, 20km to the east, on the road to Agra, ☎ (05613) 442 38 and 442 94 – 15rm. In a countryside setting and consisting of bungalows scattered over a spacious lawn, this complex provides a warm welcome. Unfortunately the rooms are damp and depressingly decorated. Expensive given the facilities, even those with air-conditioning. Great place to camp though.

Where to eat

There are any number of little places to eat around the foot of the Buland Darwaza. Those in search of more comfort may try:

Gulistan Tourist Complex (UPTDC), same address as the hotel. 6am-10pm. The only pleasant place to stop for lunch or a beer. If the weather permits, insist on being served in the courtyard-garden which is much pleasanter than the large, canteen-style dining room. If the hotel is catering to a group, you'll be able to try the buffet, otherwise the menu offers a classical selection of "chicken tikka", "dal makhani", "palak-paneer", etc.

Joshi Tourist Complex, same address as the hotel. Those travelling by car may prefer lunching out here in the countryside, under shady parasols. Tandoori cuisine as well as a few Chinese and European dishes. Try the "thali" which offers 12 different dishes.

Holidays & Festivals

Sheikh Salim Chisti Urs. "Qawwal" (Sufi chants) are sung continuously in front of the saint's "dargah".

MATHURA★

Uttar Pradesh State
Pop 455 000 – Alt 187m
144km from Delhi – 58km from Agra – 39km from Bharatpur
See map p 200

Not to be missed
The museum's sculptures.

And remember...
Combine a visit to Agra or Bharatpur with a visit to Mathura.
The Krishna Janmasthami festival in August-September is magical.
Finish off your discovery of the Braj, with a trip to Govarhan (see "Alwar").

Located in a vast fertile plain, in the heart of **Braj** (or Vraj Bhumi) country, Mathura is above all a significant religious centre, one of Hinduism's seven sacred cities. Lord **Krishna** himself was born here and spent his childhood in the surrounding countryside. An equivalent to Bethlehem for Christians, it is the object of pilgrimage all year round and pilgrims generally walk from temple to temple, sometimes trekking through the whole of the Braj region. For each morsel of earth has been sanctified by some act or other of the blue-skinned god, whether it be the pool where his swaddling clothes were washed, the wood where he played with the shepherdesses *(gopi)* or the place where he felled the terrible demon *(asura)*. The Braj conjures up a mysterious atmosphere of intense religious devotion *(bhakti)* and myth that has no parallel elsewhere in India.
From dawn until dusk, the shrines, souvenir shops and restaurants – vegetarian of course – are full of bustling pilgrims come to get closer to God. Take a stroll at the end of an afternoon down the lane next to the Yamuna and stop in one of the shrines to listen to the enthusiastic devotees chanting *bhajan* (religious hymns) to the glory of the divine cowherd. Most of all, don't miss the museum and its extraordinary sculptures which evoke Mathura's prestigious past as a former leading Buddhist centre and a political and cultural capital of the Kushan empire.

Krishna, the blue-skinned god
The life and teachings of Krishna are the object of innumerable tales, many contradictory, depending on whether they are from the "Mahabharata" (4C BC – 3C AD), the "Bhagavad Gita" (poem from the Mahabharata) or the "Bhagavata Purana" (10C). As the Earth was under threat from the demon Kamsa, king of Mathura, Vishnu decided to save it by reincarnating for the eighth time. Thus Krishna was born into the community of Yadavs. He was raised by his adoptive parents, shepherds at Vrindavan, and his exploits – and his misdemeanours and amorous adventures – rapidly made him famous throughout the region. After having slain Kamsa, he left to found the city of Dvarka (Gujarat) and served as coachman to the warrior Arjuna during the final battle related in the "Mahabharata". He died later, at Dvarka, as a result of an arrow wound to his heel, the only vulnerable part of his body.

A leading religious centre

It seems that the conflicts between local sovereigns related in Krishnuist legends have some founding in reality and it is quite probable that Krishna was in fact a historical figure. Mathura was already an important city when Buddha came to preach in the 6C BC. The new faith put down deep roots and the town became a significant cultural and religious centre, endowed with large numbers of monasteries and stupas (monumental reliquaries). Promoted to the rank of winter capital under its **Kushan** sovereigns (1-3C AD), who had converted to Buddhism, (the summer capital was Begram, in the Afghan mountains), Mathura became a melting pot of cultures. It gave birth to the famous **school of sculpture,** which reached its apogee under the **Guptas** (4-6C AD) but was killed dead by the Hun invasion towards the end of the 6C.

The sacred land of Vishnuism

Around the 12C, the *Bhagavata Purana*, a 10C text originally written in southern India, began to spread through northern India, leading to the popularisation of legends surrounding Krishna's childhood and providing an amazing impetus to the *bhakti* (devotion) movement. The Braj thus became a place of pilgrimage for Vishnuists (Krishna being a reincarnation of Vishnu), attracting large numbers of saints and poets who devoted themselves to singing his praise. The most famous among them were princess Mira Bai in the 15C *(see "Chittaurgarh", p 355)*, and thinkers such as Bengali reformist, Chaitanya (early 16C). Between the 16C and 18C, Mathura was ransacked five times, primarily by Emperor **Aurangzeb** (17C) who destroyed the majority of the region's temples. Among these was the shrine commemorating the birthplace of Krishna, in place of which Aurangzeb erected a mosque. Such past intolerance continues to undermine relations between India's two main religious communities today. In the 1990s, extremist Hindu groups planned to destroy the mosque, in its turn... A similar case having had dire consequences in Ayodhya, Rama's birthplace in Uttar Pradesh, in December 1992 *(see p 25 and 26)*, the atmosphere in the area can be strained.

The town*

Allow half a day.

The Government Museum** (B4) *(10am-5pm; closed Mondays, entrance free, tax for cameras and videos)* houses all the sculpture found in the region, most of which dates from the 1-6C. This period corresponds to the Kushan and Gupta reigns. It was also the golden age of the **Mathura School**, recognisable by its use of the red sandstone mottled with cream which is unique to Sikri's quarries, as well as by the extraordinary beauty of the faces, together with a distinctive blend of vigour and grace.

Room 1 illustrates the transition from a relatively primitive art (1C BC) to more sophisticated sculptures, such as the **young man standing**, with finely detailed treatment of necklace and hair. In Room 2, devoted to the Kushan period

Genie emerging from the mouth of a makara (Mathura museum)

JL Nou/AKG PARIS

Greco-Buddhist influence

Alexander the Great conquered Afghanistan and the northwest of what is now Pakistan in 327 BC. He left behind generals whose successors founded the Bactrian kingdom. The latter played an active role in the dissemination of Hellenistic culture throughout the region. Despite invasions by nomad Parthians and Scythians, from the 1C BC onwards, Greek script and the canons of Hellenistic sculpture took hold. The dynasty, called "Indo-Scythian" by the Romans and "Kushan" by the Indians, founded a vast empire that spread as far as the Ganges between the 1C and 3C AD. The centre of power remained the old Hellenised kingdom of Afghanistan. This was probably where the early sculptures of Buddha were produced in the 1C, by the "Greco-Buddhist" or "Gandharan" (after its main site) school. It was the easternmost of Asia's Greco-Roman schools and renowned for the realism of its expressions and the sophistication of the carving.

(1-3C AD), note the statue of **Parshavantha**, 23rd *tirthankara* (who inspired the Jain movement). At the time, the region of Mathura had Hindu, Jain and Buddhist communities, all of whom lived in harmony together. Room 3 is devoted to **Gandharan** Greco-Buddhist art (1C), which was to greatly influence Buddhist statues in northern India. Room 4 has a fine 1C **Buddha** (Kushan period) in an *abhaya* position (his right hand is raised in a sign of peace). Rooms 5 and 6 comprise a series of friezes depicting life in the royal courts, together with **naga** and **nagini** statues, aquatic and subterranean snake-like divinities. Room 7 contains a collection of Kushan pillars and stupa railings, featuring generously voluptuous *yakshini* (nymphs, guardians of the shrine). Note the blooming features of the gracious young woman in front of her mirror or the nude nymph who lavishly proffers the gift of bunches of grapes along with that of her nakedness. The **Buddha** (Guptan era) in Room 8 provides a marvellous image of serenity and harmony. The final rooms are devoted to Hindu art of the Middle Ages (7-12C) and are relatively uninteresting. There is however a very fine **four-armed Vishnu**.

The road leading to the shrine of **Shri Krishna Janmabhumi*** (*"Lord Krishna's birthplace"*) (A2) is lined with souvenir shops selling pictures of the god, as well as flutes (the instrument he used to seduce the womenfolk of Braj, including married women) and scarves marked with the legendary *mantra* "Hare Rama, Hare Krishna"... Over the entrance to the site, a statue of Krishna driving Arjuna's chariot evokes the episode of the *Mahabharata* which gave rise to the *Bhagavad Gita* *(see p 49)*. After passing through a barrage of policemen, one finds oneself within a bustling complex of temples, boutiques and administrative offices, while loudspeakers blare out hymns to the glory of Krishna. Note the 20C temple *(to the left)* beside the 17C mosque *(to the right)*.

Built in 1975, **Krishna's temple** – pink façade and red *shikhara* – is the last of a series of temples, destroyed and rebuilt over time, the last of which dates back to the 17C. Aurangzeb was not appeased by the temple's destruction and had it replaced with a mosque *(on the right)*. The actual temple is thus not located on the exact spot of the god's birth. *(Shoes must be removed before entering.)* Inside, the walls are decorated with garish paintings depicting Krishna's life and his frolics with the *gopi*. At the altar stands a statue of the divine cowherd, playing his flute. The statue is hidden behind a curtain and is revealed several times a day, at the time of *darshan* (literally "vision") (variable depending on the month), to the enthusiastic delight of the worshippers.

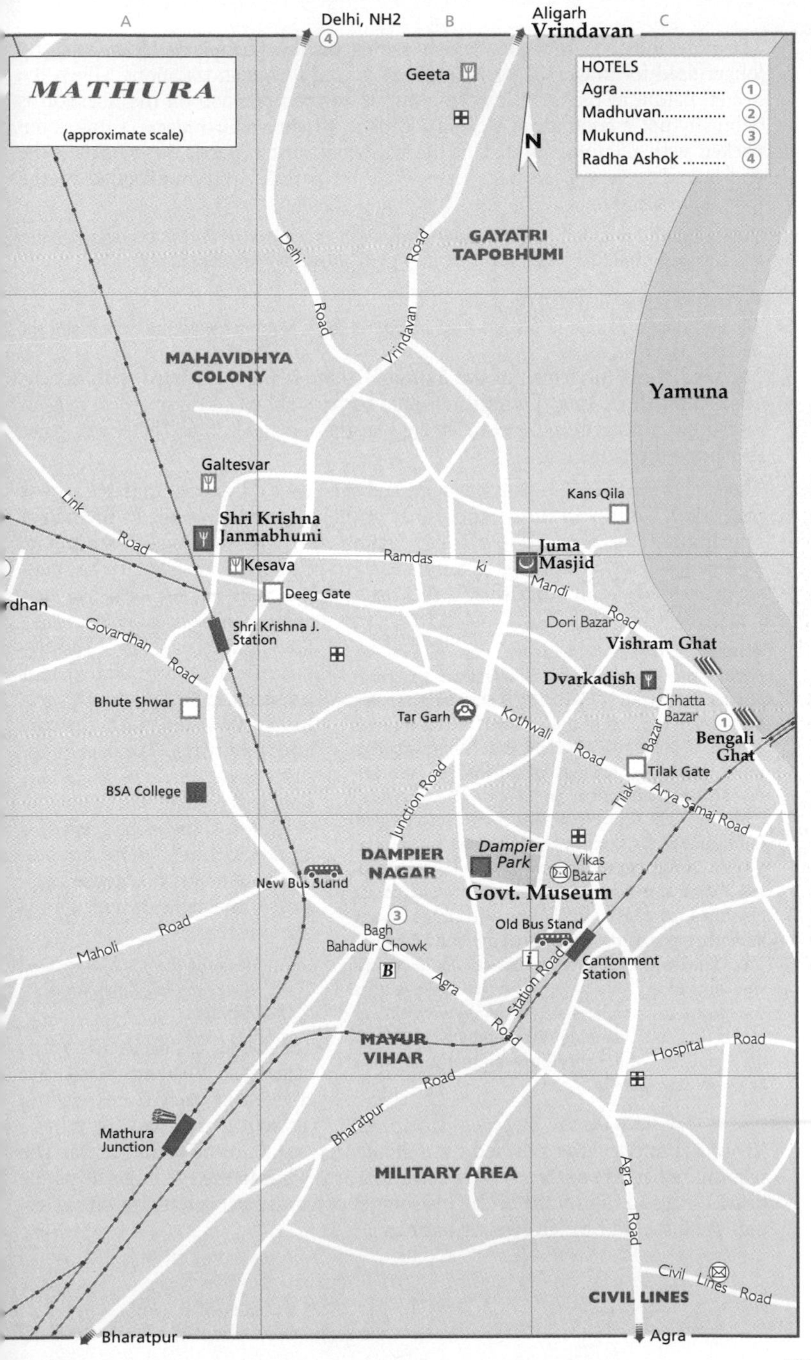
MATHURA
(approximate scale)
Delhi, NH2
Aligarh
Vrindavan
HOTELS
Agra ①
Madhuvan ②
Mukund ③
Radha Ashok ④
Geeta
GAYATRI TAPOBHUMI
Delhi Road
Vrindavan Road
MAHAVIDHYA COLONY
Yamuna
Galtesvar
Kans Qila
Link Road
Shri Krishna Janmabhumi
Juma Masjid
Ramdas ki Mandi Road
Kesava
Deeg Gate
Govardhan Road
Shri Krishna J. Station
Dori Bazar
Vishram Ghat
Dvarkadish
Chhatta Bazar
Bhute Shwar
Tar Garh
Kothwali Road
Bengali Ghat
Tilak Gate
Tilak Bazar
Arya Samaj Road
BSA College
Junction Road
DAMPIER NAGAR
Dampier Park
Vikas Bazar
Govt. Museum
New Bus Stand
Old Bus Stand
Bagh Bahadur Chowk
Cantonment Station
Maholi Road
Agra Road
Station Road
MAYUR VIHAR
Hospital Road
Bharatpur Road
Mathura Junction
MILITARY AREA
Agra Road
Civil Lines Road
CIVIL LINES
Bharatpur
Agra

The red sandstone **mosque,** which stands on the birthplace of Krishna (no longer used for prayer) is for Hindus, an affront to Indian traditions. Given the heated nature of the issue, carrying out an impromptu poll on the question is definitely not a good idea. A gallery leads to **Krishna's birthplace**, a tiny room packed with pilgrims, located in the basement, just beneath the mosque. The god is said to have been born here while his parents were imprisoned by the king-*asura* Kamsa.

On leaving the complex, take the road towards the town centre. At the crossroads, turn left, then take the first right, towards the "ghat" area on the Yamuna.

Around the Yamuna (C3)

The best time to visit is in the morning or after 4pm, when the temples are open and the streets come alive.

The road along the banks of the Yamuna *(closed to traffic)* is lined with dozens of souvenir shops mixed with traditional barber's shops and tiny grocery shops selling everything from soap or incense to the inevitable *paan* (betel nut paste that turns the gums red).

The 17C **Juma Masjid**, repainted green and surrounded by white minarets, is not particularly worthy of note. Stop rather at the **vegetable market** in the neighbouring square, then follow the pilgrims on their way to the **temple of Dvarkadish** (or Dvarkanatha), which dates from 1814 and is devoted to the "master of Dvarka", or, in other words, to Krishna. *(Open in the mornings and after 4pm. Shoes must be removed and photos are not allowed.)* The brightly-coloured façade and doors presage the flashy interior, profusely adorned with mirrors and paintings. *Darshan* takes place eight times a day *(times change depending on the month)*. Krishna's statue is then revealed to the faithful, whose spontaneous outburst of intense pleasure at the sight of their god is very moving.

Continue along the road for around 100m, then turn left down an alley to the Yamuna.

The banks of the sacred river, called the **Vishram Ghat**, are covered in *ghats* (steps leading down to the water) where Krishna is said to have purified himself after having slain the *asura* Kamsa. The pilgrims come here in the early morning to wash, while in the evenings the whole district rings to the sound of the bells announcing the *arti* ceremony (fire offering) in all the little neighbouring shrines.

Bhakti or the path to love

Among the various paths to salvation, the most popular is "bhakti" ("devotion"). It developed primarily with the cult of the young Krishna and was spread, around the 12C, by the "Bhagavata Purana". Based on feelings of an intense and unconditional affection for God, the devotee ("bhakta") chooses his or her own personal god, for example, Krishna, with whom he or she has a relationship based on mutual love. The devotee might see himself the friend of the young cowherd, as the lover of the attractive young flute player or as the mother of the child Krishna. The "bhakta's" desire to be constantly in the divine presence leads him or her to believe that they alone can see Krishna or dance with him, as in the "Ras Lila", dancing rings led by Krishna and his "gopi", in which there are as many Krishnas as there are "gopi".

Krishna and the gopis, Jaipur school of miniature painting

Around Mathura

Vrindavan★ (towards B1)

15km north of Mathura. Allow 2hr. The visit should ideally be planned to coincide with the opening times of the temples (around 5am-11am and 4.30pm-8pm).

Should the hubbub of Mathura prove too much, head out towards Vrindavan, "the basil forest", which was the scene of the young Krishna's exploits. Over the centuries, large numbers of hermits and Vishnuist thinkers withdrew here and temples and *ghats* were built (the Yamuna, whose course has altered, used to run through the area). Nowadays, this little village-like centre has several hundred temples and visitors are likely to meet more cows than humans in its peaceful bazaar. Pay no heed to Indians who may yell a somewhat jovial "Hare Krishna" in your direction. Most of the foreigners who venture this far claim to be adepts of some Hindu teaching or other.

Destroyed by Sultan Sikandar Lodi, in the 15C, the **temple of Govind Dev** *(on the left when going up the main street, to the northeast of the town)* was rebuilt in 1590 by the maharaja of Amber in an Indo-Moslem style. At that time it had seven storeys, but the upper four were destroyed the following century by Aurangzeb. Forewarned of the emperor's intended iconoclastic rampage, Maharaja Jai Singh II had the shrine's main statue of Govind Dev ("the cowherd god") transferred to his home town of Jaipur. The temple is no longer used although the object of much attention by the faithful.

The astonishing **temple of Rangaji** *(non-Hindus are not allowed inside)* is just opposite. It was built in 1851 in a most eclectic style, and priests from southern India come here to officiate.

The temple of Krishna Balaram *(some 2km from the above temples, to the southwest of the town, take a rickshaw.)* is the Indian headquarters of **ISKCON (International Society for Krishna Consciousness)**, also known as the "Hare Krishna Sect". Set in a park, it comprises offices, a guesthouse for pilgrims and a white marble **mausoleum** *(at the entrance to the complex)*, erected in honour of the founder of ISKCON, who died in 1977. The site teems with the pale skins and shaven heads of pilgrims who dance about and beat their drums and tambourines in celebration of Krishna in what feels very like a carnival atmosphere. It is unlikely that any Indian, unfamiliar with Western culture, would have the slightest idea of what kind of spiritual path is being followed by these "new Hindus" converted to Krishna.

Making the most of Mathura

GETTING THERE

By train – Mathura has three stations and the main one, ***Mathura Junction Railway Station***, lies in an outlying part of the town, some 4km from the Yamuna (A5), ☎ (0565) 40 58 30. Computerised reservations desk, 8am-8pm, Sunday 8am-2pm. Many trains run daily to Delhi: around ten "super-fast" (2hr30min) and several express trains (3hr), but the fastest is the "Radjhani" (2hr) which leaves every morning except Wednesday. All the trains arrive at New Delhi and some continue on to Nizamuddin (20min). Some twenty daily departures for Agra (1hr), 3 daily trains to Bharatpur (30min), Sawai Madhopur (3hr) and Kota (4hr30min), however for the latter two destinations, the most practical option is the morning "superfast", the "Golden Temple Mail". The "Marudhar Express" leaves daily, early in the morning for Alwar (2hr30min), Jaipur (5hr30min) and Jodhpur (11hr30min).

By bus – *New Bus Stand*, Agra Rd (B4). Timetables are not posted up and obtaining information is difficult. There are departures every hour to Delhi (it is best to take the train), as well as for Jaipur (4hr30min), Deeg (1hr) and Govardhan (25km to the west, on the road to Deeg, one bus every hour, 1hr journey).
Buses for the towns in Uttar Pradesh leave from the ***Old Bus Stand***, off Station Rd, about 1.5km from the Yamuna (C4). Access is via a little lane lined with wooden huts. Departures for Agra every 30min (2hr).

By car – Road improvements are underway between Mathura and Agra on the N.H.2, considerably slowing down traffic for the moment.

Getting about

The only pleasant place to walk about is along the banks of the Yamuna. Elsewhere, take a rickshaw, a "tempo" (group taxi) or a "tonga" (horse-drawn carriage).

By rickshaw – A trip from the station to the town centre by auto-rickshaw should cost around 25Rs and 15Rs by cycle-rickshaw.

Address book

Tourist Offices – *Uttar Pradesh Tourism*, Old Bus Stand (C4), ☎ (0565) 40 53 51. 10am-5pm; closed Saturday. Of very little practical use.

Banks/Money – *State Bank of India*, Bagh Bahadur Chowk, Station Rd (B4). Exchange cash (dollars and pounds sterling) and travellers' cheques (dollars only).

Post Office/Telephone – *GPO*, Civil Lines Rd, 4km from the centre (C5). 10am-4pm, Saturday 10am-3pm; closed Sundays. ***City Post Office***, Vikas Bazaar, 1st floor (C4). 10am-4pm, closed Sundays.

Health – *Maheshwari Hospital*, Masani Bypass, Delhi Rd. Near the Radha Ashok Hotel, on leaving Mathura (towards B1). Private clinic.

Safety – *Police*, ☎ (0565) 40 59 79. ***Fire brigade***, ☎ (0565) 40 79 79.

Where to stay

From US$7-15

Agra Hotel, Bengali Ghat, ☎ (0565) 40 33 18 – 14rm. Cooler. 3rm without bath. A traditional pilgrim inn on the banks of the Yamuna. The rooms are rather basic but not too unpleasant when overlooking the river. Residents can order-in "pure veg" meals. Radiator available in winter.

From US$15-30

Mukund Palace Hotel, Junction Rd, ☎ (0565) 41 03 16 and 41 03 26 – 29rm. 13rm. with cooler. Located in the heart of a very busy traffic area, this modern version of a pilgrim hostel has spacious communal areas covered in marble, reminiscent of a railway station, but otherwise lacks any decoration and the finishings are awful.

Madhuvan Hotel, Goverdhan Rd, Krishna Nagar, 4km from the Yamuna, ☎ (0565) 42 00 58 and 42 00 64, Fax (0565) 40 43 07 and 42 06 84 – 29rm. 10rm with cooler. An ill-kept establishment with poor quality furniture and sloppy service. It is nonetheless one of Mathura's best addresses. Also has more expensive suites.

From US$40-70

Radha Ashok Hotel (Best Western), Masani-Bypass Rd, ☎ and Fax (0565) 40 55 57 and 40 95 57 – 21rm. On the northbound exit of Mathura, in the countryside, a recent hotel with full modern facilities and spacious, airy rooms which is undoubtedly one of the few pleasant places to stay in town. Prices are however quite expensive and the walls are already dirty. Four "deluxe" rooms.

• At Vrindavan

15km to the north-east, on the road to Aligarh. Those not afraid of 'roughing' it could try one of the many "Dharmshala" (pilgrim hostels) in town, particularly on Mahatma Gandhi Rd.

Making the most of Mathura

Under US$7

Dhanuka Ashram (Durga Prasad Dhanuka Charitable Trust), Parikrama Rd, Raman Reti, 2nd lane on the left after the temple of Krishna Balaram, ☎ (0565) 44 30 18 and 44 29 25 – 31rm. Cooler. Peaceful, friendly atmosphere and sunny garden. The rooms are relatively clean and have hot running water. There is however no heating available in winter.

Shri Krishna Balaram Guest House (International Society for Krishna Consciousness), Bhaktivedanta Swami Rd, Raman Reti, in the lane alongside the temple of Krishna Balaram, ☎ (0565) 44 25 91/92, Fax (0565) 44 25 74, vrindavan@com.bbt.se – 44rm. A den for Westerners in search of spirituality. The corridors and rooms are decorated with garish paintings of Krishna and his beloved, Radha. Quiet, light and impeccably clean, what more could one ask? Hot water, but no heating in winter. The only drawback is the gloomy and somewhat unhygienic restaurant. Book at least two weeks ahead.

Where to eat

From US$3-4

Radha Ashok Hotel, Masani-Bypass Rd.. CC 6.15am-10.30pm. Varied and non-vegetarian cuisine – a rare occurrence in a pilgrim city. Clean and airy. A pleasant surprise!

Other things to do

Excursions – Excursions can be taken to ***Vrindavan***. In a "tempo" (group taxi): departures to the north of the Shri Krishna Janmabhum crossroads. By bus: a dozen buses leave every day from the Old Bus Stand, between 4.30 and 8.30am and from 4.30 to 7.30pm (in time for the "puja").

Holidays and festivals

At Barsana, Radha's native village, the festival of ***Holi*** (end of January-early February) is a particularly special day because women are allowed to take their revenge on men and for 24hr can beat men as often as they like with stout sticks.

Krishna Janmashtami, the festival which celebrates Krishna's birth, is held on the 8th and 9th days of August-September, and is a particularly festive occasion at the Janmabhumi temple at Vrindavan.

Diwali, the Vishram Ghat is the scene of intense emotion, when, as night falls, everyone entrusts his or her little oil lamp to the Yamuna.

Kamsa ka Mela, in October-November, celebrates Krishna's victory over the demon asura, Kamsa. A "Ramp Lila", theatrical production relating Krishna's exploits, is performed.

Shopping

Everyday necessities can be purchased from Tilak Bazaar (C3-4) and Vikas Bazaar (C4), which is a motley concrete construction of shops and offices on two storeys. In Chhatta Bazaar and alongside the ghats, you can buy religious souvenirs devoted to the cult of Krishna.

Pietra dura at the Taj Mahal, Agra

Exploring Rajasthan

P Ward/ANA

Camel fair
at Pushkar

S. Held

The Jal Mahal between Jaipur and Amber

The East and the North

The variety of the landscapes of this part of Rajasthan make it the least homogeneous region. To the southeast lies a plain which links Agra to Jaipur, while further north, in Mewat, the ancient Aravalli Range weaves a dense network of hills and valleys. This steppe region is the most rural, particularly around the Sariska tiger reserve: the fields are interspersed with somewhat stunted forests which turn bright green between June and September. In Dhundhar the Aravalli are more akin to rocky outcrops, sometimes just little mounds, forlornly standing as if forgotten in an otherwise completely arid landscape. The region's two sacred cities – Moslem Ajmer and Hindu Pushkar – draw a boundary with the desert lands. The sandy Shekhawati steppe lands stretch northwards. Here, the rich merchants' residences are decorated with frescoes, each vying for pride of place, providing the area with a density of decorated houses unique in India, perhaps in the world.

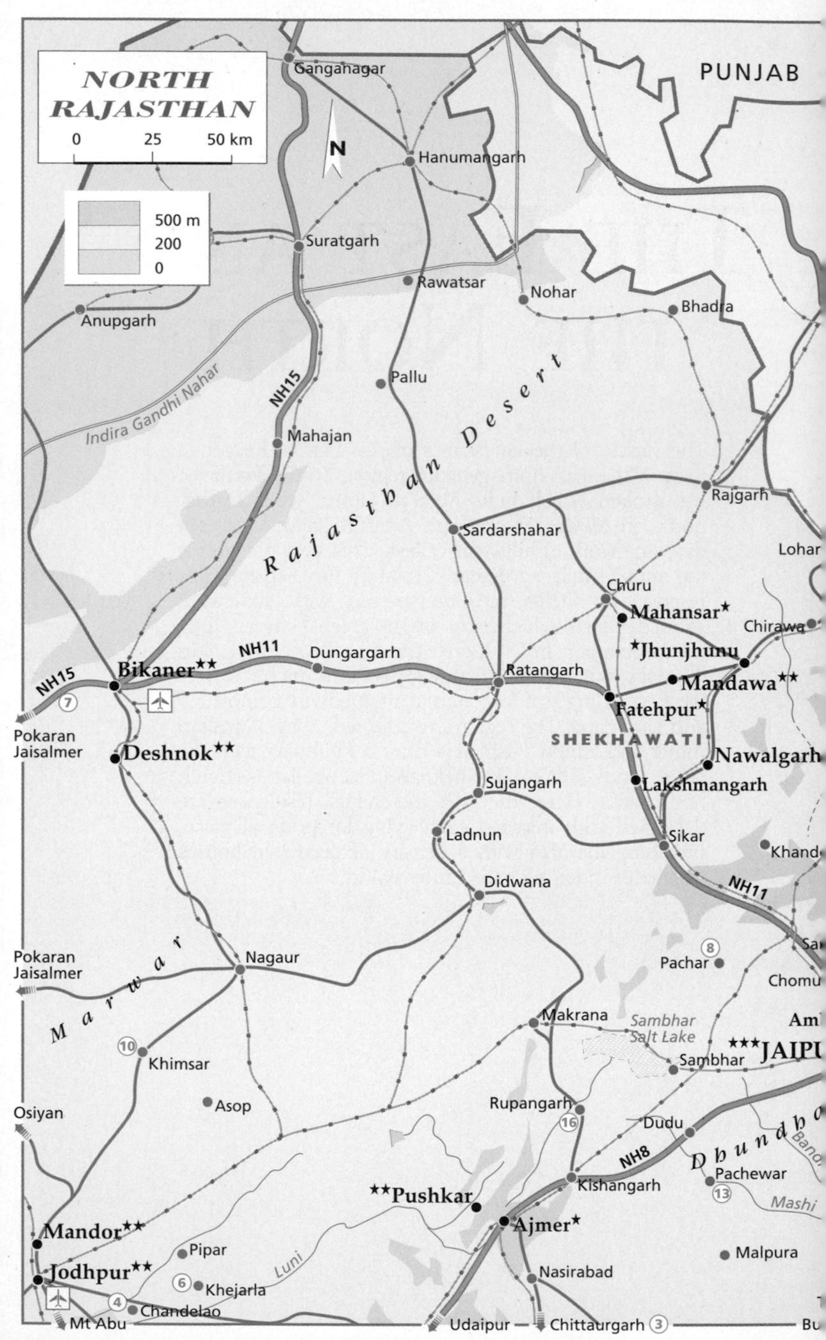
NORTH RAJASTHAN
0
25
50 km
N
500 m
200
0
PUNJAB
Ganganagar
Hanumangarh
Suratgarh
Rawatsar
Nohar
Bhadra
Anupgarh
Indira Gandhi Nahar
NH15
Pallu
Mahajan
Rajasthan Desert
Rajgarh
Sardarshahar
Lohar
Churu
Mahansar
Chirawa
Jhunjhunu
NH11
Dungargarh
Bikaner
Ratangarh
Mandawa
NH15
Fatehpur
Pokaran
Jaisalmer
SHEKHAWATI
Deshnok
Nawalgarh
Lakshmangarh
Sujangarh
Ladnun
Sikar
NH11
Didwana
Pachar
Pokaran
Jaisalmer
Nagaur
Marwar
Chomu
Makrana
Sambhar Salt Lake
Khimsar
Sambhar
Asop
Osiyan
Rupangarh
Dudu
NH8
Dhundh
Pachewar
Kishangarh
Pushkar
Mashi
Ajmer
Mandor
Pipar
Malpura
Luni
Jodhpur
Nasirabad
Khejarla
Chandelao
Mt Abu
Udaipur
Chittaurgarh

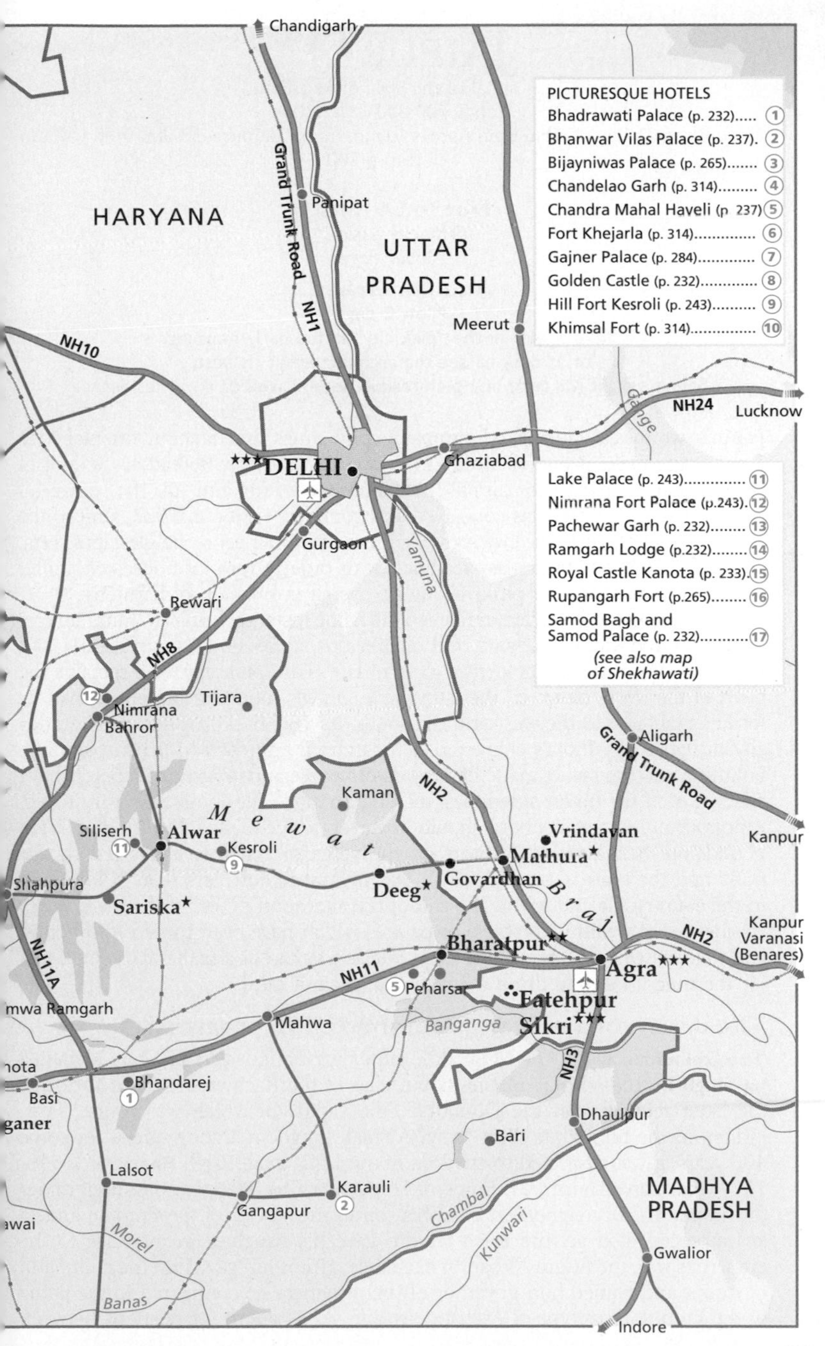

PICTURESQUE HOTELS
Bhadrawati Palace (p. 232)..... 1
Bhanwar Vilas Palace (p. 237). 2
Bijayniwas Palace (p. 265)....... 3
Chandelao Garh (p. 314)......... 4
Chandra Mahal Haveli (p. 237) 5
Fort Khejarla (p. 314).............. 6
Gajner Palace (p. 284)............. 7
Golden Castle (p. 232)............. 8
Hill Fort Kesroli (p. 243).......... 9
Khimsal Fort (p. 314)............... 10
Lake Palace (p. 243).............. 11
Nimrana Fort Palace (p.243). 12
Pachewar Garh (p. 232)........ 13
Ramgarh Lodge (p.232)........ 14
Royal Castle Kanota (p. 233). 15
Rupangarh Fort (p.265)........ 16
Samod Bagh and Samod Palace (p. 232)........... 17
(see also map of Shekhawati)
Chandigarh
HARYANA
UTTAR PRADESH
MADHYA PRADESH
Grand Trunk Road
NH1
NH10
NH24
NH8
NH2
NH11
NH11A
NH3
Panipat
Meerut
Lucknow
Ganga
Ghaziabad
DELHI
Gurgaon
Yamuna
Rewari
Tijara
Nimrana
Bahror
Aligarh
Kaman
Mewat
Siliserh
Alwar
Kesroli
Vrindavan
Mathura
Kanpur
Govardhan
Deeg
Shahpura
Sariska
Braj
Bharatpur
Agra
Kanpur Varanasi (Benares)
Peharsar
Fatehpur Sikri
Mahwa
Banganga
Bhandarej
Basi
Dhaulpur
Bari
Lalsot
Karauli
Gangapur
Chambal
Kunwari
Morel
Banas
Gwalior
Indore

JAIPUR★★★

Capital of the State of Rajasthan
Pop 1 700 000– Alt 430m
260km from Delhi – 235km from Agra – 405km from Udaipur – 337km from Jodhpur
See map p 200

Not to be missed

The city palace.
Amber Fort.

And remember...

Allow 2 days.
Take a walk in the "pink city" in the early morning or at dusk to see the architecture at its best.
Spend a night (or two) in a picturesque hotel: haveli or royal residence.

Jaipur's whimsical crenellated ramparts, pink hues and fanciful oriental-style architecture make it one of India's most appealing towns. Spread at the foot of the Aravalli Range, the capital of **Dhundhar**, kingdom of the powerful **Kachwahas** maharajas, was conceived as a complete entity, in 1727, almost like a giant chequerboard. The city is divided into seven perfect rectangles; its streets, all intersecting at right angles, are lined with orderly rows of houses of similar style and in all shades of pink, giving an overall impression of harmony.
A city of prodigiously skilled craftsmen, its name instantly brings to mind images of palaces and vibrant bazaars, full of precious stones and colourful saris, but Jaipur has lost much of its former glory of late. The "pink city" still remains the heart of the town, although the latter now sprawls much further afield than its former ramparts, to the west and the south. Its 18C backdrop has been gradually disfigured by India's characteristic anarchical approach to urban planning. Pollution and the racket made by crowds of people and swarms of scooters have affected even the tiniest side lanes, making a visit to the "pink city" very tiring. An opportunity to walk about should however not be missed, but the rush hour periods are best avoided. Visitors on the verge of collapse, exhausted by the noise and the crowds, should take a taxi to Amber Fort, less than 10km away in the countryside and spend the end of the afternoon in one of the many *haveli* (residences of wealthy notables) or palaces which have been turned into hotels, and imagine what life must have been like as a sultan or a maharaja, even if just for the time it takes to drink a cup of tea or eat a meal.

The dream of a maharaja committed to progress

The Dhundhar ally of the Mughals – Jaipur was founded in 1727 by Maharaja **Jai Singh II** (1699-1743) of the Rajput clan of the Kachwahas. From the 12C, the latter reigned over the Dhundhar, the capital of which was Amber Fort, hidden in the hills some 8km away. A small kingdom among others for some 400 years, it was projected to stardom in the 16C, when Rajah **Bhar Mal** (1548-1574) made an alliance with Emperor Humayun: Bhar Mal placed himself under the emperor's sovereignty, enrolled his son in the service of the Empire, and in an unprecedented gesture for a Hindu, gave his daughter in marriage to the emperor's son, the future Akbar. In exchange, Humayun gave him the command of troops and named him governor of the provinces he conquered in the name of the Empire. This type of exchange was to set a pattern for relations between the Great Mughals and the Kachwahas and was soon imitated by other Rajput sovereigns. From the point of the Mughals, this alliance with Amber was to their advantage, because of its strategic position on the road between Delhi and Ajmer, an important site of pilgrimage for Moslems and capital of a Mughal province. The might of Dhundhar reached its apogee under **Man Singh I** (1589-1614) and **Jai Singh I** (1621-1667), both of whom were outstanding warriors who won decisive victories for their Mughal allies.

A new capital – Jai Singh II's reign marked another pinnacle in the power of the Kachwahas. This sovereign was not only an excellent soldier and a brilliant statesman, he was also a scholar with an insatiable intellectual curiosity and an eminent astronomer who was behind the construction of no less than five revolutionary observatories. He was above all the visionary who gave Dhundhar its new capital: Jaipur.

On the death of Emperor Aurangzeb (1707), Jai Singh II seized his chance and unified the Rajput kingdoms in a defensive alliance in order to free them from their wavering Mughal sovereigns. Allied with the Sisodias of Udaipur (traditional enemies) and the Rathores of Jodhpur, he victoriously stood up to the Mughals with whom a peace treaty was signed in 1710. The city of Amber, wedged in a rocky mountain pass, had become too small for such a powerful kingdom. Jai Singh II thus decided in 1727 to build a new capital in the plain below, a capital which would be the perfect city and which he named "city of Jai", but also "city of victory". He entrusted the design to the Bengali architect-priest, **Vidyadhar Bhattacharya**, who designed a town laid out in perfect rectangles, according to the precepts of the *vastu vidya*, an ancient esoteric architectural treatise. Attracted by the exceptional peace that Dhundhar enjoyed, merchants, tradesmen, jewellers and craftsmen all flocked to the new city, where many Jains and the local nobility built impressive *haveli*.

Pink for the British – Up until the early 19C, Dhundhar remained a haven of safety and prosperity, while the Sikhs continued to paralyse trade routes through the Punjab and the incursions of the Jats and the Marathas weakened the other Rajput states, constantly riven by quarrels of succession. However, in 1818, following in the steps of the other Rajputana sovereigns, the Kachwahas also signed a treaty of alliance with the British, guaranteeing them the safety of their borders in exchange for a partial loss of independence. A Resident was installed in Jaipur and the sovereigns, taking advantage of the "Pax Britannica", launched a vast programme of public building works designed to modernise the city. In 1876, Maharaja Ram Singh II (1835-1880) had the whole city repainted in an identical shade of pink in honour of the visit of the Prince of Wales (future Edward VII). This tradition remains today: the local authorities regularly ensure that the old city is repainted, always in the same shade.

Sawai Jai Singh II

Tradition relates that when Jai Singh II, then aged 11, came to pay tribute to the Great Mughal Aurangzeb, the latter suddenly grasped the young boy's hands and asked him what good his sword was now that his hands were bound. The lad diplomatically answered: "When a bridegroom takes his future wife's hand, he promises to protect her during his life. Now that the Emperor has deemed me worthy of holding my hand, he also will protect me." Impressed by his presence of mind, Aurangzeb softened and conferred on him the hereditary title of "Sawai" ('one and a quarter') in recognition of his intellectual superiority over the other rajas.

JAIPUR
0
300
600 m
N
NH11
Sikar,
Bikaner
Amanishah Nala
Nahargarh Fo
Water Works Road
Tulsi Road
Nirwan Road
BANI PARK
Sawai Jai Singh Highway
Durga Road
Kabir Marg
Shiv Road
Kanti Chanara
Chand Pol
Bagroowalon ka Rasta
Chand
Kalyanji ka Rasta
Station Road
Geetanjali
Vanasthali Street
Chandra Road
Chaitanya
Jaipur Tower
Ganpati Plaza and Swaad
M. I. Road
Sansar
Gopinath Road
Indira Ba
Jaipur
Palace Rd
Gopal Bari
Chanakya
Mirza Ismail Road
Handi
Panch Batti Circle
(M.I. Rd
Natraj
Nirc
Khatipura Road
Ajmer Road
Raj Mandir Cinema
Ashok Road
India
Jacob Road
Malviya Road
CIVIL LINES
Sardar Patel Road
ASHOK NAGAR
Bhagwan Das Road
Mahavir Road
NH8
Ajmer
Udaipur
Prithviraj Road
Sarojini Road
Vivekananda
Ganda Nala
Statue Circle
Hospital Road
Raj Bhawan Road
Pratap Singh Road
Jamnalal Bajaj Road
Birla Planetarium and Museum
Sawai
Tilak Road
Raj Mahal
Hawa Road
Bais Godam
Bhawani Singh Road
Golf Course and Polo Ground
Sawai Ram Singh
NH12, Tonk
Sanganer
Bundi

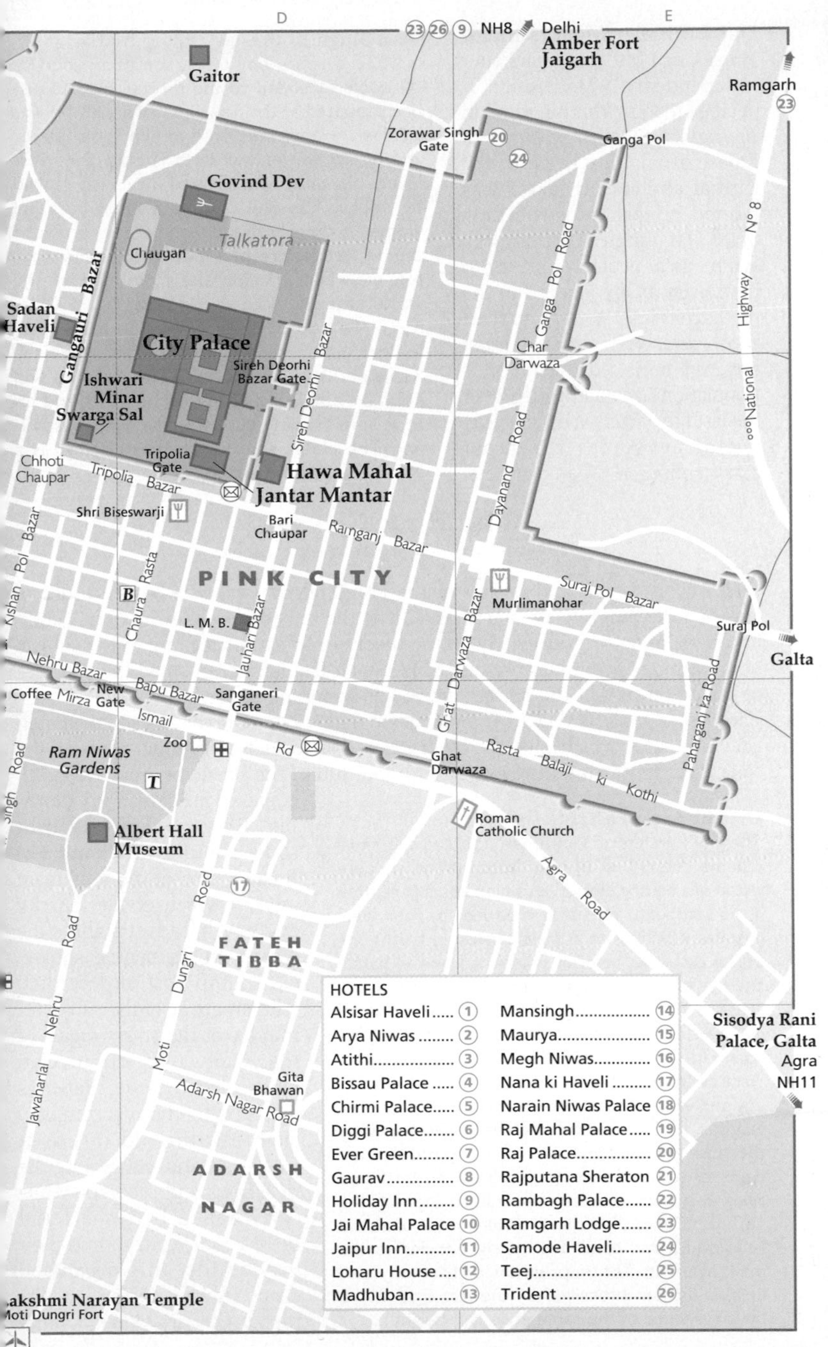

HOTELS

Alsisar Haveli	1	Mansingh	14
Arya Niwas	2	Maurya	15
Atithi	3	Megh Niwas	16
Bissau Palace	4	Nana ki Haveli	17
Chirmi Palace	5	Narain Niwas Palace	18
Diggi Palace	6	Raj Mahal Palace	19
Ever Green	7	Raj Palace	20
Gaurav	8	Rajputana Sheraton	21
Holiday Inn	9	Rambagh Palace	22
Jai Mahal Palace	10	Ramgarh Lodge	23
Jaipur Inn	11	Samode Haveli	24
Loharu House	12	Teej	25
Madhuban	13	Trident	26

One of modern India's major cities – In 1949 (two years after Independence), Man Singh II decided to found his kingdom in the newly constituted State of Rajasthan: Jaipur became the capital and its maharaja was named governor of the new State. Jai Singh II's perfectly symmetrical geometry seems to have been totally ignored in the new districts which spread south and westwards. It must however be noted that Jaipur's population has quadrupled over the last fifty years – a difficult situation, even for the most conscientious of urban planners.

Man Singh II, the last ruling maharaja
In 1922, a young boy of 11, son of a minor local noble ascended to the throne. He had just been adopted by the previous maharaja who was childless. Handsome, an excellent polo player and jet-setter, he was both famous and well-loved. His third wife, Gayatri Devi, was ranked by "Vogue" as one of the 10 most beautiful women in the world, and together they provided the perfect picture of a modern romantic couple, entertaining celebrities from all over the world in their palace at Rambagh. In 1962, Maharani Gayatri Devi was elected to India's Parliament with a record majority that made the 'Guinness Book of Records'. The maharaja was killed on a polo field in Britain in 1970, and his sons have become business men and industrialists. The eldest son, Sawai Bhavani Singh is a Member of Parliament.

The Pink City***

Allow at least half a day to walk around.

The original layout and design of the city, created in the 1720s by order of Maharaja **Jai Singh II**, is intact today. It is the only example of modern Hindu urban planning. Unfortunately all the theoretical treatises relating to the subject have been destroyed because one of Jai Singh II's descendants had the bad idea of selling off part of the palace's library as wrapping paper.
The west entrance is via **Chand Pol*** (Moon Gate) (C2), set in the city's pink crenellated ramparts, which, like the other gates, was locked every night up until the early 20C. Its surrounding neighbourhood, full of the bustle of a market town, comes to life early every morning. Fish, poultry and fruit stalls abound in **Chand Pol Bazaar**, one of the four main arteries which divide the city and which leads straight to the palace. In the central square, each lamp-post is decorated with an image of the sun, a reminder of the solar origins of the Kachwahas Rajput clan who ruled the city. Raucous blasts on the horn accompany each rattling old bus as it weaves in and out among the rickshaws and scooters, while carts pulled by camels and horses endeavour to find their way amidst this organised chaos. Ahead, to the left, the top of **Ishwari Minar Swarga**

Urbanism and astronomy
The city's architect, Vidyadhar, adopted the ritual scheme prescribed by the "vastu vidya": it consisted of a square divided into nine equal parts (ten if the southeast extension is added) by four wide avenues which cross at right angles. In truth, one of the east-west arteries is blocked by the palace and the lines are not quite perfect in the north because of the topography and because the original plan was not fully respected by Jai Singh's successors. The nine rectangles ("mohalla") thus created, were assigned to the nine planets of Hindu astrology and were allocated to different castes or professions, the two central ones being given over to the sovereign and his palace. Even today, descendents of stone-cutters or jewellers can be found living in the same district allotted to them in the 18C. Each "mohalla" is itself divided into roads and lanes which run parallel or at right-angles to the main avenues. The impression of harmony and unity is further intensified by the fact that all the buildings were of the same style and height.

Sal* (C2), a tower built within the royal palace's compound by Maharaja **Ishwari Singh**, successor to Jai Singh II, is visible. Ishwari Singh is said to have committed suicide rather than confront the besieging Maratha army. His 21 wives threw themselves onto his funeral pyre, committing *sati* *(see p 253)*.

The City Palace*** (D1-2)

This spacious palatial complex built by Jai Singh II (first half of the 18C) contains, in addition to Rajasthan's administrative buildings, the city's main tourist sites: the Palace of the Winds, the Observatory and the Palace itself, now a museum. The compound is surrounded by an 18C wall, against which have been built a collection of boutiques, private residences and small temples.

The tour starts from Sireh Deorhi Bazaar, opposite the façade of the Palace of the Winds. Photos of the façade lit up by the sun are best taken in the early morning.

The Palace of the Winds** (Hawa Mahal) *(To go inside, go to Tripolia Bazaar and take the first door on the right. 9am-4.30pm; closed Fridays, entrance fee. Extra charge for cameras and videos. Some of the resident monkeys may accompany visitors.)* is set within the palace's vast surrounding wall, but its amazing five storey **façade***** is in fact built on the street. It consists of a honeycomb of no fewer than 61 *jharokha* – covered balconies with *jali* – which capture any passing breezes and provide a view in three directions. In fact the palace's sole *raison d'être* was to enable its occupants to see without being seen themselves, and to enjoy the spectacle of the bustling city below. The Hawa Mahal is indeed little more than a façade, a sort of gigantic latticed screen, built in 1799, to ensure that the palace's womenfolk were able to respect the strict rules of *purdah*, which required them to remain unseen by foreign eyes, whilst enjoying the spectacle of the pageant of the street in a cool, refreshing breeze. Underground passages, still in use under the reign of the last ruling maharaja, provided access between the royal *zenana* and the Palace of the Winds. A climb to the top storey enables visitors to observe the hurly-burly of the city's seething street-life, whilst enjoying the refreshing flow of air created by the intricately carved *jali* screens. The top floor reveals a superb view over the city palace, the town and its surrounding hills.

Leaving the Palace of the Winds, turn right into Tripolia Bazaar and enter the City Palace complex by the first door on the right (above is Tripolia Gate, the "triple gate", for the exclusive use of the ruler in former times. It is high enough to enable an elephant bearing a howdah to pass through. The passage leads to Chandni Chowk, the Moonlit Square, where the unusual figures of the Observatory stand with the royal palace to the rear.

The strange perfectly geometrical shapes of the **Jantar Mantar**** (astronomical observatory) *(9am-4.30pm, entrance fee. Extra charge for cameras and videos. Enquire at the entrance gate about guided visits)*, are not, as may first seem, giant abstract sculptures, but colossal astronomical instruments that Jai Singh II had built between 1728 and 1733 to refine his observations and calculations on the orbits of the planets, leading to a revision of the Hindu and Moslem calendars for astrological purposes. A few years earlier, at the emperor's request, he had built similar instruments (but fewer in number) at Delhi *(see p 136)*. A genuine scientist, the maharaja was indeed very well-versed in astronomy, having read the works of all the specialists – Hindu, Arabic, Persian, Greek and European – and as a result of his invitation to two Jesuit astronomers (one French and the other Portuguese) who lived at court.

The 17 instruments, built out of stone and covered in yellow stucco, are devoid of any decoration, which further accentuates their massive presence. Just to the left of the entrance, the **Laghu Samrat Yantra** is a small sundial used, among other things, to calculate the exact time at Jaipur *(can vary from between 10 and 41min with India's official time)*. Next to this, the **Nari Valaya Yantra** consists of two hemispherical blocks. They represent the northern and southern hemisphere and enable the time to be calculated around the globe. The gigantic neighbouring metallic disk, the **Yantra Raj**, is said to have inspired Jai Singh II to write two entire books. The central hole represents the north star, while a line drawn exactly 27° above corresponds to Jaipur's latitude. This instrument was used to calculate the position of the various constellations. Near the small sundial, the **Jai Prakash Yantra,** made up of two bowls, was invented by the maharaja to check the exactitude of the other instruments' calculations. The right-hand part of the park is covered in 12 **Rashi Valaya Yantra**, small trapezoid constructions used to measure the appearance of a sign of the zodiac on the horizon. Note the **Ram Yantra**. This astrolabe, consisting of two cylindrical structures, each with 12 columns, served to calculate the stars' exact altitude and azimuth. At the rear of the garden, the enormous graduated sundial (gnomon), the **Brihat Samrat Yantra**, was used to calculate local data thanks to the shadow projected by the 27-metre long "needle".

City Palace★★★ (Maharaja Sawai Man Singh II Museum) *(9.30am-5.30pm. Tickets on sale until 4.45pm. Allow 1hr)* is part of the palace complex which still belongs to the royal family. Only the museum section can be visited, the other areas are still used as the private residence of the current maharaja, Sawai Bhawani Singh (born 1913), former Indian ambassador.

In the centre of the first courtyard stands the marble edifice of the **Mubarak Mahal** (Welcome Palace), surrounded by the graceful columns of a loggia. Maharaja Madho Singh II (ruled from 1880 to 1922) had it built in 1899 to accommodate distinguished guests. Today it contains a collection of royal clothes. Admire the rare silk saris, the beauty of the sumptuous embroidery or the know-how of the block-printing techniques of Sanganer's craftsmen. The **robe of Madho Singh I** (ruled from 1750 to 1768) made out of Benares silk is unmistakable. Its phenomenal size is due to the maharaja's own impressive corpulence: he was over two metres tall and weighed some 200kg! The luxurious Cashmere shawls, in goats' wool *(pashmina)* or antelope wool *(shahtush)* should not be missed. According to tradition, the best shawls are so fine that they can be threaded whole through the ring of a princess. In the same room is a fine collection of **musical instruments★** used during royal concerts.

The white marble **Singh Pol** (Lion's Gate) is permanently guarded by two elephant statues and two palace servants in uniform (white trousers, white or black *achkan* depending on the season and red turban). Before walking through, go upstairs to the **Maharani's Palace** *(to the left of Sing Pol)*. A series of 18C rooms now houses one of the finest collections of Hindu and Mughal weapons in India. Amidst this mass of iron, note the delicate arabesques etched onto the steel blades or the beautiful Mughal daggers *(khanjar)*, with hilts of jade inlaid with rubies or emeralds, set in gold. Some *katar* (long bladed daggers) were also equipped with two tiny pistols. Note the small cannon *(rekhla)* from Amber, which is one of the first pieces of Rajput artillery and the ruby and emerald

The Palace of the Winds

LML
vespa
RSL
412

encrusted sabre belonging to Maharaja Ram Singh II, a gift from Queen Victoria. On the walls, photos taken and developed by Ram Singh II (1835-1880) himself provide a moving picture of life at Jaipur in the 19C.

Return to the courtyard and go through Singh Pol. The Lion's Gate leads into an enclosed second courtyard, surrounded by three storeys of galleries screened by jali. In the centre stands a pleasant flat-roofed, typically Mughal, pavilion: the **Diwan-i Khas** (private audience hall). Salmon pink hues predominate, set off by touches of white marble columns and inlays. The overall effect is a superb synthesis of 18C Rajput and Mughal styles. It is here that, every year, the maharaja takes part in a religious ritual *(puja)*, celebrated with all the prescribed pomp and ceremony, royal fly-swat carriers and elephants included. Note the Lalique crystal chandeliers hanging from the beautiful ceilings of the Diwan-i Khas, painted floral arabesques in varying shades of pink. This is where the new maharaja is anointed.

Silver vessels in the Guinness Book of Records

The Diwan-i Khas houses two silver vessels, whose vast size got them into the "Guinness Book of Records" (each can contain 8 182 litres). They are a reminder of the piety of Maharaja Madho Singh II, who had them made before a voyage to England, where he was going to attend King Edward VII's coronation in 1901. They were intended to store water from the Ganges, the only water considered pure enough to be imbibed by the maharaja. During the six months of his trip, they were regularly refilled by fresh Ganges water, shipped from India by boat. It may be noted that the maharaja refused to kneel before Edward VII.

On the left-hand side of the courtyard *(with your back to Singh Pol)*, a door leads into **Pritam Niwas Chowk**, an enchanting little courtyard with four remarkably decorated doors. The Dutch gabled doors, covered in ornate copper-worked plates, seem as if they are bathed in light by the luminous painting on the surrounding porches, illustrating peacocks with fantails. The bright colours of the bird of immortality depict dancing performances which used to take place in this courtyard, dominated by the **Chandra Mahal** (Moon Palace). The façade of this white marble palace consists of six storeys of galleries, the uppermost one of which provided a panoramic view over the whole city. The only room open to visitors is the ground-floor room, the **Chandra Mandir**, decorated with ornate Mughal motifs. It dates back to the time of Jai Singh II. The rest of the palace is still occupied by the royal family.

Go back to the Diwan-i Khas courtyard which you cross to reach the opposite wing of the Pritam Niwas Chowk. In the **Diwan-i Am** (public audience hall), the maharajas used to convene their *durbar* (assembly of nobles) and receive distinguished guests. The beauty of the space and the intricacy of its brightly-painted arabesques and floral motifs, of Mughal inspiration, make it one of the finest examples of 18C reception halls. Under crystal chandeliers are exhibited superb **howdahs** (seats for riding on the back of an elephant) and palanquins, including a silver swing. 17C **carpets** from Hera, Lahore and Agra are spread over the floor. There is a very rare series of **manuscripts** and Mughal and Rajput **miniature paintings**, including an unexpected illustration of the Holy Family (Deccan School, 1627), painted in the manner of a European work of art. Mary, with the gentle features of an Indian princess, wears a *tika* (red marriage spot on the forehead) and has jet-black hair. Note also the splendid **Razm Nameh** in Persian, made for Akbar in the 1580s, as well as a richly illustrated copy of the

Gita Govinda relating the life of Krishna, a tiny copy of the *Bhagavad Gita*, and astronomical works which belonged to Jai Singh II, some of which were written in his own hand.

On leaving the palace, turn left into the passage leading to Jaleb Chowk.

The spacious courtyard of **Jaleb Chowk**, lined with the former lodges of the palace servants, now houses the State of Rajasthan's administrative offices. The courtyard was formerly the scene of military manoeuvres and reviews, but nowadays the flurry of civil servants, all sorts of animals, automobiles and carts produce a picture more akin to bedlam than to soldierly order.

To get to Govind Dev Temple, leave Jaleb Chowk via Sireh Deorhi Gate (on the right) and turn left into Sireh Deorhi Bazaar; right at the end of the bazaar is an alley which leads to Govind Dev Temple.

Govind Dev Temple (D1) is a former hunting lodge that Jai Singh II had transformed into a temple in the 1730s, at the time of Jaipur's construction, in order to provide a home for a statue of Govinda, Krishna as a young herdsman. This holy statue was formerly venerated at Vrindavan (near Mathura), where Krishna spent his childhood *(see Mathura, p 186)*. Jai Singh II rescued it from the destructive rampage of Aurangzeb's troops and it became the protective deity of Jaipur's maharajas. From that time on, and up until 1947, the latter governed in the name of Govind Dev.
The temple comprises a simple hall, which provides access to the sacred shrine where the statue is housed. The best time to visit is during **darshan** (literally "vision") which takes place seven times a day *(the times change depending on the moon, see the timetable at the entrance to the shrine)*. The most popular visiting time is at dusk. Gathered in the hall, the worshippers await the moment when the priests draw back the curtain in front of the altar, suddenly revealing the "divine herdsman's" statue, in the company of Radha, his wife, and a cow. The crowd bursts into enthusiastic shouting and sings **bhajan** (religious hymns). The intensity of this religious devotion contrasts strongly with the somewhat mercantile atmosphere that reigns in the "Pink City".

The bazaars

A stroll through the noisy, colourful bazaars of Jaipur provides a real immersion into the city's busy trade and craft industries, renowned for its precious gems and enamel work, printed fabrics, blue pottery and marble. Jaipur's bazaars are still grouped by profession and have changed little since the 18C. Do not, however, expect a massive culture shock: the lanes and roads are all relatively wide and the chequerboard construction is almost reassuring, compared to some of the twisting maze-like meanders of other towns. What's more, the continuous hooting of scooters which invade even the narrowest lanes, ensure that strollers remain constantly on their toes, ready to leap out of the way at a moment's notice. It is quite impossible to saunter at your leisure, either because of the incessant noise or the touts and hawkers despatched by neighbouring boutiques, eager to lure you into their uninteresting stores or ready with some incredible "deal" or other. Don't less this warning deter you though! The city is a magical cave with a thousand secrets for those with the curiosity to explore it. Take a deep breath and venture into the courtyards, climb the stairs…

R. Marca

Stalls and terraces

Start out from Bari Chaupar. Most shops are open from 10am-8pm; closed Sunday.

The Palace of the Winds lies to the north of **Bari Chaupar** (D2), just next-door to Rajasthan's Legislative Assembly Hall. **Ramganj Bazaar**, the territory of the cobblers and shoe merchants, lies to the east and **Jauhari Bazaar**, to the south, is the "jewellers' market", one of Jaipur's liveliest shopping centres. Like the other avenues which dissect the "Pink City" into *mohalla* (districts), Jauhari Bazaar is 35m wide and lined with houses whose terraces are also the roofs of the street-level stalls. Most of the stalls on this street sell textile products, the jewellers having been relegated to the neighbouring streets, wedged in between the confectionery shops. The quality and purity of the work of Jaipur's goldsmiths and silversmiths are quite unparalleled. These lanes are the ideal place to become better acquainted with the jewel trade: enamel work, stone polishing and the intricate skill of the tinsmiths who make *vark* (the practically translucent silver paper used to decorate sweets and *biryani*).

Walk down Jauhari Bazaar on the right-hand side and turn into the first covered passageway, **Purohitji ka Katla**, which sells everything necessary for a Hindu marriage. Red is, of course, the domi-

Terraced houses

All the buildings which line Jaipur's wide, busy avenues (bazaars) are built according to the same design: the first floor is set slightly back compared to the ground floor, thereby creating first-floor terraces which overlook the street. Here, children fly their kites while women patiently sort lentils and pilfering monkeys attempt to dart in and out of the residences. At street-level, one stall after another provides an incessant hubbub of activity and noise.

nant colour (women are married in red), but gold is also much in evidence – used on the braids and trimmings used to decorate ceremonial costumes.

Back on Bari Chaupar, go down **Tripolia Bazaar**, the avenue devoted to cooking utensils and copper objects, until you reach **Chhoti Chaupar** (C2), which runs parallel to Bari Chaupar. On the northeastern corner are two little **Vishnuist temples** whose entrance, guarded by elephant statues, opens onto a small courtyard and hall decorated with elegant murals.

The northbound avenue, **Gangauri Bazaar**, goes through a *mohalla* which is less of a shopping area than those visited up until now. Continue on to **Saras Sadan Haveli** (C1) *(ask for the "Vidhya Vihar School")* the ground floor of which houses a school. This 19C family residence built at the time of Maharaja Ram Singh was up until recently a school for courtesans. The courtyard has been disfigured by an ugly railing, but the first floor reveals a magnificent reception room covered in rare **frescoes**** in a range of reds and golds, now a jeweller's exhibition room.

Back on Chhoti Chaupar, turn right into Chand Pol Bazaar. Further down, on the left, is **Khazanawallon ka Rasta**, the road traditionally devoted to stonemasons of the Adi Gauds community, who claim to be equivalent to the Brahmins (because their vocation is to give life to sacred images, whilst respecting strict rules). Today, Adi Gauds still live in this *mohalla*, and for the most part are still stonemasons.

The new city

Allow 3hr maximum by rickshaw.

In the 19C, Jaipur's maharajas embarked on a number of building and development projects. Ram Singh II (1835-1880) provided the city with a Department of Public Works, a postal service, gas street-lighting, colleges and institutes. As the boundaries of the old city became more and more cramped, the capital crept steadily southwards.

The **Albert Hall Museum** (C3) *(10am-4.30pm, closed Friday, entrance fee, free on Monday)* is in Ram Niwas gardens. This imposing, hybrid-style pyramidal building was designed by Colonel Jacob for Maharaja Ram Singh II who wanted to offer Jaipur a museum similar to London's Victoria and Albert Museum. The first stone was laid by the future Edward VII in 1876. Some interesting showcases on the ground floor present a selection of traditional Rajasthani costumes and a glimpse of popular arts. Upstairs however, the collections are surprisingly disparate: miniature paintings stand side by side with mineralogical samples or an Egyptian mummy…

Continue southwards down Jawaharlal Nehru Avenue. Some 2km on, the fort of Moti Dungri (property of the royal family, no visits) stands perched on a mound. At its feet is the temple of Lakshmi Narayan.

Colonel Jacob's notebooks

Colonel Sir Samuel Swinton Jacob (1841-1917) spent the majority of his career in Jaipur where he settled in 1867. He was the self-proclaimed 'pope' of Indo-Sarracenic architecture, also called "colonial", "hybrid" or "Eastern Renaissance", – a sort of neo-Indo-Moslem style all the rage at the end of the 19C. The colonel meticulously recorded several thousands of decorative shapes and motifs, both Hindu and Mughal, and his well-ordered catalogue was accepted as the authoritative work on the subject for many years. The influence of Jacob's work can be seen in the buildings designed by Lutyens in the 1900s in Delhi.

Lakshmi Narayan Temple (or Birla Mandir) (towards C4) was built in the early 20C by the Birla family, industrialists originally from Shekhawati. The white marble shrine is dedicated to Narayan (another name for Vishnu) and his consort Lakshmi, the goddess of good fortune so dear to the merchant castes. A set of striking **stained-glass** windows depict Hindu gods and the outer walls are decorated with **paintings**, illustrating, among others, Christ, Zoroaster, Moses, Socrates and Saint Anthony. A perfect example of Hindu syncretism!

Take a taxi to **Rambagh Palace*** (C4), a former hunting lodge which the pious Madho Singh II had transformed into a palace in the early 20C with the help of Colonel Jacob. The last ruling maharaja, Man Singh II, grew up here and made it his main residence in 1931, extending, modernising and redecorating it in a lavish Art Deco style. After Independence, unable to maintain his former lifestyle, he was one of India's first maharajas to turn his palace into a luxury hotel *(see "Making the most of Jaipur")*. The place still evokes some of the magical aura of its former years of luxury and entertainment, as related in Gayatri Devi's autobiography *A Princess Remembers* *(see p 118)*. The solemn, white building, whose elegance is highlighted with touches of red sandstone, stands in the heart of vast lawns which lead down to a polo field. It is at its best during the monsoon season, when the peacocks take over, strutting and preening in search of mates.

Surrounding area**

While Amber, Jaigarh and Nahargarh forts evoke the glorious past of their Kachwahas sovereigns, a trip to Galta's temples, hidden deep within an unspoiled valley, takes visitors light-years away from Jaipur's noisy, polluted thoroughfares.

Amber Fort*** (in the direction of E1)

Situated 8km to the north of Jaipur, on the road to Delhi. Take a taxi or bus (no 29 in front of the Palace of the Winds). Can be combined with a visit to Gaitor (see p 219) and to Nahargarh (see p 219).

It is a real treat to leave behind the hubbub of the capital of Rajasthan and head for the peace and quiet of the outlying hills. The road borders Lake Man Sagar, which is being invaded by water hyacinths. The now practically abandoned **Jal Mahal** palace *(closed to the public)*, built in the 18C, almost seems to float in its centre. In the 19C, it was used by the maharajas for duck shoots. Further on *(on the right)*, at the end of the lake is **Kanak Vrindavan** (early 18C), a pleasant Mughal garden restored by the Birla family in the 1990s. The road winds up into a narrow gorge. Once past a wall, the road dips down into the beautiful wilderness of an enclosed valley. The great mass of the fortified Amber palace rises abruptly from the hilly slopes. The palace is overlooked by Jaigarh fort and encircled by a protective ring of fortified hills. At its feet lies a small artificial lake, Maota Sagar.

The capital of the Kachwahas – This site, strategically placed between Delhi and Rajasthan, originally belonged to the aboriginal tribe of **Meenas**, until in the 12C, the Kachhvahas prince, **Duleh Rai**, seized it, making it the capital of the emerging kingdom of Dhundhar. The origins of the name Amber are unknown: possibly in honour of the goddess Amba Mata (Durga) worshipped by the Meenas; or of Ambikeshvara (Shiva), the protective divinity of the Kachwahas. The present fortress dates back to the reign of **Man Singh I** (late 16C) and was enlarged by **Jai Singh I** (1621-1667) in the 17C. Jai Singh II lived here for a while before abandoning it, around 1773, in favour of Jaipur which he had just founded in the plain. Amber lost its status of capital but retained its strategic importance. The fort is now the property of the State of Rajasthan.

Decorative panel in the palace

Tour of the fort – *(9am-4pm, entrance fee. Extra charge for cameras and videos. Allow at least an hour.)* A steep ramp leads up to the fort – 10min on foot or on elephant-back. This is a popular spot; there are plenty of local visitors in their Sunday best, noisily enjoying their elephant ride, as well as foreign tourists sporting shorts and sun hats, whom "professional" photographers are eager to immortalise for just a few rupees.

Just after the beginning of the ramp, a path leads off to the left to an enchanting Mughal garden on an island; this is **Dilaram Bagh**, created in 1588 in order to welcome Emperor Akbar in a manner worthy of this illustrious figure. Three terraces of geometrically structured clumps of flowers and bushes each form a star-shape, through which runs a central channel leading into the lake. The ramp passes under several gates before reaching the palace. Note the military sobriety of the façades; they are bare, smooth and windowless, enlivened by just a few lookout towers. The last gate **Suraj Pol** (the sun gate), opens onto **Jaleb Chowk**, an esplanade surrounded by buildings, formerly stables, accommodation for bodyguards and servants, now tourist shops and a cafeteria.

The staircase at the rear, on the left, leads to the Temple of Kali (the most awesome aspect of Devi), which is, even today, the private shrine of the maharaja. Up until the mid-20C, a kid-goat was sacrificed daily to the image of Kali, brought back from Jessore (in Bengal) by Man Singh I.

The next-door staircase leads to a monumental gate *(where tickets are sold)*. It opens onto a terrace over which towers the **Diwan-i Am** (public audience hall), a flat-roofed, Mughal-style pavilion (early 17C) with quite wonderful marble columns. The monumental 1639 **Ganesh Pol** is a remarkable balance of strength and harmony. The façade is entirely covered in paintings (1727) and inlaid mirrors, whose motifs combine purely Mughal-inspired ornamentation with the image of Ganesha, seated on a throne in the centre of the *iwan* beneath a ribbed vault.

Take the sloping (to make it easier for horses to climb) corridor, the walls of which are coated in a soft, cool substance. This is *arayish*, a mixture of powdered marble and yoghurt, among other ingredients, used to coat walls and sometimes floors *(see p 41)*. The corridor leads to the rulers' **private apartments**, for the most part fitted out under Jai Singh I. The *mardana* (men's quarters) is set around a small garden. In the **Sukh Mahal** (Pleasure Palace) *(on the right)*, note the ingenious air-cooling device. Scented water, from a reservoir on the roof, fell in a refreshing waterfall into a small sloping channel which kept the *jali*, designed to capture and direct any breezes, permanently moist and cool. The water was then directed through the room, cooling it down even further, before reaching the channels in the garden. On the right wall, a sandalwood door still has some of its former ivory inlay, but the passing of time has partially eroded such lavish ornamentation.

Cross over to the opposite side of the garden and pause for a moment to admire the sophisticated splendour of the **Jai Mandir**, a group of three chambers surrounded by a veranda. The omnipresent glittering reflections of the tiny inlaid convex mirrors dazzle and amaze onlookers. The small *Sheesh Mahal* (Mirror Palace) is entirely studded with these little mirrors, whose flickering reflections reproduce the constellated sky. In the centre of the *Diwan-i Khas* (private audience hall) and on the veranda, the mirrors are combined with multi-coloured glass paste mosaics, with painted arabesques and with cut-out plaster shapes filled in with coloured glass. Such decorative techniques feature the full iconographical register which the Mughals imported from Iran: flasks and vases, fruit bowls and urns with lids, cypress trees and flowers. Note the superb white marble plinths, with their carved bouquets and their black stone inlay.

Spirits and lights at play

The use of small mirrors, "sheesh" is very common throughout the whole of north-western India, where they are arranged in mosaics, set in gold, sometimes combined with semi-precious stones. However such intricate work was not just for decorative purposes, because the reflections produced by the flickering candlelight, also created amazing light and dark effects. In addition, it was claimed that they kept away evil spirits, thereby explaining why "sheesh" embroidery can be found on women's clothes in western Rajasthan and in Gujarat. Not only does it embellish even the simplest clothes, it also guarantees the virtue of daughters and wives.

The southern part of the garden is blocked by a forbidding-looking wall, riddled with dark corridors. Take one of these to reach the upper gallery. The **Jas Mahal** reveals the same sophisticated and refined decorative style visible in the Jai Mandir, just underneath. The chamber overlooking the valley provides some spectacular views of Lake Maota and Dilaram gardens. Cross over to the pavilion which runs the full length of the upper storey of the Ganesh Pol. The exceptionally beautiful hexagonal motifs of the carved *jali* enabled the ladies of the court to enjoy the receptions taking place in the Diwan-i Am, without running the risk of being seen.

Go back down to the ground floor to reach the women's quarters (access via a small door set in the middle of the southern wall).

After the luxury of the royal apartments, the **zenana** (women s quarters) seems quite gloomy in comparison, if not downright sinister. A short walk around the dark corridors and tiny chambers, most of them devoid of windows or any decoration, generally suffices to impress upon visitors how morose the lives of many wives and concubines must have been. A room *(on the ground floor, to the right of the entrance)* still has a few paintings, now sorely damaged. Each wife would have had her own quarters, consisting of an independent unit, with a small courtyard and hammam. Nonetheless, the overall impression, further exacerbated by the high walls surrounding the complex's large inner courtyard, is more reminiscent of a prison than a fairytale palace fit for a royal princess.

Back in the Jaleb Chowk, enter the cafeteria *(to the left)* and walk through to the terrace from where there is a good view over the fortifications and the nearby hill, on which Jaigarh fort stands, with the old town of Amber down below.

Jaigarh Fort*

Leave Amber Fort by Suraj Pol Gate and walk down the ramp around 100m. At the first fork, continue straight on. A path of about 1km leads to Jaigarh (30min walk). If travelling by car, the visit to Jaigarh can be combined with that of Ramgarh, in which case drive back towards Jaipur. Opposite Lake Sagar, take the small road (on the right) which leads to Jaigarh and Ramgarh. Around 1.5km further on, take the right-hand fork towards Jaigarh (1km).

A modern fort – Not as interesting as Amber, Jaigarh fort is nonetheless spectacular evidence of the Kachwahas Rajputs' military might. Its foundations date back to the 12C, when the Kachwahas captured the hills from the Meenas, appointing the latter, guardians of their treasure. When Man Singh I built Amber Palace, Jaigarh was relegated to the role of dungeon, armoury and treasure-house. The present buildings date from the 18C, but have undergone innumerable transformations since.

Tour of the fort – *(9am-4.30pm, entrance fee. Extra charge for cameras and videos.)* A visit to Jaigarh provides a welcome and peaceful interlude after Amber's crowds of tourists, even if the merry-go-round of 4WDs and Ambassadors (many Indians visit the fort by car) somewhat detracts from the peace and quiet. The main gate leads into a group of courtyards, buildings and temples, most of which are in ruins. An impressive watchtower, **Diva Burj**, overlooks the ramparts.

To the right, just past the entrance, is the old **cannon foundry**, which was once the largest in India. The 18C equipment is still intact: furnace, casting moulds… but the **splendid views** of Amber and the surrounding hills are what interest most visitors in this part of the fort.

Go back to the entrance. The left-hand path takes visitors to the main buildings. **Subhat Niwas**, the first courtyard on the right, was used as a parade ground. A **hall** houses an incredible jumble of palanquins and chests.

India's first cannons

Babur, founder of the Mughal dynasty, owed his successful invasion of northern India (1526) to the superiority of his cannons, all the more so as the Rajput sovereigns had little or no conception of artillery. They were only initiated into this secret world in the early 17C, thanks to Maharaja Man Singh I who brought back his know-how from Kabul where he had been appointed governor by Akbar.

Two small 12C temples devoted to **Kali Bhairava** (Devi and Shiva's more frightening personifications) and to **Hari-Hara** (altered in the 20C) stand at the rear of the **main courtyard** *(on the right)*. Enter the second temple, which houses a statue of Hari-Hara, a divine combination, one half of which represents Vishnu, holding a discus, while the other depicts Shiva armed with his trident. Among the **weaponry collection** in the next-door room, the cannons, including a small piece with a tiger's head, are worth a pause. The buildings opposite contain objects which once belonged to the royal family (costumes, photos, maps of the fort...). The fort's water tanks are situated on the far side of the courtyard. Jai Singh II is said to have buried the Kachwahas' treasure under one of them. The next stopping-point is the legendary **Jaivan** ("arrow of Jai"), claimed to be the largest cannon-on-wheels in the whole world, cast in 1720 at Jaigarh.

From Sisodia Rani palace to the Galta temples**

(in the direction of E4)

8km east of Jaipur. By car, leave Jaipur on the road to Agra. On foot, allow at least 2hr for this pleasant hike that will take you back into Jaipur through the eastern gate.

A definite must for anyone in need of a boost of oxygen and some peace and quiet to combat the stress and pollution of Rajasthan's busy capital. A good opportunity to discover some fine architecture and frescoes in an unspoiled landscape. The contrast between the bustle of Jaipur and the peace and quiet of the stroll leaves an impression of having journeyed to another world.

After 7km, the Agra road suddenly dips down between two rows of buildings topped with *chhatri*; these were shops built close to the original fortifications. On the right, an esplanade opens onto **Vidyadhar garden** (Vidyadharji ka Bagh), created in honour of the architect who designed Jaipur. Adorned with pavilions and empty pools, it is now mainly the home of monkeys from the outlying hills.

A legendary treasure

Legend has it that, at Jaigarh, Jai Singh II buried the booty amassed by the Kachwahas during their campaigns under the Mughal banner. The secret of the burial place is said to be passed down from generation to generation by the fierce Meena warriors appointed to guard the fortune. Each maharaja of Jaipur had the right to visit this fabled site at least once in his life. He would be blindfolded and guided by the Meena guardians to the mysterious treasure. No one knows what happened to the extraordinary hoard of jewels and gems, least of all the local taxmen, for whom the hoard must have been the stuff of dreams. In the 1970s, they turned themselves into treasure hunters, embarking on excavation and digging works for several months. But to no avail...

Some 200m further on, take the small road which forks left.

Sisodia Rani palace* *(from dawn until dusk, entrance fee)* is situated on the right-hand side of the road. Built in 1710 for one of Jai Singh II's wives, a princess of the Sisodia dynasty (rulers of Mewar). The terms of this alliance between the two families stipulated that the eldest son born of this union was to become king, taking priority over the offspring of Jai Singh's other wives. This prospect gave rise to much jealousy. Fleeing the court's intrigues, the princess had this palace built where she raised her son, the future Madho Singh I. Partially restored **murals** depict hunting and courtly scenes together with some of the gods of the Vishnuist pantheon. The **garden**, encircled by hills and embellished with pavilions and water pools is a very pleasant place to wander. Opposite the palace, on the other side of the road, is a **temple to Vishnu** (1745).

Continue along the road which winds its way through the hills, amidst clusters of acacias and bougainvilleas. Turn left 1km further on. Follow the arrows to the "Vipasana Center".

300m further on is a **temple to Hanuman*** constantly invaded by *langur* monkeys. The façade, decorated with *chhatri* and *jharokha* (balconies) gives it a palace-like feel. The more modest interior contains a few interesting murals of Krishna.

The Galta temples** *(3km further on)*, built in the 18C, merge into the wild landscape of a narrow, picturesque gorge inhabited by hordes of monkeys. A spring, said to possess miraculous virtues, gushes from a rock which resembles a cow's muzzle *(gomukh)*. The spring never seems to run dry, leaving this peaceful valley eternally moist and green. **Galtav**, a pious hermit, is said to have withdrawn here to meditate at the beginning of the Christian era. Temples and a *dharmshala* (hostel for pilgrims), whose walls are decorated with **frescoes**** line the central path. Note the wall covered in paintings depicting Hanuman's army of monkeys. The spacious temples *(undergoing restoration)* provide a notable contrast between their obvious elegance and current pitiful condition. A path leads to the **pools** of holy water, cut like a staircase into the rocky flanks of the narrowest part of the gorge. The lower one is for women and the top one for men. It is said that those who bathe here in a properly reverential manner will be delivered from the cycle of reincarnation. Some of the more daring pilgrims even leap off a wall several metres high.
A partially paved path winds its way from the upper pool up through the rocks. Ten minutes further on, it opens out onto a ridge overlooking Jaipur. Before arriving at the top, admire the two tiny **shrines** devoted to Rama and Hanuman, frequented by rather "laid-back" *sadhus* (wisemen). A path *(to the left from the summit)* leads to the small 18C Surya temple, built in honour of the Sun, the Kachwahas' ancestor. *(Walk back to Jaipur from here.)*

The cenotaphs of Gaitor* (D1)

10am-4pm, no charge. Tax for cameras and videos. Located just outside Jaipur's northern wall, overlooked by Nahargarh Fort. The road leads through quiet streets lined with little white houses and patronised by the occasional wandering cow.
In the midst of trees and bushes, some twenty domed kiosks in white marble or ochre sandstone *(chhatri)* of varying sizes have been built on the cremation site of the Kachwahas princes and maharajas (the women's *chhatris* are further on, near Lake Man Sagar). The oldest cenotaph is the white marble one of **Jai Singh II**, whose **dome** is decorated with sculptures depicting 18 *apsaras* (nymphs) and *gandharva* (divine musicians). The **cenotaph of Madho Singh II**, in front of those of his children, who died during a malaria epidemic, is worth a pause.

Nahargarh Fort*

Open from dawn until dusk, entrance fee. Extra charge for cameras and videos. By car, the road to the fort is the same as that leading to Jaigarh Fort (see p 217), but the left-hand fork should be taken. The splendid ridge finishes at Nahargarh Fort (5km on). Alternatively, take a rickshaw to "below Nahargarh" ("Nahargarh Qilé keh nitche") and allow 20min to walk up the pretty hillside path.
Jai Singh II built the "Lion Fort" to protect his new capital. According to legend, this construction disturbed the spirit of the Rathore prince, Nahar Singh, a hero who died here and whose cenotaph Jai Singh had destroyed: every morning, the previous day's work was said to have been found mysteriously wrecked. A ceremony enabled the wandering spirit to be laid to rest and the building work resumed normally.

The main courtyard *(undergoing restoration)* has an attractive **baori** (well), but the most interesting item is the 19C **Madhavendra Bhawan** palace, built for Ram Singh II's wives. Its façade with its ornate kiosks can be seen from Jaipur. The interior, devoid of furniture, still has a few murals. There is a courtyard surrounded by a labyrinth of corridors, patios and chambers, some of which have stained-glass windows. The upper terrace has a wonderful view over Jaipur.

Sanganer

15km south of Jaipur, buses leave every 30min from Ajmeri Gate.

Strewn with rubbish, unsightly open drains and inhabited by colonies of black pigs, Sanganer is today a sad sight and only likely to interest textile enthusiasts. The town owes its name to the Kachwahas prince, Sangaji (17C) and its celebrity to its printed textile workshops. The textile industry took off in the 18C under the patronage of Jaipur's royal family. Today, Sanganer seems half asleep, despite the many fabric shops lining its dusty streets. The 16C Jain temple, **Shri Digambara Jain Mandir**, located in the main bazaar, next to Tripolia gate, is worth a stop. Devoted to Adinatha (the first *tirthankara,* founder of the Jain religion), it has retained some fine sculptures which provide a stunning contrast with the city's overall decrepitude. The banks of the *nala* (drainage canal) in the north of the city, where kilometres of coloured fabrics are laid out to dry, also merit a look.

Making the most of Jaipur

Getting there

By plane – *Sanganer Airport* is 15km to the south of Jaipur. There is no bus service but there are "pre-paid" taxis. Alliance Air, ☎ (0141) 55 02 22 and 72 13 33 has 1-2 daily flights to Delhi (40min), 1 daily flight to Udaipur (40min) and 1 flight, three time a week, to Jaisalmer (1hr). Jagson Airlines flies to Delhi and Udaipur four times a week. Jet Airways, ☎ (0141) 55 17 29, has 1 daily flight to Delhi. Travellers should bear in mind that flight timetables are subject to frequent changes throughout the year; flight times should be checked twice rather than once, and bookings should be made well in advance.

By train – *Jaipur Railway Station*, in the west of the city (A2). Information, ☎ 131 and 133. Central reservations desk, ☎ 135. 8am-8pm, Sunday 8am-2pm. Tourist office desk on platform n° 1. Jaipur's railway authorities demand that foreigners be present at the moment of booking. This means that it is legally impossible to have the booking made by a travel agent, and travellers have to go to the station themselves.

The fastest train to Delhi (4hr15min) is the "Shatabdi" which leaves daily (except Sundays) towards the end of the afternoon and stops at Alwar (2hr). Around 15 trains leave daily for the capital (5hr30min on the "Superfast", 8 stop at Alwar (2hr30min) and 3 go via Shekhawati (3hr30min to Churu), but they arrive in the evening or the middle of the night. Daily departures to Mathura (6hr) but no link with Agra (work is in progress), 2 daily trains to Kota (3hr30min) via Sawai Madhopur (2hr) and ten trains to Ajmer (the "Shatabdi" is faster, 2hr, everyday except Sunday). There are 3 express trains every day for Chittaurgarh (8hr) and 2 for Udaipur (13hr30min on the night train "Chetak Express"), 5 to Jodhpur (6hr30min) and 2 to Bikaner (10hr on the night train).

By bus – *Central Bus Stand*, Sindhi Camp, Station Rd (B2). 24 hours a day left-luggage office. Information about the "Silver Line" buses on platform n° 3, ☎ (0141) 20 56 21, and on platform n° 1, ☎ (0141) 38 12 77 for the express buses. Some 25 "Silver Line" buses leave daily for Delhi between 5.30am and 1.30pm, including 4 or 5 air-conditioned "Pink Line" buses (6hr). 13 buses to Agra (5hr30min) with a stop at Bharatpur, 6 to Kota (6hr) via Bundi, 3 to Chittaurgarh (7hr), 1 to Banswara, 8 to Udaipur (9hr), one of which stops at Bhilwara, 1 to Mount Abu (12hr), 7 to Jodhpur (7hr) via Ajmer (2hr30min), 1 for Jaisalmer (13hr) and 1 to Bikaner (7hr). A large number of express buses also go to other destinations. For Alwar, departures every 30min (4hr), via Sariska (3hr15min). Express buses also run services to the main tourist centres: Shekhawati (Sikar, Churu, Nawalgarh, Mukundgarh and Jhunjhunu – between 2hr30min and 4hr30min. The train is more practical when travelling to Sawai Madhopur. Private buses also leave from the Central Bus Stand.

Getting about

The modern city centre consists of two main streets: Station Rd and Mirza Ismail (M.I.) Rd. Niro's Restaurant in the east (C3), and the shopping and office complex, Ganpati Plaza, in the west are useful landmarks (B2).

By bus – Town buses, bursting at the seams, can be found on all the main roads and at major crossroads. For Amber, buses leave from the station every hour, stopping at the Palace of the Winds (Hawa Mahal). Buses also leave the station for Sisodia Palace, via Ajmeri Gate (C2).

By rickshaw – Auto-rickshaws do have meters but most drivers refuse to use them. When negotiating, it is worthwhile knowing that a reasonable price is 20Rs for 5km or 45Rs per hour (8km maximum). Cycle-rickshaws are 20 % less. "Pre-paid" rickshaw booths (red and blue signs, identical to those of the police) can be found in front of the station and Central Bus Stand.

By taxi – There are taxi ranks at the station and on M.I. Rd, between Ajmeri and Sanganeri Gates (C-D3). Taxis do not have meters. Prices are often cheaper if negotiated by an agency or a hotel. 450Rs for 4hr (40km maximum), 700Rs for 8hr (60km maximum).

Car rentals – Enquire at your hotel or at a travel agency. The minimum price is around 1 100Rs for a car with driver.

Mariam Tours, ☎ (0141) 39 96 37. A small reasonably-priced company which provides drivers who speak good English.

Europcar, G-2 Shri Gopal Tower, Ashok Rd, C-Scheme (B3), ☎ (0141) 36 26 01 and 36 27 62, Fax (0141) 36 39 93. High-quality car rentals. It is possible to rent a self-drive car, but is it really worth it?

Address book

Tourist office – *Tourist Reception Centre* (Rajasthani Government), at the station, platform n° 1 (A2), ☎ (0141) 31 57 14. Everyday 6am-8pm. Another branch at Tourist Campus Hotel, M.I. Rd, on the corner of Sardar Patel Rd (B3), ☎ (0141) 36 52 56 and 37 01 80. 10am-5pm; closed Sunday. Can provide brochures and maps of Rajasthan's main tourist centres, together with a list of guides and guesthouses in Jaipur.

Tourist Reception Centre (Indian Government), Khasa Kothi Hotel (A2), ☎ (0141) 37 22 00. 9am-6pm, Saturday 9am-1pm; closed Sunday. Information about India and list of guides.

Bank/Money – *Central Bank of India*, Sansar Chandra Rd, next to Mansingh Hotel (B2). To change cash and travellers' cheques and, in theory, to withdraw money with a Visa or MasterCard (but in practice this service is often unavailable).

Andhra Bank, M.I. Rd, west of Panch Batti (B-C3). The only place in Jaipur where withdrawing money with a Visa or MasterCard presents no problems.

State Bank of Bikaner and Jaipur, Chaura Rasta (D2). Accepts cash and travellers' cheques in dollars and pounds sterling.

The establishments below have slightly more practical opening hours than their more traditional counterparts. They can exchange cash and traveller's cheques, but are often closed on Sunday.
Bank of Rajasthan, Rambagh Palace Hotel (C4). 7am-8.30am/9am-1pm/2pm-4.30pm / 5pm-8pm.
SITA World Travel, Station Rd, corner of Sawai Jai Singh Highway (A-B2), ☎ (0141) 20 36 19 and 20 45 04, Fax (0141) 20 54 79. 9.30am-1pm/2pm-6pm, Saturday 9.30am-2pm.
Thomas Cook, A/B-2 (102) Jaipur Tower, M.I. Rd (B2). 9.30am-6pm.
LKP Merchant Financing, M.I. Rd, opposite Ganpati Plaza (B2), ☎ (0141) 36 81 75, ☎ and Fax (0141) 36 71 14. 9.30am-6pm. Represents American Express.
To receive money sent from abroad in just a few hours: **Western Union**, at SITA World Travel, LKP Merchant Financing and DHL or **Thomas Cook**.

Post office/Telephone – GPO, M.I. Rd (B2). 10am-6pm, Sunday 10am-5pm. A booth opens at 8am for stamps and mail. Registered and express mail (everyday, 10am-7.30pm). Parcels and poste restante (10am-4pm; closed Sunday). Philately (10am-6pm; closed Sunday). The other post offices open from 10am to 5pm and are closed on Sunday: **Tripolia Bazaar Post Office**, Tripolia Bazaar, just past the entrance to the Palace of the Winds (D2); **Jaipur City Post Office**, outside of Sanganeri Gate, opposite the Minerva Cinema (D3); small branch in **Rambagh Palace Hotel** (C4) for stamps and mail. Postal code: 302001.
Express mail by **EMS Speed Post**, in post offices, or by **DHL**, G-7-A Vinoba Rd, a little lane off M.I. Rd between Ever Green Hotel and Panch Batti Circle (B3), ☎ (0141) 36 11 59 and 36 28 26. 9.30am-6pm; closed Sunday. **Cargo**, at SITA World Travel and DHL.
To send and receive faxes, go to **Central Telegraph Office**, GPO.
There are several Internet booths around the station, or at **Communicator**, G-4 and 5 Jaipur Tower, ground floor, M.I. Rd (B2), ☎ (0141) 20 41 00; some guesthouses and hotels also provide Internet and e-mail services.

Health – Ambulances, ☎ 102 and 103. **Santokba Durlabhji Memorial (SDM) Hospital**, Bhawani Singh Rd (C4), ☎ (0141) 56 62 51 / 58. Private clinic. **Chemists**: There are several chemists on Station Rd, near Chand Pol (B2), and on the corner of Sawai Ram Singh and Hospital Rd (C3). Ayurvedic chemists in Kishan Pol Bazaar (C2). **Optician**: **Spectro Vision**, M.I. Rd next to the Indian Coffee House (C2-3).

Safety – Police, ☎ 100 and (0141) 56 55 54/55. **Fire brigade**, ☎ 101.

Travel agencies – Rajasthan Tourism Development Corporation (RTDC), Transport Unit, Tourist Hotel Campus, M.I. Rd, corner of Sardar Patel Rd (B3), ☎ (0141) 37 54 66. The State of Rajasthan's agency organises daily tours of Jaipur: three tours in a non air-conditioned bus (8am-1pm, 11.30am-4.30pm and 1.30pm-6.30pm; 80Rs), one in an air-conditioned mini-bus (10am-5pm; 150Rs), and one excursion in a non air-conditioned bus including Nahargarh Fort (9am-6pm; 120Rs). All include a visit to Amber but only drive past the Palace of the Winds and Gaitor. On Saturdays, dinner with a folklore show at Nahargarh Fort (170Rs). Taxi and car rentals.
Another branch at Central Reservation Office, Swagatam Hotel, Station Rd (A2), ☎ (0141) 20 25 86 and 20 35 31, Fax (0141) 20 10 45, rtdc@jp1. vsnl. net.in Reservations for RTDC hotels, including camping during Pushkar Fair and the "Palace on Wheels".
Arya Niwas, Arya Niwas Hotel, Sansar Chandra Rd (B2), ☎ (0141) 36 43 76 and 37 24 56, Fax (0141) 36 18 71, aryahot@jp1.vsnl.net.in Small well-run agency which organises excursions and reasonably-priced taxi and car rentals.
Aravali Safari & Tours, Palace Rd, opposite the Rajputana Palace Sheraton Hotel (A2), ☎ (0141) 36 53 45 and 37 31 24. Good camel and horse-back treks all over Rajasthan.
SITA World Travel, Station Rd, close to the corner of Sawai Jai Singh Highway (A2), ☎ (0141) 20 36 19 and 20 45 04, Fax (0141) 20 54 79. 9.30am-1pm/2pm-6pm, Saturday 9.30am-2pm;

closed Sunday. Reputable agency able to organise any kind of trip. Also provides taxi and car rentals, airplane tickets and cargo despatches.

Registhan Tours, E-141 Sardar Patel Rd, next to the Raj Mahal Palace Hotel (A4), ☎ (0141) 38 08 24 and 38 20 09, Fax (0141) 38 15 34. Reputable agency with the advantage of being represented all over Rajasthan. Car rentals, tickets, organisation of trips and horse or camel-back treks.

Travel Corporation India (TCI), 19-C Gopal Bari (B3), ☎ (0141) 36 32 46 and 36 79 39, Fax (0141) 36 97 67. 9am-1pm/2pm-6pm; closed Sunday. Excellent, well-represented agency throughout India. Good value car and taxi rentals. Tickets for domestic flights.

Airlines – *Air India*, Janta Travels, Ganpati Plaza, M.I. Rd (B2), ☎ (0141) 36 85 69, Fax (0141) 36 07 56. 9.30am-1pm/2pm-5.30pm, Saturday 9.30am-2pm; closed Sunday.

Air France, 201-B Jaipur Tower, M.I. Rd, ☎ (0141) 37 05 09, Fax (0141) 36 93 17.

Air Canada, 112 Jaipur Tower, M.I. Rd, ☎ (0141) 37 54 30, Fax (0141) 37 42 42.

Canadian Pacific, 101/106 Jaipur Tower, M.I. Rd, ☎ (0141) 36 05 32, Fax (0141) 36 18 86.

Indian Airlines, Nehru Place, Tonk Rd, ☎ (0141) 51 44 07 and 51 45 00, Fax (0141) 51 03 44. Daily 10am-5pm.

Jet Airways, E-4 Jaipur Tower, M.I. Rd, ☎ (0141) 37 18 32 and 37 22 10, Fax (0141) 37 38 10. Represents Air India, as well as other domestic and international companies.

Miscellaneous – To extend your visa, contact the ***Foreigners Regional Registration Office***, Police Department, next to Jantar Mantar (D2).

Press – *Jaipur Vision*, a monthly magazine with tourist information about Jaipur, on sale from bookshops.

Where to stay

A 20 % discount is often available from May to June-July.

• Around Station Rd and Sansar Chandra Rd

Less than US$7

Ever Green Guest House, Chameliwala Market, M.I. Rd, ☎ (0141) 36 24 15 and 36 34 46, Fax (0141) 20 42 34 – 80rm. Dormitory. Located in a lane off M.I. Rd, turn right before the first service station (when coming from the station), then take the next right turn. The attraction of this low-price hotel lies in its garden and lawn planted with banana trees, bougainvilleas and dwarf palm trees. The perfect place to stop, chat and exchange addresses. A friendly atmosphere, but the rooms are very basic (the ones in the new wing are better). Hot water in basins for the least expensive rooms. Cooler and water-heater in the most expensive. Rooms must be vacated by 10am.

Between US$7-15

Arya Niwas Hotel, Sansar Chandra Rd, ☎ (0141) 36 43 76 and 37 24 56, Fax (0141) 36 18 71, aryahot@jp1.vsnl.net.in – 75rm. CC Cooler. Boutique, bookshop and Internet access. This well-run and very pleasant establishment offers almost monastically sober rooms. Impeccably clean, they can be somewhat noisy due to the fanlights giving onto the corridor. Small garden and a pleasant veranda for meals.

Gaurav Hotel, Vanasthali St, ☎ (0141) 37 81 05, Fax (0141) 37 23 54 – 33rm. TV CC 19rm. with cooler. One of a whole host of small, modern, impersonal establishments, which are nonetheless well-run and comfortable, and mostly located in a small road opposite the bus station. Most rooms are windowless but are good value for money. 24hr rental. 20 % discount from March to October.

Atithi Guest House, 1 Park House Scheme, opposite All India Radio, ☎ (0141) 37 86 79, Fax (0141) 37 94 96 – 20rm. Cooler. Internet access. A pleasant family guest house with garden and terrace. Irreproachably clean and quiet, despite its central situation. Hot water in the evening and the morning.

Teej Hotel (RTDC), Sawai Jai Singh Highway, ☎ (0141) 20 31 99 and 20 54 82 – 46rm. 26rm. with cooler. Dormitory. The best of Jaipur's RTDC hotels. Clean, almost smart and quiet, even though close to the station. The only difference between the rooms is that some are air-conditioned, others not.

From US$15-30

Chirmi Palace (Heritage Hotels Association), Dhuleshwar Garden, Sardar Patel Rd, 1km from the station and 2km from the old city, ☎ (0141) 36 50 63 and 37 09 72, Fax (0141) 36 44 62, chirmi@vsnl.com – 14rm. 6rm. with cooler. An agreeable, relaxing recently restored 18C establishment. Spacious, comfortable rooms with new bathrooms. Pleasant dining room decorated with frescoes.

Bissau Palace Hotel (Heritage Hotels Association), Chand Pol, ☎ (0141) 30 43 71 and 30 43 91, Fax (0141) 30 46 28, sanjai@jp1. vsnl.net.in – 40rm. Cooler. The entrance to this elegant property, built in 1919 for the Bissau "thakur" is via an unappealing side street north of Chand Pol. It would be one of the best places to stay in Jaipur if it weren't for the unequal quality of the rooms and the disorganised, rather inattentive staff. Choose a room in the old building. Ten suites.

From US$30-45

Alsisar Haveli (Heritage Hotels Association), Sansar Chandra Rd, ☎ and Fax (0141) 36 82 90 – 30rm. A haveli tastefully restored in 1998. Protected from the street by a garden, a spacious terrace in front of the building provides an excellent spot to have breakfast or read a book. Charming inner courtyard and pretty living and dining areas with multifoil arches. The rooms are clean and tastefully decorated.

From US$45-70

Maurya Palace Hotel, S-35-A Arvind Marg, M.I. Rd, ☎ (0141) 36 76 07, 36 80 77 and 37 19 84, Fax (0141) 37 08 16 – 56rm. Beauty salon. This well-situated eight-storey establishment, close to Niro's Restaurant and the old city, has comfortable, if impersonal rooms. Ask for one with a view of the tennis club. The coffee shop and reception are notable for their garish decoration.

From US$70-140

Hotel Mansingh and ***Mansingh Towers*** (Mansinghgroup), Sansar Chandra Rd, ☎ (0141) 37 87 71, Fax (0141) 37 75 82 – 144rm. Beauty salon. Modern, comfortable establishment. The excellent, recently opened Mansingh Towers, is a little more expensive and was designed primarily for business people.

Over US$140

Rajputana Palace Sheraton (Welcomgroup), Palace Rd, ☎ (0141) 36 00 11, Fax (0141) 36 78 48, rajputana@welcomgroup.com – reservations at Delhi (see p 107) – 216rm. Shopping precinct, beauty salon. Prestigious hotel in a modern, brick building, the wings of which are spread over beautiful lawns and gardens. 17 suites.

• Bani Park

A smart residential area, some 2.5km to the west of the old city.

From US$7-15

Jaipur Inn, B-17 Shiv Marg, Bani Park, ☎ (0141) 20 11 21, Fax (0141) 20 47 96, jaipurinn@hotmail.com – 18rm. Two dormitories, camp site. Internet access. A well-run establishment catering primarily to tourists in a friendly atmosphere. Spartan comfort, but the rooms are clean and decorated in traditional cotton fabrics. The furniture is minimal: bed and chair. Ten rooms with cooler and bath are slightly more expensive. Pleasant rooftop restaurant. Rooms must be vacated by 10am.

Madhuban Guest House, D-237 Behari Marg, Bani Park, ☎ (0141) 20 00 33 and 20 54 27, Fax (0141) 20 23 44 – 20rm. Cooler. Visitors are made to feel totally at home in this pleasant family establishment run by a Rajput family. Complete with small garden and furnished in an

Anglo-Indian style, it is both clean and peaceful. Some rooms with AC are more expensive. 15 % discount from April to September.

From US$15-30

Hotel Megh Niwas, C-9 Sawai Jai Singh Highway, Bani Park, ☎ (0141) 20 20 34/35/36, Fax (0141) 20 14 20, meghniwas@hotmail.com – 22rm. Surrounded by a vast lawn, the bungalow belonging to Colonel Singh and his wife has built up a clientele of regulars. Pleasant if slightly expensive rooms. 20 % discount from April to September.

• Civil Lines

From US$15-30

Achrol House (Heritage Hotels Association), Jacob Rd, Civil Lines, ☎ (0141) 38 21 54 – 5rm. 1rm. with fan. Campsite. This large 19C family residence, surrounded by verandas offers spacious rooms furnished in an old-fashioned style. Although quite appealing, the establishment could clearly do with more care and the service is non-existent.

From US$30-40

Loharu House, Sawai Pratap Rd, Civil Lines, ☎ (0141) 38 12 51 and 38 19 45, Fax (0141) 38 32 19 – 12rm. Located in a smart residential haven, the residence of the "nawabzada" and the "begum" Aimaduddin Ahmad Khan de Loharu never fails to charm all who visit its verandas, flowery inner courtyards and cosy little rooms.

From US$70-140

Raj Mahal Palcce (Taj Group and Heritage Hotels Association), Sardar Patel Marg, ☎ (0141) 38 16 25 and 38 17 57, Fax (0141) 38 18 87; reservations at Delhi and Jaipur (see p 107) – 21rm. Bar-library for residents. This elegant early-18C property, built by Jai Singh II, founder of Jaipur, was the residence of the British Resident in the 19C, before becoming a royal residence in the 1960s. It was transformed into a hotel, without altering either its structure, or its intimate, sophisticated atmosphere. The "superior" category rooms are of very varying sizes for an identical price, n° 201 being the most spacious, with four rooms for three people. Two suites. 20 % discount from May to September.

Over US$140

Jai Mahal Palace (Taj Group), Jacob Rd, Civil Lines, ☎ (0141) 37 16 16, Fax (0141) 36 52 37, jaimahal@jp1. vsnl. net.in; reservations at Delhi and Jaipur (see p 107) – 102rm. Boutiques, beauty salon. An Indo-Moslem style palace, where Surgeon General Thomas Holbein stayed at the end of the 19C, before it became the official residence of Jaipur's prime ministers. It lost much of its charm when it was turned into a prestigious hotel. The bar is decorated with Shekhawati paintings.

• South of the old city

From US$7-15

Diggi Palace Hotel (Heritage Hotels Association), Diggi House, Shivaji Rd, 1km from the old city, ☎ (0141) 36 61 20 and 37 30 91, Fax (0141) 37 03 59 – 45rm. Ten rooms without bath under US$7 and thirty or so, a bit pricier, with cooler. The zenana of the Thakur palace of Diggi (early 18C) has been turned into a budget hotel very popular among young people travelling light. Agreeable courtyard and terrace, with a view over a large, peaceful garden, giving the impression of being in the country.

From US$15-30

Nana ki Haveli, Fateh Tiba, Moti Dungri Rd, ☎ (0141) 66 55 02, Fax (0141) 60 54 81 – 10rm. This late-19C residence, located in the craft district, 700m from the old city, is the home of a charming Rajput family. Clean, airy rooms, decorated simply but with a great deal of care, using beautiful fabrics and dhurries. New bathrooms. Five extra rooms are planned for 2000.

From US$30-40

Narain Niwas Palace Hotel (Heritage Hotels Association), Kanota Bagh, Narain Singh Rd, 2.5km from the old city, ☎ (0141) 56 12 91 and 56 34 48, Fax (0141) 56 10 45 – 31rm. Billiards. This hybrid style patriarchal residence, set in a large garden, was built in 1881 by Narain Singh of Kanota and extended in 1930 by General Amar Singh. The Kanota family runs this somewhat old-fashioned, yet charming establishment. The veranda and the living room furnished in a late-19C style and covered in family photographs are most appealing. The rooms are spacious, if a bit gloomy. Seven suites.

Over US$140

Rambagh Palace, (Taj Group), Bhawani Singh Rd, 3km from the old city, ☎ (0141) 38 19 19, Fax (0141) 38 10 98, rambagh@jp1.vsnl.net.in – reservations in Delhi and Jaipur (see p 107) – 187rm. TV CC Boutiques. This former hunting-lodge was extended by Colonel Sir Swinton Jacob in 1905 and decorated in an Art Deco style for Man Singh II. It was the latter's family residence until 1957, when he had it turned into a hotel, the first ever palace-hotel of its sort in India. The interior of this vast, elegant establishment has recently been modernised, detracting from its charm, but it is nonetheless a wonderful place. Two wings built in a U-shape around a lawn, making a wonderful setting, perfect for a quiet cup of tea. Nine suites.

• The road to Amber

All the following hotels are to the north of the old city boundary, on the road to Amber Fort and Delhi.

From US$40-70

Samod Haveli, Gangapole, ☎/Fax (0141) 63 10 68, 63 23 70 and 63 24 07, jagdish@jp1.vsnl.net.in – 21rm. CC Hidden away in a quiet little spot within the city walls, just off the road to Amber, this superb 18C haveli, belonging to the "thakurs" of Samod, is one of the best places to stay in Jaipur. Inner courtyard and garden. The reception rooms have all retained their wonderful original frescoes and the rooms are decorated with impeccable good taste. Only weak point: the buffet is very limited.

From US$70-150

Holiday Inn, Amber Rd, 500m from Zorawar Gate, ☎ (0141) 63 50 00, Fax (0141) 63 56 08, hijaiin@jp1.vsnl.net.in – 72rm. TV CC Breakfast included. Excellent modern establishment, built around an inner courtyard, in the style of a haveli. Suites. 25 % discount for single rooms.

The Trident (The Oberoi), Amber Fort Rd, Jal Mahal, ☎ (0141) 63 01 01, Fax (0141) 63 03 03 – 138rm. TV CC Opposite Lake Jal Mahal and the palace, this luxury hotel, although impersonally decorated, has a lively, pleasant atmosphere. Ask for a room with a view of the lake.

Over US$150

The Raj Palace, Chomu Haveli, Zorawar Singh Gate, Amber Rd, ☎ and Fax (0141) 63 04 84 and 63 40 77; reservations, ☎/Fax (0141) 37 31 19 – 30rm. TV CC An impressive, pale-yellow haveli built on five storeys in 1728 for the lord of Chomu is Jaipur's oldest establishment of this kind.

Where to eat

Jaipur remains a traditional town, where most of the middle-class families only eat in vegetarian restaurants. The majority of the non-veg establishments are thus mainly frequented by businessmen and tourists.

• Old city

From US$3-4

Lakshmi Mishtan Bhandar (L.M.B.), Jauhari Bazaar (D2). CC 8am-11pm. An institution! No Indian would dream of visiting Jaipur without eating at least one meal in the large, sombre room of the L.M.B. Red velvet chairs and dirty white tablecloths. The "pure-veg" menu offers a fine selection of north Indian and Rajasthani specialities. Try one of the establishment's legendary desserts to finish off your meal. For example, the "rasmalai" (semolina and condensed milk, with a lemon and cardamom flavour, served in a pistachio cream sauce). Outdoor counter and café for sweets and namkin.

• Around Mirza Ismail Rd (M.I. Rd)

This district has several places which are always popular for snacks or inexpensive meals.

Kiran Cafe, in Ram Niwas gardens, on the left on leaving the museum (C3). A series of 'multi-cuisine' eateries.

Surya Mahal, M.I. Rd, near Niro's Restaurant (C3). Two rooms which are constantly busy, serving north and south Indian dishes, together with Western and Chinese meals and ice creams.

Lassiwala, opposite the above address. Said to serve the best "lassi" in town.

Bake Hut, Arvind St, near Surya Mahal (C3). Renowned for its fresh biscuits.

Pizza Hut, Ganpati Plaza (B2). 11am-11pm. Brand-new and totally impersonal.

When waiting for the bus, try the hotel restaurants of ***Kanchandeep*** or ***Kohinoor***, on Vanasthali Street (B2).

From US$3-4

Natraj, M.I. Rd (C3). Not to be confused with Natraj Hotel, also on M.I. Rd. A cosy, clean room serving pure-veg classics of north and south Indian, together with Western and Chinese dishes. Speciality: vegetable "kofta" (minced vegetable balls, served in a spicy sauce).

Chaitanya, City Centre, Sansar Chandra St, 1st floor (B2), ☎ (0141) 36 55 84 and 37 56 24 CC 11am-11pm. Popular for family outings. Serves "pure veg" cooking. Try their "paneer gulabi" (cheese in a tomato and dried fruit sauce) or the "methi malai motia" (corn and spinach in fenugreek).

Chanakya, M.I. Rd (B3-C3), ☎ (0141) 37 61 61 and 37 84 61. CC 12noon-4pm / 7pm-11pm. Said to serve the best "pure veg" cuisine in Jaipur. Uninspiring decoration but comfortable and well-kept. Focus on north Indian and Rajasthani dishes. The "chanakya special" is an assortment of vegetables prepared with cheese and dried fruit.

From US$4-7

Handi, M.I. Rd, opposite the GPO (B3). 12.30noon-3pm/6.30pm-11pm. Good tandoori and Mughlai cooking. "Handi" specialities: meat simmered in an earthenware pot, and "roomali roti", a pancake as thin as a "handkerchief". Expensive given the setting: metal and plastic furniture and a corrugated iron awning.

Niro's, M.I. Rd (C3), ☎ (0141) 37 17 46 and 37 44 93. CC 9.30am-11pm. This establishment, one of the city's main landmarks, caters to almost equal numbers of tourists and Indians. Lively, cheerful with large wall mirrors and good Indian, tandoori and Western cooking.

Indiana, J2-34 Mahaveer Rd (C3), ☎ (0141) 37 41 37. 🍷 CC 11am-11pm. Cane armchairs and tables covered in traditional cotton fabrics, strewn over a lawn lined with Ashoka trees and two little mud huts. Taste their "Indiana chicken", baked in a tandoor oven and served in a cream, tomato and herb sauce. Folklore performances in the evenings.

Swaad, Ganpati Plaza, M.I. Rd (B2), ☎ (0141) 36 07 49/50. 🍷 CC 11am-11pm. A comfortable restaurant frequented by businessmen. The house specialities are "methi malai goli (cheese balls in fenugreek) and "murgh dhania korma" (chicken pieces, cooked in coriander).

Geetanjali, Maharani Palace Hotel restaurant, Station Rd (B2), ☎ (0141) 37 41 04. CC 7am-11pm. Spacious, comfortable carpeted and wood-panelled room. The "maharani thali" provides a taste of several of Rajasthan's specialities. "Ghazal" performances in the evenings, except Tuesdays. Barbecue dinners by moonlight on the 5th floor.

From US$7-15

Shivir, topmost floor of the Mansingh Hotel. CC 12.30noon-2.30pm/7.30pm-11pm. A comfortable place in which to taste Jaipur's best Mughlai cuisine. Taste the specialities: "paneer pudina masala" (spinach and cheese in mint) and "tarkari pappad rolls" (crunchy pancakes made out of lentil flour, stuffed with potatoes, herbs, raisins and cashew nuts). Bar next door. "Ghazal" singing in the evenings (except on Fridays).

Peshawri, Rajputana Palace Sheraton. 🍷 CC 12.30noon-3.30pm/7.30pm-11pm. The sister restaurant of the famous

Bukhara restaurant in Delhi. Similar decoration in the style of a Pakistani mountain inn and Northwestern frontier cooking, based on delicious kebabs.

- **Civil Lines**

From US$7-15

Gulab Mahal, Jai Mahal Palace Hotel. 6am-23h30. Another one of Jaipur's good restaurants. The menu has a wide selection of Western, Chinese, Indian and Rajasthani dishes, including their famous "lahsuni murgh tikka", and chicken tikka wing.

- **South of the old city**

From US$4-7

Narain Niwas Palace Hotel. 7am-11pm. Many of Jaipur's citizens reckon this to be one of the city's best restaurants. Delicious tandoori, Western and Chinese dishes in a pleasant arcaded room, or weather permitting, in the orchard. Alcohol served in the next-door room and on the veranda.

Where to go out

The Indian Coffee House, M.I. Rd (C2-3), same building as Arrow, at the rear of the courtyard.

Every day from 8am-9pm. Three tiny rooms with mildewed, flaking walls are the meeting-place of the city's intelligentsia, who spend whole days discussing current events in a warm, friendly 'pub' atmosphere. Excellent coffee and snacks at tiny prices, served by waiters wearing jaunty turbans.

Neel Mahal, Rambagh Palace Coffee-shop. Avoid the indoor room and take a seat on one of the cane sofas situated on the lofty, white marble veranda opposite the gardens. A relaxing moment not to be missed. Hot drinks, beers and snacks at reasonable prices.

Mansagar, The Trident Hotel Bar. 11am-11pm. Very pleasant stopover on the way back from Amber. Covered terrace with a view of the Lake and the Jal Mahal.

Hawa Mahal, Jai Mahal Palace. 6am-11.30pm. Enjoy the refreshing breeze of this charming tearoom, overlooking the garden. A reconstruction of the first Mughal garden in India, built for Emperor Babur at Dhaulpur.

Polo Bar, Rambagh Palace Bar. 10.30am-2.30pm/6.30pm-11.30pm. This is the only room of the palace to have escaped renovation when the palace was turned into a hotel. Comfortable armchairs and sofas covered in white loose covers, surrounding a blue tiled pool. The walls are covered in polo mallets and photos and engravings which reveal Man Singh II's passion for polo.

Other things to do

Cinema – *Raj Mandir*, Bhagwan Das Rd, Panch Batti Circle (C3), ☎ (0141) 37 93 72. The most extravagant cinema ever seen, a gleaming temple to Bombay's vigorous film industry.

Sports – *Swimming pools*, the Ever Green and Khasa Kothi hotels both admit non-residents (100Rs).

Horse riding, contact the Rajasthan Polo Club, Rambagh Palace, ☎ (0141) 36 64 92.

Polo, Polo Ground (B4). Five tournaments are held in March, during the polo season and matches are occasionally played in October and November.

Golf, Rambagh Golf Club, Rambagh Palace.

Cricket, Sawai Mansingh Stadium is an international stadium and often stages World Cup matches (only during the winter). Tickets go on sale 10 days before the match and are advertised in the English-speaking press

Excursions – *Sanganer*, 15km to the south. Buses leave every 30min from the station and stop en route at Ajmeri Gate. Good for fabric, pottery and hand-made stationery (see "Shopping").

Holidays and festivals

Makar Sankranti (January 14). Festival which marks the sun's entrance into the sign of Capricorn, at which time a kite-flying competition is held.

Elephant festival, day before Holi (March 9 2001). A festival which is marked by elephant parades, polo matches on elephants, etc.

Gangaur, 3rd and 4th days after the March-April new moon (March 28-29 2001). In honour of Spring and the goddess Gauri (Parvati), a parade, with elephants and camels, from City Palace to Tal Katora.

Teej, 3rd and 4th days after the July-August new moon (July 23-24 2001). A procession, similar to that of Gangaur, is organised to celebrate the harvest and the marriage of Teej (Parvati) with Shiva. Swings decorated with Ashoka leaves are hung up.

SHOPPING

The most modern and the best shops are all located on M.I. Rd. The modern booths and stalls of Bapur Bazaar (D3) and Nehru Bazaar (C2), within the city walls provide a transition between M.I. Rd and the more traditional bazaars in the old city. Most are closed on Sundays, with the exception of Nehru Bazaar's boutiques which close on Tuesdays.

Markets for fruit and vegetables outside Chand Pol (C2), on Chhoti Chaupar (C2) and in the south part of Jauhari Bazaar (D2-3). Note the stout stick with which the salesmen are armed and look up at the surrounding trees and roofs where hordes of rhesus monkeys eagerly await their chance to pilfer some small object.

Crafts – The old city's bazaars provide all sorts of opportunities for shopping for knick-knacks: fun jewellery, arts and crafts, etc.

The shops, where the tourist coaches stop, are lined-up one next to the other along Amber Rd, particularly around Zorawar Singh Gate (D1-E1). Open everyday, they offer jewellery, textiles, carpets, paintings, etc. Everything here is more expensive than elsewhere, because of the commission paid to the coach driver which is added onto the sales price. Make it clear you are not with a coach party to avoid this tax. Other tourist boutiques are located in the City Palace and opposite the Palace of the Winds.

Rajasthali, M.I. Rd, corner of Sawai Ram Singh Rd (C3). The State shop provides a good selection of the crafts available, together with an idea of prices.

Fabric – Jaipur's main speciality are the cotton fabrics produced at Sanganer and Bagru, block-printed and dyed with natural or synthetic dyes. Sold by the metre or by the item (tablecloths, scarves, clothes, etc). Other speciality: cotton or silk with a herringbone ("loharia") print or little white circles on a coloured background ("bandhani"), using tie-dye techniques. Can be bought by the metre or ready-made saris, "dupatta" (long scarves) and turbans.

Jauhari Bazaar, in the old city (D2), traditional centre of the textile market.

Purohitji ka Katla, covered passage to the left of Jauhari Bazaar, some 80m before Bari Chaupar. Composed entirely of boutiques specialising in wedding costumes – red fabric with gold-thread embroidery. Definitely worth a look!

Rajasthan Handloom House, M.I. Rd, next to Rajasthali (C3). Hand-woven fabrics, sold by the metre. Prices are labelled.

Textorium, M.I. Rd, between the Indian Coffee House and Ajmeri Gate (C3). Good place for silk: fabric by the metre, saris, "dupatta", scarves. A few fine-wool shawls.

Thanks to the popularity of "ethnic" fashion towards the end of the 1980s and to the simultaneous emergence of designers and dressmakers, Rajasthan's traditional textile motifs have undergone a revival and Jaipur's textile industry has become one of the most creative and successful in India. It is easy to find places to buy, at labelled prices, good-quality clothes, accessories and table and bed linen, such as quilted eiderdowns (the famous "razai", as light as a summer breeze).

Anokhi, 2 Tilak Rd, C-Scheme (B4). 10am-7pm; closed Sunday. Totally committed to defending Rajasthan's craft trade and its environment, Anokhi was one of the driving forces behind the revival of the traditional textile industry. Two branches in Delhi, but with less choice.

Soma, 5 Jacob Rd, Civil Lines, near Jai Mahal Palace (A3). 10am-8pm, Sunday 10am-6pm.

Rungeen Bazaar, Mayur Apartments, Raj Bhawan Rd, Civil Lines (A3). 10.30am-7.30pm; closed Tuesday. Less choice than the above shops. The reds and blues have a tendency to fade fast.

Rupayan Kraft Palace, G-1 Usha Plaza, M.I. Rd, next to Jaipur Tower (B2).

Nayika, M.I. Rd, opposite Niro's (C3), in the courtyard next to the jewellers' Tholia's Kuber.

Sodhi's, Amber Rd, near The Trident. The only high-quality store for tourists, but the bright colours have a tendency to fade after a few washes. High prices.

At Sanganer, it is possible to visit dying shops and printing works where the work can be purchased directly:

J.K. Arts, Main Rd. Open every day. Exports a great deal to Japan. On the "nala" quayside.

Shilpi Handicrafts, in a road parallel to the "nala". Open every day. Specialises in block-printed silks using natural dyes.

Carpets – The textile warehouses which line Amber Rd to the north of Zorawar Singh Gate (E1), offer a wide range of new carpets, knotted wool or woven cotton (dhurries). They also demonstrate the various stages in the manufacture of a carpet. Beware, many often receive coach-loads of tourists. Among the best:

Anil Exports, Old Amber Rd.

Carpet Mahal, Amber Rd, left after Zorawar Singh Gate. Woollen carpet specialist.

Arihant Arts, Amber Rd, right after Zorawar Singh Gate, in a lane which runs alongside the Raj Palace (E1). Small family enterprise unknown by tourists, only sells "dhurries".

Hand-made stationery – ***Salim's Paper***, Gramodyog Rd (right-angles to Main Rd), Sanganer. Enterprise belonging to the Kagzi family, totally focused on the export market. Before entering the shop, take a look at the different manufacturing stages of this paper made from fabric remnants and decorated with flower petals, grasses and leaves.

Blue pottery – Since the 19C, Jaipur has been famous for its predominantly blue glazed pottery, enhanced with little touches of white, yellow or green. Flowers and geometric motifs are painted onto vases, small boxes, fantasy necklaces, etc.

Kripal Singh Shekawat, Shiv Rd, Bani Park (B2).

Jaipur India Blue Art Potery, basement of the Sakshi textile shop, Main Rd, Sanganer.

Neerja International, S-19 Bhawani Singh Rd, C-Scheme Ext (B4). 9.30am-6pm; closed Sunday.

Blue Pottery Art Centre, Amber Rd, near the Holiday Inn.

Shoes – For sheepskin or kid leather "juti", embroidered with brightly coloured thread or covered in velvet, overstitched with gold thread, go to Ramganj Bazaar.

Jewellery – Jaipur is one of the world's fine and precious stone-cutting capitals, particularly emeralds. Take advantage of a visit to the Rajasthani capital to purchase any jewellery. Prices are excellent, but only reputable houses should be trusted. In case of doubt, get your stones valued at the **Gem Testing Laboratory**, set off M.I. Rd, near New Gate. Warning: firmly refuse any offer of buying wholesale gems or exporting gems on behalf of a jeweller. Jaipur's specialities: gold jewellery featuring inlaid precious, polished cut stones on one side ("kundankari") and intricate enamel work ("meenakari") on the other side. All jewellers have a few pieces of antique jewellery, but most is not on show, and only brought out on request.

Gem Palace, M.I. Rd (C3). Open Sunday. An institution! The Kasliwal family, jewellers since 1852 and suppliers to the royal family of Jaipur. Regularly supply stones to Paris, London and New York's top jewellers. Museum on the first floor, opened in 1999. Collection of vintage cars in the courtyard.

Jaipur Emporium, M.I. Rd, next to the above.

Gem Plaza, M.I. Rd (C3). Open Sundays from August to March. Gyan

Chand Dhaddha invites enthusiasts to view his personal collection of hookahs Ethnic jewellery – originals and copies – from:

Tholia's Kuber, M.I. Rd, opposite Niro's, and ***Amrapali***, Panch Batti Circle (C3).

Royal Gems & Arts, Saras Sadan, Gangauri Bazaar (C1). 10am-8pm; closed Sunday. The entrance is via a primary school. The shop is located in a beautiful room entirely painted in frescoes. A good place for jewellery, ethnic and otherwise and artefacts.

Jauhari Bazaar ("jewellers bazaar") and the nearby streets (mainly Gopalji ka Rasta and Haldiyon ka Rasta) (D2) have large numbers of jewellers, but the above-mentioned addresses are much more reputable. The traditional silver jewellers' boutiques are lined-up one next to the other on the southeastern corner of Bari Chaupar and at the beginning of Ramganj Bazaar (D2). Glass bracelets can be found on little stalls on the northwestern corner of Bari Chaupar. Brightly-coloured lacquered bracelets are made and sold in Maniharon ka Rasta.

Culinary specialities – Fans of "mithayan" (confectionery) and "namkin" (spicy or sweet and savoury snacks) will head for ***LMB*** (see "Where to eat"). The little lanes north and south of L.M.B. provide a glimpse of how "mithayan" and "paneer" (curdled milk cheese) are made. Take a look at ***Achar-wallon ki Galli***, in the "lane of achar merchants" (vegetables and preserved fruits in oil, vinegar or lemon juice, with spices).

Western clothes – Western brands are on M.I Rd: ***Lee***, Jaipur Tower (B2). ***Reebok***, at Shoe Hut, Ganpati Plaza (B2). ***Levi's*** and ***Nike***, at Marda Apparels, east of the GPO (B3). ***Arrow*** next to the Indian Coffee House (C2-3). ***Woodlands***, opposite the Gem Palace (C3).

Beauty products and treatment – Plant-based beauty care products and treatments are on sale at the legendary ***Shanaz Husain Herbal***, S-55 Ashok St (C3). Open every day. Manicures, face massages, henna designs on hands. Also see ***Biotique***, M.I. Rd, east of Niro's (C3). Face massages, but more expensive than Shanaz Husain.

Musical instruments – ***Music 'N' Sports***, 73 Chaura Rasta (D2).

Bookshops – ***Book Corner***, M.I. Rd, next to Niro's (C3). 10am-11pm. ***Bookwise***, Rajputana Palace Sheraton (A2). Every day 10am-11pm. ***Arya Niwas*** (10am-7pm) and ***Rambagh Palace hotel bookshops***.

Photography – ***Goyal Kodak***, M.I. Rd, opposite Niro's (C3). Open every day. ***Krishna Color Lab***, M.I. Rd, east of the above.

Dry cleaners – ***Smernoff***, M.I. Rd, next to Niro's. On the opposite pavement, a bit further east, ***Snowhite*** and ***De-Luxe***.

Making the most of the Jaipur area

Where to stay

• Jamwa Ramgarh

22km northeast of Jaipur. Leave Jaipur on the Amber Rd and take a right turning 1.5km after Zorawar Singh Gate. The entrance to the hotel is via the dam, on the left-hand side of the road.

From US$40-70

The Ramgarh Lodge (Taj Group and Heritage Hotels Association), Ramgarh Lake, Jamwas Ramgarh, ☎ and Fax (142) 65 22 17; reservations in Delhi and Jaipur (see p 107) – 18rm. Billiards. This royal hunting lodge, built in 1931 in a pure Art Deco style, nestles between the surrounding hills and the lake. It almost feels as if time has stood still here. An elegant lawn gracefully sweeps down from the veranda to the lake, overlooking a perfectly peaceful landscape. The walls of the wooden staircase and living room are covered in hunting trophies. The rooms are spacious and tasteful, but only the "superior" category ones have a view of the lake. Prices include half-board. 10 % discount from April to September.

• On the road to Shekhawati and Bikaner

Take the northwest bound N.H.11 and continue to Chomu (30km).

From US$15-30

Golden Castle Resort (Heritage Hotels Association), Pachar, 80km from Jaipur, ☎ (01577) 646 11; reservations in Jaipur, ☎ (0141) 38 29 55, Fax (0141) 38 05 78 and 38 28 10 – 16rm. Cooler available on request. At Chomu, turn left to Kishangarh (the road is in a terrible state), then take a right turning to Pachar, which possesses an interesting fully illuminated Jain temple. This attractive family castle, wedged in between the sand dunes and the lake, is full of character and its recent restoration has neither altered the structure nor the decoration. Jeep excursions. Booking essential.

From US$40-70

Samod Palace (Heritage Hotels Association), Samod, 40km from Jaipur, ☎ (01423) 441 14 and 441 23; reservations at Samod Haveli in Jaipur – 36rm. 8km to the east of Chomu, located in a rocky pass, this impressive fortified palace is an excellent example of Rajput architecture. Tastefully decorated, it is one of the best hotels in Rajasthan. Everything is perfect, right down to the last detail. Eleven suites. 20 % discount for single travellers. A 100Rs charge is made, unless you have lunch at the hotel, to visit the superb "rawal" hall where the Samod held their durbar. Book well ahead.

Samod Bagh (Heritage Hotels Association), Fatehpura, 3km away from the above; reservations at Samod Haveli in Jaipur – 50rm. Set in the heart of a Mughal garden, replete with water channels and pools, fountains and marble pavilions, 50 luxurious tents with real bathrooms are lined-up one next to another. The meals are cooked at Samod Palace and heated up here. Half price for single travellers.

• Pachewar

90km to the southwest of Jaipur, take the N.H.8 towards Ajmer, then, from Dudu, take the road to Malpura.

From US$15-30

Hotel Pachewar Garh (Heritage Hotels Association), Pachewar, ☎ (01437) 287 56; reservations at Jaipur, ☎ (0141) 35 64 12, ☎ and Fax (0141) 60 10 07 – 10rm. A charming rustic 17C fort currently undergoing renovation. The rooms are moderately comfortable, power cuts are frequent and the service somewhat unpredictable, the whole place nonetheless has a great deal of character and the staff are friendly. Booking advisable.

• At Kanota

15km east of Jaipur on the N.H.11.

From US$30-40

Royal Castle Kanota (Heritage Hotels Association), Kanota, 15km from Jaipur, on the right on leaving the town; reservations at Narain Niwas Palace in Jaipur – 10rm. A beautiful 19C residence set within the walls of a medieval fort. The architecture and the garden are full of charm, but the rooms are variable in quality and the overall impression is rather dishevelled. Bookings essential, 10% discount from March to August.

• **At Bhandarej**

65km out of Jaipur. Take the N.H.11 towards Agra. 9km after Dausa, turn right.

From US$15-30

Bhadrawati Palace (Heritage Hotels Association), Bhandarej, 65km from Jaipur, on the right 9km after Dausa, ☎ (01427) 83 51; reservations at Jaipur, ☎ (0141) 35 52 61 and 36 32 62, Fax (0141) 37 29 19 – 35rm. A large 16C palace with gardens and inner courtyards filled with flowers. The rooms, of varying sizes, are all pleasant and comfortable and the bathrooms are new. Rooms 128 and 129 are the best. Meals are served in the "durbar" hall, which is a blend of white marble and turquoise "arayish". Bookings advisable. Interesting "baori" in the village.

The temples of Galta

B Brillion/Michelin

BHARATPUR★★

Pop 230 000– Alt 250m
55km from Agra – 175km from Jaipur – 180km from Delhi
See map p 200

Not to be missed
The Keoladeo Ghana Ornithological Reserve.

And remember...
Avoid visiting Bharatpur at the weekends or during festivals.
Get up at dawn to make sure you're in the park the minute it opens, armed with binoculars.

In the 18C this large country town, located in a well-cultivated plain, was the capital of the only Jat kingdom of any note in India. The fort, which dates back to that period, still remains and while it is by no means spectacular, it is still worth a visit. The major attraction of the area is the bird sanctuary, one of the most varied in the world and on Unesco's world heritage list. In this lush green paradise of marshy swamps, visitors can identify – with the help of a guide – several of the sanctuary's 350 species of birds, including the endangered **Siberian crane**.

The Jat kingdom: a fleeting power

Today the Jats are still a peasant caste settled all over the northwest of India. Renowned for their agricultural expertise, they are also despised for their uncouth manners and – in former times – for the fondness of their clan leaders for banditry. The Jats' rise to power began in the late 17C, when Emperor Aurangzeb, a devout Moslem, set out to raze all the Hindu temples in the Braj region (around Mathura): the Jats immediately launched raids in Mughal territories. In the early 18C, grouped together under **Badan Singh** from Bharatpur, they forged a kingdom for themselves which spread from Delhi to Agra. Forced to recognise this *de facto* new power, the emperor granted Badan Singh the title of rajah in 1752. More audacious than their predecessors, the new rajas, **Suraj Mal** and **Jawahar Singh**, pillaged and ransacked Delhi and Agra in the 1760s. They returned with loot that was to enrich and embellish their twin capitals, Bharatpur and Deeg, and which also encouraged the Rajput clans to overlook the distaste they felt for the upstarts and form marriage alliances. Confronted with the invading Marathas and then the British, the Jats' power dwindled and in 1818, the rajah of Bharatpur was the first Rajasthani sovereign to sign a treaty with the British.

Tour of the park and the town

At least 4hr in a cycle-rickshaw.

Keoladeo Ghana National Park★★

5km south of the town. Open from dawn to dusk, entrance fee, extra charge for videos. See also "Making the most of Bharatpur – Address book".

A walk through the park provides a truly enchanting experience, enabling visitors to encounter some of the hundreds of **birds** which live in this 29 square kilometre swampland, overgrown with grass and reeds and shaded by the dense foliage of tall trees. Raised paths enable walkers to get about the reserve, even during the monsoon season, when it is almost submerged.

A national park since 1982, the sanctuary dates back to the mid-18C, when it was a hunting reserve. Maharaja Suraj Mal had it established by erecting a dike at the confluence of the two rivers, thus creating a series of ponds which would attract unsuspecting ducks and other migratory birds: Bharatpur's records have reports of former bloody duck shoots. The best period to observe the reserve's birds is from August to March, but each season provides its own treats. The first rains in July fill the park with birds who have come to breed: herons, egrets, white ibis, moorhens... Winter is when the reserve has the most guests: storks, Siberian cranes, Greylag geese, birds of prey... The park also provides a permanent home to several species of duck, as well as deer, otters, mongoose...

Mass murder

In British India, Bharatpur's duck shoots were one of the major events of the social calendar. Everyone who was anyone was invited to take part in this bloodthirsty entertainment, made doubly popular by its proximity to Delhi. Among a graceful waltz of Rolls Royces (the other passion of the maharajas of Bharatpur), VIPs accompanied by a retinue of servants, engaged joyfully in wholesale massacre. In 1914, Lord Hardinge, Viceroy of India shot 4082 birds in only one day, while in 1921 the Duke of Windsor killed 1560 in three hours. But Viceroy Lord Linlithgow holds the record with 4273 dispatched in a single day in 1930!

Lohagarh fort

North of Bharatpur Bazaar. Open from dawn until dusk. Allow 45min.

Lohagarh ("iron fort") fully deserves its nickname: built in the early 18C, it withstood several Mughal, then British assaults before being finally captured in 1826. The entrance, past the beaten earth and sand **ramparts***, surrounded by a moat, is via one of two doors which Raja Jahawar Singh brought back with loot plundered in Delhi in 1764. The northern door had already suffered a similar fate in 1303, when Sultan Ala ud-Din had it torn from Chittaurgarh's ramparts to take it back to Delhi. Inside the fort are three very decrepit palaces.

The **Government Museum** *(10am-4.30pm; closed Friday, entrance fee, extra charge for cameras)* is spread over two wings of one of the fort's palaces *(the central area is undergoing restoration)*. The **sculptures** dating from the 10C to the 18C and a pretty **hammam*** *(rear of the right wing)*, are particularly worthy of note. The terrace has a fine view over Bharatpur and its tranquil bazaar.

Making the most of Bharatpur

Getting there

By train – The ***station*** is located in the north of the city, 7km from the sanctuary, ☎ 131. Non-computerised reservations terminal (only for trains leaving Bharatpur) open every day 9am-5pm. 5 trains run daily to Delhi (4-5hr journey), stopping at Mathura (75min), and to Kota (4-5hr), stopping at Sawai Madhopur (3hr).

By bus – ***Main Bus Stand***, to the west, 4km from the sanctuary, ☎ (05644) 234 34. Around ten "Silver Line" buses stop at Bharatpur everyday, en route for Jaipur (4hr) or Agra (90min). Departures every 46min for Delhi (5hr) and Deeg (1hr), every hour for Alwar (2hr30min). 6 daily departures for Fatehpur Sikri (1hr) and 11 for Ajmer (7hr). 2 luxury buses go to Jodhpur (12hr).

Getting about

By rickshaw – To get from the station to the sanctuary by auto-rickshaw costs around 60Rs. The area around the park is the preserve of the cycle-rickshaws, almost all of which are driven by Sikhs (35-40Rs per hour). Those authorised in the sanctuary have a yellow plate.

Bicycle rentals – On Bird Sanctuary Rd or at the entrance to the sanctuary. Also ask at your hotel, which often offers very reasonable prices.

Address book

Tourist office – ***Tourist Reception Centre***, easternmost end of Bird Sanctuary Rd, 4km south of the old town. 10am-1.30pm/2pm-5pm; closed Sunday.

Keoladeo Ghana National Park – Bird Sanctuary Rd, 700m from the tourist office. Every day 6am-6pm. Entrance charge: 100Rs per person, 125Rs per car, 3Rs per bicycle, 200Rs per video camera. Guides (40Rs/hr). Cars are only allowed within a restricted area. Cycle-rickshaws (35Rs/hr), bicycles (25Rs/day) and boats.

Banks/Money – ***State Bank of Bikaner and Jaipur***, Binarayan Gate, 1st road to the right on entering the town. Can change dollars and pounds sterling (cash and travellers' cheques).

Post office and telephones – There are two post offices in the old town: ***GPO***, Gandhi Park, to the north of the fort, and ***City Head Post Office*** near Juma Masjid mosque. 10am-5pm, Saturday 10am-1pm; closed Sunday. Postal code: 321001.

Health – ***Ambulance***, ☎ (05644) 236 33.

Safety – ***Police***, ☎ (05644) 224 44, 225 26 and 225 48.

Where to stay

• In Bharatpur

Most of the town's hotels and restaurants are grouped together along Jaipur Rd. In the low season, from April to August-September, a 25% discount is often granted on hotel rooms.

Less than US$7

Pelican Hotel, Bird Sanctuary Rd, ☎ (05644) 242 21 – 9rm. 6rm with cooler. A two-storey building. Basic but clean, well-kept rooms.

Jungle Lodge, in an avenue east of Bird Sanctuary Rd, past the tourist office, ☎ (05644) 256 22 – 6rm. 4rm. with cooler. A pleasant, friendly, family guesthouse, with rooms and a veranda overlooking a very attractive little garden.

Falcon Guest House, next to the above, ☎ (05644) 238 15 and 253 06 – 8rm. Cooler. A small, very friendly, family establishment. Spacious, well-kept rooms and a pleasant flower garden.

Eagle's Nest Hotel, Bird Sanctuary Rd, ☎ (05644) 251 44/45, Fax (05644) 223 10 – 12rm. 2rm. with AC. A white ground-floor building built alongside a large lawn, bordered with hedges, where guests and non-residents can take meals. Clean rooms with plastic, but good-quality furniture.

From US$7-30

Pratap Palace Hotel, Bird Sanctuary Rd, ☎ (05644) 242 45, ☎ and Fax (05644) 250 93 – 22rm. Cooler. 6rm. with fan. Good, traditional well-cared for establishment. The decoration is somewhat gaudy, but the rooms are clean. In the winter, ask for a room with cooler, they are the same price as those with AC, but on the first floor and without a bath.

From US$30-70

Laxmi Vilas Palace, also called Kakaji ki Kothi (Heritage Hotels Association), Agra Rd, 1km from the sanctuary, ☎ (05644) 235 23, Fax (05644) 252 59 – 25rm. TV CC 11rm. with AC. This small white palace, hidden in the countryside, was built in a late-19C Indo-Rajput style. The colonial-style rooms are nothing special, but the bathrooms have been recently renovated and the whole place has a good deal of character. Good restaurant and bar in an attractive colonnaded room or in a recently redecorated inner courtyard. 50% discount in the low season.

Bharatpur Forest Lodge (Ashok), inside the sanctuary, ☎ (05644) 227 22 and 227 60, Fax (05644) 228 64 – 17rm. TV CC This hotel's appeal lies in its location, amidst trees and abundant wildlife. The rooms, refurbished and comfortable, are nonetheless somewhat ordinary and a little neglected. 30% discount for single travellers. Pleasant terrace restaurant and bar.

• In Peharsar

2km west of Bharatpur, 1km south of N.H.11, after Luharu.

From US$30-70

Chandra Mahal Haveli (Heritage Hotels Association), Peharsar, ☎ (05643) 432 38, ☎ and Fax (011) 91 38 51 84 – 17rm. CC This small, recently renovated haveli dates from 1850 and is situated in the heart of the village. A charming inner courtyard and a lovely garden overlooked by well-kept rooms (a pity the lighting is so parsimonious). 30% discount for single travellers. Excursions organised to Bharatpur and Deeg.

• In Karauli

110km south of Bharatpur and 104km to the northeast of Sawai Madhopur.

From US$15-30

Bhanwar Vilas Palace (Heritage Hotels Association), Karauli, ☎ (07464) 200 24 and 210 35; reservations at Jaipur, ☎ (0141) 21 05 12 and 21 15 32, Fax (0141) 21 05 12 – 21rm. CC This palace was built in the 1930s by the grandfather of the current maharaja, head of the Yaduvanshi Rajputs. Lack of sufficient lighting gives the place a rather melancholy, nostalgic atmosphere, particularly as it has retained its period furniture, paintings and photographs. Note the beautiful polished floors, made of crushed marble and cement in varying pastel hues. Four handsome suites which are a bit more expensive. Delicious cooking.

Where to eat

If travelling by car, there are several motels around Mahwa (see map p 200), on N.H.8. They provide a welcome halt half-way between Jaipur and Agra. The best are: ***Rajasthan Motel***, 2km before Mahwa, and ***Rajputana Country Resort***, 7km after Mahwa. Allow around US$3 per meal.

DEEG★

Pop 40 000 – Alt 260m
35km from Bharatpur – 37km from Mathura – 90km from Alwar
See map p 200

Not to be missed
The visit to the palace.

And remember...
To get a photo of the palace reflected in the lake, visit in the afternoon.
Spend the night at Bharatpur or at Kesroli castle (Alwar).

After a bumpy, dusty drive through a monotonous plain, the palace of Deeg rises like a welcome mirage, with pools, elegant pavilions and a Mughal garden. It is hard to imagine that this sleepy agricultural backwater, in the heart of which lies the royal palace, was once the summer capital of the powerful Jat kingdom.

The ransacking of Delhi
When Maharaja Suraj Mal of Bharatpur was captured and savagely killed by the emperor's soldiers, his son, Jawahar Singh, sought revenge and attacked the Mughal capital in 1764. After a six-month siege, Delhi surrendered and was ransacked. Legend tells that 2 000 horses and 500 elephants were required to transport the incredible loot to Bharatpur and Deeg.

The Jats' second capital

Enriched thanks to raids and looting, the sovereign of Bharatpur, **Badan Singh**, set about building a palace in Deeg in 1730. It was regularly extended and embellished during the 18C by its successive rajas, thanks to the spoils of incessant forays, particularly on Delhi and Agra.

Tour of the town

Allow 1hr.

Deeg palace★★

200m from the railway station. Open from dawn until dusk, no charge.
This enchanting palace invariably inspires love at first sight, its lovely pink façade flanked by two pavilions topped with "Bengali" roofs seemingly suspended over the water of the pool in which they are reflected. A walk down the main path leads into the **Mughal garden★**. Divided into four equal parts by canals, typical of the classical *chahar bagh* layout, it has 500 fountains which can only be seen in action on Saturdays in August. The garden is bordered on all sides by palaces and pavilions, the main one of which is Gopal Bhawan, on the west side.

Built in 1756 by Suraj Mal and given one of Krishna's names, **Gopal Bhawan** (palace of Gopal) *(Remove shoes before entering. Officially only the Durbar Hall can be visited, but a tip should generally persuade the caretaker to open other doors, in particular those of the first floor)*, this four-storey building (including a basement) was still inhabited by the royal family until the early 1970s, and the furniture, paintings and china still remaining give visitors the impression that the owners are expected back any minute. It is said that the two *(closed)* wings of the palace each contain a throne, one made out of black marble, the other out of white, which were part of the spoils of the ransacking of Delhi in 1764.

On leaving the palace, take a look at the two pavilions framing the palace. They are named after the two monsoon months, **Shravan** and **Bhadon**, (mid-July to mid-September), a period during which India relishes the cooler climate provided by the rain. The other buildings, undergoing restoration, are closed to the public. Walk straight across the garden towards the **Keshav Bhawan** *(opposite the Gopal Bhawan)*; this elegant summer colonnaded pavilion with a flat roof, overlooking a pool, was used for public audiences. Turning back towards the Gopal Bhawan *(along its southern flank)*, admire the view of the **Purana Mahal** (oldest part of the palace, dating from 1730), the **Kishan Bhawan**, and finally the **Suraj Bhawan**, a white marble Mughal pavilion captured at Agra during the town's pillaging by Suraj Mal in 1761, and rebuilt here, block by block.

Leave the palace by the south and take a stroll round the busy bazaar which bursts into life at the end of the afternoon.

Excursion to Govardhan

16km from Deeg on the road to Mathura.

The **royal cenotaphs*** of two of the maharajas of Bharatpur stand in the middle of the countryside by the edge of a lake, close to Govardhan, a Krishnist place of pilgrimage. Topped with the familiar kiosks and "Bengali" roofs with golden pinnacles, they face a 16C temple to Hari (another of Vishnu's names). Of the two 19C cenotaphs, **Ranjit Singh's** is the most ornate. Built on several storeys, its walls are covered in intricate carving and its painted dome depicts the siege of Bharatpur by the British.

At **Radha Kund** *(3km further on)* is the **centotaph of Suraj Mal**, built in the 18C on the edge of Lake Kusum Sarovar, the "flower lake".

Krishna lifts Mount Govardhan

From the 5C on, India's transition from Brahminism to modern Hinduism gave rise to changes in the objects of worship. Indra, a predominant figure of the Vedic pantheon, was gradually replaced by Shiva, Vishnu and Rama or Krishna. Legend relates that, incensed by this display of human fickleness, Indra triggered off a downpour of such magnitude that it threatened to engulf the Earth and all its inhabitants. Krishna, a young man at the time, who lived close by, at Vrindavan, then lifted up Mount Govardhan with his little finger, and held it aloft, like an umbrella, to protect the herdsmen and their flocks.

Making the most of Deeg

Getting there

By bus – The bus station is 200m from the palace. Buses run from 7am to 8pm, every 30 to 45min for Bharatpur (1hr) and Mathura (1hr), and every hour for Alwar (2hr30min).

Where to stay

Under US$7

Motel Deeg (RTDC), opposite the bus station, ☎ (05641) 204 30 – 3rm. Cooler. This little house set in a garden provides rooms which are just about acceptable. Pleasant welcome, but a night at Bharatpur would be a much better idea.

ALWAR

Pop 204 000– Alt 268m
125km from Jaipur – 165km from Delhi
See map p 200

Not to be missed

The museum's collection of manuscripts and miniature paintings.
Bakhtawar Singh's cenotaph.

And remember...

Treat yourself to a night in one of the nearby palace-hotels.

This small town, languorously sprawled at the foot of a circle of rocky hills, constitutes the meeting point between the rectilinear plain of Delhi and the first eastern foothills of the Aravalli Range. The northeastern flat, monotonous countryside stops dead at Alwar, replaced by rocky outcrops which paint the countryside a colourful blend of pinks. Alwar, the historic gateway to Rajasthan and the district capital, is now a quiet provincial town where India can be seen at its most traditional. Few vehicles are to be found in the narrow lanes around the palace and fewer still are the foreign tourists to adventure this far. Alwar is one of Rajasthan's few remaining cities where a quiet cup of tea can still be enjoyed on the terrace of a café, providing a pleasant picture of bygone provincial life.

The baby of the Rajput kingdoms

The city of Alwar was founded at the turn of the year 1000. Very soon, its value as a strategic observation point made it a much coveted prize. It passed from hand to hand: from the Rajputs to the Mughals, the Pathans, and then to the Jats of Bharatpur. Finally in 1771, the Rajput **Pratap Singh** (related to the Kachwahas of Jaipur) conquered Alwar and founded one of Rajasthan's most recent independent kingdoms. A subtle blend of astute diplomacy enabled the new dynasty to withstand the neighbouring Rajput and Jat kingdoms and the military might of the Maratha chiefs. In 1803, Bakhtawar Singh formed an alliance with the British, thus ensuring his kingdom's continued peace. Freed of their military duties, the town's sovereigns, turned maharajas, became active patrons of the arts and literature, investing generously, even extravagantly, as in the case of Jai Singh, maharaja from 1857 to 1933.

Deposed for cruelty to animals

Jai Singh considered himself to be an incarnation of Rama. He went so far as to have a copy of the god's crown made which he wore in place of the traditional Rajput turban. A great car enthusiast, particularly of Hispano-Suizas, he bought them three at a time, painted blue – Alwar's colour – or gold-plated, and had them buried when he felt they were past their prime. Lavish and sophisticated, he was a keen hunter and also enjoyed the company of young boys; his reputation as a cruel sadist was legendary. He was finally deposed by the British (for cruelty to animals, having had his horse burnt alive) and finished his days in Paris, dying in 1937.

Visit of the town

Allow 90min.

The City Palace* (or Vinay Vilas)

Take a taxi to Tripolia Gate. If coming from the bus station, follow the main avenue which forks left for around 200m, then turn right, in front of the "Ashok Theater" cinema. No entrance charge.

R and S Michaud/RAPHO

Chhatri along the edge of the palace reservoir

The lane leading to **Tripolia Gate** passes through a quiet bazaar, where pedestrians, cycle-rickshaws and a few scooters weave in and out among the stalls overflowing with mouth-watering pastries. The very dilapidated gate houses a small temple devoted to Shiva. A little lane, off to the left, leads past a herd of black pigs to a square frequented by public writers and civil servants during office hours. The district's administrative centre is installed in the royal palace, the façade of which, adorned with Bengali-roofed balconies, can be seen to the right of the square. The local authority's numerous employees take frequent tea breaks here, nibbling on snacks presented on leaves, fastened together by an acacia thorn to make small bowls. (The empty bowl is much appreciated by the foraging pigs and cows and the acacia thorns can frequently be found "stapled" to official administrative documents.)

The palace was built at the turn of the 18C by Pratap Singh and his successor Vinay Singh. The entrance to the **main courtyard** reveals an attractive multi-coloured marble floor. A ceremonial staircase, complete with Bengali-roofed loggia and flanked by two elegant *chhatri*, leads to the **durbar hall** (reception room) which is now entirely empty, but whose white and gold walls have kept their pristine appearance.

The somewhat old-fashioned presentation of the **Government Museum's** collections *(10am-4.30pm; closed Friday, entrance fee)*, on the top floor of the palace, *(take the staircase in the wing which opens onto the square)* rather suits the antiquated flavour of the building. Some of the timeworn, dusty old wooden showcases house quite pleasant surprises, but as most of the explanations are solely in Hindi, comprehension is not always easy. The **first room** depicts life at court: there are royal costumes, knick-knacks, ivory sandals and **musical instruments**, among them two magnificent peacock-shaped *dilruba* (stringed instruments). In the section devoted to manuscripts and miniature paintings, note the exquisitely illustrated 18C manuscripts of the *Bhagavad Gita* and the *Ramayana*, together with those of the *Babur Nameh* (Emperor Babur's memoirs) and the *Gulistan* (The "Rose-garden"), the work of a 13C Persian poet, Saadi. Among the various paintings of the Rajput schools are works by the Alwar *kalam* (Alwar's school of painting), notable for their vividly coloured borders. The **weapon** section is well-supplied with sabres, daggers and *katar*, including swords and armour worn by Muhammad of Ghor, Akbar and Aurangzeb. The terrace provides wonderful **views** over Alwar, the surrounding hills and the old fort.

Back on the square, walk past the palace to the right, to an open staircase. It leads up to a platform, on which Bakhtawar Singh's cenotaph stands.

The cenotaph of Maharaja Bakhtawar Singh, erected in 1815 by his son, is also called **Rani Mausi ki Chhatri**, in honour of the sovereign's widow, who died on her husband's funeral pyre. The red sandstone of the lower storey, dotted with kiosks contrasts pleasantly with the white marble of the upper storey *(shoes must be removed)*. Around the base of the elegant **ribbed dome** a few damaged paintings (a frieze of horsemen and camels and blue and gold motifs) and some fine **carving** (musicians, divinities and camel and elephant processions) can still be seen. Admirers of the devoted widow regularly bring flowers here, showing how much the *sati* cult remains strong, even today, in Rajput lands. The mausoleum and its surroundings have a restful atmosphere, particularly towards the end of the afternoon. Watching benevolently over the area is the rocky peak crowned by **Bala Qila Fort**, one of Rajasthan's oldest strongholds *(now a radio station, it can be visited on request)*.

The **reservoir**, surrounded by *ghats* and graceful *chhatri*, would be a perfectly idyllic spot, if not disfigured by mounds of detritus. Visitors are also advised to leave before sundown to avoid the swarms of mosquitoes.

Making the most of Alwar

Getting there

By train – *Alwar Railway Station* is at the east of the town, some 2.5km from the palace, ☎ (0144) 222 22. Computerised reservation terminal, 8am-8pm, Sunday 8am-2pm. 9 trains leave daily for Jaipur (3hr), including 1 "Shatabdi" in the morning (except Sunday). 7 trains leave for Delhi (3hr30min), 2 for Abu Road, 3 for Jodhpur (between and 8-11hr) and 1 for Mathura (3hr) and Agra (4hr).

By bus – *Roadways Bus Stand*, 1km from the palace, ☎ (0144) 222 85. No luxury buses, but express buses leave every 30min, from 6am to midnight, for Jaipur (4hr), via Sariska (45min). Departures every hour, between 5am and 9.30pm, for Delhi (4hr), as well as for Bharatpur (3hr30min), via Deeg (2hr30min). 8 buses leave daily for Agra (6hr), via Mathura (4hr).

Getting about

By rickshaw – Allow around 20-25Rs from the station to the palace.

By taxi – Taxi rank at the station.

Address book

Tourist Office – *Tourist Reception Centre*, opposite the station. 10am-1.30pm/2pm-5pm; closed Sunday. Can provide a list of guesthouses and a map of the town.

Banks/Money – *State Bank of Bikaner and Jaipur*, near the bus station. To change dollars and pounds sterling travellers' cheques.

Post Office/Telephone – *GPO*, Raghu Marg, Civil Lines. There is also a branch to the left of the station. Postal code: 301001

Safety – *Police*, ☎ (0144) 211 00 and 225 55.

Where to stay

• Town centre

From US$7-30

Hotel Aravali, near the tourist office, ☎ (0144) 33 23 16 and 33 28 83, Fax (0144) 33 23 16 – 32rm Cooler. A modern three-storey establishment run by an efficient, friendly family, but somewhat expensive. Best place in town for lunch.

• Siliserh

12km southwest of Alwar. Leave town on the road to Sariska and turn right to Siliserh.

From US$7-30

Lake Palace Hotel (RTDC), Siliserh, ☎ (0144) 863 22 and 863 31 – 10rm. This 19C royal pavilion overlooks a little lake, hidden within rambling hills. Although the site is superb, the hotel is in a sadly dilapidated state. The view from the restaurant's terrace is stunning, but it is impossible to sit and have a quiet drink, due to the maddening pestering of the local monkeys.

• Kesroli

12km east of Alwar. Take the road to Deeg, then turn left towards Delhi.

From US$30-70

The Hill Fort Kesroli (Neemrana Hotels and Heritage Hotels Association), Kesroli, ☎ (0144) 823 12; reservations in Delhi (see p 107) – 20rm. Cooler. This charming little fort with seven towers takes up the whole of the hilltop overlooking the surrounding countryside. A fixed price for one, two or three people, including breakfast. 25 % discount from April to September.

• Nimrana

75km north of Alwar, 2km from the N.H.8, between Shahjahanpur and Bahror.

From US$30-70

Nimrana Fort Palace (Neemrana Hotels and Heritage Hotels Association), Nimrana, ☎ (01494) 60 06/07 /08, Fax (01494) 60 05; reservations in Delhi (see p 107) – 42rm. This astonishing fortified palace, dating from the mid-15C, is built in an Indo-Moslem style, with eight storeys on the flanks of the rocky hill. The elegant interior decoration, the obvious care taken with the bathrooms and the sophisticated Rajasthani and French cooking all combine to make it one of the best places to stay in the region. Identical price for one, two or three people.

Sariska Tiger Reserve and National Park★

35km southwest of Alwar
See map p 200

And remember...
The best time to go is at dawn or before dusk, avoiding weekends and holiday periods. Don't forget your binoculars!

These wild rambling hills, covered in acacia trees and scattered with rocks, shelter one of Rajasthan's two tiger reserves (the other being at Ranthambore), created to protect the noble feline in danger of extinction. The site was formerly one of the favourite hunting domains of Alwar's maharajas. The capricious Jai Singh, who used to spear-hunt boar and tiger here, also had a palace built in 1902 *(now a hotel, see "Making the most of Sariska")*, whose somewhat pretentious turrets and grandiose façade contrast with the forest's wild beauty.

Tour of the reserve

7am-4pm from October to January; 6am-5pm from February to September. Entrance charge, extra for video cameras. It is possible to take cars into the reserve, but only jeeps are allowed to stray from the surfaced trails. Visitors must take a guide. Allow 3hr. Also see "Address book" in "Making the most of Sariska".

Created in the 1950s, the reserve was incorporated into the **Tiger Project** in 1978. It became a National Park in 1982. Over a third of its 866sqkm of land is still inhabited. Furthermore the Jaipur-Alwar road runs through the park and each year one or two cheetahs or leopards are run over crossing it (the reserve has some 50 cheetahs).

Boar hunting, 19C miniature

Those who want to be certain of catching sight of a **tiger** will have to brave the stifling heat of the April to June months: the dry weather of the pre-monsoon periods makes the animals dependent on the artificial water holes dug by the park's authorities near the trails. Guides and drivers are always eager to help visitors catch a glimpse of one of the 25 tigers or so that live in the reserve. But the law of the jungle prevails: some visitors have had to visit ten times before seeing even one. The cervidae (deer, chital, *sambar* bucks), antelopes (enormous *nilgai*, four-horned stags and *chinkara*), boar and peacocks are easier to spot. Within the reserve, the ruins of the 17C **Kankwari fort**, built on the water's edge are worth a stop. It is here that Emperor Aurangzeb is said to have imprisoned one of his brothers, the rightful heir to the throne.

Tiger Project

The tiger protection programme, with a total of some twenty reserves throughout India, was started jointly in 1973 by the Indian and the State governments. Despite a promising start, it was soon undermined by negligence and corruption. Hunting parties organised for wealthy city dwellers and other irregularities transformed the project into a disaster, to such an extent that in the early 1990s the number of tigers had dropped to below the figures of ten years earlier. The situation appears to have dramatically improved of late, and India's tiger population is once again on the increase.

The reserve's other "historic" vestige is **Pandu Pol** (the gate of Pandava) which dates back to the mythical era of the Mahabharata, when the five Pandava brothers and Draupadi, the wife they shared between them, were exiled in the region. One of the brothers, Bhim, of legendary strength, is said to have shattered a rock with his sword, giving birth to a waterfall that provides drinking water for the thirsty animals even today.

Making the most of Sariska

Getting there

By bus – Buses from Alwar (45min) and Jaipur (3hr) stop every half-hour at the entrance to the reserve.

Getting about

By car – It is possible to rent diesel (560Rs per day) or petrol jeeps (660Rs).

Address book

Tiger Project Reception Centre – At the entrance to the reserve, ☎ (0144) 413 33. 6am-4.30pm, 7am-4pm from February to September. Compulsory guide: 100Rs. Day entrance permit: 100Rs per person, 125Rs per car, 200Rs per video camera.

Where to stay and eat

Visitors should note that, with the exception of the Tiger Den and Sariska Palace hotels, there is nowhere to eat.

From US$15-30

Hotel Tiger Den (RTDC), Sariska, ☎ (0144) 413 42 – 28rm. Cooler. Bar. On the edge of the forest, next door to the Tiger Project Reception Centre. A modern complex with somewhat Spartan and neglected rooms.

From US$40-70

Hotel Sariska Palace (Heritage Hotels Association), Sariska, opposite the above address, ☎ (01465) 242 47, Fax (0144) 413 22, sariska@ del2.vsnl.net.in – reservations in Delhi, ☎ (011) 616 32 25/26 and 617 23 46, Fax (011) 618 88 61 – 80rm. TV CC This impressive pink and yellow palace, surrounded by spacious lawns, was built by Jai Singh, an extravagant maharaja. Far from welcoming, the service does not live up to the establishment's prices.

SHEKHAWATI★★

Tour of approximately 175km

See map p 200

Not to be missed

Sardul Singh's cenotaph at Parasarampura.

The Sone ki Dukan at Mahansar.

And remember...

Allow at least a day and a half.

Rent a jeep with a driver who knows the villages and haveli well.

Stay in one of the forts or haveli which have been turned into hotels.

On the road to Jaipur, stop at Samod for lunch and to admire the "durbar hall".

Backed by the last hills of the Aravalli Range, Shekhawati spreads out over an arid steppe region, an extension of the Thar Desert to the east. This sand-coloured land appears to have been forgotten by the passing winds of progress. On its long winding roads – more like trails in fact – visitors are more likely to encounter camels or donkeys pulling carts than motor vehicles. Trees are few and far between. Only millet, barley, lentils and oilseeds grow on the sandy plots of land, protected by thorny hedges. The towns have little more than 50 000 inhabitants – hardly more than a village by normal Indian standards. Yet this apparently forbidding, austere landscape has vast numbers of sumptuously decorated *haveli* (dwellings of wealthy merchants). Visitors are surprised – sometimes filled with wonder – at the sight of the exuberantly naïve frescoes adorning the *havelis'* walls, bringing both colour and gaiety to an otherwise sadly monochrome landscape. These works comprise one of the world's largest concentrations of mural paintings.

The heyday of the caravans

The kingdom of Shekha – The region emerged from anonymity in the 15C, when a childless local ruler, Mokul Singh, who owed allegiance to the Rajah of Amber, came on a pilgrimage to Vrindavan (near Mathura), Krishna's childhood home. A *sadhu* promised him a son on his return on condition that he undertook to care for and protect the cows so dear to Krishna. He kept his promise and, on his return home, met a pious *sheikh* (Arab Moslem) who agreed to give him a son providing that the newborn child was bathed in cow's blood. The long-awaited son, **Rao Shekha**, an ambitious, clever man, managed to free himself from the Rajah's rule and took control of nearly the whole region, which was named Shekhawati. In the 16C, *Rao* Raisal Das pledged allegiance, of his own accord, to Emperor Akbar, and his descendants loyally served in the imperial armies. Taking

An endangered heritage

Many foreign visitors admit to being disappointed by the condition of Shekhawati's monuments and quite horrified by the inhabitants' negligent attitude to their inheritance. The wealthy former owners of the haveli have long since quit Shekhawati and it would be unreasonable to ask the villagers to set about restoring these marvellous houses. However one can't help thinking that they should at least be informed and encouraged not to continue disfiguring the precious murals. With a few notable exceptions, the only people who seem interested in Shekhawati's heritage are tourists – much to the joy of local merchants who strip the buildings of their carved wood doors, lintels and window frames, to sell them to western enthusiasts.

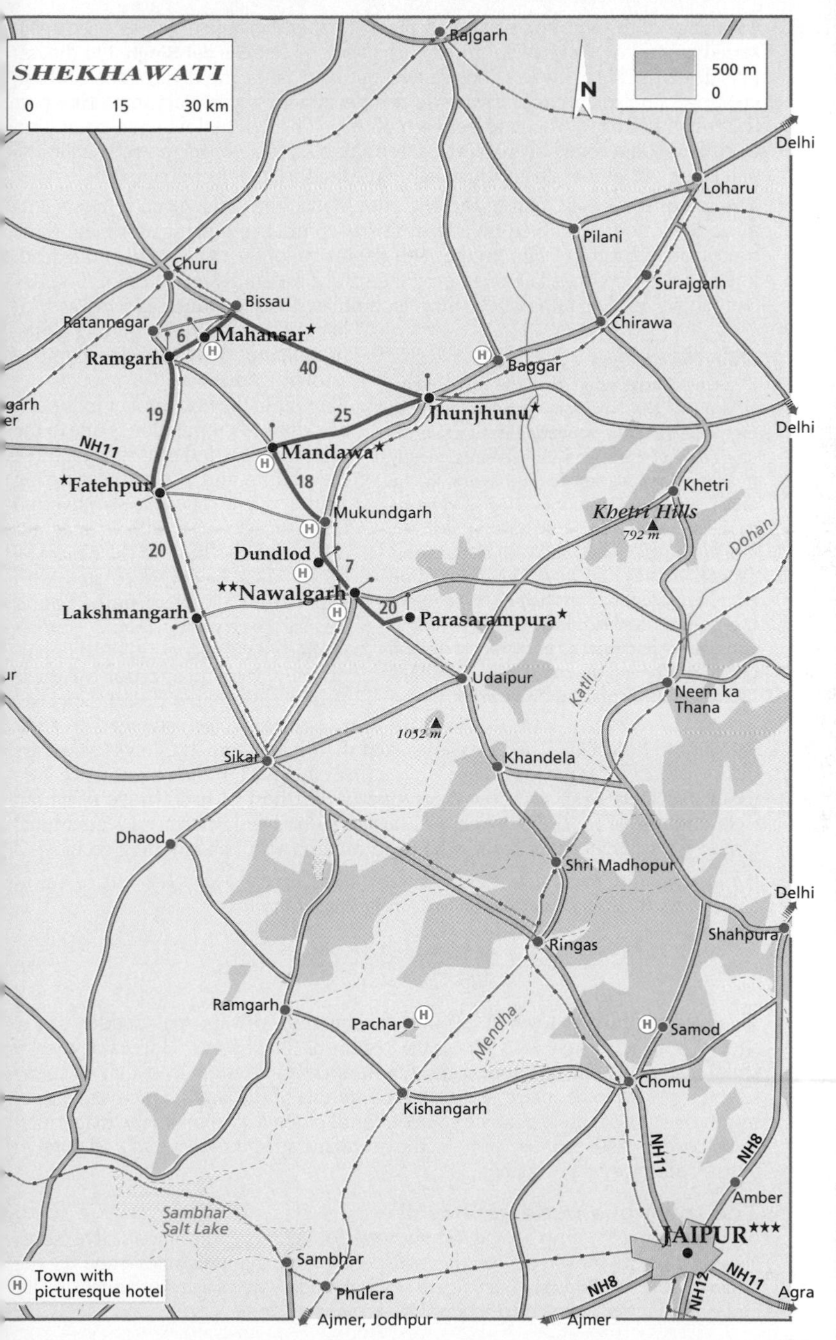
SHEKHAWATI
0
15
30 km
N
500 m
0
Rajgarh
Delhi
Loharu
Pilani
Surajgarh
Churu
Bissau
Ratannagar
6
Mahansar★
Ramgarh
40
Chirawa
Baggar
Jhunjhunu★
25
19
Delhi
NH11
Mandawa★
★Fatehpur
18
Khetri
Khetri Hills
792 m
Dohan
Mukundgarh
20
Dundlod
7
★★Nawalgarh
20
Parasarampura★
Lakshmangarh
Udaipur
Katli
Neem ka Thana
1052 m
Sikar
Khandela
Dhaod
Shri Madhopur
Delhi
Shahpura
Ringas
Mendha
Ramgarh
Pachar
Samod
Chomu
Kishangarh
NH11
NH8
Amber
Sambhar Salt Lake
JAIPUR★★★
Sambhar
Phulera
NH8
NH12
NH11
Agra
Ajmer, Jodhpur
Ajmer
Town with picturesque hotel

advantage of the empire's decline in the 18C, the Maharaja of Jaipur once again seized control of Shekhawati, ruled at the time by Rao **Sardul Singh**. On the latter's death, in 1742, his five sons carried out his wishes and divided the land up, creating a confederation of towns – a unique system within Rajasthan. However the equal division of the land between all five sons led the following generation to embark on a series of raids and interminable struggles for power, while the parcelling out of the territory inevitably resulted in its impoverishment.

The era of the haveli – From the 18C, the *baniya* (the name given to merchants in northern India) profited greatly from the commerce flowing along the trade routes radiating from Delhi. In the 19C, the arrival of the railway tolled the death knell for the caravans. The most progressive dealers emigrated to Delhi, Bombay and, above all, Calcutta, where they accumulated vast fortunes, serving as brokers with the British trading posts. In Calcutta they were inaccurately known as **marwari** (in reference to Marwar in the kingdom of Jodhpur). Shekhawati's reputation is due to the architectural undertakings of these merchants and not to its warring Rajput rulers. The *marwari* invested their substantial wealth in magnificent dwellings built in their place of birth. Their **haveli**, decorated with superb murals, were built around several courtyards *(chowk)*. India's modern day business elite still comprises a large proportion of these wealthy merchants' descendants *(see p 29)*. No longer attached to their Shekhawati homeland, they have entrusted their handsome dwellings to the care of a *chowkidar* (caretaker) who lives in the first courtyard. India's inheritance laws mean that most *haveli* are now the property of a host of heirs, none of whom feels responsible for their upkeep. Although some would never miss an annual visit to their family home, others have no qualms about abandoning them.

Nouveaux riches

It seems almost ironic that the former emigration of the "marwari" trading community appears to be repeating itself again today. Many of the region's inhabitants, mostly Moslems, are leaving to find work in the Gulf countries. The money they send home to their families is spent on building spacious modern houses, equipped with all the latest gadgets money can buy. This infatuation with new values has not helped to preserve the region's architectural legacy, which is considered antiquated, uncomfortable and out-of-touch with the standards so extolled by today's advertising and television.

For an exhaustive tour of the region's havelis, Ilay Cooper's book "The Painted Towns of Shekhawati" is very informative and can be bought locally.

▪ Nawalgarh★★

Allow half a day on foot.

This pleasant market town of 50 000 inhabitants, with its well-trodden sandy streets, is an ideal base for touring the region of Shekhawati. Hordes of cheeky children pursue visitors around the town, apparently astonished that so many foreigners seem to be interested in the old murals of the *haveli*, much less attractive to their eyes than the movie stars of Hindi cinema who make the magazines' front covers. *"One pen, one pen"* is the standard greeting to which all foreign tourists are invariably treated.

The town of a hundred haveli

Founded in 1737 by Nawal Singh, one of *Rao* Sardul Singh's five sons, Nawalgarh was the cradle of the prosperous merchant families such as the **Goenka** and the **Poddar**. Nawalgarh's *havelis* today are of very unequal quality and only the best conserved examples are worth a look.

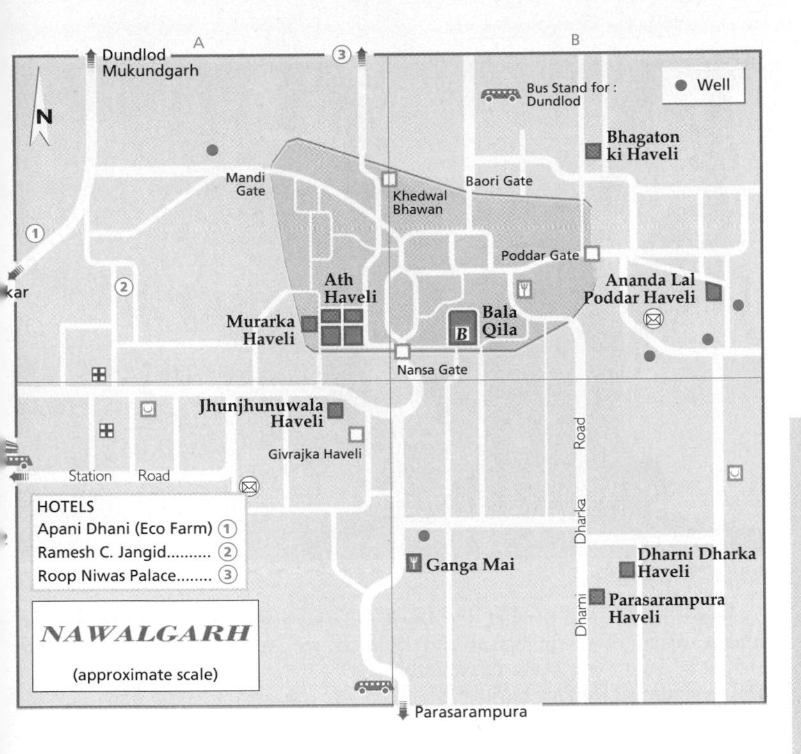

Take a taxi or rickshaw to **Nansa Gate**, a somewhat decrepit arch which formerly provided access to what used to be a fortified city. The first lane on the left leads to a group of six *haveli*, the **Ath haveli** (A1). As "ath" means eight, it is probable that the former owners left the region before completing their building projects. Most of the buildings are closed and only the paintings on the outer walls can still be admired. The prettily decorated **Murarka haveli** (A1) is also generally closed. Close by on the **Jhunjhunuwala haveli** (B2), there are particularly fine friezes representing traditional processions, with elephants, railway trains, etc.

An open-air art gallery

The artists who painted Shekhawati's havelis could not abide leaving any empty space: every single sq.cm. of the walls is covered in fantastic frescoes. Outer walls, inner courtyards ("chowk"), reception rooms, even simple corridors, all are amply and lavishly decorated. Unfortunately the sun, the monsoon rains and the sand-filled winds have faded the splendour of the original paintings. Painted advertisements and slogans, graffiti, posters and coats of whitewash have also contributed to the overall deterioration, while the interior frescoes have been blackened by the smoke from the ovens or the petrol lamps of the "chowkidar". Nor has the general neglect inflicted on most havelis by their respective owners done much to prevent the spread of damp.

Further south, **Ganga Mai Temple** (B2) (second half of the 19C), devoted to the goddess Ganga, personification of the Ganges, resembles a haveli with its elegant frescoes and mirrors. The bordering road to the north, lined with painted houses, intersects a road on which stands the early 20C **Parasarampura haveli** (B2), a rather pretentious construction covered in Europeanised statues and

B. Brillion/MICHELIN

A street in Nawalghar

paintings. In the road parallel, the **Darni Dharka haveli** (B2) (1930) provides a strange blend of mythological and political scenes: Nehru in his car and Mahatma Gandhi are easily recognisable.

The **Ananda Lal Poddar haveli*** (B1) *(9am-7pm, entrance fee)* is the only fully restored Shekhawati *haveli*. Built in 1920, it was renovated in the 1980s by the Poddar family (who now live in Bombay) and is currently a school. The flamboyant new paintings of the **outer façade** often surprise many visitors. In the **first courtyard** (where visitors would have been received), among the frescoes of dancing girls, warriors and Krishna and his adoring *gopi*, the outline of an incongruous train can be seen. Local artists were, in fact, just as excited as the rest of India by the appearance of incredible machines and novelties from Europe and took great pleasure in adding cars, bicycles, accordions, baths and other newfangled gadgets. A handsome wood and bronze door leads to the **second courtyard** (only for the family), also decorated in frescoes. A staircase leads up to the upper storey, providing a pleasant view of the whole building.

The Bhagat haveli* (Bhagaton ki haveli) (B1) has some well-preserved paintings on its **outer façade** and inner **courtyard**: they include processions, Krishna and his *gopis* (cattle girls), a steam boat. Encouraged by a tip, the old caretaker is happy to open up the upper-storey rooms where some attractive frescoes can be admired. Note the amusing depictions of Western colonists.

From natural to synthetic

From around 1880, the region's painters began using synthetic pigments. Prior to this, they would have used natural pigments: ochre for the reds and yellows, saffron and the urine of cows who were fed mango leaves for yellows, cinnabar for reddish-oranges, indigo and lapis lazuli for blues and soot for black... These pigments were applied to a damp coating (using the fresco buono technique), and each layer was polished with agate to make it more resistant. The arrival of chemical pigments from Germany enabled artists to work directly on dry surfaces (fresco secco) and the shades became both more vivid (emerald green, ultramarine...) and more varied.

A walk through Poddar Gate and along the subsequent little lanes leads to the courtyard of a small, very unmilitary-looking fort, **Bala Qila** (B1), which is now home to a market, shops and banks.

■ **Parasarampura*** – *20km southeast of Nawalgarh, along a partially surfaced dirt track.* Few visitors ever get as far as this little hamlet. It nonetheless houses the **cenotaph of Sardul Singh**** and the frescoes on its **dome** are among Shekhawati's oldest. Set in a shady garden *(the key can be obtained from Mr Banawari who lives just behind the garden)*, this *chhatri* was built in 1750 on the spot where *Rao* Sardul Singh was cremated. Note the use of natural pigments. On the lower part of the dome, various divinities are recognisable: Rama and Sita, Ganesha and the incarnations of Vishnu. Above are depicted scenes of Hindu mythology: the return of Rama to his capital Ayodhya, Krishna raising Mount Govardhan to protect mankind from the floods and the court of Dharmaraj, the god in charge of keeping tally of the *karma* (good and bad acts accomplished). Note also Sardul Singh, flower in hand, sharing out his kingdom among his five sons. The upper part is devoted to Krishna, the favourite divinity of the Rajput Shekhawats.
In 1742, shortly before his death, Sardul Singh had the little **temple of Gopinathji** (Krishna) built *(in the village)*, with pious paintings, which were never finished. The façade of **Saraf haveli** (late 18C) was repainted white (probably for a marriage), but the beautiful **inner courtyard** still has its original frescoes.

■ **Dundlod** – *7km northwest of Nawalgarh, on the road to Jhunjhunu.* Renowned for its 18C **fort**, now a hotel *(see "Making the most of Shekhawati")*, the village of Dundlod is in fact rather disappointing. A branch of the wealthy Goenka family settled in Dundlod, building a large number of haveli, before moving to Calcutta. **Goenka haveli**, built on the square opposite the fort, still has a few rather damaged frescoes.
At the end of the little lane which leaves the square is a **well**, built in a typically Shekhawati style, with a raised platform and adorned with *chhatri*. Next door, the **cenotaph**, built in 1888 to the memory of Ram Dutt Goenka, possesses a dome whose elegant paintings depict, among others, episodes from the *Mahabharata*. This edifice is a perfect illustration of the Shekhawati's inhabitants' attitude to their architectural heritage: it is now a public toilet.

Continue on the road to Jhunjhunu until you reach Mandawa (18km).

■ **Mandawa*** – A kilometre before reaching Mandawa, stop at the large **water reservoir** *(johad) (right-hand side of the road)* decorated with kiosks, where the caravaneers used to stop and bathe. Its water is now most uninviting and covered in a greenish slime. A nearby reservoir used to provide drinking water for the camels.
The main purpose of a halt in the dusty little backwater of Mandawa is a stay in its **fort** *(see "Making the most of Shekhawati")* which stands in the centre of the town and belongs to the descendants of *Rao* Shekha. Its terraces provide an interesting view over the town and its spacious *havelis*, whose walls are unfortunately often black with damp.
A walk around the streets of Mandawa alas reveals the poor upkeep of its numerous *havelis*. Many have lost part of their carved wooden doors or windows, most of which have been exported abroad. Among the most worthy of note are the **Goenka double haveli**, whose buildings are covered in faded elephants and horses and the 1890 **Saraf haveli**, of which part of the paintings still remain.

■ Jhunjhunu*

Jhunjhunu, district capital is 25km northeast of Mandawa.

With a population of 73 000, Jhunjhunu is the second city of Shekhawati (the first is Sikar). As a result of 350 years of domination by the Qaimkhani *Nawabs* (1384-1730), the city still retains a Moslem flavour. As well as a number of the usual *haveli*, it has a *dargah* (tomb of a Moslem saint), a fort and temples, thereby adding a note of variety to the region's traditional pleasures.

The dargah of Qamr ud-Din Shah (A2)

Along the road leading from the bus station. The tomb of Qamr ud-Din (1784-1859) stands on a hillside, removed from the bustle of the nearby bazaar. Qamr ud-Din was a *pir* (Moslem saint) worshipped by Hindu rulers. The latter granted him land on which to build a school and on his death had this shrine built in his honour. The tomb, topped with a **white dome**, is decorated with **paintings** depicting gardens, a lake and floral motifs – in respect of Islamic precepts which forbid any human or animal representation. Inside, the tomb, regularly strewn with rose petals, is covered in a green chador, the symbolic colour of Islamism.

Walk to Jhunjhunu bazaar and ask for directions to Khatri Mahal palace.

The bazaar*

These narrow, twisting lanes house a number of *haveli*, several of which still have their original frescoes, although this is unfortunately not the case of **Khatri Mahal** palace (A1). Built in the late 18C, it used to be one of the region's most impres-

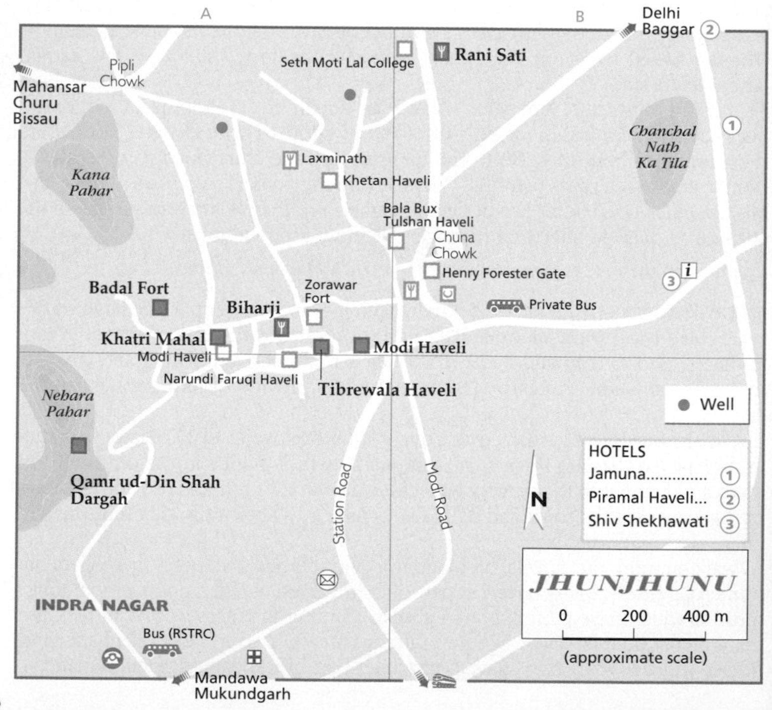

sive monuments, but its two storeys of ochre sandstone, embellished with *chhatri* and balconies, are now completely abandoned. Anyone who ventures into the evil-smelling corridors will note that the staircases have been removed, replaced by ramps. **Tibrewala haveli** (A1), which stands on a small square, possesses paintings of Krishna as a child (over the door), horsemen, a woman in a sari listening to a gramophone... Further on, the **Modi haveli*** (A1) *(on the main street)* has some very fine original frescoes, featuring in particular Krishna and Lakshmi, the goddess of prosperity, greatly favoured by the *marwari* merchant class. Also note the Englishman with his colonial hat. In a nearby lane, the little 1776 **Biharji temple*** (A1) has a number of fine old paintings, some of the earliest in Rajasthan. Overlooking the bazaar, **Badal Fort** (fort of clouds) (A1) is an unpretentious edifice, within whose imposing walls stands a statue of Sardul Singh, two uninspiring temples and a garden.

The north of the town

The **temple of Rani Sati** (B1) is an incredibly garish hotchpotch of buildings strangely reminiscent of a pink and pistachio cream cake. It comprises a *dharmshala* (hostel for pilgrims), courtyards, halls and shrines, the gaudy colours of which are further exaggerated by a myriad of mirrors, silverwork and flashy statues. The temple was erected in memory of Rani Sati, the wife of a local merchant in the late 16C, who committed *sati* by throwing herself on her husband's funeral pyre, thus becoming an object of worship by all the staunch defenders of traditional values. Such traditionalists remain legion, for it would appear that the shrine is second only to that of Tirupati (in Andhra Pradesh) in the amount of donations it receives. It also possesses branches in Hong Kong, New York... Considered to be an incarnation of Durga, Rani Sati, is worshipped in the form of a trident, complete with skirt. Pause for a moment in the **main hall** *(remove your shoes)* and admire the walls and ceiling whose frescoes illustrate the saint's sacrifice.

Sati, a chaste and faithful wife

The god Daksha was opposed to the marriage of his daughter Sati with Shiva, but ignoring her father's ban, the young goddess married the god she loved. Daksha subsequently quarrelled with his son-in-law several times. On one occasion, he – deliberately – forgot to invite Shiva to a sacrifice to which all the other gods were summoned. Sati entreated her father to invite Shiva but in vain... In proof of her love and in order to defend her husband's honour, she threw herself into the sacrificial fire. This example of marital devotion would appear to be behind the origins of the tradition whereby widows throw themselves onto their husband's funeral pyre, thus committing "sati" or suttee in English. Outlawed by the British in 1829, the custom prevails, particularly in Shekhawati, the region in India where the largest number of "sati" have taken place since 1947.

The little artificial lake, **Ajit Sagar**, to the north of the town, was created in the early 20C and adorned with **chhatri**, some of which are decorated with paintings. On the way, note the **well of Badani Chand** whose four high towers can be seen from far around.

■ **Mahansar*** – *40km to the west of Jhunjhunu, on the road to Churu, then turn left, towards Ramgarh.* Dusty lanes wind up to the ochre-coloured walls of this tumbledown **fort**, part of which has been transformed into a hotel *(see "Making the most of Shekhawati")*.

Nearby, in the main street, is a *haveli* built towards 1850 by a member of the Poddar family, an opium and precious-metal merchant. The ground-floor contains one of Shekhawati's finest examples of a painted room: the **Sone ki**

Dukan*** or "gold shop" *(the key can be obtained from the shop next door. Entrance fee)*. The reception room is entirely covered in predominantly red and gold frescoes. The ceiling features reincarnations of Vishnu (in the centre) and episodes of the lives of two of his personifications: Krishna and Rama (in particular the terrible battle during which the god Rama, assisted by Hanuman and his army of monkeys, bravely confronted the many-headed demon Ravana, king of Lanka).
Almost opposite is the **temple of Raghunatha**, built by the Poddar family at the same period. To the rear of the courtyard, decorated in floral motifs, images of Krishna and Radna, Rama and Sita, and Shiva, his wife Parvati and their son Ganesha can be seen on three altars. Note also the *linga* (phallic symbol) of Shiva.

Continue towards Ramgarh (6km).

■ **Ramgarh** – Founded in the late 18C by the Poddar family, Ramgarh enjoyed a golden age in the 19C. The Poddars built a large number of *haveli*, most of which are now closed and have been partly or completely dismantled by antique dealers. Nonetheless, Bazaar Road, entirely lined by *haveli*, the first floors of which project over the little stalls down below, still provides a lovely view. The constant toing-and-froing of villagers and peasants in carts pulled by tiny donkeys rigged out in coloured skirts makes an enchanting picture.
On the left-hand side of the street stand the **Poddars' cenotaphs*** (second half of the 19C) whose domes and "Bengali" roofs have been blackened by the monsoon rains. Further on, to the right, is the quite remarkable 1872 **chhatri of Ram Gopal Poddar***. Its dome is covered in frescoes, carried out with natural pigments, which depict the final combat of the *Ramayana*: General Hanuman is shown opening the way for Ram's chariot, while the monkeys give battle against the horned-demons of Ravana, king of Lanka, who has kidnapped the virtuous Sita.
The tour can be finished with a look at the **temple of Shani** (Saturn) *(to the northeast)*, built in the 1840s, whose decoration combines paintings and a mosaic of mirrors and multicoloured tiles.

■ **Fatehpur*** – *19km south of Ramgarh, on the road to Jaipur.* This dusty backwater was formerly the capital of the Moslem dynasty of the Qaimkhani *nawabs* up until 1731 when it fell under the control of the Hindu *raos*. Endowed with large numbers of *haveli* in a pitiful condition, some of which nonetheless still have stunning frescoes. To the north of the town, the **Jagannath Singhania haveli** features intricate predominantly blue-coloured paintings: note Lakshmi surrounded by elephants. The paintings of the 1865 **Nand Lal Devra haveli*** are well-preserved. Note the beautiful woodwork – still intact, but for how long? There is an 18C well next door. The first floor **reception room** of the **Chaudhari haveli** is a little gem, but unfortunately, is often closed. The **Mahavir Prasad Goenka haveli **** (c1865), well worth a visit, contains some of the region's finest frescoes, particularly in the first floor **reception room.**

■ **Lakshmangarh** – *20km to the south of Fatehpur.* This important market town, largely unknown by tourists, built in the 19C by the sovereign of Sikar, was designed along the same lines of the grid layout of Jaipur. Such sophistication almost brings a smile to the faces of modern day visitors, given the town's current

S. Held

The rise and fall of the haveli

rustic character. Narrow, poorly-maintained lanes plunge explorers into an almost medieval atmosphere, further amplified by the outline of a small fort *(closed)* overlooking the area. A few murals can still be seen on the **temple of Radha Murlimanohar** (Radha and Krishna) *(at the bottom of the lane leading up to the fort)*. The unfriendly welcome is indicative of the Shekhawati's approach to tourism as a whole. The frescoes of the outer walls of the vast **Char Chowk haveli** *("haveli with four courtyards")* have been worn away by time or covered over by whitewash. The **Rathi haveli**, besieged by a bazaar with little time for historical relics, is worth a look. Half-hidden under corrugated metal, the original paintings can still be made out on the outer façade. Note the way in which Western women are shown: one in a white dress is listening to music on an old gramophone while another, in a red dress, is sitting in front of a sewing machine.

Making the most of Shekhawati

Getting there

By train – The main gateways to Shekhawati are Sikar (computerised terminal) and Churu, both of which have direct links with Delhi, Jaipur and Bikaner. A few trains also run to smaller stations such as Nawalgarh, Mukundgarh or Jhunjhunu. From Jaipur, the most practical is the "Shekhawati Express" which runs between Sikar (3hr30min), Nawalgarh, Mukundgarh and Jhunjhunu. Two trains run daily between Bikaner and Churu (3hr30min), one of which continues on to Sikar (7hr). There are two express night trains from Delhi: one stops at Churu (7hr), the other at Jhunjhunu, Mukundgarh, Nawalgarh and Sikar (8hr).

By bus – This is by far the least practical way of getting to Shekhawati. The main tourist centres are linked by express buses from Jaipur (between 2hr30min and 4hr30min), Bikaner (4hr) and Delhi (7hr). It is also possible to get to Shekhawati from Ajmer (6hr), Jodhpur (9hr) and Agra (only from Sikar).

By car – The car is both the most comfortable and the fastest mode of transport. To get the most out of a tour of Shekhawati, the best option is to rent a car from Jaipur or Bikaner for two or three days. The rental agency can arrange for the car to be taken back to its departure point, while you continue on elsewhere. Another alternative is to take the bus or train to Shekhawati and then rent a car by the day from a hotel (see "Car Rental").

Getting about

Although most of the region's points of interest are relatively close to one another, the roads are more often than not in bad condition and, in urban areas, frequently strewn with potholes. To save time and energy finding one's way from one haveli to another, enquire at your hotel about a guide (250Rs per half-day and 350Rs per day).

By bus – Local buses are plentiful but generally packed. Getting about from one town to another by bus will require a lot of time and patience.

By taxi – Taxis are not a frequent sight, but it is possible to ask your hotel to send one to the station to meet you on arrival.

By group jeep – Departures leave near the bus stops.

Car rental – All the hotels can arrange for a car rental (around 950Rs per day, 300km maximum). Don't expect the driver to speak any English.

Bicycle rental – Your hotel can suggest where bicycles can be rented (30Rs per day).

Address book

• Jhunjhunu

Tourist Office –10am-1.30pm/2pm-5pm; closed every other Saturday and on Sunday.

• Mandawa

Banks/Money – ***State Bank of Bikaner and Jaipur***, in the main street, next to Binsidhar Newatia haveli. Can change travellers' cheques. In the same street (opposite the bank), two souvenir boutiques provide exchange facilities.

• Nawalgarh

Banks/Money – ***State Bank of Bikaner and Jaipur***, in the fort (B1). Travellers' cheques.

Where to stay

Shekhawati has a large number of picturesque hotels, but it is recommended to book ahead. As most don't have exact addresses, you will have to ask your way on arrival. In the low season, from April-May to June-July, a 20-25% discount is available.

• Baggar

13km northeast of Jhunjhunu.

From US$30-40

Piramal haveli (Neemrana Hotels), ☎ (01592) 222 20; reservations at Delhi (see p 107) – 8rm. Cooler. Breakfast included. This 1928 haveli built by a wealthy merchant comprises an inner courtyard with elegant columns onto which the rooms open. Tastefully decorated, colonial-style furniture. Visitors are made to feel at home. Relatively expensive given that the service, although very courteous, is limited.

• Dundlod

From US$30-40

Dundlod Fort (Heritage Hotels Association), ☎ (01594) 521 80 and 525 19; reservations at Jaipur, ☎ and Fax (0141) 21 11 18 and 21 12 76 – 45rm. Cooler. This handsome fortified 17C residence is located in the heart of the town. At the rear of the inner walled courtyard a flight of steps leads up to the "durbar" chamber. The rooms, of varying sizes, are furnished in somewhat tasteless period furniture. The overall impression suggests a lack of care which detracts from the hotel's charm. Jeep and camel excursions available.

• Fatehpur

From US$7-15

Haveli Hotel (RTDC), 400m on from the State bus stop, on the way out of the town towards Jaipur, ☎ (01571) 202 93 and 203 05 – 8rm. Cooler and 1rm with AC. Away from the bustle and dust of the town, this recently built house is located out in the fields. The rooms are airy but neglected, and once again, with a little more care, the place would be most pleasant. Dormitory.

• Jhunjhunu

From US$7-15

Shiv Shekhawati Hotel, Muni Ashram, eastbound exit to the town, ☎ (01592) 326 51 – 10rm. 3rm. with AC. This small hotel, which is clean but impersonal, is nonetheless quite acceptable. The quietest rooms are the least expensive (with cooler). The owner, Laxmi Kant Jangid, a former lawyer and a keen enthusiast of Shekhawati's culture, doubles as a guide. Car and camel excursions.

From US$15-30

Jamuna Resort, annexe of the above, ☎ (01592) 326 51 – 4rm. Cooler. The comfortable, clean rooms of this establishment are dotted about a small lawn in a relaxing, countrified atmosphere. The most expensive rooms will delight lovers of kitsch: it is entirely decorated in "old" frescoes, depicting entwined couples in the manner of the Kama Sutra.

• Mahansar

From US$15-30

Narayan Niwas Castle (Heritage Hotels Association), ☎ (01596) 643 22; reservations at Delhi, ☎ (011) 648 68 07, Fax (011) 648 68 06 – 15rm. Cooler. In the heart of a peaceful village renowned for its famous liqueur, "asha" (honey, orange, aniseed, ginger and cardamom) stands this imposing 18C dwelling with its maze of terraces and staircases. The welcome is friendly, warm and unfussy and it is the ideal place to have a try at living like a desert "thakur". The rooms are full of character and charm (columns, antique frescoes), but don't expect any great comfort. Rooms 1 and 5 are the most pleasant. Despite the charm, it remains relatively expensive, especially given that hot water comes in a basin.

• Mandawa

From US$30-40

The Desert Resort, 1km to the south, on the road to Nawalgarh, ☎ (01592) 231 51 and 235 14; reservations at Jaipur, ☎(0141) 37 11 94 and 37 41 30, Fax (0141) 37 20 84 – 62rm. The brick walls covered in adobe and thatched roofs of the resort's comfortable cottages reflect the region's traditional rustic style and the resort often caters to groups. The rooms in the main building are more ordinary and less pleasant. The manager, Mr Pandey, a lover of Shekhawati art, organises jeep or camel excursions.

Castle Mandawa (Heritage Hotels Association), in the town centre, ☎ (01592) 231 24 and 234 32, Fax (01592) 231 71; reservations at Jaipur, ☎ (0141) 37 11 94 and 37 41 30, Fax (0141) 37 20 84 – 70rm. Same prices and owners as the above. This imposing mid-18C Rajput fort is a bewildering maze of courtyards, staircases and terraces. Comfortable, tastefully decorated (a blend of Rajput, colonial and western styles), it is also superbly located. The service is carried out by discreet, smiling Nepalese men in turbans who don't speak a word of English. The dining room, decorated with original frescoes, is somewhat gloomy but the evening buffet, served in the garden or on a patio around a campfire, is a pure delight. Ten exceptional suites. Camel rides.

• Mukundgarh

From US$40-70

Mukundgarh Fort (Heritage Hotels Association), Mukundgarh, ☎ (01594) 523 96/97/98, Fax (01594) 523 95 – 46rm. This vast 18C property is composed of a mass of wings and terraces, surrounded by large lawns and high walls. Although the setting itself is pleasant, the rooms, often windowless, are neglected and the choice of furniture eclectic to say the least. The plumbing has a tendency to be on the smelly side. Four suites, one of which has a living room, four rooms and three bathrooms. Limited service. Jeep and camel excursions.

• Nawalgarh

Under US$7

Ramesh C. Jangid Tourist Pension, ☎ (01594) 240 66, Fax (01594) 224 91 and 240 61 – 5rm. Cooler. Located in a quiet neighbourhood, this unassuming house has airy, simple and extremely clean rooms, which are pleasantly decorated in an "ethnic" style. The family has adopted an ecological approach: solar-powered water heating, biological "pure veg" food. Ramesh C Jangid is keen to conserve Shekhawati's rich heritage and to show it off. He doubles as a guide and organises walking or cycling outings.

From US$15-30

Apani Dhani (also called "Eco Farm"), on the western edge of the town, on the road between Jaipur-Jhunjhunu; reservations, ☎ (01594) 240 60, Fax (01594) 224 91 and 240 61 – 9rm. Cooler. Some half-dozen houses built of cob with thatched roofs are spread around a central area, protected by an awning enabling guests to enjoy the rustic tranquillity of the spot. Pleasant "ethnic" style, attention to detail and extremely clean, the bathrooms are nonetheless basic. Similar alternative approach as the above establishment (same owner): solar-powered water heating, the milk comes direct from the buffaloes tied up behind the cottages and the vegetables all come from the hotel's garden. "Pure veg" meals. Minimal service, provided by the family.

Roop Niwas Palace (Heritage Hotels Association), 1km to the north, at the end of a dirt track, ☎ (01594) 220 08, Fax (01594) 233 88; reservations at Jaipur, ☎ (0141) 62 07 22 and 62 29 49 – 30rm. Cooler. This spacious, pale yellow residence, with its shady lawns and wide veranda is quite delightful. The rooms, furnished in an Anglo-Indian style, are of varying quality although the price is identical. Guided visits of the region by jeep or camel.

Excursions

By car – Most of the hotels organise guided visits of the region, in jeeps, "Ambassador" cars or vans. Allow 850Rs per half day for four people (80km maximum) and 1 350Rs per day (150km maximum).

By camel – Most of the hotels also organise camel rides (300-450Rs per hour and per person, 800-1 100Rs per day). Some can even arrange, on request, one- to six-day treks around Shekhawati.

By horse – The region has two excellent riding centres: The Shekhawati Brigade Horse Safari, Roop Niwas Palace at Nawalgarh and The Royal Equestrian and Polo Centre, at Dundlod (contact Mr Devendra Singh). Both organise outings (300Rs per hour, 750Rs for 3hr, 1 750Rs for 6hr, meal included) and treks in Shekhawati (4 000Rs per day and per person) or towards Pushkar (one week), Bikaner and Jaisalmer. Excursions can also be organised from Jodhpur to Udaipur and Chittorgarh (5 500 Rs per day and per person). The Dundlod Centre can also arrange for polo. Accommodation in camps or Heritage Hotels.

On foot or by bicycle – Enquire at the Ramesh Jangid Tourist Pension, at Nawalgarh. From 850Rs per day and per person (2 people) to 1 250Rs (3 or 4 people). Bed and breakfast style accommodation.

Holidays and festivals

• Dundlod

Annual Horse Show. This show, which takes place during the Gangaur festival (March-April), is intended to promote the Marwari race of horses, with their lyre-shaped ears.

• Jhunjhunu

Rani Sati Festival. In honour of Shekhawati's most famous "sati". This major festival takes place every year at the new moon of August-September, in the Rani Sati temple.

Shopping

It is not very easy to spend money in Shekhawati because tourist shops are few and far between. There are a few souvenir shops in Nawalgarh and Mandawa, along the main street and in Castle Mandawa Hotel: books, post cards, knick-knacks, local crafts, clothes. Recently, a few antique dealers have opened stalls in Mandawa and Nawalgarh, they sell mostly miscellaneous pieces of furniture and curiosities, some of which have been ripped out of local "haveli".

AJMER★

Pop 402 000 – Alt 486m
390km from Delhi – 205km from Jodhpur – 140km from Jaipur
See map p 200

Not to be missed

The dargah (tomb) of the Sufi saint Khwaja Main ud-Din Chisti.
Adhai-din ka Jhonpra mosque.

And remember...

Pushkar is much more pleasant to stay in than Ajmer.

Unfortunately, many travellers, in a hurry to reach Pushkar, only see the bus station of Ajmer. Although the town first strikes visitors as noisy and polluted, just a few hours wandering around the little lanes of its old districts are enough to change this opinion. In Ajmer, skull-caps and the call of the muezzin take the place of colourful turbans and temple bells: all year long the faithful come from all over India to commune in front of India's most venerated Moslem shrine, the *dargah* of the Sufi saint, **Khwaja Main ud-Din Chisti**. The **Urs festival**, which commemorates the saint's death and which takes place at different times according to the mobile *rajab* calendar, is even busier. The town then becomes engulfed in an impressive series of processions, as crowds flock to the *dargah*.

The stamp of Islam

A strategic site – Located in a pass in the Aravalli Range, on the road between Delhi and the ports of the Arabian sea, Ajmer has always played a significant strategic role: it is the key to the control of Rajasthan. As early as the 7C, the Rajput ruler, Ajai Pal, of the **Chauhan** dynasty, had a fort built on the peak overlooking the pass. Ajmer (a contraction of Ajai Meru, "the mountain of Ajai, the invincible") remained in the hands of the Chauhans until the invasion of Northern India by the Afghan, **Muhammad of Ghor** (late 12C). In the wake of the Moslem invaders followed pious zealots, among them **Main ud-Din Chisti** (1142-1236). The latter's saintly reputation was soon to attract large numbers of faithful pilgrims to Ajmer. The town became a thriving religious centre and the successors of Muhammad of Ghor, Qutb ud-Din, then Iltutmish, had large numbers of impressive mosques built. However the sultans of Delhi found it difficult to maintain control over the region. It was passed on from hand to hand until 1556: at this point **Akbar** annexed

Converting India to Islam

Main ud-Din Chisti, said to be a descendant of Ali, the Prophet's son-in-law, was given a divine mission when on a pilgrimage to Mecca: to preach the word of Islam in Northern India. Taking advantage of one of Muhammad of Ghor's expeditions, he settled in Ajmer in 1190 and set up the Sufi Chisti sect, already well-established in Afghanistan. Influenced by the "Upanishad" and a keen defender of the poor, he acquired the reputation of a "pir" (saint) and attracted a following, even during his life, of many Hindu disciples. Unfortunately the traditions of mysticism and tolerance of the Sufi orders appear to have had little influence on the sultans of Delhi, despite their fervent devotion to Main ud-Din. More inclined to military than to theological wisdom, their destruction of large numbers of Hindu and Jain temples inaugurated an era of intolerance.

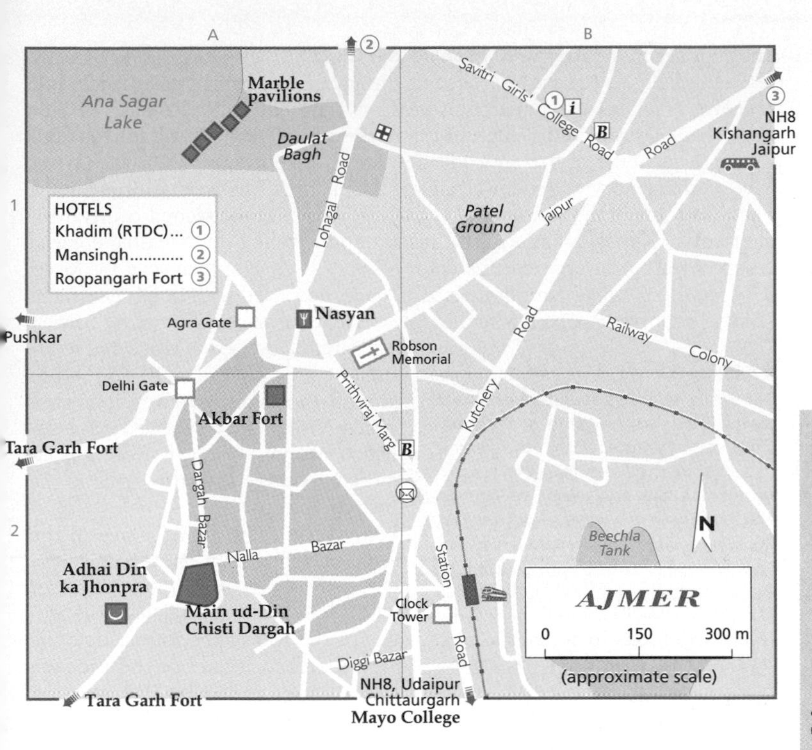

the town, creating a Moslem enclave within Rajput territories, using it as a base for his military campaigns. He had a palace built in the lower part of the town. His grandson, **Shah Jahan,** often stayed here, but with the decline of the Mughal dynasty (18C), the town was once again the prey of greedy neighbours. Both the Marathas and the Rathore rulers of Jodhpur laid claim to the area until the British arrived.

The town

Allow 3hr on foot.

Enjoy a walk through the narrow lanes of the **old town**, partially free of scooters and lined with busy little restaurants and stalls. The way in to the old town is through the impressive **Delhi Gate** (A2).Walk along Dargah Bazaar, the main street leading to the *dargah*. Shops selling basic necessities alternate with others offering pious works in Urdu, brightly-coloured chadors to lay over the *pir's* tomb and fragrant flower petals for offerings. Note the presence of little Hindu temples, which seem to symbolise India's religious context. The involuntary proximity of such diverse faiths gives rise, here as elsewhere, to ceaseless rivalries, which are nonetheless tempered in Ajmer by the presence of numerous pilgrims, and both communities seem to coexist relatively harmoniously.
It is worth taking the time to wander through the peaceful, picturesque lanes on the left, before entering the *dargah*.

The entrance to the **dargah of Main ud-Din Chisti**** (A2) *(Shoes must be left at the entrance and the head should be covered)* is through a very garish, green and white gate over which rise two minarets. Note the two gigantic cauldrons on either side of the gate, into which the pilgrims throw rice and money. During the *Urs* festival, large quantities of rice are cooked in them, the distribution of which never fails to prompt a joyful free-for-all among the pilgrims. The green **mosque** in the right hand side of the courtyard was built by Akbar. In the second courtyard is the **tomb** of Khwaja Main ud-Din Chishti, topped with a white marble dome; a group of *qawwal* sit opposite the door, ecstatically singing their love for *Khuda* (God) to the music of harmoniums. The **door**, decorated with floral motifs and Koranic inscriptions, opens into the Holy of Holies, protected by a silver barrier. The faithful, dressed in white and wearing the traditional skull-cap, walk around the tomb, covering it in rose petals. Visitors may be asked for a donation. During the *Urs* festival, it is almost impossible to get in, such is the press of the crowds.

Behind the tomb is the grave of the saint's daughter, **Bibi Hafez Jamal**, worshipped for her saintliness, together with the tomb of Shah Jahan's daughter. At the rear of the *dargah*, note the eleven-arched façade of the **mosque** built in white marble by Shah Jahan.

Wishes granted

According to tradition, any wish made during a visit to the tomb of Main ud-Din Chisti is granted within the year. It is also said that seven pilgrimages to Ajmer are the equivalent of one to Mecca. Shortly before the Urs festival, hordes of often impoverished pilgrims can be seen on the roads leading to Ajmer, marching along behind the green flag of Islam. Akbar himself carried out several pilgrimages to the saint's tomb after several of his wishes were granted.

On leaving the dargah, take the road to the left, then turn left (by the door) into a street lined with little cafés, which runs alongside the dargah and leads to the mosque of Adhai-din ka Jhonpra.

The enigmatic name of **Adhai-din ka Jhonpra mosque**** (A2) – "the hut of two and a half days" – would appear to have stemmed from the Urs festival which used to be held here and which lasted two and a half days. Another version claims that this was the time it took Muhammad of Ghor and his lieutenant, **Qutb ud-Din**, to destroy, in 1198, all the Jain buildings and to build a mosque in their place. The early 13C façade was added by Sultan **Iltutmish**.

From the road, note the impressive staircase *(on the right)* which leads to the mosque's door. At the rear of the spacious courtyard stands the superb **façade** of the prayer room, reminiscent of the Seljuk style: there are seven monumental ogee arches, the central one of which dominates the others by its size and by the presence of two minarets which used to stand on top of it, but of which only the bases remain. The screen made by these arches is entirely covered in intricately sculptured arabesques and beautifully carved Koranic inscriptions. Inside the **prayer room***, note the pillars which are made up of three superimposed columns salvaged from the 12C Hindu and Jain temples destroyed by the Moslems. Note the **five domes,** the rosette and other floral motifs.

Back on the road continue on towards the right. After a one and a half hour walk, the ruins of **Taragarh fort**, founded in 1100, appear. The superb **view** over Ajmer and the surroundings is well worth the effort of the climb.

Walk back down along Dargah Bazaar, and turn right to Akbar fort.

The entrance to the Dargah

Emperor Akbar's fort (A2) (1570) has limited interest. In the courtyard, the handsome private audience hall was the scene of the first meeting in 1616 between a Mughal emperor (Jahangir) and a representative of the British crown (Sir Thomas Roe). It resulted in an agreement whereby the East India Company was granted major trading rights in exchange for protection against Portuguese naval power – an agreement which was to provide the British with a significant advantage in the sub-continent. The **government museum** *(10am-4.30pm; closed Friday. Entrance charge)* houses sculptures from the 7C to the 14C. Only specialists are, however, likely to find it of any great interest.
The **Nasyan Jain temple** (A1) *(from dawn to dusk, entrance fee, no photos)*, built 1865, hides a surprising interior: resembling a gigantic showcase two floors high, a large room, the walls of which are covered in gilt-work and mirrors, is entirely filled by a gold-plated model depicting the **Jain cosmogony**. A flat circle represents the intermediate area in which mankind lives. In the centre is the Island of Jambu, dominated by Mount Sumeru and surrounded by alternating continents and oceans in concentric circles. The **life of Adinatha**, the first *tirthankara* (founder of the Jain religion) is related in five episodes, from his miraculous conception by the god Indra, to his "freedom from earthly life". The whole impression is rather one of a playroom for child prodigies than a place of worship. The prayer room (ground floor, closed to non-Jains) reveals an ornate façade of **murals** depicting the life of the *tirthankara.*

Finish with a walk around the lake of **Ana Sagar** (A1), created in the 12C. In the 17C, Emperor Shah added a Mughal garden, the Daulat Bagh (sorely neglected today) in which five handsome **marble pavilions** stand.

Mayo College

In the eastern suburbs, 3km from the centre of Ajmer. This "Eton of India", founded in 1875 by the viceroy, Lord Mayo, was initially created for the sons of maharajas. Since the 1950s, it has also educated children (boys and girls) from India's wealthy (900 pupils with fees at 50 000 rupees per year). The composite façades in white marble, typical of Anglo-Indian taste, are more reminiscent of a palace than a school. Inside is the large parlour, a dark hall decorated with portraits of the maharajas educated here.

Making the most of Ajmer

Getting there

By train – *Ajmer Railway Station*, Station Rd (B2), ☎ 131. Computerised reservation terminal, ☎ 132. 8.30am-1.30pm/2pm-4.30pm, Sunday 8.30am-2pm. Lots of trains for Jaipur (2hr-2hr30min), many of which continue on to Delhi (7-11hr). The fastest are the express afternoon "Shatabdi" trains (except Sundays) which stop at Alwar and the "Radjani" night train (three a week). For Chittaurgarh (5-7hr), 3 daily express trains, two of which continue on to Udaipur (10hr). Three daily trains and one "Radjani" three times a week run to Abu Road (4hr).

By bus – Buses for Pushkar (30min), often packed, leave every half-hour from ***Pushkar Bus Stand***, on Station Rd (B2). State (***Central Bus Stand***, Jaipur Rd (B1), ☎ (0145) 43 19 65; reservations, 9.30am-4.30pm) and private buses run daily to other destinations. Tickets can be purchased for the latter from the travel agents on Kutchery Rd. Tickets can also be purchased at Pushkar, in which case the shuttle between Pushkar and Ajmer is provided free by the travel agent. Jaipur (3hr), Delhi and Agra, via Bharatpur (10hr); Kota, via Bundi and Chittaurgarh (4hr); Udaipur (7hr); Abu Road (9hr); Mount Abu, only by the private bus companies (10hr); Jodhpur (5hr); Jaisalmer (10hr); Bikaner (8hr). 7 Silver Line buses run each day between Jaipur and Jodhpur, stopping at Ajmer, one of which continues on to Jaisalmer.

By taxi – There is a taxi rank at the station.

Address book

Tourist Office – *Tourist Reception Centre*, located in Khadim Hotel (B1). 8am-12noon/3pm-6pm; closed Sunday. Information about Ajmer and Pushkar, list of guest houses and taxi firms. There is a small desk at the station, open on the arrival of the main trains.

Banks/Money – *State Bank of India*, opposite the Collectorate (B1). Withdrawals with a banker's card are not possible. ***Bank of Baroda***, Prithviraj Rd, Madar Gate Circle (B2). In theory, money can be withdrawn with a banker's card…

Post Office/Telephone – *GPO*, Madar Gate Circle, Prithviraj Rd (B2), for express mail ***EMS Speed Post***. Postal code: 305006.

Where to stay

Although accommodation is much better at Pushkar (11km), a large number of small establishments for Moslem pilgrims, of varying cleanliness, can be found around Delhi Gate and on Station Rd. During the Pushkar Fair (November), prices rocket sky-high – sometimes 10 times the standard price!

• Ajmer

From US$7-15

***Khadim Hotel* (RTDC)**, Savitri Girls' College Rd, in the modern town centre, ☎ (0145) 524 90 and 525 36 – 58rm. Cooler. The building is set slightly off a quiet street, within the same complex as the tourist office. The rooms and bathrooms are poorly maintained and the restaurant is gloomy. Breakfast included in the price. Dormitory.

From US$40-70

Mansingh Palace (Mansinghgroup), Vaishali Nagar, 1km from the centre, ☎ (0145) 42 58 55 to 57, Fax (0145) 42 58 58 – 60rm. Bar, boutique. Set within pretty, peaceful flowered gardens, this modern hotel is equipped with all modern amenities and is the only one of its kind in the region. The rooms are spacious and airy. The standard rooms with a view of the lake are the best value.

• Roopangarh

50km northeast of Ajmer; 25km north of Kishangarh. A picturesque fortified village.

From US$30-40

Roopangarh Fort (Heritage Hotels Association), Roopangarh, ☎ (01463) 72 17, Fax (01463) 420 01; reservations in Delhi, ☎ (011) 641 30 00 and 335 13 01 to 04, Fax (011) 623 70 01 and 335 13 05, tis@giasdl01.vsnl.net.in – 20rm. Cooler. Ideal to get a feel of what it was like to live in a Marwari fort. Spacious rooms with views far over the plain. The "durbar" hall has been turned into a suite which can accommodate a whole family.

• Bijaynagar

67km, on the road to Chittaurgarh.

From US$15-30

Bijayniwas Palace (Heritage Hotels Association), Bijaynagar, reservations at Ajmer, ☎ (0145) 529 28, Fax (0145) 42 23 38 – 8rm. Located near a reserve, this pleasant residence set in a tranquil park has a rather surprising appearance, (half villa, half fort). Inside, the spacious rooms have retained the original floral friezes. The whole place exudes the charm of a faded country house.

Where to eat

From US$4-7

Sheesh Mahal, Mansingh Palace Hotel. 12.30noon-3pm/7.30pm-11pm. An airy, comfortable corner room with wide-reaching views over the garden and the lake beyond. Traditional northern-Indian specialities, a few Western and Chinese dishes. Drinks are served on the garden's terrace in the evening. "Ghazal" singer in the evening.

Holidays and festivals

Urs mela commemorates the death of the Sufi saint, Main ud-Din Chisti, buried in the "dargah" in Ajmer. This festival begins at the new moon of the "rajab" calendar (7th month of the Moslem calendar) and lasts 6 days. Rose petals, chadors and incense sticks are presented in offering and uninterrupted concerts of "qawwali" take place before the tomb. It is also possible to take part in all the other Moslem festivals: ***Id ul-Fitr***, ***Bakr Id***, ***Muharram***, ***Id-i Milad***, etc.

Pushkar★★

Pop 14 000 – 15km from Ajmer – See map p 200

Not to be missed

The lake and the ghats.

And remember...

If you want to be sure of enjoying the legendary tranquillity of this little town, avoid November, during the famous Camel Fair.

If you do want to see the Fair, make sure you book a room well in advance.

Pushkar is very popular among young Westerners visiting India, some staying for several months at a time. The local population has adapted to this clientele and opened terrace restaurants, cheap guesthouses and large numbers of little stalls selling poor quality "arts and crafts" at high prices (test your bargaining techniques here). This charming little town nestling at the foot of the steppes, with its picturesque lake surrounded by hills and its pedestrian-only lanes and streets is an ideal spot to stop and rest for a few days. Hindus hold Pushkar Lake to be the most sacred in India, and a purifying dip in its waters is considered to be particularly beneficial at certain dates, primarily during the full moon of October-November, when the incredible **camel fair** takes place. The fair, extolled by travel agents all over the world, now attracts vast numbers of tourists who come specially to India to attend. This notoriety has left Pushkar with a somewhat artificial atmosphere. Nonetheless, it is well worth taking the time to enjoy the tinkling bells ringing in tune to the ceremonies held in the town's numerous temples or taking a walk out of the town's bustling centre up into the quiet peace of the surrounding hills, where only the chirping of the crickets will disturb your stroll.

A major tourist event

Pushkar camel fair has undeniably lost much of its former exotic charm. Every year, at Kartik Purnima (the full moon of the month of Kartik, in October-November), the town welcomes hundreds of foreign visitors. Most of the dance, music and puppet shows put on are solely for the benefit of these tourists. Such diversity may well appear artificial to purists of Indian culture. The event is nonetheless one of the most colourful and lively in India and remains authentic despite the floods of tourists. It is in fact much better to view Pushkar camel fair as a "global festival" rather than as a step back in time to traditional rural India. To get the most out of the fair, arrive a week early and watch all the camel drivers and their herds arrive and set up camp.

A sacred city pillaged by the Moslems

In the eyes of Hindus, no more sacred city than Pushkar can be found in Rajasthan. Unfortunately however, all the old temples of this major pilgrimage centre were razed by Emperor Aurangzeb in the 17C. Pushkar's current shrines, rebuilt in the 18C and 19C, are thus of limited architectural interest.

The town

Allow 4hr on foot. No photos on the ghats.

Shoes must be removed on the ghats and before entering the temples.

The lake at Pushkar is said to have appeared when a lotus petal, falling from the hands of Brahma, dropped to the ground here. The northern and western banks of the lake are lined with *ghats* (wide staircases guarded and used by a

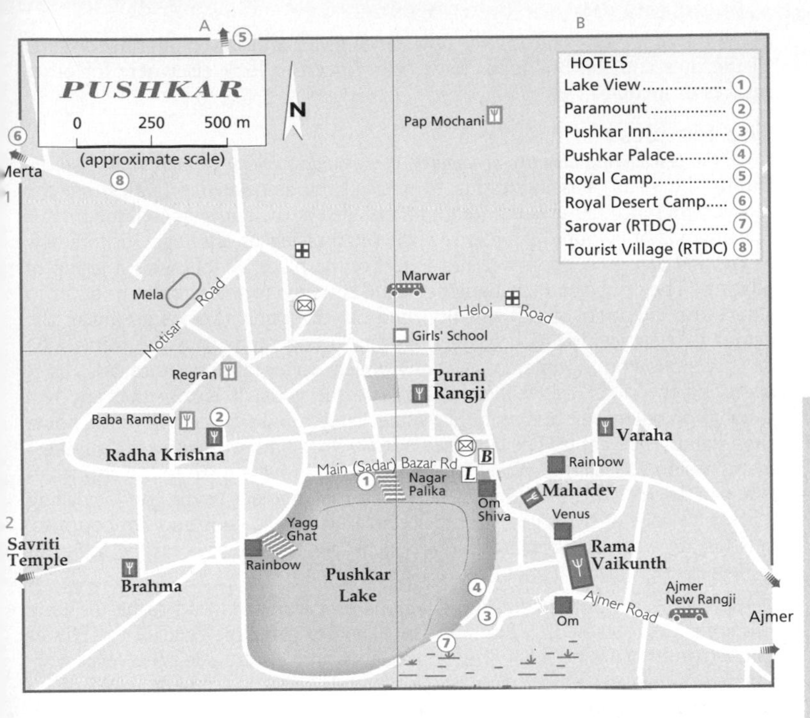

specific category of Brahmins), and the lake makes the town feel like a miniature whitewashed Benares. Early risers will be able to see pious Hindus taking their ritual bath in the lake's waters. They stand facing the rising sun and dip their hands into the water, reciting the following verses: "I take this bath to wash away the sins of my body, my mind, my words and my touch." They then plunge twice under the lake's surface, before pouring water on their heads while praying to have the strength to remain pure. They will then recite mantras, sometimes 108, including the famous *Gayatri* "Brahma is the sun". The same prayer is repeated at midday and at dusk. Walkers strolling along the *ghats* may be accosted by begging Brahmins who will offer to carry out some sort of sacrifice on their behalf in exchange for vast sums of money. Of late, times have been hard for the Brahmins: traditionally they carried out the numerous rites held at different periods

A jealous goddess

Brahma had convened an assembly of all the gods and goddesses to take part in a ritual on the banks of the lake at Pushkar. All the guests had arrived, except for Savitri (other name for Sarasvati, Brahma's wife) who was still getting herself ready. However the sacrifice demanded, as is often the case, that the sacrificer's wife be present. Brahma, angry at being made to wait, asked the gods to find him a second companion. They chose Gayatri, a shepherdess, whom he married on the spot. The furious Savitri cursed Brahma: from then on he would be forgotten by men and no new temples would be built in his honour. The curse was fulfilled: Brahma no longer has any followers and less than half a dozen temples in all India are dedicated to him. On the other hand, Savitri and Gayatri both have shrines in the region of Pushkar.

of the life of a pious Hindu, but nowadays, fewer and fewer pilgrims observe all the rites and the Brahmans have been forced to look elsewhere for other sources of income…

The temples*

Given the bewildering quantity of temples, it is pointless trying to take in all of them. During the visits, it is interesting to note all the associated activities that the temples' presence has created. Vendors, installed at the entrance, sell mountains of marigolds or coloured powder that the pilgrims use as offerings. Visitors new to Pushkar can get a good idea of the feel of the place by following a group of pilgrims. They ring the bells hanging at the entrance to the temples in order to attract the attention of the divinity, and, at the same time, scare away the demons. They set down their offerings (including money) at the feet of the divinity, following a ritual of gestures which seems almost automatic, as if observing the ritual was sufficient to please the gods. It is true that any real worship or inner searching is in fact more likely to take place before the home altar than in the temple. The latter serves to recharge the worshippers' "batteries" by the vision *(darshan)* of pious images. At dusk, crowds flock to the shrines to take part in *arti*. The officiating priest *(pujari)* pays homage to the god by waving a lamp in front of his statue, to the sound of cymbals, bells and tambourines. It is fun to watch the rigmarole of the local monkeys, always on the look out for something to snatch (hold on to your bags…).

Temple of Brahma (A2), the most famous of Pushkar, is said to be the only shrine in India devoted to Brahma. The "creative principle" god of the Hindu trinity (trimurti) has no following, unlike Shiva and Vishnu. He is however worshipped as the "great ancestor" without whom (like the sun) there would be no life on earth. The entrance to the temple stands at the top of a marble staircase. In the courtyard, all the commemorative plaques show how popular the temple is. Inside the crudely painted blue hall, note the shrine which houses a **four-headed statue of Brahma**. The four heads symbolise the four Veda. Originally, Brahma only had one head, but when he fell in love with Sarasvati, he was unable to tear his eyes away from her to such an extent that he grew three new heads to be able to follow her every movement. Sarasvati, embarrassed by such adoration, attempted to flee to the sky, but a fifth head appeared on Brahma's skull. This fifth head was later cut off by Shiva. On entering the sanctuary, note the group of *sadhu* sitting under a tree. The wisest will be lost in meditation (or perhaps just thinking?). Others beg coins from passers-by. In exchange they offer a few drags of their *shilom*, insisting that they only use "very good grass"!

Walk round the temple of Brahma to the right and take the path on the left. The path drops down into peaceful countryside, before leading up to the top of the hill *(allow at least an hour)* where the small **temple to Savitri** (towards A2) stands. From there, enjoy the superb views over the region of Pushkar, particularly towards the end of the afternoon.

Go back towards the lake. Take the first road on the left towards "Paramount Hotel".

Located in a late-19C **haveli**, the **temple of Radha and Krishna** (A2) has an amazing **façade** covered in **frescoes** depicting musicians, elephants, ox carts and even cars and an aeroplane. In theory, the family that lives there allows foreign visitors to look round, but it can't be said they encourage tourists. The temple is situated in the left-hand wing of the courtyard and is decorated with **murals** representing the life of Krishna.

Pushkar Lake

The portal of the **temple of Purani Rangji** (B2) *(north of the lake)* was formerly decorated with frescoes, which are today almost all covered in whitewash. The temple opens onto a courtyard. The **façade** of the sanctuary, which stands in the middle, has retained its paintings and bas-reliefs depicting mainly Vishnu (to whom the temple is dedicated) lying on the snake of eternity. Non-Hindus are not allowed inside.

Dedicated to Vishnu's incarnation as a boar, the **temple of Varaha** (B2) is considered to be the second most sacred temple in Pushkar, after that devoted to Brahma. Rebuilt in the 18C by Jai Singh II, the founding maharaja of Jaipur, it is now partially spoilt by successive layers of paintings. In front of the temple, a **pavilion** decorated with delicate floral motifs gives a glimpse of how beautiful the first shrine must have been.

Seen from the outside, the **temple of Mahadev** (B2) *(opposite the restaurant "Om shiva")* does not appear very tempting. It is however worth going down *(entrance to the left of the façade)* to the chapel in the basement where there is a *linga* (phallic symbol of Shiva) protected by a red sandstone cobra's hood. The atmosphere can be almost haunting in the evening during *arti*.

The temple of Rama Vaikunth (B2) *(eastern entrance to the town)* is probably the most beautiful in Pushkar but most

The earth saved from the floods

Several religious texts relate how Vishnu's incarnation as a boar came to save the earth from an evil demon who was pushing it down to the bottom of the ocean. With the help of his snout and sharp tusks, "he refloated the earth, leaving it on top of the ocean. After having flattened it, he added mountains and divided it into seven continents (...) He then took the form of the immense four-headed being (Brahma) to create life." ("Vishnu Purana", I-IV, 45-50).

of it is off limits to foreigners. The white loincloth and the distinctive hairstyle of the *pujari*, together with the five-tiered **gopuram** (tower decorated with statues) which dominates the sanctuary indicate that it is an example of a temple of southern Indian type. Note that Vaikunth is the paradise where Vishnu lives, of whom Rama is an incarnation.

Making the most of Pushkar

GETTING THERE

By bus – Links with Ajmer every half-hour (30min), leaving from ***Ajmer Bus Stand*** or ***New Ranghi Bus Stand*** (B2), ☎ (0145) 728 88 and 729 31. For other destinations, it is quicker to go to Ajmer and once there, take an RSTC or a private bus. Several travel agents in Pushkar sell tickets for the private bus companies which leave from Ajmer, providing a free shuttle service between Ajmer and Pushkar.

By taxi – Enquire at your hotel about taxis.

GETTING ABOUT

Locomotion in Pushkar revolves primarily around walking or cycling (there are lots of rental agencies). A car can be useful, but not in the town centre which is solely pedestrian.

ADDRESS BOOK

Banks/Money – ***State Bank of Bikaner and Jaipur*** (B2). Travellers' cheques.

Post Office/Telephone – ***Main Bazaar Post Office***, Main Bazaar Rd (B2). Equipped with an express service ***EMS Speed Post***. Postal code: 305022.

Safety – ***Police station***, ☎ (0145) 720 46.

WHERE TO STAY

Pushkar has a vast choice of private homes-cum-guesthouses for budget tourists and travellers. Comfort is generally pretty basic. Prices can drop between 10 and 20% between March-April and June-July. However during the seven day "mela", prices can increase ten-fold and it is impossible to find accommodation unless booked several months earlier.

Under US$7

Lake View Hotel, Main Bazaar Rd, ☎ (0145) 721 06 – 9rm. Very popular cut-price accommodation, it is located in the heart of the town and overlooks the lake. The rooms are on three storeys, set around an inner courtyard. Some are windowless but they are all clean. The pleasant terrace is an ideal spot to lie in the sun, read or chat with fellow travellers. Given its popularity, reservations are advisable.

Pushkar Palace, see below for address. This prestigious establishment also has 11 very low-price rooms. The rooms are set along the edge of a shady lawn lined with banana trees, opposite the hotel's more expensive accommodation. These tiny little cells of almost monastic comfort (bed and chair) do however have a direct view over the lake and also provide access to the hotel's pleasant setting.

Paramount Hotel, Badi Basti, behind the temple of Krishna, ☎ (0145) 724 28 – 19rm. 4rm without bath. Ideal for those in search of peace and quiet, this three-storey house, built against the hillside, is located right at the end of a cul-de-sac. The terrace restaurant and some of the rooms also have a splendid view over Krishna Temple, the town's roofs and in the distance, the lake surrounded by hills. Although the establishment has clearly attempted to improve cleanliness, the finishing remains disappointing.

Pushkar Inn Hotel, Pushkar Palace Rd, ☎ (0145) 720 10 and 724 74 – 13rm. The decoration of the rooms laid out in an L-shape pleasantly reflects the hotel's country setting, on the edge of a field of marigolds lined with Ashoka and banana trees. On one side, there are six rooms with bath and cooler, opening onto a veranda, and on the other, seven rooms, more basic but half as expensive. The ones furthest from the restaurant are less noisy.

From US$7-15

Sarovar Hotel (RTDC,) on the way in to Pushkar from Ajmer, ☎ (0145) 720 40 – 38rm. 24rm. with bath, 14 with cooler. At long last, a well-maintained RTDC establishment! The wide range of rooms and prices should enable everyone to find something to suit their budget. Half the rooms are located in the old part, three of which overlook the lake (they are the most pleasant and the most expensive). The rooms in the modern wing overlook the fields and the hills. Dormitory.

From US$15-30

Pushkar Palace (Heritage Hotels Association), Pushkar Palace Rd, ☎ (0145) 720 01 and 724 01, Fax (0145) 722 26 – 44rm. This former dwelling of the maharaja of Kishangarh is located on the banks of the lake. A perfect stopover providing you can get one of the rooms on the 1st or 2nd floor. These are airy, comfortable, pleasantly decorated with colonial furniture and overlook the lake. The ground-floor rooms are dilapidated, stifling, noisy and best avoided, especially as they are the same price as the others. Somewhat disorganised service. Jeep and camel excursions.

• **During the fair**

During the fair, a whole host of temporary camps are put up around the town. The best of these even have restaurants, a post-office and a safe. In this case, prices include full-board and bills must be paid in foreign currency. Care should be taken to choose a camp that is safe and not too far away because thefts are frequent.

From US$70-150

Tourist Village (RTDC), Mela Ground; reservations in Jaipur, ☎ (0141) 20 25 86, Fax (0141) 20 10 45 – 220rm. Hot water in basins and Turkish toilets. 5 less expensive dormitories.

Royal Camp (WelcomHeritage Hotels), north of Mela Ground; reservations in Delhi (see p 107) – 65rm. Each comfortable and tastefully decorated room is located in its own private tent.

Royal Desert Camp, Ganahera, Motisar Rd; reservations, ☎ (0145) 720 01 and 724 01, Fax (0145) 722 26 – 100rm. Camp put up by Pushkar Palace Hotel. Pleasant, comfortable tents, 50 of which have a private bathroom.

Where to eat

Given Pushkar's rank as a saintly town, meat, fish, eggs and alcohol are forbidden. This "pure veg" status has not prevented the anarchic development of cafés and restaurants, open from breakfast to dinner. Whether hidden deep in a garden or overlooking the town's streets and lake, they all contribute to Pushkar's indubitable charm and are well worth taking the time to stop and enjoy a leisurely drink or meal. Cooking is not, however, their strong-point: buffets, Western dishes and pastries are the norm. The most pleasant include: ***Om Hotel*** (B2), ***Venus*** (B2), ***Om Shiva***, above VK Tourist Palace Hotel (B2), ***Sunset Cafe***, Pushkar Inn Hotel, on the edge of the lake (B2), and the two ***Rainbow*** restaurants, on either side of the town.

Under US$3

Prince's Restaurant, Pushkar Palace Hotel (B2). 7am-10.30pm. Although the dining room is totally devoid of any sort of charm, meals can thankfully be taken on the lawn which leads down to the lake. Reasonable food but variable service. Buffets only.

Pastimes

Excursions – There is a wonderful horse trek between Pushkar and Dundlod (Shekhawati), organised by the Royal Equestrian and Polo Centre at Dundlod (see "Making the most of Shekhawati").

Holidays and festivals – ***Pushkar Fair***, now of international repute and held every year in November, begins eight days after Divali and lasts for seven days, finishing on the full moon (9-12 November 2000, 27-30 November 2001). This religious festival is noted for its cattle and camel fair. It is worth arriving a few days before the "mela's" official opening to see the camel drivers put up their camps. This period is also quieter and less commercially oriented.

Shopping

Main Bazaar Rd is primarily a long line of little shops and stalls all selling the same type of hippy clothing, decorative objects and cheap jewellery for Western tourists. However during the fair the makeshift stalls which spring up all over the town provide a wide selection of desert crafts.

Bookshops – There are three bookshops on Main Bazaar Rd, between the State Bank of Bikaner and Jaipur and the post office (B2): ***Lalchand Ram Chand***, ***Vijay Book House*** and ***The Book Worm***.

C. Pillitz/NETWORK-RAPHO

Bishnoi women at a water hole

THE NORTH-WEST

In not so distant times caravans loaded down with spices, opium and other treasures from India and Central Asia crossed over the rocky steppe lands of Marwar and the Thar Desert, enriching the towns on their route: Bikaner, Jodhpur, Jaisalmer and the bastions of the Rathore and Bhatti clans. Colourfully-dressed nomad tribes still roam over this ochre landscape with their camel and goat herds. Some continue to run contraband opium and heroin over the border between Pakistan and India, seemingly heedless of the frontier running through the desert. *Babul* (acacia tree) and *khejri* are the only trees to thrive in the burning heat of this desert landscape, home of the starving goddess, Bhukti Mata. In areas where the land is irrigated by the Indira Gandhi Canal, corn, sugar-cane and other crops flourish. Elsewhere, the few meagre crops of millet *(bajra)*, chick peas or oilseeds that manage to grow on this scrubland, regularly forgotten by the monsoon rains, are purely the result of the peasants' relentless backbreaking labour. Droughts occur every three years and famine is declared every eight.

BIKANER★★

Pop 41 500 – Alt 237m
330km from Jaipur – 328km from Jaisalmer
See map p 200

Not to be missed
A visit to Junagarh fort.
An excursion to the temple of rats at Deshnok.
And remember...
Hire a taxi to see the town and the surrounding countryside in a day.

Although far less popular than Jaisalmer or Jodhpur, Bikaner is nonetheless fully worth a visit, well off the beaten track, deep in the arid countryside of north-western Rajasthan. The town's main attraction is Junagarh fort, whose refined palaces provide a pleasant break from the harsh desert. A walk through the old town reveals an almost medieval side to Rajasthan, despite the ups and downs of India's anarchic development. Although large numbers of camels can still be seen pulling loads through the narrow lanes, the noisy invasion of scooters and cars grows daily. Visitors will soon have to rely on their imagination to catch a glimpse of this "Desert Pearl" so extolled by tourist brochures.

The impressive ramparts of Junagarh fort

A kingdom at the gateway to the desert

Wealth of the caravans – In 1488, **Rao Bika**, one of the sons of the Rathore ruler, Rao Jodha (founder of Jodhpur), decided to establish a new kingdom here. He had to compete with the desert tribes for over thirty years before definitively establishing his control over the region. From the 16C, the new dynasty then had to contend with another far more powerful rival, in the person of Emperor Akbar. Akbar conquered Bikaner's rulers militarily, but true to his policy of diplomacy, he managed to win their loyalty by granting them positions of command in the Mughal armies. The kingdom then experienced a period of peace which was to enable it to benefit from its strategic and economic position on the routes between the Middle East and northern India. The merchants' caravans began to stop in Bikaner after their desert crossing; the town prospered and its inhabitants embarked on the building of opulent *haveli* and richly carved temples.

The desert diplomat

Maharaja Ganga Singh's most illustrious work remains the creation of the "Bikaner Camel Corps", which won its renown during the British colonial wars, from China to Somalia, and also during the First World War (in France and in Egypt). The sovereign of Bikaner, a resourceful military leader, also proved himself to be a shrewd diplomat. He represented the Indian Empire during the Treaty of Versailles (1919) and was a delegate at the League of Nations from 1924 to 1930. Such was his international prestige that he played host to leading foreign statesmen, eager to taste the charms of this desert kingdom and try their luck at his famous grouse shoots in Gajner.

P. Horree/ANA

New resources – When the British took control of Rajasthan in the early 19C, Bikaner, hard pressed by the ports of Calcutta and Bombay and the establishment of new trade routes, began to decline and the region stagnated. However, at the end of the 19C, camel breeding brought a new lease of life to the region, because of the British Army's growing needs as a result of the colonial wars on the Northwest Frontier. The kingdom experienced a new golden age under the reign of **Ganga Singh** (1898-1934), who revived the region's economic activity and built the vast irrigation channel known as the "Ganga Canal" in the north of Rajasthan.

The town

Allow a day.

Junagarh fort*** (A2)

10am-4.30pm, entrance charge, extra fee for cameras and videos. Guided visits in English. Allow an hour.

One of the fort's main peculiarities is its location in a plain and not on a hilltop, as is usually the case. The desert, in fact, provides excellent natural defence and fully satisfied the local sovereigns' desire for security. The fort was built under *Raja* Rai Singh (1571-1611) to replace the one erected by Rao Bika, now destroyed (but previously within the town's ramparts). The vast **red sandstone ramparts** span a circumference of almost a kilometre. The **37 bastions** are proof of the fort's military glory, long since past, but which always lived up to its reputation: Bikaner fort never fell into enemy hands. The most spectacular features, the lavishly decorated palaces, eloquent symbols of the "India of Maharajas", lie hidden behind the ramparts. The current ruler, Narendra Singh, still resides in Bikaner with his family, but in the "modern" palace at Lalgarh *(3km to the northwest of the town centre)*.

The entrance to the fort is from the northeast. A series of three impressive gates leads into the main courtyard. Note the panels of the first gate, **Daulat Pol**. The ominous spikes riveted in the wooden gate used to deter the fighting elephants sent to batter it down. The third gate, **Suraj Pol**, is guarded by statues of two Rathore warriors riding on the backs of elephants; these young men, named Jaimal and Patta, were killed in the defence of Chittaurgarh. The gate leads to the main porch *(tickets are on sale here)*.

The visitor then enters an opulent collection of palaces, courtyards and reception halls. A ramp leads up to the **first courtyard**, paved in Italian tiles. In the centre is a **white marble kiosk** over which is a small reservoir used to provide water for the court's games during *Holi*. On the façade is a coloured fresco depicting a steam train. The arrival of the railway in the desert was a memorable event in the history of the region. In the opposite wall is a magnificent window, decorated with Delft tiles.

The ceiling and the columns of the **Diwan-i Am** (public audience hall), built in 1631 by Karan Singh, are covered in paintings and gilt paint. **Anup Mahal**, the next palace, is the fort's pride and joy. Begun under Karan Singh and finished by his successor, Anup Singh, the profusion of its decoration, the exquisite quality of its paintings, its mirror mosaics, coloured tiles and gilt paint make it quite remarkable. The maharajas were crowned here. Note the richly-worked **throne**, the beauty of which is further emphasised by inlaid coloured glass. A beautiful door carved in walnut from Kashmir leads to the neighbouring palaces.

Prior authorisation must be obtained to visit **Phul Mahal** (Flower palace) and **Chandra Mahal** (Moon palace). Some of their walls are entirely studded in tiny mirrors. The crescent-moon shaped Chandra Mahal was set aside for the court's womenfolk. Its windows overlook the fort's **gardens** *(undergoing restoration)*. In comparison with the extravagant luxury of Anup Mahal, the **Diwan-i Khas** (private audience hall) seems almost dull. Decorated with gilt paint and frescoes and mirrors from Belgium, it would nonetheless be the pride and joy of many a sovereign. The walls of **Badal Mahal** (Cloud palace) are entirely covered in blue and white **paintings of clouds**, thus reminding visitors of how essential rain is to this arid semi-desert region. Perhaps this pictorial representation sufficed to cool down the atmosphere during the stifling heat-waves before the fleeting monsoon rains brought their meagre relief ...

The first floor reveals a small **temple to Hanuman** (the monkey god and army general in the service of the god Rama in the *Ramayana*). Note the particularly fine collection of nail-studded boards and sharpened blades used by the *fakirs* during their amazing exercises. The handsome sandalwood walls of **Gaj Mandir** are partially covered in mirrors. Inside, a sophisticated swing device triggered off a merry-go-round of little statues placed around the frame. Just next door is the beautiful ivory inlaid door of the **queen's chamber**. The views from the upper terraces over the fort and the town are splendid. The walls of **Hawa Mahal** (Palace of the Winds), the only edifice built on the second floor, are covered in blue tiles. In the hot season, the maharaja would have withdrawn to this small palace – probably in "charming" company. A servant positioned outside would have worked a pulley mechanism designed to wield an enormous *panka* (fan hung from the ceiling).

Back on the ground floor, the most recent wing of the palace, **Ganga Niwas**, built under the reign of Maharaja Ganga Singh, has been turned into a **museum**. The visit begins with the familiar, very well-stocked, **armoury room**, which houses a fine collection of *katar* (large bladed daggers, some of which had two small pistols hidden on either side), a sword weighing 27kg and sabres whose hilts are inlaid in ivory and semi-precious stones. The vast **Durbar Hall** is decorated with ornate ornamental motifs finely carved into the red sandstone walls. The same motifs can be seen on the arches and the wooden **ceiling**. The work by craftsmen imported specially by Ganga Singh from Afghanistan is said to have lasted seven years. The hall houses a magnificent sandalwood throne together with objects which belonged to the maharaja. The spoon visible in a corner of the dining room was designed specially to protect the maharaja's legendary moustache. Photos of foreign politicians, diplomats and VIPs, invited to tiger hunts organised by the sovereign, are a souvenir of the diplomatic prestige enjoyed by Ganga Singh. Finally, visitors may be surprised to come upon an aeroplane in the museum's other hall. It dates from the First World War and was presented to the loyal maharaja by the British government.

The museums

Lalgarh palace* (B1) *(near the bus station, some 3km to the northeast of the town centre)* was built from 1900 onwards by Maharaja Ganga Singh on plans designed by the famous architect, Sir Swinton Jacob. This sprawling red sandstone edifice, freely inspired by the Rajput style, has been the royal family's residence since the 1920s. The family has turned one of the wings into a luxury hotel *(see "Making the most of Bikaner")*, while another section houses the **Maharaja Sadul Singh Museum** *(10am-5pm; closed Wednesday, entrance charge)* devoted to Bikaner's sovereigns. Visitors may well find that its "35 000" photos and anti-

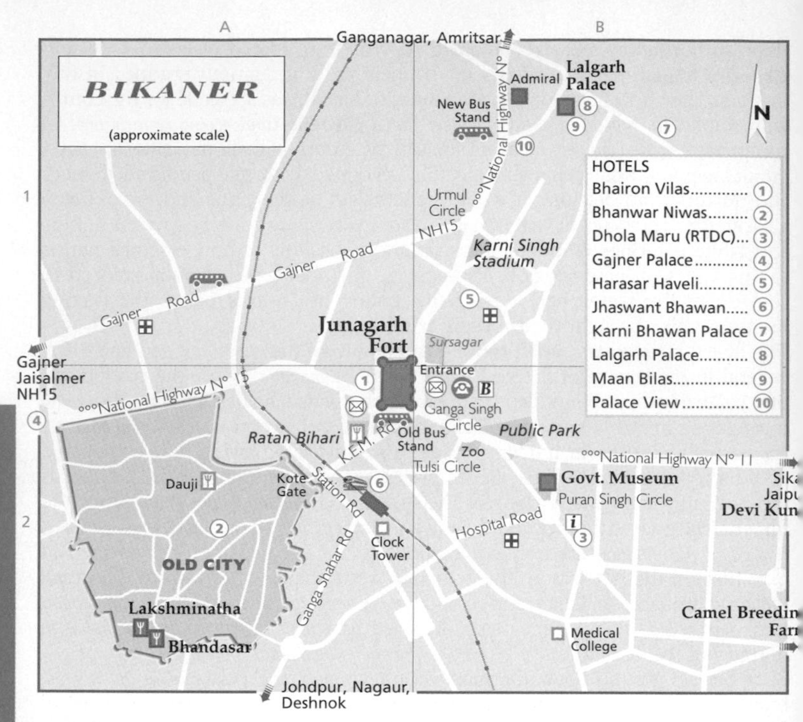

quated presentation of collections comprising objects ranging from toiletries to golfing equipment are of limited interest… Hidden within this hotchpotch of miscellanea, there is however an immense pewter vase, weighing over 100kg. Transported by camel from village to village, it served as a receptacle for collecting taxes. In the midst of the collections of uniforms, weapons and carriages is also the plough with which Ganga Singh marked the first furrow of northern Rajasthan's irrigation canal. Among the deluge of photos are large numbers of hunting trophies (mainly of tigers), including portraits of foreign politicians invited on these bloody expeditions.

The French tiger's hunting escapades

During his trip to Europe, Maharaja Ganga Singh became friends with the French prime minister, Georges Clemenceau. The latter came to India after the war and visited his friend in Bikaner when he was invited to take part in a lavish hunting party. Ganga Singh found the French politician's nickname of "tiger", particularly amusing. The sovereign thus duly set about acquiring a small figure depicting the former prime minister with a tiger's body, still to be seen in Lalgarh museum.

Near the tourist office, the **Government Museum** (Ganga Golden Jubilee Museum) (B2) *(10am-4.30pm, entrance charge)* houses, among more modest collections, a few **sculptures and earthenware objects*** of the Gupta era (4-6C), some fine miniature paintings, hunting trophies, weapons and portraits depicting the life of the maharajas. The remarkable statue of **Sarasvati** (goddess of eloquence and the arts), sculpted in the Jain style in the 11C, together with a copy of the Treaty of Versailles (1919), in which Ganga Singh is mentioned, are also worthy of note.

The temples of the old town

South-west of the 15C town, surrounded by ramparts. Take a rickshaw to the esplanade in front of the shrines. On the way, look out for several attractive red sandstone haveli with their balconies and delicately carved jali.

From the 15C onwards, Bikaner began to attract a population of bankers and merchants. Taking advantage of the town's position on the caravan route, after the Thar Desert crossing, the most astute among them quickly amassed vast fortunes. Following the pattern of other Rajasthani towns, this success enabled them to invest in magnificent sanctuaries. While those of Bikaner are no match for the priceless stone works of art of the temples of Rankapur or Dilwara (Mount Abu), they are nonetheless well worth a visit.

Bhandasar Jain temple (or Bhandeshvar) (A2) *(entrance via the courtyard opening onto the esplanade)* was begun towards the end of the 15C by the Jain merchant, Bhandasa Oswal, and completed by his daughter in 1517. The lofty white, carved **tower** *(shikhara)* can be seen far around, looming high over those of the other shrines. Enter through the 17C red sandstone door, topped by kiosks, and stop for a moment to admire the **murals** of the 18C *ranga mandapa* (hypostyle pavilion): they depict court scenes, processions, battles and notable events in the lives of the 24 *tirthankara,* the wise "ford passers". The marble statue of Sumtinatha, the 5th *tirthankara,* to whom the temple is dedicated, sits in state amidst the ornate decoration of gilt paint and mirrors of the inner shrine. The collection of **miniature** paintings on the first floor should not be missed and there is a wonderful panoramic view over the town and the surrounding plain from the third floor.

Lakshminatha Hindu temple (A2) *(behind the Jain temple, no photos)* was built in the 16C, opposite Rao Bika's fort, today destroyed. Built in white marble, it also possesses some fine **murals** and, in the inner shrine *(garbha griha)*, is an image of the goddess of good fortune and prosperity, **Lakshmi**, incarnation of Vishnu, the protective divinity of Bikaner.

The surroundings

Devi Kund*

8km east of Bikaner, first take the road to Jaipur, then turn right to Napasar. As early as the 16C, Bikaner's maharajas were cremated here, near the small artificial lake. An impressive series of **cenotaphs** mark the place of the funeral pyres of kings, princes and their families: a sun marks those of the sons of the Rathore clan and a lotus those of the daughters – occasionally with footprints of those who committed *sati*. The most impressive *chhatri* is Maharaja Surat Singh's white marble one (early 19C), decorated with frescoes.

The Camel Breeding Farm

9km to the south of the town. 3pm-5pm, no entrance charge, no photos. This farm is a research centre opened in 1960 to breed camels. A visit is of no great interest to anyone who has already seen one of these graceful beasts. Visitors may however be interested to know that there are over one and a half million dromedaries in India, most of which live in Gujarat and to a lesser extent, in Rajasthan. The Bikaner race is reputed for its strength and those of Jaisalmer are predominantly used as riding animals.

Long live the saint!

Born in 1387, Karni Mata is said to have ascended to heaven some 151 years later in a ray of divine light... It thus seems natural that she should have carried out so many miracles during her earthly life: healings, multiplying food. Many devout Hindus, including important figures of the region, came to seek her blessing. In 1457, Rao Jodha, founder of Jodhpur, asked her to grant his dynasty eternal power. Karni Mata then predicted that the family would reign for 28 generations. She announced the victory over the tribes of the region to Rao Bika. Karni Mata became the kingdom's protective divinity.

Deshnok temple**

30km south of Bikaner. Buses leave every 30min from the bus station. No entrance fee, but charge for cameras and videos. This temple owes its celebrity, not to its architecture, fine though it may be, but to its singular inhabitants, a multitude of rats swarming freely beneath the feet of the respectful pilgrims bringing them offerings. This has been the case since the 15C, when Saint **Karni Mata** of the Charans caste (community of genealogists and bards) lived here. Even during her life, she was held by the Hindus to be an incarnation of Durga. It is said that she once asked the god of death, Yama, to resuscitate a deceased Charans child. Yama was unable to fulfil her wish and the child was reincarnated as a white rat. Karni Mata then decided that all deceased Charans would escape the realm of Yama and become rats in her temple until the day of judgement and their reincarnation.

A visit to the shrine may put off the more squeamish... It may thus be reassuring to know that rats are, in principle, highly sociable creatures. They spend their time gorging themselves on the pilgrims' gifts: milk, rice and sweets on sale at the temple's entrance. It is however worthwhile watching where you put your feet, because this miniature fraternity of rats is fully at home here and not used to giving way to the human species.

An engaged couple in Deshnok temple

The shrine is one of the most popular pilgrimage centres in northern Rajasthan, and the surrounding neighbourhood overflows with stalls selling souvenirs, pious images, plastic toys and, of course, confectionery: such is the gluttonous nature of the temple's inhabitants that many confectioners have set up shop in the area. What's more, it is not considered at all sacrilegious to succumb to a delicious *laddu* (ball of flour, *ghee* and sugar) spread out temptingly on the sweet stalls. The music blasting out of the loudspeakers of the cassette sellers is not in actual fact from the latest *masala* hit movie, but rather *bhajan*, religious chants. This **festival atmosphere**, both intense and relaxed, continues right into the sanctuary itself. Swathed in their brightly-coloured saris, timorous Indian women all of a sudden find themselves obliged to pay homage to creatures not traditionally revered in most households, thereby giving rise to some amusing sights. The entrance to the temple is through a silver door, a gift from Maharaja Ganga Singh (early 20C). Seated on the white marble floor, Charans musicians perpetuate the musical traditions of their venerated caste of bards. It is possible to follow pilgrims right into the shrine itself. Watch as they place their offerings in front of the crude statue of Karni Mata, ignoring the dozy rodents sleeping lazily around the room. Only the white rats, the sight of which brings good luck, seem to make themselves scarce.

Making the most of Bikaner

Getting there

By train – ***Bikaner Railway Station*** (A2), is located close to the centre, between the old town and the fort, ☎ 131. Computerised reservation terminal, 8am-2pm/2.15pm-8pm, Sunday 8am-2pm. 2 daily links with Jaipur (7hr by day express, 10hr by night "mail train"). 3 trains for Delhi (10 to 11hr) which all arrive in Sarai Rohilla station. 1 daily departure for Churu (4hr, arrives in the night) and Sikar (7hr, arrives before dawn), 2 express trains for Jodhpur (5hr) and, three times a week, 1 train for Abu Road (11hr).

By bus – The State buses (RSTRC) leave from the ***New Bus Stand***, or the ***Central Bus Stand***, around 3km from the centre, on the Lalgarh Palace road (B1), ☎ (0151) 52 38 00. 1 "Silver Line" bus per day and a few express luxury coaches for Jaipur (7hr). 2 "Silver Line" buses for Jodhpur, via Nagaur. Express services to Delhi (11hr), Kota (11hr), Bundi (10hr) and Jaisalmer (7hr). Large number of buses to Jodhpur (6hr), but only 1 or 2 for Nagaur (3hr), Fatehpur (4hr), Jhunjhunu (5hr), Ajmer (7hr), Alwar (8hr), Abu Road (9hr) and Udaipur (12hr). The ***Old Bus Stand***, where the private bus companies leave is to the south of the fort (A2). Tickets are on sale from the ten or so companies installed in wooden huts. Departures are between 7pm and 11pm and run to Jaipur (6hr), Jodhpur (6hr), Jaisalmer (6hr), Ajmer (6hr30min), Udaipur (10hr) and Delhi (10hr).

Getting about

By auto-rickshaw – Allow around 20Rs to get from the station to Lalgarh Palace; this would seem to be a standard price in Bikaner whatever the distance travelled.

By taxi – "Tourist taxis" are available at the railway station but many often refuse to give a reasonable price. In case of difficulty, ask the tourist office to intervene on your behalf.

Car rental – Enquire at your hotel or at a travel agent.

Bicycle rental – On Station Rd.

Address book

Tourist office – ***Tourist Reception Centre*** (B2), in the grounds of Dhola

Maru Hotel, ☎ (0151) 19 13 and 54 41 25. Has a selection of brochures, list of English-speaking guides and of guest houses. Friendly and efficient service.

Banks/Money – Changing money is not necessarily easy in Bikaner. Try the ***State Bank of Bikaner and Jaipur*** (B2), Public Park, east of Junagarh fort. Cash and travellers' cheques, no ATM facilities.

Post Office/Telephone – There are three post offices in town: the ***GPO***, to the west of Junagarh fort (A2), which also has the poste restante service, ***City Post Office***, Kote Gate, within the ramparts (A2), and ***Kutchery Post Office***, near the State Bank of Bikaner and Jaipur (B2). All have an ***EMS Speed Post*** service. To send or receive a fax, enquire at the ***Telegraph Office***, Kutchery Campus, near the State Bank of Bikaner and Jaipur. Postal code: 334001.

Health – ***Ambulances***, ☎ 102. ***Kothari Medical & Research Centre***, Gajner Rd (A1).

Safety – ***Police***, ☎ 100.

Travel agents – ***Registhan Tours***, 138 Gandhi Nagar, near Narender Bhawan (B1), ☎ (0151) 52 70 72/78. This reputable agency has the advantage of having branches in several other towns in Rajasthan. Can make train, air and hotel reservations. Guides available. Car rentals. Camel rides and treks.
Rajasthan Tours, 6 Sardar Hall, Lalgarh Palace Rd (B1), ☎ (0151) 54 36 93, Fax (0151) 54 22 47. As with the above, this agency also has branches throughout Rajasthan. Prices are relatively high but the services are of excellent quality. Train and hotel reservations. Guides, car and jeep rentals. Camel rides.
Vino Desert Safari, opposite Gopeshwar temple, Ganga Shahar, towards Deshnok, ☎ (0151) 20 44 45. Organises all types of camel rides at cheap prices.
Rajasthan Safari & Treks, Bassai House, Purani Ginani, ☎ (0151) 54 37 38. Specialises in camel rides and treks.

Where to stay

During the low season, which runs from April-May to August-September, most hotels offer a 15-30 % reduction in rooms. For those on tight budgets and who don't mind a little dirt or noise, there are some extremely cheap hotels near the station, on Station Rd.

• In the modern town

From US$7-15

Jhaswant Bhawan Hotel, Daudsar House, Alakh Sagar Rd, ☎/Fax (0151) 52 18 34; reservations at Jaipur, ☎ (0141) 38 16 68 – 10rm. Cooler. A family-run establishment built in 1926 by Bikaner's last prime minister, it is located in a quiet neighbourhood, although very close to the station. Spartan rooms but with pretty printed cotton quilts. Clean and good value-for-money, although somewhat lacking in "warmth". The living and dining room areas could clearly do with more care.

Dhola Maru Hotel (RTDC), ☎ (0151) 52 96 21 – 32rm. 10rm. with cooler, 6 with AC. Hidden away in a peaceful neighbourhood, this RTDC hotel offers guests a pleasant welcome. The communal areas are quite well maintained, but the rooms are basic and very neglected, particularly in the standard category. It is however located in the same grounds as the Tourist Office. Dormitory and a few rooms under US$7.

From US$15-30

Harasar Haveli Hotel, near Karni Singh Stadium, ☎ (0151) 20 98 91 and 52 73 18, Fax (0151) 52 51 50 – 8rm. CC 6rm. with cooler, 2 with AC. Located in a recent residential area of town, this house is run by a charming Rajput family who do all they can to make your stay a pleasant one. Airy, clean rooms, simply but tastefully decorated. The cheapest are around US$10. Plans are afoot to add 12 new rooms by 2001.

From US$15-30

Bhairon Vilas Hotel, opposite Junagarh Fort the GPO, ☎ (0151) 54 47 51 and 52 04 35, Fax (0151) 54 47 51 – 18rm. CC Cooler. This late 19C dwelling with its lofty battlemented façade has become a highly picturesque hotel, with the traditional atmosphere of a Rajput nobleman's residence. The small, low-ceilinged rooms are somewhat overdone in terms of draperies and curtains, revealing a definite taste for deep reds and greens, all of which combines to make them rather oppressive. The view of the fort is however magnificent. The rooms in the building's main section are less noisy. Drinks are served on a pleasant lawn.

• **In the old town**

From US$40-70

Bhanwar Niwas (Heritage Hotels Association), Rampuria St., ☎ (0151) 710 43 and 52 93 23, Fax (0151) 618 80 – 16rm. This hotel, right in the heart of the old town, is in a 1927 haveli built by the Rampuria merchant family. Its interior decoration has recently been redone in a flashy "Bollywood" style which will delight any enthusiasts of kitsch (candelabra, stuffed toys, gilt paint). Although very popular among Bikaneris, those who prefer the refined charm of old establishments will be disappointed.

• **Around Lalgarh Palace**

The northern part of Bikaner resembles a vast wasteland in which it is difficult to find one's way. There are a few hotels, either around Lalgarh Palace, an oasis in this desert landscape, or further out, almost out of town.

From US$7-30

Palace View Hotel, Lalgarh Palace Campus, ☎ (0151) 20 34 63 and 54 36 25, Fax (0151) 52 20 41 and 52 27 41 – 14rm. Cooler. This peaceful, unpretentious hotel, which has all the charm of a Rajput family home, is located at the beginning of the small road leading to Lalgarh Palace. Friendly, attentive welcome, clean and comfortable rooms. The 1st floor rooms have a veranda which overlooks Lalgarh. Meals can be provided on request, and are served in the family living room or on the vast 1st floor terrace overlooking the palace.

From US$30-40

Maan Bilas Hotel (HRH Group), Lalgarh Palace Complex, ☎ (0151) 52 47 11/12, Fax (0151) 52 24 08; reservations in Delhi and Udaipur (see p 107) – 9rm. TV CC This red sandstone edifice which dates back to the early 20C is located in the same grounds as Lalgarh Palace, from which it is separated by flower beds. The rooms, all alike, are comfortable and pleasantly decorated in a colonial style. All have a veranda with table and armchairs, and overlook the palace gardens. Peaceful, cosy atmosphere. Elegant service. The dining room is rather ordinary, but meals can be taken on the lawn.

From US$40-70

Karni Bhawan Palace (HRH Group and Heritage Hotels Association), Gandhi Nagar, ☎ (0151) 52 47 01, Fax (0151) 52 24 08; reservations in Delhi and Udaipur (see p 107) – 20rm. TV CC Located almost outside town, this Art Deco fantasia is a must for all enthusiasts of the period. Almost nothing has been changed since it was built in the 1940s by Karni Singh, Bikaner's last ruling maharaja. The superb suites still have the original period furniture and decoration. The standard rooms are small and much less luxurious. In the living-dining area, guests can still see the screen and projector which the royal family used during their private cinema evenings.

From US$70-150

Lalgarh Palace Hotel (WelcomHeritage Hotels and Heritage Hotels Association), ☎ (0151) 52 21 05 and 52 39 63, Fax (0151) 522 22 53; reservations in Delhi (see p 107) – 40rm. TV CC An imposing palace in a majestic setting. Everything is spacious and in impeccable taste: the rooms with fireplaces and period furniture, the corridors, inner courtyards, covered swimming pool and the gardens. Unfortunately, the service is impersonal and the establishment mainly caters to groups, thus making it somewhat cold and lifeless. Windowless, rather dull dining room, but there is a bar, billiard room, games' room and smoking room.

• **Gajner**

25km to the southwest, on the N.H.15 towards Jaisalmer.

From US$40-70

Gajner Palace Hotel (HRH Group and Heritage Hotels Association), Gajner, ☎ (01534) 550 63/64/65, Fax (0151) 52 24 08; reservations in Delhi and Udaipur (see p 107) – 35rm. Cooler. Bar, billiards. This impressive pink sandstone hunting pavilion, built in the early 20C by Maharaja Ganga Singh, is set in the heart of a nature reserve, on the edge of a lake. Formerly the scene of a famous grouse shoot organised every year by the maharaja. The eleven historical suites are located in the building's main section which stands right on the lake front. The standard rooms are dotted around the wings; the right-hand wing is more pleasant and the rooms are on ground level, opening onto a flowery lawn. Meals can be taken on the terrace which overlooks the lake. Jeep excursions possible in the reserve.

Where to eat

With the exception of the hotels, Bikaner has few possibilities in terms of eating out. Near the station, on Station Rd, there are a few confectionery shops, as well as the ***Amber*** restaurant (good food, but mediocre setting). Opposite the fort, it is planned to open a terrace restaurant in the grounds of the ***Bhairon Vilas Hotel***.

• **Around Lalgarh Palace**

From US$3-4

Admiral Restaurant, opposite Urmul Dairy (B1), ☎ (0151) 25 99 03. 12.30-11.30pm. Classical north Indian cuisine, served in an impersonal, but clean, spacious room. Middle-class Indian clientele. Discreet, efficient and fast service.

Excursions

Gajner Natural Reserve, 25km to the south-west on the N.H.15. No entrance charge when arriving from Golari village (some 5km after Gajner) but 100Rs charge when entering via the Gajner Palace Hotel. Local buses from the ***Gajner Rd Bus Stand*** (A1) for Golari (40min) and Gajner. (Beware, the buses drop travellers off on the highway, at the fork to the Gajner Palace Hotel, leaving them with a 2km walk). By taxi, allow 300Rs for 4hr.

Deshnok. Local buses leave every 30min from the New Bus Stand (50min). It is also possible to take a "tempo" group taxi from the station (irregular timetable).

Camel treks. In recent years, Bikaner has become a busy camel trekking centre. The most popular destination is the region of the Bishnoi villages. Allow three to six days. "Camel safari" enthusiasts can go from Bikaner to Jaisalmer (6-13 days), and further afield, to Barmer (15 days). Departures are not in fact from Bikaner itself, but by jeep for 30km and then by camel. Similarly, the arrival into Jaisalmer itself is also by car. Book at least 15 days ahead with a travel agent and allow between 700-2 500Rs per day and per person.

Treks on horseback. There are some excellent treks available between Bikaner and Dundlod (Shekhawati) or Pushkar, organised by the Royal Equestrian and Polo Centre in Dundlod. Allow 5 500Rs per day per person (see "Making the most of Shekhawati").

Holidays and festivals

Camel Festival. Organised in January by the Rajasthan government (8-9 January 2001), this annual meeting puts on a wide range of events to do with camels (processions, races, milking, shearing, etc) together with dancing and folklore performances.

Karni Mata Festival. Every year, in March-April, the little village of Deshnok comes to life during this religious festival when pilgrims offer sweetmeats to the temple rats. Squeamish visitors should beware because the place is crawling in rodents.

Kapil Muni Fair at Kolayat (50km to the southwest of Bikaner). The pilgrimage begins 4 days before the full moon of October-November and finishes four days after (26 November-4 December 2001). The festival is in honour of Kapil Muni, a famous hermit-cum-wise man of the Vedic era, coupled with a cattle fair.

Shopping

The best stocked bazaars are located around Kote Gate (A2), on Station Rd and on Mahatma Gandhi Rd (M.G. Rd), which is still called by its former name, King Edward Memorial Rd (K.E.M. Rd).

Crafts – The region's speciality is camel skins, which are tanned and painted: the paunch is turned into bottles and flasks and the leather is used to make purses, cushion covers and lampshades. Comfortable buffalo-skin leather slippers, "mojri" are also available. Bikaner is India's largest wholesale wool market and has a thriving weaving industry: shawls, carpets, etc.

Abhivyakti, in the grounds of Junagarh fort, 9am-5pm. Direct sales, via the Urmul Association, of shirts, shawls and "mojri" made in the surrounding villages. Fixed prices. All the proceeds are reinvested in desert craft development projects and to improve the health and education of the villagers.

Culinary specialities – Bikaner's "namkin" and sweetmeats are renowned throughout northern India, as are its "bhujiya" (vegetable fritters made out of chickpea flour). On Station Rd and K.E.M. Road.

In front of Bikaner fort

R. Marca

JAISALMER★★★

Pop 40 000 – Alt 242m
328km from Bikaner – 660km from Jaipur
See inside cover map

Not to be missed
The fort.
The havelis in the lower town.

And remember...
Avoid the period between April-September, when temperatures rise to over 40°C.

The long, straight road stretches out ahead through an endless sea of sand. A single row of *babul* (acacias) provide the sole shade from the burning sun and the only touch of greenery in this ochre-coloured steppe land. Apparently free-roaming camels plod patiently along the tarmac road, stretching their neck to reach up to the top branches, heedless of the few motor vehicles which venture this far. Seemingly forsaken in the Thar Desert, Jaisalmer finally appears. Although its ochre-shades blend in perfectly with its surroundings, the imposing outline of the city in an otherwise monotonous plain, finally catches the traveller's eye. The golden sandstone ramparts, festooned with bastions, seem to merge into the city's lower walls of sand. From a distance, no outlying houses are visible, all are hidden within its protective surrounding walls.

New age camels

The golden age of the caravans is well and truly past, but the camels are still hard at work thanks to the region's thriving tourist trade. Although the locals practically all get around by bus, lorry, jeep or scooter, Western tourists can be relied on to succumb to the charm of a jolting ride astride one of these appealing creatures. "Camel safaris" provide many local travel agents with their staple income, and few foreign visitors leave the region without having tasted the joys of this back-breaking mode of transport. Some are enchanted by the experience, others simply rub their sore, aching muscles. Even if the longer treks leave the beaten track of the regular tourist traps, all the shorter excursions (several days) inevitably do the rounds of villages long since used to such visitors and well-prepared to fleece any unsuspecting tourist.

The martial era of battles and suicide charges of the Rajput warriors is well and truly past. Foreigners have taken abode here and since 1968, the railway means that Jaisalmer is no longer cut off from the rest of India. However, despite the repercussions of tourism in the region, it has retained an unspoilt feel. In the narrow streets lined with extraordinary *haveli* whose walls seem to have been sculpted by lacemakers, walking is still the preferred mode of transport. Indeed, automobiles are banned from the lower town (with the exception of the inevitable rickshaws equipped with their blaring sound systems). In the upper town ("the fort"), time seems to have stood still and all traffic is totally banned. Only the laughter of children, the muffled sounds of the lower town and the whispering wind over the seemingly infinite ochre plain interrupt the silent landscape.

A desert fortress

The caravans' fortune – Jaisalmer's foundation dates back to 1156, when **Rao Jaisal**, a Rajput sovereign of the **Bhattis** clan, decided to build his capital here. The Bhattis clan belong to the "moon race" (Chandravansh), or to be more exact, to the Yadava branch of the god **Krishna**, their ancestor. Driven from the banks of the Indus by Mahmud of Ghazi's raids (early 11C), they survived by plundering and pillaging, settling first at Tanot, then at Lodrava (15km from Jaisalmer), before finally choosing the more easily defended steep slopes of Jaisalmer. Their transformation from marauders to sovereigns was not instantaneous: for decades, they continued to play the role of local war lords, holding the merchant caravans and pilgrims on their way to Mecca to ransom. They even held up a caravan belonging to Sultan Ala ud-Din Khijli of Delhi, who retaliated by laying siege to the town in 1314. At the end of an eight-year siege, the warriors, refusing to give in, dressed in saffron robes of sacrifice and launched a suicidal counter-attack, while 24 000 women and children threw themselves into the burning fires. Only ten years after this initial horrific event, Jaisalmer was attacked for similar reasons, this time by Sultan Feroze Shah Tugluq of Delhi, prompting the Bhattis, once again, to carry out their gruesome *jauhar* rite.

Peace in the desert – After courageously resisting several Mughal offensives, Jaisalmer's *rawal* accepted imperial sovereignty in 1570. From a stronghold, Jaisalmer now became a trade centre. Rivalries between the maharawal and their prime ministers, powerful, ambitious men for the most part, did not prevent the local merchants and bankers from amassing sizeable fortunes. The arrival of the British and the advent of maritime trade routes were however to toll the death knell of the caravan era. Jaisalmer gradually became a sleepy backwater, isolated in the desert. The 1965 and 1971 wars against Pakistan however convinced India's government of the zone's strategic importance. A military base was set up with a corresponding road network, and in 1974 the region spectacularly reappeared in the headlines, when the army carried out India's first nuclear tests at **Pokaran** (110km east of Jaisalmer). Twenty-four years later (May 1998), India reasserted its position among the world's major nuclear powers, with a new series of tests at Pokaran.

Jaisalmer fortress

M Franck / MAGNUM

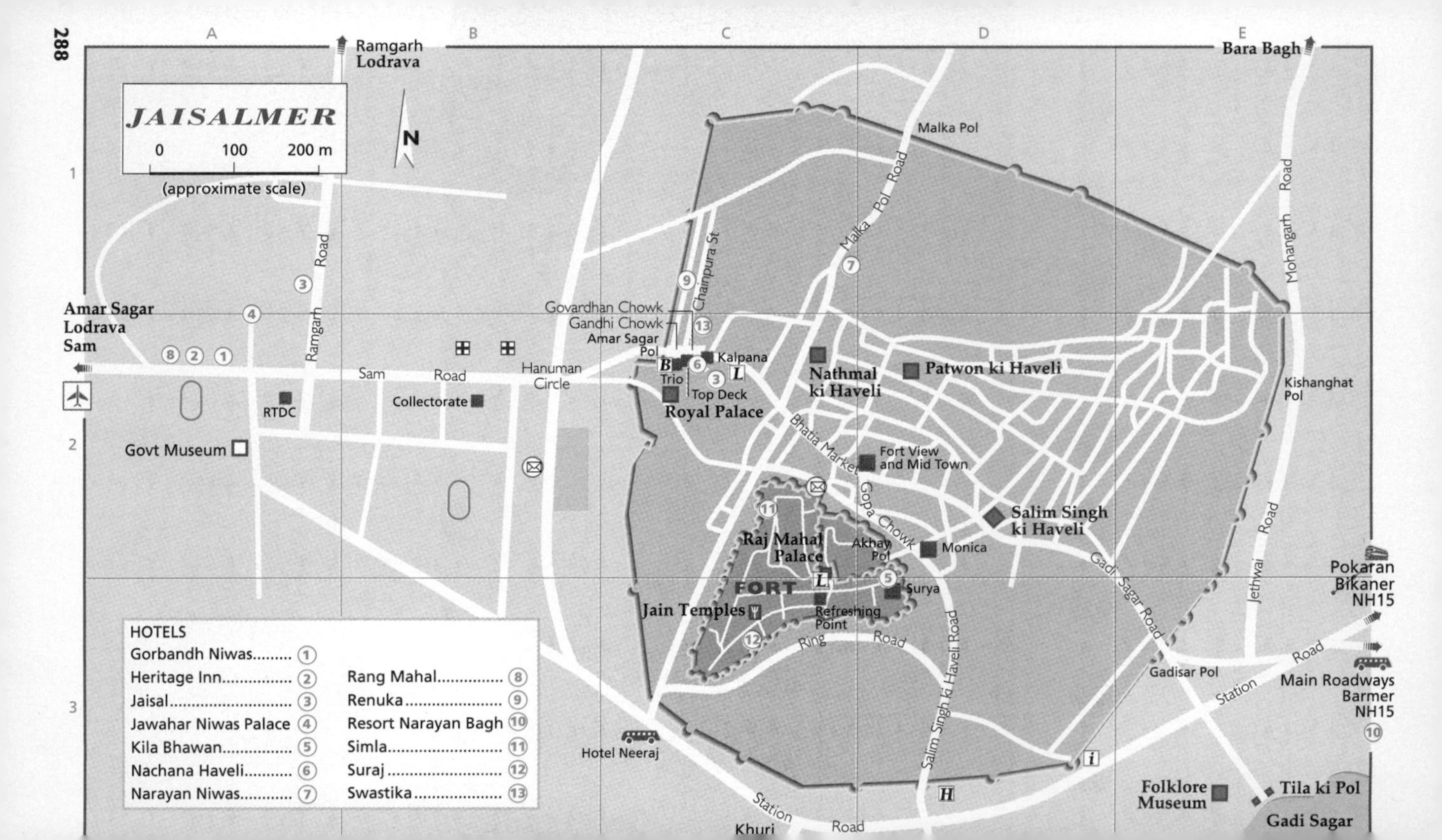
JAISALMER
0 100 200 m
(approximate scale)
N
A
B
C
D
E
1
2
3
Ramgarh
Lodrava
Bara Bagh
Amar Sagar
Lodrava
Sam
Ramgarh Road
Sam Road
Hanuman Circle
Collectorate
RTDC
Govt Museum
Govardhan Chowk
Gandhi Chowk
Amar Sagar Pol
Chainpura St
Kalpana
Trio
Top Deck
Royal Palace
Malka Pol
Malka Pol Road
Nathmal ki Haveli
Patwon ki Haveli
Bhatia Market
Fort View and Mid Town
Gopa Chowk
Salim Singh ki Haveli
Monica
Raj Mahal Palace
Akhay Pol
FORT
Surya
Jain Temples
Refreshing Point
Ring Road
Salim Singh ki Haveli Road
Gadi Sagar Road
Mohangarh Road
Kishanghat Pol
Jethwai Road
Pokaran
Bikaner
NH15
Station Road
Gadisar Pol
Main Roadways
Barmer
NH15
Hotel Neeraj
Khuri
Station Road
Folklore Museum
Tila ki Pol
Gadi Sagar
HOTELS
Gorbandh Niwas......... 1
Heritage Inn................ 2
Jaisal............................ 3
Jawahar Niwas Palace 4
Kila Bhawan................ 5
Nachana Haveli........... 6
Narayan Niwas............ 7
Rang Mahal............... 8
Renuka...................... 9
Resort Narayan Bagh 10
Simla......................... 11
Suraj 12
Swastika.................... 13

The Fort★★★

Allow 3hr on foot.

Perched on the summit of the "triangular" Trikurta hilltop, a citadel within a citadel, Jaisalmer Fort overlooks the lower town some 100m below. Up until the 17C, the whole city was located within a double ring of **battlemented ramparts★★★**. Over 10m-high and reinforced with numerous bastions, these ramparts remain a constant reminder of Jaisalmer's former bloody sieges and extravagant sacrificial fires. Today their worst enemy is the water which is slowly eroding them, because the fort is totally without a drainage system.

The first gate opens onto a steep ramp overlooked by the walls of the palace, decorated with just a few windows and balconies. This military austerity is somewhat brightened by the sophisticated music of a few *rawanata* or *sarangi* players. The low walls lining the paved track have been invaded by the little craft stalls set up by local people. Although this commercial aspect may appear out of place, it must be remembered that Jaisalmer owes its prosperity – and monuments – to the zeal of its merchant classes. Handprints of *sati* can be seen on **Suraj Pol**, the second gate. Note also the enormous round boulders standing on the ramparts, ready to be dropped onto invaders. The last gates, **Ganesh Pol** and **Hawa Pol**, lead to the fort's esplanade where the two *jauhar* took place. On the right stands the maharawals' seven-storey palace. Try and ignore the ugly overhead electric cables and admire *(opposite the palace)* **Durga temple** where the warriors came to implore the goddess to grant them her energy *(shakti)* for their combats.

The royal palace★ (Raj Mahal) (C2)

8am-5pm, entrance charge, extra fee for cameras and videos. Only a small section of the palace is open to the public. The richly ornamented **façade**, with its covered balconies *(jharokha)*, *chhatri* and *jali*, provides a perfect contrast with the fort's initial simplicity and austerity. A marble throne is set on a raised platform *(to the left of the entrance)*, from where the *rawal* presided. Inside, the palace seems modest compared with the extravagance of those of Rajasthan's other kingdoms. The rooms were fitted out during the 17C and 19C: there are faience tiles, a few mirrors and carved pillars and several fine frescoes. A small **museum** has a number of palanquins, as well as a variety of objects and documents depicting the fort's history. Note the intricate **jali**. The **grandiose panorama** over Jaisalmer and the desert from the roof-top is quite stunning. The parasol on the terrace was reserved for the *maharawal* and was a symbol of royal power.

The umbrella, a royal privilege

In Rajasthan, only sovereigns were allowed to shelter under a parasol or an umbrella, ("chhatri" or "kshatri", from the same roots as "kshatriya", the warrior caste). This privilege continued into modern India. After Independence, Vitold de Golish, author of a book on the maharajas, tells how servants of the sovereign of Bundi ripped his umbrella out of his hands during a monsoon rainstorm in order to make him conform to protocol.

The Jain temples★★ (C3)

A walk through the hushed, narrow alleyways of the fort takes visitors into a world of ochre-coloured stone. The honey hues of the sandstone dominate, whether as delicately-carved sculptures, intricate *jali* or impressive bare façades. Cars are banned, and despite the few souvenir shops and cheap hotels, the fort has retained its medieval flavour and a traditional relaxed life-style that never fails to charm. Before wandering around the alleyways in search of the best views over the lower town and the surrounding plain, you should be sure to visit the Jain temples.

The avenue alongside the southern wall leads to the Jain temples. 12noon-3pm, no entrance fee, charge for cameras and videos.

This group of shrines, linked by courtyards and galleries, was built between the 12C and the 15C by wealthy Jain merchants. Their graceful proportions and profusion of decoration, carved as if in ivory, surprise visitors, who are invariably impressed by the contrast with the fort's austerity and the desert's almost awesome simplicity.

Adinatha temple (or Rishabdev) *(on the right of the square, coming from the temple)* was built in honour of the first of the 24 *tirthankara*, inspirers of the Jain religion, who was also known under the name of Rishabdev *(see p 350)*. The peaceful atmosphere and beautiful sculptures never fail to delight visitors. The priests, in their ochre-coloured garb, go quietly about their pious tasks while a worshipper, his mouth covered by a handkerchief, stops before each *tirthankara* to anoint the statue with saffron and sandalwood paste and light an incense stick.

Chandra Prabhu temple *(just on the right, on leaving Adinatha temple)*, dedicated to the 8th *tirthankara*, dates back to 1509. Its *mandapa* (hypostyle pavilion) is covered with a **dome**, depicting the Hindu god Ganesha and *mithuna* (entwined lovers). The main shrine houses Chandra Prabhu, depicted entirely naked, in the tradition of the **digambara** sect, who are "sky-clad" *(see p 350)*. A staircase *(to the left of the temple entrance)* leads to an upper floor and a gallery with 108 illustrations of *tirthankara*.

Continue along the lane to the right. A few metres on, a door opens into a courtyard.

The 15C **Parshvanatha temple**, (23rd *tirthankara*), has a handsome **sculpted archway** *(torana)* which leads into a *mandapa* decorated with statues of dancers. Note the finely-worked **dome**, covered in mirrors and sculptures, some of which are painted.

On the right *(opposite Parshvanatha temple)*, **Sitalnatha temple** houses a statue of the 10th *tirthankara* made out of an alloy of five metals. On the left, a corridor leads to the ornately sculpted **Sambavnatha temple** (3rd *tirthankara*). In the courtyard, a staircase leads down to the library of **Gyana Bandhar temple** *(10am-11am)* whose vaults house a collection of rare 11C manuscripts.

The 16C **Shantinatha and Kunthunatha temples** *(next to the entrance to Parshvanatha temple. Closed)*, are dedicated to the 16th and 17th *tirthankara*.

The lower town and outside the walls★★

Allow a good half-day for a walk round the lower town and a rickshaw to ride to the area outside the walls.

The haveli★★

Jaisalmer prospered, like all the towns in northern Rajasthan, thanks to its position on the caravan route between Asia and the Middle-East. From the 17C, the town began to extend beyond the fort. During the 19C, a period of peace and prosperity, merchants, bankers and town councillors built sumptuous *haveli*, among the most beautiful to be found.

From the fort's first gate, take the little lane slightly to the right which takes you down into the bazaar. The blue-coloured Salim Singh haveli appears round a bend, on the left.

Salim Singh ki haveli (D2) *(8am-7pm, entrance charge. The best view of the fort is from the terrace early in the day, when it is lit up by the morning sun.)* first impresses by its unusual outline: a sort of tower, whose upper level spreads out into a projecting, covered balcony. Note the chiselled **corbels** which support the balcony and other supports in the form of peacocks. It is said that Salim Singh Mehta, an early 19C prime minister full of ambition, wanted to have his house raised two extra levels, but the *rawal* had them destroyed in order to ensure that the palace remained the town's highest building. The two stone elephant statues standing at the entrance reveal the high-ranking status of the owner. The present owners of the haveli are happy to take visitors round their home. They have opened a souvenir boutique on the first floor where it is hard to resist their sales patter. The uppermost storey houses the former **performance room** whose ceiling is covered with mirrors.

An unpopular prime minister

During the 19C, the prime ministers (diwan), descended from the merchant classes, were much richer than the "maharawal" and held the strings of the royal purse, wielding most of the power. The two sides were constantly at loggerheads... The "diwan" Swarup Singh Mehta thus had his head instantly cut off for having demanded the immediate repayment of an unpaid debt from a prince. His son, the "diwan" Salim Singh vowed to revenge his father. Both clever and ruthless, he set about ruining the royal family. The hefty taxes he collected were added to his own personal fortune and led to the departure of large numbers of craftsmen and peasants. His enemies finally banded together and had him stabbed in 1827. Legend has it that his own wife administered the poison which finished him off.

Go to Gopa Chowk and walk round to the right. Patwon ki haveli is on the right, but such is the warren of lanes and alleyways, it is perhaps best to ask your way.

Patwon ki haveli (D2) *(open from dawn to dusk, entrance charge)* is Jaisalmer's largest *haveli*, set in a quiet neighbourhood, whose silence is broken only by the melancholic tunes of a few old *sarangi* players. The construction of the building lasted the first half of the 19C. It was intended for the five sons of the rich Jain merchant, Guman Chand Patwa, who imported dried fruits from Afghanistan and exported gold threaded brocade *(Zari)*. He dealt over a vast region extending as far as China. It would be impossible to find a more elaborately decorated **façade** than this one: 60 **jharokha** of all sizes are squeezed up one against the other, rectangular and semi-octagonal, open or screened with *jali*. Every single square centimetre of wall, corbel and column has been delicately carved, producing an ornate lattice of light and shade, turning the façade into a gigantic mesh screen. Such was the skill of Jaisalmer's Silavats (Moslem stone sculptors) that the stone resembles the delicate handiwork of a lace maker. Inside, a few murals and some gilt paint in poor condition remain within the maze of dark rooms.

Walk along the façade and continue along the road to the west. Ask for Nathmal ki Haveli Road.

The unparalleled intricacy and beauty of the **façade** of **Nathmal ki haveli** (C2) *(entrance free)* built in 1885 for one of Jaisalmer's prime ministers, was the work of two Silavat brothers, each of whom was responsible for one side of the residence. Before passing through the door guarded by two elephants, note the train, bicycle and other figurative elements curiously embedded in the fine network of chiselled geometric patterns. Inside, the little courtyard has a souvenir shop.

On leaving, turn left and then right into Bhatia Market. On Gandhi Chowk, enter (on the left) the royal courtyard where the maharawal's horses roam freely.

The Royal Palace (C2) *(part of which has become a hotel and part of which is still inhabited by the royal family)* is not open to the public, but a quite incredible work of art made by the Silavats in the early 20C and offered as a gift to their royal patron can be admired: a tapering five-storey tower called **tazia** because of its shape, similar to *tazia*, which are bamboo replicas of the tomb of Hussein, the Prophet's grandson, carried aloft during Shiite processions on Muharram day.

On leaving the royal palace, hire a rickshaw to visit the area outside the walls.

Outside the walls

Although the town has sprawled beyond its ramparts since the 1950s, few constructions in fact exist outside the city walls, and what's more, all of those are built in the same honey-coloured sandstone rock of the citadel and in the same traditional style.

The Folklore Museum* (E3) *(in the avenue leading to the lake. 9am-6.30pm. Entrance charge)* and its annexe, the **Desert Cultural Centre** *(a few metres away)*, are the work of the friendly Mr Sharma, who happily guides visitors around the collections: they include crafts, musical instruments, costumes and mural decorations showing the wealth of northwest Rajasthan's traditions.

Built in the 14C, **Gadi Sagar Lake*** (E3) used to be Jaisalmer's main source of water. The road leading down to it passes under **Tila ki Pol**, a gate erected by a courtesan named Tila, a favourite of the prince. The prince's wives, consumed by jealousy, attempted to have the gate pulled down. Tila however resourcefully had the upper section transformed into a small temple dedicated to Krishna, thus saving the gate from destruction.

Go round Jaisalmer to the right and head north. Bara Bagh is 4km away.

Bara Bagh is one of the largest oases near to Jaisalmer, but its little lake is often dried up. Note the 16C **royal cenotaphs**. Their steles are still intact and the spot is ideal to watch the sun set over the citadel.

Desert proverbs

"If your donkey walks ahead of you, do not prevent it. If your wife sings, do not prevent her. If your son wants to live in freedom, show him how fragile the freedom of idiots is."

"The Lord shows the way to all those who are not afraid of seeing their shadow grow smaller."

"Just as the wise man only gives his word once, the rich man does not feed two houses."

R Mattes

Jaisalmer haveli in the lower town

B.Brillion/MICHELIN

Votive plaque inside a cenotaph

The surroundings

Allow 2 days by car for the three excursions described below.

Amar Sagar Lake and the Jain temples at Lodrava* (from A2)

7km to the west of Jaisalmer. **Amar Sagar Lake**, dry for the most part of the year (*no entrance fee, extra charge for cameras and videos*), is surrounded by *ghat*, *chhatri*, a Jain temple and a small late-17C yellow sandstone palace.

Continue northwards towards Lodrava. No entrance fee, charge for cameras and videos.

All that remains of **Lodrava**, the old capital of the Bhatti clan, is this remarkable collection of **Jain temples****. Built in the 10C, under *Rawal* Devaraja, the shrines were ransacked in the 11C by Mahmud of Ghazi's troops, and then restored in the 18C. A **torana** opens onto the **Temple of Parshvanatha**, dedicated to the 23rd *tirthankara* and surrounded by four minor temples. Inside is a fine **dome** embellished with a **rosette** carved out of a single block of stone. The inner shrine contains a statue of the wise "ford passer", covered in silver-leaf. Note the bowl of milk placed in an alcove in the outer right wall. It is for two sacred cobras said to haunt the temple, which lucky visitors may catch a glance of. The strange metal-leafed tree in the right of the courtyard depicts the **Kalpavriksha**, the heavenly tree which nourished the first humans.

The dunes of Sam

40km west of Jaisalmer. These sand dunes are a favourite destination of the "camel safaris". Visitors should however expect neither an immense Saharan landscape, nor a calm, meditative setting. Even though the light is quite fantastic towards the late afternoon, it feels more like an amusement park than a desert.

Pokaran and Ramdevra★

Allow 6hr by car. The small town of **Pokaran** *(110km east of Jaisalmer, on the road to Bikaner)* draws its fame from the nuclear tests carried out here in 1974 and 1998. The large numbers of military trucks and jeeps illustrate the zone's strategic importance. Unless on a secret mission as an undercover agent, there is no point in spending time in Pokaran: only the **fort** is of any interest *(10am-5pm, entrance fee, extra charge for cameras and videos)*. It was built in the 16C as an outpost by Jodhpur's rulers and enabled them to control the route between Jaisalmer and Bikaner. The gloomy imposing red sandstone **ramparts** and military austerity of the buildings are hardly brightened by the few murals within the courtyard. The main **palace** is now a hotel and the small **museum** houses a minor collection of weapons, costumes and traditional artefacts.

A country's pride

The nuclear tests carried out in May 1998 were a source of great pride to the majority of India's population. The rest of the world, particularly the other nuclear powers, greeted them however with far less enthusiasm. The United States began to envisage economic sanctions, while Pakistan embarked on its first nuclear tests. The turbulent relations between India and Pakistan, each of which has always been quick to accuse the other, thus came to the forefront of international news – in a climate of increased tension.

Group jeeps leave every 15min from Pokaran's bus station to Ramdevra, 10km north of Pokaran.

Together with Deshnok and its rat sanctuary, the tiny hamlet of **Ramdevra**★ is one of northern Rajasthan's most popular pilgrim centres. The devout, from all faiths, come here to venerate a local 15C hero, called **Baba Ramdevji** (or Ramdeoji) by Hindus and **Pir Ram Shah** by Moslems. A defender of the oppressed and low castes, he was miraculously found in the cradle of a Rajput family and is sometimes considered as an incarnation of Vishnu. At the time of Vishnu's festival (ten days prior to the August-September new moon), the pilgrimage is particularly lively.

It is true that the site's atmosphere is of more interest than its architectural heritage. Because of the personality of Ramdevji, the temple is mainly attended by worshippers of the lowest castes. The alleyways leading to the **shrine** are lined in ten rupee souvenir boutiques and tiny working-class restaurants, decidedly not aimed at tourists. As is often the case in pilgrimage centres, the major source of animation is provided by the cassette sellers, whose loud-speakers flood the surrounding streets with deafening music. After leaving one's shoes at the entrance, cross the paved courtyard (burning hot in the summer), flanked by halls where the pilgrims can rest. The faithful bring offerings of coconut, coloured powder and carved wooden or rag horses in honour of the hero's mount. These are placed before the altar, in front of the statue of Baba Ramdev. The sound of musicians chanting religious hymns to the accompaniment of drums and a harmonium can be heard from the nearby hall. Unlike the music-makers of Jaisalmer, these are not performing for the tourists. A small coin may however help to encourage them to compete with the blaring outdoor loud-speakers.

Making the most of Jaisalmer

Getting there

Touts and hawkers are both numerous and extremely pushy in Jaisalmer and can spoil your arrival in the town. If you have a hotel room reserved, ask them to send a vehicle to fetch you from the bus or train – free service.

By airplane – There is a military airport, 4km to the west of Jaisalmer. Flights have been resumed since December 1998, after several years of interrupted services, but for the moment only Alliance Air, subsidiary of Indian Airlines, provides a few links. 3 weekly flights for Delhi (2hr), via Jaipur (1hr) and 3 for Jodhpur (35min) and Bombay. As flight times and frequency often change and can even be suspended during the summer, check twice.

By train – The little station, in an isolated position to the east of the town, only springs to life on the arrival or departure of the two trains that run to Jodhpur (8hr day trip and 7hr night trip) ☎ (02992) 513 01 and 523 54. Computerised reservation terminal, 8am-8pm, Sunday 8am-2pm.

By bus – State and private buses depart from ***Neeraj Hotel Bus Stand***, behind Neeraj Hotel (C3), before stopping at ***Main Roadways Bus Stand***, near the station (E3), which is the official departure point. A "Silver Line" bus runs daily to Jodhpur, Ajmer and Jaipur (13hr). Once a day, an express bus leaves for Jaipur (3hr) and 3-6 buses go to Jodhpur (7hr), Bikaner (7hr) and Barmer (3hr30min). One departure for Abu Road (10hr) and for Mount Abu (11hr). Nearly all the hotels and travel agents can handle reservations for private and RSTRC companies.

Getting about

Jaisalmer is best explored on foot, taking the time to wander through the warren of lanes in the citadel.

By rickshaw – There is an auto-rickshaw station on Govardhan Chowk and at the entrance to the fort (closed from 8am to 7pm).

By taxi – Jeep taxi stations on Hanuman Circle and Govardhan Chowk, but it would be better to enquire at your hotel, the RTDC or a travel agent. Allow around 500Rs for 4hr or 4Rs per km and 5Rs per km for off-road driving.

Car rental – Enquire at your hotel or an agent. 1 150Rs per day is reasonable.

Bicycle rental – Around Amar Sagar Pol gate and near the fort's entrance. 15-20Rs per day.

Address book

Tourist office – ***Tourist Reception Centre***, Station Rd (D3), ☎ (02992) 524 06. 10am-1.30pm/2pm-5pm; closed Sunday. Can provide information and advice about "camel safaris" as well as permits for controlled zones. List of guides and guesthouses. Bookings can be made here for visits organised by the RTDC (see "Travel Agents") An information desk is open at the station when trains arrive

Banks/Change – ***Bank of Baroda***, Gandhi Chowk (C2). 10am-1pm, Saturday 10am-11am. To change travellers' cheques and make cash withdrawals with a card. A few exchange bureaux on Gandhi and Govardhan Chowk.

Post Office/sTelephone – ***GPO***, 7min walk, out of Amar Sagar Pol (B2). 10am-5pm; closed Sunday. Poste restante and express mail by ***EMS Speed Post***. Postal code: 345001.

Health – ***Ambulances***, ☎ (02992) 523 43. ***Shri Maheshwari Hospital***, opposite the Collectorate (B2), ☎ (02992) 400 24 and 504 23. Private clinic.

Safety – ***Police***, ☎ 100 and (02992) 523 22. ***Fire brigade***, ☎ (02992) 523 52.

Travel agents – With the exception of the RTDC, all the agents below can make train and bus reservations.

RTDC, Moomal Hotel, off Sam Rd (A2), ☎ (02992) 523 92. The State agent offers daily tours of the town (9am-12noon, 65Rs) and a jeep outing to Sam. Car rentals for excursions around Jaisalmer.

Safari Tours, Gandhi Chowk (C2), ☎ (02992) 510 58, Fax (02992) 511 58. Reputable agency for camel-back rides and outings at low prices. Car rental.

Thar Safari, Govardhan Chowk (C2), ☎/Fax (02992) 527 22. A dynamic team with good services at reasonable prices. Safaris, jeep excursions, car rentals.

Jaisal Tours, Narayan Niwas Palace (C1), ☎ (02992) 519 07, Fax (02992) 521 01. A "camel safari" specialist at decent prices, but their car rentals are too expensive.

Rajasthan Tours, Gandhi Chowk (C2), ☎ (02992) 518 75, Fax (02992) 525 61. This excellent agency is well represented throughout Rajasthan, even if their Jaisalmer branch is somewhat disorganised. Low price taxis, but exorbitant car rentals. High-quality camel rides. Airline bookings.

Registhan Tours, Kumhar Para (C2), ☎/Fax (02992) 524 53. This reputable agency has several branches throughout Rajasthan, but the Jaisalmer office caters mainly for groups. Reasonably-priced car rentals.

Comfort Travels & Tours, Gorbandh Palace Hotel (A1), ☎ (02992) 515 11/12/13, ext. 50, Fax (02992) 527 49. This Udaipur travel agent specialises in high-quality services. Luxury camel rides (200Rs for 4hr). Airline bookings.

Airlines – ***Alliance Air*** plans to open a branch in the new town.

Where to stay

Hotels abound in Jaisalmer, from the worst to the best. They can all organise "camel safaris" and such is the competition that certain of the smaller establishments lure tourists with the offer of ridiculously low-priced rooms, on the understanding that they will book a safari through them. However any attempt at booking with a competitor may result in being expelled from one's room. Be prudent when selecting a hotel and given the difficulty of finding accommodation, it is advisable to book ahead. During the low season, from April-May to June-July, a 20-30 % discount is available, but prices double during the Desert Festival. The smaller hotels require rooms to be vacated by 9am.

• In the fort

Those in search of peaceful, almost village-like atmosphere, will be happiest in the fort.

Under US$7

Simla Hotel, Kund Para, ☎ (02992) 530 61 – 7rm. This 16C stone-carved house has a family atmosphere. The two most expensive rooms have a bathroom and a window with a wonderful view over the town and the plain. Acceptably clean, hot water in basins.

From US$7-15

Suraj Hotel, next to the Jain temples, ☎ (02992) 516 23 – 5rm. This authentic 16C haveli, complete with inner courtyard and stone-carved walls, is quite charming. Two of the rooms have columns and are decorated with antique frescoes. The least expensive have tiny bathrooms but a gorgeous view over the countryside.

From US$15-30

Kila Bhawan Resorts, 445 Kotari Para, ☎ (02992) 512 04 – 4rm. CC Breakfast included. Tastefully decorated with much attention to detail, this smart hotel is located in a tower of the ramparts. The most expensive rooms overlook the bastions and the lower town.

• In the lower town

Gopa Chowk and the two roads leading north of Gandhi Chowk are infested with cut-price hotels. It is a pity that ***Mandir Palace Hotel***, located in part of the Royal Palace, is so negligently run, because it would otherwise be the best hotel in town.

Under US$7

Renuka Hotel, Chainpura St, ☎ (02992) 527 57 – 15rm 8rm. with bath, but 7 are windowless. This very well-run establishment has a friendly, family atmosphere. The rooms, furnished solely with a bed, are nonetheless rather spartan.

Swastika Hotel, Chainpura St, ☎ (02992) 521 52 and 524 83 – 9rm. 4rm. with bath. Same style as the above address, but slightly more comfortable.

From US$7-15

Jaisal Palace Hotel, behind the Royal Palace, ☎ (02992) 514 17 and 527 17, Fax (02992) 502 57 – 14rm. Cooler. Access is via a covered alleyway in the south-eastern corner of Govardhan Chowk. The hotel's modern façade is overgrown with bougainvillea. A perfectly run, excellent establishment. The first floor rooms with cooler, balcony and view are the best (n° 107 to 109, 112, 114 and 115).

From US$15-30

Nachana Haveli, Govardhan Chowk, ☎ (02992) 519 10 and 521 10, Fax (02992) 503 23 and 527 78 – 11rm. A young Rajput noblewoman runs this 17C haveli, and her grace and charm permeate the whole establishment. In the evening guests are invited to take dinner with her in the magnificent inner courtyard. Canopy beds, wall-hangings, carpets, animal skins and a whole bric-a-brac of disparate old-fashioned objects.

From US$30-40

Narayan Niwas Palace Hotel (Heritage Hotels Association), Malka Pol Rd, ☎ (02992) 519 01 to 04 and 524 08, Fax (02992) 521 01; bookings in Delhi, ☎ (011) 617 14 78, Fax (011) 616 24 38 – 51rm. Breakfast included. A modern section has been added to this handsome caravanserai. The rooms are somewhat disappointing, particularly the ground-floor ones, but the courtyard, with bar, boutique and library, is quite delightful. Hot water in the morning and evening.

• Outside the walls

The plain has a selection of modern, well-equipped hotels, built in the familiar yellow sandstone and in tune with the style of the haveli and the citadel. One of their attractions is the view of the fort.

From US$30-40

Jawahar Niwas Palace, Victory Pilar, 1km from Amar Sagar Pol. ☎ (02992) 522 08, Fax (02992) 526 11 – 17rm. Cooler. Bar, billiards room. This small Rajput-style palace dates back to the 19C, when it was built for the "maharawal's" guests. Renovated in 1999, it now has ten rooms in the old building and seven in the annexe.

From US$40-70

Heritage Inn Hotel, 3 Hotel Complex, Sam Rd, 2km from Amar Sagar Pol, ☎ (02992) 502 00 and 509 01 to 04, Fax (02992) 516 38 – 51rm. Bar. Of relatively little interest, all the rooms of this establishment are the same price (US$40), whether in the main building or in cottages, the latter being the more attractive.

Rang Mahal Jaisalmer Hotel, 5 Hotel Complex, Sam Rd, next to the above, ☎ (02992) 509 07 and 509 08, Fax (02992) 513 05 – 53rm. Bar. The management of this brand-new establishment is full of novel ideas. The decoration is rather flashy, but the hotel is very lively. The rooms with loggia are the most pleasant.

Gorbandh Niwas Hotel (HRH Group), 1 Hotel Complex, Sam Rd, next to the above, ☎ (02992) 501 02 to 04 and 515 11 to 13, Fax (02992) 527 49; reservations in Delhi and Udaipur, (see p 107) – 64rm. Bar. Ideal for a comfortable stay in a sophisticated setting. Tastefully decorated and excellent service. Pleasant swimming pool in the centre of the inner courtyard. Fixed price (US$50), but 50 % discount for single travellers.

• Dabla

Follow the N.H.15 for 10km towards Barmer, then turn left onto a sandy track for 600m.

From US$15-30

Narayan Bagh Resort, Barmer Rd, Dabla, ☎ (02992) 527 27, Fax (02992) 521 01; reservations in Delhi, ☎ (011) 648 68 06, Fax (011) 648 68 07 – 6rm. Cooler. An agricultural establishment belonging to one of the "maharawal's" cousins, which enables guests to get a wonderful feel of the region's rural life. The garden could do with a little more care. The first-floor rooms are the best.

Where to eat

• In the fort

Under US$3

The Refreshing Point, Rajmahal Chowk (C3). This wonderful place, run by charming Tibetans, not only serves good food but has a superb view of the "maharawal's" palace from its terrace. Simple, quite delicious international cooking, particularly the momos, moussaka and apple strudel!

Surya, near Kila Bhawan Resorts (D2-3). A magnificent view over Jaisalmer and a perfectly romantic setting, with little circular rooms, decorated Rajasthan style, in a tower.

• In the lower town

Visitors are spoilt for choice such is the variety of little terrace restaurants, most of which have a view of the fort. They all serve relatively ordinary food, Indian, Western or Chinese. For breakfast or a quick snack, ***Fort View Hotel***, and ***Mid Town*** on Gopa Chowk (C2), both vegetarian, are good, as are two tandoori restaurants, ***Kalpana***, on Govardhan Chowk (C2), and ***Monica***, Asni Rd (D2).

From US$3-4

Jaisal Palace Hotel, behind the Royal Palace (C2). Decent, although not extraordinary, vegetarian cooking, served by extremely pleasant staff.

Top Deck Restaurant, Govardhan Chowk (C2). Classical tandoori cooking.

Trio Restaurant, Gandhi Chowk (C2). The town's smartest address, although the quality is not as good as when it was first opened in the 1980s. At midday, or from 7pm in the evening, the place is always packed. Music in the evening.

From US$4-7

Nachana Haveli, Govardhan Chowk. This fine haveli has two rooms, one basement and one terrace, serving good Rajasthani cooking.

Narayan Niwas Palace Hotel, Malka Pol Rd. 7pm-11pm. A recently-opened 3rd-floor terrace room has a panoramic view over Jaisalmer, lit up at night. Tandoori cuisine and folklore performances.

• Outside the walls

From US$4-7

Rang Mahal Jaisalmer Hotel, Sam Rd. CC Fill up on desert flavours here where the accent is on good Rajasthani cooking. Taste the various "sule" (meat kebabs), accompanied by "ker sangri" (acacia pods in capers) and "bajre ki roti" (millet pancakes).

Rasoda, Gorbandh Niwas Hotel's restaurant (A2). CC Classic north-Indian, Chinese and Western cooking. A la carte and buffet. Sophisticated setting.

Excursions

Beware, access to some areas is controlled due to the proximity with Pakistan. Enquire at the tourist office.

Sam, 42km to the west. Two or three daily buses (90min). The travel agencies organise a trip to the villages, including Sam at dawn or dusk (4hr, 850Rs per jeep). RTDC excursion (3pm-7pm in winter, 4.30pm-8.30pm in the summer, 100Rs per person).

Lodurva, 16km to the south-west. Two daily buses (45min).

Khuri, 24km further on from Lodurva (1hr45min). A morning bus enables visitors to stay for 6hr, taking them back to Jaisalmer in the late afternoon.

Desert National Park, 5km after Khuri. The reserve is visited by jeep, rented from Jaisalmer. Check with the tourist office to see if you need a permit.

Camel safaris – Camel safaris are big business in Jaisalmer and you are bound to succumb. To avoid embarking on a total adventure, only contact professional agents and compare prices and services. A few hours ride around the citadel requires little preparation (200Rs for 3hr, 300Rs for 6hr). However, if considering an excursion of several or more days, check the advice on p 109 before booking anything. Allow at least 450-500Rs per day for a safari without tent or baggage cart (any less should be avoided!) and from 1 100Rs for a safari with tent and cart (group of five to ten). The most luxurious can cost as much as 3 000Rs. One of the most popular, and the most overcrowded, destinations is Sam. Avoid it if you can! Ensure that your organiser plans a trip that takes you through the least visited villages. Rides to Barmer, Pokaran, Jodhpur or Bikaner (6 to 13 days) are only a little more expensive than the 3-or 4-day rides which are confined to the region close to Jaisalmer.

Horse treks – The following are recommended for any who want to go riding in the desert: ***Resort Narayan Bagh*** (see "Where to stay") has rides from 700Rs per day, with tent, but without baggage cart. The ***Royal Equestrian and Polo Centre*** at Dundlod (see p 259) and ***Pratap Country Inn*** at Udaipur (see p 345) organise wonderful rides between Jaisalmer and the rest of Rajasthan for 5 500Rs per day, including accommodation in luxury camps or hotel-châteaux.

Holidays and festivals

Desert Festival. Created in 1979 by the Department of Tourism, the festival lasts for three days, finishing on the January-February full moon (6-8 February 2001). Various events are put on, including fire dancing, turban tying competitions, election of "Mr Desert", camel races and dances, camel polo matches, etc.

Barmer Cattle Fair, or ***Tilwara Fair***. A cattle fair organised in March-April at Tilwara (60km south of Jaisalmer), under the aegis of a local warrior-saint.

Ramdevji Fair, at Ramdevra (120km east of Jaisalmer). During the ten days prior to the August-September new moon, Hindus and Moslems celebrate Baba Ramdevji, champion of the poor and the outcast.

Shopping

The place to make your purchases is along the road that runs from outside Amar Sagar Pol up to the gate of the fort, via Gandhi Chowk, Govardhan Chowk and Bhatia Market. The choice is vast, including a selection of local arts and crafts: embroidered brocade, inlaid with mirrors, hand woven woollen blankets on white ("pattu") or black ("khes") backgrounds, soft woollen shawls, cotton fabrics printed in the reserve with indigo and red ("ajrak"), kilims from Barmer, leather goods and stone sculptures. However, picking up anything of quality requires vigilance amidst the heaps of pitiful goods on sale in the tourist shops.

Desert Handicraft, Bhatia Market (C2), ☎ (02992) 500 62. This store offers patchwork for tourists together with a few beautiful examples of antique clothes.

To get an idea of prices, take a look in the State shops:

Khadi Gramodaya, between Hanuman Circle and Amar Sagar Pol (C2). 10am-6pm. Wonderful collection of shawls. Another tiny boutique on Kela Para, to the north of Nathmal ki haveli.

Rajasthali, outside Amar Sagar Pol and on Govardhan Chowk (C2). 8.30am-1pm/2pm-8.30pm, 8.30am-8.30pm from October to February.

Bookshops – ***Bhatia News Agency***, at the beginning of Bhatia Market on the way from Govardhan Chowk (C2), and ***Students' Book Store***, on the Royal Palace square in the fort (C2), primarily second-hand novels.

Boutique Delta, Narayan Niwas Palace Hotel (C1), has some good books and novels on Rajasthan and India.

JODHPUR★★
AND OSIYAN★

Pop 700 000 – Alt 240m
335km from Jaipur – 290km from Udaipur – 300km from Jaisalmer
See map p 318

Not to be missed
Mehrangarh fort.
Mandor gardens and cenotaphs.
An outing to Osiyan.

And remember...
Visit the fort and blue city in the afternoon.
Allow at least a day and a half to visit by taxi.

The sudden appearance of the massive fortress of Mehrangarh, built on top of an impressive rocky ridge, overlooking the Thar Desert below can produce a shock. Its name, "fort of majesty", evokes the heroic past of Jodhpur's mounted princes. Within this apparently austere fort, the visitor is surprised by the sight of its interior decoration, worthy of a scene from the Arabian Nights and reminiscent of another aspect of the Rajput sovereigns' lifestyle.
Jodhpur, Rajasthan's second largest town, is now a modern city focused on economic growth. Unfortunately the usual traffic and pollution have invaded the lower town, somewhat detracting from the charm of this former capital of the **Marwar kingdom**.

A town and a fort

The town of Rao Jodha – The clan of **Rathores** to which **Rao Jodha**, founder of Jodhpur in 1459 belonged, is descended from Rama (hero of the *Ramayana*) and also belongs to the senior branch of the "race of the sun", descended from

The Fort and the blue city

the god Surya. Historically, the ruling family is said to have governed from the 6C the region of Kanauj (on the Ganges, now in the State of Uttar Pradesh). In the late 12C, the Rathore rulers, fleeing Mohammed of Ghor's troops, found refuge in the semi-arid desert of Marwar or "land of death". From their capital, established in Mandor (9km to the north of Jodhpur), they wielded their power over the kingdom of Mewar (Chittaurgarh). Suspicious of his powerful rival neighbour, in 1459 Rao Jodha decided to build a new and more easily defended capital on this rock overlooking the whole region.

The Mughal threat – In 1527, the first Mughal emperor, Babul, defeated the army of the Rathores, who had joined forces with the Sisodias (Chittaurgarh) and the Kachwahas (Amber). Following the latter's example, Jodhpur's sovereigns finally pledged allegiance to the Moslem dynasty under **Akbar** (1556-1605), who married a Rathore princess, Jodha Bai (whose residence can be seen at Fatehpur Sikri). This alliance lasted until the reign of **Aurangzeb** (1658-1707). Aurangzeb appointed Maharaja Jaswant Singh governor of Kabul – a form of exile, albeit very pleasant, where he was poisoned – and imprisoned his sons. One of these sons, Ajit Singh, finally re-established his kingdom's autonomy... before being killed by his son, Abhai Singh.

New enemies – The decline of the Mughal dynasty did not bring peace to the region. Marwar became weakened as a

Maharaja Pratap Singh's famous trousers

The legendary trousers, tight around the calves and baggy around the thighs, which enabled riders to dispense with boots, were used by all the region's riders. The enrolment of Marwari soldiers into the Mughal armies and then into the British greatly contributed to their fame. The British forces called them "leggings" adding the nickname of "jodhpurs", an affectionate allusion to Prince Pratap Singh (1845-1922), who was a keen wearer. The latter founded the Lancers Regiment of Jodhpur and fought alongside the British in Afghanistan, China and Egypt. His last exploit, in 1917 at the age of 70, was to successfully lead his Lancers against the German positions on the Western front, near Cambrai.

R Marca

result of incessant quarrels of succession, as well as having to withstand the attacks of the Marathas. In 1808, the maharaja of Jaipur unsuccessfully attacked Jodhpur *(see insert p 336)*. Finally in 1818, the region fell under **British** control. The "pax Britannica" at last enabled the kingdom to enjoy a period of unspoilt prosperity and prestige.

The town*

Allow 4hr.

Umaid Bhawan* (C3)

Take a taxi in the morning to admire the palace's sun-drenched façade. This impressive palace stands on a hill overlooking Ratanada, where most of the town's hotels are located. It is still the royal family's official residence, but most of it was turned into a luxury hotel in 1977 *(see "Making the most of Jodhpur")*. Only the right wing, now a museum, is open to the public. Built between 1927 and 1944, this residence of 350 rooms – one of the largest private homes in the world – was the brainchild of Maharaja Umaid Singh (reigned from 1918-1947) and intended to provide work for thousands of Marwaris, whom the 1920 famine had left without resources. The architect **HV Lanchester** took his inspiration from the viceroys' palaces in New Delhi (today Rashtrapati Bhawan) to which he added Art Deco touches.

The **Umaid Bhawan Museum** *(9am-5pm, entrance charge)* is disappointing, such is the meagreness of the collection (clocks, furniture, porcelain) but the grandiose setting more than compensates.

Take a taxi to Mehrangarh Fort.

Mehrangarh Fort*** (A-B2)

9am-1pm/2pm-5pm, entrance charge, extra fee for cameras and videos. From 3pm, the light over the "blue city" is quite stunning. Allow 2hr. Before arriving at the fort, note, on the right, **Jaswant Thanda** (B2): a white marble cenotaph of various styles overlooking a reservoir. It was built in 1899 on the cremation spot of Maharaja Jaswant Singh and is surrounded by other smaller cenotaphs, in memory of the last four maharajas.

The road to the fort culminates in an esplanade *(car park)* which leads to the first of seven gates, the 19C **Jai Pol** (victory gate). The cenotaph dedicated to Kiran Singh Sodha, a brave warrior who died resisting an attack by an army from Jaipur in 1808 stands just past the ticket office. A twisting lane leads to **Loha Pol** (iron gate, 15C). On the left the handprints of maharani who committed *sati*, throwing themselves onto their husband's funeral pyre, can be seen. The lane then runs alongside the fort's ramparts to the museum.

The **Mehrangarh Museum** is located in the fort's most beautiful rooms. It is run by the present maharaja, Gaj Singh II, who lives with his family in Umaid Bhawan.

Over-faithful wives...

In 1829, the British formally banned widows from committing sati by burning themselves alive on the husband's funeral pyre. However, when Maharaja Man Singh was cremated in 1843, six of his wives, the youngest of whom were scarcely over 15, threw themselves into the fire. In 1865, Maharaja Jaswant Singh watched as two of his aunts, widows of the raja of Thalamand, committed suicide. More recently, in 1952, the widow of a palace dignitary committed the banned rite, watched by a respectful crowd. "The police arrived too late..." commented the local newspaper the following day.

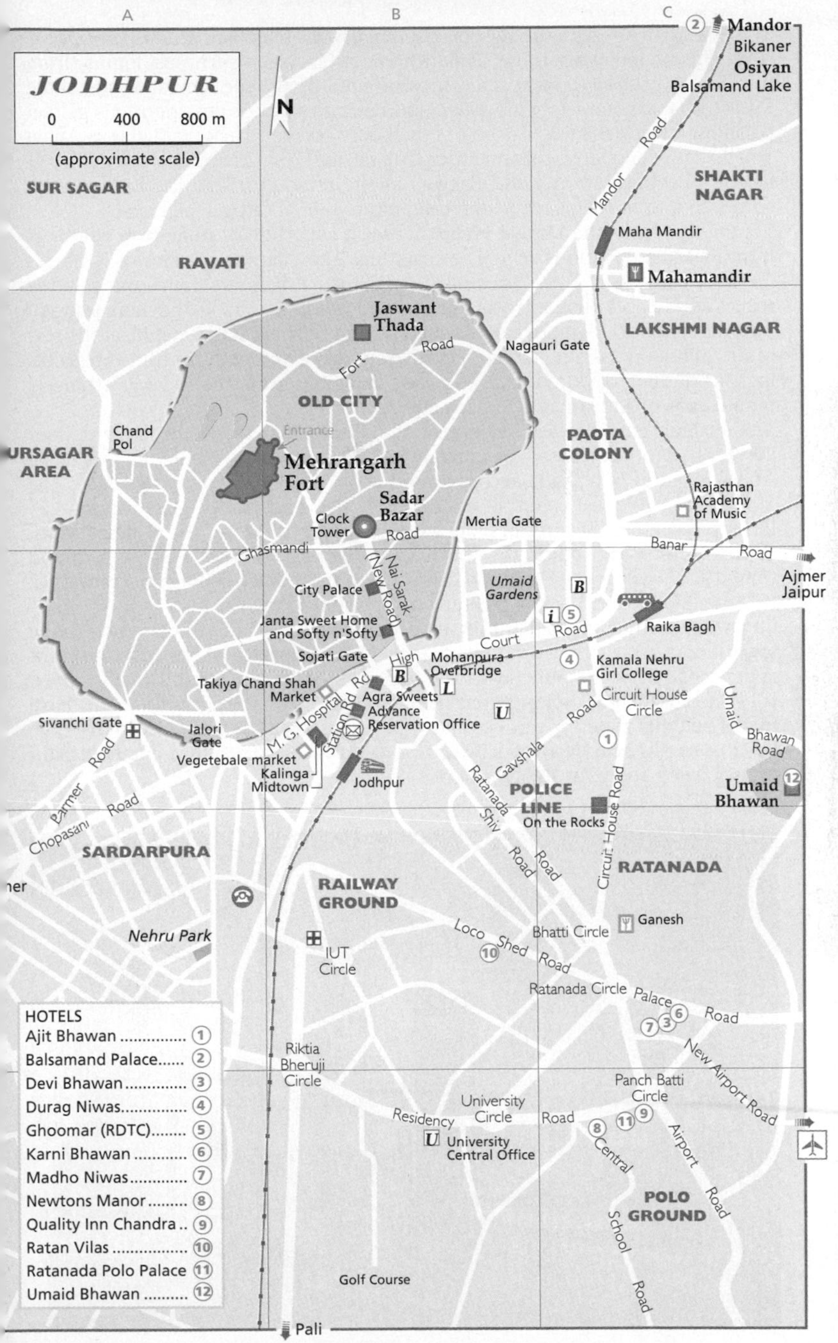
JODHPUR
0 400 800 m
(approximate scale)
N
A
B
C
Mandor
Bikaner
Osiyan
Balsamand Lake
Mandor Road
SHAKTI NAGAR
SUR SAGAR
RAVATI
Maha Mandir
Mahamandir
LAKSHMI NAGAR
Jaswant Thada
Fort Road
Nagauri Gate
OLD CITY
Entrance
Chand Pol
URSAGAR AREA
Mehrangarh Fort
PAOTA COLONY
Sadar Bazar
Clock Tower
Road
Mertia Gate
Rajasthan Academy of Music
Ghasmandi
Banar Road
Ajmer
Jaipur
Nai Sarak (New Road)
City Palace
Umaid Gardens
Janta Sweet Home and Softy n'Softy
Court Road
Raika Bagh
Sojati Gate
High Rd
Mohanpura Overbridge
Kamala Nehru Girl College
Takiya Chand Shah Market
Agra Sweets
Advance Reservation Office
Circuit House Circle
Umaid Bhawan Road
Sivanchi Gate
Jalori Gate
M. G. Hospital
Station Rd
Gavshala Road
Vegetebale market
Kalinga
Midtown
Jodhpur
Parmer Road
Chopasani Road
Ratanada Shiv Road
POLICE LINE
On the Rocks
Circuit House Road
Umaid Bhawan
SARDARPURA
RATANADA
RAILWAY GROUND
Nehru Park
Ganesh
Loco Shed Road
Bhatti Circle
IUT Circle
Ratanada Circle
Palace Road
New Airport Road
Riktia Bheruji Circle
Panch Batti Circle
University Circle
Residency Road
University Central Office
Central School Road
Airport Road
POLO GROUND
Golf Course
Pali
HOTELS
Ajit Bhawan 1
Balsamand Palace...... 2
Devi Bhawan.............. 3
Durag Niwas............... 4
Ghoomar (RDTC)........ 5
Karni Bhawan 6
Madho Niwas............. 7
Newtons Manor......... 8
Quality Inn Chandra .. 9
Ratan Vilas 10
Ratanada Polo Palace 11
Umaid Bhawan 12

The first room houses a unique collection of *howdah* (elephant saddles) in *repoussé* silver. In the following room, **Palki Khana**, are some superb palanquins (from the Hindi word *palki*). Next is a courtyard lined by the spectacular façade of the Daulat Khana, complete with *chhatri* and balconies. Inside, an enormous golden palanquin, the Mahadol, was part of the booty brought back by Maharaja Abhai Singh, who conquered the sultan of Gujarat in 1730. There is a splendid collection of sabres, swords and daggers in the armoury. Note the little cannon with a mouth in the shape of the head of an animal (a tiger perhaps?).

On the first floor, the **Umaid Mahal** houses a collection of **miniature paintings** from Rajasthan's various schools of painting. They depict episodes of Krishna's life and, of course, of the lives of the maharajas: there are court and hunting scenes and images of other royal pursuits and pastimes. One of the more unusual illustrations shows "opium eaters scared by a rat". The **Takhat Mahal**, at the rear of the miniature painting room, is profusely decorated with mirrors and paintings, including coloured balls of glass hanging from the ceiling, strangely reminiscent of Christmas tree decorations.

The magnificent gold-leaf ceiling of the **Phool Mahal** on the second floor inevitably produces gasps of amazement. This room was built for Maharaja Abhai Singh (1724-1750) and was used as a *durbar* hall (reception hall). The 19C murals, gold-leaf columns, enormous carpets and stained-glass windows all further accentuate the room's opulence. Another treasure, the **Takhat Vilas,** awaits visitors who reach the third floor. Maharaja Takhat Singh's bedroom (mid-19C) was decorated with a sandalwood marquetry ceiling and murals of Krishna, Durga and Vishnu reclining on the snake Ananta.

Opposite, on the other side of the terrace, a staircase takes visitors down to the lower floors of the other wing. From **Jankhi Mahal (palace of glances)**; the court ladies could view the outer world through the lattices of the intricately carved *jali*. The room now holds a surprising collection of royal cradles. The **Moti Mahal**, with its glittering mirrors and gold paint, is said to date back to the 16C, but it is not known whether it was used as a *Diwan-i Am* (public audience hall) or as a living room for the *zenana*.

Inside Jodhpur Fort...

S. Held

Leaving the museum, a right turn leads to a path which takes visitors up onto the ramparts. The platform with its impressive defensive lines of cannons provides a breathtaking **view** over the bustling **blue city** some 120m below and, further in the distance, of the majestic dome of Umaid Bhawan. Continue along the covered gallery to the fort's furthermost tip where there is a little **temple**, resembling a ship's figurehead, dedicated to Chamunda (other name of Durga), the royal family's protective goddess.

Blue houses

Visitors often wonder why so many of Rajasthan's houses are painted blue. Some say that blue repels mosquitoes... Others explain that the most devout Hindus, generally, but not always Brahmins, painted their houses blue, a colour traditionally associated with the gods, in order to attract divine blessing or as a sign of their piety.

The bazaars*

To reach the bazaars, take the little lanes leading down from the fort through the old town. As one gets closer to Ghasmandi Rd, the level of bustle and activity increases. Small workshop stalls appear and temple bells can be heard. The main market is the picturesque **Sadar Bazaar** (B2), whose central **clock tower** makes it easily recognisable. This was put up by the British at the same time as the surrounding buildings, which housed the local authority's administrative services up until 1947. Today, dusty files and papers have given way to sacks of lentils and rice and mounds of vegetables.

The surroundings

Allow 90min by car. The Balsamand Hotel, in a former royal palace, between the temple of Mahamandir and Mandor (see "Making the most of Jodhpur") is an ideal place to stop for a refreshing drink.

Mahamandir temple

3km to the north of the town centre, in the neighbourhood of the same name. The carved pillars and murals are the only items of interest of this fortified Shivaite shrine erected by Maharaja Man Singh (1803-1843) following his victory over Jaipur's troops in 1808. It houses a school where the uniformed pupils are always overjoyed to greet unexpected tourists.

Mandor Gardens**

9km to the north, on the road to Bikaner. Open from dawn to dusk, no entrance charge. This pleasant park, a refreshing haven of greenery, is located on the site of the former capital of the rulers of Rathore and was where the royal family was cremated up until the 19C. There are two types of **cenotaphs**: the classical *chhatri* (domed pavilion) and the *deval*, in the form of a temple. The **deval of Ajit Singh**** (1724-1750) is the most spectacular, with delicately sculpted figures of *apsaras* on the dome. At the rear of the park, the **Zenana Bagh** provides a surprising blend of greenery and red sandstone. Just to the left, an alley leads to the **hall of heroes**, where some fifteen 18C sculptures, depicting gods and local heroes, were carved into the rock-face and painted in bright colours.

Osiyan*

63km north of Jodhpur. By bus or car, allow half a day for this excursion, which can be included in a tour of the surroundings of Jodhpur. It is also possible to visit Osiyan en route to Jaisalmer (250km) or Bikaner (210km). In the latter case, stop overnight at the palace hotel of Khimsar (60km from Osiyan).

To see it now, who could believe that between the 8C and the 12C Osiyan was a thriving religious and trade centre? All that remains of the Moslem raids in the 12C and 13C are some 12 shrines, of which only two still function. These two, the Hindu temple of Sachiya Mata and the Jain shrine of Mahavira, are however the most majestic. The others, less spectacular and not yet restored, do nonetheless have a few fine sculptures which give a glimpse of the town's glorious past. A visit to Osiyan provides an interesting contrast between the relatively sober atmosphere of a Jain temple and the more lively Hindu temple.

Sachiya Mata temple★ *(on top of the hill, 300m from the bus stop)* was the first temple, dating back to the 8C, built in honour of the Hindu goddess, Sachiya Mata (a local incarnation of Devi, the mother-goddess). Ransacked by Moslem raids in the 12C, it was immediately rebuilt. Crowds of pilgrims gather here to worship and couples come to entreat Sachiya Mata to grant them a child. The steps up to the sanctuary are lined by an arbour of archways *(torana)* covered in silver leaf. The temple's interior remains beautiful, despite the garish additions of blue and green tiles which cover the hall's pillars. Note the *apsaras* on the dome. Musicians play the harmonium and the *tabla* while the devout wander round, placing their offerings in front of the black marble statue of Sachiya Mata: gifts include money, flowers, coconut and camphor balls which are burnt, releasing a bitter-acrid smell. On leaving, to the left of the tower *(shikhara)*, there are two small shrines dedicated to **Ganesha★** and **Shiva★**, both of which have pretty domes. Their outer walls are covered in carvings, which are qualified as "erotic" by the locals, although they will probably strike foreign visitors as somewhat restrained.

Mahavira temple★★ *(the officiating priest doubles as a guide. Like most of the priests who serve in the Jain temples, he is a Hindu)*, Osiyan's finest monument, is dedicated to Mahavira, the last of the 24 *tirthankara* and founder of the Jain community. Built in the 8C and extended in the 10C, it has been restored countless times, including very recently. Admire the intricate decoration on the pillars and the **domes** of the *mandapa* (halls). The inner shrine houses a **statue of Mahavira** which is said to be made from a mixture of sand and milk. It is covered in gold leaf and the eyes are reputed to be diamonds. On either side of the shrine are two chapels dedicated to Adinatha, the first *tirthankara.*

At the rear of the courtyard, a gallery houses statues found on other sites in Osiyan. The one of **Surya** (the sun god) dates back to the 6C. On the right-hand outer façade of Mahavira temple, an alcove covered in red paint is dedicated to **Bharu**, the local name for Bhairava (a forbidding incarnation of Shiva). Like Sachiya Mata, she is worshipped by couples who desire a child.

The other temples, built in the 8C and 9C, have suffered greatly from pillaging. Of modest proportions, they were built on the classic model of North Indian temples, with a porch-hall-chapel surmounted by a tower. Those most worthy of note are located close to Mahavira temple *(take the first road to the right on leaving the temple, then the first left)*. The road winds past the shrines dedicated to **Pipla** (local name for Durga), **Surya**, **Vishnu**, and **Hari-Hara** (a god combining the attributes of Vishnu and Shiva). Behind this group of temples lies a wasteland which hides a **baori** (step well). Although in poor condition, it nonetheless impresses visitors by the sophisticated design of the steps leading down to the water.

Making the most of Jodhpur

Getting there

By aeroplane – *Ratanada Airport*, 5km southeast of the town (C5). Alliance Air, ☎ (0291) 63 67 57, flies three times a week to Delhi (1hr), Udaipur (40min) and Jaisalmer (35min). Although the private airlines have ceased flights, some may well resume soon (or have already done so), such as Jagson Airlines.

By train – The main railway station, ***Jodhpur Railway Station***, is on Station Rd (B3), ☎ 131. There is a tourist information desk on platform n° 1, but travellers should be aware that it only works with hotels and taxi drivers who pay a commission. Computerised reservation desk on Station Rd, near the GPO, 8am-8pm, Sunday 8am-2pm. Three daily express trains to Jaipur (5-6.hr30min) and Alwar (9hr). The two night trains continue to Delhi (12hr), but the morning one forks off to Agra (13hr), via Mathura (12hr). Daily, two departures for Abu Road (5hr30min), but the late arrival time makes it impractical (the bus is a better option). Also two daily express trains to Jaisalmer (6hr30min on the night train, 7hr30min during the day) and two to Bikaner, the most practical being the day train (4hr30min). All trains stop at ***Raika Bagh Railway Station***, east of High Court Rd (C3), which is convenient for those staying at Ghoomar Hotel or in the Ratanada neighbourhood.

By bus – *Main Bus Stand*, east of High Court Rd (C3), ☎ (0291) 54 46 86. Reservations, 8am-7pm. Luxury RSTRC buses run to most destinations. Daily, there are 7 "Silver Line" buses to Jaipur (7hr), via Ajmer (5hr), one express to Delhi (12hr), Kota (9hr) and Jhunjhunu (9hr), 12 to Ajmer, two for Agra (14hr) via Bharatpur (12hr), and Bikaner (7hr) via Nagaur, four to Abu Road (7hr) and Jaisalmer (7hr). three daily departures to Chittaurgarh (9hr) and four to Udaipur (7hr), via Ranakpur (5hr).

Getting about

Walk around the little lanes of the old town, between the fort and Ghasmandi Rd, elsewhere, however, transport is a better idea.

By bus – Packed minibuses can be found throughout the modern town, along Station Rd and High Court Rd.

By rickshaw – Allow 30Rs from the station to Ratanada Circle by auto-rickshaw, and 40Rs to hire for an hour.

By taxi – There are taxi ranks at the station and in front of Ghoomar Hotel, but rates are better when negotiated by your hotel or a travel agency (650Rs for 8hr).

Car rental – Enquire at your hotel or in a travel agency. Expect to pay at least 1 100Rs per day.

Bicycle rental – On Station Rd, between the station and the GPO.

Address book

Tourist office – *Tourist Reception Centre*, in the grounds of Ghoomar Hotel (C3), ☎ (0291) 54 50 83. 8am-7pm, every day, except Sunday from April to July. Information about the town and the surroundings, a list of guides and guesthouses.

Money/Change – *State Bank of India*, High Court Campus (C3). Can change foreign currency and American Express and Thomas Cook travellers' cheques.

Bank of Baroda, Ratanada Rd, Sojati Gate (B3). Can change traveller's cheques in dollars and pounds sterling and cash withdrawals with a Visa or MasterCard. A ***Thomas Cook*** counter is due to open shortly in the grounds of Ghoomar Hotel on High Court Road (C3).

Post Office/Telephone – *GPO*, Station Rd (B3). 10am-6pm, Sunday 10am-4pm. Poste restante. Philately desk (10am-1pm/2pm-6pm; closed Sunday). Express mail by ***EMS Speed Post***, in GPOs or by ***DHL***, D-7 Takiya Chand Shah Market, M.G. Hospital Rd, Sojati Gate, ☎ (0291) 62 01 77. 10am-8.30pm; closed Sunday. To send and receive faxes, contact the ***Central Telegraph Office***, Sardarpura. 24 hours a day. Postal code: 342001.

Health – *Ambulances*, ☎ 102 and 103. ***Goyal Hospital***, 961/3 Residency Rd (A4), ☎ (0291) 62 59 33. Private clinic. ***Chemists***, on M.G. Hospital Rd, near Sojati Gate (B3).

Safety – *Police*, ☎ 100 or (0291) 54 71 80. ***Fire brigade***, ☎ 101.

Travel agents – With the exception of the RTDC, all the agencies below can organise car rentals, "village safaris" or camel rides, together with English-speaking guides (allow 250Rs for 4hr, 400Rs for 8hr). They can also make hotel, train and airline reservations.

RTDC, Ghoomar Hotel (C3), ☎ (0291) 450 83. 9am-5pm. Two guided tours of the town (including Mandor) at 9am and 2pm. Jeep tours to the outlying Bishnoi villages and to Dhawa reserve.

Sati-Ma Tours & Travels, A-1 Sir Pratap Colony, Airport Rd (C4), ☎/Fax (0291) 61 06 25.

Rajputana Holidays, Choudhary Bhawan, Flat 3, Ratanada Circle (C5), ☎/Fax (0291) 64 96 25.

Travel Plan, A-1 Sir Pratap Colony, Airport Rd (C5), ☎ (0291) 43 34 54, Fax (0291) 380 82.

Aravali Safari & Tours, 4 Kuchaman House Area, Airport Rd, in a lane south of Panch Batti, Ratanada (C5), ☎ (0291) 341 46, Fax (0291) 341 46.

Travel Corporation India (TCI), Madho Niwas, New Airport Rd (C4), ☎/Fax (0291) 43 02 82. Excellent services, although somewhat more expensive than its counterparts.

Airlines – *Indian Airlines*, 2 Circuit House Rd (C4), ☎ (0291) 306 16/17.

Jagson Airlines, Bhatti Circle (C4), ☎ (0291) 43 38 13.

Where to stay

During the low season, from April to August-September, a 15 % discount on rooms is granted, even 30 % on cheaper accommodation.

• Town centre

There are several low-budget hotels around the station and on Nai Sarak (B3), but accommodation in the town centre is for the most part polluted and noisy.

From US$7-15

Ghoomar Hotel (RTDC), High Court Rd, ☎ (0291) 54 40 10 and 54 80 10, Fax (0291) 54 50 10 – 75rm Bar. Slightly withdrawn from the town centre, next to the tourist office, this hotel is primarily the haunt of Indians and can be somewhat noisy. It is nonetheless superior to the average standard of RTDC establishments. Dormitory.

• Ratanada

An airy residential neighbourhood, located half-way between the station and the airport (2km).

Under US$7

Durag Niwas Guest House, 1 Old Public Park, in a cul-de-sac behind K.N. Girls College, ☎ (0291) 63 90 92 – 15rm. A pleasant, quiet, family-run establishment. The rooms are basic, but light, and the roof-top restaurant provides a wonderful view of the fort. Free shuttle to the station for those with bookings.

From US$15-30

Madho Niwas, Bhenswara House, New Airport Rd, Ratanada, ☎ (0291) 43 44 86 – 16rm. The welcome is warm and the atmosphere peaceful, even if the comfort is somewhat spartan and the decoration rather ordinary. Good Marwari cuisine served in the garden.

Ratan Vilas, Loco Shed Rd, Ratanada, ☎/Fax (0291) 61 44 18 – 9rm. Cooler. This red sandstone 1920s bungalow, set in a large garden, has spacious, comfortable and tastefully decorated rooms. Half-way between a family-run and a more sophisticated establishment. Guests are welcomed by a charming young couple and are often tempted to extend their stay, so entrancing are the "pig-sticking" tales of "Maharaja" Bharat Singh and so appealing the cooking of his wife and daughter-in-law. Excellent value-for-money.

Devi Bhawan, 1 Ratanada Area, in an avenue which runs alongside Karni Bhawan, ☎/Fax (0291) 342 15 – 8rm. CC As above, this establishment is run by a pleasant Rajput family. The comfortable rooms, well-decorated in a colonial style, are separated from the main building by a spacious shady garden. Ideal for a sophisticated, inexpensive stay.

Newtons Manor, 8 Central School Rd, Ratanada, next to Ratanada Polo Palace, ☎ (0291) 43 06 86, Fax (0291) 61 06 03 – 5rm. TV CC

A family-run hotel that lacks the prestige of the above two establishments. The impeccably clean rooms are sadly wanting in anything worthy of being deemed a window. Too expensive, but very good food.

From US$30-40

Karni Bhawan (Heritage Hotels Association), Palace Rd, ☎ (0291) 63 93 80, Fax (0291) 334 95 – 35rm. This hotel lacks the usual charm of "Heritage Hotels" and not much remains of the original 1947 villa. The upstairs' rooms and five suites are light and pleasant, but the ground floor rooms, although the same price, are small and windowless (don't be persuaded into accepting one). Negligent service and somewhat ungracious reception.

Quality Inn Chandra (Quality Inn), Panch Batti Circle, Airport Rd, ☎ (0291) 43 07 65 and 43 36 10, Fax (0291) 43 26 10 – 67rm. Breakfast included. Bar, beauty salon. A brand new hotel with spacious, light, comfortable rooms, unfortunately rather flashily decorated, which is unusual for this chain of hotels.

Ajit Bhawan Hotel (Heritage Hotels Association), Circuit House Rd, Ratanada, ☎ (0291) 43 74 10, Fax (0291) 63 77 74 – 50rm. This palace-hotel, lively, despite its austere architecture, is run by the courteous "Maharaja" Swaroop Singh. There are four rooms full of "olde worlde" charm in the main building, 41 ethnic-style individual cottages scattered around the rocky, shady grounds and five noisy suites located around the extravagant swimming pool. Rooms must be vacated by 10am.

From US$40-70

Ratanada Polo Palace, Residency Rd, Ratanada, ☎ (0291) 319 10, Fax (0291) 331 18 – 60rm. A modern hotel set in the middle of a gigantic lawn which runs alongside the polo grounds. The rooms in the main building are the most pleasant, the others are the same price, but darker and less comfortable. Delightful bar overlooking the swimming pool.

Over US$140

Umaid Bhawan Palace (WelcomHeritage Hotels), Umaid Bhawan, ☎ (0291) 43 33 16 and 43 04 60, Fax (0291) 63 53 73; reservations in Delhi (see p 107) – 86rm. Bar, billiards, shopping mall, beauty salon. This immense 1930s palace stands on top of a hill. The setting is majestic, the rooms and suites are regal, but the whole impression is somewhat overdone and melancholic. Superb Art Deco swimming pool in the basement.

- **Balsamand**

7km to the north.

From US$70-150

Balsamand Palace (WelcomHeritage Hotels and Heritage Hotels Association), Mandor Rd; reservations in Delhi (see p 107) – 36rm. The standard rooms, located in the former stables, overlook beautiful gardens, but are often booked by groups. Isolated and calmer, ten suites are located in the old pavilion which is located in the midst of a little lake, surrounded by rocky slopes. The architecture may be appealing, but the interior decoration is disappointing, as is the service.

Where to eat

- **Town centre**

For a snack or quick bite to eat without leaving the town centre, stop to the south of Nai Sarak (B3) to taste the "kachori" and other delicacies at ***Janta Sweet Home*** or the ices and "lassi" at ***Softy n'-Softy***, its neighbour. Freshly squeezed fruit juices and "lassi" outside Sojati Gate, particularly at ***Agra Sweets***, famous for its unctuous "makhaniya lassi".

Under US$3

City Palace, 32 Nai Sarak. The setting isn't very appealing, but it is a practical stopping place. It is also the only place where beer enthusiasts congregate.

From US$3-4

Midtown, in the road opposite the station. 7am-11pm. Bamboo walls and cane furniture abound in this "pure veg" establishment. South Indian snacks and a great choice of "lassi".

Kalinga, next to the above, ☎ (0291) 62 73 38. 7am-10.30pm. This pleasant restaurant is popular among the local middle-classes and travellers awaiting trains. Serves classical north Indian food in an impeccably clean setting, if somewhat lacking in originality.

• Ratanada

From US$3-4

On the Rocks, Circuit House Rd, next door to Ajit Bhawan Hotel, of which it is part (C3-4), ☎ (0291) 61 14 10. 12.30noon-3pm/7pm-11.30pm. Round tables, covered in traditional cotton fabrics, are set under trees, not too close together. There is also a woodcutter-style cabin room. Candle-lit dinners in the evening. Local, tandoori and Chinese cooking. Attentive service. Classical music at the weekends.

From US$4-7

Khamaghani, Ratanada Polo Palace (C5). CC 6am-11.30pm. Rajasthani, north Indian, western and Chinese cooking served in a spacious, lively, modern setting.

Ajit Bhawan Hotel (C3) CC Savour the flavours of a traditional Rajasthani buffet under the shade of trees, among clay ovens and little thatched out-buildings. Performances of folk music during dinner. Non-residents should book.

From US$7-15

The Pillars, the coffee-shop of the Umaid Bhawan Palace (C3). CC 6am-11.30pm. The chance to enjoy a moment of serenity in a superb setting, even if the choice is very limited (Indian and Western dishes). Guests can choose between a table on the steps overlooking the gardens or on the lawn. Next door, the Anglo-Indian style restaurant serves only Western food. Non-residents must spend at least US$7 each.

Excursions

Excursion to the villages – One of the major attractions of the area around Jodhpur are the "village safaris" in jeeps with guides, which take tourists out to the Bishnoi villages and to the camps of Rabari and Raika shepherds. Craftsmen can be seen at work (weavers, potters) and, occasionally, there is a reconstruction of an opium ceremony. All the travel agents and hotels in Jodhpur and the region offer this type of visit. Allow around 500Rs per person for a 4-5hr visit. It is not advisable to venture out alone or without an authorised guide, because the Bishnois can become aggressive towards visitors who have not paid the sacrosanct commission.

Camel-back rides – A properly organised ride, with tent and baggage cart, will cost from 1 100 to 3 000Rs per day depending on the services. Rates are a little higher for excursions towards Jaisalmer.

Horseback rides –***Rohat Garh Hotel***, at Rohat, and ***Fort Chanwa Hotel***, at Luni (see p 314), organise excursions from one to seven days around Jodhpur, with accommodation in castles or luxury camps. For a trek from Jodhpur to Udaipur (eleven days) enquire at ***Rajasthan Tours*** (see "Travel agents"), at the ***Royal Equestrian and Polo Centre*** at Dundlod (see "Making the most of Shekhawati", p 259) or at ***Pratap Country Inn*** at Udaipur (see "Making the most of Udaipur", p 345).

Holidays and festivals

Nag Panchami. On the 5th day after the July-August new moon, paper chains are hung in the streets in honour of all snakes – real and divine.

Marwar Festival. The day before and the day of the September-October full moon (31 October-1 November 2001) a festival is organised by the Rajasthani government to promote Marwari culture; there are dancing and music performances, polo matches, turban tying competitions…

Shopping

The most modern shops are situated to the west of Sojati Gate, at the end of Station Rd and in Takiya Chand Shah shopping precinct, on M.G. Hospital Rd (B3). On Nai Sarak (New Road) (B3) are all the large stores selling fabric, clothes and shoes. The traditional bazaar (B2), which is particularly lively around 5pm, consists of an unbroken line of tiny stalls along Ghasmandi Rd and a market, at the foot of the clock tower.

Most of the clothes shops are quite nondescript, with the exception of ***Bare Threads***, at the entrance to the On The Rocks restaurant (C3-4), and the ***Umaid Bhawan Palace*** boutique (shirts, dresses, shalwar-kamiz, shawls) (C3). ***Usha***, at Ajit Bhawan Hotel (C3), has an excellent choice of ethnic-style clothes and crafts.

Crafts – Jodhpur is famous for its leather and its "juti" (slippers) are said to be made from the softest leather in Rajasthan. These can be bought in ***Mochi Bazar*** (B2). The boutique of ***Shabbir Hassan***, is also reputed for its fine craftsmanship and lightweight shoes. Other town specialities are "dhurries", woven around Jodhpur, primarily at Salawas, "bandana" fabrics (tie-dye) and "loharia" turbans (herringbone motif).

Antiques – Furniture, "antiques" and miscellaneous artefacts produced in the region, pile up in mounds in a few shops and warehouses around Umaid Bhawan Rd and on High Court Rd (west of Ghoomar Hotel). Purchasers from major Western department stores come here to stock up. There are also some smaller shops to the north of Nai Sarak and the fort.

Culinary specialities – Jodhpur's "namkin" (spicy or sweet-savoury snacks) rival those of Bikaner; they can be found in the south part of Nai Sarak outside Sojati Gate. The best place however remains ***Chandra Vilas Namkin***, the 5th shop on High Court Rd, past Nai Sarak. For spices and seasonings, ***Mohanlal Verhomal***, 209-B Kirana Merchant, in Sadar Bazaar, is an institution, famous throughout the whole of Rajasthan.

Bookshops – Books on Rajasthan and postcards are on sale at the fort entrance and at ***Usha***, Ajit Bhawan Hotel. ***Rathi's Media Centre***, Ratanada Rd, on the bridge over the railway lines (B3), has books on India, novels and Indian and foreign magazines.

Making the most of the Jodhpur area

Where to stay

• Khimsar

90km northeast of Jodhpur, on the road to Nagaur.

From US$70-150

Khimsar Fort (WelcomHeritage Hotels and Heritage Hotels Association), Khimsar, ☎ (01585) 23 45; reservations in Jaipur, ☎ (0141) 38 23 14, Fax (0141) 38 11 50, khimsar@jp1.vsnl.net.in; reservations in Delhi (see p 107) – 50rm. This superb luxury 15C fort still has its ancient ramparts. The rooms in the old wing of the palace have more character than the others.

• Chandelao

45km east of Jodhpur. Take the road to Ajmer and turn right, just after Binawas.

From US$15-30

Chandelao Garh, Chandelao; reservations in Jodhpur, ☎ (0291) 54 59 73, Fax (0291) 54 66 62 – 10rm. Cooler. A small 17C fort in an area where there are many gazelles. This establishment combines a countrified atmosphere with the charm of a family hotel, notwithstanding a rather ordinary architecture. The rooms are tastefully decorated and the bathrooms are new. Booking advisable.

• Khejarla

85km east of Jodhpur. The road to Ajmer leads to Bhawi where you turn right towards Pipar. Some 5km further on, turn right.

From US$15-30

Khejarla Fort, Khejarla, ☎ (02930) 583 11 – 26rm. A rustic fort set in an area dominated by cement works. The oldest section is very impressive, consisting as it does of nine closely-spaced towers dating back to the 16C. The rooms are full of charm and character, but hot water comes in a basin and there is no heating in the winter.

• Nimaj

100km east of Jodhpur on the road to Ajmer.

From US$15-30

Jagram Durg (Heritage Hotels Association), Nimaj, ☎ (02939) 865 22 – 12rm. The "Lord" of Nimaj and his wife welcome guests in person to their fortified 18C palace, set in the heart of a picturesque town. The fine Rajput architecture and the friendly, family atmosphere add to the charm of this establishment. The cheerful rooms are whitewashed and furnished with traditional fabrics. Jeep excursions to the surrounding countryside.

• Sardarsamand

60km to the southeast of Jodhpur. Leave by the road to Pali, then turn left towards Jhalamand and Jadan.

From US$40-70

Sardarsamand Palace (WelcomHeritage Hotels and Heritage Hotels Association), Sardarsamand, ☎ (091291) 455 91, Fax (091291) 54 22; reservations in Delhi (see p 107) – 18rm. Bar. A superb 1930s hunting pavilion built for the maharaja of Jodhpur. Set on the ridge of a rocky hill, it overlooks a lake, which is now a bird sanctuary. Sophisticated, entirely Art Deco, from the cutlery down to the carpets. A pure delight!

• Luni

35km south of Jodhpur. Take the road to Pali and turn right at Kankani. The two trains which run between Jodhpur and Abu Road stop at Luni (40min from Jodhpur).

From US$30-40

Chanwa Fort (Heritage Hotels Association), Luni, ☎ (02931) 842 16; reservations in Jodhpur, ☎ (0291) 43 24 60 – 25rm. Cooler. Bar, boutique. The residence of "maharaja" Dalip Singh, this attractive little 19C palace has rooms and suites which are decorated in an exquisite Rajasthani style, with "dhurries" woven in the village. Booking advisable.

• Rohat

40km south of Jodhpur, on the road from Pali.

From US$30-40

Rohat Garh (Heritage Hotels Association), Rohat, ☎ (02936) 682 31; reservations in Jodhpur, ☎ (0291) 43 11 61, Fax (0291) 64 93 68 – 27rm. Cooler. This 17C family dwelling has a warren of hideaways where guests can pause for a drink or to read: in the living room with its handsome ceiling, on the veranda or out on the lawn… All the rooms are tiled and covered in "dhurries" and fine period furniture. Book ahead because it is often full.

• Bhadrajan

100km to the south of Jodhpur, towards Pali then, from Rohat, towards Basi and Ahor.

From US$7-15

Royal Rajwada, Bhadrajan, ☎ (02978) 282 01; reservations in Jodhpur, ☎ (0291) 308 49, and at Jaipur, Fax (0141) 20 36 56 and 31 36 56 – 12rm. A countrified fort nestling against a rocky slope which protects it on three sides. The only reasons for stopping here are the region's ethnographic diversity, as yet unspoiled by tourism, and the beauty of the view and the surroundings. The hotel otherwise provides highly Spartan comfort with absolutely no attempt at decoration. Booking essential in order to ensure that rooms and food are available.

• Bhenswara

130km to the south of Jodhpur. 3km from Ahor, on the road to Jalor.

From US$15-30

Ravla Bhenswara, Bhenswara, ☎ (02978) 220 80; reservations in Jodhpur, ☎ (0291) 344 86 – 13rm. Cooler. An attentive couple welcome guests to this modest 16C manor, set in the heart of Bhil and Rabari lands. Recently restored with an evident lack of taste, the place has sadly lost part of its charm. Uncomfortable beds. Bookings advisable.

A Bishnoi opium ceremony

C. Boisvieux/HOA QUI

B. Juge

Pilgrims at Ranakpur

The South

After the bare contours of the North and the vast arid plains of the West, the South presents the picture of a generous, carefree land of laughter. The mountain region of the Aravalli Range, inhabited by the Bhils, is the greenest, particularly around Udaipur: it has narrow, cool valleys, forests and artificial lakes. The contrast with the surrounding countryside is stark! The temperate hill station of Mount Abu, on the highest peak in Rajasthan, is a popular resort for honeymoon couples – a tropical oasis of vegetation whose lush greenery echoes the opulent carving of its Jain marble temples. The former kingdom of Mewar, more than any other, exemplifies the fiercely independent, proud nature of the Rajput rulers. Here the maharanas consistently refused to give their daughters in marriage to Moslem emperors. The atmosphere is less mercantile, the air more refreshing, the climate gentler. To the east, lies an endless vista of alternating arid and fertile plains. On the fringes of the Mewar, little known palaces, picturesque bazaars and priceless sanctuaries of peace and quiet still await adventurous travellers passing through the capitals of its legendary strongholds (Dungarpur, Bundi, Jhalawar...).

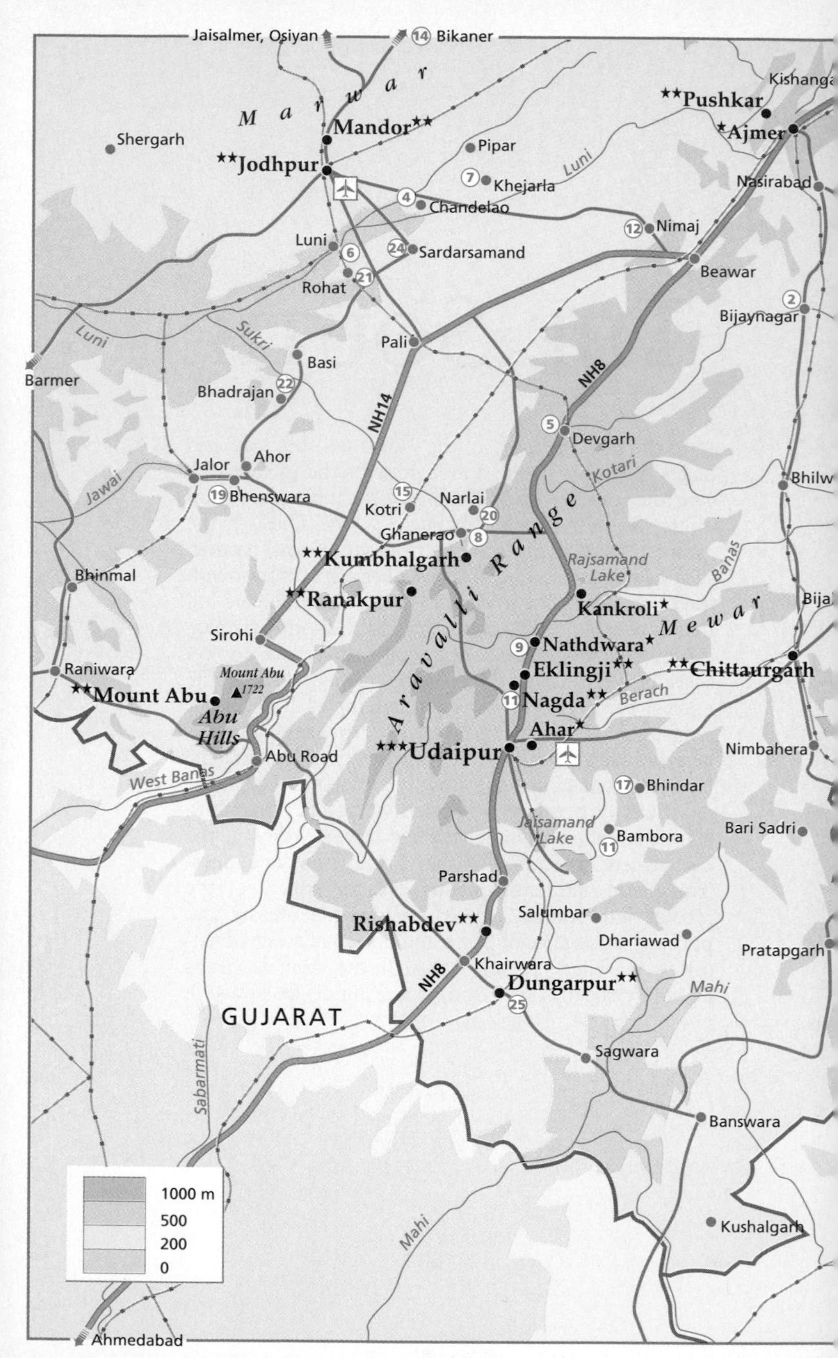

Jaisalmer, Osiyan
14 Bikaner
Marwar
Kishanga
★★Pushkar
★Ajmer
Mandor★★
Shergarh
★★Jodhpur
Pipar
7 Khejarla
Luni
Nasirabad
4 Chandelao
12 Nimaj
Luni
6
24 Sardarsamand
21
Rohat
Beawar
2
Bijaynagar
Luni
Sukri
Pali
Barmer
Basi
22
Bhadrajan
NH14
NH8
5 Devgarh
Jalor
Ahor
Jawai
19 Bhenswara
Kotari
Bhilw
15
Kotri
Narlai
20
Ghanerao
8
Aravalli Range
★★Kumbhalgarh
Rajsamand Lake
Banas
Bhinmal
★★Ranakpur
Kankroli★
Bija
Mewar
Sirohi
9 Nathdwara★
Raniwara
Mount Abu
▲1722
Eklingji★★
★★Chittaurgarh
★★Mount Abu
11 Nagda★★
Berach
Abu Hills
Ahar★
★★★Udaipur
Abu Road
Nimbahera
West Banas
17 Bhindar
Jaisamand Lake
Bambora
11
Bari Sadri
Parshad
Salumbar
Rishabdev★★
Dhariawad
Pratapgarh
Khairwara
NH8
Dungarpur★★
Mahi
25
GUJARAT
Sagwara
Sabarmati
Banswara
1000 m
500
200
0
Mahi
Kushalgarh
Ahmedabad

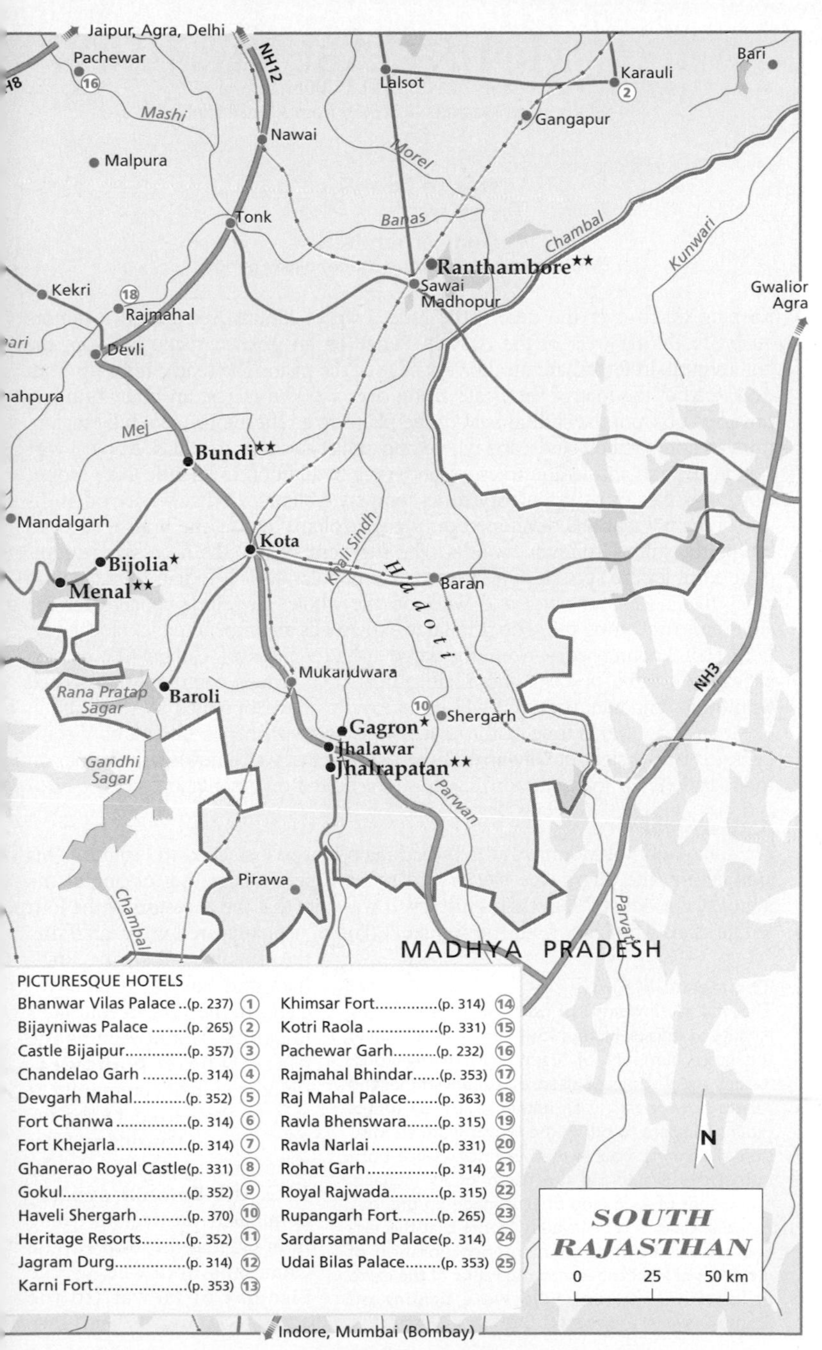

Jaipur, Agra, Delhi
Pachewar
16
NH12
Lalsot
Karauli
2
Bari
Mashi
Nawai
Gangapur
Malpura
Morel
Tonk
Banas
Chambal
Kunwari
Ranthambore★★
Sawai Madhopur
Gwalior Agra
Kekri
18
Rajmahal
Devli
Mej
Bundi★★
Mandalgarh
Kota
Khali Sindh
Hadoti
Baran
Bijolia★
Menal★★
NH3
Mukandwara
Rana Pratap Sagar
Baroli
10
Shergarh
Gagron★
Jhalawar
Jhalrapatan★★
Gandhi Sagar
Parwan
Pirawa
Chambal
Parvati
MADHYA PRADESH
PICTURESQUE HOTELS
Bhanwar Vilas Palace ..(p. 237) 1
Bijayniwas Palace ....(p. 265) 2
Castle Bijaipur..............(p. 357) 3
Chandelao Garh ....(p. 314) 4
Devgarh Mahal............(p. 352) 5
Fort Chanwa ....(p. 314) 6
Fort Khejarla................(p. 314) 7
Ghanerao Royal Castle(p. 331) 8
Gokul...........................(p. 352) 9
Haveli Shergarh ....(p. 370) 10
Heritage Resorts..........(p. 352) 11
Jagram Durg................(p. 314) 12
Karni Fort.....................(p. 353) 13
Khimsar Fort..............(p. 314) 14
Kotri Raola ....(p. 331) 15
Pachewar Garh..........(p. 232) 16
Rajmahal Bhindar......(p. 353) 17
Raj Mahal Palace.......(p. 363) 18
Ravla Bhenswara.......(p. 315) 19
Ravla Narlai ....(p. 331) 20
Rohat Garh ....(p. 314) 21
Royal Rajwada...........(p. 315) 22
Rupangarh Fort.........(p. 265) 23
Sardarsamand Palace(p. 314) 24
Udai Bilas Palace........(p. 353) 25
N
SOUTH RAJASTHAN
0 25 50 km
Indore, Mumbai (Bombay)

Mount Abu★★

Pop 16 000 – Alt 1 200m
185km from Udaipur – 220km from Ahmedabad
See map p 318

Not to be missed
The Jain temples at Dilwara.

And remember…
Avoid during the Indian school holiday period.

Keeping watch over the desert, the little town of Mount Abu lies in a remote region to the far west of the Aravalli Range on an isolated rocky outcrop, the highest peak in Rajasthan, on the very edge of the plain. The road climbs up from Abu Road at the foot of the peak, rising over 1 000m in just an hour, bringing travellers up from the stifling heat of the plains to a refreshingly cool hilly region, from an arid parched landscape where only millet survives, to a lush, tropical vegetation of palm and lemon trees, oleanders… In addition to its little lake, Mount Abu owes part of its popularity to its temperate climate. What we have here is one of the **hill stations** developed during the colonial era by the British, eager to escape the stifling summer months. The site possesses all the necessary features of an ideal leisure spot. It is also extremely popular among Indian tourists, who enjoy making lots of noise and who, on the whole, have little concern for the environment. During the school holidays, the roads are impenetrable, blocked by hordes of hooting jeeps from the large urban centres of Gujarat. Foreigners expecting a calm, peaceful mountain retreat (two virtues commonly associated with Indian mountain resorts) will undoubtedly be disappointed by the hubbub of Mount Abu at this time of the year. However a visit here will be amply compensated by the sight of **Dilwara's temples**, the most well-known Jain temples in India, famous for their extraordinarily sophisticated ornamentation.

A mythical site

The foundation of Mount Abu is buried deep in a past steeped in legends. This antique Shivaite pilgrimage site is said to have been the setting of one of the mythical episodes of Rajasthan's history. It was here that the ancestors of the four Rajput clans who comprised the **Agnikula (line of fire)** appeared in a sacred fire: the Chauhan, Pramara, Pratihara and Solanki (Chalukya) clans. In the 13C, devout Jains identified Mount Abu as the place where **Mahavira**, founder of their community, is said to have lived in the 6C BC. The site remains popular today among pilgrims. In the 11C, the **Solanki** dynasty dominated the region, ruling from Gujarat. In the 14C, the Chauhans, followed by the **Sisodias** of Mewar (to the 15C), took over. When peace

The legend of Fire

The multiple invasions of northwestern India (by Aryans, Scythians, Huns, Moslems…) were behind the large numbers of legends involving gods, heroes and demons of all sorts. An ancient legend relates how priests lit an immense fire on top of Mount Shikhara to purify the world from an invasion of demons. Four armed warriors were born out of this fire to rid the Earth of its menace. These sons of Agni (god of fire) made up the four Agnikula clans. It is believed by some that this legend evokes the enthronement/incorporation of members of local tribes into the ranks of the caste of kshatriya warriors, who were fighting off Scythian invaders in the 1C BC.

Sikh temple

HOTELS

Cama Rajputna............... ①
Chanakya....................... ②
Connaught House.......... ③
Hillock............................ ④
Hilltone.......................... ⑤
Madhuban...................... ⑥
Maharani........................ ⑦
Mount Regency.............. ⑧
Palace (Bikaner House).. ⑨
Saraswati....................... ⑩
Sunset Inn....................... ⑪

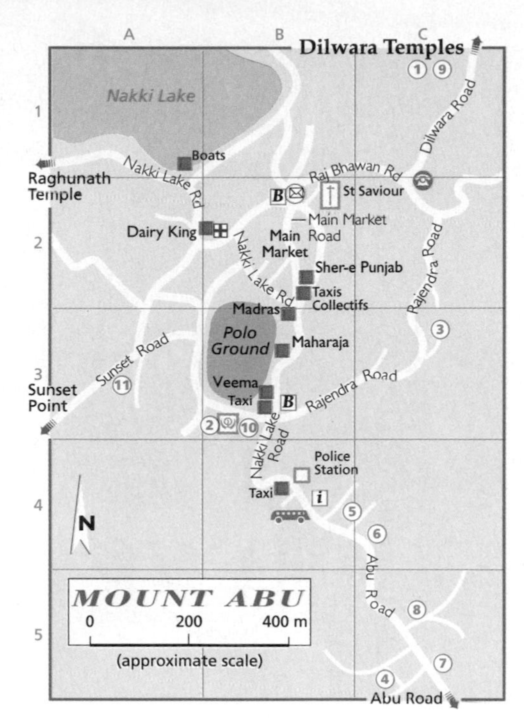

was finally established in the region in the 19C, Mount Abu experienced a new role as a hill station. It was transformed into summer quarters by the British, attracted by the temperate climate, and imitated shortly after by maharajas who built palace-like villas. With the advent of modern-day India, the town has become a retreat for the wealthy middle-classes from the plains in search of a cooler climate.

The town and its surroundings

A half day is sufficient to tour Mount Abu and its surroundings by jeep.

Mount Abu Bazaar (B2) is of little interest, but it can be fun to watch the young honeymoon couples or families of strict vegetarian Gujarati tourists, wrapped up in warm shawls and woollen jumpers, enjoying a pedalo trip on Lake Nakki or wandering through the pedestrian streets, an ice-cream in hand. If of a robust constitution and not frightened of looking ridiculous, hire the local form of transport: a tiny cart-cum-shoebox on wheels, pulled along by a driver on foot.

Dilwara's Jain temples***

3km north-east of Mount Abu. 12noon-6pm. No photos. Shoes and any leather articles must be removed before entering. Some half-dozen temples were built here from the 11C to the 15C, two of which are particularly noted for the profusion and intricacy of their interior decoration, sculpted in white marble. This fine "stone lace" was chiselled with an abrasive rope or a file by sculptors – perhaps ivory specialists – who were paid according to the amount of marble dust they produced each day. The Jain community was wealthy enough to be able to finance the astronomical cost of the purchase and transport of marble blocks, together with the upkeep, for years at a time, of several hundred craftsmen. A Moslem raid in the 14C damaged the temples, but they were immediately restored, such was the wealth and fervour of the sect.

Vimal Vasahi temple was built in the early 11C by Vimal Shah, a Jain minister of the Solanki Hindu sovereigns. Over 2 500 stonemasons, craftsmen and sculptors contributed to this work of art dedicated to Adinatha (the first of the 24 *tirthankara*, founders of the Jain community). Seen from the outside, the temple appears quite austere, but its almost bare façades hide an interior decoration of a rarely equalled luxury and opulence. In the pavilion leading up to the entrance, note the procession of elephants and, just opposite, the equestrian statue of the temple's main donor, Vimal Shah. The shrine itself stands in a courtyard surrounded by a wall in which there are 52 arched chapels, each of which contains a statue of a *tirthankara*.

The central shrine of the sanctuary, which houses the statue of Adinatha, is preceded by three hypostyle halls (*mandapa*) including the wonderful **dancing pavilion★★★** *(ranga mandapa) (the first and largest hall as you enter)*, which was added in the 12C. Note the exquisite sculptures on the pillars and consoles of the dome; the gracious outlines of musicians, dancers and divinities accentuate the architectural lines. They were carved according to the aesthetic criteria of the period, with almond-shaped eyes and aquiline nose set within a generously rounded face and an opulent feminine bosom contrasting with a tiny, supple waist. All around these human shapes, every surface however tiny, has been covered in ornate geometric and floral motifs: on the dome, chiselled and carved as if made out of lace, on the architraves, on the scrolled archways *(torana)* which open the way into the heart of the shrine.

The tirthankara

Identical statues of the "ford passers", all in a seated lotus position with expressionless faces, are endlessly repeated. The only way to tell them apart is by looking at the animal or attribute represented on the base. The bull symbolises Adinatha, the lion is for Mahavira, the elephant for Ajita, a jar for Mellinatha, the only female "tirthankara"... All these "jina" ("victorious ones") who succeeded in breaking the chain of "samsara" (endless cycle of reincarnation) are examples for the devout, and not intermediates, because there is no God. They reveal the path to those who want to overcome their "karma" (acts which lead to samsara), because the Jains do not consider life fatalistically as do the Hindus. For the Jains, every human being can free him or herself by following the teachings of Mahavira, involving absence of violence towards other forms of life ("ahimsa"), chastity, truth and poverty.

The temple of Vastupal and Tejpal (or temple of Luna Vasahi), built in the early 13C, is smaller than the above temple, but its interior decoration seems in comparison even more opulent. Vastupal and Tejpal were also powerful figures in the Solanki kingdom. They had this shrine built in memory of Luna, one of their deceased parents, dedicating it to the 22nd *tirthankara*, Neminatha. The latter was a prince who chose to give up his loved one and become an ascetic, rather than witness the sacrifice of animals at his wedding. His beloved followed his example and became a nun *(saddhvi)*.
Here too the intricacy and polish of the carving is unparalleled: there are artful *apsaras* in the company of musician consorts, elephant processions and a whole array of scrolls, stylised flowers and leaves, entwined motifs... all revealing the mastery and creativity of these 13C craftsmen. The **dancing pavilion★★★** (ranga mandapa) has a wonderful border of dancers depicted on lotus flowers, which are

Tirthankara in the temple of Vastupal and Tejpal

Exposed mandapa

"Mandapas", hypostyle chambers totally open to the outside world, are a characteristic feature of Jain architecture in Rajasthan and Gujarat. The eight pillars of the "ranga mandapa" or dancing pavilion, support an octagonal architrave on which is placed a flattened dome. The dome is entirely built using the corbel technique, whereby slabs are offset one on top of the other, climbing upwards until the central opening can be closed by a single stone. This same construction technique is found in the domes of "chhatri".

worth more than a passing glance, as is the dome's extraordinary ceiling rose placed over the octagonal chamber where the ritual dances would have been held.

Before approaching the image of Neminatha or of one of the "victorious" figures, the pilgrims, draped in their white *puja* robe, adjust the piece of fabric tied in front of their mouths in order that their breath does not indispose the saintly images and that they run no risk of inadvertently swallowing an insect. In front of the statue, they trace *swastika* signs with grains of rice. The white grains symbolise purity and cannot germinate, thus no life has been destroyed, in conformity with the sect's principle of *ahimsa*. Further on, other worshippers place flowers at the feet of a *tirthankara*, waving incense sticks in front of the face and anointing the nine sacred points on the body with their third finger, dipped in saffron and sandal paste. Each worshipper is free to proceed as he or she pleases and can join the priests, dressed in red and orange, when they anoint the statues after having delicately brushed them with a woollen duster to ensure that no living creature, however tiny, is injured.

Continue towards the northeast. 12km further on is Mount Guru Shikhara.

Apsaras and saris

F. Le Diascorn/RAPHO

The highest point in Rajasthan (1 722m), **Mount Guru Shikhara** provides some fine views of the region, particularly in the late afternoon. Indian tourists generally drive up to the summit, thereby producing a noisy toing-and-froing of vehicles which detracts from the grandeur of the site.

Making the most of Mount Abu

GETTING THERE

By train – *Abu Road Railway Station*, 29km from Mount Abu (computerised reservation terminal) is the main station. If arriving or leaving by train, you will need to catch a bus between Abu Road and Mount Abu, which not only complicates but lengthens the journey. 3 daily trains run from Ahmedabad-Abu Road-Ajmer-Jaipur-Delhi. To avoid arriving in Ajmer (6hr) or in Jaipur (8hr) in the middle of the night, take the afternoon "mail" train. If going to Delhi, take the evening "Radjhani" (11hr30min) or the Ashram Express (13hr) which stops at Alwar (10hr). An express train runs three times a week to Jodhpur (5hr) and Bikaner (10hr), but it leaves very early in the morning, before the first Mount Abu-Abu Road shuttle.

Tickets can be reserved at Mount Abu where a reservation terminal has a limited number of seats available on the main trains. Contact ***Western Railway Out Agency***, Abu Rd, ☎ (02974) 33 53 and 383 84. 9am-1pm/2pm-4pm, Sunday 9am-12noon.

By bus – Try and catch a bus that goes right to Mount Abu. Some stop at Abu Road and travellers have to change in mid-journey.

Roadways Bus Stand at Abu Road, near the station. Approximately every 20min to Mount Abu (1hr), from 5.30am to 8.30pm.

Roadways Bus Stand at Mount Abu, Abu Rd, on the way into town (B4). Bookings, ☎ (02974) 34 34, 6am-7.30pm. Ticket sales, 5.30am-8.30pm. 1 nightly "Silver Line" to Jaipur (12hr). 1 daily departure to Delhi (18hr), via Ajmer and Jaipur, and 4 to Udaipur (6hr30min), 3 via Ranakpur. 1 or 2 buses daily for Jodhpur (8hr30min), Chittaurgarh (9hr30min), Kota (14hr) and Jaisalmer (10hr). Private buses, which are faster than state buses, operate all over Rajasthan (see "Travel Agents").

By taxi – A taxi between Abu Road and Mount Abu is around 250Rs.

GETTING ABOUT

There are no auto-rickshaws in Mount Abu and walking is the best way of getting about. To transport luggage from the bus stop to your hotel, iron boxes on wheels with "pusher" can be rented for 10-30Rs. Take a taxi to the temples.

By group taxi – There is a group jeep taxi rank at the crossroads between Nakki Lake Rd and Dilwara Rd (B2).

By taxi – There is a taxi rank south of the Polo Ground (B3), but you can also enquire at your hotel or a travel agent. Allow around 40Rs for a single fare to Dilwara and 330Rs for a tour of the temples (5hr).

ADDRESS BOOK

Tourist office – *Tourist Reception Centre*, opposite the bus stop (B4), ☎ (02974) 31 51. 10am-5pm; closed Sunday. Has a list of guest houses and organises two daily guided visits, at 8.30am and 1.30pm, in Hindi to the temples at Dilwara, Achalgarh, Guru Shikhara, Nakki Lake, Adhar Devi and Om Shanti Bhawan (45Rs).

Banks/Money – Cash can be withdrawn with a Visa or MasterCard at the ***Bank of Baroda***, Nakki Lake Rd (B3). ***State Bank of India***, Raj Bhawan Rd (B2), can change cash.

Post Office/Telephone – *GPO*, Raj Bhawan Rd (B1-2). 9am-5pm; closed Sunday. Poste restante and express mail with ***EMS Speed Post***. Postal code: 307501.

Health – *J Watumull Global Hospital and Research Centre*, Dilwara Rd, ☎ (02974) 383 47 / 48. ***Chemists***, there are four or five chemists on Raj Bhawan Rd, near Government Hospital.

Safety – *Police Station*, next to the tourist office (B4), ☎ (02974) 33 33.

Travel agents – *Jain Collections*, Dilwara Rd, opposite the group jeep taxi rank (B2), ☎ (02974) 387 15. Daily 7am-10pm. Jeep rentals (in a "supari" and cheap jewellery store). ***Shobha Travels***, Nakki Lake Rd, near Samrat Hotel, ☎ (02974) 383 02. Daily 7am-10.30pm. Bus tickets, car rentals and guides.

Where to stay

The choice of hotels in Mount Abu is so vast it is almost bewildering. Accommodation out of the town centre avoids having to put up with the ear-splitting din otherwise audible 24 hours a day. The rates of Mount Abu's establishments fluctuate, increasing by 15 % to 100 % throughout the year, depending on the calendar. They are generally highest at Christmas (December 20 – January 5), in May and June, at Janmashtami (5 days in August) and at Divali (21 days in October-November. They are also at their lowest from January 5 to April 15, in September, October and November (except Divali) and from December 1-20. The monsoon period (July-August) is generally felt to be low season, but not always. Things are further complicated by the practice of increasing low season rates by 15 % at the weekends and on public holidays. To be on the safe side, call the hotel before reaching Mount Abu to check the prices when you will be staying, and don't forget to negotiate. The following prices are low season rates.

Temperatures are rarely very high in the station (34°C maximum in June) but the climate is humid, whatever the season. Most hotels require rooms to be vacated by 9am, with the exception of luxury establishments.

• South of the town

Under US$7

Saraswati Hotel, south of the Polo Ground, next to the Gurudwara, off the main street, ☎ (02974) 388 87 – 38rm. Ideal for low budget travellers. The rooms are reasonably clean. Hot water in basins in the most standard rooms. During the peak season, prices increase from between 40 to 250 %.

From US$7-15

Maharani Hotel, Abu Rd, ☎ (02974) 435 10 – 19rm. TV Pleasant welcome even if none of the staff speak English. The rooms are spacious and clean, although the cheapest are windowless. 50 % increase in peak season.

From US$15-30

Madhuban Hotel, near the bus stop, ☎ (02974) 388 22 and 388 33, Fax (02974) 389 00 – 14rm TV 8rm. with cooler. This pleasant, well-run establishment welcomes guests warmly. The main building overlooks the street and rooms are noisy until 10pm. 30 to 40 % increase in the peak season.

Mount Regency Hotel, Abu Rd, ☎ (02974) 432 00 – 21rm. TV CC Cooler. This new hotel provides clean, airy rooms with marble floors. Eight of the rooms have three beds. Allow 40 % extra in the peak season.

Sunset Inn Hotel, Sunset Rd, ☎ (02974) 431 94, Fax (02974) 40 00 00 – 40rm. TV CC 14rm with AC. A modern, seven-storey building set in the midst of a tree-lined quiet neighbourhood. Rates vary for these well-kept, identical rooms, depending on whether they have a bath, carpet or AC. 20 to 30 % increase in the high season.

From US$15-30

Hillock Hotel, Abu Rd, ☎ (02974) 384 63 to 65, Fax (02974) 384 67 – 40rm. TV CC 27rm. with AC and 9 single rooms. Bar, boutique. Perfect for those seeking a modern, impeccably managed, luxury establishment, this is the best of its sort in Mount Abu. Rooms are pleasant, light and provide a good view over the station. 60-80 % increase in the peak season.

Hilltone Hotel, Abu Rd, ☎ (02974) 383 91 to 94, Fax (02974) 383 95, hilltone@adl.vsnl.net.in – 68rm. TV CC Bar. A modern hotel off the main road. Guests have the choice between rooms in the main building or in little cottages dotted along either side of an alley. Somewhat lacking in warmth, limited service and uninspired decoration. In the peak season, expect a 25-65 % increase.

From US$30-40

Connaught House (Welcom Heritage Hotels and Heritage Hotels Association), Rajendra Rd, 300m from the centre, ☎ (02974) 385 60, Fax (02974) 54 22 40; reservations in Delhi (see p 107) – 14rm. TV CC Cooler. Two spacious bungalows built on the slopes of the hill, lost within a luxuriant garden. In this relaxing, intimate setting, the oldest bungalow, the former summer residence of Jodhpur's prime ministers, has six pretty rooms decorated with an "olde worlde" charm, if a little gloomy. Those in the more recent cottage open onto a pleasant veranda, where meals are served. Rates are fixed (no seasonal variations) and almost identical whatever the room.

• On the road to Dilwara

As these hotels are quite a distance from the town centre, a car is essential.

From US$30 to 40

Palace Hotel, also called Bikaner House (Heritage Hotels Association), 3.5km on Dilwara Rd, ☎ (02974) 386 73 and 431 21, Fax (02974) 386 74 – 35rm. CC Bar, billiards. Built in 1893 to plans by Colonel Sir Swinton Jacob, this royal residence hidden within a wooded park, provides excellent accommodation at a reasonable price. The spacious and comfortable rooms are decorated with period furniture. The suites have a loggia, office and dressing room. Rooms nos 10, 15 and 17 are the most pleasant. The standard rooms, on the ground floor, are rather dark. Prices are fixed whatever the season, but discounts are occasionally granted when business is slack.

Cama Rajputana Club Resort (Heritage Hotels Association), 2km along Dilwara Rd, ☎ (02974) 382 05 and 382 06, Fax (02974) 384 12 – 42rm. TV CC Bar, billiards, games room. This former club, built by the British around 1870, now houses old bungalows and modern cottages, dotted around a large, flowered garden. The rooms are almost identical, but the more expensive ones have a bath and balcony. The overall impression is however rather disappointing and doesn't live up to the style one might expect from such an establishment. Prices increased by 80-100 % in the peak season.

Where to eat

One is spoilt for choice, there are so many restaurants along Nakki Lake Rd, between the police station and the lake. Some have terraces, but eating outside is noisy to say the least. The predominantly Gujarati and Jain clientele means that many only serve "pure veg" cuisine. Among the best are: ***Madras Cafe*** (very good coffee), ***Maharaja*** which also serves Gujarati and tandoori thalis, and ***Veena*** which serves a few North Indian dishes. For non-vegetarian tandoori cooking, try ***Sher-e Punjab*** and for ices and milk-shakes, go to ***Dairy King***.

From US$3-4

Handi, Hilltone Hotel. 7am-3pm/5pm-11pm. Take a seat on the veranda or on the lawn and try the house specialities, "handi paneer", cheese cooked in garlic, onions and dried fruit in an earthenware dish (handi) and tandoori chicken.

Mayur, Hillock Hotel. 12noon-3pm/7pm-10.30pm. Rajasthani and North Indian cuisine, as well as a few Western and Chinese dishes, served in an elegant, comfortable setting. Attentive service.

Holidays and festivals

Summer Festival (June 1-3). Folklore dancing and "qawwali" singers.

RANAKPUR★★

65km from Udaipur – See map p 318

And remember...

Go in the afternoon (the temples are closed in the morning).
Combine a visit to Ranakpur with a trip to Kumbhalgarh.
Stay in town or in one of the palaces in the area.

Sheltered in a cool valley, on the banks of a river which widens into a lake, the temples of Ranakpur constitute one of the finest examples of Jain art, on a par with the shrines of Mount Abu (Rajasthan), Palitana and Junagadh (Gujarat). Few monuments better illustrate the expression "lacework in stone" than the temple dedicated to Adinatha, the largest Jain sanctuary in India and one of the five most sacred. Its warren of elegant halls and courtyards together comprise an amazing forest of 1 400 pillars, each different, delicately and intricately carved out of white marble. The beauty of this shrine illustrates the refinement and opulence of India's 15C elite. Today, the only residents are a coterie of *langur* monkeys and a small community of monks. The site's serene atmosphere and the charm of the surrounding countryside may well encourage you to linger in Ranakpur, one of the most alluring places on your journey through Rajasthan.

The wealth of the Jain community

In Mewar, as elsewhere in Rajasthan, Jain merchants amassed vast fortunes in medieval times and held many influential positions in the kingdom's administration. In the 15C, one of these powerful figures, **Sanghvi Dharnak Shah**, prime minister of Krana Kumbha, had a shrine built that was intended to depict the heavenly kingdom where the *tirthankara* (ford passers, and founders of the Jain religion) lived. This enterprise was entrusted to **Dipak**, a renowned architect known throughout northern India. Several other shrines were also built nearby, but a Moslem raid soon resulted in serious damage to them and they were abandoned. It was not until the 19C that the descendants of Dipak set about restoring these works of art, using the same techniques employed by their ancestor.

The temple of Adinatha

B. Brillion/MICHELIN

Visit to the temples

2pm-5pm, no entrance fee, charge for cameras and videos. Remove footwear and any other leather articles (belts, bags, etc). No photos of the statues of Adinatha in the main temple's shrine.

The temple of Adinatha***

This temple, built in the 15C by Dipak, is dedicated to Adinatha, the first of the 24 *tirthankara*, whom the Hindus call Rishabdev *(see p 350)*. The **outer façade**, studded with a host of towers *(shikhara)*, only provides a somewhat dull idea of the splendour awaiting visitors inside. The staircase up to the entrance, over which stands a three-storey pavilion, leads into a quite incredibly decorated courtyard. Every surface, however tiny, is covered in a profusion of ornamental **sculpture,** the intricate detail and perfect polished finish of which have rarely been equalled. The fluidity of the carved motifs blends in so beautifully with the overall architectural design, highlighting the latter's simple elegance, that the lavish ornamentation in fact strikes visitors as uncluttered. Wreaths, scrolls, floral motifs, animals, musicians, *apsaras* and a whole host of other petrified creatures spring gracefully to life as the sun's rays subtly reflect off and around the hundreds of pillars.

The shrine is set in the centre of the courtyard. Designed in the shape of a Greek cross, it consists of several hypostyle halls *(mandapa)* set round a central shrine whose four openings face the cardinal points. The surrounding wall houses 84 alcoves in which stand repetitive, identical sculptures of the 24 *tirthankara*. The **second dome**, in line with the first, just in front of the shrine, is one of the sanctuary's most beautiful features. Its height, intricately carved **statues** (musicians and *apsaras*) and the amazing **hanging keystone** which stands out from the background filigree work, all reveal the phenomenal mastery of its craftsmen. Mingle with the pilgrims, from simple villagers to wealthy businessmen from Mumbai (former Bombay). Some are dressed in white as a sign of their abnegation and wear a mask in front of their mouth: taking life, by inadvertently swallowing an insect, is considered to be a serious sin. The pilgrims anoint the nine sacred points (navel, plexus, third eye, etc) of the statues' bodies with their finger dipped in saffron and sandalwood or draw patterns designed to bring good luck with grains of rice. An exquisitely-carved **archway*** (torana), leads into the shrine in which stand four marble statues of Adinatha, hence the temple's name, "Chaumukha", which means four faces. On the right-hand side of the temple is a carved high-relief plaque of the 23rd *tirthankara*, **Parshvanatha**

Pious ascetics seduced by apsaras

The apsaras, stunningly beautiful dancing girls who lived in water, the air and in trees, became prostitutes due to a lack of husbands – according to the "Ramayana". They are generally depicted in the company of musicians, the "gandharva". Already present in the "Veda", before the Jain religion branched away from Brahminism, their voluptuous, generous forms can be found both in Jain temples and Hindu sanctuaries, where they lasciviously turned the heads of even the most pious of religious ascetics. The gods used the apsaras' infallible power of seduction to weaken the yogis, whose powers, achieved through meditation, could endanger that of the supreme beings. These licentious temptresses willingly gave themselves to humans. One way of conquering them is to steal their clothes while they are bathing. Beware, their ambivalent character can bring good luck… or lunacy. Fortunately, the 'Atharva Veda" contains magic formulae which can combat their evil spells.

standing up, under the shelter of a thousand-headed cobra who protects him from the rain sent by an evil demon. The sophisticated entwined motifs carved round the saint are quite breathtaking.

The other temples

Ranakpur has three other smaller temples. First go to the temple of Parshvanatha (the first on the right on leaving the temple to Adinatha).

The temple of Parshvanatha** is by far the most interesting of the three other temples. Built to the classic plan, (porch, hall and chapel with *shikhara*), it has **outer walls** with sculptures of dancers, musicians, *tirthankara*, erotic scenes...

The temple of Neminatha* *(in the centre)*, dedicated to the 22nd *tirthankara*, was built on a similar design to the above. It also has some beautiful carving, although not quite as dense.

The sculpture on the **Hindu temple of Surya** *(to the left on leaving the temple of Adinatha)* is more crudely carried out, but had it been anywhere except here, would no doubt have been deemed more than worthy of interest. The sun god Surya can be recognised by his chariot pulled by seven horses and by the full-blown lotus flowers he holds in his hands.

In front of the plaque of Parshvanatha

B. Brillion/MICHELIN

Making the most of Ranakpur

Getting there

Also see "Excursions" in "Making the most of Udaipur" p. 346.

By bus – The bus stop is to the right of the temples. Daily, 7 buses to Udaipur (2hr), 4 to Jodhpur, 3 to Abu Road... but don't expect a seat.

By taxi – Jeep service opposite the bus stop or by enquiring at the Shilpi Hotel (RTDC). For Kumbhalgarh, expect to pay around 400Rs for a single and 650Rs for a return.

Where to stay, Where to eat

A 20 % discount is available in most hotels in the low season, from May to June, possibly even from April to September in the more expensive establishments.

• Ranakpur

Under US$7

Dharmshala, in the shadow of the temples – This pilgrim hostel, run by Jains, provides accommodation for which the term Spartan is an understatement. Guests can however choose between sleeping directly on the floor or a room with a bed, cold water and a toilet. Lights out at 10pm. The restaurant serves only "pure veg" Gujarati thalis.

Shilpi Hotel (RTDC), 5min walk from the temples, ☎ (02934) 850 74 – 12rm. 6rm with cooler. A very pleasant surprise: this RTDC hotel, located on a hill overlooking the river, is reasonably clean and well-run. A desk in the lobby doubles as post office from 1pm to 4pm.

From US$7-15

The Castle, 3km northbound, on the road to Sadri, ☎ (02934) 851 33 – 20rm. 10rm with cooler. The rooms, located in two circular buildings, on the edge of a wood, are spacious and light, although minimally decorated. Tandoori cuisine.

From US$40-70

Maharani Bagh Orchard Retreat (WelcomHeritageHotels and Heritage Hotels Association), 4km on the road to Sadri, ☎ (02934) 851 05 and 851 51, Fax (0291) 54 25 40; reservations in Delhi (see p 107) – 18rm. Cooler. Bar, boutique. The ideal spot to treat oneself to quiet refuge in a refreshingly cool landscape of lemon trees, mangoes and birds. Comfortable, tastefully-decorated cottages, but avoid nos 1, 2 and 3 which are gloomy and noisy.

• Ghanerao

23km to the north of Ranakpur, between Sadri and Desuri. Bus links with Udaipur.

From US$30-40

Ghanerao Royal Castle, Ghanerao, ☎ (02934) 840 35; reservations in Udaipur, ☎ (0294) 56 08 99 and 56 18 49 – 20rm. Every evening this 17C castle turns into a palace out of the Arabian Nights, as candles and torches light up the establishment's courtyards, terraces and kiosks. Elegantly-decorated rooms and recently renovated bathrooms. Jeep excursions to the outlying Bhils and Garasiyas tribal villages.

• Narlai

30km to the north of Ranakpur, 3km from Desuri, on the road to Nadol.

From US$30-40

Ravla Narlai, Narlai, ☎ (02934) 824 25 and 824 43; reservations in Jodhpur ☎ (0291) 43 74 10, Fax (0291) 63 77 74 – 15rm. This charming 17C hunting pavilion of the maharajas of Jodhpur, built at the foot of an imposing block of granite, has some exquisitely decorated rooms, particularly nos 4, 6, 12 and 13. If travelling in a group of 4, ask for nos 9 and 10 which have a shared bathroom, living room and private veranda. A pity that the quality and variety of the buffet does not live up to the setting.

• Kotri

45km from Ranakpur, 4km south of Nadol, on the road to Sadri.

From US$15-30

Kotri Raola, Kotri, ☎ (02934) 402 24; bookings at Udaipur, ☎ (0294) 56 08 22 – 9rm. This rustic little 17C fort is worth a stay of at least a couple of days. Basic comfort and service, but ideal for anyone intending to explore the area on horseback or by jeep. Advance booking essential.

KUMBHALGARH★★

85km from Udaipur – See map p 318

And remember...

Hire a car for a day and visit Kumbhalgarh in the morning and the temples at Ranakpur in the afternoon.

Kumbhalgarh fort, lost within a wilderness of wooded hills and narrow valleys still inhabited by wolves, commands the road from the plain of Jodhpur up to the heights of Mewar. Its impressive ramparts speak eloquently of the region's love of warfare and the rivalries that were to tear Rajasthan apart until the British arrived. The isolated position and military sobriety of Kumbhalgarh fort remind visitors that the famed luxury of Rajasthan's royal courts was only a detail in its otherwise barbarous history, written in letters of blood with more accounts of merciless sieges and murderous raids than tales of courtly romance.

Today only a few peasant families still live in this lonely fort which looms threateningly over the forest below, now a wildlife sanctuary. Here in Kumbhalgarh, far more than in Jaisalmer and Jodhpur, visitors can still feel the emotional weight of centuries of bloody massacres and cruel sieges. From the first gate, the noisy bustle of the traffic and the bazaars immediately vanishes to be replaced by the fleeting memories of sword-fights which still haunt the fort's high walls.

The iron lady of Mewar

Kumbhalgarh's strategic position on the western foothills of the Aravalli Range was exploited as early as the 3C, when the first fort was built here. In the early 15C, the sovereign of Mewar, the powerful and belligerent **Rana Kumbha** (1433-1468), seized the site then under the control of a local chieftain. He enlarged it, making it one of the principal towns of his kingdom. At this time Kumbhalgarh was the second largest fort in Mewar, after the one at Chittaurgarh. The latter soon fell under the control of Emperor Akbar in 1568, who then turned towards Kumbhalgarh. In vain, however. The stronghold remained inviolable and only relinquished its military might when the British arrived, bringing peace with them to northwestern India. From their luxurious palaces at Udaipur, the region's *maharana* no longer attached any importance to its austere ramparts, with the exception of Fateh Singh (1884-1930) who fell in love with the site's majestic landscape and had a new palace built at the top of the fort.

A virtually impregnable site

Tradition holds that Kumbhalgarh never fell into enemy hands. In truth, it would appear that one of Akbar's generals, Shahbaz Khan, seized possession of it in 1578. Defeated by the Mughals at the battle of Haldighati, Maharana Pratap Singh had sought refuge here but when the imperial army began their approach, he deserted, leaving the fort in the hands of a Rajput garrison. The latter put up such a brave fight that their opponents had to resort to poisoning the water supply in order to win the battle. According to another version, Shahbaz Khan owed his victory to an explosion which destroyed the garrison's victuals. Whatever the reality, Pratap Singh was to return several years later and prise his possession back from the enemy's hands.

The fort

From dawn to dusk, no entrance charge. Allow at least one hour.

The winding road slowly snakes its way up through the hills, passing through a first gate some 2km away from the fort, which is still hidden behind its natural protection. A sudden bend in the road reveals the **ramparts**: grey, an impressive 7m thick and amply equipped with sturdy bastions. This first glimpse of the fort reminds visitors of how truly impenetrable it must have been, covering the entire plateau, with fields, wells, shops and a hundred or so temples, all surrounded by 36km of walls. After passing through the next two gates, the road finally enters the fort. Of the 300 temples and palaces which used to stand in the grounds, fewer than 10 are still intact.

The 15C **temple of Vedi** *(on the right on entering)*, Kumbhalgarh's most impressive shrine, whose austere architecture blends in perfectly with the site's military simplicity, stands on a platform. Just behind, on another esplanade, the **temple of Nilkantha**, dedicated to Shiva, seems more refined. In front of it is a pavilion which houses the bull **Nandi**, the god's steed. To the right, a small Jain temple is dedicated to the 23rd *tirthankara*, **Parshvanatha.**

Cross the entrance courtyard and go up the steep ramp leading to the palaces. Past a temple devoted to Ganesha, the path goes under three gates before reaching the **palace of Rana Kumbha**. Only the **temple to Kali** has escaped ruin. A staircase on the left leads to the **Badal Mahal** (palace of the clouds) erected by Fateh Singh in the late 19C. Built on two floors, it has a blue-walled **durbar hall** **(meeting room)** with pastel-coloured rooms – yellow, pink and green. From the terrace above, there is a **panorama** over Kumbhalgarh and the mountains in the distance. Back down on the ground floor, go to the little courtyard to the right of the durbar hall. The walls are covered in **frescoes** depicting herds of wild elephants playing in the forest or tussling with other jungle animals.

Making the most of Kumbhalgarh

Getting there

By bus – The buses stop in a wooded valley at the crossroads on the Kelwara-Desuri road and the road up to the fort (2km). There are only 2 direct buses daily from Udaipur (3hr30min) but it is possible to catch a bus from Kelwara (5km) which has more services. For Ranakpur, change at Saira (4 buses to Saira, between 9am and 5pm). See also "Excursions" in "Making the most of Udaipur".

Where to stay

From US$7-15

Ratnadeep Hotel, Kelwara, ☎ (02954) 422 17 and 422 55, Fax (02954) 423 40 – 8rm. This pleasant little establishment has clean, airy, pretty rooms overlooking the countryside. 20 % discount from June to July. Excursions to the fort and to Ranakpur.

From US$40-70

The Aodhi Hotel, Kumbhalgarh (HRH Group), ☎ (02954) 43 41 to 45, Fax (02954) 43 46; reservations in Delhi and Udaipur (see p 346) – 26rm. CC Bar. Recent extension work has unfortunately deprived this hotel of much of its former charm, but it remains a pleasant stopover. Cosy rooms, but those on the ground floor are damp and dark. 30 % discount from April to September.

Kumbhalgarh Fort Hotel, Kelwara road, 5km from the fort, ☎ (02954) 423 72, Fax (02594) 52 51 06 – 22rm. TV CC Cooler. Bar. The only attraction of this recent establishment, built on the flanks of the hillside, is its splendid view over the plain. Otherwise it is expensive and has none of the charm of the above. 30 % discount from April to September.

Pastimes

Excursions – All the hotels organise visits to the ***Kumbhalgarh Wildlife Sanctuary***, by jeep (around 2 500Rs, including entrance charge and guide), or by horse or camel-back. There is an entrance at Ghanerao, and another just 500m from The Aodhi Hotel.

UDAIPUR★★★

Pop 50 000– Alt 570m
660km from Delhi – 730km from Bombay – 405km from Jaipur
See map p 318

Not to be missed
The City Palace.
A boat ride on Lake Pichola.
The old town's bazaars..

And remember...
Take a taxi to visit the more outlying sites.
Allow two days to visit Udaipur.

The capital of **Mewar** is bathed in a mild, almost feminine aura, which contrasts greatly with the harsher tone of Rajasthan's numerous fortress towns. This state of grace is undoubtedly due to its landscape: a succession of gentle, wooded hills, providing both panoramic and more intimate views. Then again, perhaps it is due to its radiant light, transparent and fluid, ever present throughout the "city of dawn" (*udai*, named after its founder, means "dawn"). Udaipur is spread along the banks of two lakes and the constant reflection of the sun (or moon) off their surface imbues the whole town with an unusually clear, bright light. The whitewashed houses – here left white and not painted blue as in Jodhpur – and the pale yellow walls of the immense palace, further accentuate the effect of the light. Located at an altitude of 600m, the town enjoys a climate which is particularly temperate for the region: the summers are cooler and the winters warmer. The town is also less commercially oriented than that of the other major tourist centres, and the overall impression of well-being and relaxation never fails to captivate all who visit it.

The City Palace reflected in Lake Pichola

R. Mattès

The new capital of Mewar

The Sisodias dynasty – Udaipur only dates back to the 16C, whereas the origins of its founding dynasty, the **Sisodias**, can be traced back to Chief Guhil, born in a cave *(guha)* while his family was fleeing Gujarat and the Hun invaders in the 6C. His heirs, the **Guhilots**, claim to be descended from the oldest branch of the "Sun race" *(Suryavansh)*, to which Rama also belongs. They settled in Mewar in the 7C, first setting up their capital at Nagda, then at Ahar (a few kilometres from Udaipur) and adopting the name of Sisodias. In the 8C, a monarch of the youngest branch of Sisodias, **Bappa Rawal**, founded the citadel of **Chittaurgarh**, which was the capital of Mewar for eight centuries and one of the most powerful and influential cities in northern India.

A sovereign on the run seeks refuge – In 1568, Emperor Akbar besieged Chittaurgarh and laid the place to waste. *Maharana* **Udai Singh II** (ruled from 1537 to 1572) managed to escape and sought refuge in this site off the beaten track. Bewitched by the calm of its surrounding hills and the natural protection they provided, he decided to build his new capital here, following the advice of a hermit soothsayer who had predicted the emergence of a new capital in Mewar.

Resistance – The son of Udai Singh II, the legendary *Maharana* **Pratap Singh** (1572-1597) was also subjected to raids by Akbar's troops, who defeated his army at the battle of **Haldighati** (1576) (27km from Udaipur). Vanquished, Pratap Singh nonetheless managed to preserve Mewar's independent status, if only for a time: his successor Amar Singh (1597-1620) was forced to negotiate with Jahangir. But the terms of the agreement preserved the Sisodias' honour: they were saved from the ignominy of sacrificing one of their daughters to the emperor's bed. Peace and the decline of the Mughals all favoured Udaipur's development, but new enemies, the Marathas from the south, soon reared their ugly head. Incapable of preserving their independence, the *maharanas* of Udaipur finally gave in and accepted British sovereignty in 1818.

A hopeless battle

While most of the Rajputs formed alliances with the Mughal dynasty under the auspices of Emperor Akbar, reputed for his tolerance, the "maharanas" of Mewar pursued their struggle for independence. Pratap Singh personifies this hopeless combat with a bravery that made him Rajasthan's most famous hero. Supported by a few military chiefs and by archers of the Bhil tribe, he managed to hang onto his kingdom. He nonetheless never succeeded in recapturing Chittaurgarh, symbol of the lost power of the Sisodias. At the battle of Haldighati, he stood up, for the last time, to the imperial troops, who were commanded by a Rajput general, the maharaja of Amber. Hemmed in on all sides, he was saved only by his trusty steed, Chetak, who carried him out to safety before dying of its wounds. A statue of Chetak marks the place of the battle still today.

The old town★★★

Visit the city on foot. Allow 3hr.

This walled town has retained the peaceful rhythm of yesteryear, best savoured in the late afternoon, when the heat dies down and the markets spring to life. The most picturesque districts are located in the north-east, around the **Vegetable Market** and in the lanes around Dhan Mandi and Bara Bazaar. A stroll around **Gangaur Ghat** provides a glimpse of life on the banks of the lake and of white-washed houses, some of which are covered in naïve murals of horsemen, elephants, divinities, banana trees, painted on the occasion of a wedding *(see illustration p 341)*. To the south of the town are a few more or less well-cared for gardens. The most pleasant is **Manak Lal Verma Park**, terraced against the hillside, providing an unusual view of Lake Pichola.

The temple of Jagdish* (B3) was built by *Maharana* Jagat Singh 1st, in 1651, in honour of **Jagannatha** (Lord of the World) commonly known as Jagdish (contraction of *jagat* "world" and *ishvara* "God") – or in other words Vishnu. *(Go up the stairs and enter the temple grounds).* The temple's design is similar to that of those at Chittaurgarh and consists of a square courtyard with a main temple and a chapel on each corner. The main shrine is preceded by an elegant pavilion which houses a bronze statue of **Garuda**, Vishnu's winged vehicle. It is built on the classic pattern, with a porch-hall-shrine surmounted by a tower *(shikhara)*. Admire the richly carved **outer walls**, depicting dancers, elephants, *mithuna* (entwined lovers), yogis… The porch's ceiling features a fine bas-relief of Krishna (one of Vishnu's personifications) playing the flute for Radha, his favourite consort. The hall, with its dome, opens onto the shrine *(garbha griha)* and the black statue of the four-armed Vishnu-Jagannatha.

The City Palace (B4)

9am-5.30pm, entrance charge, extra fee for cameras and videos. Allow at least 1hr. Tickets are purchased at the central door in the façade (to the right when coming from Tripolia). Signposted.

This sumptuous palace, Rajasthan's largest, in fact comprises several palaces one next to the other (including the City Palace itself), all of which combine to produce a single, impressive façade nearly 500m in length. The variations in style, from north to south, also mark a chronological progression: early work started in the second half of the 16C under Udai Singh II and continued up until the early 20C. The palace combines Rajput and Mughal styles of more or less baroque inspiration. The entrance is via two successive gates, **Bari Pol** (17C) and **Tripolia** (18C). Between the two, note *(on the left)* eight marble archways *(torana)* where the *maharanas* were weighed. The equivalent of their weight in gold and silver coins was then distributed to their subjects. **Raj Angan**, the main courtyard, is the oldest part of the complex and is now a car park.

The City Palace is a warren of palaces, corridors and staircases. The first courtyard is **Amar Vilas**, designed in 1699 by Amar Singh II (1698-1710). At the rear, to the left, is **Dilkush Mahal** (palace of the joyful heart). Constructed in the early 17C, it consists of two main rooms which were decorated at a later date: Chitran ki Burj (18C) has some magnificent **miniature paintings** depicting life at court and royal pastimes; Kanch ki Burj (early 19C) is covered in tiny mirrors *(shish)*.

The heroic suicide of a 16-year-old princess

At the beginning of the 19C, Princess Krishna Kumari of Udaipur, reputed for her beauty, was promised in marriage to the maharaja of Jodhpur, but he died before their engagement was announced. The young girl's father, Maharana Bhim Singh, betrothed her to the heir prince of Jaipur. However the brother of the deceased maharaja felt he had a claim on the beautiful Krishna and demanded his due. There followed a succession of conflicts, including the siege of Jodhpur by the army of Jaipur, in 1808. Finally the maharana received an ultimatum from the pair of suitors: both promised peace if he was granted the princess's hand, war if he was thwarted. Confronted with this insoluble problem, the princess decided to silence the source of the conflict: she locked herself into Chitran ki Burj and swallowed a lethal poison prepared by her ladies-in-waiting.

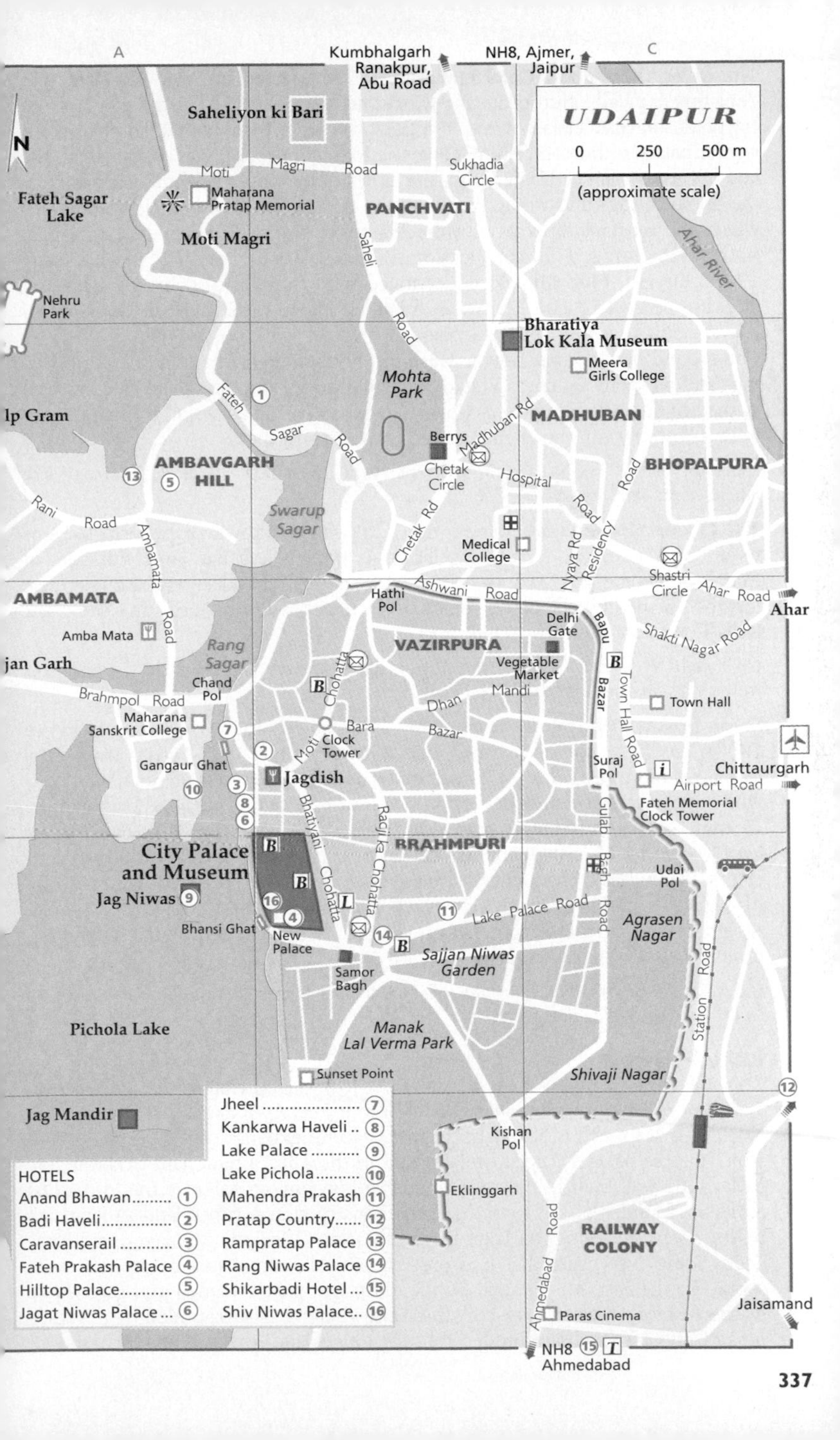
UDAIPUR
0
250
500 m
(approximate scale)
Kumbhalgarh
Ranakpur,
Abu Road
NH8, Ajmer,
Jaipur
Saheliyon ki Bari
Moti Magri Road
Sukhadia Circle
Maharana Pratap Memorial
Fateh Sagar Lake
Moti Magri
PANCHVATI
Saheli Road
Ahar River
Nehru Park
Bharatiya Lok Kala Museum
Meera Girls College
Mohta Park
Fateh Sagar Road
MADHUBAN
Madhuban Rd
Berrys
Chetak Circle
Hospital Road
BHOPALPURA
AMBAVGARH HILL
Swarup Sagar
Rani Road
Ambamata Road
Chetak Rd
Medical College
Nyaya Rd
Residency Road
Shastri Circle
Ahar Road
Ahar
AMBAMATA
Ashwani Road
Hathi Pol
Delhi Gate
Amba Mata
Rang Sagar
VAZIRPURA
Vegetable Market
Shakti Nagar Road
Chohatta
Bapu Bazar
Town Hall Road
Town Hall
Chand Pol
Brahmpol Road
Dhan Mandi
Maharana Sanskrit College
Bara Bazar
Clock Tower
Moti Chohatta
Gangaur Ghat
Jagdish
Suraj Pol
Chittaurgarh
Airport Road
Fateh Memorial Clock Tower
Bhatiyani Chohatta
Rajji ka Chohatta
Gulab Bagh Road
BRAHMPURI
City Palace and Museum
Jag Niwas
Udai Pol
Lake Palace Road
Agrasen Nagar
Bhansi Ghat
New Palace
Samor Bagh
Sajjan Niwas Garden
Station Road
Pichola Lake
Manak Lal Verma Park
Sunset Point
Shivaji Nagar
Jag Mandir
Kishan Pol
Eklinggarh
RAILWAY COLONY
Ahmedabad Road
Paras Cinema
Jaisamand
NH8
Ahmedabad
HOTELS
Anand Bhawan 1
Badi Haveli 2
Caravanserail 3
Fateh Prakash Palace 4
Hilltop Palace........... 5
Jagat Niwas Palace ... 6
Jheel 7
Kankarwa Haveli .. 8
Lake Palace 9
Lake Pichola 10
Mahendra Prakash 11
Pratap Country...... 12
Rampratap Palace 13
Rang Niwas Palace 14
Shikarbadi Hotel ... 15
Shiv Niwas Palace.. 16

The gallery next door, **Chini Mahal** (18C), is covered in Delft porcelain tiles depicting typically European and Christian themes, such as the Flight from Egypt. A staircase leads down to the floor below, to **Moti Mahal**, another extravagant palace of mirrors. **Bhim Vilas**, the following room, was decorated in the late 18C by *Maharana* Bhim Singh, the father of the brave Krishna Kumari. Note the fine paintings illustrating the life of the god Krishna, which adorn the lodge where the *maharana* appeared before his court. **Surya Chaupar** houses a gold statue of the sun god, Surya, ancestor of the Sisodias dynasty. The neighbouring 19C courtyard, **Mor Chowk,** is decorated with mosaics of coloured glass and strutting peacocks *(mor)*. The walls of **Manak Mahal** (1620) feature lavish decorative motifs in semi-precious stones.

The ground floor rooms, now a **museum**, house collections of miniature paintings and weapons. There is Pratap Singh's armour, weighing over 75kg, as well as the armour belonging to his horse, Chetak, which features an elephant trunk intended to mystify the enemy's steeds – and scare them.

Leave the palace and go into the first courtyard on the right. A door decorated with murals leads into the Queen's Palace.

The Queen's Palace *(same entrance ticket)*, otherwise known as the *zenana*, seems more sober than the former dwellings. It nonetheless has large numbers of murals and some lovely views over Lake Pichola. The collections of miniatures, together with those of palanquins and carriages, without forgetting the 1922 Rolls Royce, are the most interesting.

Go back to the main courtyard (Raj Angan) and to the rear, on the right. Go under the railings leading into the palace of Fateh Prakash.

Fateh Prakash Palace, the work of *Maharana* Fateh Singh (ruled from 1884 to 1930), has been partially turned into a luxury hotel *(see "Making the most of Udaipur")*. It is remarkable for its enormous **durbar hall** (reception room), adorned with superb crystal chandeliers and portraits of former sovereigns. Upstairs, the **Crystal Gallery** museum *(another ticket is necessary, which can be purchased in the hotel lobby)*, has an exceptional collection of crystal objects and furniture: armchairs, tables, beds, chandeliers… *Maharana* Sajjan Singh ordered them in 1877 from Osler's of Birmingham. However, the unlucky ruler was never able to admire his wonderful treasure, because he died before the shipment arrived from Britain.

Leave Fateh Prakash Palace through a door which leads directly to Lake Pichola. A road leads down to the landing stage.

Lake Pichola*

30min or 1hr boat rides around the lake leave from Bhansi Ghat. 10am-12noon/2pm-5pm from October to March; 8am-11pm/3pm-6pm from April to September.

Udaipur owes much of its charm to this peaceful expanse of water strewn with white marble palaces. Legend relates that in the 15C, a merchant of the region had a little wall built in the river to enable his convoys to cross the ford. Udai Singh II, founder of the town, had the construction fortified and other dams built thereby enlarging the lake. Despite its size (12sqkm), the lake is not very deep. Some even claim that it is possible to walk across just before the monsoons. To the east, it is flanked by the old town: palaces, *haveli* and *ghat* where washerwomen come and wash clothes. Elsewhere, it is surrounded by a wilderness of hills in which are hidden hunting lodges and fortifications in ruins.

Jag Niwas Island (A4) (1.5ha) is entirely taken up by a **palace**, whose white marble walls seem to grow out of the water – or sink into it – in perfect osmosis with the liquid landscape. The blinding whiteness of the palace seems to acquire a little of the dreamlike, changeling qualities of water. Dream or mirage? Was this incredible baroque extravagance the result of a spell? Will it disappear when the enchantment comes to an end?
It was however the work of man – and not of fairies – when in 1746 a crown prince had it built as a pleasure palace, to capture the lake's breezes and entertain amorous conquests. The **Lake Palace** is now a luxury hotel, *(see "Making the most of Udaipur")* but only hotel residents or restaurant clients can venture onto its banks.

Jag Mandir Island (A5) has another **palace**, smaller but just as charming. Built in 1620, it was enlarged some 20 years later. Twice it served as a refuge, first in 1623-24, for the future Shah Jahan, who had rebelled against his father, Emperor Jahangir, then again for Udaipur's English families in 1857 during the Mutiny: the *maharana* was said to have had all the town's boats destroyed in order to prevent the rebels from pursuing the foreigners and massacring them. The palace, built around an imposing round tower, has several fine sculptures, particularly the white elephants standing guard.

Outside the town walls

Allow a maximum of 3hr by taxi.

Lake Fateh Sagar* was created two centuries after Lake Pichola, in 1678. After floods destroyed the dam in the late 19C, it was rebuilt by *Maharana* Fateh Singh. To the south of the lake, there is a **botanical garden** on a little island *(Nehru Park, access by boat from Moti Magri jetty)*.

Moti Magri (A1) *(7.30am-7.30pm, entrance charge)*, supposedly a pleasure garden, has lost much of its charm due to the hordes of Indian tourists who have adopted the habit of driving through it. Built in terraces against the hillside, it is overlooked by a **memorial to Maharana Pratap Singh** astride his legendary Chetak, and has some fine views over Lake Fateh Sagar.

Saheliyon ki Bari* (garden of the maids of honour) (B1) *(north of Moti Magri, open from dawn to dusk)* is a delightful walled garden with all the charm of yesteryear. Designed in the early 18C for the ladies of the court, it was rebuilt under Fateh Singh (late 19C). It has a pool complete with a whole array

Statue of the goddess Gauri in Lake Pichola

B. Brillion/MICHELIN

of fountains: spurting from the trunks of four marble elephants or a fine mist of rain dropping off a *chhatri* in the centre of the pool. At the top of the dome, there is a metallic bird, whose wings were formerly made to flap by an internal device.

Indian museum of popular arts* (Bharatiya Lok Kala Museum) (B2) *(9am-6pm, entrance charge, extra fee for cameras and videos)* has interesting collections devoted to Rajasthan's folklore and arts: musical instruments, costumes, jewellery, paintings and statues depicting scenes of rural life. Some evenings, the museum puts on dance performances *(enquire at the office)*.

Excursions

Ahar* (direction of C3)

3km east of Udaipur. Archaeological excavations carried out in this village have revealed the existence of a city dating back to 2000 BC and belonging to the Indus civilisation. More recently, Ahar was the capital of the Guhilot clan before they moved to Chittaurgarh.

In a park (undergoing restoration), twenty or so **royal cenotaphs** were built on the spot where the Sisodias sovereigns were cremated. Each white marble dome houses the *linga* of Shiva, together with a commemorative plaque in honour of the *maharana* for whom the *chhatri* was built and that of his wives who committed *sati*.
A little further on, objects discovered during the excavations in this 4 000 year old city are exhibited in the **museum** *(10am-4.30pm; closed Friday, entrance charge)*.

Shilp Gram (in the direction of A2)

5km to the west of Udaipur, by the road which runs alongside Lake Fateh Sagar. 11am-7pm, entrance charge. This craft village, set in a pleasant hilly landscape, was inaugurated by Rajiv Gandhi in 1989. It presents **crafts** and **traditions** of four western Indian states: Rajasthan, Gujarat, Maharashtra and Goa. The overall impression is rather contrived, but the reconstructions of **rural dwellings** are nonetheless worth a look: they include tribal huts of the Thar Desert, the Rann of Kachchh or homes of fishermen from Goa. In the winter, some craftsmen put on demonstrations-sales in the park. A **museum** has a collection of traditional objects, musical instruments, tools, costumes, etc.

Sajjangarh (Monsoon Palace) (in the direction of A3)

8km to the west of Udaipur, at the top of a steep hill. Take a taxi at dawn or dusk. The palace is closed to the public, but a tip to the caretaker may open up part of this edifice. This fortified late-19C palace owes its name to *Maharana* Sajjan Singh who began its construction. This was finished by his successor, Fateh Singh, who often came here during the monsoon to seek refuge from the town's humid climate. The marvellous view over Udaipur and its lakes from the top of the hill (or the palace), amply justifies the effort of the excursion.

T. Bognar/LA PHOTOTHEQUE SDP

Fresco painted on a house for a wedding

Making the most of Udaipur

Getting there

By plane – ***Maharana Pratap Airport*** (or Dabok Airport) lies 25km to the east, ☎ (0294) 65 54 53. There is no shuttle service and a taxi costs around 200Rs. Alliance Air, subsidiary of Indian Airlines, has one daily flight to Delhi (2hr), via Jaipur (40min), and 1 flight, three times a week to Delhi, via Jodhpur (40min). Jagson Airlines flies to Jaipur (1hr) and Delhi (2hr30min) four times a week. Check the timetables which are subject to frequent changes, bookings also need to be made well ahead.

By train – ***Udaipur City Railway Station*** is a peaceful little, almost deserted station, in the south-east of the town, not far from Station Rd (C5), ☎ 131 or (0294) 41 29 84. Computerised reservation terminal, 8am-8pm, Sunday 8am-2pm. Tourist information desk, platform n° 1, open when trains arrive. Daily, 1 evening and 1 morning departure for Delhi (19hr and 22hr30min), via Chittaurgarh (3hr30min), Ajmer (8hr30min and 11hr) and Jaipur (12hr and 15hr). 1 express leaves every evening Udaipur for Dungarpur (4hr) and continues on to Ahmedabad, while a local (slow) train takes 12hr to get to Jodhpur!

By bus – ***Main Bus Stand***, Udai Pol (C4), ☎ (0294) 58 41 91. Reservations, 8am-1.30pm/2pm-9pm. 8 or 9 "Silver Line" buses go daily to Ajmer (7hr30min) and Jaipur (9hr30min). One stops at Chittaurgarh (3hr), another at Bhilwara. 4 luxury buses also go to these two towns. Every day, 2 luxury buses leave for Delhi (17hr), 4 for Jodhpur (7hr), via Ranakpur (2hr), for Kota (10hr), for Mount Abu (6hr30min), 3 via Ranakpur. There is also one bus for Bikaner (12hr) and, early in the morning, for Dungarpur and Banswara. Departures all day long for Eklingji (45min), Nathdwara (90min) and Lake Rajsamand (1hr45min). ***Private bus*** companies go to all the main destinations. Tickets on sale from the numerous shops and agencies around Jagdish Temple (B3).

Getting about

By rickshaw – A 2km trip costs around 15Rs. Allow 40Rs per hour in Udaipur and 170Rs for a return trip to the Monsoon Palace.

By taxi – Taxi rank on Chetak Circle (B2), as well as at the railway and bus stations. For excursions, enquire at your hotel or at a travel agents for cheaper rates.

Car rental – Enquire at your hotel or at a travel agents. Allow at least 1 100Rs per day.

Bicycle rental – Enquire in the old town.

Address book

Tourist office – ***Tourist Reception Centre***, Fateh Memorial, Suraj Pol (C3), ☎ (0294) 41 15 35. 10am-1.30pm/2pm-5pm; closed Sunday. Information, plans and brochures, together with a list of guesthouses and guides. It is possible to ask them to make bookings for RTDC excursions and visits. Information desk at the airport.

Banks/Money – In addition to large numbers of authorised exchange bureaux, there are several banks in the old town which can change cash and travellers' cheques:
Bank of Rajasthan, Moti Chohatta (B3). The entrance is through a garage. Can change dollars and pounds sterling all year round.
Vijaya Bank, in the City Palace grounds, to the right of the first gate (B4).
Thomas Cook, Comfort Travels & Tours, in the City Palace grounds (B4). Every day 9.30am-5.30pm.
LKP Merchant Financing, Lake Palace Rd, opposite Rang Niwas Palace Hotel, shop nos 3/4, (B4). 10am-5pm; closed Sunday.
Outside the old town, ***Bank of Baroda***, Town Hall Rd (C3), accepts travellers' cheques and bank cards.
To receive money from abroad in just a few hours, contact ***Western Union***, see the DHL agency (address below).

Post Office/Telephone – ***GPO***, Madhuban Rd, Chetak Circle (B2). 10am-5pm; closed Sunday. Other post offices in town: ***Shastri Circle Post Office***, Shastri Circle (C2), poste restante and philately services; ***Udaipur City Post Office***, Moti Chohatta (B3); ***Rang Niwas Post Office***, Radji ka Chohatta (B4); ***City Palace Counter***, in the City Palace (B4), stamps only. Postal code: 313001. Express mail by ***EMS Speed Post***, in post offices, or via ***DHL***, Shri Nikitan Building, 380 Ashok Nagar, Ahar Rd, ☎ (0294) 41 29 79 and 41 43 88. 9.30am-6.30pm; closed Sunday. To send and receive faxes: ***Central Telegraph Office***, GPO, open 24hr a day. Internet connections available around Jagdish Temple (B3) and ***Comfort Travels & Tours***, in the City Palace grounds (B4). Daily 9.30am-5.30pm.

Health – ***Ambulances***, ☎ 102 and (0294) 233 33. ***Udaipur Hospital***, Gulab Bagh Rd, opposite Udai Pol Rd (C4), ☎ (0294) 42 03 22 and 42 19 00. Private clinic.

Safety – ***Police***, ☎ 100. ***Fire brigade***, ☎ 101.

Travel agents – ***RTDC***, Kajri Hotel, Shastri Circle (C3). The Rajasthan State agent organises daily visits of the town (8am-1pm; 60Rs) and excursions in the region of Udaipur. Taxi and car rentals.
Travel Corporation India (TCI), Lake Palace Rd, opposite Rang Niwas Palace Hotel (B4), ☎ (0294) 52 22 39, Fax (0294) 52 23 07. High quality agency with reasonably priced car rental rates.
Travel Plan, Garden View, Lake Palace Rd (B4), ☎ (0294) 52 46 88, Fax (0294) 41 02 13. Organises guided walks and reasonably priced car rentals.

Airlines – ***Air India***, Janta Travels, Air Palace Building, shop n° 3, Nyaya Rd (C2-3). 9.30am-1pm/2pm-5.30pm, Saturday 9.30am-2pm. ***Indian Airlines***, Nyaya Rd, opposite Air India, ☎ (0294) 41 09 99 and 41 49 31. Daily 10am-1pm/2pm-5pm. ***Jagson Airlines***, Chetak Circle, behind the cinema (B2), ☎ (0294) 52 65 64 and 59 95 12.

Where to stay

Udaipur's hotels are often full and accommodation should be booked well ahead. During the low season, the hottest months from April-May to June, a 25 % discount is often possible.

• **Around the City Palace**

This is the heart of the city's tourist and historic centre. Some of the smaller establishments require rooms to be vacated by 10am.

Under US$7

Badi Haveli Hotel, Jagdish Chowk, ☎(0294) 41 25 88 – 12rm. 2rm with bath. A rather uninviting cul-de-sac leads the way to this house, with inner courtyard and terraces, inhabited by the same family since the 17C. Basic comfort, but pleasant and friendly. Ask for room n° 5 (frescoes). Classical music concerts on Saturdays. Take a sleeping bag in the winter because there is no heating.

Lake Ghat Guest House, 4/13 Lalghat, behind Jagdish Temple, ☎ (0294) 52 16 36 – 22rm. This rather old-fashioned four-storey building has two terraces overlooking the lake. All the rooms have windows, but they could be more comfortable. The higher up the establishment, the more expensive the rooms and the more "sophisticated" the bathrooms.

From US$7-15

Jheel Guest House, 52 and 56 Gangaur Ghat, ☎ (0294) 42 13 52 – 16rm. 5rm without bath. The rooms are in two buildings which are located on either side of the road. The more modern one built overlooking the lake is by far the most pleasant. The rooms are bare, but clean, the more expensive have a balcony and a wonderful view. A few rooms are available from US$3-4.

Mahendra Prakash Hotel, Lake Palace Rd, ☎ (0294) 42 20 90 and 52 29 93 – 14rm. Cooler. A rather disorganised, but friendly, hotel, with an inner courtyard and vast lawn. A few rooms from US$3-4.

Raj Palace Hotel, 103 Bhatiyani Chohatta, ☎ (0294) 41 03 64 and 52 70 92, Fax (0294) 41 03 95 – 27rm. CC 4rm. with cooler. A totally white building set in a shady courtyard full of plant pots. All that remains of the 18C haveli is the portal. The rooms are airy and well-looked after; the least expensive are the best value for money.

From US$15-30

Caravanserai Hotel (Heritage Hotels Association), 14 Lalghat, next to Lake Pichola, ☎ (0294) 41 11 03 and 52 12 52 – 24rm. CC This well-kept hotel unfortunately lacks charm. Minimal decoration and rooms which can be noisy because of the fanlights opening onto the corridor. Half of them have a view of Lake Pichola and AC, ask for those on the corner of the building (no 21, 31 and 43). Also has twelve rooms under US$15 with bath and fan.

Kankarwa Haveli, 26 Lalghat, ☎ (0294) 41 14 57, Fax (0294) 52 14 03 – 14rm. CC This handsome 19C family haveli is set on the banks of the lake. The rooms have recently been tastefully renovated. Several have a direct view over the lake. 2 rooms under US$15 with bath and fan.

Lake Pichola Hotel, slightly off the beaten track, on the north bank of Lake Pichola, ☎ (0294) 41 12 65, Fax (0294) 41 05 75 – 25rm. TV CC Cooler. Bar. 15 rooms with loggia and a superb view of the lake and the City Palace. Unfortunately the rooms are dishevelled and poorly kept. Could definitely do with some renovation.

Jagat Niwas Palace Hotel, 24-25 Lalghat, ☎ (0294) 42 01 33 and 42 28 60, Fax (0294) 52 00 23 – 21rm. CC This 17C dwelling stands right by the lakeside. Cool, well-cared for rooms, located around two inner pleasant, lively courtyards. Most of the "deluxe" rooms overlook the lake (ask for n° 101). 2 rooms under US$15 without bath but with fan.

Rang Niwas Palace Hotel (Heritage Hotels Association), Lake Palace Rd, ☎ (0294) 52 38 90/91, Fax (0294) 52 78 94 – 24rm. 8rm. with cooler. Bar, billiards. Built around 1880, this residence, the property of a member of the royal family, has two buildings which are situated on either side of an attractive garden. Its former charm is partially intact, with original tiles, Anglo-Indian furniture, old engravings and artefacts. It has six AC suites, together with four rooms for smaller budgets with bath and fan, and a dormitory. Excursions to Ranakpur and Kumbhalgarh.

Over US$70

Fateh Prakash Palace Hotel (HRH Group), City Palace, ☎ (0294) 52 80 16 to 19, Fax (0294) 52 80 06; bookings in Delhi and Udaipur (see p 107) – 16rm. Bar. This elegant establishment, recently transformed into a hotel, was one of the palaces of the City Palace. Dating from the early 20C, it is decorated in an Anglo-Indian style and has a pleasant cosy, intimate feel. Superb miniature paintings and a wonderful view of the lake, though the rooms are rather cramped.

Shiv Niwas Palace Hotel (HRH Group), City Palace, ☎ (0294) 52 80 16 to 19, Fax (0294) 52 80 06; bookings in Delhi and Udaipur (see p 107) – 34rm. Bar, billiards. Next door to the above in a magnificent late 19C palace. Ideal, providing one stays in one of the four "small suites" overlooking the lake, or in one of the nine "royal" suites, because the other 17 rooms, while spacious and decorated with beautiful miniatures of the Mewar School, are windowless!

Lake Palace Hotel (The Taj Group), Jag Niwas, Lake Pichola, ☎ (0294) 52 79 61/62/63, Fax (0294) 52 79 74; bookings in Delhi, Jaipur (see p 107) – 84rm. Bar, shopping arcade. Accessible by boat from Bhansi Ghat, this fabulous white marble palace seems to float on the lake like a mirage. It has unfortunately lost much of its former charm having chosen to adopt a more antiseptic international atmosphere. The least expensive rooms do not overlook the lake and only some have a view of the palace. 16 suites. Book well in advance.

• Around Lake Fateh Sagar

From US$15-30

Rampratap Palace Hotel, Fateh Sagar Lake, ☎ (0294) 52 87 01, Fax (0294) 52 87 00 – 24rm. A recent hotel, built in the style of a haveli, located on the banks of the lake. The "deluxe" rooms have a loggia and are quite perfect – spacious, tastefully decorated and airy – but the standard, ground floor rooms leave much to be desired. Excursions to Chittaurgarh, Ranakpur.

Anand Bhawan Hotel (Rajasthan State Hotels Corporation), Fateh Sagar Rd, ☎ (0294) 52 30 18/19 and 52 32 56, Fax (0294) 52 32 47 – 22rm. Bar. This palace was built in 1926 on a hill to receive the guests of the maharana. Its spacious verandas provide a lovely view of the lake and are perfectly secluded, but the rooms are somewhat dilapidated and dusty and the service is not all it could be.

From US$40-70

Hilltop Palace Hotel, 5 Ambavgarh, Fatehsagar, ☎ (0294) 52 19 97/98/99, Fax (0294) 52 51 06 – 65rm. Bar, shopping arcade. Built on top of a hill, this modern, luxury hotel is equipped with all the modern facilities an international traveller could desire at a reasonable price. Most of the rooms have a superb view of the lake and the surrounding landscape.

Over US$140

Laxmi Vilas Palace Hotel (Ashok Group), Fateh Sagar Rd, ☎ (0294) 52 97 11 to 15, Fax (0294) 52 55 36 and 52 62 73, lvp.hotel@gems.vsnl.net.in – 55rm. Cooler. Bar. A handsome 19C palace, just next door to Anand Bhawan Hotel, it was also built to receive guests of the royal family. Comfortable rooms, although not all have a lake view. 30 % discount from April to September.

• South of Udaipur

From US$7-30

Pratap Country Inn, 6km south-east, on the road to Jaisamand, Titardi, ☎ (0294) 58 31 38, Fax (0294) 58 30 58 – 18rm. Those who are looking for a decidedly rural, sporting environment and who would like to try horse-riding Rajput style, will love this place. Telephone when you arrive in town and they will send transport. A few more expensive rooms with cooler.

From US$40-70

Shikarbadi Hotel (HRH Group), 4km to the south on the N.H.8, Goverdhan Vilas, ☎ (0294) 58 32 01/02/ 03, Fax (0294) 58 48 41; bookings in Delhi and Udaipur (see p 107) – 34rm.

The South

This establishment provides an opportunity to stay on the royal stud farm, in the heart of the countryside where the wildlife roams almost unfettered (deer, boar...). Comfortable rooms, decorated "safari" style. Three suites in the royal pavilion and nine comfortable, less expensive, tents, only available in the winter. 50 % discount for single travellers and 30-50 % discount for all from April to September.

Where to eat

• Near the City Palace

There is no dearth of eating-places in the centre of Udaipur, which like Jaisalmer and Pushkar, abounds in roof-top café-restaurants with views of the lake. Most cater primarily to tourists and are open from 8am to 10.30pm. Pleasant, but not necessarily wonderful food: ***Roof Garden Cafe***, on Lake Palace Rd (B4), ***Lake Shore Hotel***, on the banks of Lake Pichola, next to Lake Pichola Hotel and opposite Gangaur Ghat (A3) and ***Sunset View Terrace***, on Lake Palace Rd, above the landing stage with a full 360° view of the City Palace and the lake (A-B4); 11am-7pm in winter, 3pm-5pm in summer.

From US$3 to 4

Rang Niwas Palace Hotel, Lake Palace Rd (B4). 7am-10.30pm. Visitors may be surprised by the restaurant's rather offhand decoration in what is otherwise such a pleasant hotel, but the Rajasthani food is quite delicious. Try the "lamb sula" (lamb kebabs with cloves) – order 3 hours ahead.

Berrys, Chetak Circle (B2), ☎ (0294) 52 51 32. 9am-11pm. "Multi-cuisine" restaurant catering to a middle-class clientele. Non-existent decoration but impeccably clean. House specialities of "butter chicken" and tandoori fish in tomatoes.

Samor Bagh, Lake Palace Rd (B4). 8am-11pm. This restaurant serves relatively ordinary tandoori and southern Indian food, but the spot is very pleasant and the tables and parasols are laid out on a vast tree-lined lawn. At 8pm, percussion "jal taranga" concerts on receptacles filled with water.

Jagat Niwas Palace Hotel, 24-25 Lalghat (A-B3). 8am-10.30pm. On a lovely terrace, overlooking the lake, this establishment serves delicious food. Arrive early because it is one of the pleasantest spots in Udaipur and one of the most popular.

From US$4-7

Paantya, Shiv Niwas Palace Hotel (B4). CC 6am-11pm. Not to be missed! The inner courtyard, a semicircle around a white marble swimming pool, is splendid and the cost of a meal is most reasonable. Candle-lit dinners and sitar concerts in the evenings. Quite magical, if a little formal. In the room overlooking the lake, it is possible to order from the menu, but around the pool, only a buffet is available. Try the speciality: "safed maans" (lamb in cashew nuts) quite delicious!

From US$7-15

Jharokha, Lake Palace Hotel (B4). CC Open 24 hours a day. Menu or buffet. Non-residents must book in the morning. Fresh, white decoration with touches of blue, multifoil arches. Exceptional view of the lake and the City Palace. Excellent chicken tikka with mint.

Neel Kamal, Lake Palace Hotel (B4). CC 7.30pm-10.30pm. More sophisticated than its neighbouring coffee shop. Serves Indian and Western dishes, including two quite superb specialities: "machli jaisamandi" (fish in a green sauce) and "lasanti tikka" (chicken tikka in garlic).

• Out of town

From US$3-4

Shilpi, Rani Rd, 5km to the west, next to Shilp Gram. 11am-11pm. A visit to Shilip Gram should include a pause in this open-air multi-cuisine establishment, which can serve up to 200 guests on terraces, overlooking a garden with swimming pool.

Cheetal, Shikarbadi Hotel, 4 m to the south. CC Rajasthani cuisine served on the lawn. A pleasant, relaxing meal in a countryside atmosphere, surrounded by wildlife. From 5pm, high tea is served.

WHERE TO EAT, HAVE A DRINK

The Gallery, Fateh Prakash Palace Hotel (B4). 🍸 CC 6am-11pm. A good way of discovering this magical setting without spending a fortune is to come between 3pm and 5pm for an afternoon cream tea, or from 11am to 11pm for a beer or a cocktail. Take a seat in the gallery which runs the full length of the adjacent impressive durbar hall, and has several alcoves overlooking the lake. The red velvet upholstery and muted atmosphere give the impression of being in a theatre box.

Paanera, Shiv Niwas Palace Hotel (B4). 🍸 CC 11am-11pm. Silk-upholstered sofas, royal portraits, crystal lampshades and antique carpets are all set in a sumptuous cream and turquoise colour scheme. Visitors can admire the wonderful vivid colours of the inlaid glass friezes. Loggia with view of the town. Exceptional in every respect.

PASTIMES

Theatre – *Meera Kala Mandir*, Hiran Magari, near the Paras Cinema (C5), ☎ (0294) 58 31 76. Folklore dancing performances from 7pm to 8pm; closed Sunday and from May to July. 60Rs.

Bharatiya Lok Kala Mandal, 400m north of Chetak Circle (B-C2), ☎ (0294) 52 92 96. Good quality puppet shows. From 6pm to 7pm, from September to March. 40Rs.

Shilp Gram, Rani Rd, 5km to the west. 9am-11am/5pm-7pm. Folklore performances.

Sports – *Swimming pools*. Some hotels allow non-residents to swim in their pools, such as Mahendra Prakash and Rang Niwas Palace (110Rs).

Riding. Enquire at the following hotels: Jagat Niwas Palace, Rang Niwas, Pratap Country and Shikarbadi (see "Where to stay"), and at the Rajmahal Bhindar, at Bhindar (see p 353).

HOLIDAYS AND FESTIVALS

Baneshwar Fair, at Baneshwar temple (70km to the west of Dungarpur). Three days before and after the January-February full moon, the festival of Mahadeva (Shiva) is one of the most important festivals in the Bhils calendar.

Rishabdev Festival, at Rishabdev. Lasting two days in March-April, Jains, Vishnuists and Bhils all celebrate Rishabdev (assimilated to Adhinatha), the first Jain tirthankara.

Mewar festival. Takes place during Gangaur festival (March 28-29 2001), a procession to the goddess (Parvati) takes place on Lake Pichola.

Annakut, at Nathdwara. The day after Divali (October-November new moon), the Bhils celebrate Krishna as herdsman; this is the only day of the year when they are allowed into the temple.

EXCURSIONS

Travel agents and hotels all put on various types of day trips to the region around Udaipur. For ***Ranakpur*** and ***Kumbhalgarh***, expect to pay around 1 000Rs for 9hr with a private car, and 220Rs by RTDC bus (8am-7pm). The RTDC organises daily trips to ***Haldighati***, ***Nathdwara*** and ***Eklingji*** (2pm-7pm, 90Rs), and another to ***Jagat***, ***Jai Samand*** and ***Rishbdeo*** (8am-7pm, 220Rs). To get to ***Chittaurgarh***, allow 1 000Rs for 9hr with a private car or 235Rs by RTDC bus (8am-6pm).

Excursion to the villages – All the hotels in and around Udaipur can organise a visit to the Bhil, Rawat, Banjara and Kalbeliya villages.

Walking – If you would like to go walking in the Aravalli Range, enquire at ***Travel Plan*** (see "Travel agents"). 1 500Rs per day per person (group of 5 to 9 walkers), with tent accommodation and luggage transported by van.

Riding hikes – Wonderful rides with accommodation in luxury palace hotels or in 4* tents are organised by "Maharaja" Narendra Singh Mewar across Rajasthan (from 3 to 20 days, 4 100Rs per day). Contact the ***Pratap Country Inn*** (see "Where to stay"). The ***Royal Equestrian and Polo Centre***, at Dundlod, organises rides leaving Udaipur for Jodhpur or Chittaurgarh (see "Making the most of Shekhawati").

SHOPPING

The most modern shops are on Bapu Bazaar (C3), and all the fruit and vegetable markets are around Dan Mandi (C3). The craft shops are concentrated around the City Palace and Jagdish Temple (B3-4), and on Lake Palace Rd (B4).

Crafts – "Kawad" (small portable wooden temples), commemorative earthenware plaques from Molela (north of Udaipur), brightly-coloured clay toys and all other local crafts are on sale (with price tags) at ***Rajasthali***, 2 Jagdish Temple Square, and 1 Chetak Circle.

Gas Ghar, City Palace Rd, on the corner of Bhatiyani Chohatta. A shopping arcade, located in the City Palace's former garages, specialising in high-quality arts and crafts..

Cottage Industries Exhibition (CIE), in the City Palace courtyard (B4). A gallery run by the State of Kashmir with shawls, carpets, embroidery. Not very local…

Shilp Gram, Rani Rd, 5km to the west. In what is supposed to the reproduction of a genuine village, craftsmen sell products from the States of Rajasthan, Gujarat and Maharashtra.

Paintings – "Pichhwai" from Nathdwara, "phad" from Bhilwara and above all miniatures from Udaipur on paper, silk or false ivory are on sale in shops, most of which claim to be "schools of art"; keep your wits about you and begin bartering. Most can be found around the City Palace, primarily on Lake Palace Rd.

Rajputana Art, Dilwara House, Lake Palace Rd (B4). In addition to the stereotyped pieces tourists expect, this establishment makes an attempt to present more original works of art.

Ashoka Art Palace, Shivrati Palace, 122 Ambamata Rd (A3), ☎ (0294) 52 16 74. A real school of miniature painting which sells works produced by its teachers.

Fabric and clothes – Fabric by the metre and "juti" (slippers) can be found in the stalls in Bara Bazaar.

Nagda, 59 Gadiya Devra, Chand Pol (A3). The only designer boutique in town. GK Kapoor designs clothes which are made of hand-woven silk. Collection of antique turbans.

Beauty care – ***Biotique***, 14 Bhatiyani Chohatta (B4). The largest brand of Indian body care products made from plants. Ayurvedic massages.

Hibtula Abdul Ali, 38 Bara Bazaar (B3). Traditional perfume essences ("ittar").

Bookshops – ***Mayur Book Paradise***, 60 Bhatiyani Chohatta (B4). Excellent range of books on Rajasthan and India, new and second-hand novels, good quality postcards.

AROUND UDAIPUR★

See map p 318

Not to be missed

The temples at Nagda and Eklingji.
Rishabdev temple.
Dungarpur palaces.

And remember...

Rent a car with a driver for two days.
Visit the area to the north of Udaipur one day and the area to the south the next.

North of Udaipur

140km round trip. Allow a day.

This round trip will take you from temple to temple in a pastoral landscape of hills and lakes: from tiny shrines covered in undergrowth and shrouded in silence to bustling, lively pilgrim centres. When driving through the countryside, visitors may catch a glimpse of Indian rural life, with herds of buffalo blocking the road, brightly-dressed peasant women bringing home wood or gigantic jars of water on their heads, laughing groups of boisterous school children on their way to and from some distant classroom, barefoot, but in uniform.

Leave Udaipur by the road to Ajmer. 20km further on, to the north of a little lake, turn right onto a narrow, rocky road which after 2km, reaches Nagda.

▪ **Nagda**★★ – All that remains of this 7C city are a few deserted temples, standing on a platform almost hidden by vegetation, in a landscape of gently undulating hills. Dedicated to Vishnu, these shrines date back to the 10C. The main two are called "Sas-Bahu" or "mother-in-law *(Sas)* and daughter-in-law *(Bahu)*" in reference to the queens that had them built. They still have elegant

Nagda

C. Bourzat

sculptures of a charming world of divinities, dancers, *mithuna* (entwined lovers), musicians and animals. The **mother-in-law's temple** *(to the left)*, the largest and the most richly decorated, has a lobby, a hall with a transept and inner shrine (*garbha griha*). Next door, the **daughter-in-law's temple**, seems less extravagant, except for its graceful **torana** (archway).

Continue on the road to Ajmer for 4km, until you reach the village of Eklingji which lies alongside the road.

■ **Eklingji**** – This little terraced village carved into the hillside of a rocky valley, is renowned for its **Shivaite temples** *(in the main street, on the right. 4am-7am/10.30am-1.30pm/5.30pm-8pm. No photos. Leave your shoes at the entrance)*. **Bappa Rawal**, the founder of Chittaurgarh in the 8C, is said to have followed the words of a hermit who advised him to devote his dynasty to the god Shiva in his form as Eklingji (Lord of the linga). Since that time, the *maharana* have considered themselves to be the *diwan* (prime minister) of the god of Eklingji and every Monday, the day devoted to Shiva, the current *maharana* comes to Eklingji to carry out *puja* (worship). The temples – of which there are said to be 108 – devoted to the 108 aspects of Shiva, stand next to one another. Walk through the first courtyard, where flower merchants sell garlands of carnations to be offered to the gods. Inside, the **inner courtyard** has a multitude of temples, some of which are tiny. To the rear, on the left, stands a shrine dedicated to **Vishnu***, built by Princess Mira Bai, a 16C mystical poet, who was completely devoted to Krishna (one of Vishnu's incarnations). The entrance to the **temple of Eklingji** itself is via the central avenue. *Maharana* Raimal Singh had it erected in the late 15C on the exact site of the original shrine built by Bappa Rawal. A preceding pavilion houses a bronze statue of **Nandi**, Shiva's vehicle, like the linga, a symbol of the god's regenerative powers. It is possible to join the pilgrims as they crowd in through the shrine's silver doors. Inside, in semi-darkness, stands the four-headed black marble statue of Shiva-Eklingji.

The figure 108, from Nataraja to the Virgin Mary

The figure 108 (9 times 12) crops up frequently throughout India. In the temple to Shiva Nataraja (king of dance) at Chidambaram (Tamil Nadu) there are statues of Shiva representing the 108 dance positions. Some groups of Vishnuists recite their mantras in series of 108. The "rosaries" have 108 pearls and the Jain "tirthankara" had 108 virtues... Further west, in the Middle Ages, groups of gypsies from India rekindled ancient local rites similar to those devoted to Shiva, which had been forgotten or assimilated by Christianity. The most spectacular of these is the cult of the "Black Virgins", who are related to Kali, the "Black One". The figure 108 continued its voyage through history. In 1996, during the ceremonies celebrating the christening of Clovis, traditionalist Catholics organised a procession of 108 statues of the Virgin Mary. Many pious Hindus would have felt quite at home during such a ritual.

Return to the road to Ajmer. 24km further on, you will reach the little town of Nathdwara.

■ **Nathdwara*** – In 1691, Emperor Aurangzeb decided to destroy all the Hindu temples within his territory. This prompted the *maharana* of Udaipur to move a particularly sacred statue of Krishna to Mathura (Uttar Pradesh) under the name of **Shri Nathji**, in order to remove it from Aurangzeb's destructive wrath. However the cart transporting the idol is said to have got stuck in the mud here. Attempts to free it from the mire failed, and it was decided to build a shrine at Nathji, since it was here that the divinity himself had chosen to come to rest. The festival atmosphere and the elaborate rituals surrounding the statue, rather than the beauty of the **temple** itself, whose vast white walls are covered in modern paintings *(no photos)*, make the pilgrimage to Nathdwara worthwhile. At 4pm, the *darshan* (vision) takes place, when the statue is unveiled, sparking off a collective emotional reaction among the pilgrims. Nathdwara is also famous for its wall-hangings (*pichhwai*, literally "that which is behind"), which hang behind the statue of Krishna. Formerly embroidered or printed, nowadays they are painted *(see p 74)*.

Continue towards Ajmer. 16km further on, take the right-hand fork, before Lake Rajsamand, to the village of Kankroli, 2km away.

▪ **Kankroli and Lake Rajsamand*** – The artificial lake at Rajsamand, created in the 17C by *Maharana* Raj Singh 1st, lies amidst a hilly green landscape. To mark the completion of the lake in 1671, the sovereign had a shrine built to Krishna (under the name of Dvarkadish) in the village of Kankroli. The **temple's** white walls are covered in recent **murals**. The few tourists venturing this far are always warmly welcomed. The best time to visit the shrine is at the time of the *darshan* at 4pm. To the right of the temple, a corridor and stairs lead down to the **banks of the lake**. Pilgrims come here to bathe, while jovial washerwomen gaily beat clothes clean.
On the hill overlooking Kankroli is an 18C **Jain sanctuary** built by the Prime Minister Dayal Shah *(Return to the main street and proceed to the central crossroads, near the stalls selling tea and doughnuts, and turn right)*. The 250-step climb up to the temple is well worthwhile for the splendid view of the lake.
Finish your visit on the **dam,** with a view of the *ghat*, complete with decorative *torana* (archways) and *chhatri*.

South of Udaipur

285km round trip (225km without Lake Jaisamand). See map p 318.
Allow a day, or two half-days, with a night at Dungarpur Palace.

The road to Ahmedabad (capital of Gujarat) winds its way through a network of progressively less dense hills as you get further from Udaipur. In addition, as the border with Gujarat approaches, road signs appear in Gujarati, a language close to Hindi and written with an alphabet similar to that of *devanagari* (used in Hindi and Sanskrit), but without the familiar line linking the letters into words.

65km from Udaipur, turn left and take the road (signposted) to the village of Rishabdev.

▪ **Rishabdev**** – This Jain pilgrimage site is devoted to Adinatha, the first of the 24 *tirthankara* (wise "ford passers"), who is also called Rishabdev and is worshipped both by Jains and by Hindus.

The Bull god

The "Bhagavata Purana", a sacred text with the list of the 22 incarnations of Vishnu (most standard lists only feature 10), holds King Rishabha to be the eighth incarnation of the god. Rishabha was the son of Meru (the mountain situated in the centre of the world) and of Nabhi (the navel of the world). To show his sons how to attain wisdom, he relinquished his kingdom and lived as a hermit, inflicting bodily chastisement on himself to such an extent that all that remained of him were "skin and nerves". Worshipped under the name of Rishabdev, the "bull god" (from the Sanskrit "vrishabha") he is always shown in the company of this animal. As the bull is also the vehicle of Shiva, many Hindus identify Rishabdev with Shiva.

The latter, true to their syncretic traditions, frequently worship at places held sacred by other religions; they identify Rishabdev's Adinatha as one of Vishnu's incarnations. As for the Bhils, they call the god Kalaji or Kala Baba, the "Black".

This 15C **temple** stands in the heart of the town, in a colourful **bazaar** from which cars are banned. The entrance to the courtyard passes through a gate guarded by two elephants *(Remove your shoes and any leather article. No photos)*. The temple's **outer walls** are covered in ornate carving, while **inside,** in the inner shrine, is a black marble statue of Rishabdev. To the right of the shrine is a small altar dedicated to the Hindu god, Ganesha. The pilgrims pause before each statue, placing rose petals before them and anointing the nine sacred points of the body (large toe, knee, navel...) with a finger dipped in saffron and sandalwood paste.

Continue on the road towards Ahmedabad for 27km. At Khairwara, turn left to Dungarpur (25km).

■ **Dungarpur★★** – This peaceful city, founded in the 13C by the oldest branch of the **Sisodias** dynasty, sprawls around a lake, amidst a hilly wilderness. The capital of an independent kingdom, it was too far removed from the main trade routes to have experienced the same development as Udaipur and still has a provincial feel to it. Its Rajput fort, 18C palace and lively bazaar make it ideal for tourists in search of "traditional India".
On the lake, part of which is now a bird sanctuary, the graceful white marble pavilions of a temple to Shiva seem to float on the water's surface. On the banks, the 18C **Udai Bilas palace★★** is the residence of the royal family *(most of it is now a luxury hotel, see "Making the most of Udaipur")*. In the centre of the courtyard stands an incredible baroque edifice, **Ek Thambia Mahal** (the "pillar-palace"), a strange sort of ornate extravaganza, whose walls are completely covered in carved, elaborately worked arcades, awnings, *jharoka*, and *chhatri*.

A fresco from Juna Mahal palace at Dungarpur

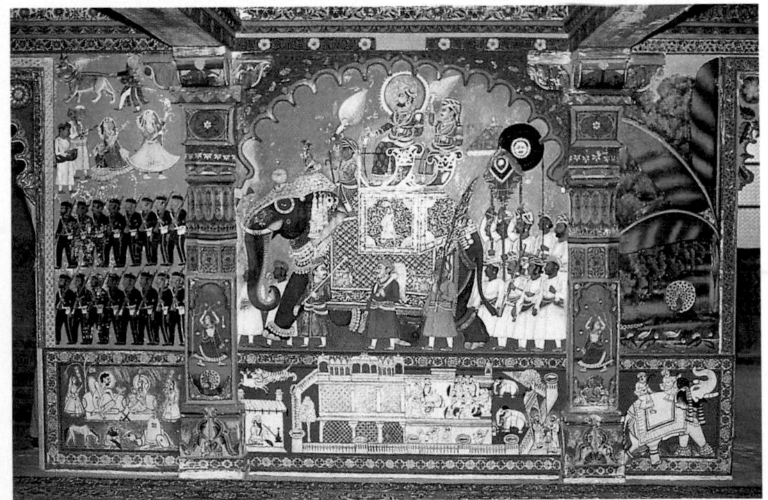

S. Held

Perched on the neighbouring hilltop, **Juna Mahal Palace**** *(entrance charge, tickets can be purchased at the reception of Udai Bilas Palace, guided tour)* has an austere external appearance, and, when it was first built, in the 13C, had an essentially military role. However behind its typically severe Rajput **façade** are hidden some wonderfully vivid **mural decorations****. A spacious, ornate **Durbar Hall** (reception hall) takes up the entire ground floor. On the walls, hunting scenes vie for pride of place next to episodes of the life of Krishna, the blue god. The sovereign's velvet throne still sits on the enormous carpet over which hang the multi-coloured reflections of lamps imported from Belgium. One can almost imagine that musicians, seated in the boxes around the sides, are going to begin playing... The fort's **five storeys** contain a thousand surprises and treasures, particularly the finely executed mural paintings, whose inspiration and vivid colours never cease to enchant modern-day visitors. In one of the first floor rooms there is a portrait of Queen Victoria painted on a gigantic wooden fan. The adjacent room has a superb mosaic of mirrors, another a collection of China plates. The palace also has other well-hidden secrets. Among them is a cupboard in a dark corridor on the top floor, lined with drawings depicting a pornographic strip cartoon.

Go back onto the road to Udaipur. Some 10km after Rishabdev, a road forks right towards Lake Jaisamand (signposted).

▪ **Lake Jaisamand** – *Maharana* Jai Singh had this vast expanse of water created in the late 17C amidst an unspoilt landscape of hills and forests, inhabited by deer. The dam is adorned with *ghat* and *chhatri* guarded by statues of elephants.

Making the most of the Udaipur area

For travel arrangements, addresses and festivals, see "Making the most of Udaipur" p 341.

Where to stay

• Nagda

20km to the north of Udaipur, on the N.H.8.

From US$40-70

Heritage Resorts, Nagda, ☎ (0294) 44 03 82 and 52 86 28, Fax (0294) 44 03 82 and 52 75 49 – 28rm. Half-board. This hotel is extremely well-located, overlooking Lake Bagela, in a wonderful landscape of green, sloping hills, close to the temples. The restaurant is open to non-residents.

• Nathdwara

50km to the north of Udaipur, on the N.H.8. Turn left on leaving Nathdwara, towards Lal Bagh.

From US$7-15

Hotel Gokul (RTDC), Nathdwara, ☎ (02953) 309 17 – 6rm. Cooler. Bar. This fine 19C dwelling, set in an exuberant garden, has large, well-kept rooms. Dormitory.

• Devgarh

135km to the north of Udaipur, on the N.H.8.

From US$40-70

Devgarh Mahal (Heritage Hotels Association), Devgarh, ☎ (02904) 525 55, Fax (02904) 527 77, devgarh@jp1.vsnl.net.in – 26rm. 9rm. with cooler or AC. Life in this impressive 17C castle takes place around the central courtyard where the "Rawat" family entertain their guests in a sophisticated atmosphere. The dining room and some of the rooms have original frescoes. Buffet open to non-residents.

• **Bhindar**
60km to east of Udaipur. Take the road to Chittaurgarh and turn right to Bhatewar, towards Kheroda and Bhindar.

From US$15-30

Rajmahal Bhindar (Heritage Hotels Association), Bhindar; bookings in Udaipur, ☎ (0294) 56 01 34 – 10rm. A small four-storey 17C Rajput castle. The decoration is somewhat unequal, but the place definitely has a lot of character. Advance booking advised.

• **Bambora**
55km southeast of Udaipur, on the road to Chittaurgarh. At Debari, turn right towards Bambora.

From US$40-70

Karni Fort, Bambora, ☎ (0291) 322 20 and 63 93 80, Fax (0291) 334 95 – 30rm. TV CC Bar. This 18C fort, perched on a hilltop in the heart of the countryside, was almost completely renovated in 1998. The rooms, decorated in a rather flashy Rajput style, are too expensive. 25 % discount from April to September. Rajasthani restaurant open to non-residents.

• **Dungarpur**
100km to the south of Udaipur, on the N.H.8, then towards Indore.

From US$40-70

Udai Bilas Palace (Heritage Hotels Association), Dungarpur, ☎ (02964) 308 08, Fax (02964) 310 08 – 18rm. The "maharawal" courteously welcomes guests to his 19C-20C palace, which stands on the banks of the lake, not far from the bird sanctuary. Three wings, added in 1940, surround an ornately and profusely carved main building. Most of the spacious, tasteful rooms, are decorated in an Art Deco style. 10 % discount from May to September.

A small Shivaite temple in the shade of a Banyan tree

CHITTAURGARH★★

Pop 72000– Alt 408m
115km from Udaipur – 320km from Jaipur
See map p 318

Not to be missed
The impressive fortress, its "tower of victory" and the temples and palaces in ruins.

And remember...
Do the visit in an auto-rickshaw.

The only claim to fame of this dusty town on the Mewar plateau is its fort, but what a fort! Overlooking the lower town and the whole region from a ridge some 160m-high, and surrounded by 12km of walls, the **former Mewar capital**, today deserted, is the largest citadel in Rajasthan. It has superb vestiges of Chittaur's former grandeur and tragic history. Despite its invincible aspect, it actually fell into enemy hands three times. Three times, it was the scene of gruesome **jauhar**, which illustrates how fiercely independent the Rajputs were. In the late afternoon, the golden rays of the setting sun add an almost romantic aura to these deserted ruins. This spell is further enhanced by the glimpse of a group of women, flitting past a ruined palace, mysteriously hidden behind their *orhni*, transporting visitors back in an instant to the era of Princess Padmini or the glorious Rana Kumbha.

Jauhar and Rajput pride
Aware that their fort was soon to be taken by the besieging Moslems, the fort's women and children threw themselves into the flames of an enormous fire. Then the soldiers, dressed in saffron-coloured robes, covered their faces with the ashes of the deceased and, drunk on opium, launched a suicidal counter attack.

Glory to the defeated

The powerful Sisodias dynasty – The foundation of Chittaurgarh dates back to the 7C, to Chittrang, chief of the Moris clan. In the next century, the fort was captured by **Bappa Rawal**, of the oldest branch of the Sisodias, who were to reign over Mewar until 1947 *(see "Udaipur", p 335)*.
The fort's strategic importance and powerful presence soon attracted the envy of the sultan of Delhi, Ala ud-Din Khilji, who was the first to claim Chittaurgarh. According to legend, he was in love with Princess **Padmini**, wife of the ruler of Chittaur. The siege led to the first *jauhar*.
The 15C was marked by the reign of **Rana Kumbha**, who encircled his kingdom with some thirty fortresses, including that of Kumbhalgarh. His grandson, **Rana Sanga**, led the Rajput coalition which attempted to drive the invader, Babul, the first Mughal, out of Rajasthan, but he died at the defeat of Khanwa (1527). Less than ten years later, the sultan of Gujarat, Bahadur Shah, seized Chittaur, provoking the second *jauhar*.

In Mughal hands – It was however the might of the Mughals which was to sign the fort's death warrant. Emperor **Akbar** launched a merciless siege on the town. While warriors, women and children sacrificed themselves rather than surrender to the Moslems, *Maharana* **Udai Singh II** managed to flee. He established a new capital at Udaipur, in the shelter of the Aravalli mountains, but he dreamt of reconquering Chittaur. Neither he nor his son, the brave **Rana Pratap**, succeeded. In the early 17C, Emperor Jahangir took control of the region and returned Chittaurgarh to the Sisodias. The latter preferred to remain in Udaipur and never returned to the heroic fort.

The citadel

From dawn to dusk, entrance charge. Allow 2hr with an auto-rickshaw.

The 15C road to the east entrance of the fort leads up a steep slope, through **seven gates**. Between the second and third gates (Behru Pol and Hanuman Pol), two *chhatri* commemorate the sacrifice of **Jaimal and Patta**, two 15- and 16-year-old Rathore warriors, who died heroically defending the fort during the siege of 1568 and who became the heroes of local ballads. The last gate, **Ram Pol** (1459), decorated with bas-relief friezes in the manner of a temple, leads into the citadel.

Just after the ticket office, the road reaches Rana Kumbha Palace.

Rana Kumbha Palace** dates back to the 14C and 15C but the last two sieges more or less destroyed it. There however remains a **façade** with balconies and *chhatri*. From the road, a small door opens onto the first floor, formerly the princess's quarters and a staircase leads down into a pretty park. On the left stands the palace's main gate, **Tripolia**, embellished with three domes. Ruins of the stables for the elephants and horses can be seen in the courtyard. All that remains of the **Diwan-i Am** (public audience hall) is a hypostyle hall. The fort's former glory becomes apparent as one walks through the buildings, linked by austere staircases and corridors.

On the other side of the road, some 200m away is Fateh Prakash palace.

Built in the early 20C, by *Maharana* Fateh Singh, **Fateh Prakash palace** *(10am-4.30pm; closed Friday, entrance charge)* is of minor architectural interest. Inside, a somewhat disappointing museum has Hindu statues of the Middle Ages, a collection of weapons and a few royal portraits. Right alongside, an ornately carved 11C **Jain temple** is dedicated to Adinatha, the first of the 24 *tirthankara*.

The following Hindu shrines, on the same esplanade, are more worthy of interest.

Kumbha Shyamaji temple*, built in the 15C on the foundations of a 9C temple, is dedicated to Varaha (Vishnu's incarnation as a boar). It is preceded by a small pavilion housing a statue of **Garuda**, Vishnu's winged vehicle. **Mira Bai temple*** was built in memory of a famous 16C princess, wife of the heir prince of Chittaur, who devoted her life to Krishna. Renouncing the luxury of court life, Mira wrote numerous poems in honour of her god, many of which are still extremely popular nowadays, and are masterpieces of *bhakti* (divine worship) *(see p 190)*. The sanctuary's remarkable **circular hall** is preceded by *chhatri* built to Mira's guru.

The stately outline of the nine storeys (37m-high) of the **tower of Victory**** (Jaya Stambha), built in the form of a richly carved pillar *(stambha)*, can be seen from far around. Erected around 1460, it celebrates the victory of Rana Kumbha over the sultan of Malwa (in southeastern Rajasthan). **Sammidheshvara temple**, a Shivaite sanctuary restored in the 15C in the same park, has some fine sculpture and houses an interesting three-faced *linga*.

The neighbouring esplanade, **Maha Sati,** was where the sovereigns of Chittaur were cremated, as well as being the scene of *jauhar*. **Lake Gaumukh**, just to the south of the tower, owes its name to the "cow's head" fountain. The surrounding **palaces** are all in ruins. The austerity of the architecture is striking with severe façades hardly relieved by the presence of a number of balconies with kiosks.

Some 300m further on is a temple dedicated to Kali, now the meeting-place of the local monkeys.

The temple to Kali (destructive incarnation of Devi) was formerly dedicated to Surya (the sun god). It is said to date back to the 8C, or in other words to the era when the Sisodias built the fort. Restored in the 14C, it has some fine carved pillars.

The road leads to the lake, where Padmini Palace, restored in the 19C, is reflected in the water.

Padmini Palace* (early 14C) is said to be where Ala ud-Din caught sight of the princess's reflection in one of the mirror's chambers. Captivated by her briefly glimpsed beauty, he did not rest until he captured Chittaur. The palace is composed of gardens (the former men's quarters) and the zenana.

The southern part of the fortress is only of minor interest, and you should go up the road along the eastern ramparts.

Suraj Pol, an impressive, well-restored gate, leads onto the paved ramp which provided access to the fort until the 15C. Below lies the plain, scene of so many bloody battles. Further to the north is the 12C **tower of fame***. Erected by a Jain merchant in honour of Adinatha, it is embellished with a large number of statues of the 24 *tirthankara*. At its feet is a small **temple** devoted to the first "ford passer".

Making the most of Chittaurgarh

GETTING THERE

By train – *Chittaurgarh Railway Station* is in the southeast neighbourhood of the town, some 7km from the fort, ☎ (01472) 401 31 and 410 09. Non-computerised reservations desk, 10am-12noon/12.30noon-5pm; advance booking only for Jaipur and Delhi, one hour in advance for other destinations. 3 daily express trains to Jaipur (8hr30min-10hr), the fastest of which is the night train "Chetak Express" which continues on to Delhi (16hr). 4 daily departures to Ajmer (5-7hr) and 2 for Udaipur (4hr30min). Every day, trains arrive in the mid-morning from Kota (4hr30min), via Bundi (3hr30min), returning in the early afternoon.

By bus – *Roadways Bus Stand*, City Rd, between the station (3km) and the fort (4km), ☎ (01472) 411 77. Reservations centre, 10am-5pm. No "Silver Line" buses leave from Chittaurgarh, but you can always take the one which runs daily from Jaipur to Udaipur. Fifteen express buses, including 3 luxury buses, for Jaipur (8hr), via Ajmer (5hr). Ten to Udaipur (2hr30min) and Kota (5hr), half of which stop at Bundi (4hr). 7 to Jodhpur (7hr) and 1 or 2 to Mount Abu (9hr30min), Nathdwara, Dungarpur.

GETTING ABOUT

Most of the tourist attractions are situated within the fort, on top of the ridge, to the east of the town. As a complete tour of the site is at least 7km long, a vehicle is recommended.

By auto-rickshaw – From the station or bus stop, allow around 100Rs for a complete tour of the fort.

By taxi – There are two taxi ranks in town: one at the railway station, the other opposite the bus station. Most drivers have a tendency to quote unrealistic prices and it is often a good idea to enlist the help of your hotel. For an excursion to Bassi and Bijaipur, allow 400Rs for 4hr.

Bicycle rentals – Bicycles can be rented near the station for around 20Rs per day. Ideal to visit the fort, once you've got up the steep slope!

Address book

Tourist office – ***Tourist Reception Centre***, Station Rd, ☎ (01472) 410 89. 10am-1.30pm/2pm-5pm; closed Sunday. A list of guides and guesthouses.

Banks/Money – ***Bank of Baroda***, Fort Rd. Can change cash (dollars and pounds sterling only) and – in principle – carry out withdrawals with a bank card.

State Bank of Bikaner and Jaipur, near the Collectorate. Changes travellers' cheques.

Post Office/Telephone – ***GPO***, Shri Gurukul Rd. 10.30am-5.30pm; closed Sunday. Express mail via ***EMS Speed Post***. Postal code: 312001.

Health – ***Ambulances***, ☎ (01472) 411 02. ***Jainani Hospital***, near the bus stop, ☎ (01472) 402 72. Private clinic. ***Chemists***: on Station Rd, around the General Hospital.

Safety – ***Police***, off City Rd, ☎ (01472) 400 88 and 410 60.
Fire brigade, ☎ (01472) 411 01.

Where to stay

Most of the hotels are located to the north of the station, at quite a distance from the old town and the fort. Chittaurgarh itself offers very little in the way of accommodation. If possible, plan on staying in Bijaipur.

• Chittaurgarh

From US$7-15

Panna Hotel (RTDC), Udaipur Rd, ☎ (01472) 412 38 – 30rm 20rm. with cooler or AC. Located in a quiet neighbourhood near the railway station. Dilapidated bathrooms, poor ventilation, and hot water in basins for the cheaper rooms. Dormitory. A few rooms available under US$7. The hotel organises visits to the fort every day at 8am and 3pm.

Pratap Palace Hotel, Bijaipur House, near the GPO, ☎ (01472) 435 63, ☎ and Fax (01472) 400 99 – 12rm. Cooler. Undoubtedly the best address in town, even if the rooms are poorly decorated, badly looked after and very noisy. The reception area remains noisy until late in the night and the bar attracts large numbers of visitors. Good cooking and a garden.

• Bijaipur

40km to the north-east of Chittaurgarh. Take the direction of Bundi then, 2km after Bassi, turn right to Baroli; 2km further on, turn right again, Bijaipur is 12km away.

From US$15-30

Castle Bijaipur Hotel (Heritage Hotels Association), Bijaipur, ☎ (01472) 762 22; bookings, ☎ (01472) 435 63, ☎ and Fax (01472) 400 99 – 12rm. This little castle, with a countrified charm and relaxed atmosphere, belongs to the owner of the Pratap Palace at Chittaurgarh. Renovated in 1998, its rooms have retained their vaults, columns and frescoes (crudely repainted), but the rooms are not all decorated in the same style, and some have somewhat antiquated furniture in not very good taste. Excursions by jeep, horse or camel back.

Where to eat

Under US$3

Ritu-Raj Vatika Restaurant, near the police station, ☎ (01472) 418 46. 8am-11pm. A popular establishment serving "pure veg" north and south Indian cooking and a wide choice of "lassi". The lawn is an attractive feature. Very pleasant when the music isn't too loud.

Hotel Pratap Palace, same address as the hotel. 7am-10.30pm. The restaurant serves tasty north Indian cooking, but the decoration lacks charm or taste and the tablecloths are often dirty. It is possible to eat in the garden. The hotel bar which overlooks the restaurant is noisy and the constant to-ing and fro-ing makes evenings there rather tiresome.

Shopping

Crafts – The town's bazaar has some interesting examples of crafts, but all the wooden toys and statues of Gangaur and Isar are carved and painted in the village of Bassi (25km to the north-east). Here, it is possible to see the local craftsmen at work and purchase directly from them.

BUNDI★★

Pop 90000– Alt 515m
160km from Chittaurgarh – 280km from Udaipur
See map p 319

Not to be missed
The Chitra Shala and its murals.

And remember...
Walk through the bazaar to discover the "baori".

Forgotten in a pass between two hills, overlooked by a fort and an impressive palace, Bundi quietly goes about its day-to-day activities, off the main tourist track. This little town has preserved its character and the medieval charm of its architecture, its bazaar and its **baori** (stepwells) – some of the finest in Rajasthan – and the frescoes which adorn the royal quarters.

A faithful Mughal ally

Bundi's birth as capital of an independent State dates back to 1342, when Deva Singh, a Rajput chieftain, forged himself a kingdom, to the detriment of the local Meena and Bhil tribes. Deva Singh called his kingdom Haravati, which later became **Hadoti**, the "kingdom of Hara". The new *rao* belonged to the **Hara** branch of the **Chauhan** clan – one of the four Rajput clans born out of the Fire, who founded Ajmer and reigned for a time over Delhi.

The *rao* of Bundi were the first sovereigns, after the *raja* of Amber, to pledge allegiance to the Mughals in 1569. This brought them a semblance of peace with their neighbours, freedom of religion and, from time to time, imperial favours, such as being nominated governor of Delhi, a singular distinction for a Rajput. However, little by little, Bundi's importance dwindled, outstripped by its neighbour, **Kota,** which had withdrawn from the alliance in the early 17C and as a result has undergone continuous expansion ever since.

The town

Allow half a day.

The palace★★

The palace of Bundi's *rao* consists of terraces of austere, sober buildings, built in the early 17C against the hilly slopes in a pure Rajput architectural style. No concession appears to have been made to the new architectural concepts introduced by the Mughals.

Within the palatial complex, a paved ramp leads through two gates: **Hazari Pol** (gate of the thousand), close to which the garrison was stationed, and **Hathi Pol**. Guarded by two elephants, whose outstretched trunks form an arch of welcome, the gate opens onto a section of the royal quarters, decorated with paintings. Unfortunately, they are in a state of neglect, victims of a legal wrangle between the *rao* and his sister, the former having sold the palace to a hotel chain against the wishes of the latter. In theory, the palace cannot be visited, but a few hotels organise private visits *(see "Making the most of Bundi")*. Only Chitra Shala is officially open.

Frescoes in the palace

Take the path up to the left (with your back to Hathi Pol) to Chitra Shala. A caretaker is generally on duty at the entrance or somewhere close by. He rarely misses an opportunity to open the building and earn a small tip.

Built by *Rao* Ummed Singh (1760-1773), the **Chitra Shala** (house of paintings), or Ummed Mahal, is located to the rear of an overgrown park, inhabited by an impressive band of monkeys. The rooms opening onto the patio are adorned with some remarkable 18C and 19C **frescoes**** depicting scenes from mythology, courtly life, hunting parties, or *raga* (melodies) and their corresponding emotions – which they express and provoke. Note the scenes depicting various episodes of Krishna's life, his exploits and his games with the shepherdesses *(gopi)* in the forest of Vrindavan.

The Bundi school of painting

Bundi's "kalam" reached its apogee in the 17C. Its distinctive miniatures and frescoes are renowned for their strength, depth and vivid colours. The figures' faces, whether in profile or face-on, stand out from a background alive with an abundance of detail; the forests swarm with wild creatures, the rivers teem with fish, ducks and lotus flowers. In the 18C, the backgrounds became simpler, adopting a single colour, green or red, sometimes enhanced with gold paint.

Leaving the Chitra Shala, take the path *(20min hard walk)* up to **Taragarh fort**. The path runs alongside the ramparts, through ruins and bushes and the undisputed kingdom of its armies of monkeys (take a stout stick). These impressive 14C ramparts were further reinforced by bastions at the four corners. The highest, **Bhim Burj**, served as a platform for an enormous cannon, the mere sound of which sufficed to strike fear into enemy hearts. If the weather is fine, the **view** extends as far as Kota. Within the ramparts, amongst the ruins, is a reservoir hollowed out of the rock. When the monsoon rains fill it to the top, an alert is given and its valves are opened, pouring the overflow down through the town's deserted streets.

Walk through the town*

Bundi is still relatively free of traffic, even its southern modern district. Take advantage of this rare occurrence and walk around, observing the inhabitants going about their daily business.

The main road, which comes down from the palace through the **old bazaar** (A2) has a few dilapidated *haveli*. Note how the houses were raised above the street level to escape the water pouring down from Taragarh reservoir and pause for a minute before the three small **temples** on the edge of the street. The first, **Lakshminatha**, is dedicated to the goddess of prosperity, Lakshmi. The inner shrine of the second houses a statue of **Jagannatha** (divinity identified with Vishnu or his incarnation Krishna), similar to the famous temple of Puri, in Orissa. The last temple, **the temple of Charbujh**, the most colourful, is covered in garish modern paintings, reflecting the religious fervour and love of the marvellous of many modern Indians.

As one descends, the stalls become more and more numerous. Jewellers, tailors and grocers work side by side shops blaring out film musical tracks or religious chants, to the accompaniment of deafening blasts of *tabla* or sweeping strings. Further down, vast displays of aluminium or beaten copper pots and pans – a speciality of the region – used to store and transport lentils, milk or other victuals indicate that you are approaching Thatera Market, the ironmongers' quarter.

Leave the old town through **Chogan Pol**, decorated with pretty paintings, to admire two pretty **baori** (stepwells). **Nagar Sagar Kund***, the first, has two symmetrical reservoirs, adorned with decorative *chhatri*.

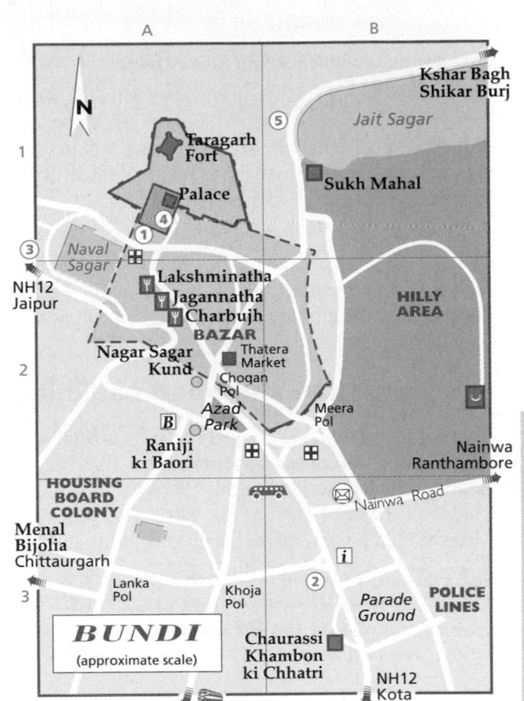

HOTELS
Haveli Braj Bhushanjee ①
Ishwari Niwas............... ②
Raj Mahal Palace.......... ③
Royal Retreat................ ④
Vrindawati (RTDC)........ ⑤

Continue along the main avenue southwards, for around 200m, to what is the finest *baori* built in the town over the last four centuries: **Raniji ki Baori**** **(Queen's well)** (A2), ordered in the 17C by *Rani* Nathavati. In a land such as Rajasthan where water is rare, digging a well for the community was a pious act. The queen had 21 built at Bundi, including this one. Sadly, the *baori's* staircase, adorned with delicately carved arches *(torana)* and statues of gods and incarnations of Vishnu, is partly disfigured by a railing. Bundi has several other stepwells and reservoirs that visitors can discover as they wander around the town.

Go to the south of the town by auto-rickshaw (which you should reserve to continue on the north of the town). Along the avenue which branches off to the right, just before the railway track, you will reach the "cenotaph of 84 pillars" (some 2km from the centre).

Built in the late 17C, to the memory of Dev Gurjar Singh, foster brother of one of Bundi's *rao*, **the 84 pillared cenotaph*** (Chaurassi Khambon ki Chhatri) (B3) has two distinctive storeys, one on top of the other. The first houses a *linga* (phallic symbol of Shiva) and a painted ceiling depicting heavenly creatures, elephants, warriors, fish, etc.

To the north of Bundi

The romantic white marble **Sukh Mahal*** (palace of pleasure) (B1), set in a pleasant park, is reflected in the waters of **Lake Jait Sagar**. Rudyard Kipling stayed here and is said to have written his poem "The last sati". Follow the path, through the park, to the ruined tower **Sukh Burj**.

Continue the lakeside road for some 2km.

Kshar Bagh* or Sar Bagh *(a caretaker will open the park's gate in exchange for a small tip)* with over 60 cenotaphs (late-16C to early-19C), was where the sovereigns of Bundi were cremated. The cenotaphs still have some fine decorations, but the vigorous undergrowth makes the visit difficult, although it does add a more romantic character to this garden of forgotten kings.

Continue the road for around 1km, as far as a small dirt track which forks off to the right. The "Hunting Tower" is slightly off the main track.

Shikar Burj, a pleasant 18C hunting lodge, features a water pool and a temple dedicated to Hanuman. Indeed, the companions of the monkey-god have colonised the spot.

On the road to Chittaurgarh

If travelling by car, don't neglect to stop at **Bijolia*** *(50km from Bundi)* where some 12C and 13C **temples** set in the heart of the countryside, outside the picturesque fortified town, await visitors. These temples constitute the last remains of Chauhan, a major city in the 10C. Two sanctuaries (dedicated to Shiva and Ganesha) have some particularly delightful and graceful sculptures.

At **Menal**** *(17km away)*, there is a complex of 12C **temples,** overshadowed by a superb shrine devoted to Shiva. Take a walk through the scattered ruins, as far as the source of the River Menal, nearby, in an impressive wooded gorge.

Making the most of Bundi

Getting there

By train – Only one train stops at the little station of Bundi (5km to the south of the town); it leaves for Chittaurgarh in the morning, returning in the evening (3hr30min).

By bus – The bus station is on N.H.12 (B3). Express buses every half-hour, including 6 "Silver Line", to Jaipur (5hr) and Kota (45min), and every hour to Ajmer (4hr). Around 6 departures to Delhi (11hr), 2 to Sawai Madhopur (4hr), 5 to Chittaurgarh (4hr) and 7 to Udaipur (8hr).

Getting about

Tourism is relatively under-developed in Bundi, and there are few hawkers, so take advantage of this rare occurrence to walk about the old town. The palace is only 20min from the bus stop (around 15Rs by auto-rickshaw).

Address book

Tourist office – *Tourist Reception Centre*, Circuit House, opposite Ishwari Niwas Hotel (B3), ☎ (0747) 226 97. 10am-5pm; closed Sunday. A list of guesthouses.

Post Office/Telephone – Nainwa Road (B3).

Health – *Sada Sukhi Nursing Home*, Indra Market (A2), ☎ (0747) 328 27. Private clinic.

Safety – *Police*, ☎ (0747) 224 25 and 224 27.

Where to stay

• In Bundi

Under US$7

Vrindawati Hotel (RTDC), to the north-east of the fort, on the banks of Lake Jait Sagar, ☎ (0747) 324 73 – 7rm. 🚿 ✕ Pleasantly secluded, it has a lovely garden and is very well-located, with a fine view of the lake, Sukh Mahal and the hills. Friendly welcome, but the upkeep is sadly in keeping with the usual low standards one expects in RTDC establishments.

From US$15-30

Braj Bhushanjee Haveli, opposite the Ayurvedic Hospital, ☎ (0747) 323 22 and 325 09, Fax (0747) 321 42 – 14rm. Cooler, boutique. In the old town, at the foot of the palace, this 19C haveli is run by the friendly descendants of several of Bundi's prime ministers. The rooms are small, but full of character and the house is decorated with large numbers of artefacts, miniatures, old photos and felt carpets from the area around Tonk. "Pure veg" meals served in a handsome dining room adorned in old frescoes or on a terrace overlooking the palace and the fort. Wide range of prices with a 15% discount from April to September. Can organise tours of the palace, including the closed sections, and excursions to the surrounding villages (potters, caves, temples).

Royal Retreat, Garh Palace, ☎ (0747) 344 26 – 7rm. Cooler, boutique. The attraction of this recent establishment lies in its location in the stables of the Royal Guard within the palace grounds. It has a spacious paved courtyard and the rooms are large and airy. The decoration is however minimal and lacks warmth. Fixed price (US$10) except for one smaller room, 20% discount from April to August. Rooms are rented for periods of 24 hours. Visits to Bundi by horse or buggy.

Ishwari Niwas, opposite the tourist office, ☎ (0747) 225 41 and 324 14, Fax (0747) 324 86 – 20rm. Cooler. Friendly, relaxed atmosphere. The rooms are decorated with crudely painted frescoes. Fixed price (US$10), 20% discount from April to July. Visit to the palace, including the closed sections, and excursions to Kota. Rooms are rented for periods of 24 hours.

• **Rajmahal**

67km to the north of Bundi. Take the N.H.12 towards Jaipur, turn left at Devli, towards Toda Rai Singh, then continue on to Rajmahal.

From US$15-30

Raj Mahal Palace Hotel (Heritage Hotels Association), Rajmahal; bookings at Narain Niwas Palace Hotel in Jaipur, ☎ (0141) 56 12 91 and 56 34 48, Fax (0141) 56 10 45 – 12rm. On the banks of River Banas, at the foot of a hill on which is perched a fort, the rustic charm of this 17C fortified residence makes a pleasant stopover on the road from Bundi to Tonk (79km) and Jaipur (160km). The rooms are spacious, tastefully decorated (with the exception of its antiquated furniture) and comfortable. Bookings essential.

Where to eat

Less than US$3

Royal Retreat, Garh Palace, ☎ (0747) 344 26. This well-run establishment serves "pure veg" cuisine from North India. Pleasant setting with a superb view of the fort and the town.

Pastimes

Excursions – Bus trips possible to ***Bijolia*** and ***Menal***, situated respectively 50km and 67km to the south-west of Bundi, on the road to Chittaurgarh (90min).

Holidays-Festivals – In August-September, on the 3rd and 4th days after the full moon, the festival of ***Kajli Teej*** features local songs and dances, as well as a procession of the goddess Teej (assimilated to Parvati) in a golden palanquin from Naval Sagar to Azad Park.

Shopping

The ***Royal Retreat*** and ***Braj Bhushanjee Haveli*** both have a Rajasthani crafts boutique in their lobby, with an excellent range of fabrics and decorative objects.

Crafts – In Thatera Market, near Chogan Pol, craftsmen produce beaten copper pots, designed to store lentils, milk and other victuals.

Kota

Pop 531 000– Alt 250m
40km from Bundi – See map p 319

Not to be missed
The palace murals.

Well-situated in a fertile plain irrigated by the Chambal (the only continuously flowing river in Rajasthan), on the main Bombay-Delhi road and railway route, Kota has become Rajasthan's leading industrial city, with chemicals, a hydro-electrical plant, and a nuclear station. It is a town of two characters: a relaxed attitude characterises its northern residential districts of the colonial era, laid out in parks and wide avenues – where the hotels are – while its southern districts reveal a busy, active get-ahead personality. Here the old town (thankfully preserved from the industrial bustle) stands next door to the modern business centre, already branded by the stigma of India's typical approach to urban development: pollution, noise, ugly architecture, billboards and garish colours. Visitors typically spend more time in the old town and the fort-palace, one of Rajasthan's largest.

Daughter of Bundi

Stronghold of the crown prince of Bundi, then of his younger brother, Kota became an independent kingdom in the early-17C, under **Madho Singh** (1625-1649). Although lacking in natural defences, the new capital expanded fast

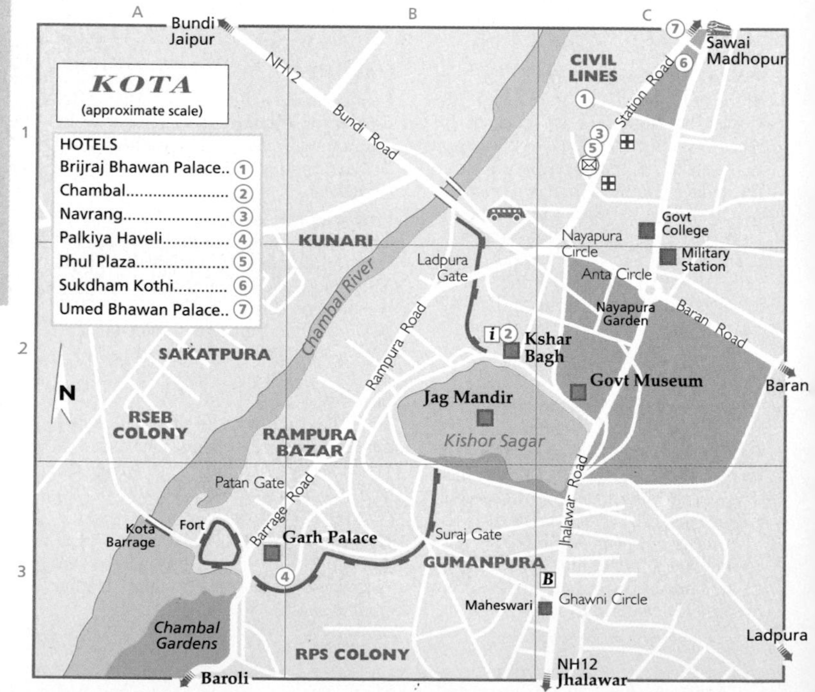

thanks to its position on the trade routes between Delhi and Gujarat and to the military and diplomatic skills of its *raja*. While Bundi remained trapped in its glorious past, Kota emerged, as early as the 19C, as the region's economic driving force.

The town

A half-day is easily sufficient.

Garh palace** (A3)

Built in the late-17C on the banks of the Chambal, which was still inhabited by crocodiles and gavials even in the 1970s, the palace has several buildings, one section of which is currently a school. Only the museum section is open to the public.

The entrance to Garh Palace is through a red sandstone door which opens onto an avenue leading into a vast courtyard. The entrance to the **Rao Madho Singh museum** *(10am-4.30pm; closed Friday, entrance charge, extra fee for cameras and videos)* is just on the right, through **Hathi Pol**, a gate guarded by two elephants, exact replicas of those at the palace of Bundi. The **Raj Mahal**, designed in the 17C under Madho Singh, provides a glittering array of colour, with mirrors edged in silver or gold, coloured-glass mosaics and above all, some wonderful **murals****, contemporaries of the most recent frescoes in Bundi palace (19C and featuring similar themes: Krishna and Radha at play, courtly life, hunting scenes... In the next room, the **Durbar Hall**, are palanquins which were carried by servants *(palki)* or by elephants *(howdah)*. Further on, is the armoury with a fine collection of sabres, together with a somewhat gruesome array of stuffed animals. The upper floor houses a rich collection of miniatures. Note the "*sadhu* tasting the joys of wine": the pious man seems just as enamoured of his pretty companion as of the liquid refreshment.

The next part of the museum is, in theory, closed, but a small extra payment will generally open the right doors. On the first floor walls are some superb **frescoes**** reproducing themes of the Raj Mahal.

Around Lake Kishor Sagar (B2)

Return to the town centre and walk along the banks of **Lake Kishor Sagar**. In the centre, the romantic 18C **Jag Mandir palace*** *(closed to the public)*, like its namesake in Udaipur, seems doomed to disappear beneath the rampant vegetation.

To the north of the lake, a pleasant, but overgrown park, **Kshar Bagh** or Sar Bagh, contains the **royal cenotaphs**, with no artistic pretensions, built on the cremation site of Kota's sovereigns.

Continue alongside the lake eastwards to the **Government Museum** (C2) *(10am-4.30pm; closed Friday, free on Monday)*. Inside are miniatures, some 9C-11C sculptures from the region, in particular from Baroli (note Vishnu reclining on the eternity snake Ananta).

Around Kota

Baroli

50km to the southwest of Kota, on the road to Lake Rana Pratap Sagar. Buses leave approximately every hour (1hr45min). Open from dawn to dusk, no entrance charge.

Located in an attractive wooded area – who could believe it was so close to a nuclear plant? – are a dozen or so of the oldest Hindu temples in Rajasthan (8C to 11C). The largest, **the temple of Ghateshvara***, dedicated to Shiva, features a graceful cluster of celestial dancing girls *(apsaras)* and entwined couples *(mithuna)*.

Making the most of Kota

Getting there

By train – *Kota Railway Station* is in an isolated part of town, to the north, far from the centre and 4km from the bus station (shuttle service) (C1), ☎ 131 and (0744) 44 11 62/64. Computerised reservation terminal, 8am-8pm, Sunday 8am-2pm. Kota is situated on the Delhi-Ahmedabad-Mumbai (Bombay) line. Daily, 7 trains to Delhi, the fastest of which is the "Rajdhani" (4hr30min) which leaves early in the morning (except on Wednesday) and stops at Mathura (3hr30min). The "Indore-Nizamuddin Express" and the "Mumbai-Dehradun Express" are slower (respectively 7hr and 10hr30min to Delhi), but they enable travellers to spend the night on board. Another day train to Mathura, the "Golden Temple Mail", also stops at Sawai Madhopur (90min) and Bharatpur (4hr). For Jaipur (3hr45min), the morning "Superfast", via Sawai Madhopur is the best option. There is also a morning train daily to Chittaurgarh (4hr30min), via Bundi (1hr), which returns in the evening.

By bus – *Roadways Bus Stand*, near the town centre (B1), ☎ (0744) 45 10 20. 6 "Silver Line" buses, from 6am to 9pm, to Jaipur (6hr), and 1 to Jodhpur (9hr). Around 7 daily services to Delhi (11hr30min), 10 to Udaipur (10hr), 5 to Ajmer (5hr) and Chittaurgarh (5hr). Departures every half-hour to Bundi (45min) and Jhalawar (2hr30min).

Address book

Tourist office – *Tourist Reception Centre*, Chambal Campus Hotel, Nayapura (B2), ☎ (0744) 32 76 95. 10am-5pm; closed Sunday. The office is in fact rarely open.

Banks/Money – *State Bank of India*, LIC Building, Chhawni Circle (C3). Changes cash (dollars and pounds sterling) and American Express travellers' cheques.

Post Office/Telephone – *GPO*, opposite MBS Hospital, Station Rd, Civil Lines (C1). 10am-5pm; closed Sunday. Poste restante, express mail by ***EMS Speed Post***, and faxes at the ***Telegraph Office***. Postal code: 324001.

Health – *Ambulance*, ☎ (0744) 45 02 41.

Safety – *Police*, ☎ 100. ***Fire brigade***, ☎ 101.

Where to stay

• Civil Lines

From US$7-15

Phul Plaza Hotel, Collectorate Circle, ☎ (0744) 32 93 50/51/52, Fax (0744) 32 26 14 – 20rm [shower] [A/C] [phone] [TV] [restaurant] [CC] 5rm. with cooler. A well-run hotel in a quiet neighbourhood, less than 1km from the bus stop and 4km from the railway station. Friendly staff. The ordinary rooms are clean, good value for money and rented for 24hr periods.

Navrang Hotel, Collectorate Circle, next to the above, ☎ (0744) 32 32 94 and 45 12 53 – 25rm. [shower] [heater] [A/C] [phone] [TV] [restaurant] [CC] Cooler. Impeccably run, this hotel has rooms painted pink or pistachio green, located on two floors around a glass-roofed patio. The top bracket rooms are rather expensive and the price is identical for one or two persons. Rooms rented for 24hr periods.

From US$15-30

Sukhdham Kothi (Heritage Hotels Association), Station Rd, ☎ (0744) 32 00 81, Fax (0744) 32 77 81 – 14rm. [shower]

The South

Located in the old colonial neighbourhood of bungalows and parks, this house, set in the grounds of a large garden, was built in 1870 as a residence for the British surgeons. Varied rooms but identical rates.

From US$30-40

Brijraj Bhawan Palace Hotel (Heritage Hotels Association), ☎ (0744) 45 05 29, Fax (0744) 45 00 57 – 7rm. The property of the British Resident up until 1900, then a palace for royal guests, this attractive white residence overlooks the Chambal and is now the home of the "maharao" of Kota. It has spacious, tastefully decorated rooms in an early 20C style. Rooms nos 1 and 6 and suites 3 and 4 are particularly delightful. The food is delicious and served under the watchful glass eyes of tigers, stags and other hunting trophies which hang in the family dining room. Coffee is served in an elegant drawing room in the company of your hosts. 30 % reduction for single travellers and 10 % discount from May to August.

From US$40-70

Umed Bhawan Palace (WelcomHeritage Hotels), Station Rd, Civil Lines, ☎ (0744) 32 52 62 to 65, Fax (0744) 45 11 10; bookings in Delhi (see p 107) – 17rm. Bar, billiards. Built by Sir Swinton Jacob in the heart of a wooded parkland, this palace is entirely decorated in Victorian style. A succession of spacious inner courtyards, corridors and galleries make it undeniably very smart, if somewhat gloomy, especially when business is slack. 40-50 % discount for single travellers. Bills to be paid in foreign currency.

• South of Lake Kishor Sagar

From US$7-15

Chambal Hotel (RTDC), Nayapura, ☎ (0744) 32 65 27 – 13rm. Cooler. Located near the lake, in a garden planted with trees. The bathrooms are recent but the rooms are neglected and devoid of all charm. Dormitory.

From US$15-30

Palkiya Haveli, Mokha Para, ☎ (0744) 32 73 75 and 32 87 97 – 6rm. A restored family haveli situated in a quiet street of the old town. The mistress of the house welcomes guests in the central courtyard, under the shade of a neem tree, an ideal spot to sit and read or have a cool drink. All the rooms are attractively decorated, with cotton fabric bedspreads and curtains from Jaipur, carpets from Tonk, pity about the antiquated furniture.

Where to eat

• Nayapura

Under US$3

Plaza, Hotel Phul Plaza, Collectorate Circle (C1). 7am-11am/1pm-3.30pm/7pm-11pm. "Pure veg" cooking from northern and southern India together with a few Chinese dishes. Minimal decoration, but the room, in the basement and windowless, is comfortable and clean. Very provincial.

Navrang Hotel, Collectorate Circle (C1). Opened in 1998, serves "mughlai" specialities, Chinese and south Indian dishes. Also in a basement and windowless.

• South of Lake Kishor Sagar

Under US$3

New Maheshwari, Chhawani Circle (C3). 8.30am-11pm. Renowned for its food, said to be the best in town, this restaurant serves "pure veg" north Indian cooking. Somewhat dreary room, but the restaurant is often full due to its location on a main road in the business district.

Shopping

Crafts – Kota's speciality is "doria sari": a very lightweight fabric (silk and cotton mixture), chequered and embroidered with fine gold thread. It can be found in Bhairon Gali in Rampura Bazaar or in the town of Khetun, where it is woven, a few kilometres southeast of Kota.

JHALAWAR

Pop 40 000 – Alt 469m
85km from Kota. – 125km from Bundi
See map p 319

Not to be missed
A trip to Jhalrapatan.

And remember…
Allow a day to see Jhalawar and its surroundings.
In October-November, go to Chandrabhaga fair at Jhalrapatan.

This sleepy, country town lies in the midst of forests, fields of poppies, and the quarries from which "Kota stone" is extracted (a bronze-coloured serpentine). In the 19C it was a flourishing economic and cultural centre. Now, ignored by tourists, Jhalawar's calm and its unusual monuments will delight all those weary of the usual tourist traps: from its amazing opera built by a music-loving sovereign, the ruins of Gagron fort or the temples of Jhalrapatan, the "city of bells", hidden behind its ramparts.

The opium trade

Without the British, Jhalawar would no doubt never have existed. It was at their instigation in the early 19C, that the sovereign of Kota designated the town of Ummedpur as capital, following the advice of **Madhan Singh Jhala**. Thanks to the enthusiasm of the new *rajah*, the city, renamed Jhalawar, rapidly grew rich due to the opium production controlled by the British. The local princes set about building a magnificent palace, inviting artists and musicians to their court, but the town's secluded position, off the main trade routes, gradually led to its decline. Nowadays it exudes a delightful perfume of faded, outmoded glory.

The town

Allow 90min.

The immense 19C **Garh Palace*** perfectly symbolises the city's former glory. Deserted by its princes, it is now the headquarters of the local administration and is steeped in a sleepy, provincial boredom. The arrival of a stranger constitutes a major distraction, and often prompts officials to take visitors on a tour of their offices, located in the former **royal apartments**. The second floor rooms still have their original murals, combining mosaics, mirrors and paintings. Mythological scenes and portraits of former rulers contrast pleasantly with the old government-issue wood furniture, swamped under mounds of mouldy files. Visitors should not miss the chance to visit the **Bhawani Natya Shala**. This opera house was built in 1921 in the courtyard of the palace by Raja Bhawani Singh, a keen music lover. With its ornate towers and multifoil arches, it is an extraordinary structure, seemingly straight out of the imagination of some capricious Italian diva, lost in India. At present, the acoustic effects of the building are heard by no-one, "neglected by the government", according to the favourite expression of local officials.

Leave by the palace's eastern door, which leads into a colourful bazaar. Anyone keen on archaeology should take a look at the museum, which is on the corner of the first road on the left.

The Government Museum *(10am-5pm; closed Friday. Entrance charge)* has a small collection of 8C-10C sculpture found in the region.

The surroundings

Jhalrapatan★★

6km south of Jhalawar. A minibus leaves the bus station every 15min.

This picturesque town, hidden behind its **fortifications**, boasts that it used to possess 108 temples (108 is a lucky number in India, *see p 349*). One can imagine what the sound of their tinkling bells used to be like, as every devout worshipper rang them on entering the shrines to attract the gods' attention. These bells are undoubtedly the reason behind Jhalrapatan's name of "city of bells". Today the little town is strewn with a few houses, painted blue. As tourists walk about they are frequently greeted and asked the ritual *"Coming from?"*, proof that very few adventure this far.

Once past the outer wall, go to **the temple of Surya★**, which is easy to recognise because of its high tower *(shikhara)*. Built in the 11C, it suffered badly from looting, but traces of its former dignity are still visible in the **hypostyle hall**, which has 52 fully-carved columns, laid out in the form of a cross. They support a flattened dome and three pavilions with awnings which were added later – making the temple look rather like a Rajput palace.

Take the lane just opposite the temple, and then turn left. Some 200m further on is the Jain temple of Shantinatha.

The temple of Shantinatha, dedicated to the 16th *tirthankara*, is surrounded by a wall on which are very garish paintings. In the centre of the courtyard are two impressive statues of elephants, with their trunks raised in greeting, obviously inspired by the temple of Surya.

Go out of the town walls and down to the banks of the sacred River Chandrabhaga, where Jain and Hindu temples, partially in ruins, mark the site of **Chandravati**, a city whose foundations are supposed to be pre 5C BC. No vestiges of this ancient site remain, of course. However the **temple of Shitaleshvara** can claim to be the oldest in Rajasthan of which the construction date (689 AD) is known for certain.

Gagron fort★

10km northeast of Jhalawar. Accessible by auto-rickshaw. No entrance fee.

The fort's romantic ruins stand in a pristine landscape at the meeting point of two rivers. Founded in the 8C by Mewar's sovereigns, Gagron was surrounded by water on three sides and a deep moat on the fourth, which didn't however prevent it from being captured three times. Each time, the fort's women carried out the terrible *jauhar* ritual, preferring to throw themselves into the fire rather than become enslaved by the Moslems. Gangron's history is not however marked only by defeats: in the early 14C, it victoriously withstood a 10-year siege, led by Sultan Ala ud-Din of Delhi.

In the middle of the ruins covered in undergrowth, the austere walls of the **old palace** can just be seen. A tottering staircase still leads upstairs, but very probably not for much longer. At the foot of the walls, a small hamlet has grown up around the tomb of a Sufi Moslem saint and a little mosque.

Chandrabhaga Fair

The cattle fair is held outside the ramparts of Jhalrapatan during the full moon of "kartik" (October-November), at the same time as the famous Pushkar fair. Not subjected to the same publicity campaigns as that of Pushkar, Chandrabhaga fair has remained totally authentic. In the midst of herds of camels, cows and horses, modest dancing performances and puppet shows provide entertainment for the onlookers. Stalls are set up, selling local crafts, knick-knacks, trimmings for camel bridles, sweetmeats, etc.

Making the most of Jhalawar

Getting there

By bus – *Roadways Bus Stand*, east of the town centre, ☎ (07432) 23 86. Buses leave for Kota every 30min (2hr30min). Several buses every day to Jaipur and Ajmer, 1 or 2 to Udaipur and Jodhpur.

Getting about

Rent rickshaws in town and hire a jeep to go to Jhalrapatan and Gagron.

Address book

Tourist office – *Tourist Reception Bureau*, Chandrawati Campus Hotel, ☎ (07432) 300 15. 10am-5pm; closed Sunday.

Post Office/Telephone – *GPO*, near the bus station.

Safety – *Police*, ☎ 100. ***Fire brigade***, ☎ 101.

Where to stay

• Jhalawar

Under US$7

Chandrawati Hotel (RTDC), south-east of Jhalawar, ☎ (07432) 300 15 – 6rm. 3rm with cooler. The best address in town (for want of anything better), located in an airy, green district.

• Shergarh

Around 50km east of Jhalawar. Take the road to Khanpur, then to Badora and turn right into Canal Road which goes to Shergarh.

From US$15-30

Shergarh Haveli (Heritage Hotels Association), Shergarh; bookings at Palkiya Haveli in Kota, ☎ (0744) 32 73 75 and 32 87 97 – 4rm. On the edge of the Sorsan bird sanctuary, overlooking River Parwan, this fortified 18C Rajput residence, complete with jharoka and multifoil arches, is ideal for those wishing to taste the romantic charm of an old-fashioned dwelling in the heart of the countryside; without running water or electricity. Bookings essential.

Holidays and festivals

Chandrabhaga Fair in Jhalrapatan, is held every year during the October-November full moon (10-12 November 2000; 29 November-1 December 2001).

C. Boisvieux/HOA QUI

Milk collection in the region of Jhalawar

8418

RANTHAMBORE NATIONAL PARK★★

7km from Sawai Madhopur – 115km from Kota – 170km from Jaipur
See map p 319

And remember...
Avoid weekends and holidays.
Visit the sanctuary by jeep.
Take binoculars and 200 or 400 asa films.

Imagine a dry forest of *dhak* ("flames of the forest") and banyan trees with, in their centre, a rocky outcrop crowned with an imposing fort in ruins. The scene is set and ready for the leading actor: Sher Khan, the lord of the jungle. With luck, you can catch a glimpse of him on the trail of a gazelle or bathing in a lake. If he fails to favour you with an appearance, the sight of stags, *nilgai* and boars will perhaps console you. There is also the possibility of exploring the ruined fort, now over-run by the jungle.
Most of the region's hotels are located out in the countryside, along the road from **Sawai Madhopur** to the park. From dusk to dawn, visitors are plunged into this unspoilt wilderness, which is undeniably one of the attractions of a visit. If given the opportunity, don't miss a visit to the outlying villages and their white-washed paintings; the local women decorate the outer walls of their mud-built dwellings with peacocks and elephants symbolising the goddess of prosperity, Lakshmi, as well as parrots, suns and, of course, tigers...

The first jauhar

Ranthambore Fort, founded in the 10C by the **Chauhan** Rajputs, is claimed to be the oldest stronghold in Rajasthan still standing, after that of Chittaurgarh. It was also the scene of the first *jauhar* in 1301, when the sultan of Delhi, Ala ud-Din Khilji, treacherously captured it after a year-long siege. All the Rajput women threw themselves into the flames, preferring death to being captured alive by the Moslems. Recaptured by the *rao* Chauhans of Bundi, the stronghold was surrendered to Emperor Akbar in 1569 almost without a struggle – the last major Rajput fort to give in to the Mughals. In the late-17C, the region fell under the control of the maharajas of Jaipur and it became one of their favourite big-game hunting grounds.

Man or tiger?

Indian environmentalists are currently faced with a dilemma since the man-tiger balance was overturned in the 1950-60s: should they promote the survival of tigers (and the forest) or that of the villagers? The creation of national parks, followed by the ban on tiger hunting (1970) and the launch of the **Tiger Project** (1973) *(see "Sariska", p 245)*, have greatly helped to protect the endangered feline... but to the detriment of the villagers living around the park lands. At Ranthambore, over 1 000 Meena peasants were expelled from their lands in order to extend the forest and the tigers' territory. Nothing was done to rehouse them. Furthermore, the peasants living around the forest's edges are growing in numbers. To find grazing for their cattle, wood for their fires or water when their village wells run dry, they have no other solution than to turn to the forest. Consequently, the forest is now receding and the villagers are forced to venture ever deeper into the forest, encroaching on the tigers' domain. Men and women are wounded, a child killed... However the peasants declare themselves willing to put up with the inconvenience of living close to a natural park, on the condition that there are at least a few compensations. They don't understand why none of them were hired by the park as guards, scouts or guides. The Ranthambore Foundation, set up in 1988 with the ambition of promoting good relations between the peasants and the tigers, has implemented various development projects, such as one aimed at replacing outdoor grazing stock by barn-fed cattle or another developing alternative sources of revenue, such as local crafts. Hope remains: the park, incorporated into the Tiger Project in 1973 and declared a National Park in 1980, only had 15 tigers when first created. It now has some 35.

From whiskers to claws

The Far East has always been partial to tigers, whether in the form of powders, lotions or other miracle remedies. An illegal traffic between Asia and India now exists that is difficult to curb: the benefits are too lucrative and the poachers too well-organised and too well-protected. It is difficult even to imagine how the park wardens themselves do not succumb to the lure of the astronomical prize money offered in exchange for a dead beast, such are their meagre salaries.

Park safaris

Two visits daily: 6.30am-10.30am and 2pm-6pm from October to March; 6am-10am and 2.30pm-6.30pm from March to June; closed from 1 July to 30 September.
See also "Making the most of Sawai Madhopur", "Address Book" and "Pastimes".

In April, when the *dhak* bursts into flower, the forest is covered in red scarlet patches. Then the torrid heat of May and June burn the dead leaves brown. This pre-monsoon period is when sightings of tigers are the most frequent: the drought makes the undergrowth less dense and forces the animals to drink at water holes created by the park's staff. What is more it is also paradoxically the

A day's shooting by the maharaja of Karoli (1930 photo)

Saola/A.Clopet/GAMMA

time when there are fewest tourists in the park's 1 330sqkm. The rest of the year visitors are likely to meet more human species than wild beasts, but the local tigers have perhaps acquired a semblance of sociability, because they have been known to appear in front of lorries packed with enthusiastic, noisy Indian tourists. Other local inhabitants you may see include the panther (called cheetah or leopard) and wild cats. Cervidae (*sambar, cheetal*) and antelopes (*chinkara* gazelles) are legion and regularly sighted. In addition, the park's lakes abound in crocodiles (introduced by the park's staff) and are also home to other species of wildlife.

The fort *(3km after the main gate into the park, but a visit is not included in the safari. Either rent a jeep or ask to be dropped-off after the morning safari. Open from dawn to dusk, no charge)* is particularly popular with tigers too, so beware! The steep path up to the fort passes by four successive gates. The impressive ramparts and bastions can still be seen, but they only contain 13C ruins, half-hidden under brambles and gigantic jungle trees. Paving stones have been forced upwards and dislodged by the vigorous underground root systems. A walk through the ruins will lead to a small **temple to Ganesha**, which is particularly popular at the time of *Ganesh Chaturthi*, the god's birthday (August-September). Ranthambore's Ganesha is also very sought-after by engaged couples and he always receives the first invitation to their wedding. This is perhaps because the elephant-god is felt to bring luck to any economic or commercial enterprise.

Ganesha, the memory of an elephant

According to the "Shiva Purana", Parvati, Shiva's wife, not wishing to be disturbed in her bath, rubbed her body, and with a little dirt, modelled a child who was posted in front of her door. Shiva was driven into a fury by the sight of such a pretty sentinel in front of his wife's door and in a fit of anger – and jealousy – cut off the creature's head. Parvati's sadness was such that Shiva promised to stick the head from the first passer-by onto the decapitated body. The first passer-by was an elephant...

Making the most of Sawai Madhopur

Getting there

By train – *Sawai Madhopur Railway Station* located in the south-east of the modern town, between the town and the entrance to Ranthambore Park (which is around 10km away), ☎ 131 and (07462) 202 22. To Jaipur, the best option is the "Superfast" morning train (2hr). Daily, 5 express trains to Delhi (6 to 9hr journey), via Bharatpur (3hr) and Mathura (3hr30min to 5hr); 4 local trains to Agra (7hr), and around ten to Kota (90min), and only one night train to Jodhpur (9hr).

By bus – To Jaipur, it is best to avoid the local buses which leave from ***Dausa-Jaipur Bus Stand***, a little hut on a road at right angles to Bazriya Market, main road of the modern town; the 3 express buses (5hr, via Tonk) which leave from ***Tonk Bus Stand***, to the west of Bazriya Market are a much better option. 1 bus to Delhi (10hr), 1 to Kota (4hr30min), 3 to Ajmer (8hr). To Bundi, only 1 express (4hr30min), but several local buses (5hr30min).

Getting about

By rickshaw – Allow 60Rs from the station to Vinayak Hotel (6km) in an auto-rickshaw.

By taxi – Jeep taxi rank at the station. Allow 90Rs to Vinayak Hotel (110Rs the other way) and 50Rs to Anurag or Ankur Hotels. Rental per day (600Rs for 200km).

Bicycle rentals – On leaving the station.

Address book

Tourist office – ***Tourist Reception Centre***, at the beginning of Ranthambore Rd, 1.5km from the station, ☎ (07462) 208 08. 10am-1.30pm/2pm-5pm; closed Sunday.

Project Tiger Reception Centre – 500m to the south-west of the tourist office, off the road into the old town, ☎ (07462) 202 23. The desk is open every day from 6am-7am/10am-5pm/6pm-8pm; closed July 1 to September 30. It is a good idea to ask for directions because it isn't easy to find.

Banks/Money – ***State Bank of Bikaner and Jaipur***, at the far eastern end of the old town (isolated to the south-east of the station). Can change cash and travellers' cheques in dollars and pounds sterling.

Post Office/Telephone – ***GPO***, in the modern town centre. 10am-5pm, Saturday 10am-2pm; closed Sunday. Postal code: 322001.

Safety – ***Police***, ☎ (07462) 204 56.

Where to stay

During the low season, from April to September, a 25 % discount (up to 50 % in the smaller hotels). Booking essential at Christmas and during the Indian school holidays.

• In the modern town

Under US$7

Rajeev Resort, 16 Indira Colony, Civil Lines, ☎(07462) 210 67 – 18rm. 4rm without bath. A private home in a residential neighbourhood, 600m from Tonk Bus Stand, with clean, basic rooms; the most expensive have three beds.

• On Ranthambore Rd

The road leading to the park is the nicest place to stay. Accommodation is out in the country, with the exception of the few hotels and other buildings along the first 3km.

From US$7-15

Anurag Hotel, Ranthambore Rd, 4km from the station, ☎ (07462) 204 51 and 207 51, Fax (07462) 204 51 – 17rm. Cooler. This pleasant establishment, surrounded by a lawn, is very friendly. Ask for the least expensive rooms, which overlook a U-shaped veranda, around an attractive courtyard-garden. Floors and bathrooms renovated in 1999. Dormitory and camp site.

Ankur Resorts, Ranthambore Rd, 3.5km from the station, ☎ (07462) 207 92, Fax (07462) 206 97 – 25rm. Cooler. A somewhat sad hotel, with damp rooms, furnished with the strict minimum, and carpeted (hence the mouldy smell). The first-floor rooms are better, quiet and with a delightful view of the countryside. The hotel can also provide full-board with two visits in a jeep to the park for US$35.

From US$15-30

Vinayak Hotel (RTDC), Ranthambore Rd, 6km from the station, ☎ (07462) 213 33, Fax (07462) 212 12 – 10rm. Bar. A pleasant, well-run hotel, situated in the countryside, on the edge of the "buffer zone" around the park. Rather expensive, the price is explained by the setting. Simple, somewhat repetitive, but decent food.

Jhoomar Baori Castle (RTDC), in the buffer zone, 1km from Ranthambore Rd and 6.5km from the station, ☎ (07462) 204 95 – 12rm. TV Cooler. Bar. Built against the hillside, hidden in the trees, this modest hunting lodge of the maharaja of Jaipur (mid-19C) has spacious and smaller rooms, most of which still have their original "arayish". Hardly in the luxury bracket, the hotel offers the usual "laid back" service found in a RTDC establishment. Its excellent position, however, means that it is often fully booked.

From US$70-140

The Sawai Madhopur Lodge (Taj Group and Heritage Hotels Association), Ranthambore Rd, 2.5km from the station, ☎ (07462) 202 47 and

205 41, Fax (07462) 207 18; bookings in Delhi and Jaipur (see p 107) – 33rm. Six tents. Bar, billiards. The communal parts of the hotel are located in a bungalow built in the 1930s by the maharaja of Jaipur: a round Art Deco living room leads onto a veranda and a wood-panelled restaurant. The rooms are situated in recent cottages, scattered around a very attractive park, but they are small and somewhat nondescript. The reception could be friendlier.

Pastimes

Excursions – A visit to ***Ranthambore National Park*** can only be done in Tiger Project vehicles: 10 5-seater jeeps (825Rs per jeep with guide) and 4 20-seater lorries, called "canters" (80Rs per person). A quota of 5 jeeps and 40 "canter" seats can be booked 1 month ahead, any remaining seats can be reserved in the morning for the afternoon visit, or in the afternoon for the following morning. It is best to reserve early as the jeeps are often fully booked. Visits leave from the Tiger Project Centre at 6.30am (6am in the summer) and 2pm (2.30pm in the summer), but those staying in hotels along Ranthambore Rd can arrange to be picked up on the way. Allow a 30min drive to reach the park, 3hr in the park and 30min return journey. Entrance charge: 100Rs per person, 200Rs per video camera.

An elephant ready to parade

X. Zimmbardo/HOA QUI

Notes

INDEX

Jaipur: curiosity, site with description
Gandhi (Indira): person
Castes: term with description
Health: practical information

E – F

G

H – I

J

K

L

M

N

O – P – Q

R

S

T

U

V-Z

MAPS

Manufacture Française des Pneumatiques Michelin
Société en commandite par actions au capital de 2 000 000 000 de francs
Place des Carmes-Déchaux – 63000 Clermont-Ferrand (France)
R.C.S. Clermont-Fd B 855 200 507

Dépôt légal novembre 2000 – ISBN 2-06-855901-3 – ISSN 0763-1383

Made in France 11-00/1.1
Compograveur : Nord Compo – Villeneuve d'Ascq
Imprimeur : I.M.E. – Baume-les-Dames
Cover photography :
Gadi Sagar Lake and Jaisalmer (T. Bognar/LA PHOTOTHÈQUE SDP)
A musician, miniature by the Jaipur School (18C) (J.L. Nou/AKG PARIS)
A Rajasthani (M. Kalensky)

Your opinion matters!

In order to make sure that this collection satisfies the needs of our readers, please help us by completing the following questionnaire with your comments and suggestions and return to:

Michelin Travel Publications
The Edward Hyde Building
38 Clarendon Road
Watford, UK

or

Michelin Travel Publications
P.O. Box 19008
Greenville, SC 29602-9008
USA

■ YOUR HOLIDAYS/VACATIONS:

1. In general, when you go on holiday or vacation, do you tend to travel... (Choose one)

- ☐ Independently, on your own
- ☐ Independently, as a couple
- ☐ With 1 or 2 friends
- ☐ With your family
- ☐ With a group of friends
- ☐ On organised trips

2. How many international holidays or vacations of 1 week or more have you taken in the last 3 years? ____________________

Last 3 destinations:	Month/Year:
______________________________	______________________________
______________________________	______________________________
______________________________	______________________________

3. What do you look for most when planning a holiday or vacation?

	Not at all	*Sometimes*	*Essential*
Somewhere new and exotic	☐	☐	☐
Real experience/meeting people	☐	☐	☐
Experiencing the wildlife/scenery	☐	☐	☐
Cultural insight	☐	☐	☐
Rest & relaxation	☐	☐	☐
Comfort & well-being	☐	☐	☐
Adventure & the unexpected	☐	☐	☐

4. When travelling, do you take a travel guide with you?

☐ Always ☐ Usually ☐ Sometimes ☐ Never

■ You and the Michelin NEOS guides

5. About your purchase of a NEOS Guide

How long was your holiday where you used the NEOS guide?
How many days? __________
For which country or countries? ____________________________
How long before your departure did you buy it? How many days? __________

6. What made you choose a NEOS Guide?

Highlight everything that applies.

- ☐ Something new and interesting
- ☐ The layout
- ☐ Easy to read format
- ☐ Cultural details
- ☐ Quality of the text
- ☐ Quality of the mapping
- ☐ Practical Information
- ☐ Michelin quality

7. Which sections did you use most during your holiday or vacation?

Score 1-4	*(1 = least used)*			*(4 = most used)*
"Setting the Scene"	☐ 1	☐ 2	☐ 3	☐ 4
"Meeting the People"	☐ 1	☐ 2	☐ 3	☐ 4
"Practical Information"	☐ 1	☐ 2	☐ 3	☐ 4
"Exploring ..."	☐ 1	☐ 2	☐ 3	☐ 4

8. How would you rate the following aspects of your NEOS guide?

Score 1-4	*(1 = Poor)*			*(4 = Excellent)*
Cover design	☐ 1	☐ 2	☐ 3	☐ 4
Chapter Order	☐ 1	☐ 2	☐ 3	☐ 4
Layout (photos, diagrams)	☐ 1	☐ 2	☐ 3	☐ 4
Ease of reading (typeface)	☐ 1	☐ 2	☐ 3	☐ 4
Style of writing	☐ 1	☐ 2	☐ 3	☐ 4
Text boxes and stories	☐ 1	☐ 2	☐ 3	☐ 4
Plans & Maps	☐ 1	☐ 2	☐ 3	☐ 4
Star ratings system	☐ 1	☐ 2	☐ 3	☐ 4
Format	☐ 1	☐ 2	☐ 3	☐ 4
Weight	☐ 1	☐ 2	☐ 3	☐ 4
Durability	☐ 1	☐ 2	☐ 3	☐ 4
Price	☐ 1	☐ 2	☐ 3	☐ 4

9. Did you use other travel guides during your trip? ☐ Yes ☐ No

If yes, which ones? ______________________________

10. Please give your NEOS guide a rating out of 20: ____/20 (with 20 as top rating)

Would you use a NEOS guide for your next trip? ☐ Yes ☐ No

If no, why not? ______________________________

Which other destinations would you like NEOS to cover? ______________

11. Any other comments or suggestions: ______________

____

____

____

____

____

____

Surname/Last Name: ______________ First Name: ______________

Address: ______________________________

Age: ______________ Sex: ☐ M ☐ F

Profession: ______________________________

Where did you purchase your NEOS Guide: What type of store?
Which country?

Data collected may be used by Michelin Travel Publications for internal purposes only and not for resale.